BASIC
FUNDAMENTALS
AND STYLE

Other titles in the Boyd & Fraser Computer Science Series

BEGINNING STRUCTURED COBOL
PASCAL
STANDARD BASIC PROGRAMMING for Business and Management Applications
PASCAL PROGRAMMING : A Spiral Approach
STRUCTURED FORTRAN 77 PROGRAMMING
STRUCTURED FORTRAN 77 PROGRAMMING for Hewlett-Packard Computers
A STRUCTURED APPROACH TO GENERAL BASIC
A STRUCTURED APPROACH TO ESSENTIAL BASIC
INTRODUCTION TO COMPUTERS AND COMPUTER SCIENCE, Third Edition
ARTIFICIAL INTELLIGENCE : Can Computers Think?

Cover Photo: David S. Hughes, Stock/Boston

BASIC
FUNDAMENTALS
AND STYLE

JAMES S. QUASNEY
JOHN MANIOTES

Purdue University/Calumet

BOYD & FRASER PUBLISHING CO.
Boston

To our wives: Linda and Mary
The Quasney tribe: Lisa, Jeff, Marci, Jodi, Amanda and Nikole
The Maniotes clan: Dionne, Sam and Andrew

Credits:

Editor: Tom Walker
Production Supervision: Dixie Clark
Development editor: Sharon Cogdill
Design/cover: Dixie Clark
Artwork: Marilyn Entwistle/Dixie Clark/Rose Design
Typesetting: Neil W. Kelley Graphic Services

Library of Congress Cataloging in Publication Data

```
Quasney, James S.
   BASIC fundamentals and style.

   Includes index.
   1. Basic (Computer program language)  I. Maniotes,
John.  II. Title.
QA76.73.B3Q37  1984          001.64'24          84-2789
ISBN 0-87835-138-8
```

CONTENTS

PREFACE

BASIC was one of the first programming languages developed for an academic environment. Subsequent to its introduction in 1963, many additional programming languages have been developed, some purporting to be the programming language to end all other languages. And yet, BASIC lives on. In fact, BASIC has emerged as one of the most widely used programming languages in the world. BASIC is so popular because it is easy to learn, it is powerful, flexible and has gained strong support from the manufacturers of timesharing and personal computer systems.

THE BASIC PROGRAMMING LANGUAGE

There are literally hundreds of books that have been written on the subject of BASIC programming. Most do a good job of presenting the repertoire of BASIC statements, but fall short in their presentation of modern day program methodology. The fact is, the attributes of a well-written program have changed considerably over the past several years. Besides the obvious characteristic that the program must work correctly, a quality program in the past was characterized by clever algorithms and tricky code; the "best" programs were those with the fewest instructions and the fastest program execution. The end result was the design and construction of BS (Bowl of Spaghetti) programs. Unfortunately, this type of programming is still prevalent in many textbooks and computer journals. Even though most instructors teach good programming techniques, students depend heavily on illustrations from their book. The end result is poorly designed and written programs and bad habits transferred to later programming courses.

NEED FOR ANOTHER BOOK

Today, the most important criterion for quality is still that the program work correctly. However, a good program now has reliability and simplicity in design; a good program is also easy to read and easy to modify. Teaching the student the design and writing of BASIC programs with these characteristics is the top priority of this book.

OBJECTIVES OF THIS BOOK

This book was developed with the following objectives:

1) To acquaint the reader with the proper and correct way to design and write programs using the BASIC language.
2) To teach good problem-solving techniques.
3) To emphasize interactive applications, the type of programming proliferating in today's world.
4) To develop a problem-oriented approach that allows the reader to learn by example.
5) To use practical problems to illustrate the application of computers to both academic and real-world environments.
6) To encourage independent study and help those working alone on their own systems.

LEVEL OF INSTRUCTION

This book is designed to be used in a one quarter or one semester course in BASIC programming or in independent study by those working alone. No previous experience with a computer is assumed, and no mathematics beyond the freshman high school level is required. The book is written specifically for the student with average ability, for whom continuity, simplicity and practicality are characteristics we consider essential. Numerous insights, based on our forty accumulated years of experience in consulting and teaching in the field of data processing, are implicit throughout the book. For the past 10 consecutive years, we have both taught introductory programming courses using BASIC.

FUNDAMENTAL TOPICS ARE PRESENTED IN DETAIL

Besides introducing students to the proper and correct way to design and write programs using structured and top-down techniques, there are fundamental topics concerning computers and programming which should be covered in any introductory programming class. These include the stored program concept, getting on the computer, editing programs, input/output operations, variables and constants, simple and complex computations, decision-making, the use of counters and running totals, rounding and truncation, looping and end-of-file tests, counter-controlled loops, the use of logical operators, string manipulation and the use of functions and subroutines. Other essential topics include data validation, control breaks, table processing, sequence checking, selection, searching, matching, merging, sorting and the differences between batch and interactive applications. Every one of these topics is covered in detail in this book.

DISTINGUISHING FEATURES

The distinguishing features of this book include the following:

Emphasis on Fundamentals and Style

Heavy emphasis is placed on the fundamentals of producing well-written and readable programs. A disciplined style is consistently used in all program examples. Thorough documentation and indentation standards illuminate the implementation of the Selection and Repetition logic structures.

Problem-oriented Approach

Over 200 BASIC programs plus many partial programs, representing a wide range of practical applications, are used to introduce specific statements and the proper and correct way to write programs.

Emphasis on the Program Development Cycle

The program development cycle is presented early in Chapter 1 and used throughout the book. Good design habits are reinforced and special attention is given to testing the design *before* attempting to implement the logic in a program.

Particular attention is given to designing proper programs using the three logic structures of structured programming: Sequence, Selection (If-Then-Else and Case) and Repetition (Do-While and Do-Until). A disciplined method for implementing the structured design is adhered to throughout the book. Major use of the IF-THEN-ELSE statement, logical operators and the WHILE and WEND statements help minimize the use of the GOTO statement.

Structured Programming Approach

Complete coverage of sequential, random and simulated indexed files provides students with knowledge central to a real programming environment. Topics include creating all three types of files, file maintenance (matching and merging operations), writing reports to auxiliary storage and an information retrieval system featuring indexed files.

Complete Coverage of File Processing

Although batch processing is discussed in detail, the primary emphasis is on interactive processing. The reader is introduced to the INPUT, PRINT and Clear Screen statements early in Chapter 2. Several menu-driven programs are illustrated to familiarize the reader with the type of programming proliferating in today's world.

Interactive Applications (Menu-Driven Programs)

The structured programming approach is sufficient to construct good programs for small problems. However, for large complex problems, another approach is needed. This book emphasizes the top-down strategy to break large complex problems into smaller, less complex problems and then breaks each one of these down—decomposes them—into even smaller solvable problems.

Top-down Approach

A flowcharting template is enclosed in the inside back cover of the book. It is a professional template with symbols based on FIPS24, ANSI X3.5 and ISO 1028.

Enclosed Flowcharting Template

Each chapter contains a succinct, list-formatted chapter summary review entitled "What You Should Know," reinforcing key concepts and data processing terminology.

What You Should Know

Dual sets of short answer exercises identified as "Self-Test Exercises" and "Test Your BASIC Skills," appear at the end of each chapter. Over 300 problems, many of which are complete programs, are included for practice. Through the use of these exercises, the reader can master the concepts presented and instructors are afforded a valuable diagnostic tool. (Answers for "Self-Test Exercises" and even-numbered "Test Your BASIC Skills" exercises are included at the end of this book.)

Self-Test and Test Your BASIC Skills

Over 80 challenging Programming Exercises with sample Input and Output are included at the end of the chapters. These problems are in order from most simple to most difficult. All the problems include sample input data and the corresponding output results. Solutions to these exercises are given in the *Instructor's Manual and Answer Book* and are also available from our publisher on an IBM PC-compatible diskette.

Programming Exercises with Sample Input and Output

Various dialects of BASIC are consistently highlighted throughout the book, which accentuates Microsoft BASIC. This approach allows the reader to overcome programming problems related to machine specificity. For the following computer systems (or lookalikes with software compatibility), we have indicated in

Machine Specificity

the presentation of the General Form or in a footnote if a statement is unavailable or is written in a different format:

Computer System	BASIC	Reference Manual
Apple	APPLESOFT II: Extended Floating Point BASIC	BASIC Programming Manual (030-0013-E)
COMMODORE	COMMODORE 64 BASIC	Programmer's Reference Guide (0-672-22056-3)
DEC Rainbow	MBASIC-86	MBASIC-86 Reference Manual (AA-P602A-TV)
DEC VAX-11	VAX-11 BASIC	VAX-11 BASIC (AA-H8667A-TE)
IBM PC	Advanced BASIC	BASIC by Microsoft (6025013)
Macintosh	MS-BASIC	Microsoft BASIC Interpreter for Apple Macintosh (014-096-001)
TRS-80 Model 4	Model 4 BASIC	TRS-80 Model 4 Disk System Owner's Manual (26-2117)

Other differences between systems, like how to get a hard copy, clearing the screen, the composition of variable names and precision, are presented in tables.

Emphasis on Data Validation

A thoroughly tested program does not guarantee its reliability once it is turned over to a user. Most abnormal terminations in a production environment are due to user errors and not programmer errors. This is especially true for programs that interact with the user or are executed on personal computers. Good programmers will attempt to trap as many user errors as possible. This book pays particular attention to illustrating various methods for ensuring that incoming data is reasonable or within limits.

Presentation of Programming Case Studies

The book contains 30 completely solved and annotated actual case studies, illuminating the use of BASIC and computer programming in the real world. Emphasis is placed on problem analysis, program design and an in-depth discussion of the program solution.

Debugging Techniques and Programming Tips

A characteristic of a good programmer is that he or she has confidence that a program will work the first time it is executed. This confidence implies careful attention has been given to the design and that the design has been fully tested. Still, errors do occur, and they must be corrected. Throughout the book, especially in Appendix C, efficient methods for locating and correcting errors are introduced. Both TRON and TROFF, as well as other techniques, are discussed in detail. The section in Appendix C dealing with Programming Tips, serves as an excellent reference, facilitating the writing of efficient, yet readable, code.

Concise Introduction to Computers

A concise discussion of data processing and how computers operate is included at the beginning of the book. Equal attention is given to timesharing and personal computers.

The BASIC Vocabulary

Data processing terms are worked into the book as naturally as possible, so that the reader can get accustomed to their use. At their first introduction, these terms are printed in boldface, to remind the reader to look them up in The BASIC Vocabulary section in the back of the book. These terms are also found in the index, so that they can be inspected in their natural linguistic setting.

Since the authors recognize flowcharting as an excellent pedagogical aid, and one of the tools of an analyst or programmer, many of the programming case studies include program flowcharts of the logic to demonstrate programming style, design and documentation considerations. For the reader's convenience, line numbers have been placed on the top left corner of the symbols to better illustrate the relationship between the flowchart and the program. Flowcharting techniques are presented in Appendix A. Alternative logic tools, including pseudocode, Nassi-Shneiderman charts, Warnier-Orr diagrams and decision tables, are presented in Appendix B.

Flowcharts Illustrating Program Design

This book introduces the PRINT USING statement in Chapter 4 and consistently uses it throughout the book. This gives students the ability to generate readable reports and gives them more control over the form of the output of the program.

PRINT USING Statement Introduced Early

The effective use of a second color throughout the book enhances readability, highlights key concepts and facilitates easy reference. This is especially important for readers using this book as a reference tool or on their own.

Use of Second Color

The *Instructor's Manual and Answer Book*, available upon request from our publisher, Boyd and Fraser, includes the following:

INSTRUCTOR'S MANUAL AND ANSWER BOOK

- Transparency masters from each chapter of the text
- Chapter-by-chapter objectives and vocabulary lists
- Lecture outlines
- Program solutions to *all* 80 programming assignments in the book
- Answers to the odd-numbered Test Your BASIC Skills exercises
- Test bank, including true/false, short answer, fill-in and multiple choice questions for quizzes and tests

An IBM PC-compatible diskette with all the program solutions to the 80 Programming Exercises is available upon request from our publisher Boyd and Fraser for those schools which adopt this book.

Solutions to Programming Exercises on IBM PC Diskette

Prior to publication, the manuscript was used and tested at Purdue University Calumet in the following courses and programs:

FIELD-TESTED

1) At the freshman level of a four-year commercial computer and information systems program leading to the degree of Bachelor of Science.
2) At the freshman level of a two-year commercial computer and information systems program leading to the degree of Associate of Applied Sciences.
3) In the first of a sequence of two courses taken by business and management students. In the first course, the students are introduced to data processing concepts, personal computers and BASIC programming.
4) In a service course taken by students interested in gaining a better understanding of the capabilities and limitations of computers.

BASIC Fundamentals and Style has been designed around the student. This book has been tested with great success; we trust others will find it to be equally successful. We would appreciate hearing from any one who has comments or suggestions on this book. Either one of us can be reached at Purdue University Calumet, 2233 - 171st Street, Hammond, Indiana 46323.

Hammond, Indiana
January, 1984

James S. Quasney
John Maniotes

ACKNOWLEDGMENTS

We would like to thank and express our appreciation to the many fine and talented individuals who have contributed to the success of this book. The original plan for this project was launched with the help of Professor James N. Haag, University of San Francisco. We were fortunate to have a group of reviewers whose critical evaluations of our first BASIC book, Standard BASIC Programming, were of great value during the preparation of this book. Special thanks goes to Professor R. Waldo Roth, Taylor University; Professor David Bradbard, Auburn University; Professor Donald L. Muench, St. John Fisher College; Professor Jerry Lameiro, Colorado State University; and Professors John T. Gorgone, J. T. Grillo and I. Englander of Bentley College for their helpful comments and suggestions.

The manuscript was reviewed and greatly improved by a very fine and talented author in her own right, Professor Marjorie Leeson.

Many other individuals contributed indirectly to this book by helping to form the authors' ideas. Particular thanks goes to our colleagues at Purdue University Calumet, Professors A. J. Adams, Jeffrey Case, Rita Fillmon, Roy Foreman, Donald Kurtz, Ty Chee Lee, Walter Miner, Steve Radosavljevic, Susan Sebok, Norman Smith, Roland Untch, Charles Winer and Ms. Diane Larson, Mr. William Dorin, Mr. Jeffrey Quasney, Ms. Janet Tigar-Kramer and Ms. Marilyn Markowicz for assisting, outlining and reviewing drafts of the manuscript.

We also wish to express our appreciation to Tom Walker, Senior Editor at Boyd and Fraser, for his encouragement, creative suggestions and assistance. Special praise is reserved for our Content/Copy Editor, Sharon Cogdill, whose editorial talents and organizational abilities added appreciably to the book.

Our last acknowledgment is reserved for Dixie Clark for diligently guiding this book through production.

1. Terms printed in **boldface** when they first appear are defined in "The BASIC Vocabulary" at the end of this book.

2. Beginning in Chapter 4, line numbers appear near symbols in flowcharts, showing the relationship between the flowchart and the corresponding program.

3. Every chapter ends with an important and useful review section called "What You Should Know."

4. The answers to all the "Self-Test-Exercises" and the even-numbered "Test Your BASIC Skills" questions are in the back of the book.

5. Appendix A, "Program Flowcharting," and Appendix B, "Pseudocode and Other Logic Design Tools," provide you with additional valuable logic design methods.

6. Appendix C, "Debugging Techniques and Programming Tips," suggests efficient methods for locating and correcting errors in a program, and it includes tips on how to write efficient, readable code.

LIST OF PROGRAMMING CASE STUDIES

COMPUTERS: AN INTRODUCTION 1

A **computer** is a machine that can accept data, process the data at high speeds by itself, and give the results of these processes in an acceptable form to the user. A more formal definition of a computer is given by the American National Standards Institute (ANSI). There a computer is defined as a device that can perform substantial computation, including numerous arithmetic or logic operations, without intervention by a human operator.*

1.1
WHAT IS A
COMPUTER?

The key phrases in the ANSI definition are "substantial computation," "logic operations," and "without intervention by a human operator." These terms point out the differences between computers and desk calculators.

Instructing a computer is known as **programming.** It involves writing precise **instructions**—in a specified form—and in a language the computer understands.

The major advantages of a computer are its speed and accuracy, and its ability, on its own, to store and have ready for immediate recall vast amounts of data. Modern computers can also accept data from anywhere via telephone line or satellite communications. They can generate usable output, like reports, paychecks, and invoices, at several thousand lines per minute.

**Advantages
of a Computer**

A release by NASA concerning the Apollo 13 mission illustrates the significance of a computer's speed and accuracy.

When America's Apollo 13 moonship ran into trouble, over 200,000 miles from earth, scientists working with computers figured out the correct return flight path for the disabled craft in just 84 minutes. The National Aeronautics and Space Administration has determined how long it would have taken before computers to figure the proper around-the-moon-and-back trajectory for astronauts James A. Lovell, Fred W. Haise, Jr., and John L. Swigert, Jr.

---

* Vocabulary for Information Processing, Report X3.12, American National Standards Institute, latest edition.

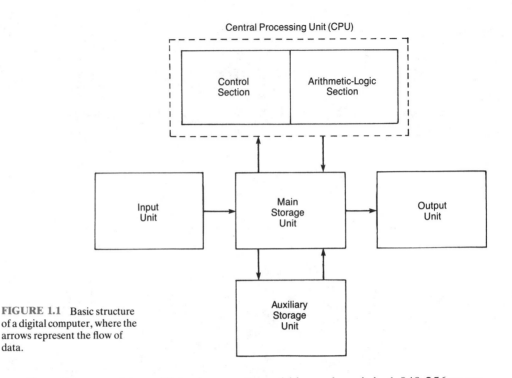

Central Processing Unit (CPU)

Control Section

Arithmetic-Logic Section

Input Unit

Main Storage Unit

Output Unit

Auxiliary Storage Unit

FIGURE 1.1 Basic structure of a digital computer, where the arrows represent the flow of data.

One person working with just a pencil would have done it in 1,040,256 years. Had a desk calculator been used, the time could have been cut to 60,480 years. This assumes that no errors and thus no recalculations had to be made during the computations.

Had all the people in the mission planning and analysis division at that time—a total of 220—been assigned the task, . . . it could have been manually computed in just under 4,730 years, or by the year 6700.*

Another example of the speed and accuracy of a computer appears in an announcement by the Ford Motor Company concerning an engine control microcomputer system. The car manufacturer says the Electronic Engine Control system (EECIV) "can read seven engine parameters and change seven engine functions in less than one engine revolution—three-hundredths of a second. The computations performed during each minute of engine operation would take a human an estimated 45 years or more using a manually operated calculator."** This microcomputer system is made up of two chips, each less than a quarter of an inch square. Ford says that a computer in 1960, with less capability than these two chips, would have filled a room and that in 1970 it would have filled a car's trunk.

The ability computers have to handle large amounts of data and tedious and time consuming work, without ever tiring, makes them indispensible for most businesses. In fact, computers have been among the most important forces in the modernization of business, industry and society since World War II. Keep in mind, however, that with all their capabilities, computers are not built to think or reason. They extend our intellect, but they do not replace thinking.

1.2 COMPUTER HARDWARE

Computer hardware is the physical equipment of a computer system. The equipment may consist of mechanical, magnetic, optical, electrical or electronic devices or combinations of devices. Although many computers have been built in different sizes, speeds, and costs, and with different internal operations, most of them have the same basic subsystems (see Figure 1.1).

---

* Quoted in *EAI Associates Newsletter*, Vol. 8, No. 17, May 7, 1971.
** News Release by Jim A. Allen, Public Affairs, Ford Motor Co., May 25, 1982.

FIGURE 1.2 CRAY X-MP computer system (Courtesy Cray Research, Inc.).

FIGURE 1.3 (Left) The IBM Personal Computer (Courtesy IBM) and (right) the DEC Rainbow Personal Computer (Courtesy Digital Equipment Corp.).

FIGURE 1.4   (Left) The Apple Macintosh Personal Computer (Courtesy Apple, Inc.) and (right) the Apple IIe Personal Computer (Courtesy Apple Inc.).

FIGURE 1.5   A DEC VAX-11/780 medium-scale computer system with interactive processing capabilities (Courtesy Digital Equipment Corp.).

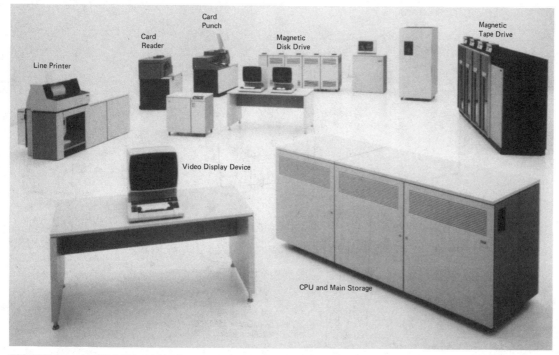

FIGURE 1.6 An IBM 4341 Model 2 large-scale computer system (Courtesy IBM).

Pictures of several types of computer systems appear in Figures 1.2 to 1.6. A brief description of each subsystem of a computer follows.

Input

An **input unit** is a device that allows **programs** (instructions to the computer) and **data** (like rate of pay, hours worked, and number of dependents) to enter the computer system. This device converts the incoming data into electrical impulses which are sent to the other units of the computer. Small computer systems usually have a **keyboard** for input. Larger systems may have at least one of each unit listed in Table 1.1 and possibly several of certain units.

Some of the input devices that BASIC programmers use are shown in Figures 1.8 and 1.9.

Main Storage

After the instructions and data have entered the computer through one of the input units, they are filed in the computer's storage unit, the **main** or **primary storage**. Since computers can process vast amounts of data in a short time and since some can perform millions of calculations in just one second, the storage unit must be able to retain large amounts of data and make any single item rapidly available for processing.

TABLE 1.1 **Some Possible Input Devices**

1) Keyboard
2) Video display device sensitive to touch
3) Magnetic disk or floppy diskette unit
4) Magnetic tape or cassette unit
5) Punched card reader
6) Optical character reader
7) Voice input
8) Joystick/Mouse

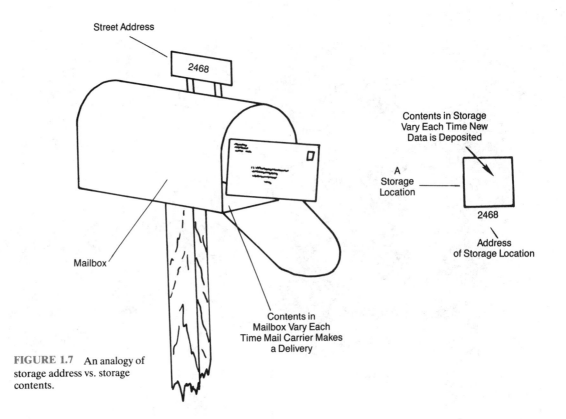

FIGURE 1.7   An analogy of storage address vs. storage contents.

The main storage unit can be compared to a series of residential mailboxes (see Figure 1.7). Each mailbox is identified by a unique street address. Each mailbox provides space to hold contents that change from day to day. Main storage in a computer is also divided into locations, each having an **address**. When instructions and data are entered, they are stored in various locations of main storage. You remove the mail from your mailbox. The computer, though, will leave data in a storage location until it is instructed to replace it with new data. And while a data item is in storage, the computer can "look it up" as often as it is needed. Thus, when data is retrieved from a storage location, the stored contents remain unaltered. When you instruct the computer to put new data in that location, it destroys the old data first.

Central Processing Unit (CPU)   The **CPU** controls and supervises the entire computer system and performs the actual arithmetic and logic operations on data as specified by the written program. The CPU is divided into the **arithmetic-logic section** and the **control section** (see Figure 1.1).

The arithmetic-logic section performs such operations as addition, subtraction, multiplication, division, transferring, storing, and setting the algebraic sign of the results. Depending on the cost and storage capacity of the computer, the speed of the arithmetic unit will range from several thousand to many millions of operations per second.

The arithmetic-logic section also carries out the decision-making operations required to change the sequence of instruction execution. These operations include testing various conditions, such as deciding the algebraic sign of a number or comparing two characters for equality. The result of these tests causes the computer to take one of two or more alternate paths through the program.

The control section directs and coordinates the entire computer system. Its primary function is to analyze and initiate the execution of instructions. This

FIGURE 1.8   A DECwriter III terminal (Courtesy Digital Equipment Corp.).

means that the control section has control over all other subsystems in the computer system. It can control the input of data and output of information and routing of data and information between auxiliary storage and main storage or between main storage and the arithmetic-logic section. This section directs the computer according to the program developed by the programmer and placed in main storage.

The function of the **auxiliary storage** unit is to store data and programs that are to be used over and over again. Common auxiliary storage devices are the **magnetic disk** or **floppy diskette**.   **Auxiliary Storage**

   Both magnetic tape and disk can be used to store programs and data for as long as desired. A new program entering the system erases the previous program and data in main memory, but the previous program and data may be permanently stored on an auxiliary storage device for recall by the computer.

   The method of storing BASIC programs and data for later use and the methods of retrieval will be discussed in Chapter 2.

   In a business, files containing employee records, customer records, accounts receivable or payable data, and inventory data are stored on magnetic tape or disks. Programs written to print paychecks, invoices and management reports are also stored on these auxiliary storage devices. Without auxiliary storage, all programs and data would have to be manually entered through an input device every single time an application is processed. To transfer a program or file to main storage from auxiliary storage, an instruction need only be inserted through the keyboard. In this manner, files or programs can be updated and restored on the auxiliary storage unit. This activity is **file maintenance**. The fact that programs and data are stored and later recalled from auxiliary storage leads many computer scientists to call auxiliary storage units input-output (I/O) units as well.

TABLE 1.2   Some Possible Output Devices

1) Video display device
2) Character printer or line printer
3) Magnetic disk or floppy diskette unit
4) Magnetic tape or cassette unit
5) Plotter
6) Card punch
7) Audio-response unit

Output   When instructed by a program, the computer can communicate the results of a program to output units. Table 1.2 lists some of the more popular output devices that may be present on computer systems.

High-speed line printers (see example in Figure 1.6), some of which can operate at speeds of more than 2000 lines per minute, can prepare invoices, checks, report cards, and other listings. If the results of a program are to be processed further, the information can also be placed on magnetic disk or diskette. The information can be used later as data for the next problem or sent over telephone lines to another computer for further processing.

The **video display device**, also called a **CRT** or **VDT**, is similar to the tube in a television set and can be used to display the output results in the form of words, numbers, graphs, or drawings (see Figure 1.9).

One of the recent breakthroughs in the development of output devices has been the **audio-response unit**. This device allows the computer to transmit replies vocally. For this to occur, the computer must have a sizable number of human voice sounds stored in active files. Such devices are used, for example, by large retail stores to check credit ratings. If you want to make a purchase on credit, a clerk first enters your credit card number on a Touch-Tone telephone connected to a computer. The credit rating is given almost instantaneously in a voice that has been mechanically assembled from pre-recorded spoken syllables.

FIGURE 1.9   A DEC VT100 visual display terminal (Courtesy Digital Equipment Corp.).

In order for a computer to take action and produce a desired result, it must have a step-by-step description of the task to be accomplished. In addition, the computer must know precisely where it can find the data (its addresses), what calculations to perform, how to arrive at a final answer, and what to do with it.

1.3
THE STORED
PROGRAM
CONCEPT

The computer is directed to perform each of these basic operations by a specific instruction. The entire series of instructions required to complete a given procedure or task is the computer program. When these instructions are placed into the main storage unit of a computer, they are called the **stored program**. The idea that instructions are stored internally in main storage is usually referred to as "the stored program concept." Main storage not only stores data but also the instructions which tell the computer what to do with the data.

The stored program gives computers a great deal of flexibility. Without it the computer's ability to handle tasks would be reduced to that of a desk calculator. Placing the instructions in the computer before it begins to process them allows the computer to execute instruction after instruction about as fast as it does individual arithmetic calculations.

Once the program is stored, in the normal sequence of computer operation, the first instruction is located and sent to the control section, where it is interpreted and executed. Then the next instruction is located, sent to the control section, interpreted and executed. This process continues automatically, instruction by instruction, until the program is completed or until the computer is instructed to halt.

In order for the computer to perform still another job, a new program must be stored in memory. Hence, a computer can be easily used to process a large number of different jobs.

Computer software is a program or a set of programs written for a computer. Included in the definition of computer programs are **systems programs**, like compilers (translators), and **application programs**, written by users.

1.4
COMPUTER
SOFTWARE

Programming languages are classified as **low-level languages** (like machine language and assembly language) and **high-level languages** (like BASIC, PASCAL, COBOL, FORTRAN and PL/I). With early generation computers, programmers were required to program in the computer's native language, called **machine language**, and this language was different for each computer manufacturer's system.

Constructing programs in machine language or assembly language is tedious and difficult, since there are many clerical details associated with the data and the instructions of the program. Constructing a program like this also requires a detailed knowledge of the computer hardware on which the program is to be processed.

Currently, most applications are programmed in one of the many popular high-level languages listed in Table 1.3. A high-level language is generally machine or computer independent; this means that programs written in a high-level language like BASIC are portable—they can easily be transferred from one computer system to another with little or no change in the programs. Furthermore, high-level languages allow the programmer to concentrate more on defining the problem and devising a solution than the machine-language requirements and details of the computer system. These are two very important characteristics that set high-level languages apart from low-level languages.

TABLE 1.3   Some Popular High-Level Languages and Their Appropriate Area of Usefulness

Language	Area of Usefulness
ADA	A programming language that encourages structured programming and is ideal for use with embedded computer systems. ADA is named in honor of Ada Lovelace, considered by many to be the world's first programmer, a close friend of Charles Babbage, a computer pioneer.*
BASIC	**B**eginner's **A**ll-purpose **S**ymbolic **I**nstruction **C**ode is a very simple problem-solving language used with personal computers or with terminals in a timesharing environment. BASIC is used for both business and scientific applications.
COBOL	The **CO**mmon **B**usiness **O**riented **L**anguage is an English-like language suitable for business data processing applications. It is especially useful for file and table handling and extensive input and output operations. COBOL is a very widely used programming language.
FORTRAN	**For**mula **Tran**slation is a problem-solving language designed primarily for scientific data processing and process control applications.
PASCAL	PASCAL, named in honor of the French mathematician Blaise Pascal, is a programming language that allows for the formulations of algorithms and data in a form which clearly exhibits their natural structure. It is primarily used for scientific applications, systems programming, and to some extent for business data processing.
PL/I	**P**rogramming **L**anguage/**I** is a problem-solving language designed for both business and scientific data processing. This language incorporates some of the best features of FORTRAN, COBOL and other languages.
RPG	**R**eport **P**rogram **G**enerator is a popular report generator designed for business data processing applications on small computer systems.

*Ada is a trademark of the United States Department of Defense (Ada Joint Program Office).

Functions of a Compiler   Computers cannot *directly* execute programs written in a high-level language like BASIC. They must first translate the high-level language instructions into equivalent machine-language instructions. Thus, when a computer is obtained from a manufacturer, it is often supplied with a number of machine-language programs, sometimes called **compilers**.

Figure 1.10 illustrates the use of a compiler to translate programs written in BASIC. When executed by a computer, a BASIC compiler will cause an entire BASIC program to be translated into machine language. This machine-language

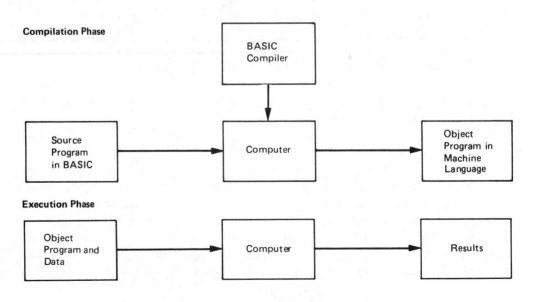

FIGURE 1.10   Compilation and execution of a BASIC program.

version of the BASIC program, often called the **object program**, is the output from the BASIC compiler. Similarly, the BASIC program, often called the **source program**, serves as input to the BASIC compiler.

When a correct BASIC program is submitted to the computer, the source program is first translated into an object program by the BASIC compiler. The conversion from a source program to an object program is **compilation**. This complete activity is the **compilation phase**.

In order to produce results or answers, the object program and data are now processed by the computer. The actual processing, such as accepting data, carrying out computations, displaying results, and so on, is the **execution**. This complete activity is the **execution phase**. The compilation and execution phases are two separate and distinct operations, as illustrated in Figure 1.10.

In the previous discussion on compilers, we assumed that the source programs and data were correct and free from error. However, in actual practice, errors can occur during the compilation process, even though a good programmer carefully reviews the program design and coding before entering it into the system. Errors necessitate modification and retrying of the program. The programmer must be able to detect and correct program errors, or **bugs**. This process is called **debugging**. Additional information on the art of debugging will be presented in subsequent chapters and in Appendix C.

Many personal computers use an **interpreter** instead of a compiler to translate programs written in BASIC. A BASIC interpreter is a machine-language program which, when executed, will cause a BASIC program to be translated and executed on a line-by-line basis to produce results or answers, all without the production of an intermediate object program.

Functions of an Interpreter

The output from an interpreter is a result or an actual answer, while the output from a compiler is an object program and not an answer of any kind. The input to the BASIC interpreter is the BASIC program, or source program.

To illustrate an application program written in the BASIC language, consider Program 1.1. This BASIC program instructs the computer to compute the average of three numbers, 17, 23 and 50.

Programming Case Study 1: Computing an Average

BASIC Program

```
100 REM PROGRAM 1.1
110 REM COMPUTING AN AVERAGE
120 REM ********************
130 LET A = (17 + 23 + 50)/3
140 PRINT "THE AVERAGE IS"; A
150 END
```

PROGRAM 1.1

System Command   `RUN`

Displayed Result   `THE AVERAGE IS 30`

The displayed answer, found below the word RUN, is 30.

Even though we are deferring detailed explanations about this program until the next chapter, Program 1.1 gives you some indication of instructing a computer to calculate a desired result using the BASIC language.

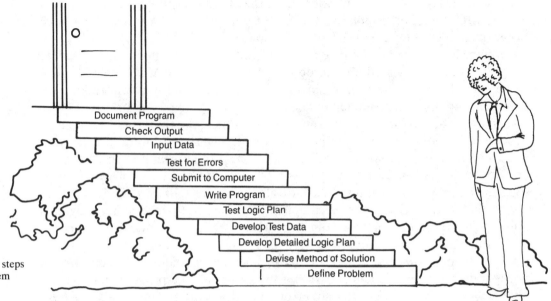

Document Program
Check Output
Input Data
Test for Errors
Submit to Computer
Write Program
Test Logic Plan
Develop Test Data
Develop Detailed Logic Plan
Devise Method of Solution
Define Problem

FIGURE 1.11 General steps required to solve a problem utilizing a computer.

1.5 PROBLEM-SOLVING AND PROGRAM DEVELOPMENT

To write a program, you must overcome two major hurdles. The first hurdle can best be described as a language barrier. That is, you must first learn the grammatical and sentence structure rules of the programming language you will use. The proper placement of commas, parentheses and statements are as critical in programming as they are in English composition. The BASIC language developed in this text is very simple. This will help you to overcome the first barrier.

The second major hurdle confronting you concerns the application of the language to the solution of a problem. Writing a composition for an English class takes experience and a certain amount of talent. The same is true if you want to write a computer program. Knowing a computer language does not mean automatic success in applying it. On the other hand, you can help yourself program well if you learn what each instruction does and how it can be used. That way you will have your tools under control before you start to work.

Every action the computer is expected to make towards solving a problem must be spelled out in detail in the program. The step-by-step procedures listed below, and shown in Figure 1.11, will help you set problems up so that the computer can solve them. These procedures make up what is called the **program development cycle**.

1) Define the problem to be solved precisely. This includes the form of the input, the form of the output and a description of the transformation of input to output. This step is called **problem analysis**.

2) Devise an **algorithm**, method of solution, the computer will use. This method must be a complete procedure for solving the specified problem, in a finite number of steps. There must be no ambiguity, no chance that something can be interpreted two ways. This step and the next three steps are called **program design**.

3) Develop a detailed logic plan using **flowcharts** or **logic diagrams** to describe each step that the computer must perform to arrive at the solution. As far as possible, the flowcharts or logic diagrams must describe *what* job is to be done and *how* the job is to be done.

4) Develop good test data. As best you can, select data that will test for erroneous input.

5) Test the logic plan. Step by step, go through the logic diagram using the test data, as if you were the computer. If the logic plan does not work, repeat steps 1 through 5.

6) Code in BASIC the logic and method of solution outlined in the logic diagram. Include program documentation. Review the code carefully before moving on to the next step.

7) Enter and submit the program to the computer.

8) Test the computer program until it is error-free and until it contains enough safeguards to ensure the desired results.

9) Run the program, using the input data to generate the results.

10) Interpret the output to see if it conforms to the problem definition. If not, steps 1 through 10 may have to be repeated until the desired results are obtained.

11) Review, and if necessary modify, the documentation within the program.

In order to solve a problem using a computer, carefully develop a method of solution and express it in great detail. It is not possible in today's technology to tell the computer to use its own judgment or, in effect to say, "If something comes up that you do not know how to handle, ask me."

A **program flowchart** is a popular logic tool used for showing an algorithm in graphic form. A program flowchart also shows how the application or job is to be accomplished by depicting a procedure for arriving at a solution.

Flowcharts

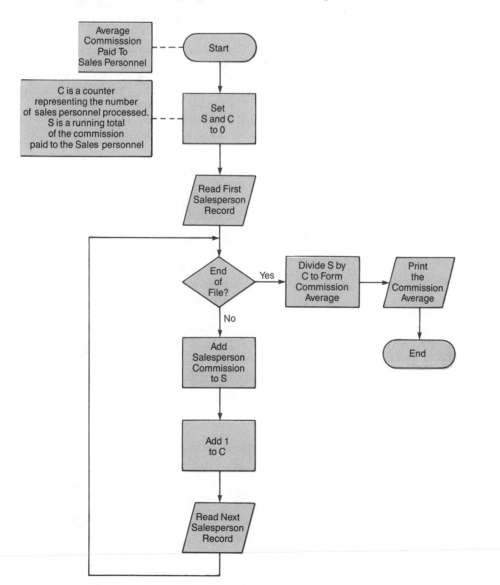

FIGURE 1.12

A programmer prepares a flowchart for a program *before* he or she begins coding it in BASIC. Eight basic symbols are used in flowcharting a program. They are given in Table 1.4 with their respective names, meanings, and some of the BASIC statements that are represented by them.

One rule that is basic to all flowcharts concerns direction. In constructing a flowchart, start at the top (or left-hand corner) of a page. The flow should be top to bottom or left to right. If the flow takes any other course, arrowheads must be used. A plastic **flowchart template** is enclosed in the back cover of this book. This template can be used to help you draw the flowchart symbols.

TABLE 1.4   Flowchart Symbols and Their Meanings

Symbol	Name	Meaning
	Process symbol	Represents the process of executing a defined operation or group of operations resulting in a change in value, form, or location of information. Examples: LET, DIM, RESTORE, RANDOMIZE, DEF and other processing statements. Also functions as the default symbol when no other symbol is available.
	Input/Output symbol	Represents an I/O function, which makes data available for processing (input) or displaying (output) of processed information. Examples: READ, INPUT, PRINT, and other I/O statements.
Left to right / Right to left / Top to bottom / Bottom to top	Flowline symbol	Represents the sequence of available information and executable operations. The lines must connect two other symbols, and the arrowheads are mandatory only for right to left and bottom to top flow.
	Annotation symbol	Represents the addition of descriptive information, comments, or explanatory notes as clarification. The vertical line and the broken line may be placed on the left as shown or on the right. Example: REM.
	Decision symbol	Represents a decision that determines which of a number of alternative paths is to be followed. Examples: WHILE, IF and ON-GOTO statements.
	Terminal symbol	The beginning, end, or a point of interruption or delay in a program. Examples: STOP, RETURN and END statements.
	Connector symbol	Any entry from, or exit to, another part of the flowchart. Also serves as off-page connector.
	Predefined Process symbol	Represents a named process consisting of one or more operations or program steps that are specified elsewhere. Examples: GOSUB and ON-GOSUB statements.

Figure 1.12 shows a flowchart which illustrates the necessary computations required to compute the average commission paid to a company's sales personnel. For an in-depth discussion on flowcharts see Appendix A, especially, for this chapter, Section A.1.

Programs are entered in one of three modes depending on the computer hardware available. First, a programmer may use a video display device connected to a central computer to enter programs, as shown in Figure 1.13. Second, a programmer may enter programs on a personal computer like the ones that appear in Figures 1.3, 1.4 and 1.14. These two modes are **interactive**, because the results will appear immediately. The third mode, **batch mode**, often entails a delay in execution from the point of submission to the time when the results are displayed. This book assumes that you are programming in one of the interactive modes.

A distinguishing feature of some interactive computer systems is their ability to provide **timesharing** between many users at terminals and the central computer.

To understand how a timesharing system works, imagine that in Figure 1.13 the computer is serving eleven users, each seated at a terminal and communicating with the system. Of these eleven users, four are running programs in the BASIC language, two in the COBOL language, one in the FORTRAN language, two in the PASCAL language; two are in the Editor, which enables them to write, correct and modify the contents in a program.

Under timesharing, two or more users can access the central computer. They all receive what seem to be simultaneous results and enjoy what seems to be total control of the computer through their terminals. In reality, the computer assigns each user a small portion or **slice** of its processing **time** and allocates service among different programs until each program has been completed. Furthermore, the computer schedules these slices of time, sometimes on a round-robin fashion, so that each user receives one at short intervals.

If a program is completely executed during the allotted slice of time, the CPU starts execution of another program. If a program is not completely executed during its allotted time, control of the CPU is given to another program and the program that was not completely executed is placed in a temporary suspended

1.6 INTERACTIVE PROCESSING

Timesharing Systems

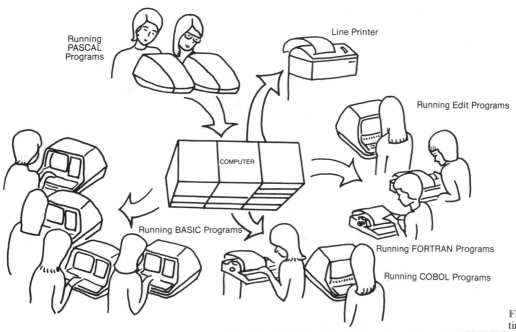

FIGURE 1.13 Users sharing time on a computer system.

FIGURE 1.14   A personal computer system.

state. The switching between many programs occurs at such a rapid rate that the user is usually unaware that execution of the program has stopped.

An interactive timesharing system must not only perform different functions for each of its users, but it must also keep these functions separate for each user and allocate and schedule the slices of time.

Personal Computers A **personal computer**, sometimes called a **microcomputer**, is a computer with a CPU which is miniaturized on a **silicon chip** typically a fraction of an inch long. The CPU, or **microprocessor**, controls the various operations of the personal computer and performs the necessary arithmetic and logic operations. Figure 1.14 illustrates the various subsystems of a personal computer.

Programs and data are normally entered through a keyboard. As Program 1.1 (Programming Case Study 1: Computing an Average) is entered through the keyboard, for example, it is transferred to main storage and displayed on the video display device.

A **printed circuit board** within the housing of the system contains the CPU, main storage, and other electronic components.

Results may be displayed on the video display device or printed on a printer. If the results and/or programs are to be saved for future reference, they may be stored in the personal computer's auxiliary storage unit, like the floppy diskette, hard disk, or cassette tape units.

Personal computers are the smallest and cheapest computers available, and they may be obtained from computer stores, department stores, and computer manufacturers. Because of their low cost and versatility, personal computers are used in a variety of business environments as well as in homes and schools.

To help you study this chapter, a summary of the topics covered in this chapter is listed below. All of these statements are true.

  1. A computer is a device that can perform substantial computation, including numerous arithmetic or logic operations, without intervention by a human operator.

  2. The major advantages of a computer are its speed and accuracy and its ability, on its own, to store and have ready for immediate recall vast amounts of data.

  3. Computers, however fast, are not built to think or reason. They extend our intellect, but they do not replace thinking.

  4. Computer hardware is the physical equipment of a computer system.

  5. A computer has five subsystems—input, output, main storage, auxiliary storage and the central processing unit.

  6. An input unit allows programs and data to enter the computer system.

  7. Main storage is the computer's storage unit, where instructions and data are stored for processing purposes.

  8. The central processing unit (CPU) controls and supervises the entire computer system and performs the actual arithmetic and logic operations on data as specified by the written program. The CPU is made up of two sections—the arithmetic-logic section and the control section.

  9. The arithmetic-logic section performs the arithmetic operations and carries out the decision-making operations required by a program.

  10. The control section directs and coordinates the entire computer system.

  11. The auxiliary storage unit stores data and programs that are to be used over and over again.

  12. An output unit is used by the computer to communicate the results of a program.

  13. A computer program is a series of instructions required to complete a procedure or task. When these instructions are placed into the main storage unit of a computer, they are a stored program.

  14. Computer software is a program or a set of programs written for a computer.

  15. Programming languages are classified as low-level languages (like machine language and assembly language) and high-level languages (like BASIC, PASCAL, COBOL, FORTRAN and PL/I).

  16. Computers cannot directly execute programs written in a high-level language like BASIC. They must first translate the BASIC instructions into equivalent machine-language instructions through the use of a BASIC compiler or interpreter.

  17. Program errors are bugs. The process of correcting errors in a program is debugging. In order to prevent bugs, good programmers carefully review the program design and coding before entering it into the system.

  18. The program development cycle is a set of step-by-step procedures used to solve a problem.

  19. During problem analysis, defining the problem is the first step in solving it.

  20. Program design is made up of four steps—devising a method of solution, drawing logic diagrams, selecting good test data and testing the logic.

  21. A BASIC program should be coded only after the design is complete and has been carefully reviewed and tested.

  22. A program flowchart is a popular logic tool used for showing an algorithm in graphic form.

  23. A distinguishing feature of some interactive computer systems is their ability to provide timesharing between many users at terminals and the central computer.

  24. Under timesharing, two or more users can access the central computer and receive what seem to be simultaneous results.

  25. A personal computer has a CPU on a single silicon chip.

1.8
TEST YOUR
BASIC SKILLS
(Even-numbered
answers in the back of
the book.)

1. State three major advantages that computers have over the manual computation of problems.
2. What are the basic subsystems of a computer system? Briefly describe the function of each subsystem.
3. What makes up the central processing unit?
4. Name two devices that serve as both input and output devices.
5. What is the difference between main storage and auxiliary storage? Name two common auxiliary storage devices.
6. What is meant by the term hardware? Software?
7. Why is its ability to store programs so critical to the success of a computer system?
8. Name and discuss briefly some of the low-level and high-level languages available to programmers today.
9. List the high-level programming languages discussed in Chapter 1 and the area of data processing applications in which they are primarily used.
10. What is the function of the compilation phase? Execution phase?
11. What is the difference between a source program and an object program?
12. Do computers think? Explain your answer.
13. Name one company in your area that has a computer. List three applications commonly run on it.
14. What have you or your family received in the mail recently that has been computer-generated?
15. Draw one flowchart which enables the Mechanical Man to accomplish efficiently the objectives in both phases 1 and 2 as illustrated in Figure 1.15.
   The Mechanical Man possesses the following properties:

   A) He does *nothing* unless given a specific instruction.
   B) His abilities are restricted to carrying out a limited repertoire of these instructions.
   C) He can carry out such instructions *one at a time*.
   D) He understands the following instructions:

   1) *Physical Movement:*
      a) Stand up (into an erect position without moving feet)
      b) Sit down (into a sitting position without moving feet)
      c) Take one step (forward only; steps are always a fixed integer length and can be made only if Man is standing up)
      d) Raise arms (into one fixed position, straight ahead)

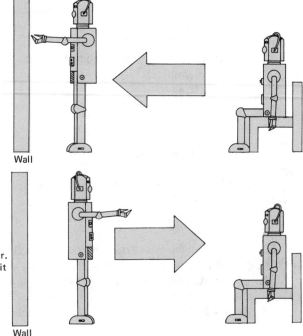

Phase 1:   The Mechanical Man is seated at an unknown integer number of steps from the wall. He will stand up and walk forward until he touches the wall with his fingertips. In a seated position with arms raised, his fingertips are aligned with the tips of his shoes.

Wall

Phase 2:   After touching the wall, the Mechanical Man will return to his chair. Since the chair is too low for him to sense by touch, he can get to it only by going back exactly as many steps as he came forward.

Wall

FIGURE 1.15

e) Lower arms (into one fixed position, straight down at his sides)
f) Turn right (in place without taking a step and can be made only if Man is
standing up; all right turns are 90 degree turns)

2) *Arithmetic:*
a) Add one (to a total that is being developed)
b) Subtract one (from a total that is being developed)
c) Record total (any number of totals can be remembered in this way)

3) *Logic:* The Man can decide what instruction he will carry out next, based on
the following:
a) Arithmetic results
   i) Is the result positive?
   ii) Is the result negative?
   iii) Is the result zero?
   iv) Is the result equal to a predetermined amount?
b) Physical status
   i) Are the raised arms touching anything?

16. Selecting test data and carefully reviewing the design before coding the program are
important steps to ensure that the program will work. Consider the flowchart in Figure
1.16 and the following list of test data items:

1, 2, 3, 2, 1, 1, 2, 2, 1, 3

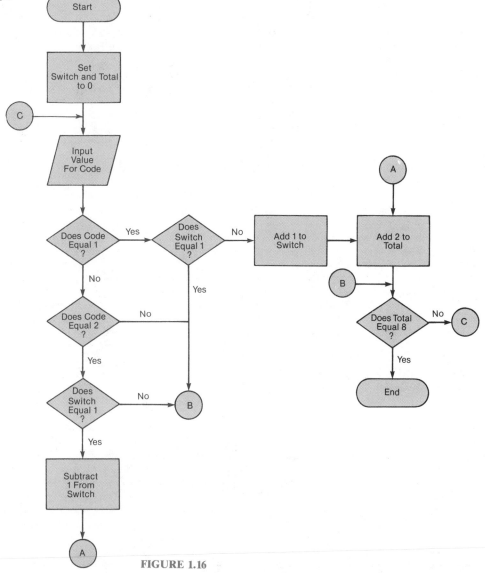

FIGURE 1.16

Assume that each time you come across the input symbol the next data item, beginning at the left, is assigned to Code.

    a) How many data items are used before the program ends?

    b) What is the value of Switch when the program ends?

    c) What is the value of Total when the program ends?

17. Construct the flowchart to calculate a weekly payroll using the following rules:

    a) Time and one half is paid for hours worked in excess of 40.

    b) $38.46 is allowed as nontaxable income for each dependent claimed.

    c) The withholding tax is 20 percent of the taxable income.

    d) Assume the end-of-file is defined as the condition where the value for the number of hours worked is negative.

For each employee input the following information:

    a) Name

    b) Hourly rate of pay

    c) Number of hours worked

    d) Number of dependents

For each employee output the following information:

    a) Name

    b) Gross pay

    c) Net pay

    d) Income tax withheld

BASIC: AN INTRODUCTION 2

The purpose of Chapter 2 is to develop some of the rules of the BASIC programming language that are common to all BASIC programs and to introduce some elementary BASIC statements. This chapter concentrates on "simple" **straight-line** program illustrations, input/output operations and system commands. A straight-line program is one in which statements are executed in sequence one after the other until the last statement of the program is reached. Upon successful completion of Chapter 2 you should be able to develop some elementary BASIC programs for submission to a computer.

2.1 COMPOSING A BASIC PROGRAM

The word BASIC is an acronym for Beginner's All-Purpose Symbolic Instruction Code. The BASIC language is a problem-solving language with wide applications in business, scientific and educational environments. It is simple and easy to learn, but it is powerful and flexible enough for most applications.

The BASIC language was developed in 1963 at Dartmouth College in a project sponsored by the National Science Foundation and directed by Professors John G. Kemeny and Thomas E. Kurtz. BASIC was originally developed to be used by non-programmers in a timesharing environment and to serve as the first programming language for beginning students in a wide spectrum of disciplines. Today, BASIC is used in a variety of computer systems, including all personal computers.

The BASIC Language

You must use a two-fold approach to master BASIC. First, you will master the grammatical rules of the language, like how to write statements. Second, you will master the **logical rules**, like which statements should precede which other statements in a program. BASIC is similar to English in that both have rules of grammar and rules of sentence and paragraph structure. The exercises in this book should be worked, therefore, with close attention both to grammatical detail and to structure—that is, to the logical position of each statement in the overall set of statements.

Mastering BASIC

General Characteristics of a BASIC Program

A BASIC program is composed of:

1) A sequence of lines
2) The last of which contains the END statement

Each line contains a unique **line number** which serves as a label for the statement (see Figure 2.1). A line number followed by a statement is a **line**, as indicated by the example below:

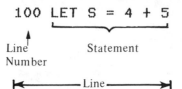

FIGURE 2.1   The general form of a BASIC program.

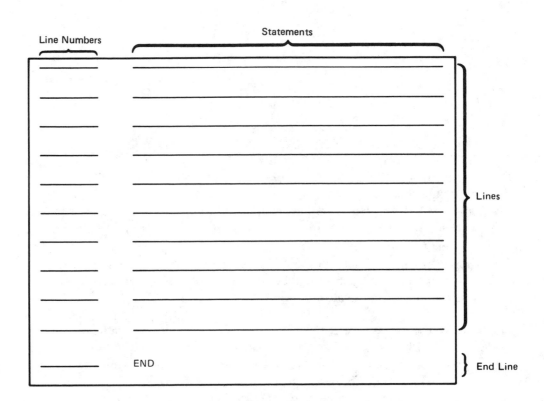

Programming Case Study 2: Determining a Salesperson's Commission

The following problem illustrates the composition of a BASIC program.

Most salespeople work on a commission basis. Their earned commissions are often determined by multiplying their assigned commission rate by the amount of dollar sales. The dollar sales amount is computed by deducting any returned sales from the sum of their weekly sales. Assuming a biweekly period, the earned commission can thus be determined from the following formula:

Earned Commission = Rate × (Week 1 Sales + Week 2 Sales − Returns)

For the biweekly period, a salesperson's assigned commision rate is 15% and sales are $1200 the first week, $1500 the second week. The returned sales are $75.

BASIC Program 2.1 instructs the system to compute the earned amount and display it on an output device. The earned commission of 393.75 is just below a **system command** RUN.

BASIC Program	`100 LET E = 0.15 * (1200 + 1500 - 75)`
	`110 PRINT E`
	`120 END`

System Command	`RUN`
Displayed Result	`393.75`

PROGRAM 2.1

There are three lines in this program. The first statement, LET E = 0.15 * (1200 + 1500 − 75), is a LET statement. The LET statement consists of the **keyword** LET, a **variable name** E, an **equal sign**, four **constants** (0.15, 1200, 1500 and 75), and three **arithmetic operators** (* , + and −).

A keyword has special meaning to BASIC. It informs BASIC of the type of statement to be executed. In Program 2.1, there are three keywords—LET, PRINT and END. Every statement in BASIC begins with a keyword.*

In programming, a **variable** is a storage location in main memory whose **value** can change as the program is executed. In Program 2.1, the variable name E references the storage location assigned to it by BASIC. The statement LET E = 0.15 * (1200 + 1500 − 75) instructs the system to complete the arithmetic operations and assign the resulting value of 393.75 to E.

All BASIC systems allow variable names to be one or two characters in length. The first character must be a letter (A–Z). If a second character is used, this character must be numeric (0–9). X, Y, E, A1, C2 and F0 are valid variable names. As you will see in Chapter 3, many BASIC systems expand on these rules to allow for more meaningful variable names.

The equal sign in any LET statement means that the value of the variable to the left of the equal sign is to be replaced by the final value to the right of the equal sign.

Constants, like 0.15, 1200, 1500 and 75, represent ordinary numbers that do not change during the execution of a program.

TABLE 2.1   The Five Arithmetic Operators

Arithmetic Operator	Meaning	Examples of Usage	Meaning of the Examples
+	Addition	3.14 + 2.9	Add 3.14 and 2.9
−	Subtraction	S − 35.4	Subtract 35.4 from the value of S
*	Multiplication	600.00 * A1	Multiply the value of A1 by 600.00
/	Division	H/10	Divide the value of H by 10
∧	Exponentiation	2 ∧ 3	Raise 2 to the third power

The plus sign (+) in Program 2.1 signifies addition between the two constants representing the weekly sales. The minus sign (−) indicates subtraction of the returned sales from the sum of the weekly sales. The asterisk (*) indicates multiplication between the rate and the actual sales. All five arithmetic operators are given in Table 2.1. As is the case in mathematics, the set of parentheses is used to override the normal sequence of arithmetic operations.

The second statement in Program 2.1 is called a PRINT statement. PRINT statements instruct the system to bring a result out from main storage and display it

---

* The keyword LET is optional on some BASIC systems.

on an output device. The statement causes the computer to display 393.75, the value of E.

The END Statement

The last line of Program 2.1, the end line, includes the END statement. When executed, the END statement instructs the system to stop executing the program. While most BASIC systems do not require an end line, it is recommended that you always include one. The end line serves the following two purposes:

1) It marks the physical end of a program.
2) It terminates the execution of the program.

Line Numbers

Every line in a BASIC program must begin with a unique line number. In this book, a line number must be an integer between 1 and 32767, though some BASIC systems allow for a greater range. A line number must not contain a leading sign, embedded spaces, commas, decimal points or any other punctuation. Line numbers are used in BASIC to:

1) Indicate the **sequence** of statement execution
2) Provide control points for branching, a topic discussed in Chapters 4 and 5
3) Add, change and delete statements

Many experienced BASIC programmers begin with 100, as in Program 2.1, and then increase each new statement's line number by 10. This leaves room to insert up to 9 possible extra statements between the numbers at a later time. Table 2.2 illustrates some valid and invalid line numbers.

TABLE 2.2   Some Valid and Invalid Line Numbers

Example	Comment
`35 LET X = 15/7`	Valid.
`035 LET C = 0`	Valid.
`+40 LET B = Q - C`	Invalid. Line number must be unsigned.
`50. LET D = 10 * E`	Invalid. Line number must not contain any decimal points.
`70.4 PRINT K`	Invalid. Line number must not contain a decimal fraction.
`80B PRINT D, X`	Invalid. Line number must not contain any letters.
`5,000 END`	Invalid. Line number must not contain any commas.
`9999 END`	Valid.

The system command RUN, found just below Program 2.1, instructs the system to execute the program. It is not part of the program itself and, therefore, it does not have a line number. A detailed discussion of the RUN command can be found in Section 2.7. For now, remember that BASIC statements have line numbers, and system commands don't!

Some Relationships Between Statements

The PRINT statement in Program 2.1 would display a result of zero if, earlier in the program, we had failed to instruct the system to assign a value to the variable E. In other words, the system cannot correctly display the value of E before it determines this value. Therefore, if Program 2.1 were incorrectly *written*, as below, it would not be correctly *executed* by the system, unless by chance the earned commission was zero.

Invalid

```
100 PRINT E
110 LET E = 0.15 * (1200 + 1500 - 75)
120 END
```

This program is incorrect for the same reason:

Invalid
```
100 LET D = 0.15 * (1200 + 1500 - 75)
110 PRINT E
120 END
```

The variable E in line 110 has not been assigned a value earlier in the program. The system will calculate a value of 393.75 for D, but display a result of zero. BASIC automatically assigns all variables in a program a value of zero when the system command RUN is issued.

The correct program can be written as Program 2.1 or as Program 2.2.

```
100 LET D = 0.15 * (1200 + 1500 - 75)
110 PRINT D
120 END
```
PROGRAM 2.2

```
RUN

 393.75
```

Using the variable name D is no different from using the variable name E, as long as the same name is used consistently. The relationship between output statements, like the PRINT statement, and other statements in the Program can now be stated as follows:

OUTPUT **Rule 1:** Every variable appearing in an output statement should appear at least once earlier in the program in such a way that its value can be determined.

You will see in later chapters that, although the flexibility of the language permits certain statements to be placed anywhere in a program, logic, common sense and **structured style** dictate where these statements are placed. Structured style is nothing more than disciplined, consistent programming. Discipline and consistency help programmers construct readable, maintainable and reliable programs. Often, the style of structured programs is determined by someone in authority, like a supervisor.

2.2
THE INPUT
STATEMENT

One of the major tasks of any computer program is to integrate the data to be processed into the program. In Program 2.1 the data was included directly in the LET statement as constants.

```
100 LET E = 0.15 * (1200 + 1500 - 75)
110 PRINT E
120 END
```
PROGRAM 2.1

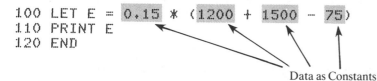

Data as Constants

Although this technique works, it has its limitations. For example, line 100 must be completely retyped for each new salesperson processed. An alternative method of integrating the data into the program is shown in Program 2.3.

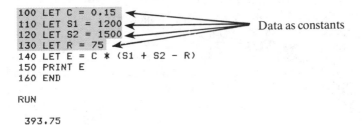

```
100 LET C = 0.15
110 LET S1 = 1200
120 LET S2 = 1500
130 LET R = 75
140 LET E = C * (S1 + S2 - R)
150 PRINT E
160 END
```
Data as constants

PROGRAM 2.3

```
RUN

   393.75
```

In this new program, data in the form of constants has been assigned to the variables C, S1, S2 and R. Line 140, used to calculate the earned commission, contains the variables that have been assigned the data in lines 100 through 130. When it executes Program 2.3, the system must be informed of the numeric values for C, S1, S2 and R before it can calculate a value for E.

Thus we have:

> **Arithmetic Rule 1:** Every variable appearing to the right of the equal sign in a LET statement should appear at least once earlier in the same program in such a way that its value is determined.

This means that the variables to the right of the equal sign should be defined before the system executes the LET statement containing their names.

This second method of integrating the data into the program has the same limitations as Program 2.1. That is, lines 100 through 130 would have to be modified in order to process a new salesperson. The only advantage to Program 2.3 is that the LET statement itself in line 140 will work for any salesperson.

A third way to integrate data into the program is through the use of the INPUT statement. The INPUT statement provides for assignment of data to variables from a source outside the program during execution. The data is supplied to the program *after* the command RUN has been executed.

Through the use of the INPUT statement, the solution to Programming Case Study 2 can be made more general for calculating the earned commission for any salesperson, no matter what his or her commission rate, weekly sales or returned sales. One version of the rewritten program is shown as Program 2.4.

```
100 INPUT C, S1, S2, R
110 LET E = C * (S1 + S2 - R)
120 PRINT E
130 END
```

PROGRAM 2.4

```
RUN

? 0.15, 1200, 1500, 75
  393.75
```

Data is entered in response to input prompt.

The input prompt displayed by line 100

The function of the INPUT statement in line 100 is to display an **input prompt** and suspend execution of the program until data has been supplied. Most BASIC systems display a question mark (?) followed by a single space for the input prompt. Then it is up to the user to supply the data. It is necessary that the carriage return key be pressed following entry of the data, as shown below.

```
? 0.15, 1200, 1500, 75   Enter
```

If the carriage return key is not pressed, the program will remain suspended indefinitely.

The key on the keyboard that functions as the carriage return key varies from one system to another. The following list indicates the name of the carriage return key on some popular computer systems.

Computer Systems	Carriage Return Key
Apple	RETURN
COMMODORE	RETURN
DEC systems	RETURN
IBM PC	←
Macintosh	RETURN
TRS-80	ENTER

Unless we are discussing specific types of computer systems, we will refer to the carriage return key as the Enter key from now on.

Once the necessary data is supplied, line 110 determines the earned commission, line 120 prints the earned commission and, finally, line 130 terminates the program.

This third alternative of integrating data into a program, by means of the INPUT statement, is far more efficient than the other two alternatives, because we can process other sales personnel without modifying statements within the program. For example, to determine the earned commission for three salespeople, we can run the program three times, as shown below.

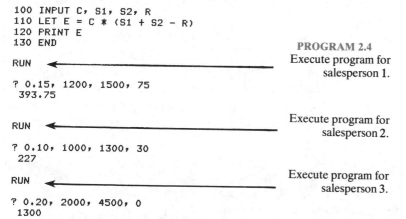

```
100 INPUT C, S1, S2, R
110 LET E = C * (S1 + S2 - R)
120 PRINT E
130 END
```

PROGRAM 2.4

```
RUN    ←
```
Execute program for
    salesperson 1.
```
? 0.15, 1200, 1500, 75
 393.75
```

```
RUN    ←
```
Execute program for
    salesperson 2.
```
? 0.10, 1000, 1300, 30
 227
```

```
RUN    ←
```
Execute program for
    salesperson 3.
```
? 0.20, 2000, 4500, 0
 1300
```

It is important that the variables in the INPUT statement and the data supplied in response to the input prompt be separated by commas. In BASIC, a comma is used to establish a **list**, which is a set of distinct elements, each separated from the next by a comma. The punctuation must be used so that the system can distinguish how many variables or data elements occur in each list. The order of the list of variables in the INPUT statement is also important. The INPUT statement in Program 2.4

```
100 INPUT C, S1, S2, R
```

may have been written as

```
100 INPUT R, S2, S1, C
```

If so, however, the data supplied for Salesperson 1 must be entered as

```
? 75, 1500, 1200, 0.15
```

To ensure that the data is entered in its proper order, most computer systems allow for an **input prompt message** to be placed in the INPUT statement. When the system executes an INPUT statement containing an input prompt message, the message is displayed on the output device. Execution is then suspended until the data is supplied. To simplify the entries, the following program requests one entry per INPUT statement:

PROGRAM 2.5

```
100 INPUT "WHAT IS THE COMMISSION RATE"; C
110 INPUT "WHAT IS THE WEEK 1 SALES"; S1
120 INPUT "WHAT IS THE WEEK 2 SALES"; S2
130 INPUT "WHAT IS THE RETURN SALES"; R
140 LET E = C * (S1 + S2 - R)
150 PRINT E
160 END

RUN

WHAT IS THE COMMISSION RATE? 0.15
WHAT IS THE WEEK 1 SALES? 1200
WHAT IS THE WEEK 2 SALES? 1500
WHAT IS THE RETURN SALES? 75
 393.75
```

When line 100 is executed in Program 2.5, the system displays the input prompt message:

WHAT IS THE COMMISSION RATE?

After displaying the input prompt message, the system suspends execution of the program until a response is entered. The system reacts the same for lines 110 through 130 as it did for line 100.

After the last data item is entered for line 130, line 140 determines the earned commission. Then line 150 displays the earned commission and, finally, line 160 terminates the program.

The quotation marks surrounding the input prompt message and the semicolon separating the message from the variable in lines 100 through 130 are required punctuation. Table 2.3 gives the general form of the INPUT statement. The INPUT statement consists of the keyword INPUT followed by an optional input prompt message followed by a list of variables separated by mandatory commas. Here is the rule for determining the placement of the INPUT statement in a program:

> INPUT **Rule 1:** Every variable appearing in the program whose value is directly obtained through input must be listed in an INPUT statement before it is used elsewhere in the program.

TABLE 2.3   The INPUT **Statement**

General Form: INPUT variable, . . . , variable
    or
    INPUT "input prompt message"; variable, . . . , variable

Purpose: Provides for the assignment of values to variables from a source external to the program.

Examples:	*Input Statements*	*Data from an External Source*
	100 INPUT A	23.5
	115 INPUT X, Y, Z	2, 4, 6
	300 INPUT A$, B	GROSS, -2.73
	400 INPUT "PLEASE ENTER THE SALES TAX"; T	0.05
	500 INPUT "WHAT IS YOUR NAME"; N$	JOHN
	600 INPUT "ENTER PART NUMBER"; P	1289

Note: In the second General Form, a question mark is displayed when a semicolon is used after the INPUT prompt message. In Microsoft BASIC, using a comma instead of a semicolon suppresses the question mark.

The INPUT statement allows the user complete interaction with the computer while the program is executed. The main use of the INPUT statement is found in applications that involve:

1) Small amounts of data to be entered into a program

2) Data input that is dependent on the output or conditions of previous parts of a program

3) The processing of data as it occurs in an interactive or on-line processing environment

This section on the INPUT statement has introduced you to one method of assigning values to variables in a program. In later chapters we will discuss two other methods that are used to process data, the READ-DATA statements in Chapter 4 and the use of data files, presented in Chapter 8.

One of the functions of the PRINT statement is to display the values of variables defined earlier in a program. You should understand by now that the following:

2.3
THE PRINT AND CLEAR SCREEN STATEMENTS

```
100 LET X = 10
110 PRINT X
```

displays 10, the *value* of X, and not the letter X. The PRINT statement can also be used to display messages that identify a program result, as it is here:

```
100 INPUT "WHAT IS THE COMMISSION RATE"; C
110 INPUT "WHAT IS THE WEEK 1 SALES"; S1
120 INPUT "WHAT IS THE WEEK 2 SALES"; S2
130 INPUT "WHAT IS THE RETURN SALES"; R
140 LET E = C * (S1 + S2 - R)
150 PRINT "THE EARNED COMMISSION IS"; E
160 END

RUN

WHAT IS THE COMMISSION RATE? 0.15
WHAT IS THE WEEK 1 SALES? 1200
WHAT IS THE WEEK 2 SALES? 1500
WHAT IS THE RETURN SALES? 75
THE EARNED COMMISSION IS 393.75
```

PROGRAM 2.6

Line 150 in Program 2.6 instructs the computer to display the message THE EARNED COMMISSION IS followed by the value of E. As with the INPUT statement, it is necessary in a PRINT statement to begin and end a message with quotation marks. The quotation marks in a PRINT statement serve to inform BASIC that the item to be displayed is a message rather than a variable.

The semicolon following the message in line 150 instructs the system to keep the **cursor** on the same line instead of positioning it on the next line. The cursor is a movable, blinking marker (like a line or block) on the video screen that indicates where the next point of character entry, change or display will be. For example, the contents of line 150 can be written on two separate lines:

```
150 PRINT "THE EARNED COMMISSION IS"
155 PRINT E
160 END
```

The system displays the message found in line 150 and positions the cursor on the left margin of the next line. The value of E is then displayed on the line below the message:

```
THE EARNED COMMISSION IS
 393.75
```

BASIC displays a numeric value which consists of a sign, the decimal representation and a **trailing space**. Appearing immediately before the number, the sign is a **leading space** if the number is positive and a leading minus sign if the number is negative.* The space following the message displayed by line 150 in Program 2.6 represents the sign of the variable E.

```
THE COMMISSION EARNED IS 393.75
```

⌐─────────────A space here indicates that 393.75 is positive.

One of the responsibilities of the programmer is to ensure that the prompt messages and results are meaningful and easy to read. This is especially true of video display devices found on personal computer systems. A cluttered screen on a video display device can make it difficult for you to locate necessary information. Most personal computer systems include a BASIC statement to clear the screen, which erases all the information on the screen and places the cursor in the upper left corner of the screen.

TABLE 2.4   The Clear Screen Statement

General Form:	Depends on the computer system you have.

Computer	General Form
Apple	HOME
COMMODORE	PRINT "Press Shift and CLR HOME keys"
DEC Rainbow	PRINT CHR$(27); "[H"; CHR$(27); "[OJ"
DEC VAX-11	PRINT CHR$(27); "[H"; CHR$(27); "[OJ"
IBM PC	CLS
Macintosh	CLS
TRS-80	CLS

Purpose:	Erases all the information on the screen and places the cursor in the upper left corner of the screen.
Examples:	For the IBM, Macintosh and TRS-80:

```
100 CLS
600 CLS
```

The general form of the Clear Screen statement is found in Table 2.4. As shown in Table 2.4, different computer manufacturers use different statements to clear the screen. The following program incorporates the Clear Screen statement, CLS.

```
100 CLS
110 INPUT "WHAT IS THE COMMISSION RATE"; C
120 INPUT "WHAT IS THE WEEK 1 SALES"; S1
130 INPUT "WHAT IS THE WEEK 2 SALES"; S2
140 INPUT "WHAT IS THE RETURN SALES"; R
150 LET E = C * (S1 + S2 - R)
160 PRINT
170 PRINT "THE EARNED COMMISSION IS"; E
180 END

RUN

WHAT IS THE COMMISSION RATE? 0.15
WHAT IS THE WEEK 1 SALES? 1200
WHAT IS THE WEEK 2 SALES? 1500
WHAT IS THE RETURN SALES? 75

THE EARNED COMMISSION IS 393.75
```

PROGRAM 2.7

When the RUN command is issued for Program 2.7, the system clears the screen and then displays the input prompt message WHAT IS THE COMMISSION RATE on line 1. After obtaining a response through the keyboard, the

---

*The Apple computer does not display a leading space when the number is positive; nor does it automatically display a trailing space after the number.

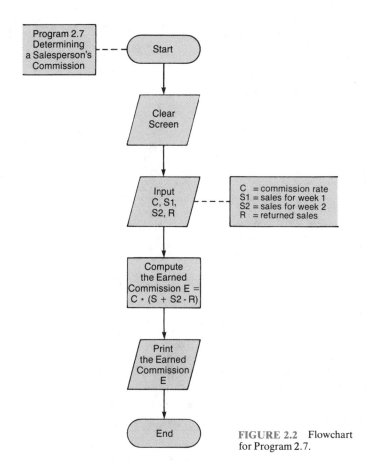

FIGURE 2.2 Flowchart
for Program 2.7.

system displays the next input prompt message on line 2, and the rest of the
program is executed.

The Clear Screen statement clears the screen, but it does not clear main
memory. After you have entered the RUN command and the output results are
displayed, you may again display the program by entering the LIST command. A
detailed discussion of the LIST command can be found in Section 2.7.

Line 160, which contains a PRINT statement without a list, shows how to instruct the system to display a blank line to separate the input prompt messages from
the results. A **null list** like this causes the PRINT statement to display a blank line.

The flowchart that corresponds to Program 2.7 is shown in Figure 2.2. The
flowchart does not have to include a symbol for each statement in the program. the
four INPUT statements are logically illustrated by the single I/O symbol just after
the symbol representing the action which clears the screen.

The PRINT and CLS statements were introduced in this section. In Chapter 4,
the PRINT statement will be presented in greater detail, along with the PRINT
USING statement. Together, these two statements allow greater flexibility in
selecting the type of format to display output.

In the preceding programs, only one BASIC statement is written on each line, and
the first letter in each statement is always written under the first letter of the
statement above it. A program written in such a form is usually easier to read and
debug; as you will discover now, however, this is—in certain respects—only an
optional practice.

**2.4
CODING AND
DOCUMENTING**

CODING FORM WITH PROGRAM 2.8

1	2	3	4	5	6	7	8	9	10	11	12	13	14	15	16	17	18	19	20	21	22	23	24	25	26	27	28	29	30	31	32	33	34	35	36	37	38	39	40	41	42	43	44	45	46	47	48	49	50	51	52	53

```
100 REM PROGRAM 2.8
110 REM J. S. QUASNEY
120 REM DETERMINING A SALESPERSON'S COMMISSION
130 REM ****************************************
140 REM CLEAR SCREEN
150 CLS
160 REM REQUEST DATA FROM OPERATOR
170 INPUT "WHAT IS THE COMMISSION RATE"; C
180 INPUT "WHAT IS THE WEEK 1 SALES"; S1
190 INPUT "WHAT IS THE WEEK 2 SALES"; S2
200 INPUT "WHAT IS THE RETURN SALES"; R
210 REM CALCULATE THE EARNED COMMISSION (E)
220 LET E = C * (S1 + S2 - R)
230 REM DISPLAY THE EARNED COMMISSION
240 PRINT
250 PRINT "THE EARNED COMMISSION IS"; E
260 END
```

FIGURE 2.3

Coding Techniques

A BASIC program may be written on an ordinary sheet of paper. However, it is sometimes more convenient to write it on a specially printed sheet of paper called a **coding form**. Figure 2.3 shows Program 2.8 written on a coding form.

The coding form is divided into columns identified by the numbers near the top of the form. When constructing a BASIC statement, place the first digit of the line number in column one. The first letter in each statement, like the L in LET is customarily printed after spacing over one position from the line number. For clarity, all programs in this book will be printed as though, with respect to **position**, they were hand-printed on a coding form, even though the coding form will not be shown.

The **space**, or **blank**, is also a character. It is obtained on a keyboard by pressing the space bar once for each blank character desired. The blank character may be used freely to improve the appearance of the program. A useful rule of thumb for blank characters is this: leave spaces in a BASIC statement in the same places that you would leave spaces in an English sentence. Spaces in line 100 of Program 2.1 yield

```
100 LET E = 0.15 * (1200 + 1500 - 75)
```

which is much more readable than:

```
100 LETE=0.15*(1200+1500-75)
```

Spaces should not appear at the beginning of a line, within line numbers, within keywords, within numeric constants or within variable names.

Documenting a Program—The REM Statement

Documentation is the readable description of what a program or procedure within a program is supposed to do. More often than not, programmers are asked to support the programs they write by means of **internal comments**. Documentation is used to identify programs and clarify parts of a program that would otherwise be difficult for others to understand. In this section the means by which a BASIC program can be internally documented will be discussed.

The REM Statements, in Program 2.8, lines 100 through 140, 160, 210 and 230, are called **remark lines**. The remark line consists of some comment or explanation intended solely for humans. The keyword REM, when present after a line number, designates the line as a remark line. A REM statement can be located anywhere before the END statement.

```
100 REM PROGRAM 2.8
110 REM J. S. QUASNEY
120 REM DETERMINING A SALESPERSON'S COMMISSION
130 REM ****************************************
140 REM CLEAR SCREEN
150 CLS
160 REM REQUEST DATA FROM OPERATOR
170 INPUT "WHAT IS THE COMMISSION RATE"; C
180 INPUT "WHAT IS THE WEEK 1 SALES"; S1
190 INPUT "WHAT IS THE WEEK 2 SALES"; S2
200 INPUT "WHAT IS THE RETURN SALES"; R
210 REM CALCULATE THE EARNED COMMISSION (E)
220 LET E = C * (S1 + S2 - R)
230 REM DISPLAY THE EARNED COMMISSION
240 PRINT
250 PRINT "THE EARNED COMMISSION IS"; E
260 END

RUN

WHAT IS THE COMMISSION RATE? 0.15
WHAT IS THE WEEK 1 SALES? 1200
WHAT IS THE WEEK 2 SALES? 1500
WHAT IS THE RETURN SALES? 75

THE EARNED COMMISSION IS 393.75
```

PROGRAM 2.8

REM statements have no effect on the execution of a BASIC program. Note that Program 2.8, which includes REM statements, and Program 2.7, which does not, both produce the same results.

The general form for the REM statement is found in Table 2.5.

TABLE 2.5 **The REM Statement**

General Form:	REM comment
Purpose:	To insert explanatory comments in a program for documentary purposes.
Examples:	110 REM J. S. QUASNEY 160 REM DETERMINE THE BALANCE DUE 200 REM PROGRAM 2.7 250 REM 300 REM ************************

Another method of documenting a program is to place remarks or comments on the right-hand side of a BASIC statement. In order to distinguish between a BASIC statement and a comment on the same line, some BASIC systems require the insertion of an apostrophe (') or an exclamation point (!) before the comment. For example, line 220 in Program 2.8 may be written as follows:

```
220 LET E = C * (S1 + S2 - R)      ' E IS THE EARNED COMMISSION
                                   ↑
                        Indicates the beginning of a comment
```

When the BASIC system encounters an apostrophe in a line, it stops processing that line and ignores any comments that follow. This book uses REM statements to provide internal documentation for the majority of the programs.

Shown below are a few basic suggestions for including explanatory remarks in a program.

Tips on Internal Documentation of a Program

1) Write and include your remarks as you code the program.

2) Write a prologue, including the program name, date, author and any other desirable remarks, at the beginning of each program. See the Introduction to the Programming Exercises at the end of Chapter 2.

3) Remark lines should come before any major procedure in a program. It is better for the remarks to be clear than terse and cloudy.

4) Remark lines should not duplicate codes. They should explain the purpose of a section of code.

5) Variables should be defined when it is not apparent what they represent.

6) Remark lines should be inserted into areas of a program only where the code is not self-explanatory. Do not insert remarks for the sake of remarks. Insert remarks to make your program readable.

7) For the sake of appearance, highlight a group of remark lines by adding a series of asterisks or other special characters as the last remark line.

Multiple Statements Per Line   Most BASIC systems allow you to write multiple statements per line. That is, Program 2.1 can be rewritten as the following:

```
100 REM PROGRAM 2.1
110 LET E = 0.15 * (1200 + 1500 - 75) : PRINT E : END
```

Note that the statements in line 110 are separated by colons. The purpose of the colon is to inform the system that a statement has ended and that a new statement follows on the same line.

Do not precede any statement with a REM statement when using multiple statements per line. BASIC considers all characters following the keyword REM to be a comment, including of course, the colon. The following one line program would be considered a comment by BASIC.

```
100 REM PROGRAM 2.1 : LET E = 0.15 * (1200 + 1500 - 75) : PRINT E : END
```

For the purpose of readability, it is recommended that you use this technique sparingly.

2.5 GETTING ON THE COMPUTER

To enter a BASIC program like Program 2.8 into the computer system, you must first familiarize yourself with the procedures for **getting on** (**logging on**) the computer. In most instances, the input device will be a keyboard. As a program is entered, not only is it transmitted to main storage, but the program is also displayed on the output device associated with the keyboard.

Logging on a Timesharing System   In Section 1.6 we discussed timesharing. Recall that in such an environment there are many terminals connected to the same computer system. Most timesharing systems are designed so that only authorized people can use them. Authorized users are assigned an account number and password.

Table 2.6 presents a summary of the log-on procedures that are common to most timesharing systems.

TABLE 2.6   The Typical Log-on Procedures Found with Timesharing Systems

1) Turn ON the power to the terminal.
2) Press the Enter key
3) Enter your account number and press the Enter key.
4) Enter your password and press the Enter key. The password is not normally displayed on the output device.

Following a successful log-on, the system displays on your terminal a special character, like a dollar sign ($), which is called the **system prompt**. When you see the special character on your terminal, type the word BASIC and press the Enter key.

$ BASIC

System prompt   You enter

The system responds by displaying the word READY. To key in a new program, enter the command NEW and the name you wish to call the program and press the Enter key.

NEW PROG1

You enter this

The system responds with READY and you can begin entering the lines of your BASIC program.

Figure 2.4 illustrates a program entered and executed via a terminal in a timesharing environment.

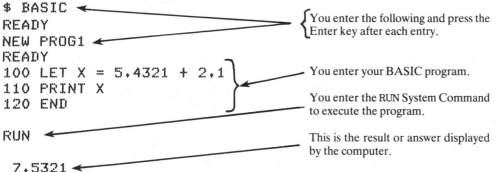

```
$ BASIC
READY
NEW PROG1
READY
100 LET X = 5.4321 + 2.1
110 PRINT X
120 END

RUN

7.5321
```

You enter the following and press the Enter key after each entry.

You enter your BASIC program.

You enter the RUN System Command to execute the program.

This is the result or answer displayed by the computer.

FIGURE 2.4 Entering and executing a BASIC program using a terminal in a time-sharing environment.

Start-Up Procedures for Personal Computer Systems

The initial start-up procedures for nearly all personal computer systems are similar in that the user initially turns the power on and, depending on the form of auxiliary storage, inserts a cassette or diskette as per the instructions in the user's manual. The steps that follow vary slightly and depend on the system under which the personal computer operates. For example, if you are using an Apple personal computer, you can immediately begin entering a BASIC program as soon as the cassette or diskette is loaded. On the other hand, many personal computers have an **operating system** like CP/M or MS-DOS. An operating system is a program that controls the activities performed by a computer. Operating systems require that you enter BASIC by issuing a command, like BASIC or BASICA. If you are using a personal computer system, read the operating instructions in the user's manual before you begin to enter BASIC programs.

2.6 EDITING BASIC PROGRAMS

Most BASIC programs are entered one line at a time into the computer system via a keyboard. Pressing the Enter key signals to the system that a line is complete. During the process of entering a program, you will quickly learn that it is easy to make many **grammatical errors** because of your inexperience with the BASIC language and your unfamiliarity with the keyboard. **Logical errors** can also occur in a program if you have not considered all the details associated with the problem.

Some of these errors can be eliminated by using coding forms and flowcharts and carefully reviewing your design and program before you enter it into the computer system. The remaining errors are resolved by editing the BASIC program. Table 2.7 illustrates the most common features used for editing BASIC programs. You will find these features to be powerful and easy to use.

TABLE 2.7 Commonly Used Features in Editing BASIC Programs

1) *Correct an error* in the line being keyed before pressing the Enter key	Press the key assigned to delete a character. Each time it is pressed, a character is deleted. Complete the line after the erroneous characters have been deleted. (or) Press the key assigned to delete a line and reenter the line from the beginning.*
2) *Replace a line* in an existing program.	Key in the new statement, using the line number of the line to be replaced.
3) *Insert a line* in an existing program.	Key in the statement using a line number that will cause BASIC to place the statement in the desired sequence.
4) *Delete a line* in an existing program.	Key in the line number and press the Enter key.

* The keys that are assigned for deleting a character or a line are not standardized and vary from system to system. Check the specifications on your BASIC system in the user's manual.

2.7 SYSTEM COMMANDS

As indicated earlier, two types of instructions are used with BASIC systems. One type is the BASIC statement itself, like the LET statement, the PRINT statement and the INPUT statement. The second type is the system command associated with the BASIC system, like the RUN command.

The RUN and LIST Commands

Perhaps the most important system command to a beginner is the command RUN. If this command is not issued, the BASIC program will not be executed.

Another useful system command is the LIST command. It instructs the computer to display all or part of the BASIC program. This command is especially useful in those circumstances where changes have been made to statements in the BASIC program and a new listing of the program is desired. Programs 2.9a and 2.9b illustrate the use of the RUN and LIST system commands.

```
100 REM PROGRAM 2.9
110 INPUT A, B
120 LET C = A - B
130 PRINT "THE DIFFERENCE IS:"; C
140 END
```

PROGRAM 2.9a

```
RUN

? 159, 62
THE DIFFERENCE IS: 97
```

If line 120 is changed by entering the following statement

```
120 LET C = B - A
```

this new line 120 replaces the original line 120. If a LIST command is issued followed by RUN, Program 2.9 appears:

```
LIST
100 REM PROGRAM 2.9
110 INPUT A, B
120 LET C = B - A
130 PRINT "THE DIFFERENCE IS:"; C
140 END

RUN

? 159, 62
THE DIFFERENCE IS:-97


LIST 130
130 PRINT "THE DIFFERENCE IS:"; C


LIST 120-140
120 LET C = B - A
130 PRINT "THE DIFFERENCE IS:"; C
140 END
```

PROGRAM 2.9b

The command LIST can be used to list a program at a point other than the first statement of the program. LIST 130 lists line 130 only. LIST 120−140 lists lines 120 through 140, inclusive.

Another command that is of considerable importance is the command NEW. This command instructs the system to erase or delete the last program keyed into the main storage. Without this command, statements from the old program may mix with the statements of the new one.

The NEW Command

Table 2.8 summarizes the system commands discussed thus far.

TABLE 2.8 Summary of Some Common System Commands Found with BASIC Systems

System Command	Function
LIST	Causes all or part of the BASIC program currently in main storage to be displayed.
NEW	Causes deletion of the BASIC program currently in main storage and indicates the beginning of a new program to be created in main storage.
RUN	Causes the BASIC program currently in main storage to be executed.

The system commands summarized in Table 2.8 are common to all BASIC systems. The syntax of the remaining commands varies from system to system. Several **system functions** are listed in Table 2.9. A system function is the action taken by the computer when a system command is entered. Also listed in Table 2.9 are the system commands that correspond to most BASIC system functions. A column has been left blank for you to fill in the system commands for your BASIC system. You will have to rely on your instructor or find in the user's manual the exact syntax of the system commands that correspond to the functions listed.

Additional System Commands

Two of the more important system functions listed in Table 2.9 are saving BASIC programs into auxiliary storage for later use and loading BASIC programs from auxiliary storage into main storage.

Programs are not always finished during a single session with the computer. As Figure 2.5 illustrates, it is possible with BASIC systems to store an incomplete program into auxiliary storage and at a later time retrieve the program.

TABLE 2.9   Additional System Functions

System Command Used with Microsoft BASIC	System command on Your BASIC System (You may write them in this column.)	Common System Function
SAVE "filename"		Saves or files the current program into auxiliary storage for later use. Most BASIC systems require that a filename be 8 characters or less and begin with a letter.
LOAD "filename"		Loads a previously stored program from auxiliary storage into main storage.
KILL "filename"		Deletes a previously stored program from auxiliary storage.
FILES		Lists the names of all programs and files in auxiliary storage that belong to the user.
SYSTEM		Terminate your session with BASIC.
LLIST		Lists the current program on the line printer (valid only if you have a personal computer with a line printer attached).
RENUM start,, increment		Renumbers the entire current program uniformly.
AUTO start, increment		Automatically starts a BASIC line with a line number. Each new line is assigned a systematically incremented line number.
NAME "f-1" AS "f-2"		Changes the name of a file in auxiliary storage to a new name.
Press both CTRL key and Break key		Terminates a system activity, such as execution of a program, listing of a program or automatic line numbering.

2.8 PROGRAMMING TIPS

Having read the first seven sections of this chapter, you are ready to write your first program to use a computer for solving a problem. At the end of Chapter 2 are several Programming Exercises. Each exercise includes a short statement of the problem, suggested input data and the corresponding output results. Collectively, these items are the **program specifications.** Following the sample Programming Exercise below, we have suggested a step-by-step procedure showing how to solve the problem. You will find this helpful when you begin solving problems on your own. You will also find it helpful to review Section 1.5, Problem-Solving and Program Development.

Sample Programming Exercise: Computation of State Tax

Problem: Construct a program that will compute the state tax owed by a taxpayer. The state determines the amount of tax by taking a person's yearly income, subtracting $500.00 for each dependent and then multiplying the result by 2% to determine the tax due. Use the following formula:

$$Tax = 0.02 * (Income - 500 * Dependents)$$

Code the program so that it will request the taxpayer's income and the number of dependents.

Input Data: Use the following sample input data:

Taxpayer's income — $73,000.00
Number of dependents — 8

Output Results: The following results are displayed:

```
WHAT IS THE TAXPAYER'S INCOME? 73000
WHAT IS THE NUMBER OF DEPENDENTS? 8

THE STATE TAX DUE IS 1380
```

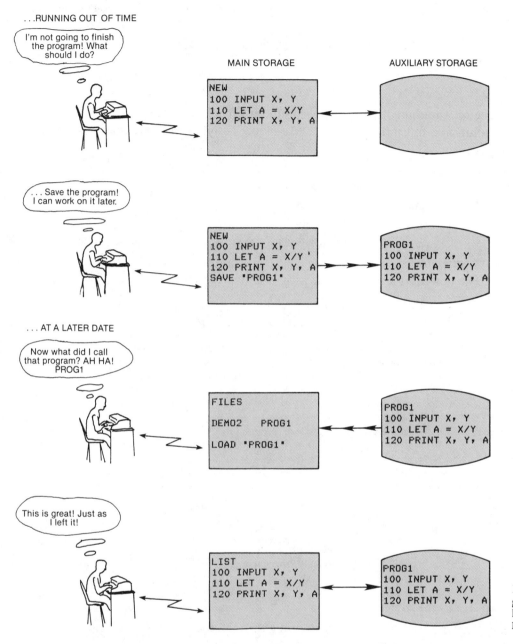

FIGURE 2.5 Storing a program into auxiliary storage and later loading the program PROG1 into main storage.

The following systematic approach to solving this exercise as well as the other programming exercises in this textbook is recommended. In essence, this list is the same as the program development cycle outlined in Section 1.5. Some steps have been combined.

Step 1: Problem Analysis

Review the program specifications until you thoroughly understand the problem to be solved. Ascertain the form of input, the form of output and the type of processing that must be performed. For this exercise, you should have determined the following:

Input—The program must allow for the user to supply the data through the use of INPUT statements. There are two data items—taxpayer's income and number of dependents.

Processing—The formula Tax = 0.02 * (Income − 500 * Dependents) will determine the state tax.

Output—The required results include the input prompt messages and the state tax due.

Step 2: Program Design

Develop a method of solution the computer will use. One way to develop a method of solution is to list the program tasks sequentially. For this exercise, the program tasks are:

1) Clear screen.
2) Prompt the user for the necessary data.
3) Calculate the state tax.
4) Display the state tax.

Next, draw a program flowchart that shows how the program will accomplish the program tasks.

The flowchart for the sample programming exercise is shown in Figure 2.6.

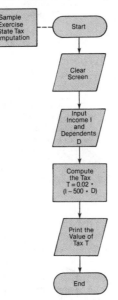

FIGURE 2.6 Flowchart for Sample Programming Exercise.

Step 3: Test the Design

Carefully review the design by stepping through the program flowchart to ensure that it is logically correct.

Step 4: Code the Program

Code the program, as shown in Figure 2.7, according to the program design.

Step 5: Review the code

Carefully review the coding. Put yourself in the position of the computer and step through the program. This is sometimes referred to as **desk checking** your code. Be sure the syntax of each instruction is correct. Check to be sure that the sequence of the instructions is logically correct. *You want to be confident that the program will work the first time it is executed.*

Step 6: Enter the Program

Enter the program into the computer system, as shown in Figure 2.8. Before starting this step, you should be familiar with the system commands and the method for getting on the computer.

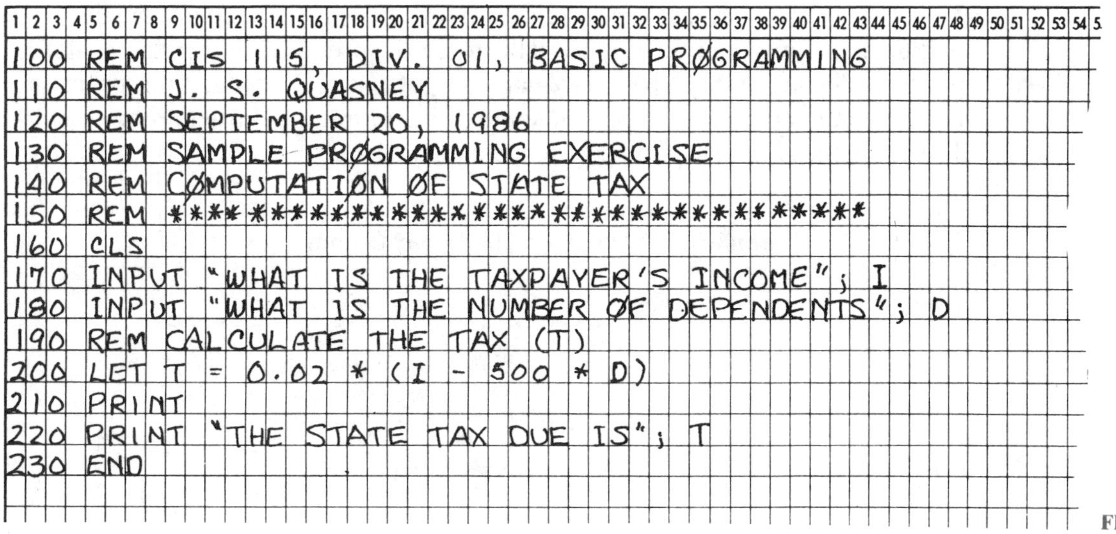

FIGURE 2.7 Sample Programming Exercise on coding form.

```
100 REM CIS 115, DIV. 01, BASIC PROGRAMMING
110 REM J. S. QUASNEY
120 REM SEPTEMBER 20, 1986
130 REM SAMPLE EXERCISE
140 REM COMPUTATION OF STATE TAX
150 REM ***********************************
160 CLS
170 INPUT "WHAT IS THE TAXPAYER'S INCOME"; I
180 INPUT "WHAT IS THE NUMBER OF DEPENDENTS"; D
190 REM CALCULATE THE TAX (T)
200 LET T = 0.02 * (I - 500 * D)
210 PRINT
220 PRINT "THE STATE TAX DUE IS"; T
230 END
```

FIGURE 2.8 Sample Programming Exercise entered in the computer system.

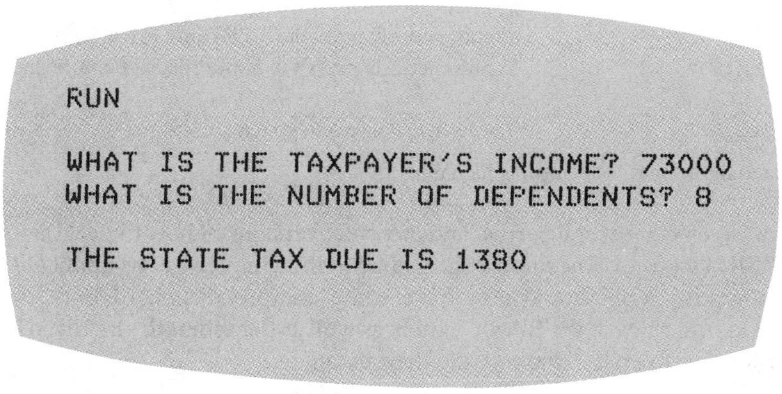

```
RUN

WHAT IS THE TAXPAYER'S INCOME? 73000
WHAT IS THE NUMBER OF DEPENDENTS? 8

THE STATE TAX DUE IS 1380
```

FIGURE 2.9 The display from executing the Sample Programming Exercise.

Step 7: Test the Program

Test the program by executing it, using the RUN command, as shown in Figure 2.9. If the input data does not produce the expected results, the program must be reviewed and corrected.

Step 8: Formalize the Solution

Obtain a **hard copy**, a listing, of the source program and the output results. If the program logic was modified in Steps 4 through 6, redraw the program flowchart to include the modifications.

2.9 HARD COPY OUTPUT

Most BASIC programmers use a keyboard for input and a video display device for output. In many instances, it is desirable to list the program and/or the results on a printer. A listing of this type is **hard copy output**. Table 2.10 illustrates procedures for obtaining hard copy output for some of the more popular computer systems. The procedures involve issuing system commands.

TABLE 2.10   Procedures for Obtaining Hard Copy Output

Computer Systems	List the Program	List the Program and Output Results
Apple	PR#1 LIST PR#0	PR#1 LIST RUN PR#0
COMMODORE	OPEN 4, 4 CMD 4 LIST PRINT# 4 CLOSE 4	OPEN 4, 4 CMD 4 LIST RUN PRINT# 4 CLOSE 4
DEC Rainbow	LLIST	Simultaneously press the CTRL and P keys. LIST RUN Simultaneously press the CTRL and P keys.
DEC VAX-11*	SAVE LAB1.BAS EXIT PRINT LAB1.BAS	SAVE LAB1.BAS EXIT PRINT LAB1.BAS BASIC LAB1 LINK LAB1 ASSIGN/USER LAB1OUT.LIS SYS$OUTPUT RUN LAB1 PRINT LAB1OUT
IBM PC	LLIST	Simultaneously press the CTRL and Prt Sc keys. LIST RUN Simultaneously press the CTRL and Prt Sc keys.
Macintosh	LLIST	Simultaneously press the Shift, Special Feature and key 4.
TRS-80	LLIST	Varies from system to system.

*Check the user's manual for the rules regarding filenames.

2.10 WHAT YOU SHOULD KNOW

In this chapter there have been several correct and incorrect versions of how to program a computer in the BASIC language. The knowledge gained in this chapter will be applicable to most BASIC programs. You should now have some comprehension of both the grammatical and the logical rules of the BASIC syntax as well as the **semantics** involved—that is, the relationships between the symbols and their meanings.

1. In a straight-line program, statements are executed in sequence until the END statement is reached.

2. BASIC is an acronym for *B*eginner's *A*ll-Purpose *S*ymbolic *I*nstruction *C*ode.

3. A BASIC program is composed of a) a sequence of lines; b) the last of which contains the END statement.

4. A keyword informs BASIC of the type of statement to be executed. LET, PRINT and END are keywords.

5. In programming, a variable is a storage location in main memory whose value can change as the program is executed.

6. The LET statement is used to assign a value to a variable on the left-hand side of the equal sign.

7. The equal sign in any LET statement means that the value of the variable to the left of the equal sign is to be replaced by the final value to the right of the equal sign.

8. Constants represent ordinary numbers that do not change during the execution of a program.

9. The PRINT statement instructs the system to bring a result out from its storage area and display it on an output device.

10. The line containing the END statement marks the physical end of a program and terminates its execution.

11. Each program should physically terminate with an END statement.

12. Every line in a BASIC program must begin with a unique line number.

13. Each succeeding line must begin with a line number greater than the line number of the preceding statement.

14. Every variable appearing in an output statement should appear at least once earlier in the program in such a way that its value can be determined.

15. Although most BASIC statements can be placed anywhere in a given program, logic, common sense and structured style dictate where these statements are placed.

16. Every variable appearing to the right of the equal sign in a LET statement should appear at least once earlier in the same program in such a way that its value can be determined.

17. The INPUT statement provides for assignment of data to variables from a source outside the program during execution.

18. The function of the INPUT statement is to display an input prompt and to suspend execution of the program until data has been supplied.

19. In response to an INPUT statement it is important that the Enter key be pressed following entry of the data.

20. A comma is used to establish a list, which is a set of distinct elements. Each element is separated from the next by a comma.

21. Every variable appearing in the program whose value is directly obtained through input must be listed in an INPUT statement before it is used elsewhere in the program.

22. In a PRINT statement, like 110 PRINT X, the system displays the value of X and not the letter X.

23. The PRINT statement can be used to display messages as well as the values of variables.

24. The Clear Screen statement, like CLS, causes all the information on the screen to be erased and places the cursor in the upper left corner of the screen.

25. In a PRINT statement, the semicolon separator instructs the system to maintain the current position of the cursor.

26. After displaying the list of items, a PRINT statement causes the cursor to return to the leftmost position on the next line unless the list ends with a semicolon. If the PRINT statement ends with a semicolon, the system keeps the cursor on the same line.

27. A null list in a PRINT statement causes the system to display a blank line.

28. A BASIC program should be written on a coding form. The use of a coding form encourages good formatting of code.

29. A line in a program can contain multiple statements separated by colons.

30. Spaces can appear in a BASIC statement in the same places that spaces appear in an English sentence, except, for some systems, at the beginning of a line, within line numbers, within keyboards, within numeric constants or within variable names. Blanks are required around keywords.

31. The REM statement, used to document a program, has no effect on the execution of the program.

32. Before you can enter a program into the computer, you must familiarize yourself with how to get on the computer.

33. Grammatical and syntactical errors can be corrected by editing the BASIC program. For example, you can correct errors while keying in a line. Lines can also be replaced, inserted or deleted.

34. BASIC statements have line numbers; system commands do not.
35. The RUN command is used to execute a BASIC program.
36. The LIST command is used to display all or part of a BASIC program.
37. The NEW command deletes the current BASIC program and indicates the beginning of a new program to be created in main storage.
38. Most BASIC systems include additional system commands to facilitate program development, such as ones used to store a program into auxiliary storage and to load a stored program into main storage.

**2.11
SELF-TEST
EXERCISES**
(Answers in the back of
the book)

1. Put yourself in the place of the computer and record for each line number the current values of W, X, and Y.

```
100 LET W = 4
110 LET X = 2
120 LET Y = 6
130 PRINT Y, X, W
140 LET W = W + 1
150 LET X = W * Y
160 PRINT X
170 LET X = 9
180 LET Y = Y - 2
190 PRINT X, Y
200 LET X = X/100
210 PRINT X
220 END
```

W	X	Y	Displayed

(*Hint:* The value of a variable does not change until the program instructs the computer to change it.)

2. What will be displayed when the following program is executed?

```
100 PRINT "CALCULATE DISCOUNT"
110 LET P = 4162.50
120 LET D = 0.10
130 LET N = D * P
140 LET S = P - N
150 PRINT "ORIGINAL PRICE"; P
160 PRINT "DISCOUNT"; N
170 PRINT "SALE PRICE"; S
180 PRINT "END OF PROGRAM"
190 END
```

3. Write LET statements for each of the following:
   a) Assign T the value of 3.
   b) Assign X the value of T less 2.
   c) Assign P the product of T and X.
   d) Triple the value of T.
   e) Assign A the quotient of P divided by X.
   f) Increment X by 1.
   g) Cube the value of R.

4. Given the following:

   `100 LET A = B + C`

   a) The number 100 is called a _____ .
   b) The term LET is called a _____ .
   c) The letters A, B and C represent _____ .
   d) The equal sign means _____ .

5. Identify the BASIC arithmetic operators for the following:
   a) Addition
   b) Subtraction
   c) Multiplication
   d) Division
   e) Exponentiation

6. Indicate what is displayed if the following program is executed.

```
110 PRINT "THE SUM OF ";
120 PRINT "A AND B IS"
130 END
```

7. Describe the results that are displayed when the following program is executed.

```
100 LET A = -2
110 LET B = -3
120 LET C = A * B
130 PRINT "THE VALUE OF A IS"; A
140 PRINT "THE VALUE OF B IS "; B
150 PRINT
160 PRINT "THE VALUE OF C IS"; C
170 END
```

8. What is wrong with each of the following programs?

a)
```
100 LET X = Y * Z
110 INPUT Y, Z
120 PRINT Y, Z, X
130 END
```

b)
```
100 INPUT A, L, W
110 LET A = L * W
120 PRINT "THE AREA IS"; A
130 END
140 RUN
```

9. What does the following program display when the values 10 and 8, respectively, are entered in response to the INPUT statements?

```
100 INPUT "WHAT IS THE LENGTH"; L
110 INPUT "WHAT IS THE WIDTH"; W
120 LET A = L * W
130 PRINT "A RECTANGLE WITH DIMENSIONS"; L; "AND"; W
140 PRINT "HAS AN AREA OF"; A; "."
150 END
```

10. Indicate three techniques which were presented in Chapter 2 for integrating data into a program.

11. In the following program indicate which lines are superfluous and if deleted, will still generate the same results?

```
100 REM CHAPTER 2 SELF-TEST 11
110 REM CALCULATE THE SALES TAX
120 INPUT A
130 LET T = 0.04 * A
140 PRINT "THE SALES TAX IS"; T
150 END
```

12. If the following program is entered as shown, would it be accepted or rejected by a BASIC system?

```
130 END
120 PRINT X
110 LET X = 4 * 5 * 6
100 REM CHAPTER 2 SELF-TEST 12
```

13. Assume you enter and execute the following program:

```
100 REM CHAPTER 2 SELF-TEST 13
110 LET X = 2.456 * 3.456 * 716
120 PRINT "THE PRODUCT IS"; X
130 END
```

After executing the program, you decide to enter the following *new* program:

```
105 LET Y = 5 ^ (1/2)
115 PRINT "THE SQUARE ROOT IS"; Y
125 END
```

What is displayed, when you issue the command LIST after entering the second program?

2.12
TEST YOUR
BASIC SKILLS
(Even-numbered
answers in the back of
the book.)

1. Which of the following are invalid line numbers for BASIC programs?

   a) 3½   c) 9999.   e) 1,321   g) 1.000   i) +10
   b) 10   d) 0   f) 100033   h) 10.   j) −10

2. Record for each line number the current values of D, E and F as well as the values displayed by the PRINT statements. See Self-Test Exercise 1.

```
100 LET D = 9
110 LET E = 2
120 LET D = D + 1
130 LET D = D - 1
140 LET F = D^E
150 LET E = D + F + E
160 LET F = F - D
170 REM OUTPUT PORTION OF PROGRAM
180 PRINT F
190 PRINT D
200 PRINT E
210 END
```

3. For each program below, construct a table similar to the one in Exercise 2. Record for each line number the current values of the variables and the results displayed by the PRINT statements.

   a)
```
100 LET A = 1
110 LET B = 3
120 PRINT A, B
130 LET A = A + 1
140 LET B = B - 1
150 PRINT A, B
160 LET A = A + 1
170 LET B = B - 1
180 PRINT A, B
190 END
```

   b) Assume A and B are assigned the values 4 and 2, respectively.
```
100 LET C = 4
110 PRINT C
120 INPUT A, B
130 LET C = A/B + C
140 LET A = A - 3
150 LET B = C^A
160 PRINT A, B
170 END
```

   c) Assume A and B are assigned the values 7 and 2, respectively.
```
100 INPUT A, B
110 LET C = A^B
120 PRINT C
130 LET D = A - B
140 PRINT D
150 LET E = 1
160 PRINT E
170 LET D = D - 3
180 LET X = E/D
190 PRINT X
200 END
```

   d) Assume P and R are assigned the values 500 and 10, respectively.
```
100 INPUT P, R
110 LET R = R/100
120 LET D = P * R
130 LET R = R * 100
140 REM PRINT RESULTS
150 PRINT "DISCOUNT RATE"; R; "%"
160 PRINT "PRICE"; P; "DOLLARS"
170 PRINT "DISCOUNT"; D; "DOLLARS"
180 END
```

4. Supply the missing output statement which will instruct the computer to output the value of R. Make certain that the variable is consistent with the rest of the program.
```
100 LET R = 6.2345 + 9.001
110 END
```

5. Fill in the missing word in each of the following:

   a) An output statement must contain the word _____ .
   b) Every BASIC program must have as its last the _____ line.
   c) Every LET statement must contain an _____ sign.

6. Correct the errors in the following programs.

   a)
```
100 PRINT Y
110 END
120 LET Y = 21.0
```

   b)
```
100 LET S = 3/5000
110 PRINT
120 END
```

   c)
```
100 LET X = 3003 * 4004
110 PRINT X
```

   d)
```
100 LET S = 23 - 901
95  PRINT S
110 END
```

   e)
```
100 LET A1 = 999/888
110 PRINT S
120 DEND
```

   f)
```
100 LET Z = 1
110 PRINT Z1
120 END
```

7. Is a line containing 10 REM with the rest of the line blank valid?

8. Is it possible to key in a BASIC program beginning with the last statement first and the first statement last? (*Hint:* Assume the line numbers decrease rather than increase with each statement).

9. Which key is used by your system to delete a line you are in the process of keying in? Which key is used to erase characters on a line you are in the process of keying in?

10. Explain in one sentence each the purpose of the following system commands: RUN, LIST, NEW.

11. How many times can you retype a BASIC line?

12. Is it possible to issue a RUN command more than once for the same program?

13. How do you instruct the computer to display two consecutive blank lines in a program?

14. A program requests the user to input the hours worked (40) and the rate of pay ($6.75). The program determines the gross pay by multiplying the two values together and displays the gross pay. Is the following program solution *logically* correct for the problem stated?

```
100 INPUT "WHAT ARE THE HOURS WORKED? 40"; H
110 INPUT "WHAT IS THE RATE OF PAY? 6.75"; R
120 LET G = R * H
130 PRINT "THE GROSS PAY IS 270"
140 END
```

15. What is wrong with the following program?

```
100 INPUT X
110 LET X = A/B
120 PRINT "THE ANSWER IS"; X
130 END
```

16. How would you delete line 150 from a BASIC program?

17. How do you correct the following statement in your program if the error is detected after the Enter key is pressed? Assume the statement

    20 LET X = (6 + A) * 3   should read as   20 LET X = (5 + A) * 3

18. Given the following statement:

```
30 LET Y = A + B * 9
```

Assume that you have not pressed the Enter key and you realize that the statement should read:

```
30 LET Y = A + B/9
```

How do you correct the statement?

In order to document computer programs properly, the following identification format may be used at the beginning of each BASIC source program:

2.13 PROGRAMMING EXERCISES

```
100 REM DEPARTMENT, COURSE NUMBER, DIVISION, COURSE NAME
110 REM YOUR NAME
120 REM DATE
130 REM PROBLEM OR EXERCISE NUMBER
140 REM A SHORT DESCRIPTION OF THE PROBLEM
150 REM ***************************************************
```

Upon completion of each exercise, turn in to your instructor:

1) A logic diagram
2) A listing of the source program
3) The output results

Whenever possible, meaningful variable names should be used in all the programs. Each major section of the source program should be documented with appropriate remark lines.

> **NOTE:** All Programming Exercises in this book include partial or complete sample output results and, when applicable, sample input data. Learn to select good test data to evaluate the logic of your program. Check your design and program against the sample output, and also select your own data for additional testing purposes.

Exercise 1:
Determining the
Selling Price

Purpose: To become familiar with elementary uses of the INPUT, PRINT and LET statements.

Problem: Merchants are in the retail business to buy goods from producers, manufacturers and wholesalers and to sell the merchandise to their customers. To make a profit they must sell their merchandise for more than the cost plus the overhead (taxes, store rent, upkeep, salaries, and so forth). The margin is the sum of the overhead and profit. The selling price is the sum of the margin and cost. Write a program that will determine the selling price of an item that costs $48.27 and has a margin of 25%. Use the formula:

$$\text{Selling Price} = \left(\frac{1}{1 - \text{Margin}} \right) \text{Cost}$$

Input Data: Use the following data in response to INPUT statements:

Cost—$48.27
Margin—25%

Output Results: The following results are displayed:

```
WHAT IS THE COST? 48.27
WHAT IS THE MARGIN IN PERCENT? 25

THE SELLING PRICE IS 64.36
```

Exercise 2:
The Optimal
Investment

Purpose: To familiarize the student with the use of the INPUT, PRINT and LET statements and to perform multiple runs on the same program.

Problem: Three local banks have undertaken an advertising campaign to attract savings account customers. The specifics of their advertisements are shown in Table 2.11.

Construct a single program that will be executed three times, once for each bank. The program is to compute and display the amount of a $500 investment for a period of 1 year. A comparison of the results will show the optimal investment. Use the following formula:

$$\text{Amount} = \text{Principal} * (1 + \text{Rate}/T)^T$$

where T = number of times the investment is compounded per year (i.e., the conversions).

TABLE 2.11

Bank 1	Bank 2	Bank 3
Compounded annually Interest 6⅞%	Compounded semiannually Interest 6¾%	Compounded quarterly Interest 6⅝%

Input Data: Enter the data found in Table 2.11 in response to INPUT statements. For example, for Bank 1 enter:

Bank—1
Principal—$500.00
Rate—0.06875
Conversions—1

Output Results: The following results are displayed for Bank 1:

```
WHAT IS:
        THE BANK NUMBER? 1
        THE PRINCIPAL? 500
        THE RATE IN DECIMAL? 0.06875
        THE NUMBER OF CONVERSIONS? 1

AMOUNT OF INVESTMENT AFTER ONE YEAR IS $ 534.375 FOR BANK 1
```

Purpose: To become familiar with some of the grammatical and logical rules of BASIC and to demonstrate the basic concepts of executing a BASIC program.

Problem: Construct a program that will compute and display the gross pay for an employee working 80 hours during a biweekly pay period at an hourly rate of $12.50.

Version A: Insert the data, 80 and 12.50, directly into a LET statement that determines the gross pay.

Version B: Assign the data, 80 and 12.50, to variables in LET statements and then compute the gross pay in a separate LET statement.

Version C: Enter the data, 80 and 12.50, in response to INPUT statements.

Output Results: The following results are displayed for Version B.

```
HOURS===> 80
RATE OF PAY====> 12.5
GROSS PAY======> 1000
```

**Exercise 3:
Payroll Problem I—
Gross Pay
Computations**

PROGRAMS WITH CALCULATIONS AND STRINGS 3

3.1 INTRODUCTION

In Chapter 2, you were introduced to some simple computer programs that showed some of the grammatical rules of the BASIC language. Also presented were examples of programs that interact with the user through the use of the INPUT and PRINT statements. This chapter continues to develop straight-line programs, with more complex computations and manipulation of data.

This chapter concentrates on constants, variables, expressions, functions, rounding and truncation techniques, and statements which assign values. This chapter also expands on the type of data that can be assigned to variables by introducing string values, examples of which include a word, phrase or sentence. Upon successful completion of this chapter you should be able to write programs that manipulate string expressions and numeric expressions.

Programming Case Study 3: Tailor's Calculations

Program 3.1 determines the average neck, hat and shoe sizes of a male customer. The program uses the following formulas:

$$\text{Neck Size} = 3 \left(\frac{\text{Weight}}{\text{Waistline}} \right)$$

$$\text{Hat Size} = \frac{\text{Neck Size}}{2.125}$$

$$\text{Shoe Size} = 50 \left(\frac{\text{Waistline}}{\text{Weight}} \right)$$

Program 3.1 computes the average neck size (15.8333), hat size (7.45098) and shoe size (9.47368) for Mike, who has a 36-inch waistline and weighs 190 pounds. Not used in the computations, the customer name helps identify the measurements when more than one set of computations is involved.

Program 3.1 contains a sequence of LET statements (lines 180 through 200) with expressions that are more complex than those encountered in Chapter 2. Furthermore, line 150 contains a variable N$ that is assigned a string of letters MIKE rather than a numeric value. The value of N$ is displayed along with the results because of lines 220 through 240. The following pages introduce some formal definitions and special rules for constructing LET statements and manipulating strings.

```
100 REM PROGRAM 3.1
110 REM TAILOR'S COMPUTATIONS
120 REM H = HAT SIZE,  S = SHOE SIZE
130 REM N = NECKSIZE, N$ = CUSTOMER'S NAME
140 REM *********************************
150 INPUT "CUSTOMER'S FIRST NAME"; N$
160 INPUT "WAISTLINE"; W
170 INPUT "WEIGHT"; P
180 LET N = 3 * P/W
190 LET H = N/2.125
200 LET S = 50 * W/P
210 PRINT
220 PRINT N$; "'S NECK SIZE IS"; N
230 PRINT N$; "'S HAT SIZE IS"; H
240 PRINT N$; "'S SHOE SIZE IS"; S
250 END

RUN

CUSTOMER'S FIRST NAME? MIKE
WAISTLINE? 36
WEIGHT? 190

MIKE'S NECK SIZE IS 15.8333
MIKE'S HAT SIZE IS 7.45098
MIKE'S SHOE SIZE IS 9.47368
```

PROGRAM 3.1

3.2 CONSTANTS

Recall from Chapter 2 that constants are values that do not change during the execution of a program. Two different kinds of constants are valid for use in BASIC programs, **numeric constants** and **string constants**.

Constants are common in the LET statement and the PRINT statement. Numeric constants represent ordinary numbers. A string constant is a sequence of letters, digits, and special characters enclosed in quotation marks. They are used for such non-numeric purposes as representing an employee name, social security number, address or telephone number.

Numeric Constants

A numeric constant can have one of these three forms in BASIC:

1) **Integer:** a positive or negative whole number with no decimal point, like -174 or 5903 or 0 or -32768.

2) **Fixed Point:** a positive or negative real number with a decimal point, like 713.1417 or 0.0034 or 0.0 or -35.1 or 19235475957463.34.

3) **Floating Point:** a positive or negative real number written in **exponential form**. A constant written in this form consists of an integer or fixed point constant, followed by the letter E and an integer.* E stands for "times ten to the power." The allowable range for floating point constants is 10^{-38} to 10^{+38}. Valid floating point constants include 793E19, 62E-23, 1E0, -2.3E-3, $+12.34$E$+7$.

Examples of numeric constants in Program 3.1 are 3, 2.125 and 50, found in lines 180, 190 and 200. A line number like 220 is not considered to be a constant in BASIC.

```
180 LET N = 3 * P/W


190 LET H = N/2.125               Numeric constants


200 LET S = 50 * W/P
```

To write the constant three and one-half in a BASIC program, you may *not* use 3½ or 3&½ or 3 and ½ or three & ½. You may validly write 3.5 or 3.50 or 3.50000 or 3.5E0 or 0.35E1 or 35E-1.

---

*Some systems, like the DEC Rainbow and IBM PC, allow the E to be replaced by a D for double-precision.

Table 3.1 lists some ordinary numbers and shows how they may be expressed as valid numeric constants in BASIC. Examples 1, 3 and 9 of Table 3.1 show that special characters like $, ¢, and @ are not allowed in numeric constants.

TABLE 3.1 **Examples of Numeric Constants**

Ordinary Numbers	Numeric Constants in BASIC
1) $3.14	3.14 or 3.140
2) 512.71	512.71 or 512.710 or 0512.71
3) 4¢	4 or 4. or 4.00 or 04 or 4E0
4) 1.7321	1.7321 or 1.73210
5) −29.7822	−29.7822
6) 0	0 or 0. or 000 or 0E0
7) −39.5	−39.5 or −39.50 or −0039.50 or −.395E2
8) 12,768.5	+12768.5 or 12768.5
9) 100,000@	100000 or 100000. or 1.E5 or 1E5
10) 6.02257×10^{23}	6.02257E23 or +6.02257E+23

Examples 3 and 6 show that you may write an integer in any of the three forms. However, if you include the decimal point or write the integer in floating point form, most BASIC systems will require additional storage to store the constant in main memory.

If a number is negative, the minus sign must precede the number. If a number is positive, the plus sign is optional.

Examples 8 and 9 also indicate that *commas may not be inserted into numeric constants.* Example 7 illustrates that high order zeroes (to the left of the first significant digit) have no effect on the number. Finally, spaces should not occur in numeric constants.

Programming Case Study 4: Banker's Simple Interest

Program 3.2 uses the formula:

$$\text{Banker's Interest} = P \times R \left(\frac{\text{Exact No. of Days}}{360} \right)$$

to determine the ordinary simple interest for a loan of $4,850 at 15.6% for 90 days.

The answer resulting from the execution of this program is 189.15 (dollars). Lines 130 and 160 each include a numeric constant. In line 130, the variable R, the rate of interest, is set equal to the value of 0.156. In line 160 the numeric constant 360 is used to determine the time factor. The numeric data items, 4850 and 90 days, entered in response to the INPUT statements in lines 140 and 150, must take the form of numeric constants. This leads to the following rule:

> INPUT **Rule 2:** Numeric data assigned to numeric variables through the use of the INPUT statement must take the form of numeric constants.

A number entered in response to the INPUT statement may have as many digits as required, up to a maximum of 38. However, only the first several digits are significant. The exact number of digits that is significant is dependent on the precision of the computer system and the type of numeric variable being assigned the value. The different types of numeric variables in BASIC will be discussed shortly.

Program 3.2 could have been made more general if R had been assigned the interest rate through the use of the INPUT statement. A LET statement was used to assign R the value 0.156 to illustrate the makeup of a numeric constant.

```
100 REM PROGRAM 3.2
110 REM BANKER'S SIMPLE INTEREST
120 REM ************************
130 LET R = 0.156
140 INPUT "PRINCIPAL"; P
150 INPUT "TIME IN DAYS"; T
160 LET I = P * R * T/360
170 PRINT
180 PRINT "THE INTEREST IS $"; I
190 END

RUN

PRINCIPAL? 4850
TIME IN DAYS? 90

THE INTEREST IS $ 189.15
```

PROGRAM 3.2

Computer Precision

Some constants can be internally represented with exact or infinite precision. Other values, like 1/3, which may be written as .333333333333333333, can be internally represented only approximately, with finite precision. When the maximum number of **significant digits** is six, as it is in some systems, the equivalent value of 1/3 is .333333, with an error of .000000333333333333.

Numeric values, like constants, are stored in main storage in one of two forms, **integer** or **single-precision**. Some systems also have a third form, **double-precision**. Numeric values that are stored as integers take up less room in main storage than do values stored in single-precision. Likewise, numeric values stored in single-precision take up less room than values stored in double-precision.

We tell BASIC how to store a value, like a numeric constant, by the way we write it. For example, a numeric constant is stored as an integer if it is between −32768 and +32767 and it does not contain a decimal point. A numeric constant is stored in single-precision if it is outside the range for an integer, or contains a decimal point, or is written in exponential form. Some systems that allow for double-precision store a numeric constant in this form if the number of significant digits exceeds that of single-precision. Table 3.2 shows the **precision** with which a numeric constant may be stored and the **accuracy** with which it may be displayed.

Table 3.3 shows several examples of constants and the form used to store them.

TABLE 3.2 Numeric Precision and Accuracy of Some Computer Systems

Computer System	Single-Precision		Double-Precision	
	Stored With a Precision of	Displayed With a Accuracy Up To	Stored With a Precision of	Displayed With a Accuracy Up To
Apple	10 digits	9 digits	Not Available	
COMMODORE	10 digits	9 digits	Not Available	
DEC Rainbow	7 digits	6 digits	16 digits	16 digits
DEC VAX-11	7 digits	6 digits	16 digits	16 digits
IBM PC	7 digits	7 digits, last digit may not be accurate	17 digits	16 digits
Macintosh	6 digits	6 digits	14 digits	14 digits
TRS-80	7 digits	6 digits	16 digits	16 digits

TABLE 3.3   Numeric Constants and the Form Used to Store Them

Numeric Constant	Stored in a Form of
4.67	Single-Precision
−128	Integer
3E−4	Single-Precision
125678	Single-Precision
348.91366789	Double-Precision. On systems without double-precision as 348.9136678 (Single-Precision).
−6.1382E4	Single-Precision
5125	Integer

The precision with which numeric values are stored can also play a role in determining the type of arithmetic that the system will use to compute the value of an expression. Generally speaking, integer arithmetic is faster than single-precision arithmetic, which in turn is faster than double-precision. Some BASIC systems allow for an alternative method for indicating one form over another.*

For the most part, you can let the computer handle the precision with which it stores numeric values. However, you should be aware that not all computers store values to the same precision, and for this reason, identical programs executed on different computers will not always generate identical results.

Numeric Constants in Exponential Form

Numeric constants may also be written in **exponential (E-type)** or **scientific notation**. This form is a shorthand way of representing very large and very small numbers in a program. If a result exceeds the precision under which it is stored, the system displays it in exponential form. For these two reasons it is important to have some idea of how to read and write numbers in this form.

Using exponential notation, a number, regardless of its magnitude, is expressed as a value between 1 and 10 times a power of 10. That is, the decimal point is placed to the right one place after the high order nonzero digit.

For example, 1,500,000 can be expressed as 1.5×10^6 in exponential notation or written as an E-type constant in the form of 1.5E6. The *positive* power of ten in the exponential notation of 1.5×10^6 shows that the decimal point was previously moved 6 places to the *left*. That is,

1.500000.

6 places to left

In order to write 1.5×10^6 as an E-type constant in BASIC, the letter E, which stands for "times ten to the power" is substituted for the "× 10." Hence, the E-type constant is 1.5E6. Exponential notation illustrates how a "compact" number can be represented, since it eliminates the great many zeroes used to define the number in the first place.

In the same way, a small number like 0.000000001234 can be expressed in exponential notation as 1.234×10^{-9} or 1.234E−9. The *negative* power of ten in 1.234×10^{-9} represents that the decimal point was previously moved 9 places to

---

*Ending a numeric value with a percent sign (%) causes it to be stored as an integer. Ending a numeric value with an exclamation point (!) causes it to be stored in single-precision. Ending a numeric value with a number sign (#) causes it to be stored in double-precision. 19.34% is stored as an integer (19) rather than in single-precision. 25! is stored in single-precision rather than as an integer. 21.2# is stored in double-precision rather than single-precision.

the *right*. That is,

0.000000001 . 234

9 places to right

When a number is written in exponential notation, the value to the left of the E is the **mantissa**, and the value to the right of the E is the **exponent**.

1.23456E + 8

mantissa   exponent

Program 3.3 represents the use of exponential notation in computing the Banker's Interest for a 90-day loan of $1,500,000. This program is nearly the same as Program 3.2, except that it shows the principal entered in E-type form.

```
100 REM PROGRAM 3.3
110 REM BANKER'S SIMPLE INTEREST ON A LOAN OF $1,500,000
120 REM ****************************************************
130 LET R = 0.156
140 INPUT "PRINCIPAL"; P
150 INPUT "TIME IN DAYS"; T
160 LET I = P * R * T/360
170 PRINT
180 PRINT "THE INTEREST IS $"; I
190 END

RUN

PRINCIPAL? 1.5E6
TIME IN DAYS? 90

THE INTEREST IS $ 58500
```

PROGRAM 3.3

{ Principal of $1,500,000 entered in E-type form.

Table 3.4 lists some ordinary numbers and shows how they may be expressed in scientific notation and as E-Type constants in BASIC.

TABLE 3.4   Examples of Scientific Notation and E-Type Constants

Ordinary Numbers	Scientific Notation	Possible E-Type Constants
10,000,000	1×10^7	1E7 or 1.E+7 or 0.01E9
0.0000152	1.52×10^{-5}	1.52E−5 or +152E−7
0.001	1×10^{-3}	1E−3 or 0.001E0
−6000000000000	-6×10^{12}	−6E+12 or −6E12 or −0.6E13
−0.005892	-5.892×10^{-3}	−5.892E−3 or −5892E−6
186,000	1.86×10^5	1.86E+5 or .186E6

A string constant has as its value the string of all characters between surrounding quotation marks. In this book we will adopt the rule that the length of a string constant may be from 0 to 255 characters. Some BASIC systems are more restrictive, while others allow for string constants to be longer. The quotation marks indicate the beginning and end of the string constant and are not considered to be part of the value.

String Constants

The messages that have been incorporated in INPUT statements to prompt for the required data and in PRINT statements to identify results are examples of string constants. For example, lines 140, 150 and 180 of Program 3.3 each contain a string constant. A string with a length of zero is a **null** or **empty string.**

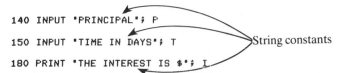

```
140 INPUT "PRINCIPAL"; P
150 INPUT "TIME IN DAYS"; T                    String constants
180 PRINT "THE INTEREST IS $"; L
```

String constants can be assigned to variables in a LET statement, as is shown in the following program.

```
100 REM PROGRAM 3.4
110 REM EXAMPLES OF STRING CONSTANTS
120 REM ****************************
130 LET M$ = "Q1937A"
140 LET P$ = "12AB34"
150 LET D$ = "NYLON, DISC"
160 PRINT "MODEL NUMBER: "; M$
170 PRINT "PART NUMBER: "; P$
180 PRINT "DESCRIPTION: "; D$
190 END

RUN

MODEL NUMBER: Q1937A
PART NUMBER: 12AB34
DESCRIPTION: NYLON, DISC
```

PROGRAM 3.4

In line 130 of Program 3.4, the variable M$ is assigned the value Q1937A. In line 140, P$ is assigned the value 12AB34, and in line 150, D$ the value NYLON,DISC.

String constants are used in a program to represent values that name or identify a person, place or thing. They are also used to represent report and column headings and output messages. The ability to manipulate data of this type is important in the field of business data processing. As you will see later in this chapter, BASIC includes **string functions**, for manipulating strings.

Table 3.5 lists sequences of letters, digits and special characters and shows how they may be expressed as valid string constants.

TABLE 3.5   Examples of String Constants

String of Characters	Corresponding String Constant in BASIC
1) 844-0520 (telephone number)	"844-0520"
2) NIKOLE ZIGMUND	"NIKOLE ZIGMUND"
3) blank (space)	" "
4) EMPLOYEE FILE LIST	"EMPLOYEE FILE LIST"
5) 310386024 (social security no.)	"310386024"
6) A null or empty string	""

Be careful not to include a quotation mark within a string. For example,

Invalid   `100 LET S$ = "SHE SAID, "NO""`

is invalid because the second quotation mark ends the string. An apostrophe is recommended for cases where a quotation mark is needed in a string. For example,

Valid   `100 LET S$ = "SHE SAID, 'NO'"`

is valid. Another alternative is to use the concatenation operator and the function CHR$. The concatenation operator is discussed later in Section 3.5 and the function CHR$ in Chapter 9.

Recall from Chapter 2 that, in programming, a **variable** is a storage location in main memory whose value can change as the program is executed. In a program, the variable is referenced by a variable name. Variables are declared in a BASIC program by incorporating variable names in statements. For example the LET statements,

```
100 LET A = 15
110 LET B$ = "PURDUE"
```

instruct BASIC to set up independent storage areas for A and B$ as well as the constants 15 and PURDUE.

Although it may appear to you that A is being assigned the value 15 when you enter the statement through your keyboard, this does not occur until the program is executed. Recall from Chapter 1 that a BASIC program must be translated into equivalent machine-language instructions before it can be executed. During this translation, the variables and numeric constants of a program are assigned particular storage areas in main storage. Figure 3.1 illustrates the storage areas for A and B before and after execution of lines 100 and 110 in the partial program above.

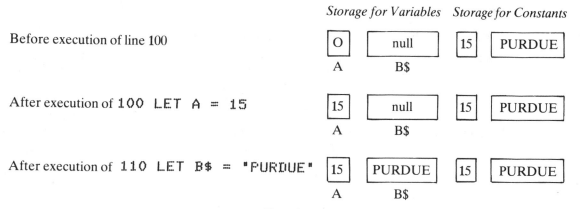

FIGURE 3.1   The assignment of values to variables in main storage.

Unlike a constant, a variable may be redefined (that is, its value may be changed) during the execution of a program. However, its value may remain unchanged in a BASIC program if you so desire. For example, if in the previous partial program another line is added after line 110,

```
100 LET A = 15
110 LET B$ = "PURDUE"
120 LET A = 20
```

the value of A which is assigned the value 15 by line 100 changes to 20 when line 120 is executed. BASIC recognizes that the two variable names are the same and during translation does not attempt to create an independent storage location for the second variable name A. In other words, there can only be one variable in a program with the name A; however, it can be referenced and the value changed as often as needed.

Two categories of variables are valid for use in a BASIC program. These are **simple variables** and **subscripted variables**. Simple variables are used to store single values, while subscripted variables are used to store groups of values, like one- or two-dimensional arrays. Our discussion here concerns simple variables. Subscripted variables will be discussed in Chapter 7.

As with constants, there are two types of simple variables: **numeric** and **string**. A numeric variable may only be assigned a number and a string variable may only be assigned a string of characters.

When the system command RUN is issued for a program, all numeric variables are assigned an initial value of zero and all string variables are assigned a null value. The LET statement may be used to assign a variable a constant value or the result of a calculation. Variables may also be assigned values through INPUT statements.

Selection of Variable Names

All BASIC systems allow variable names to be one or two characters in length. The first character must be a letter (A–Z). If the second character is used, it must be numeric (0–9). String variables always end with a dollar sign ($). Valid numeric variable names include A, D, T, Z, A0 and A3. Valid string variables names include A$, D$, S$, W$, A0$ and F5$.

Some examples of numeric and string variable names, invalid if written as given, are listed in Tables 3.6 and 3.7.

Although all BASIC systems allow variable names to be one or two characters in length, many allow them to be considerably longer. Table 3.8 illustrates the rules regarding the composition of variable names for some of the more popular computer systems.

TABLE 3.6   Invalid Numeric Variables and the Corresponding Valid Forms

Invalid Numeric Variables	Type of Error	Valid Numeric Variables
1P	First character must be a letter	P1 or P
Z@	Optional character must be digit or omitted	Z1 or Z
Q*	Special characters are invalid	Q3 or Q
)I	Special characters are invalid	I5 or I
A$	Optional character must be digit or omitted	A or A1

TABLE 3.7   Invalid String Variables and the Corresponding Valid Forms

Invalid String Variables	Type of Error	Valid String Variables
A	Appended dollar sign necessary	A$
$X	First character must be a letter followed by a dollar sign	X$
Y $	Blank character not permitted	Y$

When you compose variable names, make them as meaningful as possible. It is far easier to follow the various statements in a program if meaningful names are used. For example, assume the formula for gross pay is given by:

Gross Pay = Rate × Hours

The following BASIC statement represents the formula:

```
150 LET A = B * C
```

However, it is more meaningful to write:

```
150 LET G = R * H
```

And if your BASIC system allows it, it is even more meaningful to say:

```
150 LET GROSS = RATE * HOURS
```

Develop a structured style for choosing variable names in a program. During the design stage, establish guidelines for how variable names will be selected and rigorously follow these guidelines when coding the program. Of course, you must

TABLE 3.8 **Variable Naming Conventions for Some of the More Popular Computer Systems**

Computer System	Naming Convention	Valid Forms	Invalid Forms and Reason	
Apple COMMODORE TRS-80	A variable name begins with a letter and may be of any length. The letter may be followed by letters and digits. However, only *the first two characters* of the variable name are used to distinguish one name from another. Keywords like LET, PRINT and END or any other word that has special meaning to BASIC may not be included in the variable name. It is important to note that the variable name *COUNT* and *COT* represent the same variable.	S D1 SUM COUNTER NAME\$ CUST\$ DAYNAME\$ G6\$	IFTAL F T\$ FILET VALUE\$ 1AB	IF is a keyword. Blank character not allowed. LET is a keyword. VAL is a function name and has special meaning to BASIC. Must begin with a letter.
DEC Rainbow IBM PC Macintosh In general, any system running Microsoft BASIC.	A variable name begins with a letter and may be of any length. The letter may be followed by letters, digits and decimal points. Only *the first 40 characters* are significant. A variable name may not be a keyword or any other word that has special meaning to BASIC, but the variable name may contain embedded keywords or words that have special meaning to BASIC.	D F4 CUST.COUNT WEEK.1.SALES TOTAL FILET\$ F5\$	GOTO %RATE\$ A B 1AB IF\$	GOTO is a keyword. Must begin with a letter. Blank character not allowed. Must begin with a letter. IF is a keyword.
DEC VAX-11 In general, any system running BASIC-PLUS-2.	A variable name begins with a letter followed by up to 29 letters, digits, underscores and decimal points. For a string variable name, the \$ at the end counts as one of the 29 characters.	S J3 SUMMATION TOTAL.COUNT CUST_NAME\$ SALESPERSON\$ DO\$ J\$	1AB A#B _S	Must begin with a letter. Number sign is invalid. Must begin with a letter.

abide by the rules that may restrict or enhance the ways you make up variable names.

This book abides by the more stringent rules for constructing variable names to ensure that, with respect to variable names, all programs in this book will execute properly on your system.

Nearly every serious BASIC program, when first written, contains errors. BASIC systems will detect many of the more common types of BASIC statement errors, and they will display appropriate diagnostic messages.   **Undefined Variables**

One of the most common errors beginners make is not to define variables for computation. An **undefined variable** has no value assigned to it by the programmer during the execution of the program. Undefined variables are not detected by the BASIC system during the process of translating a BASIC program into its equivalent machine-language instructions. All numeric variables are assigned a value of zero and all string variables the null string when the system command RUN is issued for the program.

It is recommended that all variables be assigned valid values through the use of the LET or INPUT statements, rather than relying on BASIC to **initialize** them for you. Assigning variables a valid value before they are used for computation purposes will decrease your debugging effort and increase your confidence in the program. Furthermore, defining variables is an excellent habit, because few other programming languages automatically initialize variables to a valid value.

Program 3.5 represents a program with an undefined variable X in line 150 and 160.

```
            100 REM PROGRAM 3.5
            110 REM EXAMPLE OF A PROGRAM
            120 REM WITH AN UNDEFINED VARIABLE
            130 LET A = 4
            140 LET B = 6
            150 LET C = A + B + X
            160 PRINT "THE VALUE OF X IS"; X
            170 PRINT "THE VALUE OF C IS"; C
            180 END

            RUN

            THE VALUE OF X IS 0
            THE VALUE OF C IS 10
```

PROGRAM 3.5

To avoid problems brought on by undefined variables in a program, make sure all variables are assigned initial values.

Declaring Variable Types

The name of a variable determines whether it is string or numeric, and if numeric, what its precision is.

As the last character in a variable name, the dollar sign ($) declares that the variable will represent a string. If the dollar sign is absent at the end of the variable name, then the variable is declared to be numeric. The presence or absence of the dollar sign also informs BASIC what must be allocated for the variable by the system.

An integer variable is declared by ending the variable name with a percent sign (%). Valid integer variable names include A%, S3%, F9% and D9%. Integer variables take up less room in main storage and for that reason are often used in programs to count the number of times something has occurred. Integer variables can only hold an integer value, typically between $-32,768$ and $+32,767$. If you assign an integer variable a non-integer value BASIC will round the non-integer value to an integer.* For example,

```
            100 LET A% = 3.7
```

results in A% being assigned the value 4. Likewise the following partial program

```
            100 LET D = 5.4345
            110 LET S% = D
```

is valid and results in S% being assigned a value of 5.

If the variable type is not explicitly declared, then BASIC assumes it to be a single-precision variable.‡ Examples of single-precision variables are A, G, E4 and Y7. Table 3.9 illustrates the precision and accuracy with which values assigned to single-precision variables are stored and displayed for some of the popular computer systems.

TABLE 3.9   Precision and Accuracy of Some Computer Systems

Computer System	Values are Stored with a Precision of	Values Displayed with an Accuracy Up to
Apple	10 digits	9 digits
COMMODORE	10 digits	9 digits
DEC Rainbow	7 digits	6 digits
DEC VAX-11	7 digits	6 digits
Macintosh	14 digits (default double precision)	14 digits
IBM PC	7 digits	7 digits, the last digit may be inaccurate.
TRS-80	7 digits	6 digits

*Some BASIC systems, like DEC VAX-II BASIC, truncate the decimal portion of the non-integer value to form an integer.

‡ Variables not explicitly declared on the Macintosh are by default declared as double precision.

A numeric value, assigned to a single-precision variable in a LET statement or in response to an INPUT statement, may contain up to 38 digits. However, as illustrated in Table 3.9, only the first 7 digits for some systems are considered significant. The remaining digits are not retained, but the magnitude of the number is. For example, the statement 100 LET A = 1234567898 is stored as .1234567E+10 and displayed as .123457E+10 by a statement like 110 PRINT A. When displaying a value that is stored to the maximum precision, most computer systems round off the last digit.

Some BASIC systems allow for double-precision variables. Like single-precision variables, a double-precision variable may be assigned up to 38 digits. The value may be positive or negative. The difference between the two types of variables is in the precision. A double-precision variable can store a value with 16 or 17 digits of precision, depending on the computer system being used.

Some computer systems do not allow for double-precision variables. In Microsoft BASIC, a double-precision variable is declared by appending a number sign (#) to the variable name. On large computer systems, a variable is declared as double-precision in a DECLARE statement. Examples of double precision variables in Microsoft BASIC are S#, X1# and V#.

The following program illustrates the difference, in terms of the results displayed, between assigning the constant 10,023,457,656 to a single-precision variable S and a double-precision variable D#.

```
100 LET S = 10023457656
110 LET D# = 10023457656
120 PRINT "THE VALUE IN SINGLE PRECISION IS"; S
130 PRINT "THE VALUE IN DOUBLE PRECISION IS"; D#
140 END

RUN

THE VALUE IN SINGLE PRECISION IS 1.00235E10
THE VALUE IN DOUBLE PRECISION IS 10023457656
```

Although single-precision variables are adequate for most applications, real world applications, especially in finance, may require the use of double-precision variables for accuracy.

The following program requests that string data be entered in response to the INPUT statements.

Assigning String Variables Values Through the INPUT **Statement**

```
100 REM PROGRAM 3.6
110 REM ENTERING STRING DATA IN
120 REM RESPONSE TO THE INPUT STATEMENT
130 REM *******************************
140 INPUT "MODEL NUMBER"; M$
150 INPUT "PART NUMBER"; P$
160 INPUT "DESCRIPTION"; D$
170 PRINT
180 PRINT "THE MODEL NUMBER IS "; M$
190 PRINT "THE PART NUMBER IS "; P$
200 PRINT "THE DESCRIPTION IS "; D$
210 END

RUN

MODEL NUMBER? "Q1937A"
PART NUMBER? "345123"
DESCRIPTION? "NYLON, DISC"

THE MODEL NUMBER IS Q1937A
THE PART NUMBER IS 345123
THE DESCRIPTION IS NYLON, DISC
```

Quoted string data entered in response to the program's INPUT statements

PROGRAM 3.6

In Program 3.6 the string variables M$, P$ and D$ are assigned quoted strings following the rules for string constants. In general, surrounding a string with quotation marks is optional when using an INPUT statement to assign the string to a string variable. Examine the following output from Program 3.6 when quoted and unquoted strings are entered.

```
RUN

MODEL NUMBER? Q1937A                            Unquoted strings
PART NUMBER? 345123
DESCRIPTION? "NYLON, DISC"                       Quoted strings

THE MODEL NUMBER IS Q1937A
THE PART NUMBER IS 345123
THE DESCRIPTION IS NYLON, DISC
```

The first two string data items Q1937A and 345123 are entered as unquoted strings. The third data item NYLON,DISC is entered within quotes because it contains an embedded comma. Quotation marks are only necessary if one of the following characteristics is true of the string data item:

1) The string contains leading or trailing blanks.
2) The string contains a comma.

The following rule summarizes the assignment of string data items through the use of the INPUT statement.

> INPUT **Rule 3:** String data assigned to string variables through the use of the INPUT statement may be entered with or without surrounding quotation marks, provided the string contains no leading or trailing blanks or embedded commas. If the string contains leading or trailing blanks or embedded commas, it must be surrounded with quotation marks.

In Chapter 9 we will discuss the LINE INPUT statement, which assigns any character entered, including the space, comma and quotation marks, to the string variable in question.

**Displaying
String Variables**

BASIC does not add leading or trailing spaces when it displays a string value. Therefore, when the semicolon is used as the separator between string items in a PRINT statement, a space should be included to separate the values displayed. Line 180 of the following partial program includes a space following the word IS in the string constant. This causes the system to display the value of M$ one space after the word IS.

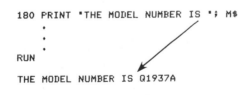

```
180 PRINT "THE MODEL NUMBER IS "; M$
      .
      .
      .
RUN

THE MODEL NUMBER IS Q1937A
```

If the space after IS is omitted, the system displays the value of M$ right next to it, as shown here:

```
180 PRINT "THE MODEL NUMBER IS"; M$
      .
      .
      .
RUN

THE MODEL NUMBER ISQ1937A
```

The LET statement in BASIC is used to assign a value to a variable. The general form of the LET statement is given in Table 3.10. Each LET statement consists of the keyword LET, followed by a variable, followed by an equal sign, and then by an expression.

TABLE 3.10   The LET **Statement**

General Form:	LET numeric variable = numeric expression
	or
	LET string variable = string expression
Purpose:	Causes the evaluation of the expression, followed by the assignment of the resulting value to the variable to the left of the equal sign.
| *Examples:* | ```
100 LET H = A + 7
150 LET Q = (B + A)/2 - Q + R
200 LET C = C + 1
250 LET X = -X
300 LET A(Y, 4) = 0
350 LET D$ = "PRICE"
400 LET F$ = G$
450 LET P(I) = C(K) + P(J)
500 LET E = M * C^2
550 LET A$ = B$ + "001"
``` |
| *Note:* | The keyword LET is optional. |

TABLE 3.11   Invalid LET **Statements and the Corresponding Valid** LET **Statements**

Invalid LET *Statements*	*Reason for Error*	*Valid* LET *Statements*
`100 LET X/Y = 10`	Expression not permitted to left of the equal sign.	`100 LET Z = 10`
`100 LET 1984 = Z`	Constant not permitted to left of the equal sign.	`100 LET Z = 1984`
`100 LET -X(K) = 20 * D`	Arithmetic operator not permitted to the left of the equal sign.	`100 LET X(K) = -20 * D`
`100 LET X - 1 = A + B`	Expression not permitted to left of the equal sign.	`100 LET X = A + B + 1`
`100 LET #S = M * N`	Invalidly formed variable name to the left of the equal sign.	`100 LET S = M * N`
`100 LET A = "CREDIT"`	Variable to the left of the equal sign must be of the same type (string) as the constant.	`100 LET A$ = "CREDIT"`

`100 LET A$ = X - 4`	Same as previous example.	`100 LET A = X - 4`
		OR
		`100 LET A$ = "X - 4"`

Table 3.11 lists some invalid LET statements and their possible valid counterparts. Constants and expressions involving arithmetic operations are not permitted to the left of the equal sign.

The execution of the LET statement is not a one-step process for the processor. The execution of a LET statement requires two steps, evaluation and assignment.

Although the = sign is employed in BASIC, it does not carry all the properties of the = sign in mathematics. For example, the = sign in BASIC does not allow for the symmetric relationship. That is,

```
100 LET A = B
```

cannot be written as

```
100 B = LET A
```
```

The = sign in BASIC can best be described as meaning "is replaced by." Therefore in Program 3.3

```
160 LET I = P * R * T/360
```

means: replace the old value of I with the value determined from the expression to the right of the equal sign.

Since the equal sign has this unique meaning in BASIC, the statement

```
100 LET Y = Y + 1
```

has a valid meaning in the BASIC language, while in algebra the statement

$$Y = Y + 1$$

is meaningless.

Programming Case Study 5: Finding the Single Discount Rate

Program 3.7 determines the single discount rate equal to the series of discount rates of 25%, 10% and 10% using the following formula:

$$R = 1 - (1 - r_1)(1 - r_2)(1 - r_3)\cdots(1 - r_n)$$

where R is the single discount rate, and r_1, $r_2 \ldots r_n$ is the series of discount rates. The number of factors of $(1 - r_n)$ that are used to determine the single discount rate is dependent on the number of discounts. Program 3.7 is written to find the single discount rate of a series of *three* discount rates.

```
100 REM PROGRAM 3.7
110 REM FINDING THE SINGLE DISCOUNT RATE
120 REM R = SINGLE DISCOUNT RATE
130 REM ********************************
140 PRINT "ENTER IN DECIMAL FORM THE:"
150 INPUT "            FIRST DISCOUNT"; R1
160 INPUT "            SECOND DISCOUNT"; R2
170 INPUT "            THIRD DISCOUNT"; R3
180 LET R = 1 - (1 - R1) * (1 - R2) * (1 - R3)
190 PRINT
200 PRINT "THE SINGLE DISCOUNT IS"; R
210 END

RUN

ENTER IN DECIMAL FORM THE:
            FIRST DISCOUNT? 0.25
            SECOND DISCOUNT? 0.10
            THIRD DISCOUNT? 0.10

THE SINGLE DISCOUNT IS .3925
```

PROGRAM 3.7

After the three discount rates are assigned their decimal values, the LET statement in line 180 determines the value of the single discount from the expression found to the right of the equal sign. Specifically, the expression is evaluated and the final value 0.3925 is assigned to the variable R. Line 200 displays the value for R before the program ends.

When dealing with rates that usually occur in percent form, it is often preferable to have the program accept the data and display the results in percent form. Program 3.8 shows how you can write a solution to Programming Case Study 5 that accomplishes this task.

In Program 3.8, the INPUT statements (lines 150 through 170) prompt the user to enter the discount rates in percent form. In lines 180 through 200, the rates are changed from percent form to decimal form by dividing R1, R2 and R3 by 100. The single discount is then determined by line 210. Line 220 replaces the assigned value of R (0.3925) with 100 times R. In other words, line 220 changes the value of R from decimal form to percent form. Line 240 then displays the value of R. The string constant % found at the end of line 240 helps identify the result as a percent value.

```
100 REM PROGRAM 3.8
110 REM FINDING THE SINGLE DISCOUNT RATE
120 REM R = SINGLE DISCOUNT RATE
130 REM ********************************
140 PRINT "ENTER IN PERCENT FORM THE:"
150 INPUT "          FIRST DISCOUNT"; R1
160 INPUT "          SECOND DISCOUNT"; R2
170 INPUT "          THIRD DISCOUNT"; R3
180 LET R1 = R1/100
190 LET R2 = R2/100
200 LET R3 = R3/100
210 LET R = 1 - (1 - R1) * (1 - R2) * (1 - R3)
220 LET R = 100 * R
230 PRINT
240 PRINT "THE SINGLE DISCOUNT IS"; R; "%"
250 END

RUN

ENTER IN PERCENT FORM THE:
          FIRST DISCOUNT? 25
          SECOND DISCOUNT? 10
          THIRD DISCOUNT? 10

THE SINGLE DISCOUNT IS 39.25 %
```

PROGRAM 3.8

Program 3.8 includes two concepts that many beginners have difficulty understanding. The first is that the same variable—R1, for example, in line 180—can be found on both sides of the equal sign. The second concerns the reuse of a variable that had been assigned a value through computations in an earlier LET statement. In Program 3.8, R1, R2 and R3 are reused in line 210 after being assigned values in earlier LET statements. There are several exercises at the end of this chapter that will help you to better understand these important concepts.

3.5 EXPRESSIONS

Expressions may be either numeric or string. **Numeric expressions** consist of one or more numeric constants, numeric variables and numeric function references, all of which are separated from each other by parentheses and arithmetic operators.* **String expressions** consist of one or more string constants, string variables and string function references separated by the **concatenation operator** (+).

A programmer must be concerned with both the formation and the evaluation of an expression. It is necessary to consider what an expression is, as well as what constitutes validity in an expression, before it is possible to write valid BASIC statements with confidence.

Formation of Numeric Expressions

The definition of a numeric expression dictates the manner in which a numeric expression is to be validly formed. For example, it may be perfectly clear to you that the following *invalid* statement has been formed to assign A twice the value of B.

```
100 LET A = 2B
```

However, the computer will reject the statement because a constant and a variable within the same expression must be separated by an arithmetic operator. The statement can validly be written

```
100 LET A = 2 * B
```

An example of another invalidly formed numeric expression is shown in the following statement:

```
100 LET A = B + -2 * A
```

This statement is invalid because no two successive characters may be arithmetic

---

* Function references are discussed at the end of Section 3.5.

TABLE 3.12   Invalidly Formed Numeric Expressions Due to the Misuse of Arithmetic Operators

Invalid Numeric Expression	Valid Numeric Expression
1) 2 * −4	2 * (−4) or −2 * 4
2) B + −3	B + (−3) or B − 3
3) D − +25	D − (+25) or D − 25
4) − +1984	−1984
5) − −1984	+1984
6) + −1984	−1984
7) 50T	50 * T
8) 2J + 10	2 * J + 10
9) A/−E	A/(−E) or −A/E
10) (5I) ∧ (2K)/+500	(5 * I) ∧ (2 * K)/500

operators in a numeric expression. That is, the "+ −" makes the above expression invalid, which makes the entire statement invalid. The numeric expression must be rewritten either as B − 2 * A or as −2 * A + B in order to be validly formed. To state this in another way, we can say that the arithmetic operators must always be separated from each other by constants, variables, function references or parentheses in a numeric expression. Table 3.12 shows a number of invalidly formed numeric expressions, together with one or more corresponding valid expressions in each case.

A numeric expression may consist of only one constant, like 1984, or of only one variable, like B. In Table 3.12 examples 4, 5 and 6 show that, if an expression has only one constant, the constant may be preceded by a minus or a plus sign. This is also true for a variable. Even though

−1984
+1984
−B
+B

are four valid numeric expressions, all of the following are invalid and meaningless numeric expressions in BASIC:

* 1984
/ 1984
* B   } Invalid
/ B
∧ B

Finally, it is invalid to use a string variable or string constant in a numeric expression. The following are invalid numeric expressions:

```
6 + "DEBIT"/C    }  Invalid
A$/B + C$ - 19   }
```

Pay close attention to the formation of valid numeric expressions. Remember that a machine is dealing with the program in its translation and execution stages and is not some sort of electronic human being. As a result, you may assert your individuality by selecting one variable name over another, but not by using − −2 * A instead of +2 * A or 2 * A in a numeric expression.

Evaluation of Numeric Expressions

Formation of complex expressions involving several arithmetic operations can sometimes create problems. For example, consider the statement:

```
100 LET A = 8/4/2
```

Does this assign a value of 1 or 4 to A? The answer depends on how the BASIC system evaluates the expression. If it completes the operation 8/4 first and only then 2/2, the expression yields the value 1. If the system completes the second operation, 4/2, first and only then 8/2, it yields 4.

In BASIC the **evaluation** of an expression—the assigning of a value to that expression—follows the normal algebraic rules. Therefore, the expression 8/4/2 yields a value of 1.

The order in which the operations in an expression are evaluated is given by the following rule:

> **Precedence Rule 1:** Unless parentheses dictate otherwise, reading from left to right in a numeric expression, all exponentiations are performed first, then all multiplications and/or divisions, and finally all additions and/or subtractions.

This order of operations is sometimes called the **rules of precedence**, or the **hierarchy of operations**. The meaning of these rules can be made clear with some examples.

For example, the expression $18/3 \wedge 2 + 4 * 2$ is evaluated as follows:

$$
\begin{aligned}
18/3 \wedge 2 + 4 * 2 &= 18/9 + 4 * 2 \\
&= 2 \quad + 4 * 2 \\
&= 2 \quad + 8 \\
&= 10
\end{aligned}
$$

If you had trouble following the logic behind this evaluation, use the following technique. Whenever a numeric expression is to be evaluated, "look" or "scan" from *left* to *right* three different times applying the Precedence Rule 1. On the first scan, every time you encounter an $\wedge$ operator, you perform exponentiation. In this example, 3 is raised to the power of 2, yielding 9.

On the second scan, moving from left to right again, every time you encounter the operators $*$ and $/$, you perform multiplication and division, respectively. Hence, in the previous example, 18 is divided by 9, yielding 2, and 4 and 2 are multiplied, yielding 8.

On the third scan, moving again from left to right, every time you detect the operators $+$ and $-$, you perform addition and subtraction, respectively. In this example, 2 and 8 are added to form 10.

The expression below yields the value of -2.73, as follows:

$$
\begin{aligned}
2 - 3 * 4/5 \wedge 2 + 5/4 * 3 - 2 \wedge 3 &= 2 - 3 * 4/25 + 5/4 * 3 - 8 \text{ (at end of first scan)} \\
&= 2 - 0.48 + 3.75 - 8 \text{ (at end of second scan)} \\
&= -2.73 \text{ (at end of third scan)}
\end{aligned}
$$

When necessary, BASIC will convert a value from one precision to another. That is, you may mix variable and constant types within an expression. BASIC evaluates the following statement

```
100 LET A = D/C% + 4
```

by converting the variables and constant in the expression D/C% + 4 to the same precision, that of the most precise variable, D. The result is computed in single-precision and then assigned to the variable A, which in this case is also single-precision.

In the following statement

```
100 LET C% = F/E%
```

the system evaluates the expression F/E% in single-precision. It then converts the single-precision result to an integer upon assigning the result of the expression to C%.

The Effect of Parentheses in the Evaluation of Numeric Expressions

Parentheses may be used to change the order of operations. In BASIC parentheses are normally used to avoid ambiguity and to group terms in a numeric expression; they do *not* imply multiplication. The order in which the operations in an expression containing parentheses are evaluated is given in the following rule:

> **Precedence Rule 2:** When parentheses are inserted into an expression, the part of the expression within the parentheses is evaluated first and then the remaining expression is evaluated according to Precedence Rule 1.

If the first example contained parentheses, as $(18/3) \wedge 2 + 4 * 2$ does, then it would be evaluated in the following manner:

$$
\begin{aligned}
(18/3) \wedge 2 + 4 * 2 &= 6 \wedge 2 + 4 * 2 \\
&= 36 + 4 * 2 \\
&= 36 + 8 \\
&= 44
\end{aligned}
$$

Note the different value for the numeric expression. The rule is: *make three scans from left to right within each pair of parentheses and only after this make the standard three passes over the entire numeric expression.*

The expression below yields the value of **1.41**, as follows:

$$
\begin{aligned}
(2 - 3 * 4/5) \wedge 2 + 5/(4 * 3 - 2 \wedge 3) &= (2 - 3 * 4/5) \wedge 2 + 5/(4 * 3 - 8) \\
&= (2 - 2.4) \wedge 2 + 5/(12 - 8) \\
&= (-0.4) \wedge 2 + 5/4 \\
&= 0.16 + 5/4 \\
&= 0.16 + 1.25 \\
&= 1.41
\end{aligned}
$$

A rule of thumb for utilizing parentheses in your first programs is: *use parentheses freely when in doubt as to the formation and evaluation of a numeric expression.* For example, if you wish to have the computer divide $8 * D$ by $3 \wedge P$, the expression may correctly be written as $8 * D/3 \wedge P$, but you may also write it as $(8 * D)/(3 \wedge P)$ and feel more certain of the result.

For more complex expressions, BASIC allows parentheses to be contained within other parentheses. When this occurs, the parentheses are said to be **nested**. In this case the BASIC system evaluates the innermost parenthetical expression first and then goes on to the outermost. Thus, $18/3 \wedge 2 + (3 * (2 + 5))$ would be broken down in the following manner:

$$
\begin{aligned}
18/3 \wedge 2 + (3 * (2 + 5)) &= 18/3 \wedge 2 + (3 * 7) \\
&= 18/3 \wedge 2 + 21 \\
&= 18/9 + 21 \\
&= 2 + 21 \\
&= 23
\end{aligned}
$$

Table 3.13 illustrates the rules discussed above. Study each expression and the methods used to evaluate them. Two of the most common errors beginners make are surrounding the wrong part of an expression with parentheses and not balancing the parentheses, as shown in Table 3.14. Be sure that an expression has as many closed parentheses as open parentheses. When operations of the same

TABLE 3.13   Evaluation of Numeric Expressions

Numeric Expression	Interpretation and Evaluation of Numeric Expression
1) $6 + 4 * 2$	$6 + (4 * 2) = 6 + 8 = 14$
2) $5 - 3 - 2$	$(5 - 3) - 2 = 2 - 2 = 0$
3) $32/8/2$	$(32/8)/2 = 4/2 = 2$
4) $40/10 * 3$	$(40/10) * 3 = 4 * 3 = 12$
5) $6 * 8 - 7 * 2$	$(6 * 8) - (7 * 2) = 48 - 14 = 34$
6) $5 * ((6 + 4) - 2)$	$5 * (10 - 2) = 5 * 8 = 40$
7) $2 \wedge (2 + 3) - 4$	$2 \wedge 5 - 4 = 32 - 4 = 28$
8) $5 \wedge 2 \wedge 2$	$(5 \wedge 2) \wedge 2 = 25^2 = 625$

TABLE 3.14   Invalidly Formed Numeric Expressions Due to the Misuse of Parentheses

Mathematical Expression	Invalid Numeric Expression	Valid Numeric Expression
1) $Y(B^3)$	$(Y * B) \wedge 3$	$Y * B \wedge 3$
3) $\dfrac{A}{B - 4}$	$A/B - 4$ or $(A/B) - 4$	$A/(B - 4)$
3) $\dfrac{3 * 4 - E}{5}$	$(3 * 4) - E/5$ or $3 * 4 - E/5$	$(3 * 4 - E)/5$
4) $8(I - 6.66)$	$8 * I - 6.66$ or $(8 * I) - 6.66$	$8 * (I - 6.66)$
5) $A^{(B^C)}$	$(A \wedge (B \wedge C)$	$A \wedge (B \wedge C)$

TABLE 3.15   BASIC Equivalent of Algebraic Statements

Algebraic Statements	BASIC Equivalent LET Statement
1) $H = \sqrt{X^2 + Y^2}$	`130 LET H = (X^2 + Y^2)^0.5`
2) $S = AL^P K^{1-P}$	`170 LET S = A * L^P * K^(1 - P)`
3) $Q = \dfrac{-b + \sqrt{b^2 - 4ac}}{2a}$	`220 LET Q = (-B + (B^2 - 4 * A * C)^0.5)/(2 * A)`
4) $A = F\left[\dfrac{r}{(1 + r)^n - 1}\right]$	`350 LET A = F * (R/(((1 + R)^N) - 1))`
5) $P = \sqrt[3]{(x - p)^2 + y^2}$	`600 LET P = ((X - P)^2 + Y^2)^(1/3)`
6) $Z = \dfrac{ab}{x + \sqrt{x^2 - a^2}}$	`810 LET Z = A * B/(X + (X^2 - A^2)^0.5)`

precedence are encountered, Precedence Rule 1 applies. For example,

$A - B - C$ is interpreted as $(A - B) - C$
$A/B/C$ is interpreted as $(A/B)/C$
$A \wedge B \wedge C$ is interpreted as $(A \wedge B) \wedge C$

Table 3.15 gives examples of the BASIC equivalent of some algebraic statements.

To illustrate the order of operations and the use of parentheses, here is still a third solution to Programming Case Study 5.

Program 3.9 is similar to Program 3.8 in that both the data entered and the result displayed are in percent form. The major difference is that in this new solution all the computations have been incorporated into a single LET statement. Lines 180 through 210 in Program 3.8 have been replaced by a new line 180 in Program 3.9.

```
100 REM PROGRAM 3.9
110 REM FINDING THE SINGLE DISCOUNT RATE
120 REM R = SINGLE DISCOUNT RATE
130 REM *********************************
140 PRINT "ENTER IN PERCENT FORM THE:"
150 INPUT "            FIRST DISCOUNT"; R1
160 INPUT "           SECOND DISCOUNT"; R2
170 INPUT "            THIRD DISCOUNT"; R3
180 LET R = 1 - (1 - R1/100) * (1 - R2/100) * (1 - R3/100)
190 LET R = 100 * R
200 PRINT
210 PRINT "THE SINGLE DISCOUNT IS"; R; "%"
220 END

RUN

ENTER IN PERCENT FORM THE:
            FIRST DISCOUNT? 25
           SECOND DISCOUNT? 10
            THIRD DISCOUNT? 10

THE SINGLE DISCOUNT IS 39.25 %
```

PROGRAM 3.9

The programmer's ability to control the sequence of operations with the use of parentheses is obvious in Program 3.9. If you have a mathematical background you will surely find the method employed in Program 3.9 to your liking. If you have less confidence in your mathematical ability you may find it easier to use the technique of using multiple LET statements, as shown in Program 3.8.

The following rules summarize the arithmetic rules discussed in this section.

Arithmetic Rule 2: A numeric expression is a sequence of one or more numeric constants, numeric variables and function references, separated from each other by parentheses and arithmetic operators.

Arithmetic Rule 3: A numeric expression may not contain two consecutive arithmetic operators.

Arithmetic Rule 4: The formation and evaluation of numeric expressions follow the normal algebraic rules.

Construction of Error Free Numeric Expressions

Once you have written a numeric expression observing the precedence rules, the system is capable of translating it. No error messages will be generated. However, this is no guarantee that the system will actually be able to execute the instructions. In other words, although a numeric expression may be validly formed, a system may not be able to evaluate it because of the numbers involved. In situations where error conditions arise, the system will do one of two things, depending on the type of error. The **fatal error** causes the system to terminate execution of the program. The **non-fatal error** causes the system to supply a value to the expression which depends on the type of non-fatal error. Listed below are some rules that will help you to avoid such hazards. In your program:

   1) Do not attempt to divide by zero.
   2) Do not attempt to determine the square root of a negative value.
   3) Do not attempt to raise a negative value to a non-integral value.
   4) Do not attempt to compute a value that is greater than the largest permissible value or less than the smallest non-zero permissible value of the BASIC system.

It is also important that you understand that the evaluation of a numeric expression gives as a value a *processor approximation of the mathematical value* represented by each operation in a numeric expression. Depending upon the particular processor involved, the value assigned to 2/3 might be 0.666666, 0.666667, or 0.666665, and the value assigned to $2 \wedge 2$ might be 4.00000, 4.00001, or 3.99999. Many computers are capable of "being correct" to within 1 in the last significant digit for certain of their evaluations. On the other hand, in some cases this departure from the mathematical value can be much larger. Consult your user's manual or other references if you need to know these details.

By way of a dramatic summary, Figure 3.2 illustrates some of the combinations that should be avoided in numeric expressions written in a BASIC program.

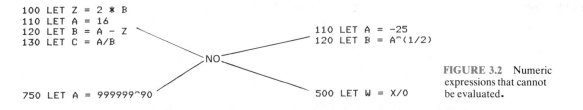

```
100 LET Z = 2 * B
110 LET A = 16
120 LET B = A - Z
130 LET C = A/B

750 LET A = 999999^90
```

NO

```
110 LET A = -25
120 LET B = A^(1/2)

500 LET W = X/0
```

FIGURE 3.2 Numeric expressions that cannot be evaluated.

String Expressions

The ability to process strings of characters is an essential part of any programming language that is to be used for business applications. Letters, words, names, and a combination of letters and numbers can play an important role in generating readable reports and easing communication between non-data-processing personnel and the computer.

In BASIC, string expressions include string constants, string variables, string function references and a combination of the three separated by the concatenation operator $(+)$. Consider the following program:

```
100 REM PROGRAM 3.10
110 REM EXAMPLES OF STRING EXPRESSIONS
120 REM *****************************
130 INPUT "AREA CODE"; A$
140 INPUT "LOCAL NUMBER"; T$
150 LET B$ = A$
160 LET C$ = "TELEPHONE NUMBER "
170 LET D$ = A$ + "-" + T$
180 PRINT
190 PRINT C$; D$
200 PRINT "AREA CODE "; B$
210 END

RUN

AREA CODE? 219
LOCAL NUMBER? 844-0520

TELEPHONE NUMBER 219-844-0520
AREA CODE 219
```

PROGRAM 3.10

Examples of string expressions in Program 3.10 include:

1) The string variable A$ in line 150, which is assigned to B$.
2) The string TELEPHONE NUMBER in line 160, which is assigned to C$.
3) The expression A$ + "−" + T$ in line 170, which is assigned to D$.

In line 170 the plus sign is the concatenation operator. When strings are concatenated, the resultant expression combines the value of each term in the order they are found in the expression to yield a single string. The value of D$, which is displayed by line 190, is illustrated in the output results of Program 3.10.

TABLE 3.16   **Some Common String Functions**

Function	Function Value
LEFT$(X$, N)	Returns the leftmost N characters of the string argument X$
LEN(X$)	Returns the number of characters in the value associated with the string argument X$
MID$(X$, P, N)	Returns N characters of the string argument X$ beginning at P
RIGHT$(X$, N)	Returns the rightmost N characters of the string argument X$

Where X$ is a string expression, and N and P are numeric expressions.

Use of LEFT$, LEN, MID$ **and** RIGHT$ **String Functions**

Although concatenation is the only valid string operation, most BASIC systems include functions that allow for additional string manipulation. The string functions most commonly found in BASIC systems are presented in Table 3.16.

The following program illustrates the use of the functions found in Table 3.16.

```
100 REM PROGRAM 3.11
110 REM EXAMPLE OF REFERENCING STRING FUNCTIONS
120 REM ********************************
130 REM *****REQUEST TELEPHONE NUMBER*****
140 INPUT "COMPLETE TELEPHONE NUMBER"; T$
150 LET A$ = LEFT$(T$, 3)
160 LET P$ = MID$(T$, 5, 3)
170 LET N$ = RIGHT$(T$, 4)
180 LET N = LEN(T$)
190 PRINT
200 PRINT "THE AREA CODE IS "; A$
210 PRINT "THE PREFIX NUMBER IS "; P$
220 PRINT "THE LAST FOUR DIGITS ARE "; N$
230 PRINT "THE NUMBER OF CHARACTERS IN "; T$; " IS"; N
240 END

RUN

COMPLETE TELEPHONE NUMBER? 219-844-0520

THE AREA CODE IS 219
THE PREFIX NUMBER IS 844
THE LAST FOUR DIGITS ARE 0520
THE NUMBER OF CHARACTERS IN 219-844-0520 IS 12
```

PROGRAM 3.11

In Program 3.11, the function LEFT$ in line 150 assigns the three leftmost characters of T$ to A$. A$ is assigned the string 219. In line 160, the MID$ function assigns 3 characters beginning with the fifth character 8 in T$ to P$. P$ is assigned the string 844. In line 170, the function RIGHT$ assigns the last four characters of T$ to N$. N$ is assigned the string 0520. Finally, in line 180, the numeric variable N is assigned a value equal to the number of characters in T$. N is assigned the numeric value 12.

For a more detailed discussion on the operation of concatenation and the LEFT$, LEN, MID$ and RIGHT$ functions, see Section 9.2.

3.6 ROUNDING, TRUNCATION AND THE INT **FUNCTION**

Many applications often require that computation results be **rounded** or **truncated** before being displayed. Consider again Program 3.2, which determines the Banker's Simple Interest, and the following revised loan data:

Principal — $4,850
Rate   — 15.6%
Time   — 95 days

Since the result 199.658 represents a monetary amount, it should be displayed in terms of dollars and cents, that is, to the nearest hundredths place—rounded to 199.66 or truncated to 199.65. There are various ways to round or truncate a result in BASIC. In this section, a generalized procedure for rounding and truncating will be developed. Later in Chapter 4, the PRINT USING statement will be used to display a result in rounded form.

```
100 REM PROGRAM 3.2
110 REM BANKER'S SIMPLE INTEREST
120 REM ***********************
130 LET R = 0.156
140 INPUT "PRINCIPAL"; P
150 INPUT "TIME IN DAYS"; T
160 LET I = P * R * T/360
170 PRINT
180 PRINT "THE INTEREST IS $"; I
190 END

RUN

PRINCIPAL? 4850
TIME IN DAYS? 95

THE INTEREST IS $ 199.658
```

PROGRAM 3.2

**Developing a
Rounding and
Truncation Procedure**

Recall from your earlier years in school that the rounding operation involves two steps. Assuming you are dealing with positive numbers, you first add five to the digit to the right of the digit to be retained. For example,

$$199.658 + 0.005 = 199.663$$

Second, you truncate the digits to the right of the digit to be retained. For example,

$$199.663 = 199.66$$

This second step of the rounding operation is the most complex part of the procedure for a beginner to grasp. However, we can handle this in the following way:

1) Multiply the value 199.663 by 100: $199.663 \times 100 = 19966.3$

2) Truncate the digits to the right of the decimal: $19966.3 = 19966$

3) Divide the resultant value by 100: $19966 \% 100 = 199.66$ (rounded result)

Combining the steps we may write the BASIC code in the following way:

Step 1 —— `161 LET I = I + 0.005`

Step 2 ——
```
162 LET I = I * 100
163 LET I = INT(I)
164 LET I = I/100
```

Line 163 in this code makes reference to the Integer function (INT). The Integer function is one of the numeric functions that is available in BASIC to handle mathematical calculations that are needed frequently. These functions are discussed in detail in Chapter 9.

Table 3.17 lists some examples of the function INT. The expression following the function name INT and surrounded by parentheses is called the **argument**. The Integer function, INT, returns the largest integer not greater than the argument.

With parentheses the BASIC code can be rewritten as a single statement for rounding a value.

```
165 LET I = INT((I + 0.005) * 100)/100
```

TABLE 3.17   Examples of the Function INT

Value of Variable	The Statement	Results In
Q = 10.8	`100 LET Q = INT(Q)`	Q = 10
X = 1.6543	`110 LET X = INT(X + 0.5)`	X = 2
Y = −3.45	`120 LET W = INT(Y)`	W = −4

Similarly, the BASIC code can be rewritten as a single statement for truncating a value.

```
185 LET I = INT(I * 100)/100
```

Recall from our earlier discussions that the operations found in the innermost set of parentheses are completed first. Therefore, in line 165 the number 0.005 is added to the value of I first, and only then is the sum multiplied by 100. The INT function returns the largest integer not greater than the argument—this integer, in turn, is divided by 100.

Program 3.12, which is similar to Program 3.2 except for the inclusion of lines 165, 185 and 190, illustrates the use of the procedures developed for rounding and truncating to the nearest hundredth, before displaying them.

```
100 REM PROGRAM 3.12
110 REM BANKER'S SIMPLE INTEREST WITH ROUNDING AND TRUNCATION
120 REM ********************************************************
130 LET R = 0.156
140 INPUT "PRINCIPAL"; P
150 INPUT "TIME IN DAYS"; T
160 LET I = P * R * T/360
165 LET I = INT((I + 0.005) * 100)/100
170 PRINT
180 PRINT "THE INTEREST IS $"; I; "(ROUNDED)"
185 LET I = INT(I * 100)/100
190 PRINT "THE INTEREST IS $"; I; "(TRUNCATED)"
200 END

RUN

PRINCIPAL? 4850
TIME IN DAYS? 95

THE INTEREST IS $ 199.66 (ROUNDED)
THE INTEREST IS $ 199.65 (TRUNCATED)
```

PROGRAM 3.12

3.7
WHAT YOU
SHOULD KNOW

1. Constants are values that do not change during the execution of a program.
2. There are two types of constants—numeric constants and string constants.
3. Numeric constants represent ordinary numbers.
4. String constants represent strings of characters enclosed in quotation marks.
5. The only special characters allowed in a numeric constant are a leading sign (+ or − or blank), the decimal point and the letter E.
6. The letter E is used in E-type constants and stands for "times ten to the power."
7. In programming, a variable is a storage location in main memory whose value can change as the program is executed and that can be referenced by a variable name.
8. There are two types of variables in BASIC, simple variables and subscripted variables. Simple variables are used to store single values. Subscripted variables are used to store groups of values like one- or two-dimensional arrays. Either of the two can have a data type of numeric or string.
9. All BASIC systems allow variable names to be one or two characters in length. The first character must be a letter (A–Z). If the second character is used, it must be numeric (0–9).
10. Although you are sometimes limited in your selection of variable names, develop a structured style for choosing variable names in a program.
11. All variables used in a program should be assigned an initial value.
12. The name of a variable determines whether it is string or numeric, and if numeric, what its precision is.
13. As the last character in a variable name, the dollar sign declares that the variable will represent a string.
14. An integer variable is declared by ending the variable name with a percent sign.
15. A single-precision variable may be assigned up to 38 digits. The value may be positive or negative. A single-precision variable can store a value with 6 to 10 digits of precision, depending on the computer system.

16. Like a single-precision variable, a double-precision variable may be assigned a positive or negative value and up to 38 digits. A double-precision variable can store a value with 16 or 17 digits of precision, depending on the computer system.
17. Numeric data assigned to numeric variables through the use of the INPUT statement must take the form of numeric constants.
18. String data assigned to string variables through the use of the INPUT statement must be surrounded with quotation marks if the string contains leading or trailing blanks or an embedded comma.
19. The LET statement causes evaluation of the expression to the right of the equal sign, followed by assignment of the resulting value to the variable to the left of the equal sign.
20. The = sign in BASIC can best be described as meaning "is replaced by."
21. It is invalid to assign a string expression to a numeric variable or a numeric expression to a string variable.
22. A numeric expression is a sequence of one or more numeric constants, numeric variables and numeric function references separated from each other by parentheses and arithmetic operators.
23. A string expression is a sequence of one or more string constants, string variables or string function references separated by the concatenation operator.
24. The formation and evaluation of numeric expressions follow the normal algebraic rules.
25. Unless parentheses dictate otherwise, reading from left to right in a numeric expression, all exponentiations are performed first, then all multiplications and/or divisions, and finally all addition and/or subtractions. This order is called the "hierarchy of operations" or the "rules of precedence."
26. When parentheses are inserted into an expression, the part of the expression within the parentheses is evaluated first and then the remaining expression is evaluated according to the rules of precedence.
27. No numeric expression can be evaluated if it requires a value that is not mathematically defined. For example, do not divide a number by zero in your program.
28. Concatenation generates a single string value which is the result of combining the values of each of the terms in the order that they are found in the expression.
29. Most BASIC systems include the string functions LEFT$, LEN, MID$ and RIGHT$. These functions allow you to access and manipulate groups of characters (substrings) within a string.
30. The Integer function, INT, returns the largest integer not greater than the argument.
31. To round a number to the nearest hundredths place, use this formula:

    INT((I + 0.005) * 100)/100.

32. To truncate a number to the nearest hundredths place, use this formula:

    INT(I * 100)/100.

1. Consider the valid programs listed below. What is displayed if each is executed?

**3.8
SELF-TEST
EXERCISES**

a)
```
100 REM CHAPTER 3 SELF-TEST 1A
110 LET A = 4
120 LET B = 2
130 LET C = -3
140 LET A = A + B
150 LET B = B + C
160 LET C = A + B + C
170 PRINT "A ="; A
180 PRINT "B ="; B
190 PRINT "C ="; C
200 END
```

b)
```
100 REM CHAPTER 3 SELF-TEST 1B
110 REM FINDING THE AVERAGE OF 5 NUMBERS
120 LET A = 4 + 6 + 5 + 6 + 10/5
130 LET B = (4 + 6 + 5 + 6 + 10)/5
140 PRINT "IS THE AVERAGE"; A
150 PRINT "OR IS THE AVERAGE"; B
160 END
```

c) Assume X, Y and Z are assigned the values 2, 4 and 5, respectively.

```
100 REM CHAPTER 3 SELF-TEST 1C
110 INPUT "VALUES OF X, Y, Z"; X, Y, Z
120 LET W = X^3 + (Y + Z)/3 + 6 * Y - 9
130 PRINT "W ="; W
140 END
```

d) Assume that P and R are assigned the values 100 and 15, respectively.

```
100 REM CHAPTER 3 SELF-TEST 1D
110 INPUT "PRINCIPAL"; P
120 INPUT "RATE IN %"; R
130 LET R = R/100
140 LET A = P + R * P
150 PRINT "THE AMOUNT IS"; A
160 END
```

e)
```
100 REM CHAPTER 3 SELF-TEST 1E
110 LET X = 4
120 LET Y = 2
130 LET A = X + Y
140 PRINT A
150 LET B = Y - X
160 PRINT B
170 LET C = A + B - X
180 PRINT C
190 LET D = 2 * (A + B + C)/4
200 PRINT D
210 END
```

f) Assume X is assigned the value 1.

```
100 REM CHAPTER 3 SELF-TEST 1F
110 INPUT "ENTER SEED NUMBER"; X
120 LET X = X * (X + 1)
130 PRINT X
140 LET X = X * (X + 1)
150 PRINT X
160 LET X = X * (X + 1)
170 PRINT X
180 LET X = X * (X + 1)
190 PRINT X
200 END
```

2. Find the errors in the following programs.

a)
```
100 CHAPTER 3 SELF-TEST 2A
110 INPUT, A, B$
120 LET (A + B$/4) * 2 = C
130 PRINT THE ANSWER IS; C
140 END
```

b)
```
100 REM CHAPTER 3 SELF-TEST 2B
110 LET X = 42,000
120 LET B = $5.00
130 LET #A = X + B
140 PRINT #A
150 END
```

3. Categorize the following variables as numeric, string or invalid.
   a) A¢   b) X$ c) C   d) B   e) $Y   f) C$ g) Z0   h) %$ i) X9

4. Evaluate each of the following:
   a) $4 * 5 * 3/6 - 7 \wedge 2/3$ b) $(2 - 4) + 5 \wedge 2$ c) $12/6/2$

5. Calculate the numeric value for each of the following valid numeric expressions if
   $A = 3$, $B = 4$, $C = 5$, $W = 3$, $T = 4$, $X = 1$ and $Y = 2$.

   a) $(A + B/2) + 6.2$ b) $3 * (A \wedge B)/C$

   c) $(A/(C + 1) * 4 - 5)/2$ d) $X + 2 * Y * W/3 - 7/(T - X/Y) - W \wedge T$

6. Write the following ordinary numbers in E-type format.
   a) .00000001   b) 356123000

7. Given the expression: $4 + (X - (3 * Y)) \wedge 3/6$
   a) Determine the first operation performed.
   b) Determine the third operation performed.
   c) Determine the fifth operation performed.

8. Write a valid LET statement for each of the following statements.
   a) $X = \sqrt{Y + 8}$

   b) Assign Y$ the string END OF REPORT

   c) $S = \dfrac{I}{\left(1 + \dfrac{P}{50}\right)^H}$

9. Which of the following strings must be surrounded by quotation marks when entered
   in response to an INPUT statement?

   a) LISA ANN   d) Q13A9

   b) 14621   e) RELIANT

   c) 9946 REDBUD ROAD, CR. PT.   f) PLYMOUTH, RELIANT

10. Given the LET statement:

    ```
    100 LET B$ = "BASIC IS NOT EASY"
    ```

    write a LET statement that will assign A$ the following substrings:

    a) BASIC   b) IS NOT   c) EASY   d) BASIC IS EASY

11. Rewrite the LET statement for Exercise 10 using only the MID$ function.

12. Write a LET statement that will assign L the length of the string assigned to B$ in Exercise 10.

13. If necessary, insert parentheses so that each numeric expression results in the value indicated.

    a) $8/2 + 2 + 12 \longrightarrow 14$

    b) $8 \wedge 2 - 1 \longrightarrow 8$

    c) $3/2 + 0.5 + 3 \wedge 1 \longrightarrow 5$

    d) $1 \wedge 2 + 1 * 2 * 3/4 - 3/2 \longrightarrow 0$

    e) $12 - 2 - 3 - 1 - 4 \longrightarrow 10$

    f) $7 * 3 + 4 \wedge 2 - 3/13 \longrightarrow 28$

    g) $3 * 2 - 3 * 4 * 2 + 3 \longrightarrow -60$

    h) $3 * 6 - 3 + 2 + 6 * 4 - 4/2 \wedge 1 \longrightarrow 33$

3.9 TEST YOUR BASIC SKILLS

1. Which of the following are invalid constants if each appeared exactly as written in a valid location in a BASIC statement?

   a) 6.4   e) 1,976   i) 1E1

   b) 7/8   f) 1792164   j) 987.6E-25

   c) +.319   g) 9.613

   d) 0   h) $1.75

2. Write the number 8,962,482,176 to the greatest possible accuracy using a precision of 7 significant digits. What is the error in this value?

3. Which arithmetic operation is performed first in the following numeric expressions?

   a) $9/5 * 6$

   b) $X - Y + A$

   c) $3 * (A + 8)$

   d) $(X * (2 + Y)) \wedge 2 + Z \wedge (2 \wedge 2)$

   e) $X/Y/Z$

   f) $(B \wedge 2 - 4 * A * C)/(2 * A)$

4. Which of the following represents X divided by Y correctly in BASIC?

   a) X/Y

   b) $X \div Y$

   c) Y/X

   d) $Y\sqrt{X}$

   e) $(1/X)/(1/Y)$

   f) $(1/Y)/(1/X)$

5. Write the value of 128.829% in E-type form with a decimal point present. Without a decimal point present.

6. Which of the following are invalid variables in BASIC? Why?

   a) A   c) #E   e) 39   g) 7F   i) Q$

   b) %C   d) P1   f) (h) B   j) Q9

7. Consider the valid programs below. What is displayed if each is executed?

   a)
   ```
   100 REM EXERCISE 3.7A
   110 LET A = 2.5
   120 LET B = 4 * A/2 * A + 5
   130 PRINT B
   140 LET B = 4 * A/(2 * A + 5)
   150 PRINT B
   160 LET A = -A
   170 PRINT A
   180 LET A = -A
   190 PRINT A
   200 END
   ```

   b)
   ```
   100 REM EXERCISE 3.7B
   110 LET E = 0
   120 LET E = E + 1
   130 PRINT E
   140 LET E = E + 1
   150 PRINT E
   160 LET E = E + 1
   170 PRINT E
   180 LET E = E - 3
   190 PRINT E
   200 END
   ```

   c)
   ```
   100 REM EXERCISE 3.7C
   110 LET Y = 50
   120 LET A$ = "INDIANA"
   130 LET B = 4 * Y * (Y - 10)
   140 LET C = (B - Y + 5 * Y)/(Y - 39 + B/2000)
   150 LET B$ = A$
   160 PRINT Y
   170 PRINT B
   180 PRINT C
   190 PRINT B$
   200 END
   ```

   d)
   ```
   100 REM EXERCISE 3.7D
   110 LET A$ = "A"
   120 LET T$ = "T"
   130 LET B$ = "B"
   140 LET W$ = B$ + A$ + T$
   150 PRINT W$
   160 LET W$ = T$ + A$ + B$
   170 PRINT W$
   180 END
   ```

8. What is the distinction between the formulation of a numeric expression and the evaluation of a numeric expression?

9. Can a validly formed numeric expression always be executed by a computer?

10. Calculate the numeric value for each of the following valid numeric expressions if $X = 2, Y = 3$ and $Z = 6$.

    a) $X + Y \wedge 2$ c) $12/(3 + Z) - X$ e) $X * Y + 2.5 * X + Z$

    b) $Z/Y/X$ d) $X \wedge Y \wedge Z$ f) $(X \wedge (2 + Y)) \wedge 2 + Z \wedge (2 \wedge 2)$

11. Repeat Exercise 10 for the case of $X = 4, Y = 6, Z = 2$.

12. Write a valid LET statement for each of the following algebraic statements.

    a) $q = (d + e)^{1/3}$

    b) $d = (A^2)^{3.2}$

    c) $b = \dfrac{20}{6 - S}$

    d) $Y = a_1x + a_2x^2 + a_3x^3 + a_4x^4$

    e) $e = X + \dfrac{X}{X - Y}$

    f) $S = 19.2X^3$

    g) $V = 100 - (2/3)^{100-B}$

    h) $t = \sqrt{76,234}/(2.37 + D)$

    i) $V = 0.12340005M - \left[\dfrac{(0.123458)^3}{M - N}\right]$

    j) $Q = \dfrac{(F - M\,1000)^{2B}}{4M} - \dfrac{1}{E}$

13. Write a correct mathematical statement for each LET statement.

    a) `100 LET A = (X + Y)/C + B2`

    b) `200 LET A1 = B2/(B3 + B4) - B1`

14. Which of the following are invalid LET statements?

    a) `100 LET X = 9/B(A + C)`

    b) `200 LET X + 5 = Y`

    c) `0    LET X = 17`

    d) `750 LET P = 4 * 3-+6`

    e) `260 LET US = GO`

    f) `140 LET X = -X * (((1 + R)^2 - N)^2 + (2 + X)`

    g) `300 GET Q = R^S^Q^T`

    h) `400 LET P = +4`

    i) `500 LET G = 4(-2 + A)`

    j) `120 LET X = X + 1`

15. Calculate the numerical value for each of the following validly formed LET statements if $A = 2$ and $B = 3$.

    a)
    ```
    100 LET D = (A^6/A * B) - (8 * B/4)
    110 LET D = D + 1
    ```

    b)
    ```
    100 LET E1 = A * B
    110 LET E1 = A^(6/E1)
    120 LET E2 = B * 8
    130 LET E3 = 4 + 1
    140 LET E2 = E2/E3
    150 LET A = E1 - E2
    ```

16. Repeat Exercise 15 for the case where the value of A is 1 and the value of B is 2.

17. Correct the syntax errors in the following programs.

    a)
    ```
    100 REM EXERCISE 3.17A
    1I0 PRINT, VALUES FOR A AND B;
    120 INPUT B, A
    130 GET AB = AB
    140 PRINT 'THE PRODUCT' IS'; AB
    150 DONE
    ```

    b)
    ```
    100 EXERCISE 3.17B
    110 LET 3 = X
    120 LET B = X&Y
    130 LET C = 4 * (X + B/3)/3 + Y
    140 C PRINT
    150 END
    ```

18. Correct the logic errors in the following programs.

    a)
    ```
    100 REM EXERCISE 3.18A
    110 LET A = 3
    120 LET B = 6
    130 LET A = A - 3
    140 LET C = B/A
    150 PRINT C
    160 END
    ```

    b)
    ```
    100 REM EXERCISE 3.18B
    110 LET X = -2
    120 LET Y = 0.5
    130 LET Z = X^Y
    140 PRINT Z
    150 END
    ```

19. If the string   JOHN R. BLAKELY   is entered in response to the INPUT statement, what is displayed by the following program?

```
100 REM EXERCISE 3.19
110 INPUT S$
120 LET A$ = LEFT$(S$, 4)
130 LET B$ = RIGHT$(S$, 7)
140 LET C$ = MID$(S$, 6, 2)
150 LET D$ = LEFT$(S$, 1) + MID$(S$, 7, 1)
160 LET D$ = D$ + " " + MID$(S$, 6, 3) + RIGHT$(S$, 7)
170 LET E = LEN(S$)
180 PRINT S$
190 PRINT A$
200 PRINT B$
210 PRINT C$
220 PRINT D$
230 PRINT E
240 END
```

Purpose: To become familiar with the use of constants and variables and the INPUT, PRINT and LET statements.

Problem: Write a program to determine the new service charge. Use the formula:

New Service Charge = Old Service Charge + 2% × Old Service Charge

Input Data: Use the following sample data in response to the appropriate INPUT statement:

Old Service Charge — 114.26

Output Results: The following results are displayed:

```
OLD SERVICE CHARGE? 114.26
NEW SERVICE CHARGE  116.575
```

Purpose: To become familiar with entering data items in response to an INPUT statement and calculating an average.

Problem: Construct a program to input the last 10 Dow-Jones closings, compute the average from these ten numbers and print the average.

Input Data: Use the following sample data:

Week 1 Closings: 1285.45, 1276.45, 1260.50, 1263.80, 1267.95
Week 2 Closings: 1269.34, 1275.29, 1280.34, 1287.46, 1290.58

Output Results: The following results are displayed:

```
FIRST WEEK FIVE CLOSINGS
? 1285.45, 1276.45, 1260.50, 1263.80, 1267.95
SECOND WEEK FIVE CLOSINGS
? 1269.34, 1275.29, 1280.34, 1287.46, 1290.58

THE TWO WEEK DOW-JONES AVERAGE IS 1275.72
```

Purpose: To become familiar with the concepts associated with arithmetic operations, parentheses in expressions and the use of INPUT, LET and PRINT statements.

Problem: Write a program to determine the maturity value of an investment of P dollars for N years at I percent converted quarterly. Use the formula:

$$S = P \left(1 + \frac{I}{M}\right)^{NM}$$

where

S = Maturity value
P = Investment
I = Nominal rate of interest
N = Time of years
M = Number of conversions per year

Input Data: Use the following sample data in response to the appropriate INPUT statements:

Investment — $10,500
Interest   — 11.5%
Time   — 4 years 6 months
Conversions — 4

(*Hint:* The program must include a statement to change the rate from percent form to decimal form.)

Output Results: The following results are displayed:

```
PLEASE ENTER THE:
        INVESTMENT? 10500
        NOMINAL RATE IN %? 11.5
        TIME IN YEARS? 4.5
        NO. OF CONVERSIONS? 4

THE MATURITY VALUE IS $ 17489
```

**Exercise 4:
Present Value of
an Annuity Fund**

Purpose: To become familiar with the hierarchy of operations in a complex LET statement and the procedures for rounding and truncating.

Problem: The present value of an annuity fund is defined as the amount of money required on hand to pay out a given sum of money (for example, to a beneficiary) over a period of years where interest is earned on the amount left after each payment. The following formula determines the present value of an annuity:

$$A = R \left[\frac{1 - \left(1 + \frac{J}{M}\right)^{-MN}}{P\left[\left(1 + \frac{J}{M}\right)^{M/P} - 1\right]} \right]$$

where

A = Present value of the annuity
R = Payment per year
P = Number of payments per year
M = Conversions per year
N = Duration of payments in years
J = Nominal interest rate

Write a program that determines the amount of money to be placed in an annuity fund for a beneficiary to receive $300 a month for 15 years. An interest rate of 11.85% is earned on the annuity fund converted quarterly. Round and display the final result to the nearest dollar. Truncate and display the result to the nearest dollar.

(*Hint:* The generalized expression INT(N * 10 ^E + 0.5)/10 ^E rounds a positive value N to E decimal places. The generalized expression INT(N * 10 ^E)/10 ^E truncates any positive value N to E decimal places.)

Input Data: Use the following sample data in response to the appropriate INPUT statements.

Payment per year	— $3600
Number of payments per year	— 12
Duration of payments	— 15 years
Conversions per year	— 4
Interest	— 11.85%

Output Results: The following results are displayed:

```
WHAT IS:
        THE PAYMENT PER YEAR? 3600
        NUMBER OF PAYMENTS PER YEAR? 12
        DURATION OF PAYMENTS? 15
        CONVERSIONS PER YEAR? 4
        INTEREST RATE? 11.85

THE PRESENT VALUE OF THE ANNUITY IS $ 25356 (ROUNDED)
THE PRESENT VALUE OF THE ANNUITY IS $ 25355 (TRUNCATED)
```

**Exercise 5:
Determining the
Monthly Payment
on a Loan**

Purpose: To become familiar with the hierarchy of operations in a LET statement and the use of the INPUT and PRINT statements.

Problem: Write a program to determine the monthly payment for a loan where the annual interest rate (expressed in *percent*), the amount of the loan, and the number of years are entered via INPUT statements. The monthly payment for the loan is computed from the following relationship:

$$P = \left(\frac{r(1 + r)^n}{(1 + r)^n - 1} \right) \times L$$

where

P = Payment
L = Amount of the loan
r = Monthly interest
n = Number of payments

Display the payment rounded to the nearest cent. Also determine the total interest paid by using the following formula:

Total Interest Paid = nP − L

Input Data: Use the following sample data:

Loan   — $8000.00
Annual Interest — 12.8%
Time   — 4 years

(*Hint:* The annual interest must be divided by 1200 and the time must be divided by 12.)

Output Results: The following results are displayed:

```
LOAN? 8000
INTEREST? 12.8
TIME IN YEARS? 4

THE MONTHLY PAYMENT IS $ 213.82
THE TOTAL INTEREST PAID WILL BE $ 2263.36
```

Purpose: To become familiar with the use of the INT function and the procedure for rounding.

**Exercise 6:
English to
Metric Conversion**

Problem: Write a program to convert an English measurement in miles, yards, feet and inches to a metric measurement in kilometers, meters and centimeters. Use the following formula to change the English measurement to inches:

Total Inches = 63360 * Miles + 36 * Yards + 12 * Feet + Inches

Use the following formula to determine the equivalent meters.

$$\text{Meters} = \frac{\text{Total Inches}}{39.37}$$

Use the INT function to determine the number of kilometers, meters and centimeters. Round the centimeters to two decimal places.

(*Hint:* Once the number of meters has been determined, the maximum number of kilometers can be computed from: Kilometers = INT(Meters/1000). Next, the remaining meters can be determined from: Remaining Meters = Meters − 1000 * Kilometers. The number of integer meters in Remaining Meters can then be determined from: Integer Meters = INT(Remaining Meters). Continue with the same technique to compute the number of centimeters.)

Input Data: Use the following sample data:

Miles — 3
Yards — 2
Feet   — 2
Inches — 6

Output Results: The following results are displayed:

```
MILES? 3
YARDS? 2
FEET? 2
INCHES? 6

KILOMETERS: 4
METERS: 830
CENTIMETERS: 63.28
```

Exercise 7:
Extracting Substrings

Purpose: To become familiar with the string functions.

Problem: Construct a program to prompt you to enter the alphabet and assign it to a string variable. Using the MID$ string function and concatenation operator, have the program string the selected letters from the alphabet together to form and display your name and determine the number of characters in your name.

Input Data: Prepare and use the following data:

ABCDEFGHIJKLMNOPQRSTUVWXYZ

Output Results: The following results are displayed for a person with the first name John:

```
MY FIRST NAME IS: JOHN
THE NUMBER OF LETTERS IN MY FIRST NAME IS: 4
```

(*Note:* Answers will vary.)

Exercise 8:
Payroll Problem II —
Federal Withholding
Tax Computations

Purpose: To become familiar with executing a program a multiple number of times and the procedure for rounding.

Problem: Modify Payroll Problem I in Programming Exercise 2.3 to accept by means of INPUT statements an employee number, number of dependents, hourly rate of pay and hours worked during a biweekly pay period. Use the following formulas to compute the gross pay, federal withholding tax and net pay:

1) Gross pay = hours worked × hourly rate of pay
2) Federal withholding tax = 0.2 × (gross pay − dependents × 38.46)
3) Net pay = gross pay − federal withholding tax

Round the gross pay and federal withholding tax following their computation. Execute the program for each employee described under Input Data.

Input Data: Use the following sample data:

Employee Number	Number of Dependents	Hourly Rate of Pay	Hours Worked
123	2	$12.50	80
124	1	8.00	100
125	1	13.00	80
126	2	4.50	20

Output Results: The following results are displayed for employee number 123:

```
EMPLOYEE NUMBER? 123
NUMBER OF DEPENDENTS? 2
HOURLY RATE OF PAY? 12.50
HOURS WORKED? 80

GROSS PAY=================> 1000
FEDERAL WITHHOLDING TAX===> 184.62
NET PAY===================> 815.38
```

MORE ON INPUT/OUTPUT PROCESSING 4

The programs discussed in the previous chapters are classified as straight-line coding programs. Up to this point, therefore, we have not utilized the complete power of the computer. We have merely used the computer to function essentially as a high-speed calculator. However, the power of a computer is derived both from its speed and its ability to deviate from sequential execution. One of the purposes of this chapter is, thus, to introduce you to a statement, the GOTO statement, that allows the computer to branch backward or forward to other statements in a program.

The programs developed in Chapters 2 and 3 also processed only small amounts of input. In this chapter we will present a technique for integrating data into a program through the use of the READ and DATA statements. The READ and DATA statements are usually preferred over the INPUT statement when a program has to process large amounts of data that are part of the program itself. An even better technique is the use of data files presented in Chapter 8.

The third topic to be discussed in this chapter is the generation of tabular reports. To write programs that can produce meaningful information in an easily readable and understandable form, you need to know more about the PRINT statement and the PRINT USING statement, a statement that gives you even more control over the output than the PRINT statement does. Both statements are discussed in detail in this chapter.

Upon successful completion of this chapter you should be able to write programs that can process data that is part of the program itself and generate readable reports.

Programming Case Study 6A: Determining the Sale Price

Program 4.1 computes the discount amount and sale price for each of a series of products. The discount amount is determined from the following formula:

$$D = \frac{R}{100} \times P$$

where

D = discount amount
R = discount rate in percent
P = original price

The sale price S is determined from the following formula:

$$S = P - D$$

The product data includes a product identification number, original price and discount rate, as shown below:

Product Number	Original Price	Discount Rate in Percent
112841A	$115.00	14
213981B	100.00	17
332121A	98.00	13
586192X	88.00	12
714121Y	43.00	8

The flowchart that corresponds to Program 4.1 is given in Figure 4.1. For your convenience in following the logic, line numbers have been placed on the top left-hand corner of the symbols to illustrate the relationship between the flowchart and the program.

```
100 REM PROGRAM 4.1
110 REM DETERMINING THE SALE PRICE
120 REM N$ = PRODUCT NO.    P = ORIGINAL PRICE
130 REM R  = DISCOUNT RATE  D = DISCOUNT AMOUNT
140 REM S  = SALES PRICE
150 REM ******************************************
160 PRINT "PRODUCT", "ORIGINAL", "DISCOUNT", "DISCOUNT", "SALE"
170 PRINT "NUMBER", "PRICE", "RATE IN %", "AMOUNT", "PRICE"
180 REM ************PROCESS A RECORD************
190 READ N$, P, R
200 REM DETERMINE THE DISCOUNT AMOUNT AND SALE PRICE
210 LET D = R/100 * P
220 LET S = P - D
230 PRINT N$, P, R, D, ,S
240 GOTO 190
250 REM *************DATA FOLLOWS***************
260 DATA 112841A, 115, 14
270 DATA 213981B, 100, 17
280 DATA 332121A, 98, 13
290 DATA 586192X, 88, 12
300 DATA 714121Y, 43, 8
310 END
```

PROGRAM 4.1

```
RUN

PRODUCT      ORIGINAL    DISCOUNT    DISCOUNT    SALE
NUMBER       PRICE       RATE IN %   AMOUNT      PRICE
112841A      115         14          16.1        98.9
213981B      100         17          17          83
332121A      98          13          12.74       85.26
586192X      88          12          10.56       77.44
714121Y      43          8           3.44        39.56

---OUT OF DATA LINE 190
```

Lines 100 through 150 of Program 4.1 are remark lines, which simply give information about the program to the reader. Lines 160 and 170 are PRINT statements which display the column headings. Note that all but the last of the three PRINT statements in Program 4.1 contain a separator, the comma (,), after each string constant or variable, instead of the semicolon separator used in previous programs. The use of the comma separator in PRINT statements causes the system to produce output that is automatically positioned in a tabular format. These concepts are described in detail in Section 4.4.

Line 190 is a READ statement which instructs the computer to assign values to N$, P, and R from the sequence of data created from DATA statements that begin at line 260. Note that this data is part of Program 4.1 itself. The rules regarding the READ and DATA statements are presented in Section 4.3.

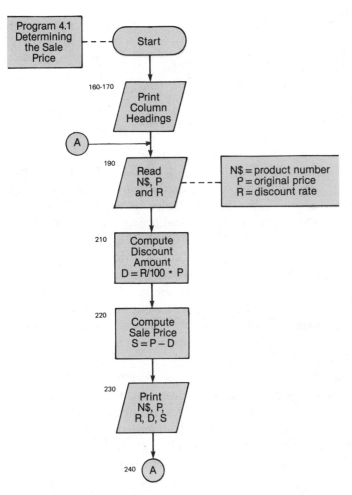

Program 4.1
Determining
the Sale
Price

Start

160-170
Print
Column
Headings

A

190
Read
N$, P
and R

N$ = product number
P = original price
R = discount rate

210
Compute
Discount
Amount
D = R/100 * P

220
Compute
Sale Price
S = P − D

230
Print
N$, P,
R, D, S

240 A

FIGURE 4.1 Flowchart for
Program 4.1.

Lines 210 and 220 are LET statements which assign values to the variables D and S. Line 230 causes the display of the output in tabular format. Later in Section 4.5, the PRINT USING statement will be used to display monetary values to the nearest cent.

Lines 190 through 240 establish a **loop**. In looping, a control statement, like that represented by line 240, is used to return control to the first of a series of statements that are executed repeatedly until a specified condition is met or satisfied. One execution of the loop is called a **pass**.

By now the potential of the GOTO statement should be apparent. In Program 4.1, after the first three values in line 260 are read by the READ statement and the values of the discount amount and sales price are computed and displayed along with the product number N$, the assigned price P and the discount rate R, the system executes the GOTO 190 statement represented by line 240. This in turn causes line 190, the READ statement, to be executed next.

As a result, the system reads in the next three values represented by line 270. These newly read values for N$, P, and R therefore replace the three original values in the main storage unit. Next, the system calculates values for D and S, displays them along with the values of N$, P and R, and executes the GOTO 190 statement for the second time, which again transfers control back to line number 190. The system continues this looping operation until all the values in the DATA statements have been read by the READ statement and all the computations and output have been completed.

**4.2
THE
UNCONDITIONAL
GOTO
STATEMENT**

TABLE 4.1   **The Unconditional** GOTO **Statement**

General Forms:	GOTO line number
Purpose:	Causes the execution of the program to be continued starting at the specified line number.
Examples:	500 GOTO 300
	700 GOTO 900
	800 GOTO 100

Lines 260 through 300 contain data for only five products. When the system branches back to the READ statement for the sixth time, there are no data items left in the DATA statements to be assigned to the three variables in the READ statement. Therefore, the program terminates execution after printing a diagnostic message regarding the unavailability of additional data, like ---OUT OF DATA LINE 190.

Later, in Chapter 5, you will be introduced to some additional concepts that cause this particular class of diagnostic message from being displayed.

In Program 4.1 a discount amount and sale price can be calculated for almost an unlimited number of products by adding more DATA statements after line 300. Each pass through the loop, lines 190 through 240, produces the desired product information from the data processed. The general form of the unconditional GOTO statement is given in Table 4.1.

Upon the execution of the GOTO statement, this statement interrupts the sequential execution of statements in a program by transferring control to a line number in that same program. For this reason, the GOTO statement is sometimes called a **transfer statement** or an **unconditional branch statement.**

There are several important points to watch for in the application of the GOTO statement. For example, if Program 4.1 is rewritten by changing the READ statement to

    188 READ N$, P, R

then the GOTO statement in line 240 must be changed to

    240 GOTO 188

Avoid having a GOTO statement reference itself, like this:

    240 GOTO 240

If this error is not detected, a never-ending loop develops. There is no way to stop the endless program execution except by manual intervention. Check the specifications of your BASIC system in the user's manual to find the key on the keyboard that terminates the current activity.

A GOTO statement can transfer control to any statement in a BASIC program, regardless of whether the statement has a higher or lower line number than the GOTO statement itself. When control transfers to a statement with a higher line number, the intervening statements skipped will not be executed. Additional statements must be included in the program to execute the statements skipped and also to prevent the occurrence of never-ending loops. The use of the GOTO statement to branch forward in programs is illustrated in greater detail in Chapters 5 and 6.

As with the other BASIC statements, there may be any number of GOTO statements in the program. As we will discover in Chapter 5, a more complex program might include several GOTO statements, like the partial program with three GOTO statements shown below:

```
         .
         .
         .
100 GOTO 800
         .
         .
         .
140 GOTO 920
         .
         .
         .
170 GOTO 920
         .
         .
         .
800 LET A = B + C
         .
         .
         .
920 LET A = B - C
         .
         .
         .
999 END
```

There are two GOTO 920 statements in this example since sometimes there may be two or more locations in a program where it is desirable to transfer control to the same line number. Consequently, although not more than one statement can be labeled with the same line number, more than one GOTO statement may refer to the same line number.

Recent trends in modern programming minimize the use of the GOTO statement in programs. Experience has shown that good, error-free and reliable programs can be constructed by avoiding heavy use of the GOTO statement. There are some situations in which the GOTO statement is desirable, but in general in this book, we will endeavor to use it sparingly. See Chapters 5 through 9 for examples of programs that contain loops without the use of the GOTO statement.

When you flowchart the branch called for by the GOTO statement, you may wish to use a connector symbol, like the circled A in Figure 4.1, rather than long flowlines, an example of which can be seen in Figure A.3 of Appendix A.

In Section 4.1 the READ and DATA statements were briefly introduced. This section will illustrate the rules of the READ, DATA and RESTORE statements and will give further examples of their use, as well as their limitations.

4.3 THE READ, DATA AND RESTORE STATEMENTS

The DATA Statement

The DATA statement provides for the creation of a sequence of data items for use by the READ statement. The general form of the DATA statement and some examples are given in Table 4.2.

The DATA statement consists of the keyword DATA followed by a list of data items separated by mandatory commas. The data items may be numeric or string and formulated according to the following rules:

> **DATA Rule 1:** Numeric data items placed in a DATA statement must be formulated as numeric constants.

> **DATA Rule 2:** String data items placed in a DATA statement may be formulated with or without surrounding quotation marks, provided the string contains no trailing or leading blanks or embedded commas. If the string contains a trailing or leading blank or an embedded comma, it must be surrounded with quotation marks.

TABLE 4.2 The DATA **Statement**

General Form:	DATA data item, . . . , data item where each data item is either a numeric constant or a string constant.
Purpose:	Provides for the creation of a sequence of data items for use by the READ statement.

Examples (with READ statements):

```
110 DATA 2, -3.14, 0.025, -95
120 READ A, B, C, D2
_____

130 DATA 0.24E33, 0, -2.5E-12
140 READ E, F, G(J)
_____

150 DATA 15, CENTS, ",", "YES", "2 + 7", NO, 2.2, "15.47"
160 READ H(3), A$, B$, C$, D$, E$, I, F$
```

Data items from all DATA statements in a program are collected in main storage into a single **data sequence holding area**. The order in which the data items appear among all DATA statements determines the order of the data items in the single data sequence (see Figure 4.2). In other words, the ordering of the data items is based on:

1) The ascending line numbers of the DATA statements
2) The order from left to right of the data items within each DATA statement

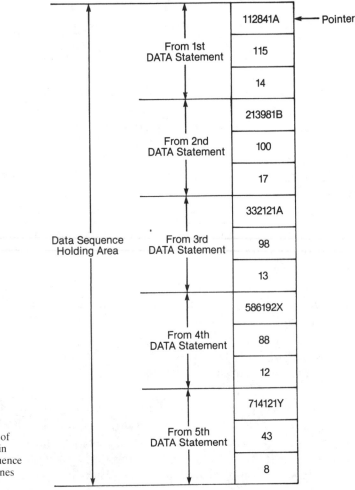

FIGURE 4.2 The order of data items as represented in main storage from the sequence of DATA in Program 4.1, lines 260–300.

The number of data items that can be represented in a DATA statement depends not only on the type of problem but also on the programming style adopted by the programmer. Some prefer to write one DATA statement for each data item, like this:

```
110 DATA 310386024
120 DATA "JOE NIKOLE"
130 DATA -3.85
140 DATA -1E-15
150 READ S$, N$, A, B
```

Others prefer to write as many data items in a DATA statement as there are variables in the READ statement that refers to that DATA statement. For example, the previous DATA and READ statements can be re-written as:

```
140 DATA 310386024, "JOE NIKOLE", -3.85, -1E-15
150 READ S$, N$, A, B
```

The DATA statement, like the REM statement, is a **non-executable statement**; that is, if the execution of a program reaches a line containing a DATA statement, it proceeds to the next line with no other effect.

> DATA **Rule 3:** The DATA statement may be located anywhere before the end line in a program.

The DATA statement permits a great deal of leeway in its placement in the program. Some BASIC programmers prefer to place all of the program's DATA statements first. Others prefer to place the DATA statement immediately after the first READ statement that refers to it, so that it is easier to see the connection between the READ statement and the DATA statement. We prefer to place all the program's DATA statements just before the end line, as shown in Program 4.1.

The READ Statement

The READ statement provides for the assignment of values to variables from a sequence of data items created from DATA statements. The general form of the READ statement is given in Table 4.3. The READ statement consists of the keyword READ followed by a list of variables separated by mandatory commas. The variables may be numeric or string variables.

Table 4.4 lists some invalid READ and DATA statements and their possible valid counterparts. Commas are required to separate both the variables in the READ list and the data items in the DATA list.

The READ statement causes the variables in its list to be assigned specific values, in order, from the data sequence formed by all of the DATA statements. In order to visualize the relationship between the READ statement and its associated DATA statement, you may think of a **pointer** associated with the data sequence holding area as shown in Figure 4.2. When a program is first executed, this pointer points to the first data item in the data sequence. Each time a READ statement is executed, the variables in the list are assigned specific values from the data

TABLE 4.3 The READ Statement

General Form:	READ variable, . . . , variable where each variable is either a numeric variable or a string variable.
Purpose:	Provides for the assignment of values to variables from a sequence of data items created from DATA statements.
Examples (with DATA statements):	See Table 4.2.

TABLE 4.4   Invalid READ **and** DATA **Statements and Their Corresponding Valid Forms**

Invalid Statement	Reason for Error	Valid Statements
100 READ, A, B, C	Comma is not permitted after the keyword READ.	100 READ A, B, C
150 DATA, 2, 4, 6	Comma is not permitted after the keyword DATA.	150 DATA 2, 4, 6
180 READ X, Y,	Comma is not permitted after the last variable in the READ list.	180 READ X, Y
200 DATA 1, 2,	Comma is not permitted after the last value in the DATA list.	200 DATA 1, 2
300 READ V V W 310 DATA 10, 20, 30	Commas are required between variables in the READ list. (Note that the double appearance of the variable V in the valid list is legal. The final value assigned to V is 20.)	300 READ V, V, W 310 DATA 10, 20, 30
400 READ J; K; L	Semicolons are not permitted in the READ list.	400 READ J, K, L

sequence beginning with the data item indicated by the pointer, and the pointer is advanced one value per variable, in a downward fashion, to point beyond the data used.

Program 4.2 illustrates the data sequence holding area and pointer for a program containing multiple READ and multiple DATA statements. The pointer initally points to the location of 565.33 in the holding area. When line 150 is executed, the value of 565.33 is assigned to the variable M, the pointer is advanced to the location of the next value 356.45, which is assigned to the variable T, and the pointer is advanced to the location of the next value 478.56. When line 160 is executed, the variable W is assigned the value of 478.56, T1 the value of 756.23, and F the value of 342.23.

As this assignment occurs, the pointer advances one value per variable to point to a location beyond the data used, which is recognized by the system as the end of the data sequence holding area.

```
100 REM PROGRAM 4.2
110 REM DETERMINING THE AVERAGE DAILY SALES
120 REM WITH MULTIPLE READ AND
130 REM MULTIPLE DATA STATEMENTS
140 REM ***********************************
150 READ M, T
160 READ W, T1, F
170 LET A = (M + T + W + T1 + F)/5
180 PRINT M, T
190 PRINT W, T1, F
200 PRINT A
210 REM ***********DATA FOLLOWS***********
220 DATA 565.33, 356.45, 478.56
230 DATA 756.23, 342.23
240 END

RUN

565.33        356.45
478.56        756.23        342.23
499.76
```

PROGRAM 4.2

Data Sequence Holding Area

565.33	356.45	478.56	756.23	342.23	Undefined

↑ Pointer *before* the execution of line 150.   ↑ Pointer *after* the execution of line 150.   ↑ Pointer *after* the execution of line 160.

In Program 4.2, the system is unable to calculate A correctly until it has the value of M, T, W, T1 and F. The READ statement should occur somewhere *before* the LET statement in the program. This example can be generalized to give the following:

> READ **Rule 1:** Every variable appearing in the program whose value is directly obtained by a READ should be listed in a READ statement before it is used elsewhere in the program.

Program 4.2 can be incorrectly written in violation of this rule, as shown in the following:

```
145 LET A = (M + T + W + T1 + F)/5
150 READ M, T
160 READ W, T1, F
180 PRINT M, T
190 PRINT W, T1, F
200 PRINT A
210 REM ************DATA FOLLOWS*************
220 DATA 565.33, 356.45, 478.56
230 DATA 756.23, 342.23
240 END

RUN

   565.33            356.45
   478.56            756.23            342.23
   0
```

Incorrectly written program

While the placement of the DATA statements in a program is immaterial, the placement of the READ statement is important. Furthermore, more than one DATA statement may be used to satisfy one READ statement and more than one READ statement may be satisfied from one DATA statement.

> READ **Rule 2:** A program containing a READ statement must also have at least one DATA statement with values to be assigned to the variables listed in the READ statement.

If there is an insufficient number of data items to be assigned to the variables of a READ statement, a diagnostic message appears, as shown in Program 4.3. However, an excessive number of data items is ignored, as shown in Program 4.4.

```
100 REM PROGRAM 4.3
110 REM INSUFFICIENT DATA ITEMS
120 REM IN A DATA STATEMENT
130 REM *********************
140 READ A, B, C, D
150 PRINT A, B, C, D
160 REM ****DATA FOLLOWS******
170 DATA 1, 2, 3
180 END
```

PROGRAM 4.3

```
RUN

----OUT OF DATA LINE 140
```

```
100 REM PROGRAM 4.4
110 REM EXCESSIVE DATA ITEMS
120 REM IN A DATA STATEMENT
130 REM ********************
140 READ A, B, C
150 PRINT A, B, C
160 REM ****DATA FOLLOWS****
170 DATA 1, 2, 3, 4, 5
180 END

RUN

1            2            3
```

PROGRAM 4.4

Finally, the type of data item in the data sequence must correspond to the type of variable to which it is to be assigned. That is, numeric variables in READ statements require numeric constants as data items in DATA statements, and string variables require quoted strings or unquoted strings as data.

The RESTORE Statement

Usually data items from a DATA statement are processed by a READ statement only once. If you want the system to read these same data items later, you must use the RESTORE statement to restore the data.

TABLE 4.5   **The RESTORE Statement**

General Form:	RESTORE
Purpose:	Allows the data in the program to be reread.
Example:	**500 RESTORE**
Note:	On the IBM PC, Macintosh and in general with Microsoft BASIC, a line number may optionally follow the keyword RESTORE. If a line number is present, the data pointer is reset to the first data item in the DATA statement with that line number.

The RESTORE statement allows the data in a given program to be reread as often as desired by other READ statements. The general form of the RESTORE statement is given with an example in Table 4.5. The RESTORE statement consists simply of the keyword RESTORE.

The RESTORE statement causes the pointer to be moved back to the beginning of the data sequence holding area. This is done so that the next READ statement executed will read the data from the beginning of the sequence once again.

The RESTORE statement is generally used when it is necessary to perform several types of computations on the same data items. Program 4.5 illustrates the use of the RESTORE statement.

```
100 REM PROGRAM 4.5
110 REM USE OF THE RESTORE STATEMENT
120 REM ****************************
130 READ A, B, C
140 LET U = A * B * C
150 RESTORE
160 READ D, E, F
170 LET V = F/E/D
180 RESTORE
190 READ G, H, I
200 LET W = G^H^I
210 PRINT A, B, C
220 PRINT U, V, W
230 REM ********DATA FOLLOWS********
240 DATA 2, 4, 8
250 END

RUN

2            4            8
64           1            4.29497E+09
```

PROGRAM 4.5

When the first READ statement in line 130 is executed in Program 4.5, A is assigned the value of 2, B the value of 4, and C the value of 8. After a value for U is computed in line 140, the RESTORE statement in line 150 is executed. This resets the pointer to the beginning of the data sequence holding area so that it points at the value of 2. When the second READ statement in line 160 is executed, the values of 2, 4 and 8 are assigned to D, E and F, respectively.

After a value of V is calculated in line 170, the RESTORE statement in line 180 is executed and the pointer is reset accordingly. When the third READ statement in line 190 is executed, 2, 4 and 8 are assigned to G, H and I. Finally, the value of W is calculated in line 200, and the values of all the variables used in the program are displayed. See Programming Exercises 6 and 11 at the end of Chapter 5 on how the RESTORE statement is used.

The execution of the PRINT statement generates a string of characters for transmission to an external device like a video display device. The PRINT statement is commonly used to display the results from computations, to display headings and labeled information, and to plot points on a graph. In addition, the PRINT statement allows you to control the spacing and the format of the desired output.

Only values defined in main storage can be displayed. These may be supplied to the program by having been previously read by a READ or INPUT statement or calculated in the program by a LET statement.

The general form of the PRINT statement is given with examples in Table 4.6. The PRINT statement consists of the keyword PRINT. It may also have an optional list of **print items** separated by mandatory commas and/or semicolons. The print items may be numeric or string constants, variables, expressions, or null items. In addition, the print items may include useful function references, like the Integer function, INT, described in Chapter 3.

**4.4
THE** PRINT
STATEMENT

TABLE 4.6   The PRINT **Statement**

General Form:	PRINT item pm item pm . . . pm item where each item is one of the following: 1) Constant 2) Variable 3) Expression 4) Function reference 5) Null and where each punctuation mark pm is one of the following: 1) Comma 2) Semicolon
Purpose:	Provides for the generation of labeled and unlabeled output or of output in a consistent tabular format from the program to an external device.
| *Examples:* | ```
100 PRINT
110 PRINT X
120 PRINT A, B, C
130 PRINT A; B; C; D, E, F
140 PRINT H, I; J(2), A$, B$
150 PRINT "THE ANSWER IS"; M
160 PRINT "X = "; X, "Y = "; Y, N
170 PRINT (M + N)/4,,, P; Q, B * B - 4 * A * C
180 PRINT TAB(5); A$; TAB(40); B$; "END"
190 PRINT TAB(37); 16, INT(A)
200 PRINT ","; R, 3, S; 19, T
210 PRINT " ",,, Y, Z
220 PRINT A, B,
230 PRINT A; B;
240 PRINT TAB(5 * I + 1); I;
``` |

The most common use of the PRINT statement is to output values defined earlier in a program. Every sample program presented thus far has included a PRINT statement. Listing several variables separated by commas within a PRINT statement, like this line

**Print Zones and
Print Positions**

```
230 PRINT N$, P, R, D, S
```
```

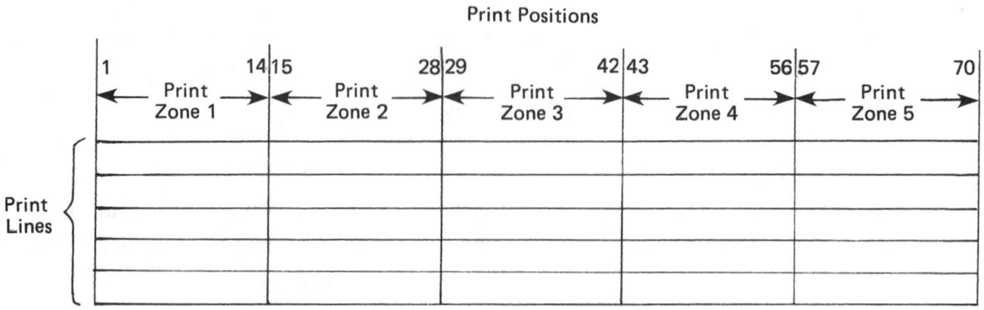

Print Positions

FIGURE 4.3 The print line is divided into five print zones.

in Program 4.1, causes the values of N$, P, R, D and S to be displayed on a *single* line. BASIC displays the values of N$, P, R, D and S into **print zones**. On most computer systems, there are five print zones per line. Each print zone has 14 positions, for a total of 70 positions per line. The print positions are numbered consecutively from the left, starting with position one, as shown in Figure 4.3.

Representation of Numeric Output   Numeric constants, variables, expressions, and function references are evaluated to produce a string of characters consisting of:

1) a sign
2) the decimal representation of the number
3) a trailing space

In other words, a number is represented on output as:

Sign	Decimal representation of number	Trailing Space

The sign is a leading space if the number is positive or a leading minus sign if the number is negative.*

Use of the Comma Separator   Punctuation marks like the comma and the semicolon are placed between print items. In this section the role of the comma, or **comma separator**, as it is formally called, is examined. The comma separator allows you to produce output that is automatically positioned in a tabular format determined by the print zones.

Commas with Numbers. Some possible formats for the decimal representation of numeric expressions like constants and variables are shown by Program 4.6 in Figure 4.4. Each PRINT statement executed displays one line of information, unless one of the following conditions prevails:

1) The number of print zones required by the PRINT statement exceeds 5. In Figure 4.4 line 250, the value of C is displayed twice on the next line as −4.56789E-12. If a PRINT statement contains more than 5 numeric expressions separated by commas, then the first 5 print on one line, the next 5 on the next line, and so on, until all items in the list are displayed.
2) The PRINT statement ends with a punctuation mark like a comma or semicolon. In Figure 4.4, line 260 illustates that when a PRINT statement ends with a comma, the items in the next PRINT statement (line 270) display on the same line but at the next print zone.

---

*The Apple computer does not display a leading space when the number is positive, nor does it display a trailing space.

```
100 REM PROGRAM 4.6
110 REM COMMAS WITH NUMERIC EXPRESSIONS
120 REM ******************************
130 LET X = -10
140 LET Y = -2.3
150 LET Z = -369.246
160 LET A = -1.234
170 LET B = -999999
180 LET C = -4.56789E-12
```

	Print Zone 1	Print Zone 2	Print Zone 3	Print Zone 4	Print Zone 5
190 PRINT X	-10				
200 PRINT X, Y	-10	-2.3			
210 PRINT X,, Y, -987654	-10		-2.3	-987654	
220 PRINT X,, Y, Z, -3 * 2	-10		-2.3	-369.246	-6
230 PRINT X,,,, Y	-10				-2.3
240 PRINT X, Y, Z, A, B	-10	-2.3	-369.246	-1.234	-999999
250 PRINT X, Y, Z, A, B, C, C	-10 / -4.56789E-12	-2.3 / -4.56789E-12	-369.246	-1.234	-999999
260 PRINT X, Y, / 270 PRINT Z, A	-10	-2.3	-369.246	-1.234	
280 PRINT C, C, C, C, C	-4.56789E-12	-4.56789E-12	-4.56789E-12	-4.56789E-12	-4.56789E-12
290 END					

Print Positions (header above print zones)

RUN

FIGURE 4.4 The effect of commas with numeric expression in PRINT statements.

All the numbers displayed in Figure 4.4 are negative, and therefore a leading minus sign is automatically produced as the first character in the various print zones. When a number is positive, a leading space is produced in the first position of the print zone. Two or more consecutive commas may be included in a PRINT statement (lines 210, 220 and 230 of Figure 4.4) as a means of tabulating over several print zones.

Commas with Strings. The PRINT statement may also be used to display string expressions for report and column headings and other messages. Many of the program examples that you have already studied illustrate the use of the PRINT statement to display string expressions for report and column headings.

Some possible formats for the representation of strings are also shown by Program 4.7 in Figure 4.5. Line 140 displays the heading of the report. Line 160 displays column headings in each of the 5 print zones. The first letter of each string appears in the first print position of each print zone. A complete zone is used for

```
100 REM PROGRAM 4.7
110 REM COMMAS WITH STRING EXPRESSIONS
120 REM *****************************
130 LET A$ = "REGISTER"
140 PRINT "          PAYROLL CHECK REGISTER"
150 PRINT
160 PRINT "HOURS", "RATE", "GROSS PAY", "DEDUCTIONS", "NET PAY"
170 PRINT 40, 3, 120, 15, 105
180 PRINT " ", "END OF", "PAYROLL", A$
190 END
```

RUN

Print Zone 1	Print Zone 2	Print Zone 3	Print Zone 4	Print Zone 5
	PAYROLL CHECK REGISTER			
HOURS	RATE	GROSS PAY	DEDUCTIONS	NET PAY
40	3	120	15	105
	END OF	PAYROLL	REGISTER	

FIGURE 4.5 The effect of commas with string expressions in PRINT statements.

each string whether or not it contains 1 or 14 characters. Unused print positions in a zone are left blank. Line 180 illustrates the use of a blank character surrounded by quotation marks to tabulate over to the second print zone and the output of the value of the string variable A$ assigned earlier in line 130.

The message enclosed within the quotation marks displays the exact spelling and spacing of the PRINT statement. If the message is too long to fit in a given PRINT statement, it must be broken into two or more PRINT statements.

Commas with Strings and Numbers. PRINT statements may contain a mixed list of both string and numeric expressions as shown by Program 4.8 in Figure 4.6.

```
100 REM PROGRAM 4.8
110 REM COMMAS WITH NUMERIC
120 REM AND STRING EXPRESSIONS
125 REM *********************
130 PRINT "GROSS PAY =", 3 * 32
140 PRINT "DEDUCTIONS =",
150 PRINT 10
160 PRINT "NET PAY =", 86
170 END

RUN
```

FIGURE 4.6 The effect of commas with numeric and string expressions in PRINT statements.

Print Zone 1	Print Zone 2
GROSS PAY =	96
DEDUCTIONS =	10
NET PAY =	86

In line 130, the string GROSS PAY = appears starting in print position 1 of the first print zone, followed by the positive numeric value 96 in the second print zone. Line 140 illustrates that when a comma terminates a PRINT statement, the items in the next PRINT statement (line 150) display on the same line but starting at the next print zone. Hence, the string DEDUCTIONS = displays in the first zone followed by the positive value of 10 in the second zone. Like line 130, line 160 displays NET PAY = starting in print position 1 of the first print zone, followed by the positive numeric value 86 in the second print zone.

Creating Blank Lines. If a PRINT statement contains a **null list**, then a blank line results. In other words,

```
140 PRINT
```

contains no print items and results in a blank line. Program 4.9 in Figure 4.7 illustrates what happens when several PRINT statements with null print items are used to create blank lines for the purpose of improving the appearance of the output.

Use of the Semicolon Separator

In this section, the role of the **semicolon separator** in the PRINT statement is examined.* The semicolon does not allow you to tab to a fixed print position as the comma does. Instead, the evaluation of the semicolon separator in a PRINT statement generates a string of zero length. The use of the semicolon enables you to display more than 5 items on a line.

Semicolons with Numbers. Some possible formats for the decimal representation of numeric expressions like constants and variables are shown by Program 4.10 in Figure 4.8. Each numeric representation is preceded by a leading sign and followed by a trailing space. Hence, the statement

```
190 PRINT A; B; C; D; E
```

---

* With Microsoft BASIC, typing one or more spaces has the same effect as typing a semicolon.

```
100 REM EXERCISE 4.9
110 REM PRINT STATEMENTS WITH NULL LISTS
120 REM ******************************
130 PRINT "              ***PAYROLL DEDUCTIONS***"
140 PRINT
150 PRINT
160 PRINT "FICA", "FIT", "SIT", "UNION", "MISC"
170 PRINT "----", "---", "---", "-----", "----"
180 PRINT
190 PRINT 15, 50, 4, 3, 2
200 END

RUN
```

Print Zone 1	Print Zone 2	Print Zone 3	Print Zone 4	Print Zone 5
	PAYROLL DEDUCTIONS			
FICA	FIT	SIT	UNION	MISC
----	---	---	-----	----
15	50	4	3	2

2 Blank Lines
1 Blank Line

FIGURE 4.7 Creating blank lines with PRINT statements.

```
100 REM PROGRAM 4.10
110 REM SEMICOLONS WITH NUMERIC EXPRESSIONS
120 REM ***********************************
130 LET A = -10
140 LET B = -20
150 LET C = -30
160 LET D = -40
170 LET E = -50
180 PRINT A, B, C, D, E
190 PRINT A; B; C; D; E
200 PRINT A, B; C; D, E
210 PRINT A; B; C; D; E; -60; -70; -80; -90
220 PRINT " ", A, B; C
230 PRINT A, B;
240 PRINT C; D, E, -4 * 15
250 END

RUN
```

Print Zone 1	Print Zone 2	Print Zone 3	Print Zone 4	Print Zone 5
-10	-20	-30	-40	-50
-10 -20 -30 -40 -50				
-10	-20 -30 -40	-50		
-10 -20 -30 -40 -50 -60 -70	-80 -90			
	-10	-20 -30		
-10	-20 -30 -40	-50	-60	

FIGURE 4.8 The effect of semicolons with numeric expressions in PRINT statements.

can be used to generate numeric output in a compressed form without having the numeric representations run into one another.

Lines 180 and 190 illustrate the difference between using a comma and a semicolon as a separator. Line 180, which contains comma separators, displays the values of A, B, C, D, and E into the 5 print zones. Line 190, which contains semicolon separators, compresses the values of A, B, C, D, and E starting at print position 1. Comma and semicolon separators can be mixed in a PRINT statement, as shown by lines 200, 220, 230, and 240. If a PRINT statement ends with a semicolon, as in line 230, the first item in the next PRINT statement (line 240) displays on the same line in compressed form.

The use of semicolons with numeric expressions in PRINT statements may cause the numeric output not to line up in neat, vertical columns. If you want the output aligned, use commas between the items in the PRINT statements.

```
100 REM PROGRAM 4.11
110 REM SEMICOLONS WITH STRING EXPRESSIONS
120 REM **********************************
130 LET B$ = "OUT"
140 PRINT "HOURS", "RATE", "GROSS PAY", "DEDUCTIONS", "NET PAY"
150 PRINT "HOURS"; "RATE"; "GROSS PAY"; "DEDUCTIONS"; "NET PAY"
160 PRINT "FICA", "FIT", "SIT", "UNION", "MISC"
170 PRINT "FICA", "FIT"; "SIT", "UNION"; "MISC"
180 PRINT "END", "OF", B$;
190 PRINT "PUT"
200 END

RUN
```

Print Zone 1	Print Zone 2	Print Zone 3	Print Zone 4	Print Zone 5
HOURS	RATE	GROSS PAY	DEDUCTIONS	NET PAY
HOURSRATEGROSSPAYDEDUCTIONSNET PAY				
FICA	FIT	SIT	UNION	MISC
FICA	FITSIT	UNIONMISC		
END	OF	OUTPUT		

FIGURE 4.9   The effect of semicolons with string expressions in PRINT statements.

Semicolons with Strings. As stated earlier, the PRINT statement may also be used to display string expressions for report and column headings and other messages. Some possible formats for the representation of strings are shown by Program 4.11 in Figure 4.9. When the semicolon is used to separate strings, no trailing space occurs between the strings in the output, as shown by line 150. As you can see in Program 4.11, the semicolon works the same way for string expressions as it does for numeric expressions. (See Program 4.10 for comparison.)

Semicolons with Strings and Numbers. Recall from Chapters 2 and 3 that the semicolon can be used in PRINT statements containing a mixed list of numeric and string expressions. Consider Program 4.12 in Figure 4.10. In this program, line 130 displays the message:

    ENTER EMPLOYEE NUMBER, HOURS, AND RATE

The INPUT statement in line 130 also displays the input prompt consisting of a question mark and a single space on the same line. The user responds by entering the following values

    1234, 38, 4.50

and pressing the Enter key. Line 160, which contains comma separators, displays the information in the 5 print zones. Line 180, which contains semicolon separators, displays the same information in packed form.

```
100 REM PROGRAM 4.12
110 REM SEMICOLONS WITH NUMERIC AND STRING EXPRESSIONS
120 REM ***************************************************
130 INPUT "ENTER EMPLOYEE NUMBER, HOURS, AND RATE"; N, H, R
140 REM ****COMPUTE THE GROSS PAY*****
150 LET G = H * R
160 PRINT "EMPLOYEE", N, "EARNED $", G, "THIS PERIOD"
170 PRINT "EMPLOYEE"; 1234,, "EARNED $"; 38 * 4.50,, "THIS PERIOD"
180 PRINT "EMPLOYEE"; N; "EARNED $"; G; "THIS PERIOD"
190 END

RUN
```

Print Zone 1	Print Zone 2	Print Zone 3	Print Zone 4	Print Zone 5
ENTER EMPLOYEE NUMBER, HOURS, AND RATE? 1234, 38, 4.50				
EMPLOYEE	1234	EARNED $	171	THIS PERIOD
EMPLOYEE 1234		EARNED $ 171		THIS PERIOD
EMPLOYEE 1234	EARNED $ 171	THIS PERIOD		

FIGURE 4.10   The effect of semicolons with numeric and string expressions in PRINT statements.

Thus far, PRINT statements have contained the comma and semicolon as separators among numeric and string expressions in order to display the values of these expressions in a readable format with correct spacing. Compact and exact spacing of output results can also be achieved by the use of the TAB function.

The TAB function is used in the PRINT statement to specify the exact print positions for the various output results on a given line. In effect, the TAB function allows you to move the cursor to a specified position. The positions are numbered from left to right starting with position one. The TAB function is similar to the tabulator key on a typewriter.

The form of the TAB function is:

TAB (numeric expression)

where the numeric expression, the argument, may be a numeric constant, variable, expression, or function reference. The value of the argument determines the position on the line of the next character to be displayed.

```
100 REM PROGRAM 4.13
110 REM PRINT STATEMENTS WITH THE TAB FUNCTION
120 REM **************************************
130 LET A = 27
140 LET B = 4
150 LET C = 14
160 PRINT TAB(25); "ABC COMPANY"
170 PRINT
180 PRINT
190 PRINT TAB(5); "EMP NO"; TAB(21); "RATE"; TAB(36); "HOURS"
200 PRINT TAB(5); 12345; TAB(21); 3.25; TAB(36); 40
210 PRINT
220 PRINT TAB(A/B + C); "RATE"
230 PRINT
240 PRINT "COLUMN 1"; "    "; "COLUMN 2"; "    "; "COLUMN 3"
250 PRINT "--------"; "   "; "--------"; "    "; "--------"
260 PRINT TAB(3); A; TAB(13); B; TAB(24); C
270 PRINT
280 PRINT "END OF JOB"
290 END
RUN
```

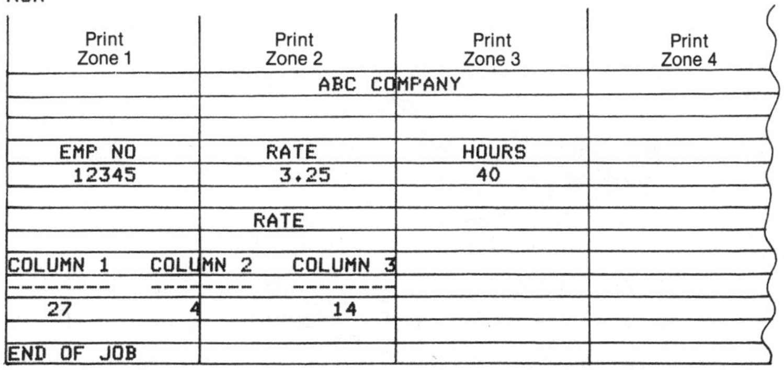

Print Zone 1	Print Zone 2	Print Zone 3	Print Zone 4
	ABC COMPANY		
EMP NO	RATE	HOURS	
12345	3.25	40	
	RATE		
COLUMN 1	COLUMN 2	COLUMN 3	
--------	--------	--------	
27	4	14	
END OF JOB			

FIGURE 4.11 The use of the TAB function in PRINT statements.

Consider line 160 of Program 4.13 in Figure 4.11:

`160 PRINT TAB(25); "ABC COMPANY"`

The function TAB (25) causes the system to tab to print position 25 and display the string ABC COMPANY in positions 25 to 35.

Multiple TAB functions are allowed in a PRINT statement. Line 190, for example:

`190 PRINT TAB(5); "EMP NO"; TAB(21); "RATE"; TAB(36); "HOURS"`

displays the strings EMP NO, beginning at print position 5, RATE beginning at print position 21, and HOURS beginning at print position 36, displaying three centered column headings. Line 200 illustrates the printing of three numeric values under these column headings.

The argument of the TAB function may be a numeric expression as indicated by line 220:

```
220 PRINT TAB(A/B + C); "RATE"
```

Since A = 27, B = 4, and C = 14, the argument is first evaluated (27/4 + 14 = 20.75) and then rounded to the integer value, which is 21. This causes the system to tab to position 21 and display the string RATE in positions 21 to 24.

The TAB function can also be used in PRINT statements for graphic purposes. Test Your Basic Skills Exercises 18 and 19 are designed to illustrate this point.

Backspacing is not permitted on most BASIC systems.

```
500 PRINT TAB(50); 2.56; TAB(21); -1.24
```

causes the system to tab to position 50 and print the number 2.56 in positions 51 to 54. However, TAB(21) does not cause the system to backspace on the same line and print the number −1.24. Instead this number is displayed in the next line starting in print position 21.

Calculations Within the PRINT Statement

BASIC systems permit calculations to be made within the PRINT statement as is clear from many examples in this section. For instance, the sum, difference, product, quotient, and exponentiation of two numbers, like 2 and 4, may be made in the conventional way by using LET statements or by using the PRINT statement, as is done in Program 4.14.

```
100 REM PROGRAM 4.14
110 REM CALCULATIONS WITHIN THE PRINT STATEMENT
120 REM *****************************************
130 PRINT 2 + 4; 2 - 4; 2 * 4; 2/4; 2^4
140 END

RUN

 6 -2  8  .5  16
```

PROGRAM 4.14

Using the Immediate Mode in BASIC

Many BASIC systems have an **immediate mode** or a **calculator mode** of operation which permits the computer to appear to the user as a powerful desk calculator. When you are in the immediate mode, BASIC statements like the PRINT statement can be executed individually without being incorporated into a program. You merely enter the keyword PRINT followed by any numeric expression. As soon as you press the Enter key, the BASIC system immediately computes and displays the value of the expression. Line numbers are not used in the immediate mode.

The following example of calculating a complex expression uses the immediate mode of a BASIC system:

```
PRINT (2 - 3 * 4/5)^2 + 5/(4 * 3 - 2^3)
```

The value printed is 1.41. This expression was previously computed in Section 3.5 to illustrate the effect of parentheses and the rules of precedence on the evaluation of numeric expressions.

BASIC also allows you to use the immediate mode to debug programs. For example, if a fatal error occurs, the PRINT statement can be used to display the values of variables used in the program that terminates. It is important that no other commands be issued between the time the program stops and the time the PRINT statement is entered. There are methods for debugging a program that has errors; see Appendix C for a discussion of debugging.

Programming
Case Study 7A:
Determining the
Accounts Receivable
Balance

This problem and its program solution incorporate much of the information discussed in this section.

Problem

Ron's Family Discount House would like its computer to generate a management report for the accounts receivable balance for a monthly billing period. The following formula is used to determine the balance:

$$E = B - P + P1 - C + S$$

where

   E = end of the month balance
   B = beginning of the month balance
   P = payments
   $P1$ = purchases
   C = credits
   S = service charge on the ending unpaid balance — 19.5% annually, or
      $S = 0.01625 * (B - P - C)$ per month, rounded to the nearest cent.

The input data for each customer includes customer number, beginning of the month balance, payments, credits and purchases.

The program should generate a report that includes report and column headings and a line of information for each customer. Each line is to include customer number, beginning of the month balance and end of the month balance.

The following accounts receivable data is to be processed:

Customer Number	Beginning Balance	Payment	Purchases	Credit
14376172	$1,112.32	$35.00	$56.00	$ 0.00
16210987	30.00	30.00	15.00	0.00
18928384	125.50	25.00	0.00	12.50
19019293	120.00	12.00	12.00	23.00
19192929	10.00	7.00	2.50	1.50

A list of the program tasks, flowchart and a program solution follow:

Program Tasks

1) Display report and column headings.
2) Read an accounts receivable record.
3) Compute the unpaid balance from the formula: $U = B - P - C$.
4) Compute the service charge S from the formula: $S = 0.01625 * U$.
5) Round the service charge to the nearest cent using the formula:
   $S = INT(S * 100 + 0.5)/100$.
6) Compute the end of the month balance E from the formula:
   $E = U + P1 + S$.
7) Display the customer number, beginning of the month balance and end of the month balance.
8) Repeat steps 2 through 7 until there are no more records in the accounts receivable file.

```
100 REM PROGRAM 4.15
110 REM DETERMINING THE ACCOUNTS RECEIVABLE BALANCE
120 REM N$ = CUSTOMER NUMBER   B  = BEGINNING BALANCE   P = PAYMENTS
130 REM C  = CREDITS            P1 = PURCHASES      U = UNPAID BALANCE
140 REM S  = SERVICE CHARGE     E  = ENDING BALANCE
150 REM ******************************************************
160 PRINT "CUSTOMER", "BEGINNING", "ENDING"
170 PRINT "NUMBER", "BALANCE", "BALANCE"
180 REM ******************PROCESS A RECORD*******************
190 READ N$, B, P, P1, C
200 LET U = B - P - C
210 LET S = 0.01625 * U
220 LET S = INT(S * 100 + 0.5)/100
230 LET E = U + P1 + S
240 PRINT N$, B, E
250 GOTO 190
260 REM ******************DATA FOLLOWS**********************
270 DATA 14376172, 1112.32, 35, 56, 0
280 DATA 16210987, 30, 30, 15, 0
290 DATA 18928384, 125.5, 25, 0, 12.5
300 DATA 19019293, 120, 12, 12, 23
310 DATA 19192929, 10, 7, 2.5, 1.5
320 END
```

PROGRAM 4.15

```
RUN

CUSTOMER        BEGINNING       ENDING
NUMBER          BALANCE         BALANCE
14376172        1112.32         1150.83
16210987        30              15
18928384        125.5           89.43
19019293        120             98.38
19192929        10              4.02

---OUT OF DATA LINE 190
```

```
100 REM PROGRAM 4.16
110 REM DETERMINING THE ACCOUNTS RECEIVABLE BALANCE
120 REM N$ = CUSTOMER NUMBER  B  = BEGINNING BALANCE   P = PAYMENTS
130 REM C  = CREDITS           P1 = PURCHASES      U = UNPAID BALANCE
140 REM S  = SERVICE CHARGE    E  = ENDING BALANCE
150 REM ******************************************************
160 PRINT TAB(21); "ACCOUNTS RECEIVABLE REPORT"
170 PRINT TAB(21); "--------------------------"
180 PRINT
190 PRINT "CUSTOMER"; TAB(10); "BEGINNING"; TAB(50); "SERVICE";
200 PRINT TAB(60); "ENDING"
210 PRINT "NUMBER"; TAB(10); "BALANCE"; TAB(20); "PAYMENT";
220 PRINT TAB(30); "PURCHASES"; TAB(40); "CREDIT";
230 PRINT TAB(50); "CHARGE"; TAB(60); "BALANCE"
240 PRINT
250 REM ******************PROCESS A RECORD*******************
260 READ N$, B, P, P1, C
270 LET U = B - P - C
280 LET S = 0.01625 * U
290 LET S = INT(S * 100 + 0.5)/100
300 LET E = U + P1 + S
310 PRINT N$; TAB(10); B; TAB(20); P; TAB(30); P1; TAB(40);
320 PRINT C; TAB(50); S; TAB(60); E
330 GOTO 260
340 REM ******************DATA FOLLOWS**********************
350 DATA 14376172, 1112.32, 35, 56, 0
360 DATA 16210987, 30, 30, 15, 0
370 DATA 18928384, 125.5, 25, 0, 12.5
380 DATA 19019293, 120, 12, 12, 23
390 DATA 19192929, 10, 7, 2.5, 1.5
400 END
```

PROGRAM 4.16

```
RUN

                    ACCOUNTS RECEIVABLE REPORT
                    --------------------------

CUSTOMER BEGINNING                           SERVICE  ENDING
NUMBER   BALANCE   PAYMENT   PURCHASES CREDIT CHARGE   BALANCE

14376172 1112.32   35        56        0      17.51    1150.83
16210987 30        30        15        0      0        15
18928384 125.5     25        0         12.5   1.43     89.43
19019293 120       12        12        23     1.38     98.38
19192929 10        7         2.5       1.5    .02      4.02

---OUT OF DATA LINE 260
```

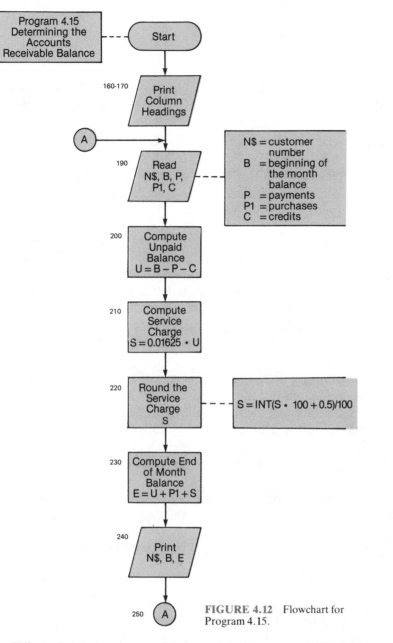

FIGURE 4.12   Flowchart for Program 4.15.

When the RUN command is issued for Program 4.15, the system executes the two PRINT statements (lines 160 and 170) that display the column headings in print zones 1, 2 and 3. The system next reads the first accounts receivable record found in line 270. The record is processed and the information is displayed by line 240 in tabular format. The GOTO 190 in line 250 instructs the system to branch back to line 190 to read the next accounts receivable record. The second record is processed and displayed before the system branches back to read the next record. This process continues until all of the accounts receivable records have been processed.

The report generated by Program 4.15 can be enhanced if, along with the current output, the payment, purchases, credits and service charge are displayed. If such a report is generated, it will contain a total of seven columns of information instead of the three generated by Program 4.15. Since there are only five print zones per line, the comma separating the seven items in a PRINT statement would cause the computer to display the first five values on one line and the last two values on the next line. One way to get more than five items to a line in columnar format is to use the TAB function, which is demonstrated in Program 4.16.

Program 4.16 displays four additional items of information (payment, purchases, credit and service charge) that are not part of the report generated by

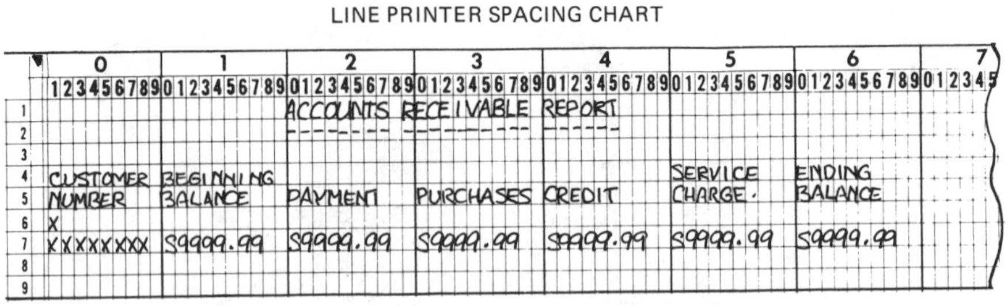

LINE PRINTER SPACING CHART

FIGURE 4.13 Output for Program 4.16 designed on a printer spacing chart.

Program 4.15. Furthermore, a report title and some vertical spacing has been added to make this new report easier to read.

To determine the TAB positions in the new program, a skeleton of the report is first designed on a **printer spacing chart**, as shown in Figure 4.13. Lines 1 through 5 of the printer spacing chart define the report and column headings. Line 7 defines the **detail line** that is to be displayed for each record processed: the row of Xs on line 7 describes an area for a string value, and the groups of 9s preceded by the letter S describe areas for numeric values.

From the printer spacing chart, the argument for each TAB function can easily be determined. The arguments for the TAB functions in lines 160 and 170 in Program 4.16 reflect the position of the report title in the printer spacing chart. The arguments for the TAB functions in lines 190 through 230 reflect the positions of the column headings in the printer space chart; and the arguments for the TAB functions in lines 310 and 320 reflect the printer space chart positions for the columns themselves.

As illustrated in Program 4.16, the TAB function is useful in generating reports that require more control over the output than the fixed format supplied by the comma separator. BASIC allows even more control of the format in which information is displayed through the use of the PRINT USING statement, which will be explained in the next section.

4.5
THE PRINT USING STATEMENT FOR FORMATTED OUTPUT

Similar to the PRINT statement, the PRINT USING statement is far more useful in exactly controlling the format of a program's output.* In Section 4.4 you were introduced to the comma, semicolon and TAB function for print control purposes. For most applications, these print control methods will suffice. However, when you are confronted with generating readable reports for non-data-processing personnel, more control over the format of the output is essential. The PRINT USING statement gives you the desired capabilities to display information according to a predefined format instead of the free format provided by the PRINT statement. Through the use of the PRINT USING statement, you can:

1) Specify the exact image of a line of output.
2) Force decimal point alignment when printing numeric tables in columns.
3) Control the number of digits displayed for a numeric result.
4) Specify that commas be inserted into a number. (Starting from the units position of a number and progressing toward the left, digits are separated into groups of 3 by a comma).
5) Specify that the sign status of the number be displayed along with the number (+ or blank if positive, − if negative).
6) Assign a fixed or floating dollar sign ($) to the number displayed.

---

*The PRINT USING statement is not available on the Apple and COMMODORE systems.

TABLE 4.7 The PRINT USING Statement

General Form:	PRINT USING string expression; list
	where string expression (sometimes called the format field) is either a string constant or a string variable. The format field is an exact image of the line to be displayed.
	list is a list of items to be displayed in the format specified by the format field.
Purpose:	Provides for controlling exactly the format of a program's output by specifying an image to which that output must conform.
Examples:	150 PRINT USING "THE ANSWER IS #,###.##"; Y
	200 PRINT USING "## DIVIDED BY # IS #.#"; A, B, C
	200 LET A$ = "THE TOTAL IS $$,###.##-" 210 PRINT USING A$; T
	350 LET C$ = "**,###.##" 360 PRINT USING C$; X;
	900 PRINT USING "\ \"; Q$
	950 PRINT USING "!, !, \ \"; F$, M$, L$
	999 PRINT USING "#.##^^^^"; S$,
Caution:	The PRINT USING statement is not available on Apple and COMMODORE systems. Large timesharing systems, like the DEC VAX-11, use a comma instead of a semicolon after the string expression in the PRINT USING statement.

7) Force a numeric result to be displayed in exponential notation.
8) **Left-** or **right-justify** string values in a formatted field (i.e., align the left- or rightmost characters, respectively).
9) Specify that only the first character of a string be displayed.
10) Round a value automatically to a specified number of decimal digits.

The general form of the PRINT USING statement is given with examples in Table 4.7.

To control the format of the values displayed, the PRINT USING statement is used in conjunction with a string expression that specifies the desired format of the print line. The string expression is placed immediately after the words PRINT USING in the form of a string constant or string variable. If the format is described by a string variable, then the string variable must be assigned the format by a LET statement before the PRINT USING statement is executed in the program. Consider the two methods shown below.

Declaring the Format of the Output

Method 1:
```
100 REM FORMAT SPECIFIED AS A STRING IN THE PRINT USING STATEMENT
110 PRINT USING "EMPLOYEE ### HAS EARNED $#,###.##"; I, B
```
Method 2:
```
100 REM FORMAT SPECIFIED EARLIER AND ASSIGNED TO A STRING VARIABLE
110 LET A$ = "EMPLOYEE ### HAS EARNED $#,###.##"
      .
      .
      .
170 PRINT USING A$; I, B
```

In Method 1, the string constant following the keywords PRINT USING in line 110 instructs the system to display the values of I and B using the format found in that statement. In Method 2, the string constant has been replaced by the string variable A$ which was assigned the desired format in line 110. If I is equal to 000105 and B is equal to 4563.20, then the results displayed from the execution of line 110 in Method 1 or line 170 in Method 2 are:

```
EMPLOYEE 105 HAS EARNED $4,563.20
```

Format Symbols   Table 4.8 includes the **format symbols** available on most BASIC systems. One or more consecutive format symbols appearing in a string expression is a **descriptor field**, or **field format**.

TABLE 4.8   Format Symbols

Symbol	Function	Examples
#	The number sign defines a numeric field. Grouped number signs indicate how many positions are desired in a numeric result during output. For each # in the field, a digit (0 to 9) or sign is substituted.	# ### ###.## #.#
.	The period is used for decimal point placement. The internal value is automatically aligned with the assigned format.	#.## ###.
,	A comma in the descriptor field places a comma in the output record at that character position unless all digits prior to the comma are zero. In that case, a space is displayed in that character position.	#,### ###,###.##
+ or −	A single plus or minus sign to the right or left in the descriptor field causes the sign status (positive or negative) of the number to be displayed. A plus or minus sign to the left in the descriptor field causes the sign status to be displayed to the left of the first significant nonzero digit.	+## −### #,###.##+ $$#.##−
$	A single dollar sign as the first character in the descriptor field causes a dollar sign to be displayed in that position. Two dollar signs ($$) cause a dollar sign to be placed to the left of the first significant nonzero digit. One of the two dollar signs reserves a position for a digit.	$$,###.## $$##.##− $##.##
**	Two leading asterisks cause the number to be displayed with leading asterisks filling any unused positions to the left in the displayed result. Each asterisk reserves a position for a digit.	**,###.## **###.### **.##−
∧∧∧∧	Four consecutive circumflexes to the right of a set of grouped number signs indicate that the numeric value is to be displayed in exponential notation.	##∧∧∧∧ ##.##∧∧∧∧ #.###∧∧∧∧
&	The ampersand specifies a variable length descriptor field for a string value. The string value is aligned in the descriptor field left-justified. If the string value has more than one character, the ampersand causes expansion to the right to display the entire string value in the output line. (DEC VAX-11 uses the characters 'L in place of the ampersand.)	&
\\	Two backslashes separated by n spaces reserves a fixed number of positions (n + 2) for a string value. The internal string value is aligned left-justified with the assigned format. If the string value is made up of more characters than the number specified in the descriptor field, the rightmost characters in the string value are truncated. If the string value has fewer characters than the number specified in the descriptor field, the result is filled on the right with spaces. (The TRS-80 uses percent signs instead of backslashes.)	\ \ \\
!	An exclamation point specifies a one-character field for a string value. The exclamation point causes the first character of a string value to be displayed. (The DEC VAX-11 uses the characters 'E in place of the exclamation point.)	!

The number sign (#) is the format symbol used to define a numeric field. Grouped number signs indicate exactly how many positions are desired in a numeric result during output. A number sign reserves space for a digit or sign. For example,

#	indicates one position in a numeric result
##	indicates two positions in a numeric result
####	indicates four positions in a numeric result
####.##	indicates six positions, two of which are decimal fractional positions

It is your responsibility to ensure that enough number signs are in the descriptor field to fit the output results in the prescribed format.

Consider the following example, where A = 10, B = −11, C = 12.75, and D = 4565.

```
100 REM FORMAT SPECIFIED EARLIER AND ASSIGNED TO A STRING VARIABLE
110 LET S$ = ' ####      ####      ##       ###'
       .
       .
       .
190 PRINT USING S$; A, B, C, D
```

The results that are displayed from the above sequence are as follows:

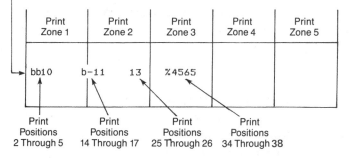

The fields are spaced exactly as indicated in the string expression. The value of A, which is 10, is displayed right-justified as bb10 with leading spaces b. The value of B, which is −11, is displayed with the minus sign positioned next to the first significant digit.

The value of C, 12.75, is automatically rounded to 13 in order to agree with the ## field format. In other words, the value of C is rounded to an integer. The value of D, 4565, is too large to be displayed using the ### field format. Hence, the value is displayed but preceded by a percent sign (%) to indicate that an insufficient number of positions were reserved for this field.

Table 4.9 summarizes the use of the number sign in various descriptor fields, or field formats. Program 4.17 gives examples of the use of the number sign.

TABLE 4.9 Use of the Number Sign (#) in a Descriptor Field

Field Format	Data	Output	Remarks
####	10	bb10	Right-justify the digits in the field with leading spaces.
####	−11	b−11	
##	12.75	13	The data is rounded to an integer, since only integers are represented by the specified format.
###	4565	%4565	Since the data is too large for the specified format, the value is displayed but preceded by a percent sign (%) to indicate that an insufficient number of positions were reserved for this field.

The Number Sign
Symbol

The Decimal Point (Period) Symbol

The period (.) in a descriptor field places a decimal point in the output record at that character position in which it appears, and the format of the numeric result is aligned with the position of the decimal point. When number signs (#) precede the decimal point in a descriptor field, any leading zeros appearing in the data are replaced by spaces, except for a single leading zero immediately preceding the decimal point.

When number signs follow the decimal point, unspecified decimal fractional positions are filled with trailing zeros. When the data contains more decimal fractional digits than the descriptor field allows, the decimal fraction is rounded to the limits of the field.

Table 4.10 and Program 4.17 illustrate the use of the decimal point in various descriptor fields.

TABLE 4.10   Use of the Decimal Point (Period) in a Descriptor Field

Field Format	Data	Output	Remarks
####.##	217.5	b217.50	Unspecified decimal fraction positions are filled with trailing zeros.
#####.##	40	bbb40.00	
#####.##	23.458	bbb23.46	Decimal fractional digits are rounded.
#####.##	0.027	bbbb0.03	The last leading zero before the decimal point is not suppressed.

```
100 REM PROGRAM 4.17
110 REM EXAMPLES OF THE USE OF THE NUMBER SIGN,
120 REM DECIMAL POINT AND COMMA IN A DESCRIPTOR FIELD
130 REM ***********************************************
140 LET A$ = "####    #,###    #,###.##"
150 READ X
160 PRINT USING A$; X, X, X
170 PRINT USING "####"; X
180 PRINT USING "#,###"; X
190 PRINT USING "#,###.##"; X
200 DATA 1234.56
210 END

RUN

1235    1,235    1,234.56
1235
1,235
1,234.56
```

PROGRAM 4.17

The Comma Symbol

A comma (,) in a descriptor field places a comma in the output record at that character position unless all digits before the comma are zero. In that case, a space is printed in that character position. Table 4.11 and Program 4.17 illustrate the use of the comma in various descriptor fields.

If the descriptor field containing a comma has too few number signs, the comma is replaced by a digit.

The Plus and Minus Sign Symbols

A single plus sign (+) as either the first or last character in a descriptor field causes a + to be displayed if the data item is positive, or a − if the data item is negative. If the plus sign is the leftmost character, the sign is displayed immediately to the left

TABLE 4.11   Use of the Comma (,) in a Descriptor Field

Field Format	Data	Output	Remarks
#,###	4000	4,000	Comma displayed
###,###	999999	999,999	Comma displayed
#,###.##	30.5	bbb30.50	Space displayed for comma with leading digits blank.

TABLE 4.12   Use of the Plus (+) or Minus (−) in a Descriptor Field

Field Format	Data	Output	Remarks
Fixed Signs			
###.##+	20.5	b20.50+	
###.##−	000.01	bb0.01b	The last leading zero before the decimal point is not
###.##+	−8.236	bb8.24−	suppressed.
###.##−	−456.0	456.00−	
Floating Signs			
+##.##	40.5	+40.50	
+##.##	7.07	b+7.07	
−##.##	−0.236	b−9.24	
−##.##	−456.0	%−456	Since the data is too large for the specified format, the result is displayed but preceded by a percent sign to indicate that an insufficient number of positions were reserved for this field.

of the most significant nonzero digit of the output item. This is a **floating** plus sign. A plus sign to the right of the last character in a descriptor field (**fixed** plus sign) causes the sign to be displayed in that position. A minus sign (−) has the same effect as a plus sign, except that a space is displayed for a positive value while a minus sign always appears when the value is negative.

Table 4.12 gives examples of the use of the plus and minus sign symbols in various descriptor fields.

The Dollar Sign Symbol

A single dollar sign, or fixed $ sign, appearing as the first character in the descriptor field causes a $ to be displayed in that position of the output record.

Two dollar signs, or floating $ sign, at the left of the descriptor field causes the dollar sign to float. The dollar sign will appear at the left of the first digit. Table 4.13 gives examples of the use of the $ in various descriptor fields.

TABLE 4.13   Use of the Dollar Sign ($) in a Descriptor Field

Field Format	Data	Output	Remarks
Fixed Dollar Sign			
$###.##	123.45	$123.45	
$###.##	98.76	$b98.76	
$###.##−	40.613	$b40.61b	
$###.##−	−40.613	$b40.61−	
$###.##+	−40.613	$b40.61−	
Floating dollar Sign			
$$###.##	1.23	bbb$1.23	
$$,###.##	1234.68	$1,234.68	Second $ sign replaced by digit.
$$##.##−	−1.0	bb$1.00−	

TABLE 4.14   Use of the Asterisk Sign (∗) in a Descriptor Field

Field Format	Data	Output	Remarks
∗∗,###.##	10.15	∗∗∗∗10.15	Asterisk displayed for comma when leading digits are zero.
∗∗##−	−6.95	∗∗∗7−	Data is rounded to an integer.
∗∗#.##	4.58	∗∗4.58	

The Asterisk Symbol

Two asterisks (∗∗) starting at the left side of the descriptor field cause the value to be displayed in asterisk-filled format. The left side of the numeric field will be filled with leading asterisks rather than leading spaces.

Leading asterisks are often used in place of number signs when printing checks or when the result must be protected. This prevents someone from adding digits to the left side of a number. Table 4.14 gives examples of the use of the asterisk in various descriptor fields.

Formatted Character String Output

Descriptor fields for string values are defined in terms of the ampersand (&), two backslashes (\\) or the exclamation point (!), rather than the number sign (#). Some systems use other characters to define these functions. Table 4.8 summarizes these three symbols.

As a descriptor field, the ampersand represents a variable-length string field. The number of positions used to display the string is dependent on the internal size of the string. The ampersand indicates the beginning position in which the string is displayed, and expansion is to the right in the line. Table 4.15 summarizes the use of the ampersand. Program 4.18 gives examples of the use of the ampersand.

TABLE 4.15   Use of the Ampersand (&) as a Descriptor Field

Field Format	Data	Output	Remarks
&	ABC	ABC	The character A is placed exactly in the line at the location specified by the ampersand. The B and C are placed in &+1 and &+2 positions of the line, respectively.
&	ABCDE	ABCDE	
&	A	A	

```
100 REM PROGRAM 4.18
110 REM USE OF THE AMPERSAND AS A DESCRIPTOR FIELD
120 REM ******************************************
130 LET A$ = "REM"
140 LET B$ = "REMARK"
150 LET C$ = "REMARKABLE"
160 PRINT USING "THE KEYWORD  &"; A$
170 PRINT USING "REPRESENTS   &"; B$
180 PRINT USING "ISN'T THAT   &"; C$
190 END

RUN

THE KEYWORD REM
REPRESENTS  REMARK
ISN'T THAT  REMARKABLE
```

PROGRAM 4.18

The exact number of positions to use for displaying a string value can be specified by using two backslashes separated by zero or more spaces. The number of positions in the descriptor field, including the two backslashes, indicate how many positions are to be used to display the string value. The string value is aligned in the descriptor field left-justified. If the internal value of the string contains fewer characters than the descriptor field, the string value is filled with spaces on the right in the print line. If the internal value of the string contains more characters than the descriptor field, the string value is truncated on the right. Table 4.16 summarizes the use of the backslash, and Program 4.19 gives examples of its use.

TABLE 4.16   Use of the Backslash (/) in a Descriptor Field

Field Format	Number of Spaces Between Backslashes	Data	Output	Remarks
\ \	3	ABCDE	ABCDE	Size of descriptor field and string value the same.
\ \	1	ABCDE	ABC	The last two characters are truncated.
\\	0	ABCDE	AB	The last three characters are truncated.
\ \	6	ABCDE	ABCDEbbb	Three spaces are appended to the right of the string value in the print line.

```
100 REM PROGRAM 4.19
110 REM USE OF TWO BACKSLASHES IN A DESCRIPTOR FIELD
120 REM ******************************************
130 PRINT     "NAME       ADDRESS       CITY-STATE       ZIP CODE"
140 PRINT     "_____   _____    _____    _____"
150 LET A$ = "\      \  \       \  \            \  \        \"
160 READ N$, D$, C$, Z$
170 PRINT USING A$; N$, D$, C$, Z$
180 REM ****************DATA FOLLOWS****************
190 DATA JONES J, 451 W 173, "GARY, IN", 46327
200 END
```
                                                           PROGRAM 4.19

```
RUN

NAME        ADDRESS        CITY-STATE        ZIP CODE
_____    _____     _____    _____
JONES J    451 W 173    GARY, IN           46327
```

Study closely the method used in lines 130 through 150 in Program 4.19 to align the fields. The string constants in lines 130 and 140 are purposely started five positions to the right of the keyword PRINT so that the column headings align with the string constant in line 150. This technique will be used throughout this book.

The exclamation point is used as a descriptor field to specify a one-position field in the print line. If the internal value of the string to be displayed is longer than one character, only the left-most character is displayed. Table 4.17 summarizes the use of the exclamation point, and Program 4.20 illustrates its use.

TABLE 4.17   Use of the Exclamation Point (!) as a Descriptor Field

Field Format	Data	Output	Remarks
!	JOE	J	First initial of name displayed.
!	XYZ	X	

```
100 REM PROGRAM 4.20
110 REM USE OF THE EXCLAMATION POINT AS A DESCRIPTOR FIELD
120 REM *****************************************************
130 READ F$, M$, L$
140 PRINT USING "! ! \          \"; F$, M$, L$
150 REM ********DATA FOLLOWS********
160 DATA  GEORGE , ALFRED , SMITH
170 END

RUN

G A SMITH
```

PROGRAM 4.20

Programming Case Study 7B: Determining the Accounts Receivable Balance Using a PRINT USING Statement

Program 4.21 presents the following useful techniques for formatting a report:

1) Aligning the detail lines with the column headings
2) Forcing decimal point alignment
3) Controlling the number of digits displayed in a result
4) Specifying that commas and decimal points be appropriately displayed in numeric results.

Program 4.21 generates a far more acceptable report than the one produced by Program 4.16. The report shows that this new program displays all monetary

```
100 REM PROGRAM 4.21
110 REM DETERMINING THE ACCOUNTS RECEIVABLE BALANCE
120 REM N$ = CUSTOMER NUMBER  B  = BEGINNING BALANCE  P = PAYMENTS
130 REM C  = CREDITS              P1 = PURCHASES       U = UNPAID BALANCE
140 REM S  = SERVICE CHARGE   E  = ENDING BALANCE
150 REM *****************REPORT FORMAT************************
160 PRINT "             ACCOUNTS RECEIVABLE BALANCE"
170 PRINT
180 PRINT "CUSTOMER  BEGIN               PUR              SERV    ENDING"
190 PRINT "NUMBER    BALANCE PAYMENT   CHASES   CREDIT  CHARGE   BALANCE"
200 LET D$="\        \ #,###.## ####.## ####.## ####.## ##.## #,###.##"
210 PRINT
220 REM *****************PROCESS A RECORD*********************
230 READ N$, B, P, P1, C
240 LET U = B - P - C
250 LET S = 0.01625 * U
260 LET S = INT(S * 100 + 0.5)/100
270 LET E = U + P1 + S
280 PRINT USING D$; N$, B, P, P1, C, S, E
290 GOTO 230
300 REM *****************DATA FOLLOWS************************
310 DATA 14376172, 1112.32, 35, 56, 0
320 DATA 16210987, 30, 30, 15, 0
330 DATA 18928384, 125.5, 25, 0, 12.5
340 DATA 19019293, 120, 12, 12, 23
350 DATA 19192929, 10, 7, 2.5, 1.5
360 END

RUN

          ACCOUNTS RECEIVABLE BALANCE

CUSTOMER  BEGIN               PUR              SERV    ENDING
NUMBER    BALANCE PAYMENT   CHASES   CREDIT  CHARGE   BALANCE

14376172 1,112.32   35.00    56.00     0.00   17.51 1,150.83
16210987    30.00   30.00    15.00     0.00    0.00    15.00
18928384   125.50   25.00     0.00    12.50    1.43    89.43
19019293   120.00   12.00    12.00    23.00    1.38    98.38
19192929    10.00    7.00     2.50     1.50    0.02     4.02

---OUT OF DATA LINE 230
```

PROGRAM 4.21

values rounded to the nearest cent, with decimal points aligned and right-justified below the column headings. The customer number, which is defined to be a string item, is displayed left-justified.

The significance of taking the time to lay out the report on a printer spacing chart should be apparent in this Case Study. Once the printer spacing chart is complete, the format of the report can be copied directly into the program, as shown in lines 160 through 210 of Program 4.21. With the output techniques discussed in this chapter you may now begin to dress up the output. Programmers often forget that the majority of people using the results of computer-generated reports are unfamiliar with computers and are confused by poorly formatted output. You now have the capability in BASIC to produce reports that are meaningful and easy to read.

While the PRINT and PRINT USING statements display results on your video display device, the LPRINT and LPRINT USING statements print the results on the line printer of your personal computer system. Everything that has been presented with respect to the PRINT and PRINT USING statements in this chapter applies to the LPRINT and LPRINT USING statements as well. Obviously, to use these two statements you must have a line printer attached to your personal computer. Furthermore, it must be plugged in and turned on.

LPRINT and LPRINT USING Statements

4.6 WHAT YOU SHOULD KNOW

1. A loop is a repeating process in which a control statement at the end of a series of instructions returns control to the first statement of that series.
2. One execution of a loop is a pass.
3. The GOTO statement is called "a transfer statement" or an "unconditional branch statement."
4. The DATA statement provides for the creation of a sequence of data items for use by the READ statement.
5. The DATA statement consists of the keyword DATA followed by a list of data items which can be either numeric or string. If string data contains a leading or trailing blank or an embedded comma, the data must be enclosed in quotation marks.
6. The DATA statement is a non-executable statement. The placement of DATA statements has no bearing on the execution of the program.
7. Data items from all DATA statements are collected and placed into one single data sequence holding area. The order in which the data items appear among all DATA statements determines the order of the data items in the single data sequence.
8. The READ statement provides for the assignment of values to variables from a sequence of data items created from DATA statements.
9. The READ statement consists of the keyword READ followed by a list of variables separated by mandatory commas.
10. Every variable appearing in the program whose value is directly obtained by a READ must be listed in a READ statement before it is used in the program.
11. A program containing a READ statement must also have at least one DATA statement. The values in the DATA statement will be assigned to the variables listed in the READ statement.
12. The RESTORE statement allows the data in a given program to be reread as often as desired by READ statements.
13. The RESTORE statement consists simply of the keyword RESTORE.
14. The PRINT statement consists of the keyword PRINT. It may also have an optional list of print items separated by mandatory commas and/or semicolons. The print items may be numeric or string constants, variables, expressions or null items. In addition, the print items may include useful functions like TAB.

15. On most computer systems, there are five print zones per line. Each print zone is 14 positions.

16. The comma separator in a PRINT statement allows you to produce output that is automatically positioned in a tabular format determined by the five print zones.

17. If a PRINT statement contains no list of print items, if it is a null list, then a blank line results.

18. The semicolon separator can be used to generate output in a packed format.

19. The TAB function is used in the PRINT statement to specify the exact print positions for the various output results on a given print line. The TAB function should always be followed by a semicolon separator.

20. BASIC allows calculations to be made within the PRINT statement.

21. In immediate mode, BASIC permits the system to be used as a powerful desk calculator.

22. The PRINT USING statement is useful in controlling the output format.

23. One or more consecutive format symbols appearing in a string expression are a descriptor field, or field format.

24. Depending on the type of editing desired, numeric descriptor fields can include a number sign, decimal, comma, dollar sign, asterisk, and four consecutive circumflexes.

25. Descriptor fields for string values use the exclamation point, ampersand, and two backslashes separated by n spaces (which reserve n + 2 positions in the line) to display a string value.

26. While the PRINT and PRINT USING statements display results on a video display device, the LPRINT and LPRINT USING statements print the results on a printer.

4.7 SELF-TEST EXERCISES

1. Consider the valid programs listed below. What is displayed if each is executed?

a)
```
100 REM CHAPTER 4 SELF-TEST 1A
110 READ A, B, C
120 LET D = A + B/C - B
130 PRINT A; B; C; D
140 GOTO 110
150 REM ***DATA FOLLOWS***
160 DATA 1, 6, 3
170 DATA 4, 2, 1
180 DATA 8, 9, 3
190 END
```

b)
```
100 REM CHAPTER 4 SELF-TEST 1B
110 READ X, Y
120 PRINT "OLD VALUE OF X ="; X
130 PRINT "OLD VALUE OF Y ="; Y
140 LET X = Y
150 LET Y = X
160 PRINT "NEW VALUE OF X ="; X
170 PRINT "NEW VALUE OF Y ="; Y
175 PRINT
180 GOTO 110
190 REM ***DATA FOLLOWS***
200 DATA 4, 6
210 DATA 3, 7
220 END
```

c)
```
100 REM CHAPTER 4 SELF-TEST 1C
110 READ X, Y
120 PRINT "OLD VALUE OF X ="; X
130 PRINT "OLD VALUE OF Y ="; Y
135 LET T = X
140 LET X = Y
150 LET Y = T
160 PRINT "NEW VALUE OF X ="; X
170 PRINT "NEW VALUE OF Y ="; Y
175 PRINT
180 GOTO 110
190 REM ***DATA FOLLOWS***
200 DATA 4, 6
210 DATA 3, 7
220 END
```

d)
```
100 REM CHAPTER 4 SELF-TEST 1D
110 LET A = 0
120 LET B = 0
130 LET C = 0
140 READ X, Y
150 LET A = A + X
160 LET B = B + Y
170 LET C = C + 1
180 PRINT C; A; B
190 GOTO 140
195 REM ***DATA FOLLOWS***
200 DATA 4, 9
210 DATA 6, 10
220 DATA 8, 12
230 END
```

2. Find the errors in the following programs:

a)
```
100 REM CHAPTER 4 SELF-TEST 2A
110 READ A, B, C,
120 LET D = (A + B + C/3
130 GOTO 110
140 PRINT "THE AVERAGE IS"; D
150 END
```

b)
```
100 REM CHAPTER 4 SELF-TEST 2B
110 READ A$, 6
120 DATA A, 4, B, C, 2
130 PRINT A$, "=", B
140 GOTO 150
150 END
```

3. Given the list of string data items below, which of the items can be placed in a DATA statement without surrounding quotation marks. (The letter b represents a leading or trailing space.)

a) 1134
b) Q-156
c) OAKLAND, CA
d) NO

e) END OF REPORT
f) 614 317 219
g) bbbYES
h) HUNT

4. Indicate the errors, if any, in the following independent statements:

```
a) 100 PRINT
b) 110 READ, A, B, C
c) 120 PRINT TAB(5); "PRINT A"; "     "; X,, A/B
d) 130 READ M, X, N,
e) 140 PRINT TAB(B - K*J); "TAB"
f) 150 READ
g) 160 INPUT G, H, I,
h) 170 READ A1, A2 * 2, B
i) 180 DATA 2, X, "DATA", ";"
j) 190 DATA
```

5. Write a single PRINT statement to replace the sequence of statements following line 100.

```
100 REM CHAPTER 4 SELF-TEST 5
110 LET A = 8 + 4
120 LET B = 6
130 LET C = B^A
140 LET D$ = "ABC"
150 PRINT A, B, C, D$
```

6. Write a two-statement program to input values of A, B and C and print the value of the first variable A, the sum of the first and second variable A + B, and the sum of all three variables A + B + C.

7. Write a sequence of PRINT statements that use the TAB function to center the following column headings.

```
            BASIC COMPANY
            -------------

VALUE OF A     VALUE OF B     VALUE OF C
----------     ----------     ----------
```

8. Given the following PRINT statements, indicate the position in which the value of each variable will begin.

```
a) 100 PRINT TAB(10); A; TAB(35); B
b) 110 PRINT TAB(20); B, C; TAB(66); D
c) 120 PRINT TAB(35);
   130 PRINT A
```

9. Consider the following program:

```
100 REM CHAPTER 4 SELF-TEST 9
110 READ A
120 LET A1 = 0.2*A
130 PRINT USING "###.##-"; A1
140 GOTO 110
150 REM ********DATA FOLLOWS********
160 DATA -20, 20, 500.3, 500.6, 1.9, 3.84
170 END
```

a) What values of A1 are displayed on each of the resulting six lines?
b) What is displayed after these six lines?

10. Which of the following descriptor fields will produce the edited result $2,148.67 from the value 2148.67?

a) $, $##.##
b) **,###.##
c) #,###.##

d) $$,###.##
e) $$,###.##-

11. Write a PRINT USING statement that includes a string constant for the purpose of displaying the message THE ANSWER IS followed by the value of A. Include a descriptor field with the following characteristics:

    a) Five digit positions, two to the right of the decimal point
    b) A floating dollar sign
    c) A sign status to the right of the number

12. Assume A has a value of 1525.83. Match the descriptor field in the left column with the displayed results in the right column.

Descriptor Field		Result
a) ####	1)	1,525.83
b) #,###.##	2)	$1,525.83
c) $$,###.##	3)	**1,525.83
d) **#,###.##	4)	%1525.83
e) ###	5)	1526
f) #.##∧∧∧∧	6)	1.53E+03

13. Write a PRINT USING statement that displays the value of A$ beginning in position 1, as follows:

    a) Only the first character of A$ is displayed.
    b) All of A$ is displayed.
    c) The first six characters of A$ are displayed.

4.8
TEST YOUR
BASIC SKILLS

1. Consider the valid programs listed below. What is displayed if each is executed?

a)
```
100 REM EXERCISE 4.1A
110 REM MPG COMPARISON
120 READ C$, M, G
130 LET A = M/G
140 PRINT "VEHICLE "; C$
150 PRINT "MILES"; M
160 PRINT "GALLONS"; G
170 PRINT "MPG"; A
180 PRINT
190 GOTO 120
200 REM ****DATA FOLLOWS****
210 DATA A, 1275, 41.7
220 DATA B, 685, 23.2
230 DATA C, 1650, 62.5
240 END
```

b)
```
100 REM EXERCISE 4.1B
110 REM DETERMINING PRODUCTS
120 READ X, Y
130 LET C = X * (Y + 1)
140 PRINT "C IS EQUAL TO C"
150 PRINT "C IS EQUAL TO"; C
160 GOTO 120
170 REM ****DATA FOLLOWS****
180 DATA 3, 4
190 DATA 3
200 DATA 2, 1
210 DATA 7, 8
220 END
```

c)
```
100 REM EXERCISE 4.1C
110 REM ACCUMULATED LOAN PAYMENTS
120 LET C = 0
130 LET A = 0
140 READ N$
150 PRINT "NAME "; N$
160 READ P
170 LET C = C + 1
180 LET A = A + P
190 PRINT
200 PRINT "WEEK"; C
210 PRINT "PAYMENT"; P
220 PRINT "ACCUMULATED PAYMENTS"; A
230 GOTO 160
240 REM ****DATA FOLLOWS****
250 DATA LAURA GOODLY, 120, 50
260 DATA 30, 60, 500.25
270 END
```

d)
```
100 REM EXERCISE 4.1D
110 REM DETERMINING SQUARE FOOTAGE
120 PRINT "ROOM", "SQ FT", "ACC SQ FT"
130 LET T = 0
140 READ R$, L, W
150 LET A = L * W
160 LET T = T + A
170 PRINT R$, A, T
180 GOTO 140
190 REM ****DATA FOLLOWS****
200 DATA KITCHEN, 13, 15
210 DATA FAMILY ROOM, 25, 17.5
220 DATA HALL 1, 6, 12.5
230 DATA HALL 2, 6.5, 8
240 DATA WASHROOM, 8, 9
250 DATA BEDROOM 1, 16, 18
260 DATA BEDROOM 2, 13, 15
270 DATA FRONT ROOM, 20, 18
280 END
```

2. Correct the errors in the following programs:

a)
```
-95 REM EXERCISE 4.2A
100 READ S, B,
110 LET D = S - B
120 PRANT D
130 END
140 DATA 4, 6
```

b)
```
100 REM EXERCISE 4.2B
110 DATA 1, 2, 5, 6, 8, 7, 1, 3, 2
120 READ X, Y, Z
130 LET X1 = X * Y
140 LET X1 = X1 * Z
150 GOTO 130
160 PRINT X2
170 END
```

3. How many values will be read from a DATA statement by the following READ statement?
   a) `100 READ Q, R, S, T, U`
   b) `110 READ A, B`
   c) `120 READ J, K, K, J`
   d) `130 READ U * V - W, S, X`

4. Write valid DATA statements for the READ statements in 3.

5. Write a correct PRINT statement to display your name in the first position of:
   a) The first print zone
   b) The third print zone

6. Write a sequence of PRINT statements that will display the value of A on the first line and the value of B on the fourth line.

7. Write a single PRINT statement to compute and display:
   a) $\sqrt{Y}$
   b) $\sqrt[3]{Y}$
   c) $\sqrt[4]{Y}$

8. Which of the following are true?
   a) Every PRINT statement displays one line of information.
   b) The END statement is mandatory.
   c) Every program must have a PRINT statement.
   d) The semicolon causes spacing to the next print zone.
   e) It is invalid to have more data items in a DATA statement than required by a READ statement.

9. Write two PRINT statements; one that will head the 5 print zones as COLUMN1, COLUMN2, etc., and one that will underline each heading. Use minus signs in the second PRINT statement for underlining purposes.

10. What will the following statement display if B is equal to 5 and C is B squared?
    ```
    100 PRINT "THE ANSWER TO"; B; "SQUARED IS"; C; "."
    ```

11. Write an INPUT statement that is comparable to the READ statement in line 110.
    ```
    100 REM EXERCISE 4.11
    110 READ A, B, C
    ```

12. Explain, briefly, the differences between the use of the READ and DATA statements and the INPUT statement.

13. Explain what is meant by the statement, "The DATA statement is non-executable."

14. Rewrite the following invalid program.
    ```
    100 REM EXERCISE 4.14
    110 INPUT "WHAT VALUE DO YOU WISH TO SQUARE" W
    120 PRINT W "SQUARED IS" W^2
    130 END
    ```

15. Write a PRINT statement that would precede an INPUT statement that raises the question:
    WHAT ARE THE TWO VALUES?

16. What does this program display?
    ```
    100 REM EXERCISE 4.16
    110 PRINT "NET"; "    "; "PAY"
    120 PRINT TAB(11); "NET PAY"
    130 PRINT
    140 PRINT "N"; "   "; "E"; "   "; "T"; "      "; "P";
    150 PRINT "  "; "A"; "   "; "Y"
    ```

17. What does this program display?
    ```
    100 REM EXERCISE 4.17
    110 PRINT "HOURS", "GROSS", "FICA", "FIT"
    120 PRINT "HOURS"; "GROSS"; "FICA"; "FIT"
    130 PRINT
    140 PRINT -10, -20, -30, -30-10
    150 PRINT -10; -20; -30; -30-10
    160 PRINT
    170 PRINT TAB(10); "HOURS"
    180 PRINT "HOURS"; TAB(40); "GROSS"
    190 END
    ```

18. What kind of graphic output displays from this program?

```
100 REM EXERCISE 4.18
110 PRINT TAB(34); "VVVVV"
120 PRINT TAB(33); "X"; TAB(39); "X"
130 PRINT TAB(32); "X"; TAB(35); "O"; TAB(37); "O"; TAB(40); "X"
140 PRINT TAB(32); "X"; TAB(40); "X"
150 PRINT TAB(32); "X"; TAB(36); "U"; TAB(40); "X"
160 PRINT TAB(32); "X"; TAB(34); "("; TAB(38); ")"; TAB(40); "X"
170 PRINT TAB(32); "X"; TAB(36); "-"; TAB(40); "X"
180 PRINT TAB(33); "X"; TAB(39); "X"
190 PRINT TAB(34); "XXXXX"
200 END
```

19. Write a program that will generate the following graphic output.

```
*************
* B A S I C *
B L       N B
A   E   R   A
S       A   S
I   E   R   I
C L       N C
* B A S I C *
*************
```

20. Study the following program. Give your interpretation of what the program does when executed.

```
100 REM EXERCISE 4.20
110 READ A, B
120 LET C = A * B
130 PRINT C,
140 GOTO 120
150 REM ***DATA FOLLOWS***
160 DATA 2, 4, 6, 3
170 END
```

21. For each of the following descriptor fields and corresponding data, indicate what the computer displays. Use the letter b to indicate the space character.

	Descriptor Field	Data	Output
a)	###	25	
b)	#,###.##	38.4	
c)	$$,###.##−	−22.6	
d)	$#,###.##−	425.89	
e)	**#,###.##	88.756	
f)	#,###.#	637214	
g)	##.##−	3.975	
h)	###.##	−123.8	
i)	##,###.###	12.6143	
j)	#.##∧∧∧∧	265.75	
k)	!	ABCD	
l)	&	ABCD	
m)	\\ (zero spaces)	ABCD	
n)	\ \ (2 spaces)	ABCD	

4.9 PROGRAMMING EXERCISES

Exercise 1: Determining the P/E Ratio

Purpose: To become familiar with I/O statements and the GO TO statement.

Problem: Construct a program to print the Price/Earnings (P/E) ratio for companies whose current stock prices and earnings per share are known. The P/E ratio is a useful tool employed by stock market analysts in evaluating the investment potential of various companies. The P/E ratio is determined by dividing the price of a share of stock by the company's latest earnings per share.

Input Data: Prepare and use the following sample data:

Stock Name	Price per Share	Latest Earnings
DIGITAL	113.5	5.98
DATAGN	57	1.06
IBM	121.75	8.12
APPLE	34	1.42
TANDY	54.5	2.51

Output Results: The following results are displayed:

```
STOCK          PRICE PER     LATEST       P/E
NAME           SHARE         EARNINGS     RATIO
-----          ---------     --------     -----

DIGITAL        113.5         5.98         18.9799
DATAGN         57            1.06         53.7736
IBM            121.75        8.12         14.9939
APPLE          34            1.42         23.9437
TANDY          54.5          2.51         21.7132
```

Output Results Formatted: Use the PRINT USING statement to display all numeric fields to the nearest hundredth place. Right-justify and align all numeric fields on the decimal point. The fields must also be centered under the column headings.

Purpose: To become familiar with looping and the use of the READ and DATA statements.

Problem: If a principal of $1 is invested at 8% compounded annually, the actual interest earned at the end of the year is $0.08, the same as the rate. However, if the rate quoted is 8% compounded semiannually, the actual interest earned at the end of the year would be $0.0916 or 9.16%. In this case the stated rate of 8% is called the nominal rate. The corresponding rate of 9.16% is called the effective rate. The effective rate can be determined from the following formula:

$$R = \left(1 + \frac{J}{M}\right)^M - 1$$

where

    R = Effective rate
    J = Nominal rate
    M = Number of conversions per year

Write a program to compute the effective rate in percent equivalent to a given nominal rate for a given number of conversions.

Exercise 2: Nominal and Effective Interest Rates

Input Data: Use the following sample data:

Nominal Rate in %	Number of Conversions
10.55	6
11.65	12
12.75	2
15.65	4
17.85	3

Output Results: The following results are displayed:

```
NOMINAL        NUMBER OF       EFFECTIVE
RATE IN %      CONVERSIONS     RATE IN %
---------      -----------     ---------
10.55          6               11.0246
11.65          12              12.2923
12.75          2               13.1564
15.65          4               16.5926
17.85          3               18.9331
```

Output Results Formatted: Use the PRINT USING statement to display the first and third columns to the nearest hundredth place right-justified. Center and right-justify the second column under its heading.

**Exercise 3:
Inflation Gauge**

Purpose: To become familiar with gauging inflation and the use of the PRINT statement.

Problem: Write a program to input today's current price, the previous price and the number of weeks between price quotes. Compute the sample *annual* inflation rate and the expected price of the item one year from today's current price. Round the annual inflation rate and expected price to the nearest hundredth place. For each item processed, display the item, current price, computed annual inflation rate and expected price in one year.

Input Data: Prepare and use the following sample data:

Item	Current Price	Previous Price	Number of Weeks
1 dozen eggs	$0.93	$0.92	13
1 lb. butter	2.59	2.50	15
1 gal. milk	1.92	1.85	18
1 loaf bread	1.10	1.07	6

Output Results: The following results are displayed:

```
                CURRENT      INFLATION     EXPECTED
ITEM            PRICE        RATE IN %     PRICE IN 1 YR
----            -------      ---------     -------------
1 DOZEN EGGS    .93          4.3           .97
1 LB BUTTER     2.59         12.05         2.9
1 GAL MILK      1.92         10.53         2.12
1 LOAF BREAD    1.1          23.64         1.36
```

Output Results Formatted: Use the PRINT USING statement to align the decimal points and display all numeric results to the nearest hundredth place right-justified under their column headings.

**Exercise 4:
Determining the Point
of Intersection**

Purpose: To become familiar with using the computer to solve systems of equations and generate readable reports.

Problem: Maximum profit or minimum cost can often be determined from equations based on known facts concerning a product. The point of intersection of the equations is significant. Write a program to find the point of intersection for two first-degree equations in two variables (that is, two equations and two unknowns). The general form for two equations is:

$$a_1x + b_1y = c_1$$
$$a_2x + b_2y = c_2$$

Its solutions are expressed as:

$$x = \frac{c_1b_2 - c_2b_1}{a_1b_2 - a_2b_1}$$

$$y = \frac{c_2a_1 - c_1a_2}{a_1b_2 - a_2b_1}$$

The program should read the coefficients (a_1, b_1, c_1, a_2, b_2 and c_2 in this order) from a DATA statement, solve for x and y, display the values of a_1, b_1 and c_1 on one line, a_2, b_2, c_2, x and y on the next line. The program should loop back to read a set of data for the next system of equations.

Input Data: Prepare and use the following sample data:

System	Equation 1 Coefficients			Equation 2 Coefficients		
	a	b	c	a	b	c
1	1	1	5	1	−1	1
2	2	−7	8	3	1	−8
3	.6	−.75	−8	.6	−.125	2

Output Results: The following results are displayed:

```
<--------------------EQUATIONS-------------------->       <----INTERSECTION----->
COEFF A         COEFF B         COEFF C               X VALUE         Y VALUE
--------        --------        --------              --------        --------
   1               1               5
   1              -1               1                      3               2

   2              -7               8
   3               1              -8                  -2.08696        -1.73913

  .6             -.75             -8
  .6             -.125             2                   6.66667          16
```

Output Results Formatted: Use the PRINT USING statement to display the results of x and y to the nearest thousandth place, right-justified with the decimal points aligned.

Purpose: To become familiar with calculating the annual straight-line depreciation charges or allowances on potential or present capital investments.

Exercise 5: Straight-Line Depreciation Calculations

Problem: As a corporate accountant you have been asked to write a program that calculates the annual depreciation expense under the straight-line method using the following formula:

$$\text{Depreciation} = \frac{\text{Asset Cost} - \text{Salvage Value}}{\text{Service Life}}$$

Input Data: Prepare and use the following sets of data:

	Data	
Description	Set 1	Set 2
I.D. No.	1486	2173
Asset Cost in $	325,000	42,000
Salvage Value in $	45,000	12,000
Years of Service Life	14	10

Execute the program with data from Set 1 and then replace the corresponding DATA statement with one incorporating the data from Set 2.

Output Results: The following results are displayed for Set 1 (Final results for Set 2 are not shown):

```
ITEM 1486 HAS AN ANNUAL DEPRECIATION OF $ 20000
FOR AN INVESTMENT OF $ 325000 FOR 14 YEARS
WITH A SALVAGE VALUE OF $ 45000.
```

Output Results Formatted: Use the PRINT USING statement to float the dollar sign, insert a comma and display each monetary amount to the nearest cent. The following formatted results are displayed for Set 1:

```
ITEM 1486 HAS AN ANNUAL DEPRECIATION OF  $20,000.00
FOR AN INVESTMENT OF  $325,000.00 FOR 14 YEARS
WITH A SALVAGE VALUE OF  $45,000.00.
```

Purpose: To become familiar with annuity formulas and the hierarchy of operations in a complex LET statement.

Exercise 6: Determining the Eventual Cash Value of an Annuity

Problem: An annuity or installment plan is a series of payments made at equal intervals of time. Examples of annuities are pensions and premiums on life insurance. More often than not, the interest conversion period is unequal to the payment interval. The following formula determines the eventual cash value of an annuity of R dollars paid per year in P installments for N years at an interest rate of J percent converted M times a year:

$$S = R \left[\frac{\left(1 + \frac{J}{M}\right)^{MN} - 1}{P\left[\left(1 + \frac{J}{M}\right)^{M/P} - 1\right]} \right]$$

where

S = Eventual cash value
R = Payment per year
P = Number of installments per year
N = Duration of the annuity in years
J = Nominal interest rate
M = Conversions per year

Write a program to determine the eventual cash value of an annuity. After processing the first annuity, branch back to process the next annuity. Use the TAB function to help display the results, six columns per line.

Input Data: Prepare and use the following sample data:

Description	Data Set 1	Set 2	Set 3
Payments per year	$2000	$3000	$4000
Installments per year	12	12	12
Time in years	20	20	20
Interest rate in %	13	14	15
Conversions per year	2	4	6

Output Results: The following results are displayed:

PAYMENT PER YEAR	INSTALLMENTS PER YEAR	TIME IN YEARS	INTEREST RATE IN %	CONVERSIONS PER YEAR	CASH VALUE
2000	12	20	13	2	180330.4
3000	12	20	14	4	318119.8
4000	12	20	15	6	492591.7

Output Results Formatted: Use the PRINT USING statement to insert a decimal point and comma in the Payment Per Year and Cash Value results and display these results right-justified to the nearest cent. Center the Time, Interest and Conversion results under their appropriate column headings.

Exercise 7: Check Digit Calculation

Purpose: To become familiar with elementary check digit calculations.

Problem: Companies that issue credit cards often use algorithms to create credit card numbers that people will have difficulty generating at random. One approach is to add the digits of a number and add 0 or 1 to make the sum of the digits even. For example, whereas the number 45931 would be acceptable (i.e., $4 + 5 + 9 + 3 + 1 = 22$ and even) the number 37230 (i.e., $3 + 7 + 2 + 3 + 0 = 15$ and odd) would not be acceptable. The last digit in the number, either a 1 or a 0, is called the check digit. Write a program that accepts a four digit number, generates the check digit, and displays the original number, check digit number and five digit credit card number.
(*Hint:* Use the function INT to determine the individual digits that make up the four digit number and the check digit.)

Input Data: Prepare and use the following sample data: 4631, 4737, 2222, 9998

Output Results: The following output results are displayed:

FOUR DIGIT NUMBER	CHECK DIGIT	CREDIT CARD NUMBER
4631	0	46310
4737	1	47371
2222	0	22220
9998	1	99981

Purpose: To become familiar with looping and the use of the READ and DATA statements.

Problem: Modify Payroll Problem II in Programming Exercise 3.8 to generate a report with column headings and a line of information for each employee. Each line is to include employee number, gross pay, federal withholding tax and net pay.

Input Data: Use the sample data found in Programming Exercise 3.8.

Output Results: The following results are displayed:

```
EMPLOYEE
NUMBER         GROSS PAY      FED. TAX       NET PAY
--------       ---------      --------       -------
   123         1,000.00        184.62        815.38
   124           800.00        152.31        647.69
   125         1,040.00        200.31        839.69
   126            90.00          2.62         87.38

---OUT OF DATA LINE 170
```

LOOPING AND DECISION-MAKING 5

5.1 STRUCTURED PROGRAMMING

It is appropriate at this time to introduce you to some important concepts related to **structured programming**.

Structured programming is a methodology according to which all program logic can be constructed from a combination of the following three basic logic structures: *

1) **Sequence.** The most fundamental of the logic structures. It provides for two or more actions to be executed in the order they appear.
2) **If-Then-Else** or **Selection.** Provides a choice between two alternative actions.
3) **Do-While** or **Repetition.** Provides for the repeated execution of a loop.

The following are two common extensions to these logic structures:

4) **Do-Until** or **Repeat-Until.** An extension of the Do-While logic structure.
5) **Case.** An extension of the If-Then-Else logic structure in which the choice includes more than two alternatives.

Structured programming allows programs to be written with little or no use of the GOTO statement.

The use of these logic structures will be illustrated via algorithms and various BASIC statements. However, you should be aware that, because of the limitations of the BASIC language, it will not always be possible to write programs completely free of GOTO statements.

There are definite advantages to using structured programming. Computer scientists have found that when structured programming is applied correctly in the construction of programs,

1) Programs are clearer and more readable.
2) Less time is spent debugging, testing, and modifying the program.
3) The programmer's productivity is increased.
4) The quality, reliability, and efficiency of the program are improved.

Hence, there are important payoffs in using structured programming.

---

* In the discussion of these terms, IF-THEN-ELSE refers to a BASIC statement and If-Then-Else to the selection logic structure.

FIGURE 5.1 Sequential structure.

In the previous chapter, the programs performed precisely the same computation for every set of data items processed. Except for some elementary looping described in Chapter 4, the flow of control was sequential, as it is here in Figure 5.1. It is not always desirable to process each set of data items exactly the same way. For example, in a program that computes gross pay, some employees may be eligible for overtime, the number of hours they worked is greater than 40, while others may not. Therefore, in a payroll computation, a decision must be made concerning which of two gross pay formulas to use.

The sequential flow of control used in previous programs and shown in Figure 5.1 is not sufficient to solve problems that involve **decision-making**. To develop an algorithm that requires deviation from sequential control we need another logic structure. This new structure, called If-Then-Else, is shown in Figure 5.2 and is described in Appendix A, Section 3.

The flowchart representation of a decision is the diamond-shaped symbol. One flowline will always be shown entering the symbol and two lines will always be shown leaving the symbol. A condition which must be true or false is written within the decision symbol. Such a condition asks, for example, if two variables are equal or if an expression is within a certain range. If the condition is true, one path is taken; if not, the other path is taken.

To instruct the computer to select actions based on the values of variables, as illustrated in Figure 5.2, BASIC includes three statements which are classified as decision statements: IF (IF-THEN and IF-THEN-ELSE), ON-GOTO and ON-GOSUB. This chapter presents both forms of the IF statement and the ON-GOTO. The ON-GOSUB will be discussed in Chapter 6.

Logic Structures

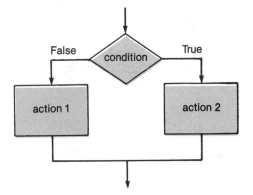

FIGURE 5.2 If-Then-Else structure.

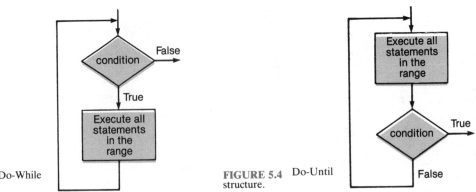

FIGURE 5.3   Do-While
structure.

FIGURE 5.4   Do-Until
structure.

Another common feature of many problems is the necessity to repeat execution of a range of instructions. This repeated execution is looping. Most programs perform only simple calculations but repeat these calculations again and again until certain conditions are satisfied.

It is necessary to include within the repeatedly executed process a decision to terminate the loop after a sufficient number of repetitions has occurred. Most computer scientists agree that the decision to terminate a loop should be located at the very top or very bottom of the loop. A loop that has the termination decision at the top is called a Do-While structure (see Figure 5.3). A loop that has the termination decision at the bottom is called a Do-Until structure (see Figure 5.4). See Appendix A, Section 3 for additional information on the Do-While and Do-Until logic structures.

BASIC has the following three pairs of statements to control the looping process illustrated in Figures 5.3 and 5.4:

1) IF-THEN and GOTO
2) WHILE and WEND *
3) FOR and NEXT

This chapter is concerned with the first two pairs of statements. The FOR and NEXT statements will be discussed in Chapter 6.

Upon successful completion of this chapter, you should be able to develop algorithms and write programs that include decisions, controlled loops, accumulators, control breaks, summary results and menus.

**5.2
THE IF-THEN AND
IF-THEN-ELSE
STATEMENTS**

The IF statements are commonly regarded as the most powerful statements in the BASIC language. They have two primary functions in BASIC:

1) They perform selection.
2) They facilitate looping.

In selection, a statement is used to let a program choose between two alternative paths, as illustrated in Figure 5.2. The IF statements are used to specify conditional control, decision-making, in a program. Looping is illustrated in Figures 5.3 and 5.4. BASIC has two types of IF statements.† One is the IF-THEN statement and is illustrated in Table 5.1. The second is the IF-THEN-ELSE statement and is illustrated in Table 5.3.

---

* The WHILE and WEND are not available on the Apple and COMMODORE systems. The DEC VAX-11 uses NEXT rather than WEND.

† Some BASIC systems allow for a third type of IF statement, the IF-GOTO. This type of IF statement will not be used in this book.

TABLE 5.1   The IF-THEN Statement

General Form:	IF condition THEN $\left\{\begin{array}{l}\text{line number}\\ \text{statement}\end{array}\right\}$ where braces { } signify choice between line number and statement; condition is a relationship that is either true or false.
Purpose:	Causes execution of a specified line number or statement if the condition is true. If the condition is false, control passes to the line following the IF-THEN statement.
| *Examples:* | ```
125 IF X >= 0 THEN 50
190 IF Y + 5 > 8 THEN LET A = A + 1
290 IF C + B/A <= X + 9 THEN IF S >= 50 THEN 560
300 IF A$ = "YES" THEN GOTO 100
400 IF C$ <> B$ THEN PRINT C$
500 IF C * (X - Y) + 8 < 45.7 THEN READ D, E$, F
``` |

As indicated in Table 5.1, the IF-THEN statement is used to specify a decision. The **condition** appears between the keywords IF and THEN. The condition specifies a relationship between expressions that is either true or false. The relationship is a comparison between one numeric expression and another or between one string expression and another. If the condition between IF and THEN is true and a *line number* follows the keyword THEN, control transfers to the stated line number. If the condition is true and a *statement* follows the keyword THEN, the statement is executed and control passes to the line following the IF-THEN. If the condition is false, regardless of what follows the keyword THEN, execution continues to the next line following the IF-THEN statement.

The condition between the keywords IF and THEN is made up of two expressions and a relational operator. Expressions may be associated with either numeric or string values. In determining whether a condition is true or not, BASIC first determines the single value of each expression and then evaluates them both with

TABLE 5.2   Relational Operators Used in Conditions

Relations	Math Symbol	BASIC Symbol	Examples
Equal to	$=$	=	`400 IF A = B THEN 200 ELSE 1400`
Less than	$<$	<	`500 IF A$ < "4" THEN 900 ELSE PRINT A`
Greater than	$>$	>	`600 IF X - Y > 9 THEN LET P = X * Y`
Less than or equal to	$\leqq$	<=	`700 IF X$ <= B$ THEN READ A$ ELSE READ A`
Greater than or equal to	$\geqq$	>=	`800 IF X + Y/Z >= C THEN 150`
Not equal to	$\neq$	<>	`900 IF S$ <> "NO" THEN READ A, B`

TABLE 5.3   The IF-THEN-ELSE Statement

General Form:	IF condition THEN $\left\{\begin{array}{l}\text{line number}\\ \text{statement}\end{array}\right\}$ ELSE $\left\{\begin{array}{l}\text{line number}\\ \text{statement}\end{array}\right\}$ where braces { } signify choice between line number and statement; condition is a relationship that is either true or false.
Purpose:	Causes execution of a line or statement following the keyword THEN if the condition is true. Causes execution of a line or statement following the keyword ELSE if the condition is false.
| *Examples:* | ```
200 IF F > T THEN 210 ELSE 250
300 IF D$ = "Y" THEN LET A = A + 1 ELSE GOTO 310
400 IF X + Y <> S * Q THEN 450 ELSE LET C = C * 2
500 IF A * (B + C) <= S/G THEN LET G = G + 2 ELSE LET G = G + 1
600 IF L >= INT(L) THEN PRINT "THE VALUE IS"; L ELSE PRINT 2 * L
700 IF LEN(T$) < 5 THEN 710 ELSE 750
800 IF Z = Y THEN IF S > T THEN LET F = F + 1 ELSE 500 ELSE 750
900 IF D <= R THEN IF G = 5 THEN PRINT D ELSE PRINT R
``` |
| *Caution:* | This statement is not available on the Apple and COMMODORE systems. |

respect to the relational operator. Table 5.2 lists the six relational operators that are used to indicate this type of comparison.

As is clear in Table 5.3, the IF-THEN-ELSE statement is similar to the IF-THEN statement. If the condition between IF and THEN is true, the system acts upon the line number or statement following the keyword THEN.

There is an important difference, however, between the IF-THEN-ELSE statement and the IF-THEN statement, which passes control to the next line when the condition is false. When the condition is false in the IF-THEN-ELSE statement, the system acts upon the line number or statement following the keyword ELSE. If a line number follows THEN or ELSE, control transfers to that line number. If a non-transfer statement follows the keyword THEN or ELSE, the statement is executed and control passes to the line following the IF-THEN-ELSE.

Figure 5.5 illustrates the use of the If-Then-Else structure to resolve a gross pay computation in which employees are paid a fixed rate per hour for hours worked less than or equal to 40 and time-and-a-half for hours worked greater than 40.

The gross pay computation illustrated in Figure 5.5 may be written in BASIC as follows:

```
100 REM GROSS PAY COMPUTATIONS
110 REM H = HOURS WORKED, R = RATE OF PAY, G = GROSS PAY
    .
    .
    .
200 IF H <= 40 THEN LET G = R * H ELSE LET G = R * H + 0.5 * R * (H - 40)
210 .
    .
    .
    .
```

Line 200 selects a LET statement to compute the gross pay G. If H (hours worked) is less than or equal to 40, the gross pay is computed using the LET statement immediately following the keyword THEN. If the condition, H ≤ 40, is false, then the gross pay is computed using the LET statement following the keyword ELSE. In either case, control passes to line 210.

Comparing Numeric Expressions

If the condition includes two numeric expressions, the comparison is based on the algebraic values of the two expressions. That is, the system evaluates not only the magnitude of each resultant expression, but also its sign. Table 5.4 illustrates several examples of statements that include conditions made up of numeric expressions.

Comparing String Expressions

If the condition includes two string expressions, the system evaluates the two strings from left to right, one character at a time. Two string expressions are considered equal if the two expressions have the same length and contain an

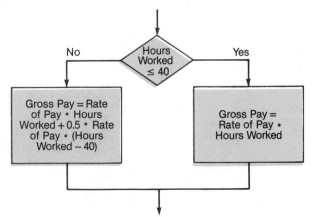

FIGURE 5.5 Use of the If-Then-Else structure.

TABLE 5.4   IF Statements with Numeric Expressions

Example	The statement	Value of variables	Result
1. Numeric variable compared against numeric constant.	`100 IF A = 3.25 THEN 230 ELSE 500`	A = 1.28	Line 500 is executed.
2. Numeric variable compared against numeric variable.	`150 IF X < Y THEN PRINT A ELSE PRINT B`	X = 7 Y = 9	The value of A is displayed and control passes to the line following 150.
3. Numeric variable compared against numeric expression.	`200 IF D <> A - B - 6 THEN PRINT S`	D = 23 A = 14 B = −15	Line following 200 is executed.
4. Numeric constant compared against numeric constant.	`250 IF 5 < 7 THEN PRINT F ELSE 300`		The value of F is displayed and control passes to the line following 250.
5. Numeric constant compared against numeric variable.	`300 IF 12.8 <= S THEN 100 ELSE PRINT Y`	S = 12.7	The value of Y is displayed and control passes to the line following 300.
6. Numeric constant compared against numeric expression.	`350 IF -1.25 > Z^X * (C - 4) THEN 370`	Z = 2 X = 4 C = −0.1	Line 370 is executed.
7. Numeric expression compared against numeric constant.	`400 IF A + B >= 2 THEN LET A = A + 1`	A = 3 B = 2	A is incremented by 1 and control passes to the line following 400.
8. Numeric expression compared against numeric value.	`450 IF (X - Y)/3 > LEN(C$) THEN 100`	X = 9 Y = 3 C$ = "AB"	Line following 450 is executed.
9. Numeric expression compared against numeric expression.	`500 IF A * B - 3 = A/C THEN PRINT A * B`	A = 3 B = 7 C = 3	Line following 500 is executed.
10. Numeric variable compared against string variable.	`600 IF A = A$ THEN 700 ELSE 800`	A = 5 A$ = "YES"	Invalid comparison. The expressions must be both of the same type, i.e., in this case, both numeric.

identical sequence of characters. As soon as one character in an expression is different from the corresponding character in the other expression the comparison stops and the system decides which expression has a lower value, based in general on numerical and alphabetical order. In other words, the system evaluates two string expressions like you would. For example,

"DOE" is less than "JOE"
"JEFF" is greater than "JAFF"
"YES" is equal to "YES"
"TAPE" is greater than "TAP"

BASIC determines which characters are "less" than others based upon the code used to store data in main memory. Most minicomputers and personal computers use the **ASCII** code (**American Standard Code for Information Interchange**). The ASCII code and the **collating sequence** are shown in Table 5.5. The collating code is the position of a character in relation to other characters. As indicated in Table 5.5, numbers are less than letters in value, and the null character is considered to have the least value in the collating sequence.

TABLE 5.5   The BASIC Character Set and the Corresponding ASCII Decimal Numeric Code Representation*

	BASIC CHARACTER	ASCII DECIMAL CODE	BASIC CHARACTER	ASCII DECIMAL CODE	BASIC CHARACTER	ASCII DECIMAL CODE
Low	NULL	00	A	65	d	100
	CTRL. CHARS.	01-31	B	66	e	101
	SPACE	32	C	67	f	102
	!	33	D	68	g	103
	"	34	E	69	h	104
	#	35	F	70	i	105
	$	36	G	71	j	106
	%	37	H	72	k	107
	&	38	I	73	l	108
	'	39	J	74	m	109
	(	40	K	75	n	110
	)	41	L	76	o	111
	*	42	M	77	p	112
	+	43	N	78	q	113
	,	44	O	79	r	114
	–	45	P	80	s	115
	.	46	Q	81	t	116
	/	47	R	82	u	117
	0	48	S	83	v	118
	1	49	T	84	w	119
	2	50	U	85	x	120
	3	51	V	86	y	121
	4	52	W	87	z	122
	5	53	X	88	{	123
	6	54	Y	89	|	124
	7	55	Z	90	}	125
	8	56	[	91	~	126
	9	57	\	92	DELETE	127
	:	58	]	93	High	
	;	59	^	94		
	<	60	_	95		
	=	61	`	96		
	>	62	a	97		
	?	63	b	98		
	@	64	c	99		

* Some BASIC systems have 128 different characters, while others have up to 256 characters. The term CTRL. CHARS. represents a series of control characters that have special meaning to a given system. These control characters are represented by the ASCII decimal codes 01 through 31. Check the user's manual on your BASIC system for the meaning of these control characters.

Table 5.6 illustrates several examples of IF-THEN and IF-THEN-ELSE statements that include conditions made up of string expressions.

Termination of a Loop Using an IF-THEN Statement

A useful function of the IF-THEN statement is to perform an end-of-file (**EOF**) test to terminate a looping process. An IF-THEN statement following a READ statement can be used to test for a final data item that is distinguishable from all the rest of the data assigned to a variable. This final data item is put in a **trailer record** that is placed in the last DATA statement. Since it guards against reading past the end-of-file, the extra record is also called a **sentinel record**. The data item selected for the EOF test is called the **sentinel value**. When the sentinel value is detected by the IF-THEN statement, control transfers to an end-of-job routine. This technique for terminating a program prevents the diagnostic messages which occurred in programs in Chapter 4 from being displayed at the conclusion of the programs, and it allows for final totals to be displayed prior to termination.

Programming Case Study 6B: Determining the Sale Price With an EOF Test

Consider again the program solution presented for Programming Case Study 6A in Chapter 4 (p. 83). Recall that the program read a record consisting of a product number, original price and discount rate. A discount amount and sale price were computed and displayed. The program then processed the next record and proceeded in this fashion until all the records were processed. Program 5.1 is similar to Program 4.1 except that it employs an EOF test and prevents a diagnostic message from being displayed upon termination.

TABLE 5.6   IF Statements with String Expressions

Example	The statement	Value of variables	Result
1. String variable compared against string constant.	`100 IF A$ = "NO" THEN PRINT A$`	A$ = "YES"	Line following 100 is executed.
2. String variable compared against string variable.	`150 IF X$ <> Y$ THEN 180 ELSE PRINT X$`	X$ = "1" Y$ = "2"	Line 180 is executed.
3. String variable compared against string expression.	`200 IF B$ <= H$ + J$ THEN LET S = S - 1`	B$ = "ABX" H$ = "A" J$ = "BY"	S is decremented by 1 and control passes to the line following 200.
4. String constant compared against string variable.	`250 IF "SH2" < V$ THEN READ A ELSE READ B`	V$ = "SH1"	B is assigned a value and control passes to the line following 250.
5. String constant compared against string constant.	`300 IF "X" > "Y" THEN 120 ELSE 130`		Line 130 is executed
6. String constant compared against string expression.	`350 IF "AB" = "A" + MID$(S$, 3, 1) THEN 6700`	S$ = "PAB"	Line 6700 is executed.
7. String expression compared against string constant.	`400 IF LEFT$(Z$, 2) + RIGHT$(Z$, 1) = "XYZ" THEN 10`	Z$ = "XYACZ"	Line 10 is executed.
8. String expression compared against string variable.	`450 IF "X100" + MID$(F$, 1, 1) <> B$ THEN 350`	F$ = "Y" B$ = "X100Y"	Line following 450 is executed.
9. String expression compared against string expression.	`500 IF A$+B$ < C$ + MID$(A$, 1, 2) THEN READ A, B`	A$ = "12" B$ = "12" C$ = "12"	Line following 500 is executed.

To incorporate an EOF test, a variable must be selected and a trailer record added to the data. In Program 5.1, the authors selected the product number as a test for the end-of-file and the sentinel value of EOF. The input data for Program 5.1 is the same as that processed by Program 4.1 except for the addition of the trailer record as shown below.

	Product Number	Original Price	Discount Rate in Percent
	112841A	$115.00	14
	213981B	100.00	17
	332121A	98.00	13
	586192X	88.00	12
	714121Y	43.00	8
Trailer Record →	EOF	0	0

Note that for the trailer record the authors arbitrarily assigned zero values to the remaining data items.

Side by side, Program 5.1 and its flowchart in Figure 5.6 show that a Do-While structure is used to establish the looping process. The algorithm includes the use of two READ statements. The first READ statement before the loop is executed only once and is used to read the first record. The product number is then tested to determine if the loop should be executed. The second READ statement located at the bottom of the loop is used to read the remaining records. Each time the second READ statement is executed, control passes back to the decision statement to determine if the trailer record has been read. If the trailer record is read, the

```
100 REM PROGRAM 5.1
110 REM DETERMINING THE SALE PRICE WITH AN EOF TEST
120 REM N$ = PRODUCT NO.    P = ORIGINAL PRICE
130 REM R  = DISCOUNT RATE  D = DISCOUNT AMOUNT  S = SALES PRICE
140 REM ***********************************************************
150 PRINT    "PRODUCT    ORIGINAL    DISCOUNT    DISCOUNT    SALE"
160 PRINT    "NUMBER     PRICE       RATE IN %   AMOUNT      PRICE"
170 PRINT    "-------    --------    ---------   --------    -----"
180 LET A$ = "\      \   #,###.##       ###      #,###.## #,###.##"
190 REM READ THE FIRST RECORD
200 READ N$, P, R
210 REM **************PROCESS A RECORD**************
220 IF N$ = "EOF" THEN 290
230    LET D = R/100 * P
240    LET S = P - D
250    PRINT USING A$; N$, P, R, D, S
260    READ N$, P, R
270 GOTO 220
280 REM **************EOF ROUTINE******************
290 PRINT
300 PRINT "END OF REPORT"
310 REM ***************DATA FOLLOWS*****************
320 DATA 112841A, 115, 14
330 DATA 213981B, 100, 17
340 DATA 332121A, 98, 13
350 DATA 586192X, 88, 12
360 DATA 714121Y, 43, 8
370 DATA EOF, 0, 0
380 END

RUN

PRODUCT    ORIGINAL    DISCOUNT    DISCOUNT    SALE
NUMBER     PRICE       RATE IN %   AMOUNT      PRICE
-------    --------    ---------   --------    -----
112841A     115.00        14         16.10     98.90
213981B     100.00        17         17.00     83.00
332121A      98.00        13         12.74     85.26
586192X      88.00        12         10.56     77.44
714121Y      43.00         8          3.44     39.56

END OF REPORT
```

PROGRAM 5.1

program terminates; otherwise, the loop is re-entered and the record is processed further. The statements in the loop, other than the first and last, should be indented by three spaces for the purpose of readability (see lines 230 through 260 in Program 5.1).

Some Words of Caution for Constructing Conditions

In Chapter 3, it was pointed out that an expression is evaluated by the system, which calculates an *approximation* to the true mathematical value of the expression. Since the internal binary representation of the value is sometimes less than the true mathematical value, some values cannot be represented exactly in a computer system. Consider the following three algebraic equations:

$$x = 1/3$$
$$y = 3x$$
$$z = y - 1$$

When these equations are evaluated by a person, $y = 1$ and $z = 0$. When they are evaluated by a computer, z may not equal 0 because BASIC requires all fractions to be in decimal form. If these equations are expressed as BASIC statements, together with the IF-THEN statement that follows,

```
   .
   .
   .
110 LET X = 1/3
120 LET Y = 3 * X
130 LET Z = Y - 1
140 IF Z = 0 THEN 200
150 .
```

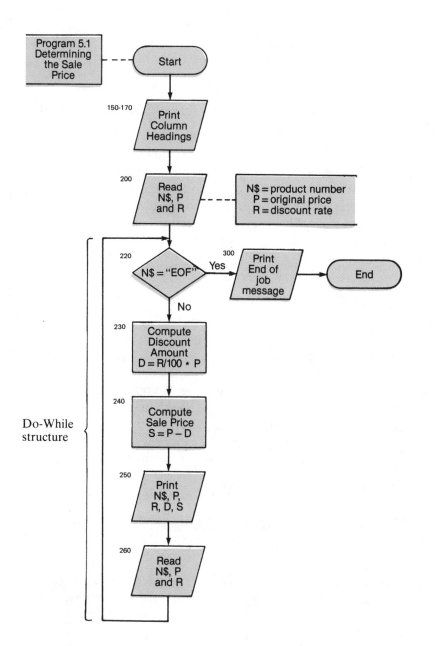

FIGURE 5.6   Flowchart for Program 5.1.

line 150, not line 200, is executed after the IF-THEN statement, since 1/3 yields 0.333333 instead of an infinitely long 0.3333333333. When line 120 LET Y = 3 * X, is evaluated, Y is assigned the value of 0.999999 instead of 1. Z, then, is assigned the value of -0.000001, which is certainly not zero.

Once you get the hang of them, computer aproximations should present no difficulties whatsoever. In order to make this partial program work, line 140 should be rewritten as:

```
140 IF Z <= 0 THEN 200
```

Most programs require the inclusion of accumulators. **Accumulators** are often used to develop totals. Accumulators are initialized to a value of zero before the execution of a loop, incremented within the loop and then manipulated or displayed after the looping process is complete. Although BASIC automatically initializes numeric variables to zero, good programming practice demands that it

5.3 ACCUMULATORS

be done in the program. There are two types of accumulators—counters and running totals. Both types are discussed in the sections that follow.

Counters   A **counter** is an accumulator used to count the number of times some action is performed. For example, the statement

```
230 LET C = C + 1
```

appropriately placed within a loop causes a counter C to increment by one each time the loop is executed. Associated with a counter is a statement placed prior to the execution of the loop that initializes the counter to some value. In most cases the counter is initialized to zero. The following partial program illustrates the initialization and incrementation of a counter called C:

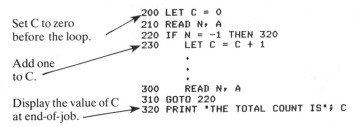

```
200 LET C = 0
210 READ N, A
220 IF N = -1 THEN 320
230     LET C = C + 1
        .
        .
        .
300     READ N, A
310 GOTO 220
320 PRINT "THE TOTAL COUNT IS"; C
```

Set C to zero before the loop.

Add one to C.

Display the value of C at end-of-job.

You may write programs that increment counters based upon decision-making statements. The following partial program tests S$. If S$ is equal to M, the counter M1 is incremented by 1, otherwise F1 is incremented by 1.

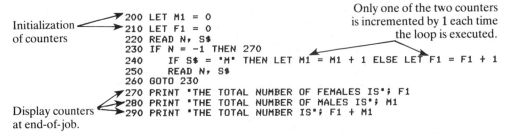

```
200 LET M1 = 0
210 LET F1 = 0
220 READ N, S$
230 IF N = -1 THEN 270
240     IF S$ = "M" THEN LET M1 = M1 + 1 ELSE LET F1 = F1 + 1
250     READ N, S$
260 GOTO 230
270 PRINT "THE TOTAL NUMBER OF FEMALES IS"; F1
280 PRINT "THE TOTAL NUMBER OF MALES IS"; M1
290 PRINT "THE TOTAL NUMBER IS"; F1 + M1
```

Initialization of counters

Only one of the two counters is incremented by 1 each time the loop is executed.

Display counters at end-of-job.

Lines 200 and 210 initialize the counters M1 and F1, respectively. Each time a record is read, line 240 increments M1 or F1, depending on the value of S$. When the trailer record is read, control passes to line 270, and the values of F1, M1 and F1 + M1 are displayed.

Running Totals   A **running total** is an accumulator used to sum the different values that a variable is assigned during the execution of a program. For example, the statement

```
230 LET T = T + S
```

appropriately placed within a loop causes the variable T to increase by the value of S. T is called a running total. If a program is processing an employee file and the variable S is assigned the employee salary, then variable T in line 230 represents the running total of the salaries paid to all the employees in the file. As with a counter, a running total must be initialized to some predetermined value prior to the execution of the loop.

The following partial program illustrates the initialization and incrementation of a running total. Assume the variable S is assigned the monthly salary of an employee each time the READ statement is executed. Since the variable T is incremented by the employee salary S, at end-of-job T will represent the total monthly salary paid to all the employees in the file.

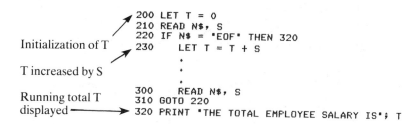

Initialization of T

T increased by S

Running total T
displayed

```
200 LET T = 0
210 READ N$, S
220 IF N$ = "EOF" THEN 320
230     LET T = T + S
         .
         .
         .
300     READ N$, S
310 GOTO 220
320 PRINT "THE TOTAL EMPLOYEE SALARY IS"; T
```

Think carefully about the placement of an IF-THEN statement to facilitate looping. Poorly placed IF-THEN statements may introduce too many GOTO statements in your program, making the program highly unstructured. In addition, too many GOTO statements may make the program difficult to modify and maintain after the program is put into production use.

For an illustration of these points, the following program computes and displays the sum of the following series:

$$1 + 2 + 3 + \ldots + 99 + 100$$

Programs 5.2, 5.3 and 5.4 display correctly the sum of the series. Note carefully the placement of the IF-THEN statement in each program and the introduction of the GOTO statement in Programs 5.2 and 5.4.

Program 5.2 shows the use of the Do-While structure where the decision to terminate is at the top of the loop. This solution is similar to that used in Program 5.1.

Program 5.3 shows the use of the Do-Until structure, in which the decision to terminate is at the bottom of the loop. This solution contains no GOTO statement. Notice how the IF-THEN statement in line 180 returns control to the top of the loop until I is greater than 100. Program 5.4 is a less desirable solution; the decision to terminate in the middle of the loop gives the program a poor structure. Although the third solution generates the correct answer, it lacks the clarity associated with Programs 5.2 and 5.3.

5.4 PLACEMENT OF THE IF-THEN STATEMENT TO FACILITATE LOOPING

Do-While
Structure

```
100 REM PROGRAM 5.2
110 REM SUMMING A SERIES OF INTEGERS FROM 1 TO 100
120 REM USING A DO-WHILE STRUCTURE
130 REM ********************************************
140 LET S = 0
150 LET I = 1
160 IF I > 100 THEN 200
170     LET S = S + I
180     LET I = I + 1
190 GOTO 160
200 PRINT "THE SUM IS"; S
210 END

RUN

THE SUM IS 5050
```

PROGRAM 5.2

Do-Until
Structure

```
100 REM PROGRAM 5.3
110 REM SUMMING A SERIES OF INTEGERS FROM 1 TO 100
120 REM USING A DO-UNTIL STRUCTURE
130 REM ********************************************
140 LET S = 0
150 LET I = 1
160     LET S = S + I
170     LET I = I + 1
180 IF I <= 100 THEN 160
190 PRINT "THE SUM IS"; S
200 END

RUN

THE SUM IS 5050
```

PROGRAM 5.3

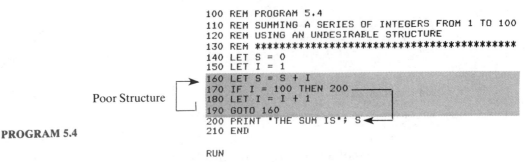

```
100 REM PROGRAM 5.4
110 REM SUMMING A SERIES OF INTEGERS FROM 1 TO 100
120 REM USING AN UNDESIRABLE STRUCTURE
130 REM *******************************************
140 LET S = 0
150 LET I = 1
160 LET S = S + I
170 IF I = 100 THEN 200
180 LET I = I + 1
190 GOTO 160
200 PRINT 'THE SUM IS'; S
210 END
```

Poor Structure

PROGRAM 5.4

```
RUN

THE SUM IS 5050
```

5.5
THE WHILE
AND WEND
STATEMENTS

The second method for controlling a looping process in BASIC is through the use of the WHILE and WEND statements, which define a loop called a **While loop**. Like the IF-THEN and GOTO statements illustrated in the first four programs of this chapter, the WHILE and WEND statements can be used to implement the Do-While structure. The general forms of the WHILE and WEND statements are given in Tables 5.7 and 5.8, respectively.

To illustrate the similarity in programming between the looping concepts discussed in the previous sections of this chapter and the WHILE and WEND statements, recall Program 5.2 and look at Program 5.5, which includes a While loop. Both programs compute and display the sum of the first 100 integers.

TABLE 5.7 **The** WHILE **Statement**

General Form:	WHILE condition
Purpose:	Causes the statements between WHILE and WEND to be executed repeatedly while the condition is true. When the condition is false, control transfers to the line following the corresponding WEND statement.
Examples:	100 WHILE C = 0 200 WHILE M$ <> "EOF" 300 WHILE A + B > S 400 WHILE X >= 0 500 WHILE D < C * D + 4/S 600 WHILE F <= 0
Caution:	This statement is not available on the Apple or COMMODORE systems.

TABLE 5.8 **The** WEND **Statement**

General Form:	WEND
Purpose:	Identifies the end of a While loop.
Examples:	500 WEND 700 WEND
Caution:	The DEC VAX-11 uses the keyword NEXT rather than WEND to identify the end of a While loop. This statement is not available on the Apple or COMMODORE systems.

```
100 REM PROGRAM 5.5
110 REM SUMMING A SERIES OF INTEGERS FROM 1 TO 100
120 REM USING A WHILE LOOP
130 REM *******************************************
140 LET S = 0
150 LET I = 1
160 WHILE I <= 100
170     LET S = S + I
180     LET I = I + 1
190 WEND
200 PRINT 'THE SUM IS'; S
210 END
```

While loop

PROGRAM 5.5

```
RUN

THE SUM IS 5050
```

Program 5.2 employs the IF-THEN and GOTO statements to control the looping process. Lines 140 and 150 initialize the running total S to 0 and the counter I to 1, respectively. Line 160 tests to determine if the value of I is greater than 100. If the condition is false, control passes to line 170 where lines 170 and 180 are executed and control transfers back to line 160. When the condition in the IF-THEN statement is true, the program terminates the loop and displays the running total S in line 200.

Program 5.5 facilitates the construction of the loop by use of the WHILE and WEND statements. In executing the While loop in Program 5.5, the following occurs:

1) When the WHILE statement is executed for the first time, the While loop (lines 160 to 190) becomes activated.
2) Next, the condition is tested to determine if the statements in lines 170 and 180 in the loop should be executed. This test occurs *before* the first pass.
3) If the condition is true, the statements within the loop are executed. If the condition is false, control transfers to line 200, which follows the corresponding WEND.
4) The WEND statement is the last statement of a While loop. As long as the condition is true, control *automatically* returns to the top of the loop.

Note that the statements in the loop are indented to make the program more readable. In our opinion, Program 5.5 is easier to read and code than Program 5.2. With a While loop, you need not concern yourself with a GOTO as the last statement of a loop. Furthermore, as indicated in Chapter 4, recent trends in modern programming minimize the use of the GOTO statement, and the use of the While loop makes it unnecessary.

A While loop may also be used to process data until a sentinel value is read. For example, the following partial program illustrates a loop that executes until the sentinel value EOF is assigned to N$:

```
      .
→ 200 READ N$, A
  210 WHILE N$ <> "EOF"
           .
           .
           .
  400    READ N$, A
  410 WEND
  420 .
```

Line 200 reads the first record. If the first record contains the sentinel value EOF, then the loop is not executed and control passes to line 420. If the first record does not contain EOF, then control passes into the loop. Line 400 reads the next record and control passes back to line 210. Line 210 again tests the value of N$ and the process continues.

Instead of READ and DATA statements, the While loop may use INPUT statements so that the user interacts with the program. Consider the following partial program which initializes the variable found in the condition of the WHILE statement to YES to ensure that control passes into the body of the loop.

```
300 LET A$ = "YES"
310 WHILE A$ = "YES"
320    INPUT "PAYMENT"; P
         .
         .
         .
390    PRINT "DO YOU WANT TO PROCESS ANOTHER PAYMENT"
400    INPUT "ENTER 'YES' OR 'NO'"; A$
410 WEND
```

Line 300 assigns A$ the value YES just prior to the WHILE statement in line 310. This ensures that lines 320 through 410 execute at least one time.

In line 400 the user enters YES to process another payment or NO to cause the loop eventually to terminate. (Actually, any value assigned to A£ other than YES causes the WHILE statement in line 310 to transfer control to the statement following WEND in line 410.) The following rules can be formulated about the placement of the WHILE and WEND statements:

> WHILE **Rule 1:** The WHILE statement may be located anywhere before the corresponding WEND statement.

> WEND **Rule 1:** The WEND statement may be located anywhere after the corresponding WHILE statement and before the end line.

Programming Case Study 8A: Weekly Payroll and Summary Report

The following example incorporates both a counter and a running total, as well as some of the concepts discussed earlier in this section. An analysis of the problem, a flowchart, and a BASIC program follow.

Problem

A payroll application requires that the employee number, the hours worked, the rate of pay and the gross pay be displayed for each employee shown below.

Employee Number	Hours Worked	Rate of Pay
124	40	$5.60
126	56	5.90
128	38	4.60
129	48.5	6.10

Also, the total gross pay, the total number of employees, and the average gross pay for this payroll are displayed. The gross pay is determined by multiplying the hours worked by the hourly rate of pay. Overtime (hours in excess of 40) is paid at 1½ times the hourly rate.

Program Tasks

Consider the following analysis for this problem.

1) Display report and column headings.
2) Initialize a counter C and running total T to 0. Use the counter C to determine the total number of employees processed. Use the running total T to determine the total gross pay.
3) Read a record.
4) Test for end-of-file. If end-of-file, compute and display the average gross pay. If not end-of-file, proceed to the next step.
5) Establish a loop and do the following within the loop:
   a) Increment counter C by 1.
   b) Determine the gross pay.
   c) Increment the running total T by the gross pay.
   d) Read the next record.

The solution to the Weekly Payroll Report as represented by the flowchart in Figure 5.7 and the corresponding Program 5.6 includes a few significant points which did not appear in previous programs. They are:

1) The loop (lines 260 through 330) is defined by the WHILE and WEND statements. The condition in line 260 tests for the sentinel value EOF. When E$ is assigned the value EOF by line 320, control passes to the EOF routine begining at line 350.

2) The use of a counter C and a running total T are initialized to zero (lines 220 and 230). Both variables are incremented in the loop. The counter is used to keep track of the total number of employees and is incremented in line 270. The running total is used to sum the gross pay and is incremented by the individual employee gross pay in line 300.

3) A decision is made in line 290 to determine which of two formulas is to be used to compute the gross pay.

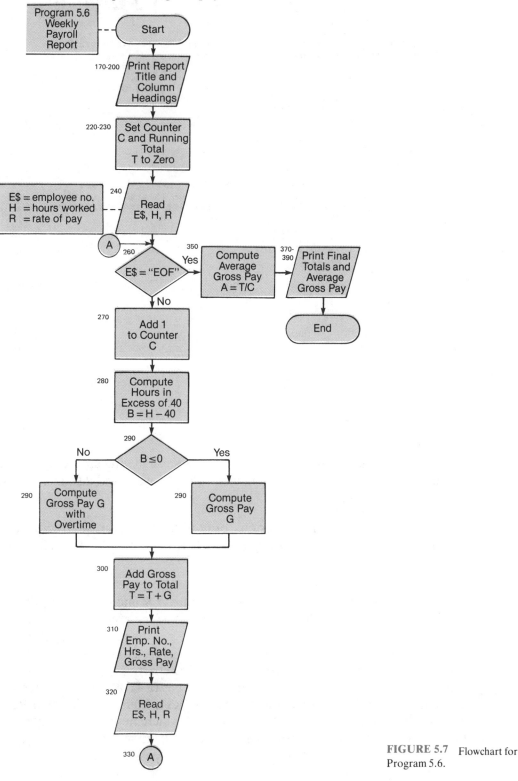

FIGURE 5.7 Flowchart for Program 5.6.

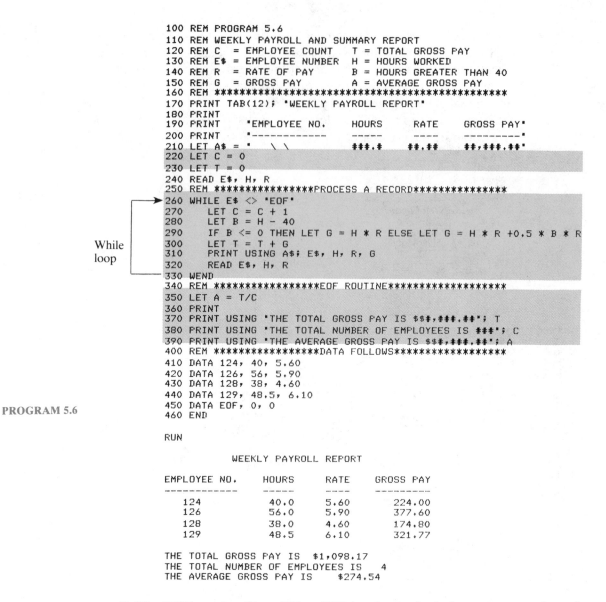

```
100 REM PROGRAM 5.6
110 REM WEEKLY PAYROLL AND SUMMARY REPORT
120 REM C  = EMPLOYEE COUNT    T = TOTAL GROSS PAY
130 REM E$ = EMPLOYEE NUMBER   H = HOURS WORKED
140 REM R  = RATE OF PAY       B = HOURS GREATER THAN 40
150 REM G  = GROSS PAY         A = AVERAGE GROSS PAY
160 REM ***********************************************
170 PRINT TAB(12); "WEEKLY PAYROLL REPORT"
180 PRINT
190 PRINT       "EMPLOYEE NO.    HOURS     RATE     GROSS PAY"
200 PRINT       "-----------    -----    -----    ---------"
210 LET A$ = "   \    \         ###.#    ##.##    ##,###.##"
220 LET C = 0
230 LET T = 0
240 READ E$, H, R
250 REM *****************PROCESS A RECORD***************
260 WHILE E$ <> "EOF"
270    LET C = C + 1
280    LET B = H - 40
290    IF B <= 0 THEN LET G = H * R ELSE LET G = H * R +0.5 * B * R
300    LET T = T + G
310    PRINT USING A$; E$, H, R, G
320    READ E$, H, R
330 WEND
340 REM ******************EOF ROUTINE******************
350 LET A = T/C
360 PRINT
370 PRINT USING "THE TOTAL GROSS PAY IS $$#,###.##"; T
380 PRINT USING "THE TOTAL NUMBER OF EMPLOYEES IS ###"; C
390 PRINT USING "THE AVERAGE GROSS PAY IS $$#,###.##"; A
400 REM ******************DATA FOLLOWS*****************
410 DATA 124, 40, 5.60
420 DATA 126, 56, 5.90
430 DATA 128, 38, 4.60
440 DATA 129, 48.5, 6.10
450 DATA EOF, 0, 0
460 END

RUN

              WEEKLY PAYROLL REPORT

EMPLOYEE NO.    HOURS     RATE     GROSS PAY
-----------    -----    -----    ---------
    124         40.0     5.60        224.00
    126         56.0     5.90        377.60
    128         38.0     4.60        174.80
    129         48.5     6.10        321.77

THE TOTAL GROSS PAY IS  $1,098.17
THE TOTAL NUMBER OF EMPLOYEES IS    4
THE AVERAGE GROSS PAY IS    $274.54
```

While loop

PROGRAM 5.6

4) The EOF routine (lines 350 to 390) involves calculating an average based on the total gross pay and the number of employees and displaying these totals and the average.

**5.6
IMPLEMENTING
THE IF-THEN-ELSE
STRUCTURE**

This section will be a discussion of various forms of the If-Then-Else structure and their implementation in BASIC using the IF-THEN and IF-THEN-ELSE statements.

**Simple Forms of the
If-Then-Else Structure**

Consider the If-Then-Else structure in Figure 5.8 and the corresponding methods of implementing the logic in BASIC. Assume that R$ represents a person's voter registration status. If R$ is equal to "Y," the person is registered to vote. If R$ does not equal "Y," the person is not registered to vote. R1 and R2 are counters that are incremented as specified in the flowchart.

In the first method of solution in Figure 5.8 an IF-THEN-ELSE statement resolves the If-Then-Else structure in one line. If R$ is equal to "Y," then R2 is incremented by 1. If R$ is not equal to "Y," then R1 is incremented by 1. Regardless of the counter incremented, control passes to line 210. Line 210 is said to be the **structure terminator**, since both the true and false tasks pass control to this line.

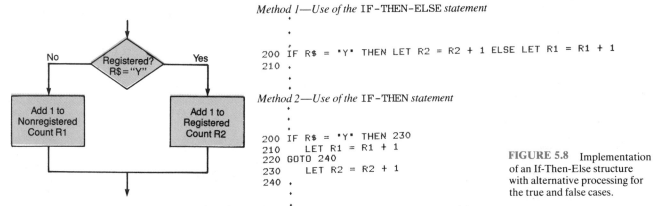

Method 1—Use of the IF-THEN-ELSE *statement*

```
200  IF R$ = "Y" THEN LET R2 = R2 + 1 ELSE LET R1 = R1 + 1
210  .
```

Method 2—Use of the IF-THEN *statement*

```
200  IF R$ = "Y" THEN 230
210      LET R1 = R1 + 1
220  GOTO 240
230      LET R2 = R2 + 1
240  .
```

FIGURE 5.8 Implementation of an If-Then-Else structure with alternative processing for the true and false cases.

In the second method shown in Figure 5.8, an IF-THEN and a GOTO combine to implement the structure. Line 200 compares R$ to "Y." If R$ is equal to "Y," control transfers to line 230 and R2 is incremented by 1. If R$ does not equal "Y," control passes to line 210 and R1 is incremented by 1. Following execution of line 210, the GOTO 240 in line 220 transfers control to the structure terminator.

Although both methods satisfy the If-Then-Else structure, the first method is more straightforward, involves fewer lines of code and does not use the GOTO statement. Therefore, this method is usually recommended. In this second method, the alternative tasks (lines 210 and 230) are indented by 3 positions for readability. We shall use this style of indentation when alternative tasks are listed on separate lines.

As shown in Figures 5.9, 5.10 and 5.11, the If-Then-Else structure can take on a variety of appearances. In Figure 5.9, there is a task only if the condition is true.

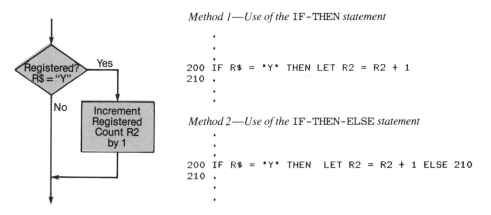

Method 1—Use of the IF-THEN *statement*

```
200  IF R$ = "Y" THEN LET R2 = R2 + 1
210  .
```

Method 2—Use of the IF-THEN-ELSE *statement*

```
200  IF R$ = "Y" THEN  LET R2 = R2 + 1 ELSE 210
210  .
```

FIGURE 5.9 Implementation of an If-Then-Else structure with alternative processing for the true case.

In Figure 5.9, both methods of implementation of the If-Then-Else structure involve one line of code. The first method is preferred over the second, since the IF-THEN automatically passes control to the next higher line number following execution of the statement after the keyword THEN.

The If-Then-Else structure in Figure 5.10 illustrates the incrementation of a counter R1 when the condition is false. Included in Figure 5.10 are three methods that may be used to implement the logic.

In method 1, the relation in the condition found in the partial flowchart has been negated. The condition, R$ = "Y" has been modified to read R$ < > "Y" in the BASIC code. Since we often develop algorithms using positive thought patterns, negating relations in IF statements is a common and necessary practice and should always be considered when there is alternative processing for only one of the two cases.

In method 2, an IF-THEN-ELSE statement is used to implement the structure. If R$ is equal to "Y," then control transfers to line 210. If R$ does not equal

Method 1—Use of the IF-THEN *statement with the relation negated.*

```
200 IF R$ <> "Y" THEN LET R1 = R1 + 1
210 .
```

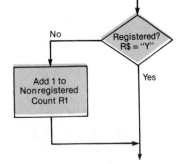

Method 2—Use of the IF-THEN-ELSE *statement.*

```
200 IF R$ = "Y" THEN 210 ELSE LET R1 = R1 + 1
210 .
```

FIGURE 5.10 Implementation of an If-Then-Else structure with alternative processing for the false case.

Method 3—Use of the IF-THEN *statement.*

```
200 IF R$ = "Y" THEN 220
210     LET R1 = R1 + 1
220 .
```

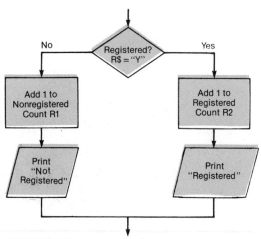

FIGURE 5.11 Implementation of an If-Then-Else structure with multiple statements for both the true and false cases.

Method 1—Use of the IF-THEN-ELSE *statement.*

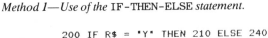

```
            200 IF R$ = "Y" THEN 210 ELSE 240
True      { 210     LET R2 = R2 + 1
task      { 220     PRINT "REGISTERED"
            230 GOTO 260
False     { 240     LET R1 = R1 + 1
task      { 250     PRINT "NOT REGISTERED"
            260 .
```

Method 2—Use of the IF-THEN *statement.*

```
            200 IF R$ = "Y" THEN 240
False     { 210     LET R1 = R1 + 1
task      { 220     PRINT "NOT REGISTERED"
            230 GOTO 260
True      { 240     LET R2 = R2 + 1
Task      { 250     PRINT "REGISTERED"
            260 .
```

"Y," the system executes the statement following the keyword ELSE and then passes control to line 210.

The third method of implementing the If-Then-Else structure in Figure 5.10 is the least preferred, since it involves a branch forward around a statement and an additional line of code. If R$ is equal to "Y," control transfers to line 220. If R$ does not equal "Y," then control passes to line 210 and R1 is incremented by 1 before passing control to the structure terminator, line 220.

The If-Then-Else structure in Figure 5.11 includes alternative tasks for both the true and false cases. Each task is made up of multiple statements.

In method 1 of Figure 5.11, the IF-THEN-ELSE statement is used to implement the structure. If the condition R$ = "Y" is true, control transfers to line 210 and the true task (lines 210 and 220) is executed. The GOTO statement in line 230 transfers control to line 260, thereby branching forward past the false task (lines 240 and 250). If the condition is false, control transfers to line 240 and the false task is executed.

The second method in Figure 5.11 is similar to the first, except that an IF-THEN statement has replaced the IF-THEN-ELSE statement of method 1, and the false task is positioned just below the decision statement. As illustrated in both methods of solution, when alternative tasks include multiple statements, each statement is placed on a separate line and indented three positions. The GOTO that divides the two tasks is not indented. Method 1 is preferred over method 2 in Figure 5.11 primarily because the IF-THEN-ELSE statement allows you to position the true task immediately below the decision statement. This style helps make the program easier to read.

In summary, the following may be stated regarding the implementation of simple If-Then-Else structures in BASIC:

1) Use the IF-THEN-ELSE statement when there are alternative tasks for both cases.
2) Use the IF-THEN statement when there is an alternative task for only one of the two cases.
3) If there are multiple statements in a task, place each statement on a separate line. Indent each statement by three positions. If there are alternative tasks for both cases, divide the two tasks with a GOTO statement that is not indented. The GOTO statement should reference the line designated as the structure terminator.

Nested Forms of the If-Then-Else Structure

A **nested** If-Then-Else structure is one in which the action to be taken for the true or false case includes yet another If-Then-Else structure. The second If-Then-Else structure is considered to be **nested** or **layered** within the first.

Study the partial program that corresponds to the nested If-Then-Else structure in Figure 5.12. If the condition A $> = 18$ is true, control transfers to line 210. If the condition is false, control transfers to line 280. Line 300 serves as the structure terminator. The true task, lines 210 through 260, contains a second IF-THEN-ELSE statement which corresponds to the inner If-Then-Else structure in the flowchart. As with the previous IF-THEN-ELSE statement, the true and false tasks are indented by three positions. Note in Figure 5.12 that only one of the three alternative tasks is executed for each record processed. It is impossible to process a record that increments two or more counters (M, R1 and R2) in the partial program shown. Here, for instance, it is clear that only one counter is incremented for each record.

Record	Age	Registered	Add 1 to Counter
1	18	Y	R2
2	25	N	R1
3	17	N	M

If-Then-Else structures can be nested to any depth, but readability decreases as nesting increases.

Consider the nested structure in Figure 5.13 and the corresponding BASIC statements. Figure 5.13 contains three nests of If-Then-Else structures and six counters. The counters can be described in the following manner:

M1 totals the number of males not eligible to register.

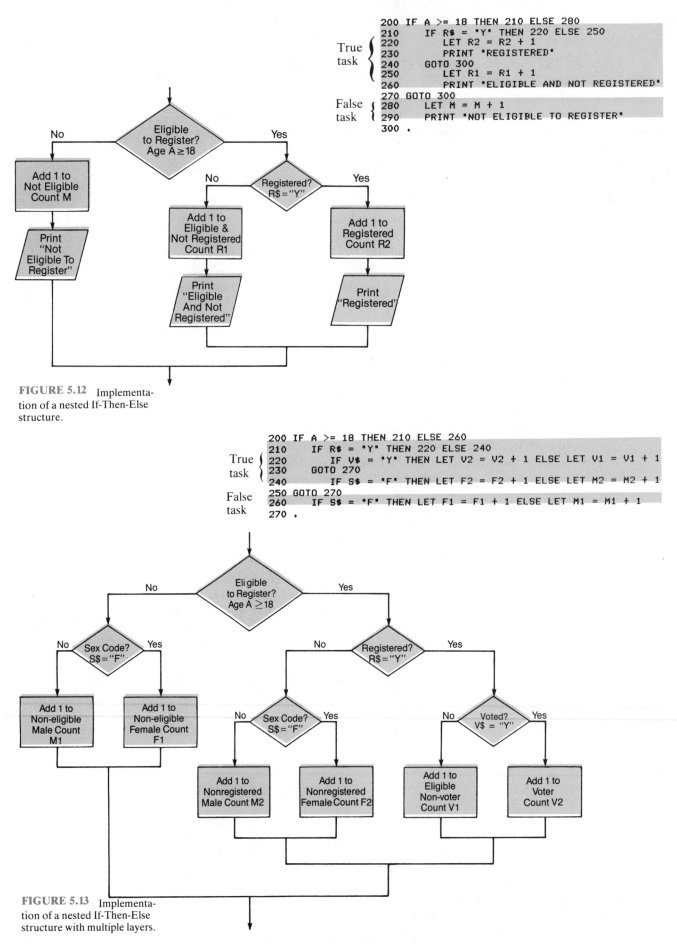

```
200 IF A >= 18 THEN 210 ELSE 280
210     IF R$ = "Y" THEN 220 ELSE 250
220         LET R2 = R2 + 1
230         PRINT "REGISTERED"
240     GOTO 300
250         LET R1 = R1 + 1
260         PRINT "ELIGIBLE AND NOT REGISTERED"
270 GOTO 300
280     LET M = M + 1
290     PRINT "NOT ELIGIBLE TO REGISTER"
300 .
```

True task { 210–260

False task { 280–290

FIGURE 5.12 Implementation of a nested If-Then-Else structure.

```
200 IF A >= 18 THEN 210 ELSE 260
210     IF R$ = "Y" THEN 220 ELSE 240
220         IF V$ = "Y" THEN LET V2 = V2 + 1 ELSE LET V1 = V1 + 1
230     GOTO 270
240         IF S$ = "F" THEN LET F2 = F2 + 1 ELSE LET M2 = M2 + 1
250 GOTO 270
260     IF S$ = "F" THEN LET F1 = F1 + 1 ELSE LET M1 = M1 + 1
270 .
```

True task { 210–240

False task { 260

FIGURE 5.13 Implementation of a nested If-Then-Else structure with multiple layers.

144

F1 totals the number of females not eligible to register.

M2 totals the number of males who are old enough to vote but have not registered.

F2 totals the number of females who are old enough to vote but have not registered.

V1 totals the number of individuals who are eligible to vote but did not vote.

V2 totals the number of individuals who voted.

In the partial BASIC program in Figure 5.13, line 200 corresponds to the decision at the very top of the flowchart. Lines 210 through 240 implement the true case to the right in the flowchart. Line 260 fulfills the false case to the left in the flowchart. Incorporating the logic and concepts found in Figure 5.13 into a complete program is left as an exercise for you at the end of this chapter in Programming Exercise 3.

This problem requires the use of a nested If-Then-Else structure. An analysis of the problem, a flowchart, and a BASIC program follow.

Programming Case Study 9A: Employee Analysis and Summary Report

Problem

Records in an employee file that meet the following criteria are to be displayed:

1) Sex code is male.
2) Age is greater than or equal to 35 years.
3) Service is less than 10 years.

A summary of the total number of employees who meet the criteria and the average salary paid to these selected employees are to be displayed at end-of-job. The employee file is as follows:

Name	Sex	Service	Age	Annual Salary
Babjack Bill	M	3	41	$19,500.00
Knopf Louis	M	19	53	29,200.00
Taylor Jane	F	12	38	26,000.00
Droopey Joe	M	4	36	28,000.00
Lane Lyn	F	9	44	19,800.00
Lis Frank	M	1	44	21,000.00
Bye Ed	M	1	42	15,000.00
Braion Jim	M	19	35	26,500.00

Program Tasks

This problem can be analyzed in the following way:

1) Display appropriate report title and column headings.
2) Use a counter C to determine the total number of employees who meet the criteria.
3) Use T as a running total to sum the selected salaries.
4) Calculate the average salary by using T and C.
5) The name N$, sex code S$, service S, age A and annual salary M are values read from DATA statements.
6) If the record represents an employee who is male (S$ = "M"), who is at least 35 years old (A ≥ 35) and who has fewer than 10 years' service (S < 10), then the counter C is incremented by 1, the running total T is incremented by the salary M, and the record is displayed.

7) Since there is no action to be taken when a record fails to pass the criteria, it is easiest to negate or reverse the relational operators in each of the decision statements.

8) A sentinel value EOF as an employee name determines when the data for all the employees have been processed.

The flowchart in Figure 5.14 and the corresponding Program 5.7 represent a solution to the Employee Analysis and Summary Report. The nested If-Then-Else structure in the flowchart illustrates the advisability of negating the relational operators. The conditions are constructed so the flow bypasses the prescribed

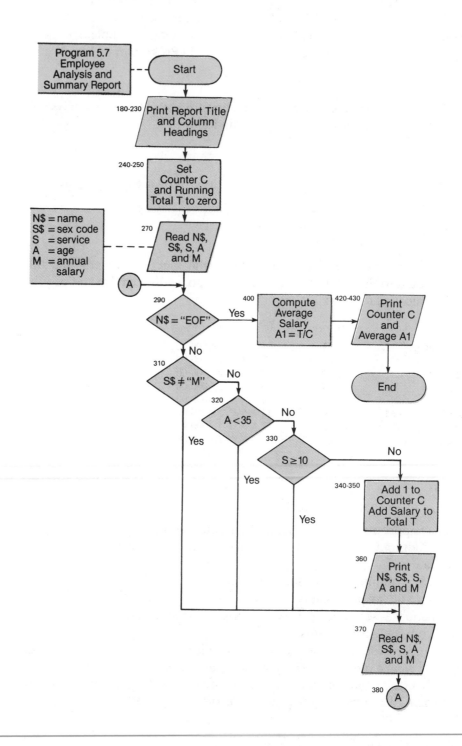

FIGURE 5.14

action when any of the conditions are *true*. Lines 310 through 330 in Program 5.7 show the implementation of that logic. If the conditions in the decision statements are written as specified in the problem, each IF-THEN statement (lines 310 through 330) would have been followed by a GOTO statement.

In Chapter 6, the use of logical operators (AND, OR and NOT) in IF statements will be discussed. The ability to link conditions through logical operators will reduce the nested If-Then-Else structure in Figure 5.14 to a simple one. This in turn would eliminate two of the three nested IF-THEN statements in Program 5.7. Programming Case Study 9B in Chapter 6, (p. 186), uses logical operators to solve this problem.

```
100 REM PROGRAM 5.7
110 REM EMPLOYEE ANALYSIS AND SUMMARY REPORT
120 REM N$ = NAME   S$ = SEX CODE   S = YEARS OF SERVICE
130 REM A  = AGE    M  = ANNUAL SALARY
140 REM C  = TOTAL NUMBER OF EMPLOYEES WHO MEET CRITERIA
150 REM T  = TOTAL ANNUAL SALARY OF EMPLOYEES WHO MEET CRITERIA
160 REM A1 = AVERAGE ANNUAL SALARY OF EMPLOYEES WHO MEET CRITERIA
170 REM *********************************************************
180 PRINT TAB(15); "EMPLOYEE ANALYSIS AND SUMMARY REPORT"
190 PRINT TAB(16); "SEX = MALE, AGE >= 35, SERVICE < 10"
200 PRINT
210 PRINT TAB(57); "ANNUAL"
220 PRINT "NAME", "SEX", "SERVICE", "AGE", "SALARY"
230 PRINT "----", "---", "--------", "---", "------"
240 LET C = 0
250 LET T = 0
260 REM *****READ FIRST RECORD*****
270 READ N$, S$, S, A, M
280 REM *******************PROCESS A RECORD*********************
290 WHILE N$ <> "EOF"
300     REM *****TEST RECORD AGAINST CRITERIA*****
310     IF S$ <> "M" THEN 370
320        IF A < 35 THEN 370
330           IF S >= 10 THEN 370
340              LET C = C + 1
350              LET T = T + M
360              PRINT N$, " "; S$, "  "; S, A, M
370     READ N$, S$, S, A, M
380 WEND
390 REM ********************EOF ROUTINE************************
400 LET A1 = T/C
410 PRINT
420 PRINT "NUMBER OF EMPLOYEES MEETING CRITERIA"; C
430 PRINT "AVERAGE ANNUAL SALARY OF EMPLOYEES MEETING CRITERIA $"; A1
440 REM *******************DATA FOLLOWS************************
450 DATA BABJACK BILL, M,  3, 41, 19500
460 DATA KNOPF LOUIS,  M, 19, 53, 29200
470 DATA TAYLOR JANE,  F, 12, 38, 26000
480 DATA DROOPEY JOE,  M,  4, 36, 28000
490 DATA LANE LYN,     F,  9, 44, 19800
500 DATA LIS FRANK,    M,  1, 44, 21000
510 DATA BYE ED,       M,  1, 42, 15000
520 DATA BRAION JIM,   M, 19, 35, 26500
530 DATA EOF,          " ", 0,  0,  0
540 END
```

PROGRAM 5.7

```
RUN

             EMPLOYEE ANALYSIS AND SUMMARY REPORT
                SEX = MALE, AGE >= 35, SERVICE < 10


                                                   ANNUAL
NAME            SEX         SERVICE       AGE       SALARY
----            ---         --------      ---       ------

BABJACK BILL    M              3          41        19500
DROOPEY JOE     M              4          36        28000
LIS FRANK       M              1          44        21000
BYE ED          M              1          42        15000

NUMBER OF EMPLOYEES MEETING CRITERIA 4
AVERAGE ANNUAL SALARY OF EMPLOYEES MEETING CRITERIA $ 20875
```

A nested IF statement is one in which another IF statement immediately follows the keyword THEN or ELSE. The following statement has multiple ELSEs following multiple IF-THENs:

```
400 IF X > Y THEN IF A = B THEN LET S = S + 1 ELSE LET T = T + 1 ELSE 500
```

If X is greater than Y, the condition A = B is evaluated. If A equals B, S is incremented by 1. If X is greater than Y and A does not equal B, T is incremented by 1. If X is not greater than Y, control transfers to line 500.

The relationship between a specific IF-THEN and the ELSE to which it is paired can be determined from the following rule:

> **Nested IF-THEN-ELSE Rule 1:** Each ELSE is matched with the closest previous unmatched IF-THEN.

In this example, line 400, reading from left to right, the first ELSE belongs to IF A = B THEN. The second ELSE is paired with IF X > Y THEN. It is not necessary that a nested IF statement have as many ELSE as IF-THEN statements. For example, the statement:

```
550 IF X = Y THEN IF A = B THEN IF C = D THEN 700 ELSE LET S = S + 1
```

contains three IF-THENs and one ELSE. The ELSE belongs to IF C = D THEN 700. Therefore, if all three conditions are true, control transfers to line 700. If the first two conditions are true and the third is false, S is incremented by 1 and control passes to the line following 550. If either of the first two conditions is false, control passes to the line following 550.

On the other hand, it is invalid to have more ELSEs than IF-THENs in a single nested IF statement. Thus, the following nested IF statement is invalid:

```
Invalid due
to unbalanced  }  750 IF S > T THEN GOTO 200 ELSE PRINT A ELSE PRINT B
ELSE
```

Nested IF statements tend to increase the complexity of a program significantly. This is especially true if more than two IF statements are located on the same line. Compare, for example, the following implementation of the earlier nested IF statement in line 400:

```
400 IF X > Y THEN 410 ELSE 500
410     IF A = B THEN LET S = S + 1 ELSE LET T = T + 1
```

In our opinion, this partial program is easier to read and understand. The same can be said for the following partial program which is logically equivalent to the earlier nested IF statement in line 550:

```
550 IF X = Y THEN 560 ELSE 580
560     IF A = B THEN 570 ELSE 580
570         IF C = D THEN 700 ELSE LET S = S + 1
```

**Logical versus
Physical Lines**

Some BASIC systems differentiate between a logical line and a physical line. A **logical line** is composed of a line number followed by one or more **physical lines** which have no line numbers. On such systems you may write our example, line 400, as follows:

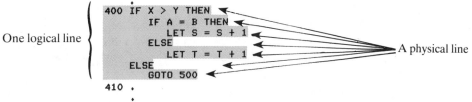

In this partial program, line 400 (a logical line) is made up of 7 physical lines. Note how much easier it is to read than the earlier nested IF statement. This is especially true because each statement has been indented and the keyword ELSE placed on a separate physical line. Line 400 may also be written as follows:

```
         .
         .
         .
400 IF  X > Y
        THEN IF A = B
                 THEN LET S = S + 1
                 ELSE LET T = T + 1
        ELSE GOTO 500
410 .
    .
    .
```

Note how the THENs and ELSEs pair under each respective IF statement.

At the conclusion of all physical lines, except for the last one, a special key (or keys), like a Line Feed key or CTRL and Enter, is pressed to go to the next physical line. The last physical line is terminated by pressing the Enter key. Some BASIC systems limit the number of characters allowed in a logical line. Check the specifications on your BASIC system to see whether it differentiates between a logical line and physical line. If your system does, it is recommended that you make use of it when writing BASIC code for a nested If-Then-Else structure, or when multiple statements must be executed for the true or false task in any type of If-Then-Else structure.

Read

Most businesses today are divided into smaller units for the purpose of better management. A retail company that is doing business on a national scale may have several levels of management, with the levels headed by such people as a district manager, store manager and department manager. To evaluate the performance of the units within each level, managerial reports are generated that show summaries or minor totals for each sub-unit. For example, a sales-by-salesperson report generated for the manager of a store often shows a summary sales total for each department within the store as well a grand sales total for the store. This type of report also permits a rapid appraisal of each salesperson's performance.

5.8 CONTROL BREAKS

Programs that are written to generate levels of subtotals use a technique involving **control fields** and **control breaks**. A control field contains data to be compared from record to record. A control break occurs when the data in the control field changes.

A control break may be used to display a summary line each time a selected data item, common to all records in the file, changes value. The variable assigned the selected data item is called the **control variable**. For this technique to work successfully, it is essential that the records be processed in sequence according to the data item that determines the break. For example, to generate the Sales by

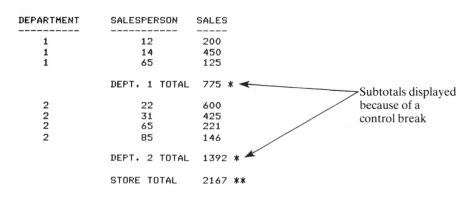

FIGURE 5.15 Sales by department within store report. (A report with a single level control break.)

Department Within Store report shown in Figure 5.15, all the records that belong to department 1 must precede all the department 2 records.

In order to generate the report illustrated in Figure 5.15, the program solution must check each record to see if it is the first record of a new department. If the record represents a salesperson from the old department (that is, if the current salesperson and the previous one belong to the same department), then selected contents of that record are displayed, and the system adds the amount of sales credited to that salesperson to a department sales accumulator.

When a record that belongs to a salesperson from a new department is read, a control break occurs and the current value of the department sales accumulator is displayed. In addition, asterisks are usually printed to the right of the totals to indicate a summary. One asterisk indicates the lowest level, two asterisks the next level, and so on. Before processing the record that caused the control break, the system must add the department sales to the store sales total, which is displayed after all records in the file have been processed. Furthermore, the variable used to sum the department sales must be reset to zero after each control break so that it can be used to sum the sales for the next department. Finally, the control variable must be assigned the value of the next department number before processing of the record is resumed.

Programming Case Study 10: Sales By Department Within Store—Single Level Control Break

The following Programming Case Study pertains to generating the report found in Figure 5.15. An analysis of the problem, a flowchart, and a program follow.

Problem

The sales analysis department has requested that a program be written to generate the Sales by Department Within Store report shown in Figure 5.15. Each record in the file includes a department number, salesperson number, and the sales amount as shown below:

Department	Salesperson	Sales
1	12	$200.00
1	14	450.00
1	65	125.00
2	22	600.00
2	31	425.00
2	65	221.00
2	85	146.00

In column form, the department, salesperson and sales for each record read are to be displayed. Also to be displayed are the sales total for each department prior to processing a new department and the sales total (i.e., *final* sales total) for the store after all records have been processed.

Program Tasks

1) The records defined by DATA statements must be in ascending order by department number D$.
2) Two accumulators are necessary. T1 is used to sum the individual department sales and T2 is used to sum the store sales.
3) Two READ statements are utilized. The first READ statement reads only the first record. The control variable V$ is initialized to the first department number and the department sales accumulator is incremented by the salesperson's sales. The second READ statement is used to read the remaining records.
4) A "EOF" value for the department number indicates an EOF condition.
5) A test for a control break follows the EOF test. The test determines if the record just read belongs to the same department as the previous record or to a new department. If no control break occurs, the department sales accumulator is incremented and the data items in the record are displayed. If a control break occurs, the program must:
   a) Increment the store sales accumulator by the department sales accumulator.
   b) Display the department sales accumulator.
   c) Assign the control variable the value of the new department number.
   d) Initialize the department sales accumulator to zero.
   e) Process the record that caused the control break by incrementing the department sales accumulator and display the data items in the record.
6) In the EOF routine, the store sales accumulator is incremented and displayed accordingly.

The following points should be noted concerning Program 5.8:

1) The READ statement in line 220 is executed only once. Its function is to read the first record followed by the initialization of the control variable V$ to the first department number. The sales relating to the first record is added to the department sales accumulator (line 360) and displayed (line 370) before the second record is read in line 380.
2) The LET statement in line 230 initializes the control variable V$ to the first department number. Thereafter, line 330 resets the control variable to the new department number when a control break occurs.
3) The IF-THEN statement in line 270 determines if there is a control break.
4) If a control break occurs, the store sales accumulator is incremented, the department total is displayed, the control variable is set to the new department number and the department sales accumulator is set to 0 before the record that caused the break is processed.
5) The EOF routine includes a LET statement (line 410) that increments the store total by the last department total.

Multilevel Control Breaks

The single level control break can be extended to multilevel control breaks. There are four classifications of control breaks: minor, intermediate, major, and multiple (for more than three). A report may include one break (minor), as was the case in the previous example, two breaks (minor within major), three breaks (minor within intermediate within major), or multiple breaks.

Figure 5.17 illustrates a Sales Analysis Report generated with three control breaks. The control breaks include department within store within district. Each control break causes a number of summaries to be displayed, dependent on the

```
100 REM PROGRAM 5.8
110 REM SALES BY DEPT. WITHIN STORE SINGLE LEVEL CONTROL BREAK
120 REM T1 = TOTAL DEPT. SALES    T2 = TOTAL STORE SALES
130 REM V$ = CONTROL VARIABLE     D$ = DEPT. NUMBER
140 REM N$ = SALESPERSON NUMBER   S  = SALESPERSON SALES
150 REM ***************************************************
160 PRINT "DEPARTMENT", "SALESPERSON", "SALES"
170 PRINT "-----------", "-------------", "-----"
180 REM *****INITIALIZE DEPT. AND STORE ACCUMULATORS*****
190 LET T1 = 0
200 LET T2 = 0
210 REM ***READ FIRST RECORD AND INITIALIZE CONTROL VARIABLE**
220 READ D$, N$, S
230 LET V$ = D$
240 REM ****************PROCESS A RECORD********************
250 WHILE D$ <> "EOF"
260     REM *****TEST FOR A CONTROL BREAK*****
270     IF D$ = V$ THEN 360
280         REM *****PROCESS A CONTROL BREAK*****
290         LET T2 = T2 + T1
300         PRINT
310         PRINT TAB(16); "DEPT. "; V$; " TOTAL", T1; "*"
320         PRINT
330         LET V$ = D$
340         LET T1 = 0
350     REM ****PROCESS NEXT RECORD*****
360     LET T1 = T1 + S
370     PRINT "      "; D$, "      "; N$, S
380     READ D$, N$, S
390 WEND
400 REM ******************EOF ROUTINE**********************
410 LET T2 = T2 + T1
420 PRINT
430 PRINT TAB(16); "DEPT. "; V$; " TOTAL", T1; "*"
440 PRINT
450 PRINT TAB(16); "STORE TOTAL", T2; "**"
460 REM ********************DATA FOLLOWS*******************
470 DATA 1, 12, 200, 1, 14, 450, 1, 65, 125, 2, 22, 600
480 DATA 2, 31, 425, 2, 65, 221, 2, 85, 146, EOF, 0, 0
490 END
```

PROGRAM 5.8

```
RUN

DEPARTMENT      SALESPERSON    SALES
-----------     -------------  -----
    1               12          200
    1               14          450
    1               65          125

            DEPT. 1 TOTAL   775 *

    2               22          600
    2               31          425
    2               65          221
    2               85          146

            DEPT. 2 TOTAL   1392 *

            STORE TOTAL     2167 **
```

level of the break. A department change (minor) causes one summary to be displayed. A store change (intermediate) causes both the last department total as well as the store total to be displayed. A district change (major) causes the last department total within the last store total as well as the district total to be displayed.

When the sentinel value is read, all summaries relating to the last department, store and district are displayed, along with the grand total sales for the company. The logic employed in a program involving multilevel control breaks is similar to that shown in Program 5.8. It makes little difference if there are two, three, or more levels to consider. The program need only include additional IF-THEN comparisons and accumulators. The comparison should be structured so that the major level is considered first, and so forth then on down to the minor level. The flowchart and coding for Figure 5.17 is left as an exercise at the end of this chapter (see Programming Exercise 13).

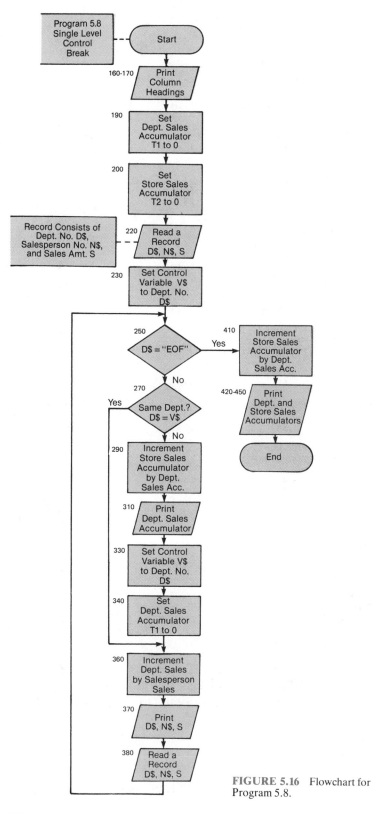

FIGURE 5.16 Flowchart for Program 5.8.

The program flowcharts presented thus far in this chapter are common to so many applications which require the generation of information in the form of reports that there is a standard form for organizing the program. This standard form is a sequence of programming steps:

1) Initialize
2) Input first record
3) Test for end-of-file

5.9
A STANDARD
FORM OF
PROGRAM
ORGANIZATION

```
                              SALES ANALYSIS REPORT
                              ---------------------

                                                           AMOUNT
                 DISTRICT    STORE     DEPARTMENT     ITEM  OF SALE
                 --------    -----     ----------     ----  -------
                 1           1         12             2039     4.00
                 1           1         12             3849   500.00
                 1           1         12             7641     3.98

                             TOTAL SALES FOR DEPT. 12          507.98 *

                 1           1         17             3453     9.96
                 1           1         17             1302    15.00

                             TOTAL SALES FOR DEPT. 17           24.96 *
                             TOTAL SALES FOR STORE 1           532.94 **

                 1           2         23             5543     5.00
                 1           2         23             1130    30.00

                             TOTAL SALES FOR DEPT. 23           35.00 *

                 1           2         24             2765     4.00

                             TOTAL SALES FOR DEPT. 24            4.00 *
                             TOTAL SALES FOR STORE 2            39.00 **
                             TOTAL SALES FOR DISTRICT 1        571.94 ***

                 3           1         17             2223    25.00
                 3           1         17             3435    13.00

                             TOTAL SALES FOR DEPT. 17           38.00 *

                 3           1         34             2039    14.00

                             TOTAL SALES FOR DEPT. 34           14.00 *
                             TOTAL SALES FOR STORE 1            52.00 **

                 3           5         40             5543    12.00
                 3           5         40             9562    16.00

                             TOTAL SALES FOR DEPT. 40           28.00 *
                             TOTAL SALES FOR STORE 5            28.00 **
                             TOTAL SALES FOR DISTRICT 3         80.00 ***
                             TOTAL SALES FOR COMPANY           651.94 ****
```

FIGURE 5.17   A report with three levels of control breaks.

4) Process
5) Output
6) Input next record
7) Finalize

More specifically, the pattern can be thought of as follows:

1) Initialize
   a) Display report titles and column headings.
   b) Set accumulators (counters and running totals) to a predetermined value.
2) Input first record
3) Test for an end-of-file condition
   a) Test for the sentinel value.
   b) If the sentinel value is detected, proceed to the Finalization step (7); otherwise, continue to the next step (4).
4) Process
   a) Complete all computations.
   b) Increment all counters and running totals.
5) Output
   a) Display any intermediate detailed results.
6) Input next record
   a) Read next record.
   b) Return to step 3 to test for end-of-file.

7) Finalize
a) If necessary, compute summaries and round or truncate numeric values accordingly.
b) Display final totals.
c) Terminate processing.

Stop

Recall in Section 4.2 the GOTO statement was defined as an **unconditional** GOTO statement because each time such a statement is executed, control is always transferred to the line number following the keyword GOTO, regardless of any conditions existing in the program.

On the other hand, the ON-GOTO statement is called a **conditional** GOTO statement. Depending on the current value of the numeric expression associated with this statement, control will be transferred to one of two or more different lines.

The ON-GOTO statement can be used to implement an extension of the If-Then-Else structure in which execution of one of many alternatives is to be selected based on an integer test. This extended version of the If-Then-Else structure is called the Case structure; it is illustrated in Figure 5.18 and described in Appendix A, Section 3.

5.10 THE ON-GOTO STATEMENT

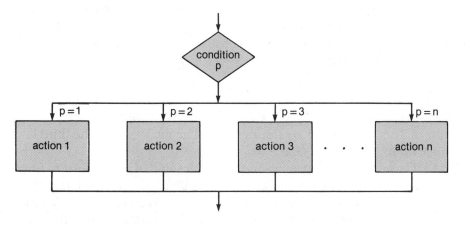

FIGURE 5.18   The Case structure.

The condition in the ON-GOTO statement may be a numeric variable or a numeric expression. The condition is placed between the keywords ON and GOTO. Depending on the value of the condition, control transfers to one of several line numbers appearing in a list following the keyword GOTO. Commas are mandatory punctuation in the list of line numbers in the ON-GOTO statement. It is also mandatory that the variables for the expression be defined in the program before the ON-GOTO is executed. The general form of the ON-GOTO statement is given in Table 5.9.

When the ON-GOTO statement is executed, control transfers to one of the line numbers in the list following the keyword GOTO. The system reads the line numbers in the ON-GOTO statement from left to right, beginning with the first one in the list. If the value of the condition is 1, then control is transferred to the first line number in the list; if 2, then the second, and so on. Consider the following example:

```
200 ON X GOTO 300, 300, 300, 400, 400, 500, 300, 600
```

Condition   List of line numbers to which control is transferred depending on the value of the condition.

TABLE 5.9 **The** ON-GOTO **Statement**

General Form:	ON numeric expression GOTO k_1 , k_2 , . . . , k_n
Purpose:	Causes control to be transferred to a selected line number k_i , where i is the current value of the numeric expression.
Examples:	300 ON Y GOTO 400, 100, 600 500 ON K/10 + 1 GOTO 600, 1200, 3300, 100 750 ON A + B*C/D GOTO 850, 650, 1400, 5000, 650
Note:	A number of GOTO statements are required to implement the ON-GOTO statement. In Chapter 6, these GOTO statements will be eliminated by the ON-GOSUB statement.

If the value of X is 1 at the instant of the execution of line 200, control will be transferred to line number 300 and the statement with this indicated line number will be the next statement executed after the ON-GOTO statement. The same thing will take place whenever X has the integer value of 2, 3 or 7. When X has the integer value of 4 or 5, control will pass to line number 400. When X has the value of 6, control will pass to line number 500. Finally, when X has the value of 8, control will be transferred to line number 600. The number of line numbers that can follow the keyword GOTO is limited only by the length of the line.

On most BASIC systems, the numeric expression in an ON-GOTO statement is evaluated and any decimal portion is rounded to obtain an integer whose value is then used to select a line number from the list following the keyword GOTO.* Consider the following example:

```
300 ON A * B - C/D + E GOTO 400, 600, 800
```

If the value of the expression A * B − C/D + E is 2.64, it will be rounded to an integer value of 3 and control will be transferred to line number 800, the third line number in the list following the GOTO.

In a BASIC program, you must never permit the value of an expression in an ON-GOTO statement to be negative or zero, or to attain a value that is larger than the total number of line numbers in the list of the ON-GOTO statement. A value that is too large, zero or negative cannot be used to select a line number from the list. An IF-THEN statement may be used to prevent an error condition like this from happening by validating the value of the expression just before the ON-GOTO statement is executed. Thus, the following portion of a program can be used to test for all of the non-permissible values of X:

```
200 INPUT "ENTER A ONE DIGIT JOB CODE BETWEEN 1 AND 8"; X
210 IF X < 1 THEN 230
220 IF X <= 8 THEN 250
230    PRINT "JOB CODE "; X; "IS INVALID"
240    GOTO 200
250 ON X GOTO 260, 300, 350, 400, 450, 500, 550, 600
     .
     .
     .
```

In this program, each such non-permissible value of X will cause a diagnostic message to be displayed before control is transferred back to line 200, which requests a valid value for X.

The restrictions on the value of the expression in an ON-GOTO may be summarized as:

---

*Some BASIC systems truncate rather than round the value of the expression.

ON-GOTO **Rule 1:** At the instant of execution of the ON-GOTO statement, the integer obtained as the value of the expression must never be
negative, zero, or greater than the total number of line numbers in the
list of the statement.

In addition, the ON-GOTO statement, like the GOTO and IF statements, must refer
to an existing line number in the program; otherwise an error condition will exist.

The more common errors that must be avoided in using the ON-GOTO statement are:

1) Neglecting to insert the mandatory commas between the line numbers in
the list, as in 600 ON Y GOTO 20406080

2) Neglecting to assign all of the line numbers in the list to executable
statements or to existing line numbers

3) Neglecting to define the values of the variables for the numeric expression
before the execution of the ON-GOTO statement

4) Neglecting to ensure that the integer value of the numeric expression is not
negative, zero, and does not exceed the total number of line numbers in the
list

The reasons for using an ON-GOTO statement are not complex. An ON-GOTO
statement is used when the design of a program includes a Case structure, as
illustrated in Figure 5.18 and the condition in the decision symbol can be equated
to an integer test. Consider the following Case structure in Figure 5.19, and the two
alternative methods of implementing the structure in BASIC.

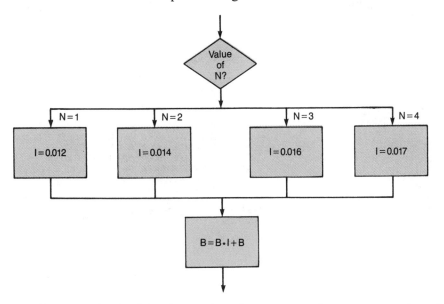

FIGURE 5.19 Use of the
Case structure to determine
the value of 1.

One method of implementing the structure is to use a series of IF-THEN
statements, as shown below.

```
200 IF N = 1 THEN 240
210 IF N = 2 THEN 260
220 IF N = 3 THEN 280
230 IF N = 4 THEN 300
240     LET I = 0.012
250 GOTO 310
260     LET I = 0.014
270 GOTO 310
280     LET I = 0.016
290 GOTO 310
300     LET I = 0.017
310 LET B = B * I + B
```

The four IF-THEN statements can be replaced by a single ON-GOTO statement, as shown below.*

```
230 ON N GOTO 240, 260, 280, 300
240    LET I = 0.012
250 GOTO 310
260    LET I = 0.014
270 GOTO 310
280    LET I = 0.016
290 GOTO 310
300    LET I = 0.017
310 LET B = B * I + B
```

The ON-GOTO statement will transfer control to line numbers 240, 260, 280 or 300, depending on whether N has the value of 1, 2, 3 or 4.

Programming Case Study 11: A Menu-Driven Program

Programs are often characterized as being batch or interactive in mode. A **batch program** is one that generates information based on data that has been collected over a period of time. The data is placed in DATA statements or into a file and made available to the program via READ statements.†The majority of programs presented in Chapter 4 and thus far in Chapter 5 can be classified as batch programs. An **interactive program** is one that generates information based on data as it occurs; the data is usually entered into the program by the operator via INPUT statements in response to questions. Most of the programs presented in Chapters 2 and 3 were of the interactive type.

```
    MENU FOR COMPUTING AREAS
    ---------------------------

    CODE      FUNCTION
    ----      --------
     1   -    COMPUTE AREA OF A SQUARE
     2   -    COMPUTE AREA OF A RECTANGLE
     3   -    COMPUTE AREA OF A PARALLELOGRAM
     4   -    COMPUTE AREA OF A CIRCLE
     5   -    COMPUTE AREA OF A TRAPEZOID
     6   -    COMPUTE AREA OF A TRIANGLE
     7   -    END PROGRAM

    ENTER A CODE 1 THROUGH 7?
```

FIGURE 5.20   A menu of program functions.

It is not at all uncommon for interactive programs to have multiple functions. A **menu**, a list of the functions that a program can perform, is often used to guide an operator through a multi-function interactive program. When a menu-driven program is first executed, it displays a menu of functions like the one illustrated in Figure 5.20. The operator can then choose the desired function from the list by entering a corresponding code. Once the request is satisfied, the program again displays the menu. As illustrated in Figure 5.20, one of the codes (in this case 7) terminates execution of the program.

---

* Note the number of GOTO statements in both illustrations. As you can see, a number of GOTO statements are required to implement both these IF-THEN and ON-GOTO statements. In Chapter 6, these GOTO statements will be eliminated by the ON-GOSUB statement.

† The use of files is discussed in Chapter 8.

The following problem uses the menu illustrated in Figure 5.20. An analysis of the problem, a flowchart and a program follow.

Problem

A menu-driven program is to compute the area of a square, rectangle, parallelogram, circle, trapezoid and triangle. The program should display the menu shown in Figure 5.20. Once a code is entered, the program must validate it to ensure that the code corresponds to one of the menu functions. After the selection of the proper function, the program should prompt the operator for the necessary data, compute the area, and display it accordingly. The displayed results are to remain on the screen until the Enter key on the keyboard is pressed. After that, the program should display the menu again.

Use the following formulas for the areas:

1) Area of a square:
$$A = S * S$$
where S is the length of a side of the square.

2) Area of a rectangle:
$$A = L * W$$
where L is the length and W is the width of the rectangle.

3) Area of a parallelogram:
$$A = B * H$$
where B is the length of the base and H is the height of the parallelogram.

4) Area of a circle:
$$A = 3.14159 * R * R$$
where R is the radius of the circle.

5) Area of a trapezoid:
$$A = \frac{H(B1 + B2)}{2}$$
where H is the height, B1 is the length of the primary base, and B2 is the length of the secondary base of the trapezoid.

6) Area of a triangle:
$$B = \frac{B * H}{2}$$
where B is the base and H is the height of the triangle.

Program Tasks

1) Clear the screen and display the menu shown in Figure 5.20.
2) Request the operator to enter a code.
3) Validate the code. If the code is invalid, display an appropriate diagnostic message and again request the operator to select a function.
4) When a valid code is entered, clear the screen and use an ON–GOTO statement to transfer control to that portion of the program that carries out the requested function.
5) Request the data using one or more INPUT statements.
6) Compute the area and display the results.
7) Use the following prompt message to re-display the menu:
   PRESS ENTER KEY TO RETURN TO THE MENU
8) Repeat steps 1 through 7 as necessary.
9) Enter a code of 7 to terminate the program.

The flowchart in Figure 5.21 illustrates the six independent functions of Program 5.9. Each function includes its own input, processing and output statements.

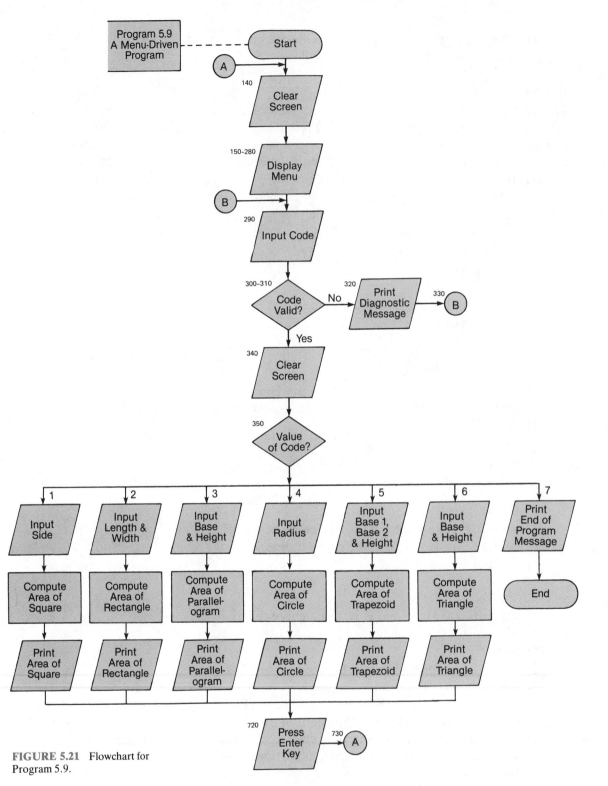

FIGURE 5.21 Flowchart for Program 5.9.

When Program 5.9 is first executed, line 140 clears the screen, and lines 150 through 290 display the menu as illustrated in Figure 5.20. Assume function 3 is selected, as shown in the lower right corner of Figure 5.22.

When the Enter key is pressed, lines 300 and 310 validate the code and transfer control to line 340.

Line 340 clears the screen of the menu, and line 350, the ON-GOTO statement, transfers control to line 480. Figure 5.23, for example, shows a base of 10 units and

```
100 REM PROGRAM 5.9
110 REM A MENU-DRIVEN PROGRAM
120 REM C = FUNCTION CODE        A = AREA
130 REM **********************************************
140 CLS
150 PRINT
160 PRINT "        MENU FOR COMPUTING AREAS"
170 PRINT "        --------------------------"
180 PRINT
190 PRINT "   CODE     FUNCTION"
200 PRINT "   ----     --------"
210 PRINT "    1   -   COMPUTE AREA OF A SQUARE"
220 PRINT "    2   -   COMPUTE AREA OF A RECTANGLE"
230 PRINT "    3   -   COMPUTE AREA OF A PARALLELOGRAM"
240 PRINT "    4   -   COMPUTE AREA OF A CIRCLE"
250 PRINT "    5   -   COMPUTE AREA OF A TRAPEZOID"
260 PRINT "    6   -   COMPUTE AREA OF A TRIANGLE"
270 PRINT "    7   -   END PROGRAM"
280 PRINT
290 INPUT "   ENTER A CODE 1 THROUGH 7"; C
300 IF C < 1 THEN 320
310 IF C <= 7 THEN 340
320    PRINT "   CODE OUT OF RANGE, PLEASE"
330    GOTO 290
340 CLS
350 ON C GOTO 370, 420, 480, 540, 590, 660, 750
360 REM ***********COMPUTE AREA OF A SQUARE***************
370 INPUT "LENGTH OF SIDE OF SQUARE"; S
380 LET A = S * S
390 PRINT "AREA OF SQUARE IS"; A; "SQUARE UNITS"
400 GOTO 710
410 REM **********COMPUTE AREA OF A RECTANGLE*************
420 INPUT "LENGTH OF RECTANGLE"; L
430 INPUT "WIDTH OF RECTANGLE"; W
440 LET A = L * W
450 PRINT "AREA OF RECTANGLE IS"; A; "SQUARE UNITS"
460 GOTO 710
470 REM **********COMPUTE AREA OF A PARALLELOGRAM*********
480 INPUT "BASE OF PARALLELOGRAM"; B
490 INPUT "HEIGHT OF PARALLELOGRAM"; H
500 LET A = B * H
510 PRINT "AREA OF PARALLELOGRAM IS"; A; "SQUARE UNITS"
520 GOTO 710
530 REM ************COMPUTE AREA OF A CIRCLE**************
540 INPUT "RADIUS OF CIRCLE"; R
550 LET A = 3.14159 * R * R
560 PRINT "AREA OF CIRCLE IS"; A; "SQUARE UNITS"
570 GOTO 710
580 REM **********COMPUTE AREA OF A TRAPEZOID*************
590 INPUT "PRIMARY BASE OF TRAPEZOID"; B1
600 INPUT "SECONDARY BASE OF TRAPEZOID"; B2
610 INPUT "HEIGHT OF TRAPEZOID"; H
620 LET A = H * (B1 + B2)/2
630 PRINT "AREA OF TRAPEZOID IS"; A; "SQUARE UNITS"
640 GOTO 710
650 REM **********COMPUTE AREA OF A TRIANGLE*************
660 INPUT "BASE OF TRIANGLE"; B
670 INPUT "HEIGHT OF TRIANGLE"; H
680 LET A = B * H/2
690 PRINT "AREA OF TRIANGLE IS"; A; "SQUARE UNITS"
700 REM ******************RETURN TO MENU****************
710 PRINT
720 INPUT "PRESS ENTER KEY TO RETURN TO THE MENU"; A$
730 GOTO 140
740 REM ******************EOF ROUTINE******************
750 PRINT
760 PRINT "END OF PROGRAM"
770 END
```

PROGRAM 5.9

a height of 4 units to have been entered, which results in an area of 40 square units for the parallelogram. After line 520 transfers control to line 710, the last line is displayed in Figure 5.23. Once the Enter key is pressed, control returns to line 140, the screen is cleared, and the menu is again displayed.

Figure 5.24 shows an out-of-range code generating a diagnostic message. The diagnostic message is displayed by line 320. Line 330 transfers control back to line 290 so that another code may be entered. After a valid code is entered (see the

```
          MENU FOR COMPUTING AREAS
          --------------------------

     CODE      FUNCTION
     ----      --------
       1   -   COMPUTE AREA OF A SQUARE
       2   -   COMPUTE AREA OF A RECTANGLE
       3   -   COMPUTE AREA OF A PARALLELOGRAM
       4   -   COMPUTE AREA OF A CIRCLE
       5   -   COMPUTE AREA OF A TRAPEZOID
       6   -   COMPUTE AREA OF A TRIANGLE
       7   -   END PROGRAM

     ENTER A CODE 1 THROUGH 7? 3
```

FIGURE 5.22 The menu displayed by Program 5.9, lines 150 through 290.

```
     BASE OF PARALLELOGRAM? 10
     HEIGHT OF PARALLELOGRAM? 4
     AREA OF PARALLELOGRAM IS 40 SQUARE UNITS

     PRESS ENTER KEY TO RETURN TO THE MENU?
```

FIGURE 5.23 The display from the selection of code 3 (compute area of a parallelogram).

```
          MENU FOR COMPUTING AREAS
          --------------------------

     CODE      FUNCTION
     ----      --------
       1   -   COMPUTE AREA OF A SQUARE
       2   -   COMPUTE AREA OF A RECTANGLE
       3   -   COMPUTE AREA OF A PARALLELOGRAM
       4   -   COMPUTE AREA OF A CIRCLE
       5   -   COMPUTE AREA OF A TRAPEZOID
       6   -   COMPUTE AREA OF A TRIANGLE
       7   -   END PROGRAM

     ENTER A CODE 1 THROUGH 7? 9
     CODE OUT OF RANGE, PLEASE
     ENTER A CODE 1 THROUGH 7? 5
```

FIGURE 5.24 Diagnostic message displayed by line 320 due to the invalid code 9.

```
     PRIMARY BASE OF TRAPEZOID? 18
     SECONDARY BASE OF TRAPEZOID? 9
     HEIGHT OF TRAPEZOID? 5
     AREA OF TRAPEZOID IS 67.5 SQUARE UNITS

     PRESS ENTER KEY TO RETURN TO THE MENU?
```

FIGURE 5.25 The display from the selection of code 5 (compute area of a trapezoid).

last line of Figure 5.24), the screen is again cleared and the ON-GOTO statement in line 350 transfers control to that portion of the program (lines 590 through 640) that computes the area of a trapezoid.

Figure 5.25 shows that for a trapezoid with primary base 18, secondary base 9, and height 5, the area is 67.5 square units.

To terminate execution of Program 5.9, a code of 7 is entered. The ON-GOTO statement in line 350 transfers control to line 750 and the end of program message is displayed.

The preceding problem could have been solved by replacing the ON-GOTO statement with a series of consecutive IF statements. Usually, however, when a series of three or more tests is to be performed in succession, the ON-GOTO statement is the better alternative.

The flowchart in Figure 5.21 illustrates the logic used in Program 5.9. Many menu-driven programs call for similar logic. That is, the same general pattern can be found in most menu-driven programs. These steps will handle most problems requiring a menu-driven program:

1) Clear the screen.
2) Disply a menu.
3) In a friendly manner, prompt the operator to enter a response code.
4) Validate the response.
5) If the response is valid, transfer control to the appropriate function or to another menu.
6) If the response is invalid, in a clear and courteous manner notify the operator of the incorrect response and request the operator to enter a new response code.
7) Perform the function chosen.
   a) If the function is another menu, repeat steps 1 through 6.
   b) If the function is interactive, input the data and execute the function accordingly. When the function is completed, prompt the operator to enter a response to the code for:
      i) The main menu
      ii) Another menu
   c) If the function is batch, follow the general logic pattern in Section 5.9. Steps 8 and 9 below may not apply in this case.
8) Repeat steps 1 through 7 as necessary.
9) Enter a response to terminate the program.

5.11 A STANDARD FORM OF PROGRAM ORGANIZATION FOR A MENU-DRIVEN PROGRAM

5.12 WHAT YOU SHOULD KNOW

1. The If-Then-Else structure is used in program design to specify a selection between two alternative paths.
2. Most computer scientists agree that the decision statement to terminate a loop should be located at the top or bottom of the loop.
3. A loop that has the termination decision statement at the top is called a Do-While structure.
4. A loop that has the termination decision statement at the bottom is called a Do-Until structure.
5. IF statements have two primary functions in BASIC: they perform selection and facilitate looping.
6. A condition is a relationship that is either true or false. Conditions may be used in the IF-THEN, IF-THEN-ELSE and WHILE statements.
7. In an IF-THEN statement, if the condition is true and a line number follows the keyword THEN, control transfers to the line number following THEN. If the condition is true and a non-transfer statement follows the keyword THEN, the system executes the statement and control passes to the line following the IF-THEN. If the condition is false, execution continues to the next line following the IF-THEN statement.
8. In an IF-THEN-ELSE statement, if the condition is true and a line number follows the keyword THEN, control transfers to the line number following THEN. If the condition is true and a non-transfer statement follows THEN, the statement is executed and control passes to the line following the IF-THEN-ELSE. If the condition is false and a line number follows ELSE, then control transfers to that line number. If the condition is false and a non-transfer statement follows ELSE, the statement is executed and control passes to the line following the IF-THEN-ELSE.
9. A counter is an accumulator used to count the number of times some action is performed.

10. A running total is an accumulator used to sum the different values that a variable is assigned during the execution of a program.

11. All accumulators should be initialized to some value before they are used in a statement that tests the accumulator or adds to its value.

12. A loop defined by the WHILE and WEND statements is a While loop.

13. The statement WEND identifies the end of a while loop.

14. Depending on the problem to be solved, an If-Then-Else structure can have alternative processing for both the true case and false case, alternative processing only for the true case or alternative processing only for the false case.

15. Negating the relation in the condition of an If-Then-Else structure can sometimes eliminate an unwanted GOTO statement and shorten the coding accordingly.

16. A nested If-Then-Else structure is one in which the action to be taken for the true or false case includes yet another If-Then-Else structure.

17. Programs written to generate levels of subtotals use control fields and control breaks. A control field contains data to be compared from record to record. A control break occurs when the data in the control field changes.

18. The Case structure is used in program design to specify a selection between many alternatives.

19. The ON-GOTO can be used to implement a case structure, provided the decision is based on an integer test.

20. The condition in the ON-GOTO statement may be a numeric variable or numeric expression. Depending on the value of the condition, control transfers to one of several line numbers following the keyword GOTO.

21. In a BASIC program, you must never permit the value of an expression in an ON-GOTO statement to be negative or zero, or to attain a value that is larger than the total number of line numbers in the list of the ON-GOTO statement.

22. A batch program is one that generates information based on data that has been collected over a period of time.

23. An interactive program is one that generates information based on data as it occurs; the data is usually entered into the program by the operator via INPUT statements in response to questions.

24. A menu is a list of the functions which a program can perform. When a menu-driven program is first executed, it displays a menu of functions. Each time a requested function is satisfied the program redisplays the menu.

5.13 SELF-TEST EXERCISES

1. Consider the valid programs listed below. What is displayed if each is executed?

a)
```
100 REM CHAPTER 5 SELF-TEST 1A
110 REM N$ = EMPLOYEE NUMBER
120 REM G  = GROSS PAY    F = FEDERAL TAX
125 REM ********************************
130 LET C = 0
140 LET P = 0
150 LET T = 0
160 READ N$, G, F
170 WHILE N$ <> 'EOF'
180    LET C = C + 1
190    LET P = P + G
200    LET T = T + F
210    READ N$, G, F
220 WEND
230 PRINT 'NUMBER OF EMPLOYEES'; C
240 PRINT 'TOTAL GROSS PAY'; P
250 PRINT 'TOTAL FEDERAL TAX'; T
260 REM *****DATA FOLLOWS*****
270 DATA 132, 582.58, 156.24
280 DATA 135, 625.25, 175.52
290 DATA 142, 857.65, 256.25
300 DATA 145, 225.56, 58.75
310 DATA 151, 138.43, 22.55
320 DATA EOF, 0, 0
330 END
```

b)
```
100 REM CHAPTER 5 SELF-TEST 1B
110 REM A = AGE    W = WEIGHT
115 REM ***********************
120 LET C = 0
130 LET D = 0
140 READ A, W
150 IF A < 0 THEN 220
160    LET C = C + 1
170    IF A < 21 THEN 200
180       IF W < 120 THEN 200
190          LET D = D + 1
200    READ A, W
210 GOTO 150
220 PRINT "THE NUMBER OF PEOPLE EVALUATED IS"; C
230 PRINT "THE NUMBER OF ADULTS ";
240 PRINT "WEIGHING 120 POUNDS OR MORE IS"; D
250 REM *****DATA FOLLOWS******
260 DATA 10, 125, 24, 130, 21, 150, 30, 120
270 DATA 51, 225, 47, 175, 18, 130, -1, 0
280 END
```

c)
```
100 REM CHAPTER 5 SELF-TEST 1C
110 REM N$ = EMPLOYEE NUMBER    S$ = SEX CODE
120 REM A  = AGE                H  = HIRE YEAR
125 REM **********************************
130 READ N$, S$, A, H
140 WHILE N$ <> "EOF"
150    IF S$ <> "F" THEN 190
160       IF A < 40 THEN 190
170          IF H < 75 THEN 190
180             PRINT N$, S$, A, H
190    READ N$, S$, A, H
200 WEND
210 PRINT
220 PRINT "END OF REPORT"
230 REM *****DATA FOLLOWS******
240 DATA 196, M, 56, 76
250 DATA 204, F, 62, 80
260 DATA 310, M, 30, 78
270 DATA 516, F, 40, 65
280 DATA 612, F, 38, 78
290 DATA 613, F, 43, 77
300 DATA EOF, " ", 0, 0
310 END
```

d)
```
100 REM CHAPTER 5 SELF-TEST 1D
110 LET X = 0
120 LET Y = 0
130 WHILE X < 7
140    LET X = X + 1
150    LET Y = Y + X
160 WEND
170 PRINT "THE SUM IS"; Y
180 END
```

e) Assume that the following data items are entered in sequence, as requested: 1, 40, 3, 25, 2, 15, −1, 0.
```
100 REM CHAPTER 5 SELF-TEST 1E
110 INPUT "JOB CODE AND HOURS, SEPARATED BY A COMMA"; J, H
120 WHILE J <> -1
130    ON J GOTO 140, 160, 180
140       LET G = 4.75 * H
150    GOTO 190
160       LET G = 5.70 * H
170    GOTO 190
180       LET G = 6.50 * H
190    PRINT "GROSS PAY ="; G
200    INPUT "JOB CODE AND HOURS, SEPARATED BY A COMMA"; J, H
210 WEND
220 END
```

2. Find the logic error(s) in the following programs:

a)
```
100 REM CHAPTER 5 SELF-TEST 2A
110 LET S = 0
120 READ A
130 IF A = -999999 THEN 170
140    LET S = S + A
150    READ A
160 GOTO 120
170 PRINT "THE TOTAL IS"; S
180 DATA 6, 12, 2, 4, 9, 8, -999999
190 END
```

b)
```
100 REM CHAPTER 5 SELF-TEST 2B
110 REM N = NEGATIVE COUNT    P = POSITIVE COUNT
120 REM Z = ZERO COUNT
125 REM ******************************************
130 LET N = 0
140 LET P = 0
150 LET Z = 0
160 READ X
170 WHILE X <> -999999
180    IF X > 0 THEN 220
190       IF X < 0 THEN 210
200          LET Z = Z + 1
210       LET N = N + 1
220    LET P = P + 1
230    READ X
240 WEND
250 PRINT Z, P, N
260 DATA 4, 6, 0, -2, -4, 3, 0
270 DATA -8, -9, -6, 2, 0, -999999
280 END
```

3. Find the syntax error(s) in the following program:
```
100 REM CHAPTER 5 SELF-TEST 3
110 LET C = 0
120 LET A = 170
130 READ X, Y
140 WHILE X >= 0
150    IF X > Y THEN A
160       LET C = C + 1
170    READ X, Y
180 GOTO 140
190 PRINT C
200 DATA 4, 6, 9, 2, 3, 6, -3, 0
210 END
```

4. For each of the following, construct an equivalent partial program without using GOTO statements.

a)
```
100 IF A > B THEN 120
110 GOTO 130
120 LET A = A + 1
130 READ X, Y
```

b)
```
100 IF X <> Y THEN 120
110 GOTO 150
120 IF Y >= Z THEN 140
130 GOTO 150
140 IF C = S THEN 250
150 LET A = A + 1
```

5. Which of the following are invalid? Why?

a) `100 IF X EQUALS Y THEN 300`

b) `110 IF A$ = 15 THEN 300`

c) `120 IF 15 = B THEN PRINT A, S`

d) `130 IF (X + Y)/Z <> C + D THAN 300`

e) `140 IF <X THEN READ S, F`

f) `150 IF A^3 >= B * C THEN X`

g) `160 WHEREAS A > B THEN 300`

h) `170 IF S = "EOF" THEN LET A = 2 * A`

i) `180 IF A > B > C > D THEN 300`

j) `190 IF LEFT$(T$, 3) = "219" THEN 300`

6. Determine the value of X that will cause the condition in the IF-THEN statements below to be true.

a) `100 IF X > 9 THEN LET D = D/4`

b) `110 IF X/8 + 2 < 4 THEN LET X = X + 5`

c) `120 IF -X <> 5 THEN 300`

7. Construct a partial program for the following logic structure:

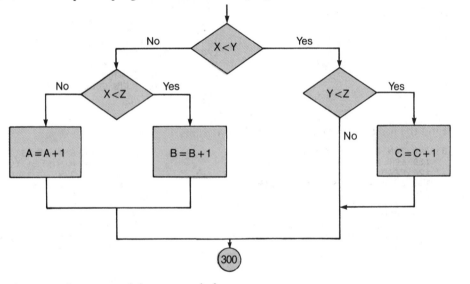

8. Compare the two partial programs below:

a)
```
100 REM CHAPTER 5 SELF-TEST 8.1
110 REM ASSIGN L THE LARGEST VALUE
120 REM BETWEEN X, Y AND Z.
130 REM **************************
    .
    .
    .
300 IF X >= Y THEN 310 ELSE 330
310     IF X >= Z THEN LET L = X ELSE LET L = Z
320 GOTO 340
330     IF Y >= Z THEN LET L = Y ELSE LET L = Z
340 .
    .
    .
```

b)
```
100 REM CHAPTER 5 SELF-TEST 8.2
110 REM ASSIGN L THE LARGEST VALUE
120 REM BETWEEN X, Y AND Z.
130 REM **************************
    .
    .
    .
300 LET L = X
310 IF Y >= L THEN LET L = Y
320 IF Z >= L THEN LET L = Z
330 .
    .
    .
```

Do both partial programs accomplish the same task? If so, which is better, and why?

9. Construct a partial program for the following logic structure:

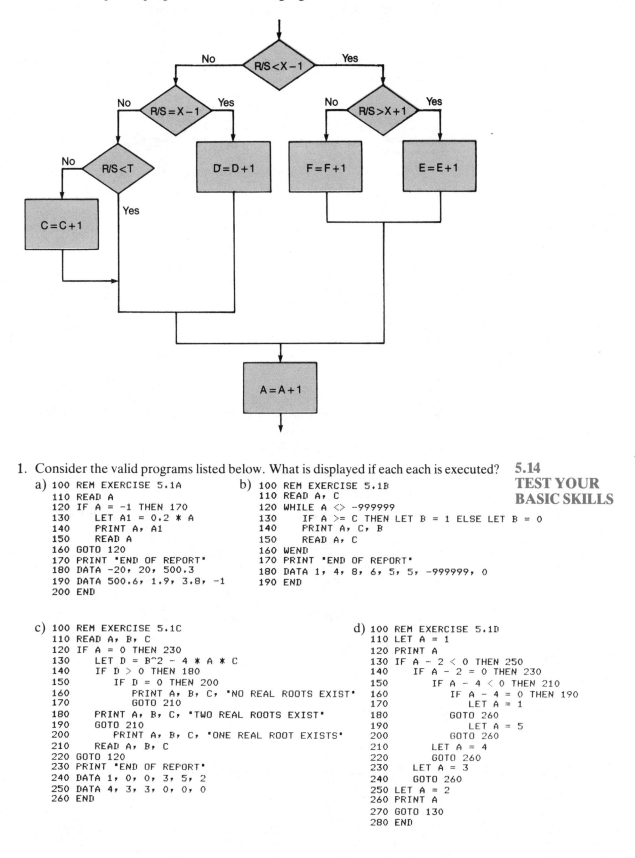

1. Consider the valid programs listed below. What is displayed if each each is executed?

5.14
TEST YOUR
BASIC SKILLS

a)
```
100 REM EXERCISE 5.1A
110 READ A
120 IF A = -1 THEN 170
130     LET A1 = 0.2 * A
140     PRINT A, A1
150     READ A
160 GOTO 120
170 PRINT "END OF REPORT"
180 DATA -20, 20, 500.3
190 DATA 500.6, 1.9, 3.8, -1
200 END
```

b)
```
100 REM EXERCISE 5.1B
110 READ A, C
120 WHILE A <> -999999
130     IF A >= C THEN LET B = 1 ELSE LET B = 0
140     PRINT A, C, B
150     READ A, C
160 WEND
170 PRINT "END OF REPORT"
180 DATA 1, 4, 8, 6, 5, 5, -999999, 0
190 END
```

c)
```
100 REM EXERCISE 5.1C
110 READ A, B, C
120 IF A = 0 THEN 230
130     LET D = B^2 - 4 * A * C
140     IF D > 0 THEN 180
150         IF D = 0 THEN 200
160             PRINT A, B, C, "NO REAL ROOTS EXIST"
170             GOTO 210
180     PRINT A, B, C, "TWO REAL ROOTS EXIST"
190     GOTO 210
200         PRINT A, B, C, "ONE REAL ROOT EXISTS"
210     READ A, B, C
220 GOTO 120
230 PRINT "END OF REPORT"
240 DATA 1, 0, 0, 3, 5, 2
250 DATA 4, 3, 3, 0, 0, 0
260 END
```

d)
```
100 REM EXERCISE 5.1D
110 LET A = 1
120 PRINT A
130 IF A - 2 < 0 THEN 250
140     IF A - 2 = 0 THEN 230
150         IF A - 4 < 0 THEN 210
160             IF A - 4 = 0 THEN 190
170                 LET A = 1
180             GOTO 260
190                 LET A = 5
200             GOTO 260
210         LET A = 4
220         GOTO 260
230     LET A = 3
240     GOTO 260
250 LET A = 2
260 PRINT A
270 GOTO 130
280 END
```

2. Write a BASIC statement that will initialize X to 0 and another that will initialize T to 10. Also, write additional BASIC statements that will consecutively increment these variables by:

   a) 1   b) 7   c) 2   d) double each value   e) minus 1

3. Write an IF statement which will perform the test and branch operations indicated below for each example:

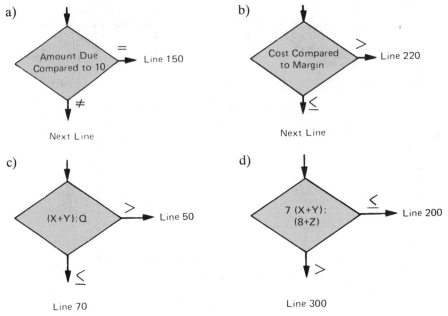

4. Determine the value of Q that will cause the condition in the IF-THEN statements below to be true.

   a) 100 IF Q > 8 THEN LET Z = Z/10
   b) 110 IF Q + 10 >= 7 THEN PRINT "THE ANSWER IS"; A
   c) 120 IF Q/3 < 9 THEN 300
   d) 130 IF Q<> 3 THEN LET S = S + A

5. Write a series of statements to perform the test and branching operations indicated below:

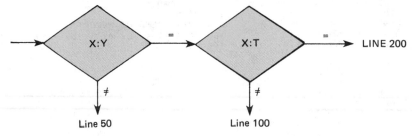

6. Construct partial programs for each of the logic structures found below. Do not use any GOTO statements.

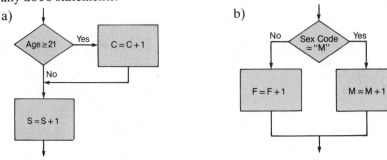

7. Construct partial programs for each of the logic structures found below. Use at most one GOTO statement in 7a. Do not use any GOTO statements in 7b or 7c.

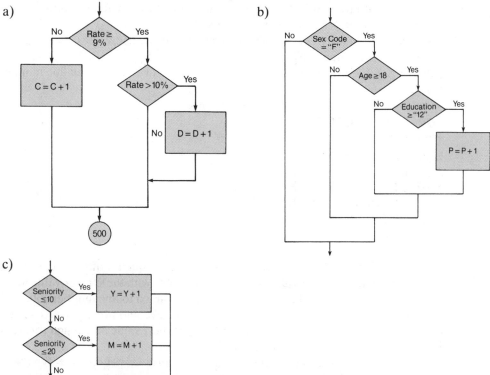

a)

b)

c)

8. Construct an equivalent program for each of the following without using any GOTO statements.

a)
```
100 REM EXERCISE 5.8A
110 INPUT "ENTER AMOUNT"; A
120 LET B = 0.04 * A
130 LET C = A + B
140 PRINT A, B, C
150 PRINT "DO YOU WANT TO ENTER ";
160 INPUT "ANOTHER AMOUNT (YES OR NO)"; D$
170 IF D$ <> "YES" THEN 190
180 GOTO 110
190 PRINT "END OF JOB"
200 END
```

b)
```
100 REM EXERCISE 5.8B
110 INPUT A, B, C, D
120 IF A > B THEN 140
130 GOTO 190
140 IF B > C THEN 160
150 GOTO 190
160 IF C > D THEN 180
170 GOTO 190
180 PRINT "VALUES O.K."
190 END
```

9. The five data items in the DATA statement are read by the following program. What single numeric value will be displayed?

```
100 REM EXERCISE 5.9
110 LET T = 0
120 READ S
130 WHILE S >= 0
140     IF S <= 1000 THEN 160
150         LET T = T + S
160     READ S
170 WEND
180 PRINT T
190 DATA 1000, 120000, 80000, 22, -12345
200 END
```

10. If the condition S < = 1000 in line 140 of Exercise 9 is changed to S < 999.9 and no other changes are made, what result is displayed for this set of data?

11. If the statement in line 140 of Exercise 9 is changed to IF S < 1000 THEN 160 what single result is displayed for the same set of data?

12. If the original program in Exercise 9 is unchanged except for the different output statement 180 PRINT T, S what is displayed?

13. Given four variables W, X, Y and Z with previously defined values, write a sequence of IF-THEN statements to execute line number 200 if all four variables have the exact value of 100. If one or more variables have a different value, execute line number 300 instead.

14. What is the final sum of P in the example below?

```
100 REM EXERCISE 5.14
110 LET P = 0
120 LET R = 0
130 LET R = R + 1
140 LET P = P + R
150 IF R < 6 THEN 130
160 PRINT P
170 END
```

15. Given two positive valued variables A and B, write a sequence of statements to assign the variable with the larger value to G and the variable with the smaller value to S. If A and B are equal, assign either to E. After completion, go to line number 150.

16. The values of three variables U, V and W are positive and not equal to each other. Using IF statements, determine which has the smallest value and assign this value to S. After completion, go to line number 270.

17. The symbol N! represents the product of the first N positive integers: $N! = N * (N - 1) * (N - 2) * \ldots * 1$. When a result is defined in terms of itself, we call it a **recursive definition**. Construct a program that will accept from the keyboard a positive integer and compute its factorial. The recursive definition is as follows: If $N = 1$, then $N! = 1$; otherwise $N! = N(N - 1)!$.

18. Consider the following program:

```
100 REM EXERCISE 5.18
110 LET C = 0
120 LET S = 0
130 READ X, Y, Z
140 WHILE X > 0
150     IF X < Y + 2 THEN 160 ELSE 180
160        LET C = C - 1
170     GOTO 240
180        IF X < Z + 1 THEN 190 ELSE 210
190           LET C = C - 2
200        GOTO 240
210           LET S = S + X * Y * Z
220           LET C = C + 1
230           PRINT X, Y, Z, C, S
240     READ X, Y, Z
250 WEND
260 PRINT S, C
270 PRINT "END OF REPORT"
280 DATA 4, 1, 3, 12, 7, 1, 8, 4, 7
290 DATA 6, 2, 3, 3, 7, 2, -1, 0, 0
300 END
```

a) Which variable is used to test for end-of-file?

b) What are the values of C and S just prior to the third time line 240 is executed?

c) How many lines are displayed by the program?

d) What is the maximum value of S displayed?

e) What is the maximum value of C displayed?

19. The sequence of Fibonacci numbers begins with 1, 1 and continues endlessly, each number being the sum of the preceding two:
1, 1, 2, 3, 5, 8, 13, 21, 34, . . .

Construct a program to compute the first X numbers of the sequence where the value of X is entered in response to an INPUT statement.

20. Write a partial program to set A = −1 if C and D are both zero, set A = −2 if neither C nor D is zero and set A = −3 if either, but not both, C or D is zero. After completion go to line number 150.

21. The WESAVU NATIONAL BANK computes its monthly service charge on checking accounts by adding 25¢ to a value computed from the following:

$0.09 per check for the first ten checks

$0.08 per check for the next ten checks

$0.07 per check for the next ten checks

$0.06 per check for all the rest of the checks

Write a sequence of statements that includes an ON-GOTO statement and a PRINT statement to display the account number A, the number of checks cashed C, and the computed monthly charge B. Assume the account number and the number of checks cashed are entered via an INPUT statement prior to the execution of the ON-GOTO statement.

22. Study the following program and fill in the table below describing the value of the variables each time line 240 is executed.

```
100 REM EXERCISE 5.22
110 LET A = 0
120 LET B = 0
130 LET C = 0
140 LET D = 3
150 LET E = -4
160 LET F = 0
170 LET F = F + 1
180 ON F GOTO 230, 210, 190, 260
190    LET A = A + E
200 GOTO 240
210    LET B = B + D + F
220 GOTO 240
230    LET C = A + B + E
240 PRINT D; E; A; B; C; F
250 GOTO 170
260 END
```

Line 240 Executed	VALUE OF VARIABLES					
	D	E	A	B	C	F
1st Time	___	___	___	___	___	___
2nd Time	___	___	___	___	___	___
3rd Time	___	___	___	___	___	___

5.15 PROGRAMMING EXERCISES

Exercise 1: On-Line Sales Tax Computation

Purpose: To become familiar with the concepts of looping and testing for the last value in a set of data.

Problem: Construct an efficient program that will prompt the user to input the purchase price; from that input, the program is to compute a 4% sales tax, output the sales tax, prompt the user to input the next purchase price and loop back to compute and display the sales tax. The system is to display the message JOB FINISHED when a −1 is entered for the purchase price.

Input Data: In response to the question WHAT IS THE PURCHASE PRICE? key in each value individually as found below:

Purchase Price

$39.00

16.50

25.50

−1

Output Results: The following results are displayed:

```
WHAT IS THE PURCHASE PRICE ? 39.00
THE SALES TAX IS 1.56
WHAT IS THE PURCHASE PRICE ? 16.50
THE SALES TAX IS .66
WHAT IS THE PURCHASE PRICE ? 25.50
THE SALES TAX IS 1.02
WHAT IS THE PURCHASE PRICE ? -1
JOB FINISHED
```

Exercise 2:
Employee Average
Yearly Salary

Purpose: To illustrate the concepts of counter and running total initialization, counter and running total incrementation, looping, and testing for the last value in a set of data.

Problem: Construct a program to read, count records, accumulate salaries, and display a sequence of data consisting of employee numbers and salaries for various employees in a payroll file. After the sentinel value ("EOF") is processed, display the total number of employees and the average yearly salary of all the employees processed.

Input Data: Prepare and use the following sample data:

Employee Number	Employee Salary
123	$16,000
148	8,126
184	14,800
196	17,400
201	18,950
EOF	0

Output Results: The following results are displayed:

```
EMPLOYEE      EMPLOYEE
NUMBER        SALARY
--------      --------

   123        16,000.00
   148         8,126.00
   184        14,800.00
   196        17,400.00
   201        18,950.00


THE NUMBER OF EMPLOYEES IS   5
THE AVERAGE SALARY IS $15,055.20
```

Exercise 3:
Voter Analysis

Purpose: To become familiar with nested If-Then-Else structures.

Problem: Construct a program that will analyze a citizen file and generate the following totals:

1) Number of males not eligible to register
2) Number of females not eligible to register
3) Number of males who are old enough to vote but have not registered
4) Number of females who are old enough to vote but have not registered
5) Number of individuals who are eligible to vote but did not vote
6) Number of individuals who did vote
7) Number of records processed

(*Hint:* See Figure 5.13.)

Input Data: Prepare and use the following sample data:

Number	Age in Years	Sex Code	Registered	Voted
1614	18	F	N	N
1321	21	M	N	N
1961	33	M	Y	Y
1432	46	F	Y	Y
1721	25	M	Y	Y
1211	16	M	N	N
1100	38	F	Y	Y
4164	34	M	Y	N
2139	19	M	Y	N
8647	25	F	Y	Y
9216	13	M	N	N
7814	15	F	N	N

Output Results: The following results are displayed:

```
***************** VOTER ANALYSIS *****************

MALES NOT ELIGIBLE TO REGISTER==================> 2
FEMALES NOT ELIGIBLE TO REGISTER================> 1

MALES OLD ENOUGH TO VOTE BUT NOT REGISTERED=====> 1
FEMALES OLD ENOUGH TO VOTE BUT NOT REGISTERED===> 1

INDIVIDUALS ELIGIBLE TO VOTE BUT DID NOT VOTE===> 2

INDIVIDUALS WHO VOTED===========================> 5

TOTAL NUMBER OF RECORDS PROCESSED===============> 12

END OF REPORT
```

Purpose: To become familiar with the If-Then-Else structure and methods used to determine a stockbroker's commission.

Exercise 4: Stockbroker's Commission

Problem: Write a program that will read a stock transaction and determine the stockbroker's commission. Each transaction includes the following data: the stock name, price per share, number of shares involved and the stockbroker's name.

The stockbroker's commission is computed in the following manner: if price per share P is less than or equal to $40.00 the commission rate is 15¢ per share; if P is greater than $40.00 the commission rate is 25¢ per share. If the number of shares sold is less than 125, the commission is 1.5 times the rate per share.

Each line of output is to include the stock transaction data set and the commission paid the stock broker. Test the stock name for the EOF. Display the total commission earned.

Input Data: Prepare and use the following sample data:

Stock Name	Price per Share	Number of Shares	Stockbroker Name
CRANE	$32.50	200	Baker, G.
FSTPA	17.50	100	Smith, J.
GENDYN	56.25	300	Smith, A.
HARRIS	40.00	125	Lucas, M.
BELLCD	48.00	160	Soley, K.
BELLHOW	22.00	300	Jones, D.

Output Results: The following results are displayed:

```
STOCK          PRICE        NUMBER       STOCKBROKER
NAME           PER SHARE    OF SHARES    NAME           COMMISSION
-----          ---------    ---------    ------------   ----------
CRANE          32.50        200          BAKER, G.      30.00
FSTPA          17.50        100          SMITH, J.      22.50
GENDYN         56.25        300          SMITH, A.      75.00
HARRIS         40.00        125          LUCAS, M.      18.75
BELLCD         48.00        160          SOLEY, K.      40.00
BELLHOW        22.00        300          JONES, D.      45.00

TOTAL COMMISSION EARNED IS   $231.25

END OF REPORT
```

**Exercise 5:
Utility Billing
Computations**

Purpose: To devise an efficient branching pattern for computational purposes.

Problem: The Northern Indiana Public Service Company computes the electrical bills for its customers by multiplying a factor times the number of kilowatt hours used each month. The rate, or factor, varies with the amount of electricity consumed. The customer is billed according to the following table:

Kilowatts Used	Cost per Kw/Hr.	Formula Used
1–50	.1123	.1123 (Kw)
50–200	.09409	.09409 (Kw − 50) + 5.615
200 and up	.07275	.07275 (Kw − 200) + 19.7285

The minimum payment is $5.88.

Write an efficient program using this table to compute the payment and totals as illustrated in the output below. Round the payment to the nearest cent.

Input Data: Prepare and use the following sample data:

Customer Number	Kilowatts Consumed
46189	168
57129	221
68647	14
71285	428

Output Results: The following results are displayed:

```
CUSTOMER       KILOWATTS
NUMBER         CONSUMED        PAYMENT
---------      ---------       -------
46189          168             16.72
57129          221             21.25
68647          14               5.88
71285          428             36.31

TOTALS         831             80.16
```

**Exercise 6:
Average Class Score
and Deviations**

Purpose: To become familiar with processing a file more than once using the RESTORE statement.

Problem: Write a program that will read a group of student numbers and test scores and compute and display the average score rounded to two decimal places. The program should then read the file again and display the student number, student score and deviation from the average. A student number of EOF indicates end-of-file.

Input Data: Prepare and use the following sample data:

Student Number	Score	Student Number	Score
1	96	7	70
2	84	8	61
3	67	9	97
4	48	10	83
5	82	11	56
6	85	12	63

Output Results: The following results are displayed:

```
THE CLASS AVERAGE IS 74.33

STUDENT
NUMBER        SCORE        DEVIATION
------        -----        ---------
   1           96           21.67
   2           84            9.67
   3           67            7.33-
   4           48           26.33-
   5           82            7.67
   6           85           10.67
   7           70            4.33-
   8           61           13.33-
   9           97           22.67
  10           83            8.67
  11           56           18.33-
  12           63           11.33-

END OF REPORT
```

Purpose: To illustrate the concepts of replacement and looping.

Problem: The WESAVU National Bank pays 5½% interest compounded quarterly on savings accounts. Inflation amounts to 4% annually. If you put $1,000 in a savings account, how many years will it take for your savings to grow to the equivalent of $10,000 in today's money?

Hint: The annual interest rate (effective rate) can be computed from the compounded rate (nominal rate) by using the formula discussed in Programming Exercise 4.2.

Input Data: Use the following input data:

    Principal—$1000
    Interest—5½%
    Rate of Inflation—4%

Output Results: The following results are displayed:

```
WHAT IS THE PRINCIPAL? 1000
WHAT IS THE INTEREST? 5.5
WHAT IS THE INFLATION RATE? 4.0
THE NUMBER OF YEARS IS 144
```

Exercise 7:
Interest on Savings with a Built-In Inflation Factor

Purpose: To illustrate the concepts of multiple loops and data validation.

Problem: Construct a program that will make change from a one-dollar bill on a sale of less than or equal to one dollar. Have the program request the amount of the sale. If the sale amount is less than 1 cent or greater than 100 cents, display a diagnostic message and request that the amount of the sale be re-entered. The program is to display the number of half-dollars, quarters, dimes, nickels and pennies that are to be returned to the customer. Have the program return as many half-dollars as possible, then as many quarters as possible, and so on. A sale amount of -99 indicates end-of-job.

Exercise 8:
Money Changer

Input Data: Prepare and use the following sample data:

13¢, −29¢, 0¢, 72¢, 104¢, 25¢, 100¢, 1¢ and 47¢.

Output Results: The following results are displayed for sale amounts of 13¢ and −29¢:

```
MONEY CHANGER

ENTER AMOUNT OF SALE AS A WHOLE NUMBER
BETWEEN 1 CENT AND 100 CENTS INCLUSIVE? 13

RETURN TO THE CUSTOMER - 1 HALF-DOLLAR
                         1 QUARTER(S)
                         1 DIME(S)
                         0 NICKEL(S)
                         2 PENNIES

ENTER AMOUNT OF SALE AS A WHOLE NUMBER
BETWEEN 1 CENT AND 100 CENTS INCLUSIVE? -29

AMOUNT MUST BE BETWEEN 1 PENNY AND 1 DOLLAR, PLEASE

ENTER AMOUNT OF SALE AS A WHOLE NUMBER
BETWEEN 1 CENT AND 100 CENTS INCLUSIVE? -99

END OF JOB
```

**Exercise 9:
Checking the
Sequence of
Customer Numbers**

Purpose: To devise an efficient method of checking the sequence in ascending order for a given field of an input file.

Problem: A customer input file must be checked on the customer number field to ensure that all records are in sequence. Construct an efficient program that will sequence check in ascending order the customer number field. The program *must not* compare the first customer number against the customer number of 0 or 1 or any predetermined fixed number. Beginning with the second record, each customer number should be compared to the previous customer number in sequence.

If a customer number is out of order, the following is to be displayed: OUT OF ORDER XXXXX where the Xs represent the customer number out of order. If a duplicate customer number is detected, the following is to be displayed: DUPLICATE XXXXX.

If the customer number is in ascending order, processing continues. Duplicate customer numbers are not out of order. When the last value of an input file is processed, display the total customer numbers that have been sequence checked in ascending order.

Input Data: Prepare and use the following sample data for the customer number field.

Input File	Input File Continued	Input File Continued
03000	03035	03067
03012	03039	03068
03013	03042	03079
03015	03043	03077
03014	03043	03076
03016	03043	03076
03017	03042	03075
03018	03043	03078
03018	03044	03080
03019	03063	03081
03020	03062	03094
03034	03064	03096
03038	03065	03095
03037	03066	
03036	03066	

Output Results: The following partial results are shown when the file is processed:

```
OUT OF ORDER 3014
DUPLICATE 3018
OUT OF ORDER 3037
        .
        .
        .
OUT OF ORDER 3078
OUT OF ORDER 3095
CUSTOMER NUMBERS IN SEQUENCE EQUAL 31
JOB FINISHED
```

Purpose: To become familiar with the concepts of developing an amortization schedule for a loan.

Exercise 10:
Loan Problem

Problem: Write a program that will use the amount of a loan, the annual interest rate expressed in percent, and the amount of the monthly payment to calculate and display an amortization schedule in tabular form as shown below. The last line of output contains the amount of refund if the last payment results in an overpayment. The interest for each month is equal to 1/12 the annual interest times the balance. All monetary amounts are to be rounded to the nearest cent.

Input Data: Prepare and use the following sample data:

Amount of Loan—$1000
Annual Interest Rate—10%
Amount of Monthly Payment—$150

Output Results: The following results are displayed:

```
                MONTHLY   MONTHLY
PAYMENT         INTEREST  PRINCIPAL  BALANCE
NUMBER          PAID      PAID       OWED
-------         --------  ---------  -------
   1             8.33      141.67     858.33
   2             7.15      142.85     715.49
   3             5.96      144.04     571.45
   4             4.76      145.24     426.21
   5             3.55      146.45     279.76
   6             2.33      147.67     132.09
   7             1.10      132.09       0.00

REFUND DUE===>    $16.81
```

Purpose: To become familiar with exchanging the values of string variables and using the RESTORE statement.

Exercise 11:
Selecting the
Best and Worst
Salesperson

Problem: Write a program that will determine and display the best and worst salesperson based on total sales from a salesperson file.

Input Data: Prepare and use the following sample data:

Salesperson Name	Total Sales
DOOLITTLE, FRANK	$11,316.00
FRANKLIN, ED	96,185.00
SMITH, SUSAN	18,421.00
RUNAW, JEFF	32,146.00
RAY, KATHY	13,467.00
ZACHERY, LOUIS	48,615.00
STANKIE, JIM	97,856.00

Output Results: The following results are displayed:

```
THE BEST SALESPERSON IS STANKIE, JIM
TOTAL SALES  97,856.00

THE WORST SALESPERSON IS DOOLITTLE, FRANK
TOTAL SALES  11,316.00
```

Exercise 12:
Computing the
Average Age of
Employees With a
Minor Control Break

Purpose: To become familiar with the decision-making function of the IF statement and a method of testing for a control break in a file.

Problem: Construct a program that will find the average age of those employees less than 40 years old and the average age of those greater than or equal to 40 years old. The program should do the following:

1) Read a department number and a person's age.
2) Test to see if the department number is the same as the previous one was.
3) If it is the same, determine if the age is greater than or equal to 40 or less than 40. Use an IF statement to transfer control so that the age is added to an appropriate total and a variable representing a counter has its value incremented by one.
4) If the department number changes (control break occurs), transfer control to determine the average ages of those employees below 40 and of those 40 and above, display a summary line, then reset counters and the control variable and continue processing the next department.
5) Use a −1 sentinel value to terminate the program.

Input Data: Prepare and use the following sample data:

Dept. No.	Age	Dept. No. (Continued)	Age
1	26	2	18
1	38	2	37
1	22	2	41
1	40	2	43
1	51	2	25
1	64	3	21
1	19	3	23
1	38	3	34
2	46	3	56
2	48		
2	65		

Output Results: The following results are displayed:

```
           BELOW     AVERAGE AGE   40 AND   AVERAGE AGE
DEPT. NO.  40        BELOW 40      ABOVE    40 AND ABOVE
---------  -----     -----------   ------   ------------
    1        5          28.6         3          51.7
    2        3          26.7         5          48.6
    3        3          26.0         1          56.0

END OF REPORT
```

Exercise 13:
Sales Analysis Report
with Multilevel
Control Breaks

Purpose: To become familiar with the concepts of multilevel control breaks.

Problem: Write a program that generates the sales analysis report shown in Figure 5.17.

Input Data: Prepare and use the following sample data:

District	Store	Dept.	Item	Amt. of Sales
1	1	12	2039	$ 4.00
1	1	12	3849	500.00
1	1	12	7641	3.98
1	1	17	3453	9.96
1	1	17	1302	15.00
1	2	23	5543	5.00
1	2	23	1130	30.00
1	2	24	2765	4.00
3	1	17	2223	25.00
3	1	17	3435	13.00
3	1	34	2039	14.00
3	5	40	5543	12.00
3	5	40	9562	16.00

Output Results: The output results are shown in Figure 5.17.

Purpose: To become familiar with a multi-function program and the use of a menu.

**Exercise 14:
A Menu-Driven
Program with
Multi-Functions**

Problem: Write a menu-driven program to compute the volume of a box, cylinder, cone, and sphere. The program should display the menu which is shown under Output Results. Once a code is entered, it must be validated. After the selection of the proper function, the program should prompt the operator for the necessary data, compute the volume, and display it accordingly. The displayed results are to remain on the screen until the Enter key on the keyboard is pressed. After that the program should re-display the menu.

Use the following formulas for the volumes V:

1) Volume of a box: $V = L * W * H$ where L is the length, W is the width, and H is the height of the box.
2) Volume of a cylinder: $V = \pi * R * R * H$ where π equals 3.14159, R is the radius, and H is the height of the cylinder.
3) Volume of a cone: $V = (\pi * R * R * H)/3$ where π equals 3.14159, R is the radius of the base, and H is the height of the cone.
4) Volume of a sphere: $V = 4 * \pi * R * R * R$
   where π equals 3.14159, and R is the radius of the sphere.

Input Data: Use the following sample data:

Code — 3, Radius = 7, Height = 9
Code — 4, Radius = 10
Code — 1, Length = 4.5, Width = 6.7, Height = 12
Code — 2, Radius = 8, Height = 15
Code — 7 (This code should return a diagnostic message.)

Output Results: The following menu is displayed:

```
    MENU FOR COMPUTING VOLUMES
    ------------------------------

 CODE     FUNCTION
 ----     --------
   1  -   COMPUTE VOLUME OF A BOX
   2  -   COMPUTE VOLUME OF A CYLINDER
   3  -   COMPUTE VOLUME OF A CONE
   4  -   COMPUTE VOLUME OF A SPHERE
   5  -   END PROGRAM

 ENTER A CODE 1 THROUGH 5?
```

**Exercise 15:
Payroll Problem IV–
Weekly Payroll
Computations with
Time-and-One-Half
for Overtime**

Purpose: To become familiar with decision making and some payroll concepts.

Problem: Modify Payroll Problem III in Programming Exercise 4.8 to include the following conditions:

1) Overtime (hours worked > 80) is paid at 1.5 times the hourly rate.
2) Federal withholding tax is determined in the same manner as indicated in Payroll Problem III. However, assign a value of $0.00 if the gross pay less the product of the number of dependents and $38.46 is not positive.
3) After processing the employee records, display the total gross pay, federal withholding tax and net pay.

Input Data: Use the sample data found in Payroll Problem II in Programming Exercise 3.8. Modify the DATA statement representing employee 126 so that the number of dependents equals 9.

Output Results: The following results are displayed:

```
EMPLOYEE
NUMBER         GROSS PAY        FED. TAX        NET PAY
--------       ---------        --------        -------
  123          1,000.00          184.62         815.38
  124            880.00          168.31         711.69
  125          1,040.00          200.31         839.69
  126             90.00            0.00          90.00

TOTAL GROSS PAY=========>       3,010.00
TOTAL WITHHOLDING TAX===>         553.24
TOTAL NET PAY===========>       2,456.76

JOB COMPLETE
```

MORE ON LOOPING, DECISION-MAKING AND PROGRAM CONSTRUCTION 6

Up to now, we have been working with relational operators, like >, < and =, and relational expressions, or conditions. **Logical operators**, like AND, OR and NOT, may also be used to combine conditions. Logical operators reduce the number of IF statements required to implement certain If-Then-Else structures.

For example, the following partial program

```
100 IF A > 30 THEN 200
110 IF B > 15 THEN 200
    .
    .
    .
200 LET C = C + 1
```

increments the counter C by 1 if A is greater than 30 *or* if B is greater than 15. The logical operator OR combines the two conditions found in lines 100 and 110 into one IF statement:

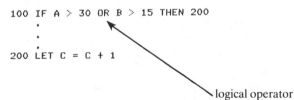

```
100 IF A > 30 OR B > 15 THEN 200
    .
    .
    .
200 LET C = C + 1
```

logical operator

It is often necessary for a program to verify that the data entered by the operator is within the range that will generate valid results when the program is run. Logical operators are often used for this **data validation**. For example, a program may only generate proper results if a sex code is assigned a value of "M" or "F." The following partial program validates the sex code S$:

```
100 INPUT "SEX CODE (M OR F)"; S$
110 IF S$ = "M" OR S$ = "F" THEN 140
120    PRINT "SEX CODE "; S$; " IS INVALID, PLEASE RE-ENTER"
130    GOTO 100
140 .
    .
    .
```

Line 110 transfers control to line 140 only if S$ is equal to "M" *or* "F." An invalid sex code results in the display of a diagnostic message and the return to the INPUT statement.

In Chapter 5, loops were implemented (coded) using the IF–THEN and GOTO statements or the WHILE and WEND statements. In this chapter, loops will be implemented using a third method of controlling loops, FOR and NEXT statements. This chapter also presents internal **subroutines**, which can be an effective tool for designing and implementing algorithms. Finally, this chapter presents the **top-down** approach, which is used to divide large, complex problems into many manageable ones.

**6.2
LOGICAL
OPERATORS**

There are many instances in which a decision to execute one alternative or another is based upon two or more conditions. In previous examples that involved two or more conditions, we tested each condition in a separate decision statement. In this section, we will discuss combining conditions within one decision statement using the logical operators AND, OR, XOR, EQV and IMP.* When two or more conditions are combined by logical operators, the expression is called a **compound condition**. The logical operator NOT allows you to write a condition in which the truth value is **complemented**, or reversed.

**The AND Logical
Operator**

The AND operator requires that both conditions be true for the compound condition to be true. Consider the following IF–THEN statement:

```
200 IF S$ = "M" AND A > 20 THEN 210 ELSE 400
210 .
    .
    .
```

If S$ is equal to "M" *and* A is greater than 20, then control transfers to line 210. If either one of the conditions is false, the compound condition is false and control passes to line 400.

Like a single condition, a compound condition can only be true or false. To determine the truth value of the compound condition, the system must evaluate and assign a truth value to each individual condition. Then the truth value is determined for the compound condition, which contains a logical operator like AND.

For example, if X equals 4 and Y equals 0, the system evaluates the following compound condition like this:

```
300 IF X = 3 AND Y = 0 THEN 310 ELSE 400
```

1. false   2. true

3. false

The system first determines the truth value for each condition, then it concludes that the compound condition is false because of the AND operation.

A compound condition can be made up of several conditions separated by AND operators. The flowchart in Figure 6.1 indicates that all three variables (T1, T2 and T3) must equal zero to increment the counter A by 1. Line 400 in Figure 6.1 illustrates the implementation of the logic using a compound condition. The AND operator requires that all three conditions be true for A to be incremented by 1. If any one of the three conditions is false, control is transferred to line 410, and A is not incremented by 1.

---

*Logical operators are not available on the Apple. The EQV and IMP are not available on the COMMODORE.

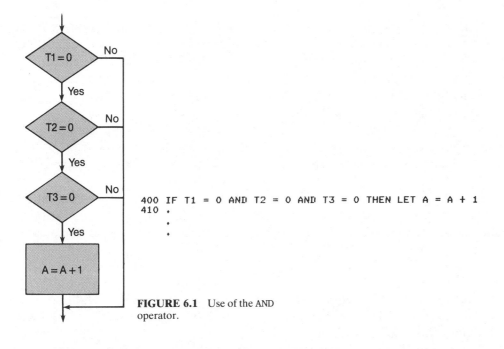

```
400 IF T1 = 0 AND T2 = 0 AND T3 = 0 THEN LET A = A + 1
410 .
    .
    .
```

FIGURE 6.1 Use of the AND operator.

The following rule summarizes the use of the logical operator AND:

Logical Operator Rule 1: The logical operator AND requires that all conditions be true for the compound condition to be true.

The OR Logical Operator

The OR operator requires that only one of the two conditions be true for the compound condition to be true. If both conditions are true, the compound condition is also true. The use of the OR operator is illustrated below.

```
500 IF W = 4 OR Q < 5 THEN 510 ELSE 530
510     LET S = S + 1
520     PRINT "W = 4 OR Q < 5"
530 .
    .
    .
```

In line 500, if either W equals 4 *or* Q is less than 5, control transfers to line 510. If both conditions are true, control also transfers to line 510. If both conditions are false, control passes to line 530.

As with the logical operator AND, the truth values of the individual conditions are first determined, and then the truth values for the conditions containing the logical operator OR are evaluated. For example, if C equals 4, X equals 4.9 and Y equals 4.8, the following condition is true:

```
600 IF C = 3 OR C = 5 OR X > Y THEN 610 ELSE 650
```

   1. false   2. false   3. true

        4. false

           5. true

In line 600, the system first evaluates the individual conditions (steps 1, 2 and 3). The first and second conditions are false and the third condition is true. Next, the system evaluates the leftmost OR (step 4). Since the truth values of the first two conditions are false, the truth value of C = 3 OR C = 5 is also false.

Finally, the system evaluates the truth value of the condition resulting from step 4 and the condition resulting from step 3 for the rightmost logical operator OR. Since the condition resulting from step 3 has a truth value of true, the entire condition is determined to be true.

The following rule summarizes the use of the logical operator OR:

> **Logical Operator Rule 2:** The logical operator OR requires that *only one* of the conditions be true for the compound condition to be true. If both conditions are true, the compound condition is also true.

The NOT Logical Operator

A relational expression preceded by the logical operator NOT forms a condition which is false when the relational expression is true. If the relational expression is false, then the condition is true. Consider the following IF–THEN–ELSE statement:

```
700 IF NOT A > B THEN 710 ELSE 800
710 .
    .
    .
```

If A is greater than B (the relational expression is true), then the condition NOT A > B is false. If A is less than or equal to B (the relational expression is false), then the condition is true.

Because the logical operator NOT can increase the complexity of the decision statement significantly, use it sparingly. As illustrated in Table 6.1, in BASIC you may write the complement, or reverse, of a condition by using other relations.

TABLE 6.1   Use of Other Relations to Complement a Condition

| Condition | Complement of Condition | |
	Method 1	Method 2
A = B	A <> B	NOT A = B
A < B	A >= B	NOT A < B
A > B	A <= B	NOT A > B
A <= B	A > B	NOT A <= B
A >= B	A < B	NOT A >= B
A <> B	A = B	NOT A <> B

The following rule summarizes the use of the logical operator NOT:

> **Logical Operator Rule 3:** The logical operator NOT requires that the relational expression be false for the condition to be true. If the relational expression is true, then the condition is false.

Combining Logical Operators AND, OR and NOT

The logical operators AND, OR and NOT can be combined in a decision statement to form a compound condition. The formation of compound statements involving more than one type of logical operator can create problems unless you fully understand the order in which the system evaluates the entire condition. Consider the following decision statement:

```
800 IF X > Y OR T = D AND H < 3 OR NOT Y = R THEN 810 ELSE 900
```

Does the system evaluate operators from left to right or right to left or one type of operator before another?

The order of evaluation is a part of what is sometimes called the **rules of precedence**. Just as we have rules of precedence for arithmetic operations (see Section 3.5), we also have rules of precedence for logical operations.

Precedence Rule 3: Unless parentheses dictate otherwise, reading from left to right, conditions containing relational operators are evaluated first, then those containing NOT operators, then those containing AND operators, and finally those conditions containing OR operators.

This same compound condition, then, is evaluated as follows. Assume that D = 3, H = 3, R = 2, T = 5, X = 3 and Y = 2:

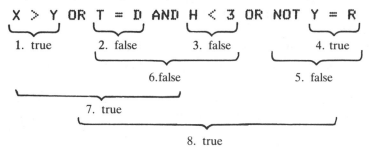

If you have trouble following the logic behind this evaluation, use this technique. Applying the rules of precedence, look or scan from *left* to *right* four different times. On the first scan, evaluate the truth value of each condition containing a relational operator. On the second scan, moving from left to right again, evaluate all conditions containing NOT operators. Y = R was true and NOT true is false. On the third scan, moving again from left to right, evaluate all conditions containing AND operators. T = D was false, as was H < 3; therefore, T = D AND H < 3 is false. On the fourth scan, moving from left to right, evaluate all conditions containing OR operators. The first OR yields a truth value of true. The second OR yields, for the entire condition, a final truth value of true.

Parentheses may be used to change the order of precedence. In BASIC, parentheses are normally used to avoid ambiguity and to group conditions with a desired logical operator. When there are parentheses in a compound condition, the system evaluates that part of the compound condition within the parentheses first and then continues to evaluate the remaining compound condition according to the rules of precedence. For example, suppose a variable C has a value of 6 and D has a value of 3. Consider the compound condition:

The Effect of Parentheses in the Evaluation of Compound Conditions

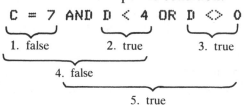

Following the order of precedence for logical operators, the compound condition yields a truth value of true. If parentheses surround the latter two conditions in the compound condition, then the OR operator is evaluated before the AND condition is, and the compound condition yields a truth value of false, as shown below:

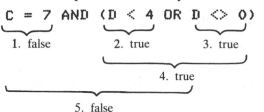

Parentheses may be used freely when the evaluation of a compound condition is in doubt. For example, if you wish to evaluate the compound condition

```
C > D AND S = 4 OR X < Y AND T = 5
```

you may incorporate it into a decision statement as it stands. You may also write it as

```
(C > D AND S = 4) OR (X < Y AND T = 5)
```

and feel more certain of the outcome of the decision statement.

The XOR, EQV and IMP Logical Operators

Three logical operators that are not used very often, but that are part of most BASIC systems, are XOR (exclusive OR), EQV (equivalence) and IMP (implication).

The XOR operator requires that one of the two conditions be true for the compound condition to be true. If both conditions are true, the compound condition is false. For example, if C = 3 and D = 4, then the following compound condition is false.

```
C = 3 XOR D > 3
```
1. true   2. true
3. false

The EQV operator requires that both conditions be true or both conditions be false for the compound condition to be true. For example, if C = 4 and D = 3, then the following compound condition is true.

```
C = 3 EQV D > 3
```
1. false   2. false
3. true

The IMP operator requires that both conditions be true or both conditions be false or the first condition be false and the second condition be true for the compound condition to be true. For example, if C = 4 and D = 5, then the following compound condition is true.

```
C = 3 IMP D > 3
```
1. false   2. true
3. true

The six logical operators discussed in this section are summarized in Table 6.2 and 6.3. The logical operators may be used in IF-THEN, IF-THEN-ELSE and WHILE statements.

Programming Case Study 9B: Employee Analysis and Summary Report

Turn again to Program 5.7, Programming Case Study 9A: Employee Analysis and Summary Report, presented in Section 5.6. However, let us modify the criteria used to select employee records to the following:

1) Sex code is female and service is greater than 10 years

or

2) Sex code is male and age is greater than or equal to 35 years and service is less than 10 years.

Program 6.1 is similar to 5.7 except that the three IF-THEN statements (lines 310 through 330 in the old program) have been replaced by a single IF-THEN-ELSE

TABLE 6.2 **Summary of All Operators**

	Operator	Order of Precedence
Arithmetic Operators	$\wedge$ * or / + or −	Highest
Relational Operators	=, >, >=, <, <= or <>	
Logical Operators	NOT AND OR or XOR IMP EQV	↓ Lowest

Caution: Logical operators are not available on the Apple. The EQV and IMP are not available on the COMMODORE.

TABLE 6.3 **Truth Tables for Logical Operators**

Logical Operator NOT			Logical Operator XOR		
Value of A	Value of NOT A		Value of A	Value of B	Value of A XOR B
T	F		T	T	F
F	T		T	F	T
			F	T	T
			F	F	F

Logical Operator AND			Logical Operator IMP		
Value of A	Value of B	Value of A AND B	Value of A	Value of B	Value of A IMP B
T	T	T	T	T	T
T	F	F	T	F	F
F	T	F	F	T	T
F	F	F	F	F	T

Logical Operator OR			Logical Operator EQV		
Value of A	Value of B	Value of A OR B	Value of A	Value of B	Value of A EQV B
T	T	T	T	T	T
T	F	T	T	F	F
F	T	T	F	T	F
F	F	F	F	F	T

where A and B represent conditions
      T represents True
      F represents False

statement with a compound condition. Line 310 in Program 6.1 evaluates these employee characteristics. If the employee has the desired characteristics, then control transfers to line 340 and the system increments the accumulators and displays a line before reading the next record. (To maintain similarity between the two programs, line numbers 320 and 330 are purposely omitted from Program 6.1.) If an employee record fails to pass the criteria specified in line 310, control transfers to line 370 and the next record is read.

Line 310 illustrates the capabilities of both the IF-THEN-ELSE statement and compound conditions. Not only does Program 6.1 have fewer lines of code than Program 5.7, but the logic is more straightforward and, therefore, easier to read and understand. The parentheses in line 310 are optional: if they are removed, the program will still generate the same report. The parentheses are inserted solely for the purpose of clarity.

```
100 REM PROGRAM 6.1
110 REM EMPLOYEE ANALYSIS AND SUMMARY REPORT
120 REM N$ = NAME     S$ = SEX CODE     S = YEARS OF SERVICE
130 REM A  = AGE      M  = ANNUAL SALARY
140 REM C  = TOTAL NUMBER OF EMPLOYEES WHO MEET CRITERIA
150 REM T  = TOTAL ANNUAL SALARY OF EMPLOYEES WHO MEET CRITERIA
160 REM A1 = AVERAGE ANNUAL SALARY OF EMPLOYEES WHO MEET CRITERIA
170 REM ***************************************************************
180 PRINT TAB(15); "EMPLOYEE ANALYSIS AND SUMMARY REPORT"
182 PRINT TAB(19); "SEX = FEMALE, SERVICE > 10"
184 PRINT TAB(32); "OR"
190 PRINT TAB(15); "SEX = MALE, AGE >= 35, SERVICE < 10"
200 PRINT
210 PRINT TAB(57); "ANNUAL"
220 PRINT "NAME", "SEX", "SERVICE", "AGE", "SALARY"
230 PRINT "----", "---", "-------", "---", "------"
240 LET C = 0
250 LET T = 0
260 REM *****READ FIRST RECORD*****
270 READ N$, S$, S, A, M
280 REM ********************PROCESS A RECORD********************
290 WHILE N$ <> "EOF"
300    REM *****TEST RECORD AGAINST CRITERIA*****
310    IF (S$="F" AND S>10) OR (S$="M" AND A>=35 AND S<10) THEN 340 ELSE 370
340       LET C = C + 1
350       LET T = T + M
360       PRINT N$, " "; S$, "  "; S, A, M
370    READ N$, S$, S, A, M
380 WEND
390 REM ********************EOF ROUTINE********************
400 LET A1 = T/C
410 PRINT
420 PRINT "NUMBER OF EMPLOYEES MEETING CRITERIA"; C
430 PRINT "AVERAGE ANNUAL SALARY OF EMPLOYEES MEETING CRITERIA $"; A1
440 REM ********************DATA FOLLOWS********************
450 DATA BABJACK BILL, M,  3, 41, 19500
460 DATA KNOPF LOUIS,  M, 19, 53, 29200
470 DATA TAYLOR JANE,  F, 12, 38, 26000
480 DATA DROOPEY JOE,  M,  4, 36, 28000
490 DATA LANE LYN,     F,  9, 44, 19800
500 DATA LIS FRANK,    M,  1, 44, 21000
510 DATA BYE ED,       M,  1, 42, 15000
520 DATA BRAION JIM,   M, 19, 35, 26500
530 DATA EOF,          " ", 0,  0, 0
540 END
```

PROGRAM 6.1

```
RUN

              EMPLOYEE ANALYSIS AND SUMMARY REPORT
                  SEX = FEMALE, SERVICE > 10
                             OR
                 SEX = MALE, AGE >= 35, SERVICE < 10


                                                    ANNUAL
NAME            SEX            SERVICE       AGE     SALARY
----            ---            -------       ---     ------
BABJACK BILL    M                 3          41      19500
TAYLOR JANE     F                12          38      26000
DROOPEY JOE     M                 4          36      28000
LIS FRANK       M                 1          44      21000
BYE ED          M                 1          42      15000

NUMBER OF EMPLOYEES MEETING CRITERIA 5
AVERAGE ANNUAL SALARY OF EMPLOYEES MEETING CRITERIA $ 21900
```

6.3
DATA
VALIDATION
TECHNIQUES

Data validation is a technique used to ensure that valid data is assigned to a program. You were briefly introduced to a form of data validation in Program 5.9, Programming Case Study 11: A Menu-Driven Program. Recall that in Program 5.9, the variable C, representing the function code, is tested before the ON–GOTO statement is executed. If C is between 1 and 7, inclusive, the ON–GOTO statement is executed. If C is outside this range, a diagnostic message is displayed and control transfers back to the INPUT statement so that a valid value of C may be re-entered.

It should be apparent that the information produced by a computer is only as accurate as the data it processes. In data processing, the phrase "GIGO" (Garbage In—Garbage Out, pronounced GIG-OH) is often applied to the generation of inaccurate information from the input of invalid data. A good program always validates the data at initial input, especially when the INPUT statement is used.

In this section some definitions and techniques for data validation will be formalized so that you will write programs that are characterized by "GDGI" (Garbage Doesn't Get In) rather than "GIGO." The data validation techniques used are:

1) The reasonableness check
2) The range check
3) The code check
4) The digit check

The remainder of this section describes each of these techniques.

A **reasonableness check** ensures that data items entered from an external source are legitimate. For example, a program may check a string variable to be sure a specific number of characters is assigned to it. Or a program may check a numeric variable representing a person's age to ensure that it is positive. If the data is not reasonable, the program can request that the data be re-entered or it can note the error in a report.

The following partial program requests that the user enter a 5-character part number. If the string data item does not contain 5 characters, a diagnostic message displays, and the part number must be re-entered.

The Reasonableness Check

```
200 INPUT "FIVE CHARACTER PART NUMBER"; P$
210 IF LEN(P$) = 5 THEN 240
220     PRINT "PART NUMBER "; P$; " IN ERROR, PLEASE RE-ENTER"
230     GOTO 200
240 .
    .
    .


RUN

FIVE CHARACTER PART NUMBER? 436A
PART NUMBER 436A IN ERROR, PLEASE RE-ENTER
FIVE CHARACTER PART NUMBER? 436A2
```

An invalid part number

Line 200 requests that the user enter a part number. Line 210 tests the length of the entry using the LEN function. If the length of P$ is 5, control transfers to line 240. If the length of P$ is not 5, a diagnostic message displays and the part number must be re-entered.

A **range check** is a technique used to ensure that data items entered from an external device fall within a range of valid values. A company may have a rule that all purchase order amounts be less than $500.00. If so, then the program processing the purchase order should check the amount on the order to verify that it is greater than zero and less than $500.00. This range check is shown in the following partial program.

The Range Check

```
200 INPUT "PURCHASE ORDER AMOUNT ($0.00 < AMOUNT < $500.00)"; A
210 IF A > 0 AND A < 500 THEN 240
220     PRINT "PURCHASE ORDER AMOUNT"; A; "IS IN ERROR, PLEASE RE-ENTER"
230     GOTO 200
240 .
    .
    .


RUN

PURCHASE ORDER AMOUNT ($0.00 < AMOUNT < $500.00)? 525.45
PURCHASE ORDER AMOUNT 525.45 IS IN ERROR, PLEASE RE-ENTER
PURCHASE ORDER AMOUNT ($0.00 < AMOUNT < $500.00)? 425.45
```

An out of range purchase order amount

The range check in line 210 verifies that the value of the purchase order amount is positive and less than $500.00. If the purchase amount is out of range, line 220 displays a diagnostic message. If the purchase order amount is within the acceptable range, control transfers to line 240.

The Code Check   A **code check** ensures that codes entered from an external source are valid. In a school registration system, for example, the value for class standing may be "F" for freshman, "S" for sophomore, "J" for junior and "G" for senior. All other codes are considered invalid.

The following partial program requests that the user enter the class standing.

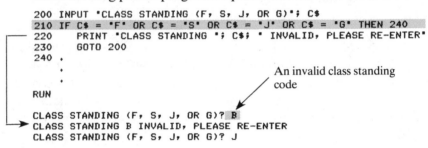

```
200 INPUT "CLASS STANDING (F, S, J, OR G)"; C$
210 IF C$ = "F" OR C$ = "S" OR C$ = "J" OR C$ = "G" THEN 240
220     PRINT "CLASS STANDING "; C$; " INVALID, PLEASE RE-ENTER"
230     GOTO 200
240 .
    .
    .
RUN

CLASS STANDING (F, S, J, OR G)? B
CLASS STANDING B INVALID, PLEASE RE-ENTER
CLASS STANDING (F, S, J, OR G)? J
```

An invalid class standing code

As illustrated in line 210, since the codes are seldom contiguous (they seldom follow one another in the alphabet or, for that matter, in sequence), the logical operator OR is normally used to form the compound condition. If C$ equals "F," "S," "J" or "G," control transfers to line 240. Any other value assigned to C$ causes the diagnostic message in line 220 to display and the class standing to be re-entered.

The Digit Check   A **digit check** verifies the assignment of a special digit to a number. A company may use a procedure whereby all part numbers of items sold begin with the digit 2. The partial program below illustrates how the string function LEFT$ can be used to accept only part numbers that begin with a 2.

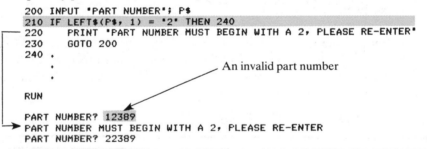

```
200 INPUT "PART NUMBER"; P$
210 IF LEFT$(P$, 1) = "2" THEN 240
220     PRINT "PART NUMBER MUST BEGIN WITH A 2, PLEASE RE-ENTER"
230     GOTO 200
240 .
    .
    .
RUN

PART NUMBER? 12389
PART NUMBER MUST BEGIN WITH A 2, PLEASE RE-ENTER
PART NUMBER? 22389
```

An invalid part number

In line 210, the expression LEFT$ (P$, 1) is equal to the first character of P$. If the first character in P$ is a "2," control transfers to line 240. If the first character is not a "2," control passes to line 220, which displays a diagnostic message. Line 230 returns control to the INPUT statement so the part number may be re-entered.

One of the most interesting uses of the digit check technique is the **check digit**. A check digit is an addition to a number that requires validation; this addition can be used to verify the rest of the digits. A check digit is effective in catching the most common mistakes made in entering a number.

For example, an elementary way to compute a check digit involves adding all the digits of the original number. From this sum, the number in the units position is retained (7 is in the units position in 27, 4 in 104, 9 in 9, and so on). This number is then appended at the end of the original number, and it is that number's check digit.

To illustrate this process, let us validate a company's part number 567432 by computing its check digit. If the digits are added,

$$5 + 6 + 7 + 4 + 3 + 2 = 27$$

the sum is 27. The number in the units position of this sum is 7, the check digit.

The part number, then, is created by appending the check digit to the number, to form 5674327. A program that requests a part number verifies it by summing the first 6 digits. If the part number 5674327 is entered as 4674327, the program will reject this number, because the sum of the 6 leftmost digits is 26, which yields a check digit of 6 instead of 7.

Program 6.2 verifies a 5-digit part number by summing the first 4 digits, develops a check digit, and compares this to the fifth digit. Lines 170 through 210 in Program 6.2 determine the individual 5 digits from the part number through the

```
100 REM PROGRAM 6.2
110 REM CHECK DIGIT VERIFICATION
120 REM ***********************
130 LET R$ = "Y"
140 WHILE R$ = "Y"
150    PRINT
160    INPUT "PART NUMBER"; P
170    LET D5 = INT(P/10000)
180    LET D4 = INT((P - D5 * 10000)/1000)
190    LET D3 = INT((P - D5 * 10000 - D4 * 1000)/100)
200    LET D2 = INT((P - D5 * 10000 - D4 * 1000 - D3 * 100)/10)
210    LET D1 = INT(P - D5 * 10000 - D4 * 1000 - D3 * 100 - D2 * 10)
220    LET S = D5 + D4 + D3 + D2
230    IF S = D1 OR S - 10 * INT(S/10) = D1 THEN 240 ELSE 260
240       PRINT "PART NUMBER IS VALID"
250    GOTO 270
260       PRINT "PART NUMBER IS INVALID - PLEASE RE-ENTER"
270    PRINT
280    INPUT "TO CONTINUE ENTER 'Y', ELSE 'N'"; R$
290    IF R$ = "Y" OR R$ = "N" THEN 320
300       PRINT "INVALID RESPONSE - PLEASE RE-ENTER"
310       GOTO 270
320 WEND
330 PRINT
340 PRINT "JOB COMPLETE"
350 END
```

PROGRAM 6.2

```
RUN


PART NUMBER? 33332
PART NUMBER IS VALID

TO CONTINUE ENTER 'Y', ELSE 'N'? Y

PART NUMBER? 98792
PART NUMBER IS INVALID - PLEASE RE-ENTER

TO CONTINUE ENTER 'Y', ELSE 'N'? Y

PART NUMBER? 98793
PART NUMBER IS VALID

TO CONTINUE ENTER 'Y', ELSE 'N'? J
INVALID RESPONSE - PLEASE RE-ENTER

TO CONTINUE ENTER 'Y', ELSE 'N'? Y

PART NUMBER? 87950
PART NUMBER IS INVALID - PLEASE RE-ENTER

TO CONTINUE ENTER 'Y', ELSE 'N'? Y

PART NUMBER? 87959
PART NUMBER IS VALID

TO CONTINUE ENTER 'Y', ELSE 'N'? N

JOB COMPLETE
```

use of the INT function. Line 220 sums the four leftmost digits. Line 230 tests to see if the sum S is equal to the rightmost digit. The first condition in line 230, $S = D1$, transfers control to line 240 when the sum S of the first four digits is less than 10 and equals the rightmost digit D1 of the part number. The second condition, $S - 10 * INT(S/10) = D1$, transfers control to line 240 when S is greater than 9 and equal to D1.

The first part number entered for Program 6.2, 33332, is valid since the sum of the first 4 digits is 12, which yields a check digit of 2. On the other hand, the second part number, 98792, is invalid because the sum of the first 4 digits is 33, which yields a check digit of 3, not 2.

Although the check digit technique illustrated in Program 6.2 will not catch all input errors, it is one of the more common techniques used in business data processing. The number of invalid entries—made, for example, by reversing the digits—can be reduced considerably by using more sophisticated algorithms than the simple computation of the sum of the first four digits (see Programming Exercise 13 at the end of this chapter).

**6.4
THE FOR AND
NEXT
STATEMENTS**

The FOR and NEXT statements make it possible in BASIC to execute a section of a program repeatedly, with automatic changes in the value of a variable between repetitions.

In previous sections of this chapter as well as in Chapter 5, the WHILE and WEND statements were used to implement a loop structure that executed a section of a program repeatedly. Whenever a While loop is developed to execute a **counter-controlled loop**, to execute a specified number of times, the coding requires statements for initializing, incrementing and testing of a counter. Any While loop involving this type of coding may be rewritten as a **For loop** using the FOR and NEXT statements and still perform the same tasks. The FOR and NEXT statements provide for the construction of counter-controlled loops.

**The While Loop
Versus the For Loop**

To illustrate the similarity between the While loop and For loop, consider Programs 6.3 and 6.4. Both programs compute the sum of the integers from 1 to 10.

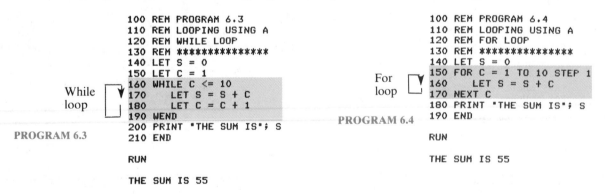

```
100 REM PROGRAM 6.3
110 REM LOOPING USING A
120 REM WHILE LOOP
130 REM ***************
140 LET S = 0
150 LET C = 1
160 WHILE C <= 10
170     LET S = S + C
180     LET C = C + 1
190 WEND
200 PRINT "THE SUM IS"; S
210 END

RUN

THE SUM IS 55
```

```
100 REM PROGRAM 6.4
110 REM LOOPING USING A
120 REM FOR LOOP
130 REM **************
140 LET S = 0
150 FOR C = 1 TO 10 STEP 1
160     LET S = S + C
170 NEXT C
180 PRINT "THE SUM IS"; S
190 END

RUN

THE SUM IS 55
```

PROGRAM 6.3

PROGRAM 6.4

Program 6.3 uses the While loop. Lines 140 and 150 initialize the running total S to 0 and the counter C to 1. Line 160 tests to determine if the value of C is less than or equal to 10. If the condition is true, the running total S is incremented by the counter C, the counter C is incremented by 1 before control transfers back to line 160. When the condition is false, the program terminates the loop and line 200 displays the running total S.

Program 6.4 incorporates the FOR and NEXT statements to define the For loop (lines 150 through 170). Read through Program 6.4 carefully and note how compact it is and how superior it is to Program 6.3. Using a single FOR statement, as in line 150 of Program 6.4, we can delete two statements (lines 150 and 180) in Program 6.3.

The execution of the For Loop in Program 6.4 involves the following:

The Execution of a For Loop

1) When the FOR statement is executed for the first time, the For loop becomes "active" and C is set equal to 1.

2) The statements in the For loop, in this case line 160, are executed.

3) Control returns to the FOR statement where the value of C is incremented by value of 1 following the keyword STEP.

4) If the value of C is less than or equal to 10, execution of the For loop continues.

5) If the value of C is greater than 10, control transfers to the statement (line 180) following the NEXT C statement.

The general forms of the FOR and NEXT statements are given in Tables 6.4 and 6.5.

TABLE 6.4   The FOR Statement

General Form:	FOR k = m_1 TO m_2 STEP m_3 *or* FOR k = m_1 TO m_2 where k is a simple numeric variable called the **control variable**, and m_1, m_2, and m_3 are each numeric expressions, called, respectively, the **initial parameter**, the **limit parameter**, and the **increment parameter**. In the absence of the keyword STEP m_3, the value of the increment is 1.
Purpose:	Causes the statements between the FOR and NEXT statements to be executed repeatedly until the value of k exceeds m_2. When k exceeds m_2, control transfers to the line just after the corresponding NEXT statement.

Examples:	```250 FOR X = 1 TO 20```
	```350 FOR A = 5 TO 15 STEP 2```
	```400 FOR C = 10 TO -5 STEP -3```
	```450 FOR Y = 1 TO 10 STEP 0.1```
	```500 FOR T = A TO B STEP C```
	```550 FOR S = A + 5 TO C/D STEP F * B```

A **control variable** is a variable used in FOR and NEXT statements. The control variable is the variable to the left of the equal sign in FOR statements—it appears between the keyword FOR and the equal sign. The control variable also appears after the keyword NEXT in NEXT statements. **Parameter** means "value" in this context, but its use is restricted here to special values—those of the initial, limit and increment values—which appear to the right of the equal sign in FOR statements.

TABLE 6.5   The NEXT Statement

General Form:	NEXT k where k is the same variable as the control variable in the corresponding FOR statement.
Purpose:	Identifies the end of a For loop.
Examples:	```300 NEXT X``` ```380 NEXT A```

The terminology used to describe the FOR statement is shown below:

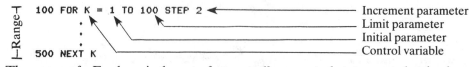

```
100 FOR K = 1 TO 100 STEP 2  ←———————————— Increment parameter
     .                                      ←——— Limit parameter
     .                                      ←——— Initial parameter
500 NEXT K                                  ←——— Control variable
```

The **range** of a For loop is the set of repeatedly executed statements beginning with the FOR statement and continuing up to and including the NEXT statement with the same control variable.

Flowchart Representation of a For Loop

The flowchart representation for a For loop corresponds to a Do-While structure (see Figure 6.2). In the first process symbol, the control variable k is assigned the initial parameter (or value) m_1. If the condition is true, the loop is terminated and control transfers to the statement following the Do-While structure.

If the condition is false, control passes into the body of the For loop. After the statements in the For loop are executed, the control variable k is incremented by the increment parameter m_3, and control transfers back up to the decision symbol again to test if the control variable k exceeds the limit parameter m_2.

Figure 6.3 illustrates a flowchart that corresponds to Program 6.4.

General Form of For Loop
FOR k = m_1 TO m_2 STEP m_3

⋮   statements within the For loop

NEXT k

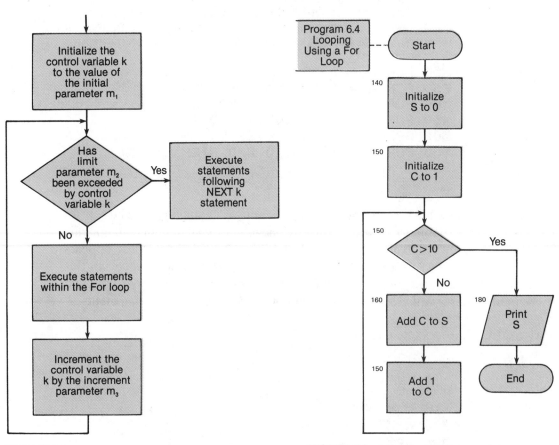

FIGURE 6.2   General form and flowchart representation for a For loop.

FIGURE 6.3   A flowchart for Program 6.4.

The examples presented in Table 6.3 indicate that the parameters of a FOR statement can take on a variety of representations. This section is divided into subsections which illustrate these representations.

Valid Parameters in the FOR Statement

Stepping by 1. Many applications call for incrementing or **stepping** the control variable **by 1** each time the For loop is executed. You may write a FOR statement like this as:

```
170 FOR R = 1 TO 12 STEP 1
```

or

```
170 FOR R = 1 TO 12
```

Program 6.5 computes the amount of an investment A, compounded annually, for interest rate R between 1 and 12 percent, inclusive.

Line 130 in Program 6.5 requests the operator to enter the principal P. Line 170 activates the For loop and assigns R a value of 1 (1%). Line 180 computes the amount of the investment, and line 190 displays the interest rate and amount. The control variable R is incremented by 1, and the loop is executed repeatedly until the control variable exceeds 12. When this occurs, control transfers to line 210.

The statements in the For loop, except for the first and last, should be indented by three spaces for the purposes of readability (see lines 180 and 190). This style allows you to scan a For loop quickly, and it simplifies the debugging effort.

```
100 REM PROGRAM 6.5
110 REM STEPPING BY 1 IN A FOR STATEMENT
120 REM *******************************
130 INPUT "INVESTMENT"; P
140 PRINT
150 PRINT    "RATE        AMOUNT"
160 LET A$ = "  ##     ##,###.##"
170 FOR R = 1 TO 12
180    LET A = P * (1 + R/100)
190    PRINT USING A$; R, A
200 NEXT R
210 PRINT "JOB COMPLETE"
220 END
```

Loop → (lines 170–200)

PROGRAM 6.5

```
RUN

INVESTMENT? 500

RATE        AMOUNT
  1         505.00
  2         510.00
  3         515.00
  4         520.00
  5         525.00
  6         530.00
  7         535.00
  8         540.00
  9         545.00
 10         550.00
 11         555.00
 12         560.00
JOB COMPLETE
```

```
100 REM PROGRAM 6.6
110 REM STEPPING BY OTHER THAN 1
115 REM IN A FOR STATEMENT
120 REM ************************
130 INPUT "INVESTMENT"; P
140 PRINT
150 PRINT    "RATE        AMOUNT"
160 LET A$ = "  ##     ##,###.##"
170 FOR R = 1 TO 12 STEP 3
180    LET A = P*(1 + R/100)
190    PRINT USING A$; R, A
200 NEXT R
210 PRINT "JOB COMPLETE"
220 END
```

PROGRAM 6.6

```
RUN

INVESTMENT? 1000

RATE        AMOUNT
  1        1,010.00
  4        1,040.00
  7        1,070.00
 10        1,100.00
JOB COMPLETE
```

Stepping by a Value Other Than 1. Some applications call for the control variable to be incremented by a value other than 1. Program 6.6 is similar to Program 6.5, but it computes the amount of an investment, compounded annually, for interest rates of 1%, 4%, 7% and 10%. The loop terminates when the control variable R becomes 13, since this exceeds the value of the limit parameter, 12.

Initializing the Control Variable to a Value Other Than 1.   It is not necessary to initialize the control variable to 1. Program 6.7 generates a report that computes the amount of an investment compounded annually for even integer interest rates between 8 and 16 percent, inclusive.

Some applications may call for the initialization of the control variable to zero or some negative value. For example, the statements

```
500 FOR X = 0 TO 10
        .
        .
        .
600 NEXT X
```
and
```
700 FOR Y = -6 TO 12
        .
        .
        .
900 NEXT Y
```

are both valid. Line 500 will cause the corresponding For loop to execute 11 times. Line 700 will cause the For loop to execute 19 times.

```
100 REM PROGRAM 6.7
110 REM STARTING AT A VALUE OTHER THAN 1
115 REM IN A FOR STATEMENT
120 REM ******************************
130 INPUT "INVESTMENT"; P
140 PRINT
150 PRINT    "RATE       AMOUNT"
160 LET A$ = "  ##      ##,###.##"
170 FOR R = 8 TO 16 STEP 2
180    LET A = P * (1 + R/100)
190    PRINT USING A$; R, A
200 NEXT R
210 PRINT "JOB COMPLETE"
220 END
```
PROGRAM 6.7

```
RUN

INVESTMENT? 2000

RATE       AMOUNT
  8       2,160.00
 10       2,200.00
 12       2,240.00
 14       2,280.00
 16       2,320.00
JOB COMPLETE
```

```
100 REM PROGRAM 6.8
110 REM DECIMAL FRACTION PARAMETERS
115 REM IN A FOR STATEMENT
120 REM ***************************
130 INPUT "INVESTMENT"; P
140 PRINT
150 PRINT    "RATE       AMOUNT"
160 LET A$ = "##.#      ##,###.##"
170 FOR R = 11.5 TO 12.5 STEP 0.1
180    LET A = P * (1 + R/100)
190    PRINT USING A$; R, A
200 NEXT R
210 PRINT "JOB COMPLETE"
220 END
```
PROGRAM 6.8

```
RUN

INVESTMENT? 1500

RATE       AMOUNT
11.5      1,672.50
11.6      1,674.00
11.7      1,675.50
11.8      1,677.00
11.9      1,678.50
12.0      1,680.00
12.1      1,681.50
12.2      1,683.00
12.3      1,684.50
12.4      1,686.00
12.5      1,687.50
JOB COMPLETE
```

Decimal Fraction Parameters in a FOR Statement. The parameters in a FOR statement can be decimal fraction numbers. Program 6.8 computes the amount of an investment compounded annually for interest rates between 11.5 and 12.5 percent, inclusive, in increments of one-tenth of a percent.

Be careful with decimal fraction parameters, since the computer may not always store the exact binary representation of a decimal number. Stepping by a decimal number can, in some instances, result in one less or one more time through the loop than you expect.

Negative Parameters in a FOR **Statement.** The parameters in a FOR statement may be negative. Program 6.9 generates a report in which the interest rates are decremented from 8 to 0 percent. the negative value step in the FOR statement is necessary to be sure that the control variable attains the value assigned to the limit parameter.

The following FOR statement creates an infinite loop (an endless loop) because the increment parameter would never allow the value of the control variable to exceed that of the limit parameter.

Invalid⟶ 500 FOR C = 15 TO 6 STEP 2

Variable Parameters in a FOR **Statement.** Program 6.10 shows that the parameters in a FOR statement can be variables as well as numeric constants. Lines 130 through 150 request the user to enter the initial, terminal and increment parameters. Many people make mistakes with the parameters of FOR statements, and many of these mistakes cause endless loops. You are likely to do the same, so make a point of checking to be sure that R1, R2 and S have values that allow the control variable to reach the value of the limit parameter.

```
100 REM PROGRAM 6.9
110 REM NEGATIVE PARAMETERS IN A FOR STATEMENT
120 REM ***************************************
130 INPUT "INVESTMENT"; P
140 PRINT
150 PRINT    "RATE       AMOUNT"
160 LET A$ = "##.#     ##,###.##"
170 FOR R = 8 TO 0 STEP -1
180    LET A = P * (1 + R/100)
190    PRINT USING A$; R, A
200 NEXT R
210 PRINT "JOB COMPLETE"
220 END                                      PROGRAM 6.9
```

```
RUN

INVESTMENT? 2500

RATE       AMOUNT
 8.0      2,700.00
 7.0      2,675.00
 6.0      2,650.00
 5.0      2,625.00
 4.0      2,600.00
 3.0      2,575.00
 2.0      2,550.00
 1.0      2,525.00
 0.0      2,500.00
JOB COMPLETE
```

```
100 REM PROGRAM 6.10
110 REM VARIABLE PARAMETERS IN A FOR STATEMENT
120 REM *****************************************
130 INPUT "INITIAL INTEREST RATE (IN PERCENT)"; R1
140 INPUT "LIMIT INTEREST RATE (IN PERCENT)"; R2
150 INPUT "INTEREST RATE INCREMENT (IN PERCENT)"; S
160 INPUT "INVESTMENT"; P
170 PRINT
180 PRINT    "RATE       AMOUNT"
190 LET A$ = "##.#     ##,###.##"
200 FOR R = R1 TO R2 STEP S
210    LET A = P * (1 + R/100)
220    PRINT USING A$; R, A
230 NEXT R
240 PRINT "JOB COMPLETE"
250 END                                      PROGRAM 6.10
```

```
RUN

INITIAL INTEREST RATE (IN PERCENT)? 10
LIMIT INTEREST RATE (IN PERCENT)? 12.5
INTEREST RATE INCREMENT (IN PERCENT)? 0.5
INVESTMENT? 3000

RATE       AMOUNT
10.0      3,300.00
10.5      3,315.00
11.0      3,330.00
11.5      3,345.00
12.0      3,360.00
12.5      3,375.00
JOB COMPLETE
```

Expressions as Parameters in a FOR **Statement.** The parameters in a FOR statement may be complex numeric expressions. For example, the following FOR statements are valid:

```
500 FOR X = A * B TO S^T STEP C * 2
        .
        .
        .
550 NEXT X

600 FOR Y = (A + B)/C TO P * (F - G)^C STEP 5 * V
        .
        .
        .
800 NEXT Y
```

Again, care must be taken to ensure that the variables are assigned logically correct values so that the For loop terminates correctly. If C is zero, what do you think happens in line 500 and line 600 above?

Branching Within a For Loop

You may branch forward or backward within a For loop. Quite often, branching forward involves bypassing the remaining statements in the For loop by branching to the NEXT statement. Program 6.11 reads from a DATA statement (line 220) the number of data items a For loop will process. After line 150 reads the first data item, line 160 tests if X is less than zero. If the condition is true, control passes to line 170, otherwise control transfers to the NEXT statement, bypassing lines 170 and 180. In other words, the counter S is incremented by 1 and the value of X is displayed only if X is negative. When the value of I exceeds the value of L, control automatically transfers to line 200.

```
100 REM PROGRAM 6.11
110 REM BYPASSING STATEMENTS IN A FOR LOOP
120 REM ***********************************
125 LET S = 0
130 READ L
140 FOR I = 1 TO L
150     READ X
160     IF X < 0 THEN 170 ELSE 190
170         LET S = S + 1
180         PRINT X; "IS NEGATIVE"
190 NEXT I
200 PRINT
210 PRINT "THE NUMBER OF NEGATIVE DATA ITEMS IS"; S
220 DATA 7
230 DATA 5, -3, -2, 0, 4, -6, 3
240 END

RUN

-3 IS NEGATIVE
-2 IS NEGATIVE
-6 IS NEGATIVE

THE NUMBER OF NEGATIVE DATA ITEMS IS 3
```

PROGRAM 6.11

Normal and Transferred Exits from a For Loop

There are two ways control can transfer outside the range of a For loop. The **normal exit** occurs when the FOR statement is satisfied, at the completion of the number of executions of the range specified by the parameters m_1, m_2 and m_3 (see Program 6.4). When this happens, control passes to the statement following the NEXT statement. At this time, the value of the control variable is greater than the limit parameter, and the value of the control variable is available for any other purpose or computation.

Control can also get outside the range of a For loop by a transfer or control statement, like an IF or GOTO statement. Control transferred outside the range of a For loop before the FOR statement is satisfied is a **transferred exit**. When this happens, the value of the control variable retains its current value, and this value is also available for any other purpose or computation.

Program 6.12 illustrates the use of a decision statement to transfer control outside the For loop to line 190 whenever L or W is less than or equal to zero. The control variable B retains its value when the transfer is complete.

```
100 REM PROGRAM 6.12
110 REM TRANSFERRED EXIT FROM A FOR LOOP
120 REM ********************************
130 FOR B = 1 TO 5
140     READ L, W
150     IF L <= 0 OR W <= 0 THEN 190
160         PRINT B, L, W, L * W
170 NEXT B
180 GOTO 220
190 PRINT "NEGATIVE NUMBER IN DATA SET";
200 PRINT B; "-L ="; L; "AND W ="; W
210 DATA 5, 6, 4, 3, -1, 6, 8, 2, 4, 3
220 END
```

PROGRAM 6.12

```
RUN

1               5               6               30
2               4               3               12
NEGATIVE NUMBER IN DATA SET 3 - L =-1 AND W = 6
```

Initial Entry into a For Loop

Control must not transfer into the range of a For loop from any statement outside its range. You cannot use a GOTO or an IF statement to transfer into the range of a For loop without executing the FOR statement itself.

The following partial program is invalid, since control is transferred into the range of a For loop, which means that the FOR statement is not executed to define the control variable I correctly.

```
200 GOTO 410
    .
    .
    .
400 FOR I = 1 TO 50
410     PRINT I
420 NEXT I
```
Invalid

Redefinition of the Control Variable and Parameters in a For Loop

No statement within the range of a For loop may alter or redefine the values of control variable k or the parameters m_1, m_2 and m_3 of a FOR statement. The control variable and parameters may be used in any way that does not alter their value.

The following partial program is invalid since the control variable I is redefined.

```
300 FOR I = 1 TO 100 STEP 2
    .
    .
    .
350     LET I = 3
    .
    .
    .
400 NEXT I
```
Invalid

Listed below are rules that summarize the preceding material on the FOR and NEXT statements.

NEXT **Rule 1:** The NEXT statement must have a higher line number than its corresponding FOR statement.

FOR **Rule 1:** The FOR statement may be located anywhere before the corresponding NEXT statement.

FOR **Rule 2:** The value of the increment parameter must not be zero.

FOR **Rule 3:** A valid initial entry into a For loop can only be accomplished by transferring control to the FOR statement.

FOR **Rule 4:** A normal exit from a For loop leaves the current value of the control variable greater than the limit parameter.

FOR **Rule 5:** A transferred exit from a For loop leaves the current value of the control variable preserved without change.

FOR **Rule 6:** No statement located in the range of a For loop may be used to change the value of the control variable or the initial, limit and increment parameter values.

Determining the Number of Iterations in a For Loop

The number of repetitions or iterations specified by a FOR statement with the general parameters m_1, m_2 and m_3 may be computed using the following formula:

$$\text{No. of Iterations} = \frac{m_2 - m_1}{m_3} + 1$$

where the ratio is performed in integer arithmetic so that the quotient is truncated to the next lowest integer.

How many iterations are performed by the following For loop?

```
400 FOR I = -73 TO 987 STEP 7
          .
          .
          .
800 NEXT I
```

Using the formula, the number of iterations is:

$$\frac{987 - (-73)}{7} + 1$$

or $151 + 1 = 152$

Note that the initial quotient was 151.42, but the decimal fraction 0.42 was truncated.

Nested For Loops

When two or more For loops are used so that the statements of one For loop lie within the range of another For loop, the loops are said to be **nested** or embedded. Furthermore, the outer For loop may be nested in the range of still another For loop, and so on.

Program 6.13 utilizes two nested For loops. The inner For loop, formed by lines 150 through 170, is written so that all the statements in its range also lie within the range of the outer For loop, lines 130 through 190.

When line 130 is executed, the outer For loop becomes active. The control variable X is set to 1 and line 140 displays that value. When line 150 is executed, the inner For loop becomes active. The control variable Y is set to 1 and line 160 displays the values of both X and Y. With X equal to 1, control remains within the inner loop, which is executed three times, until Y exceeds 3. At this point, the inner loop is satisfied and control passes to the outer For loop, which executes line 180.

Control then passes to line 130, where the control variable X is incremented by 1 to become 2. After line 140 displays the new value of X, line 150 is executed and the inner For loop becomes active again. The control variable Y is initialized to 1 and the process repeats itself.

When the outer loop is satisfied, control passes to line 200. In Program 6.13, the outer For loop executes a total of 4 times and the inner For loop executes a total of 3 * 4 or 12 times.

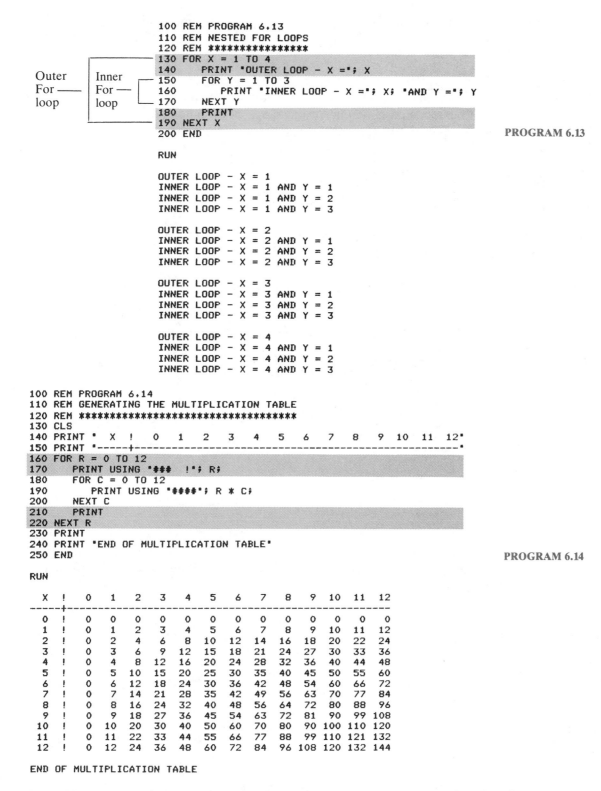

```
                    100 REM PROGRAM 6.13
                    110 REM NESTED FOR LOOPS
                    120 REM ****************
                    130 FOR X = 1 TO 4
                    140    PRINT "OUTER LOOP - X ="; X
                    150    FOR Y = 1 TO 3
                    160       PRINT "INNER LOOP - X ="; X; "AND Y ="; Y
                    170    NEXT Y
                    180    PRINT
                    190 NEXT X
                    200 END
```

Outer For loop / Inner For loop

PROGRAM 6.13

```
RUN

OUTER LOOP - X = 1
INNER LOOP - X = 1 AND Y = 1
INNER LOOP - X = 1 AND Y = 2
INNER LOOP - X = 1 AND Y = 3

OUTER LOOP - X = 2
INNER LOOP - X = 2 AND Y = 1
INNER LOOP - X = 2 AND Y = 2
INNER LOOP - X = 2 AND Y = 3

OUTER LOOP - X = 3
INNER LOOP - X = 3 AND Y = 1
INNER LOOP - X = 3 AND Y = 2
INNER LOOP - X = 3 AND Y = 3

OUTER LOOP - X = 4
INNER LOOP - X = 4 AND Y = 1
INNER LOOP - X = 4 AND Y = 2
INNER LOOP - X = 4 AND Y = 3
```

```
100 REM PROGRAM 6.14
110 REM GENERATING THE MULTIPLICATION TABLE
120 REM *********************************
130 CLS
140 PRINT "  X !  0   1   2   3   4   5   6   7   8   9  10  11  12"
150 PRINT "-----+-------------------------------------------------------"
160 FOR R = 0 TO 12
170    PRINT USING "###  !"; R;
180    FOR C = 0 TO 12
190       PRINT USING "####"; R * C;
200    NEXT C
210    PRINT
220 NEXT R
230 PRINT
240 PRINT "END OF MULTIPLICATION TABLE"
250 END
```

PROGRAM 6.14

```
RUN

  X !  0   1   2   3   4   5   6   7   8   9  10  11  12
-----+-------------------------------------------------------
  0 !  0   0   0   0   0   0   0   0   0   0   0   0   0
  1 !  0   1   2   3   4   5   6   7   8   9  10  11  12
  2 !  0   2   4   6   8  10  12  14  16  18  20  22  24
  3 !  0   3   6   9  12  15  18  21  24  27  30  33  36
  4 !  0   4   8  12  16  20  24  28  32  36  40  44  48
  5 !  0   5  10  15  20  25  30  35  40  45  50  55  60
  6 !  0   6  12  18  24  30  36  42  48  54  60  66  72
  7 !  0   7  14  21  28  35  42  49  56  63  70  77  84
  8 !  0   8  16  24  32  40  48  56  64  72  80  88  96
  9 !  0   9  18  27  36  45  54  63  72  81  90  99 108
 10 !  0  10  20  30  40  50  60  70  80  90 100 110 120
 11 !  0  11  22  33  44  55  66  77  88  99 110 121 132
 12 !  0  12  24  36  48  60  72  84  96 108 120 132 144

END OF MULTIPLICATION TABLE
```

Program 6.14 generates the multiplication table. Each time the control variable in the outer For loop (lines 160 through 220) is assigned a new value, the inner For loop (lines 180 through 200) computes and displays one row of the table. The PRINT USING statements in lines 170 and 190 end with the semicolon separator. From Chapter 4 recall that when a PRINT statement ends with a semicolon, the cursor remains on that same line. Each time the inner loop is satisfied, the PRINT statement in line 210 prints blanks and moves the cursor to the beginning of the next line.

Valid and Invalid Nests of For Loops

When nesting occurs, all statements in the range of the inner For loop must also be in the range of the outer For loop. The situation in which the range of an inner For loop extends past the end of the range of an outer For loop is prohibited. An example of this kind of invalid nest of For loops is shown below:

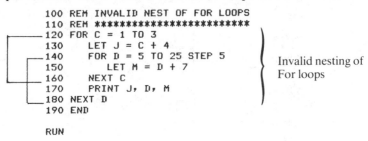

```
100 REM INVALID NEST OF FOR LOOPS
110 REM ************************
120 FOR C = 1 TO 3
130     LET J = C + 4
140     FOR D = 5 TO 25 STEP 5        Invalid nesting of
150         LET M = D + 7             For loops
160     NEXT C
170     PRINT J, D, M
180 NEXT D
190 END

RUN

---INVALID NESTING AT LINE 180
```

The inner loop which begins at line 140 extends past the NEXT statement that corresponds to the outer loop. The invalid nest of For loops may be rewritten, validly, as:

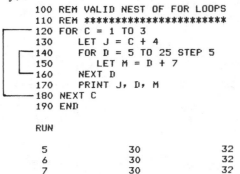

```
100 REM VALID NEST OF FOR LOOPS
110 REM **********************
120 FOR C = 1 TO 3
130     LET J = C + 4
140     FOR D = 5 TO 25 STEP 5
150         LET M = D + 7
160     NEXT D
170     PRINT J, D, M
180 NEXT C
190 END

RUN

5               30              32
6               30              32
7               30              32
```

When one For loop is nested within another, the name of the control variable for each For loop must be different. Figure 6.4 illustrates proper nesting of For loops and the naming of control variables.

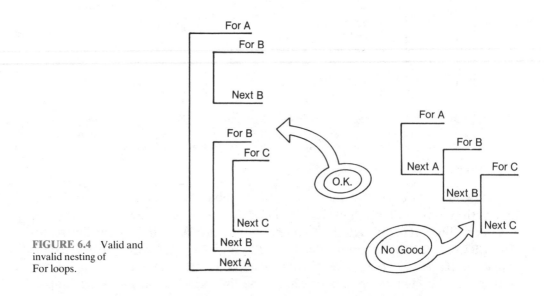

FIGURE 6.4   Valid and invalid nesting of For loops.

The usefulness of the FOR and NEXT statements for looping purposes should be apparent from the examples and illustrations presented thus far. However, you will see an even greater use for them in applications involving the manipulation of arrays, which are discussed in the next chapter. The material in this section can be summarized in the following rules:

> FOR **Rule 7:** If the range of a For loop includes another For loop, all statements in the range of the inner For loop must also be within the range of the outer For loop.

> FOR **Rule 8:** When one For loop is within another, the name of the control variable for each For loop must be different.

Programming Case Study 12: Determining the Effective Rates of Interest Using Nested For Loops

Most financial institutions quote a nominal rate of interest—that is, an annual interest rate that is compounded a number of times per year. For example, if a principal of $1.00 were invested for one year at 6%, compounded annually, the actual interest earned would be 6¢. However, if the rate quoted were 6% compounded semiannually, the interest for the first half year would be 3¢. The new principal would be $1.03 and the interest earned for the second half year would be 1.03 * .03 = 3.09¢. The actual interest earned annually would be 6.09¢. In this case, the nominal rate is 6%. The corresponding 6.09% is called the effective or true rate. If R represents the effective rate, C the number of conversions per year, and J the nominal rate, then the effective rate can be derived from the following formula:

$$R = \left(1 + \frac{J}{C}\right)^C - 1$$

Problem

The WESAVU National Bank wants a program that requests the loan officer to enter a range of nominal rates and an increment value. For each nominal rate, compute the effective rate for an investment compounded 2, 4, 6, 8, 10 and 12 times per year, as shown below.

Nominal Rate	Effective Rates Compounded					
	2	4	6	8	10	12
5.5%	—	—	—	—	—	—
6.5%	—	—	—	—	—	—
7.5%	—	—	—	—	—	—
8.5%	—	—	—	—	—	—
9.5%	—	—	—	—	—	—

Validate the data as follows:

   1) The initial nominal rate must be greater than zero and less than or equal to 25%.

   2) The limit nominal rate must be greater than the initial nominal rate and less than or equal to 25%.

   3) The increment value must be greater than zero.

An analysis of the problem, a flowchart, and a program follow.

Program Tasks

1) Clear the screen and display the report title.

2) Enter and validate the initial nominal rate I, limit nominal rate T and increment value S.

3) Display appropriate column headings.

4) Using nested For loops, generate and display the table entries. The outer For loop should display the nominal rate J for each row. The inner For loop should compute and display the effective rate R for investments compounded 2, 4, 6, 8, 10 and 12 times per year for the corresponding nominal rate.

5) The outer For loop should consist of a control variable, like J, and the parameters I, T, and S. The value of J should display as the first entry of each line within this loop. The PRINT statement that displays J should terminate with a semicolon to display the corresponding effective rates on the same line.

6) The inner For loop should consist of a control variable, like C, and the parameters of 2, 12 and 2. The effective rate R is computed and displayed for each conversion within this loop. The following LET statement computes the effective rate

$$LET\ R = 100 * ((1 + (J/100)/C) \wedge C - 1)$$

The variable J is divided by 100 to change the nominal rate from percent to a decimal fraction. The PRINT statement that displays the effective rate should also terminate with a semicolon to display the effective rates on the same line.

7) When the inner For loop is satisfied, use a PRINT statement with a null list to move the cursor to the beginning of the next line.

8) The message "Table Complete" should display before the program terminates.

```
100 REM PROGRAM 6.15
110 REM DETERMINING THE EFFECTIVE RATES OF INTEREST
120 REM J = NOMINAL RATE   C = NO. OF CONVERSIONS   S = INCREMENT VALUE
130 REM ***********************************************************
140 CLS
150 PRINT "<--------NOMINAL RATE TO EFFECTIVE RATE CONVERSION--------->"
160 PRINT
170 PRINT "ENTER INITIAL NOMINAL RATE"
180 INPUT "BETWEEN 0 AND 25 INCLUSIVE"; I
190 IF I >= 0 AND I <= 25 THEN 220
200    PRINT "INITIAL VALUE OUTSIDE RANGE - PLEASE"
210    GOTO 160
220 PRINT
230 PRINT "ENTER LIMIT NOMINAL RATE BETWEEN"; I
240 INPUT "AND 25 INCLUSIVE"; T
250 IF T > I AND T <= 25 THEN 280
260    PRINT "LIMIT VALUE OUTSIDE RANGE - PLEASE"
270    GOTO 220
280 PRINT
290 INPUT "ENTER POSITIVE INCREMENT VALUE"; S
300 IF S > 0 THEN 330
310    PRINT "INCREMENT VALUE NOT GREATER THAN ZERO - PLEASE"
320    GOTO 280
330 PRINT
340 PRINT TAB(25); "EFFECTIVE RATES COMPOUNDED"
350 PRINT TAB(16); "<--------------------------------------------->"
360 PRINT "NOMINAL RATE      2       4       6       8       10       12"
370 PRINT "---------------   --------------------------------------------"
380 FOR J = I TO T STEP S
390    PRINT USING " ###.##%      "; J;
400    FOR C = 2 TO 12 STEP 2
410       LET R = 100 * ((1 + (J/100)/C)^C - 1)
420       PRINT USING " ###.###"; R;
430    NEXT C
440    PRINT
450 NEXT J
460 PRINT
470 PRINT "TABLE COMPLETE"
480 END

RUN
```

PROGRAM 6.15

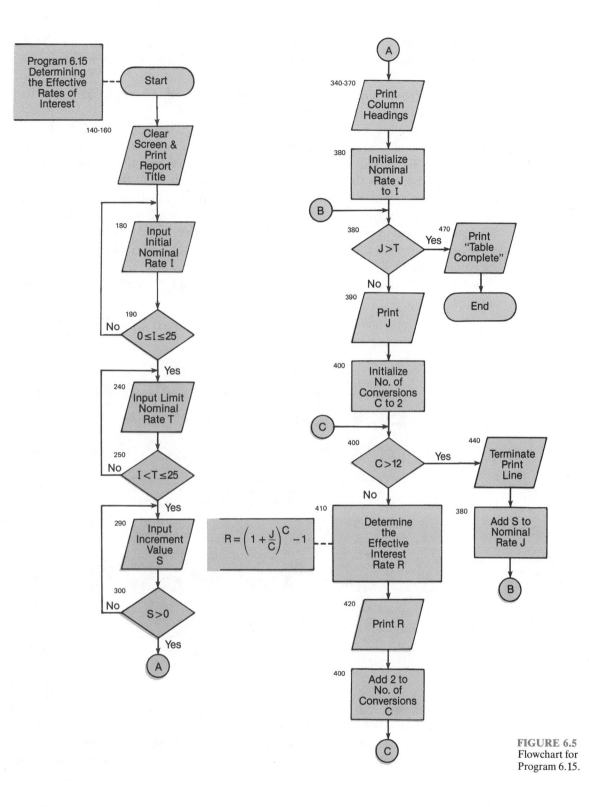

FIGURE 6.5
Flowchart for
Program 6.15.

Here is a summary of how the program tasks and the flowchart in Figure 6.5 relate to Program 6.15.

1) Lines 140 and 150 clear the screen and display the report title.

2) Lines 170 through 210 request and validate the initial nominal rate I. The range test in line 190 transfers control to line 220 when the value of I is greater than or equal to zero and less than or equal to 25. If the value of I is outside this range, a diagnostic message displays and control transfers back to line 160.

3) Lines 220 through 270 request and validate the limit nominal rate T. Line 230 illustrates how a limit previously entered via an INPUT statement may be displayed.

4) Lines 280 through 320 request and validate the increment value S. The test in line 300 ensures that S is greater than zero.

5) The nested For loops in lines 380 through 450 determine and display the table entries. Line 380 activates the outer loop and initializes J to the value of I (5.5%). Line 390 displays the value of J. Line 400 activates the inner loop, which computes and displays the 6 effective rates that correspond to the current value of J. When the inner loop is satisfied, line 440 terminates the displayed line and moves the cursor to the beginning of the next line of the report. Control then returns to the FOR statement in line 380, and J is incremented by S to 6.5%. The nested loops are then executed for the new nominal rate. This process continues until J exceeds the value of T (9.5%).

6) Line 470 displays the message TABLE COMPLETE and the program terminates.

The results displayed from the execution of Program 6.15 are shown in Figure 6.6 for nominal rates between 5.5% to 9.5%.

```
<--------NOMINAL RATE TO EFFECTIVE RATE CONVERSION-------->

ENTER INITIAL NOMINAL RATE
BETWEEN 0 AND 25 INCLUSIVE? 5.5

ENTER LIMIT NOMINAL RATE BETWEEN 5.5
AND 25 INCLUSIVE? 9.5

ENTER POSITIVE INCREMENT VALUE? 1

                        EFFECTIVE RATES COMPOUNDED
                  <-------------------------------------------->
NOMINAL RATE       2       4       6       8      10      12
----------------------------------------------------------------
     5.50%       5.576   5.614   5.627   5.634   5.638   5.640
     6.50%       6.606   6.660   6.679   6.688   6.693   6.697
     7.50%       7.641   7.714   7.738   7.751   7.758   7.763
     8.50%       8.681   8.775   8.807   8.823   8.832   8.839
     9.50%       9.726   9.844   9.884   9.904   9.916   9.924

TABLE COMPLETE
```

FIGURE 6.6 The display from the execution of Program 6.15.

6.5 INTERNAL SUBROUTINES (MODULES)

In this section, internal **subroutines** are presented. A subroutine is a *group of statements* within a BASIC program associated with a single programming task. Internal subroutines, or **modules**, as they can also be called, are useful in solving large, complex problems, because they allow a problem to be subdivided into smaller and more manageable subproblems, which can then be solved with appropriate subroutines.

The idea of solving a large problem by dividing it into smaller subproblems is not new. In his *Discourse on Method*, some three hundred years before the first computer was built, René Descartes made this very same point. In essence, he says that we can understand the truth of a problem if we:

1) Divide each of the difficulties into as many parts as possible.

2) Think in an orderly fashion, beginning with the things which are simplest and easiest to understand, and gradually work toward the more complex.

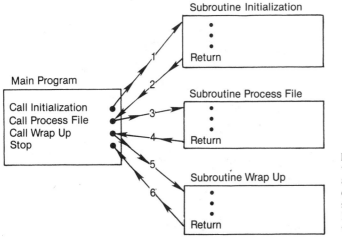

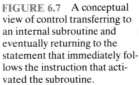

FIGURE 6.7   A conceptual view of control transferring to an internal subroutine and eventually returning to the statement that immediately follows the instruction that activated the subroutine.

An internal subroutine is executed only if referenced, **called**, by an explicit instruction from some other part of the program, as illustrated in Figure 6.7. Following execution of the internal subroutine, control passes back to the statement immediately following the instruction that activated the subroutine.

A subroutine may be called by either a GOSUB or an ON-GOSUB statement. The GOSUB statement is similar to the GOTO statement in that the keyword GOSUB is immediately followed by a line number to which control is transferred. The ON-GOSUB statement is similar to the ON-GOTO in that a series of line numbers follow the keyword GOSUB, and the system selects which line to transfer control based on the integer value of the numeric expression between the keywords ON and GOSUB. Hence, the GOSUB and RETURN statements allow for subroutine calls, and the ON-GOSUB and RETURN statements allow for *selected* subroutine calls. The last statement executed in a subroutine must be the RETURN statement. A subroutine, therefore, can only exit through a RETURN statement.

The major difference between a GOSUB and a GOTO statement, or between an ON-GOSUB and an ON-GOTO statement, lies in the execution of a subroutine. For a GOSUB or ON-GOSUB,

The GOSUB, ON-GOSUB and RETURN **Statements**

1) The Main program calls or transfers control to the subroutine.

2) The called subroutine executes and performs a particular or recurring task for the Main program.

3) The RETURN statement of the subroutine transfers control back to the statement immediately following the GOSUB or ON-GOSUB which referenced the subroutine.

The general forms for the GOSUB, ON-GOSUB and RETURN statements are shown in Tables 6.6, 6.7 and 6.8.

TABLE 6.6   **The GOSUB Statement**

General Form:	GOSUB line number where the line number represents the first line of a subroutine.
Purpose:	Causes control to transfer to the subroutine represented by the specified line number. Causes also the line number of the next statement following the GOSUB to be retained.
Examples:	250 GOSUB 600 900 GOSUB 2000

TABLE 6.7   **The** ON-GOSUB **Statement**

General Form:	ON numeric expression GOSUB k_1 , k_2 , . . . , k_n where k, the line number, represents the first line of a subroutine, and where k_1 , k_2 , . . . , k_n collectively represent a list of line numbers of one or more subroutines.
Purpose:	Causes control to transfer to the subroutine represented by the selected line number k_i , where i is the current value of the numeric expression. Causes also the line number of the next statement following the ON-GOSUB to be retained.
Examples:	``` 300 ON X GOSUB 400, 500, 600, 700 800 ON F - D/Y GOSUB 850, 900, 1000, 900 ```

TABLE 6.8   **The** RETURN **Statement**

General Form:	RETURN
Purpose:	Causes control to transfer from the subroutine back to the statement immediately following the corresponding GOSUB or ON-GOSUB statement.
Examples:	``` 700 RETURN 900 RETURN ```

A subroutine does not have a unique *initial* statement to differentiate it from other subroutines or from the Main program, sometimes called the **Main module**. In order to highlight the beginning of a subroutine, a remark or comment line is often used before the first executable statement of a subroutine (see lines 500, 510 and 520 of Figure 6.8). This boxed in remark should define the purpose of the subroutine and indicate to the reader that a subroutine follows.

The last statement of a subroutine should always be the RETURN statement. Any attempt to execute a RETURN statement without executing a prior corresponding GOSUB or ON-GOSUB statement results in the display of a diagnostic message and the termination of the program. This can be summarized by the following rule:

RETURN **Rule 1:** The execution of a RETURN statement must be preceded by the execution of a corresponding GOSUB or ON-GOSUB statement.

In the partial program in Figure 6.8, lines 100 through 120 highlight the Main module and lines 500 to 520 highlight the subroutine defined as the Display Menu module. When the RUN command is issued, the Main module (lines 100 to 490) executes and calls the subroutine (lines 500 to 720) from lines 410 and 450. Line 440 refers to the location of other subroutines not shown in Figure 6.8.

So that subroutines can be located easily, for debugging purposes, they should be placed near the end of the program but before any DATA statements and the END line. Assigning distinctive line numbers, like 1000, 1100, 1200, and so on, to subroutines would also be helpful.

Figure 6.8 also illustrates the flow of control from the Main module of the program to the subroutine and the eventual transfer from the subroutine back to the line immediately following the corresponding GOSUB statement.

When line 410 transfers control to line 530 of the subroutine, the subroutine displays a menu and requests a code to be entered. Once the code is entered and verified, the RETURN statement in line 720 causes control to transfer back to line 420.

As long as the code C is not 7, control enters the While loop. Line 430 clears the screen, and the ON-GOSUB in line 440 selects to transfer control to one of six

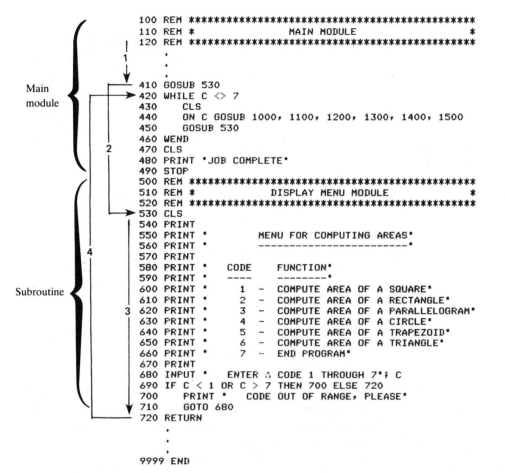

```
                100 REM ************************************************
                110 REM *                   MAIN MODULE                 *
                120 REM ************************************************
                   .
                   .
                   .
                410 GOSUB 530
                420 WHILE C <> 7
                430     CLS
                440     ON C GOSUB 1000, 1100, 1200, 1300, 1400, 1500
                450     GOSUB 530
                460 WEND
                470 CLS
                480 PRINT "JOB COMPLETE"
                490 STOP
                500 REM ************************************************
                510 REM *              DISPLAY MENU MODULE              *
                520 REM ************************************************
                530 CLS
                540 PRINT
                550 PRINT "           MENU FOR COMPUTING AREAS"
                560 PRINT "           -------------------------"
                570 PRINT
                580 PRINT "   CODE     FUNCTION"
                590 PRINT "   ----     --------"
                600 PRINT "    1   -   COMPUTE AREA OF A SQUARE"
                610 PRINT "    2   -   COMPUTE AREA OF A RECTANGLE"
                620 PRINT "    3   -   COMPUTE AREA OF A PARALLELOGRAM"
                630 PRINT "    4   -   COMPUTE AREA OF A CIRCLE"
                640 PRINT "    5   -   COMPUTE AREA OF A TRAPEZOID"
                650 PRINT "    6   -   COMPUTE AREA OF A TRIANGLE"
                660 PRINT "    7   -   END PROGRAM"
                670 PRINT
                680 INPUT "    ENTER A CODE 1 THROUGH 7"; C
                690 IF C < 1 OR C > 7 THEN 700 ELSE 720
                700     PRINT "   CODE OUT OF RANGE, PLEASE"
                710     GOTO 680
                720 RETURN
                   .
                   .
                   .
              9999 END
```

FIGURE 6.8 The flow of control from the Main module of a program to a subroutine and the eventual return of control to the Main module.

subroutines, depending upon the value of C. Any one of the subroutines selected by line 440 eventually transfers control back to line 450, which again displays the menu. The While loop (lines 420 to 460) continues to execute until C is assigned a value of 7 in line 680 of the subroutine.

The STOP Statement

The STOP statement halts the execution of the program. The STOP statement also causes the following or an equivalent message to be displayed:

    BREAK IN 490

In Figure 6.8, line 490, the STOP statement is the last statement executed and it causes the program to halt. Note that by placing the STOP statement at line 490, we prevent the Display Menu module from being executed again, as a part of the end-of-job routine. The general form of the STOP statement is shown in Table 6.9.

TABLE 6.9 The STOP Statement

General Form:	STOP
Purpose:	Causes termination of execution of the program after displaying the message BREAK IN k, where k represents the line number of the STOP statement.
Examples:	500 STOP 700 STOP
Note:	The STOP statement differs from the END statement in that it halts or suspends execution of the program, rather than terminating it. Execution of the program will resume if the system command CONT is entered.

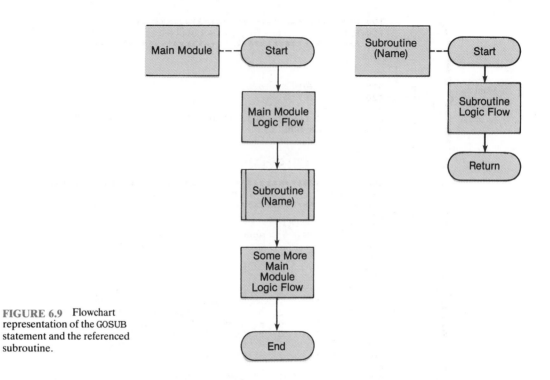

FIGURE 6.9 Flowchart representation of the GOSUB statement and the referenced subroutine.

Flowchart Representation of GOSUB, ON-GOSUB, RETURN **and Referenced Subroutine**

The program flowchart representation of the GOSUB statement and the referenced subroutine is shown in Figure 6.9. The GOSUB statement, which calls the subroutine, is represented by the **predefined process symbol**, which was defined in Table 1.4 (p. 14). The predefined process symbol consists of a set of vertical lines in the left and right sides of a rectangle and indicates that the program steps of the subroutine are specified elsewhere. In Figure 6.9, the subroutine is represented by the flowchart to the right of the Main module and the RETURN statement is represented by the terminal symbol.

The ON-GOSUB statement is represented by the decision symbol and each case is illustrated by a predefined process symbol, as shown in Figure 6.10.

FIGURE 6.10 Flowchart representation of the ON-GOSUB statement and the referenced subroutine.

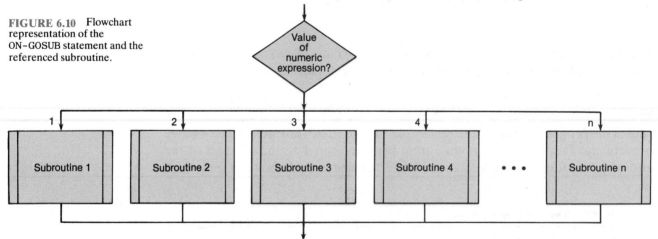

Nested Subroutines

Just as there are nested For loops, there are nested subroutines. In a nest of subroutines, one subroutine may call another subroutine, which may in turn call another, and so on. However, each subroutine must terminate with a RETURN statement. Figure 6.11 illustrates the flow of control from the Main module to the nested subroutines. The lines and numbers represent the flow of control.

It might help you understand nested subroutines if you thought of a stack of line numbers. Before the execution of the first GOSUB or ON–GOSUB statement, the stack is empty. Each time one of these statements is executed, its line number is put on the stack. The next line executed is the one *specified* by the GOSUB or ON–GOSUB statement, but each time a RETURN statement is executed the top number is taken off the stack. The execution cannot begin again with the number that is left on top of the stack, since that would put the program back into the subroutine; therefore, execution begins again with whatever number *follows* the top one in the stack.

```
         100 REM *********************************************
         110 REM *                MAIN MODULE                *
      ┌  120 REM *********************************************
      │1     .
      │      .
      ▼      .
   ┌─── 410 GOSUB 530
   │ ┌─► 420 WHILE C <> 7
   │ │   430    CLS
   │ │   440    ON C GOSUB 1000, 1100, 1200, 1300, 1400, 1500
   │ │   450    GOSUB 530
   │ │2 460 WEND
   │ │   470 CLS
   │ │   480 PRINT "JOB COMPLETE"
   │ │   490 STOP
   │ │   500 REM *********************************************
   │ │   510 REM *             DISPLAY MENU MODULE           *
   │ │   520 REM *********************************************
   │ └── 530 CLS
   │     540 PRINT
   │     550 PRINT "         MENU FOR COMPUTING AREAS"
 7 │     560 PRINT "         ------------------------"
   │     570 PRINT
   │     580 PRINT "   CODE      FUNCTION"
   │     590 PRINT "   ----      --------"
   │ 3   600 PRINT "    1  -  COMPUTE AREA OF A SQUARE"
   │     610 PRINT "    2  -  COMPUTE AREA OF A RECTANGLE"
   │     620 PRINT "    3  -  COMPUTE AREA OF A PARALLELOGRAM"
   │     630 PRINT "    4  -  COMPUTE AREA OF A CIRCLE"
   │     640 PRINT "    5  -  COMPUTE AREA OF A TRAPEZOID"
   │     650 PRINT "    6  -  COMPUTE AREA OF A TRIANGLE"
   │     660 PRINT "    7  -  END PROGRAM"
   │     670 PRINT
   │ ┌── 680 GOSUB 730
   └─┼─► 690 RETURN
     │   700 REM *********************************************
   4 │   710 REM *             ACCEPT CODE MODULE            *
     │   720 REM *********************************************
 6 └─► 730 INPUT "    ENTER A CODE 1 THROUGH 7"; C
       740 IF C < 1 OR C > 7 THEN 750 ELSE 770
     5 750    PRINT "    CODE OUT OF RANGE, PLEASE"
       760    GOTO 730
       770 RETURN
           .
           .
      9999 END
```

FIGURE 6.11 The flow of control in a program with nested subroutines.

6.6 THE TOP-DOWN APPROACH

The attributes of a well-written program have changed considerably over the past several years. Besides the obvious characteristic that the program must work correctly, a quality program in the past was characterized by clever algorithms and tricky code; the "best" programs were those with the fewest instructions and the fastest program execution. The end result was the construction of BS (Bowl of Spaghetti) programs, like the one shown in Figure 6.12, that were nearly impossible to read and modify.

Today, the most important criterion for quality is still that the program work correctly. However, a good program now has reliability and simplicity in design; a good program is also easy to read and easy to maintain, or modify.

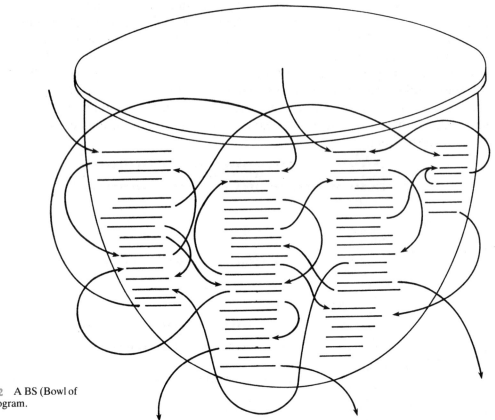

FIGURE 6.12   A BS (Bowl of Spaghetti) program.

Up to this point, we have emphasized programming techniques like documentation, indentation and data validation. The structured programming approach, which we have also emphasized, encourages you to use these techniques to produce readable programs. These techniques are sufficient to construct good programs that work for small problems. However, for large and complex problems, another approach is required.

Top-Down Versus Structured

In this section, you will study top-down design and top-down programming. Do not confuse structured programming with top-down programming. They are *not* the same.

For now, you should know that whenever "structured" is appended to any data processing task associated with analysis, design, programming, testing, debugging, maintenance and documentation, it is used to describe a task that is well organized, rigorous, and formal. Structured programming increases the clarity and reduces the complexity associated with the given task.

When "top-down" is used with any of these data processing tasks, it describes a strategy for solving large complex problems. To solve a problem top-down, you divide and conquer.

For example, **top-down design** is a design strategy that breaks large, complex problems into smaller, less complex problems and then breaks each one of these down—**decomposes** them—into even smaller problems. In **top-down programming**, high-level modules are coded as soon as they are designed, generally before the low-level modules have been designed.

Two graphical representations of the top-down approach are a **top-down chart** (a **hierarchy** or VTOC chart) and an outline. Figure 6.13 represents a top-down chart of a task that is broken down into subtasks. If necessary, the subtasks are further refined into smaller subtasks. The overall task and each of the subtasks are represented by a process symbol with a short description written inside the symbol. The top-down chart is read from top to bottom, and in general from left to right.

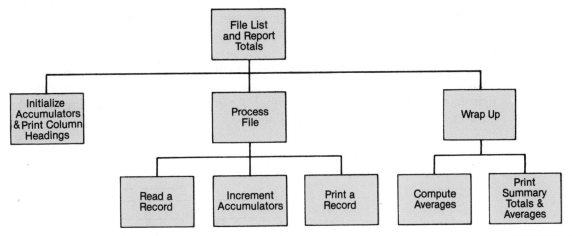

FIGURE 6.13   A general view of a top-down chart.

A top-down chart differs from a program flowchart in that it does not show decision-making logic or flow of control. A program flowchart shows procedure, but a top-down chart shows *organization*.

A top-down chart allows you to concentrate on defining *what* needs to be done in the program before deciding *how* and *when* it is to be done, which is represented in a program flowchart. We will use both a top-down chart and an outline in the solution of complex problems.

A top-down chart is very similar to a company's organization chart: each subtask carries out a function for its superior. Think of the higher level subtasks as vice presidents of the organization, who perform the *controlling* functions for that organization. Also think of the lower level sub-subtasks as workers of the organization, who perform the *repetitive* kinds of work for that organization.

In the top-down approach, both the design and programming are done beginning with the general and moving to the specific. Consider a problem in which a file must be processed. Each time a record is read, accumulators are incremented and a record is displayed. At the end-of-job, averages and summary totals are also displayed. To design a solution to this problem, use a top-down chart like the one in Figure 6.13.

As you design from top to bottom (general to specific), the subtasks are connected to their superior tasks by vertical lines. Each subtask is subordinate to the one above it and superior to any below it.

Top-down programming is based on the idea that the subtasks, especially the higher level ones, are implemented into the program as internal subroutines, or modules. For example, the Main module at the top in Figure 6.13 may be implemented in a BASIC program as three GOSUB statements. The function of the first GOSUB is to call upon the Initialization module. At the completion of its prescribed task, the Initialization module returns control to the Main module. The second GOSUB references the Process File module, which maintains control until the file is processed. The final GOSUB in the Main module references the Wrap Up module, which computes the averages and displays the summary totals and averages. Upon completion of its task, the Wrap Up module returns control to the Main module and the program terminates.

Not all lower level subtasks in a top-down chart become subroutines in a program. A top-down chart attempts to illustrate *what must be done* and *not necessarily how to implement it.* A subtask that ends up being one or two lines of code is usually placed in its superior module. If the subtask Print a Record in Figure 6.14 is one line of code, then the subtask may be implemented directly into the Process File module.

The same subtask may be subordinate to more than one superior task. This is illustrated in Figure 6.14. Recurring subtasks are identified by darkening the upper right-hand corner of the process symbol. At implementation, recurring subtasks are coded once and called as often as needed.

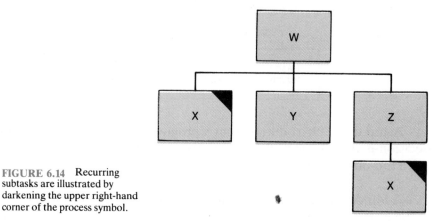

FIGURE 6.14   Recurring subtasks are illustrated by darkening the upper right-hand corner of the process symbol.

A top-down chart is *not* a program flowchart, nor does it replace the program flowchart in designing algorithms. A top-down chart is a tool, used early in the design stage, to decompose, in an orderly fashion, a large task into sub-tasks, and to some extent to show the flow of control between these sub-tasks. The result is a graphical view of what must be done to solve the overall problem.

The emphasis in the top-down approach is on careful analysis. Seldom is the first top-down chart the one that is implemented. Typically, a top-down chart is reviewed and refined several times before it is considered acceptable. In many companies, top-down charts are submitted to a **peer review group**, composed of programmers and analysts, for further review and refinement before a programmer is allowed to proceed with the next step of program development. This process of review and refinement is sometimes referred to as a **structured walk-through.**

A program flowchart, on the other hand, resolves the question of *how* to implement each of the subtasks. Emphasis is placed on decision-making and looping. Many programmers use the program flowchart or some other intermediate technique to develop algorithms for the more complex modules, but an experienced programmer may or may not construct a program flowchart for each sub-task.*

---

* Another popular logic tool is **pseudocode**, which allows a programmer to express thoughts in a form that uses regular English. It serves as an alternative to program flowcharts and is presented in Appendix B.

The following programming case study is solved using top-down charts and subroutines. An analysis of the problem, top-down charts, program flowcharts and a program follow.

Problem

The Inventory and Control department of company PUC wants a program to display, on command, either summary totals or all the records in inventory and the summary totals. The manager should be able to select one of the two alternatives from a menu. Each of the inventory records located in DATA statements includes the following items:

Data Item	Data Type	Data Item Size
Item Number	String	XX
Quantity on Hand	Numeric	999
Unit Cost	Numeric	9.99
Margin Code	Numeric	9 (1, 2, 3, or 4)

When a detailed listing of the inventory records is requested, then display the following:

			Inventory Analysis			Page 99
Item	Quantity	Unit Cost	Margin Code	Retail Value	Wholesale Value	Profit Potential
XX	999	9.99	9	99,999.99	9,999.99	9,999.99

The formulas for determining the retail value, wholesale value and profit potential are:

Retail value:
$$S = \left(\frac{1}{1 - M}\right) C$$

where S = retail value
C = wholesale value
M = margin as follows:

Margin Code	Margin Value
1	0.35
2	0.45
3	0.55
4	0.65

Wholesale value: $C = U * Q$

where C = wholesale value
U = unit price
Q = quantity on hand

Profit potential: $Z = R - C$

where Z = profit potential
R = retail value
C = wholesale value

Display at most six records per page. Use the following prompt message to display the next page:

PRESS ENTER KEY TO VIEW NEXT PAGE . . . . . ?

Clear the screen before displaying the report title and a page number.
Display the following summary totals with respect to all items in inventory:

1) Total retail value
2) Total wholesale value

3) Total profit potential
4) Total number of pieces
5) Average retail value
6) Average wholesale value
7) Average profit potential

Before processing any records, display the following menu so that the user may choose the type of report desired:

MENU FOR INVENTORY ANALYSIS
Code   Function
  1 —DISPLAY RECORDS AND SUMMARY TOTALS
  2 —DISPLAY SUMMARY TOTALS
ENTER A CODE OF 1 OR 2?

Verify that the code is a 1 or 2.

Program Tasks

Consider the following outline and the corresponding top-down chart (in Figure 6.15) of the tasks that must be accomplished to solve this problem.

1. Initialization
    1.1   Display menu
        1.1.1   Clear screen
        1.1.2   Print menu screen
        1.1.3   Accept user request F
        1.1.4   Validate user request
    1.2   Initialize accumulators to zero
        1.2.1   Page count P
        1.2.2   Total wholesale value T1
        1.2.3   Total profit potential T2
        1.2.4   Total retail value T3
        1.2.5   Total item count T
    1.3   Print report and column headings
        1.3.1   Add 1 to page count
        1.3.2   Print report title
        1.3.3   If function code F is equal to 1, then print column headings and initialize line count L to zero
2. Process File
    2.1   Read a record I\$, Q, U, K
    2.2   Test for end-of-file. If end-of-file, then transfer control to Wrap-Up
    2.3   Compute
        2.3.1   Compute item wholesale value C
        2.3.2   Compute item retail value S
        2.3.3   Compute item profit potential Z
    2.4   Increment accumulators
        2.4.1   Add C to total wholesale value T1
        2.4.2   Add Z to total profit potential T2
        2.4.3   Add S to total retail value T3
        2.4.4   Add Q to total item count T
    2.5   If function code F is equal to 1, then do 2.5.1 and 2.5.2
        2.5.1   If line count L is greater than or equal to 6, then do 1.3
        2.5.2   Print a record I\$, Q, U, K, S, C, Z
    2.6   Read a record I\$, Q, U, K
    2.7   Return to 2.2

3. Wrap Up
   3.1 Compute averages
      3.1.1 Compute average wholesale value A1
      3.1.2 Compute average profit potential A2
      3.1.3 Compute average retail value A3
   3.2 Print summary totals and averages
      3.2.1 Print totals T3, T1, T2 and T
      3.2.2 Print averages A3, A1 and A2
      3.2.3 Print end-of-job message

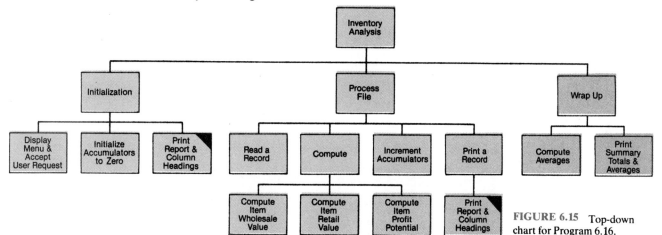

FIGURE 6.15 Top-down chart for Program 6.16.

Implementation

Figures 6.16, 17, 18, 19 and 20 illustrate the implementation of the tasks into modules. The program flowchart in Figure 6.16 shows that the Main module is made up of three subroutine calls and the STOP statement.

Figure 6.17 illustrates the program flowcharts for the Initialization module and the three modules called by the Initialization module.

Figure 6.18 depicts the logic of the Process file module, Compute module and Compute Item Retail Value module. Note in Figure 6.18 that three of the original subtasks are crosshatched to show that they were directly incorporated into their superior module instead of implemented as subroutines.

Figure 6.19 shows the program flowcharts for the Increment Accumulators and Print a Record modules.

Finally, Figure 6.20 illustrates the logic of the Wrap Up module and the two modules called by the Wrap Up module.

When the RUN command is issued for Program 6.16, the GOSUB statement in line 1180 transfers control to the Initialization module beginning at line 2070. Line 2070 transfers control to the Display Menu module beginning at line 2240. The Display Menu module displays the menu shown in Figure 6.21 and requests a function code from the user to indicate the type of report desired.

When control returns from the Display Menu module, the Initialization module calls upon the Initialize Accumulators module and the Print Report and Column Heading module. When a function code of 1 is entered (see Figure 6.21), the Print Report and Column Headings module displays both the report title and column headings. Control then returns to the Initialization module and Z\$ is assigned the format used to display a detail line (see line 3690). The system need not reassign the format Z\$ each time the Print a Record module is executed because the format is assigned in the Initialization module rather than in the Print a Record module.

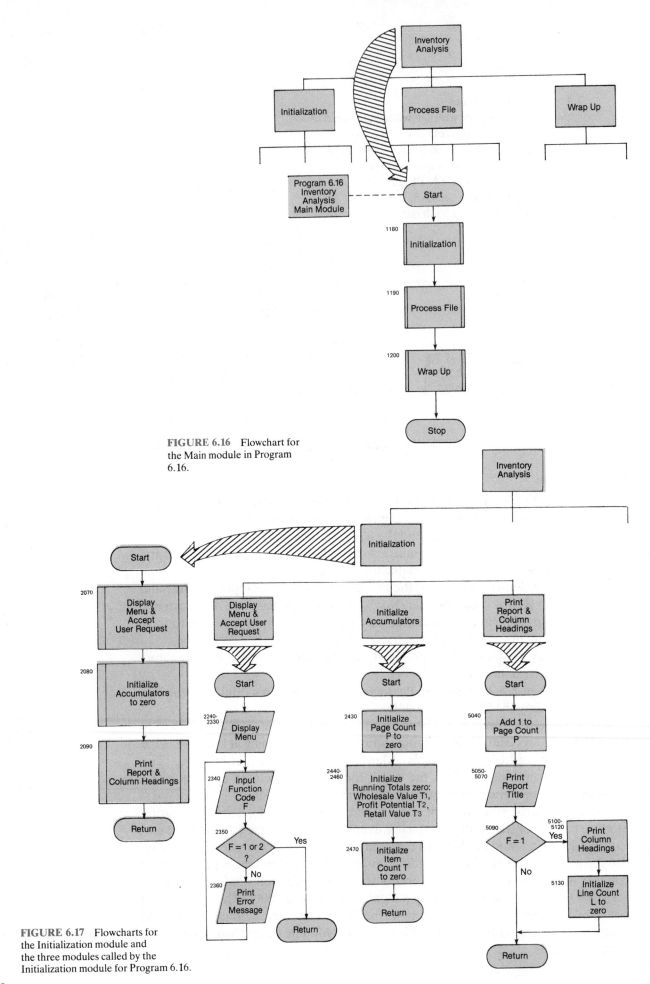

FIGURE 6.16 Flowchart for the Main module in Program 6.16.

FIGURE 6.17 Flowcharts for the Initialization module and the three modules called by the Initialization module for Program 6.16.

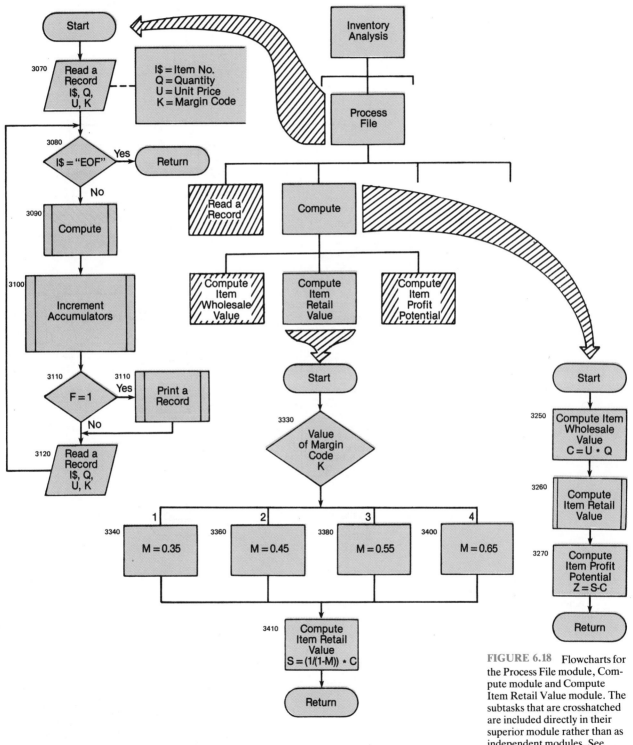

FIGURE 6.18 Flowcharts for the Process File module, Compute module and Compute Item Retail Value module. The subtasks that are crosshatched are included directly in their superior module rather than as independent modules. See Figure 6.19 for the flowcharts of the Increment Accumulators module and Print a Record module.

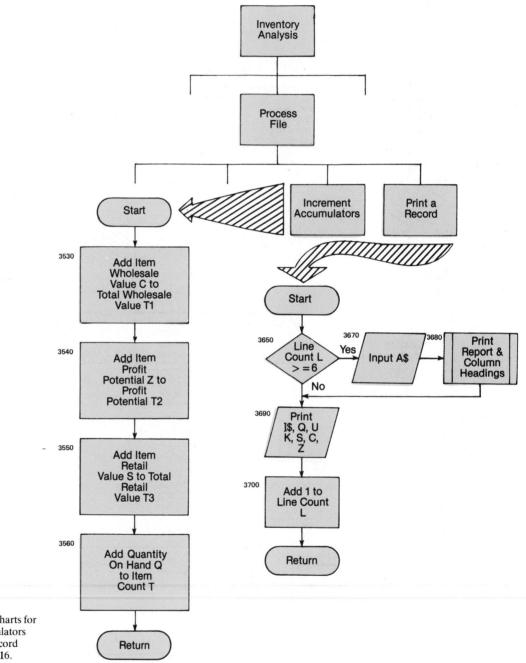

FIGURE 6.19   Flowcharts for the Increment Accumulators module and Print a Record module for Program 6.16.

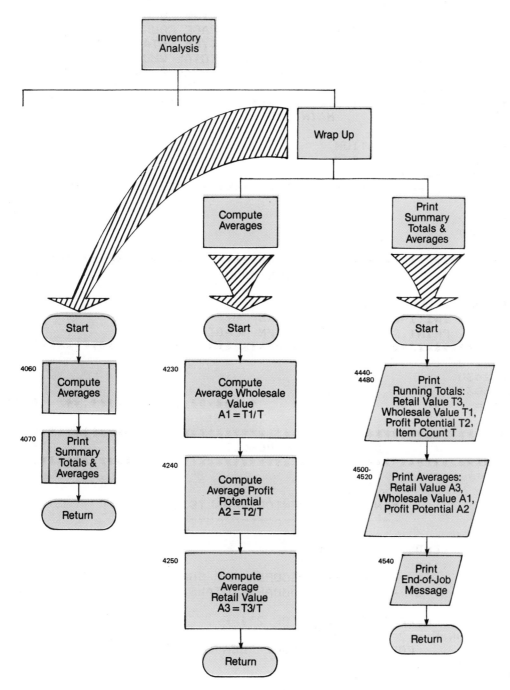

FIGURE 6.20 Flowcharts for the Wrap Up module and the two modules called by the Wrap Up module for Program 6.16.

```
1000 REM PROGRAM 6.16
1010 REM INVENTORY ANALYSIS
1020 REM A1 = AVERAGE WHOLESALE VALUE, A2 = AVERAGE PROFIT POTENTIAL
1030 REM A3 = AVERAGE RETAIL VALUE,    C  = ITEM WHOLESALE VALUE
1040 REM F  = PROGRAM FUNCTION CODE,   I$ = ITEM NUMBER
1050 REM K  = ITEM MARGIN CODE,        L  = LINE COUNT
1060 REM M  = ITEM MARGIN IN %,        P  = PAGE COUNT
1070 REM Q  = QUANTITY ON HAND,        S  = ITEM RETAIL VALUE
1080 REM T  = ITEM COUNT,              T1 = TOTAL WHOLESALE VALUE
1090 REM T2 = TOTAL PROFIT POTENTIAL,  T3 = TOTAL RETAIL VALUE
1100 REM U  = ITEM UNIT PRICE,         Z  = ITEM PROFIT POTENTIAL
1110 REM ***************************************************************
1120 REM *                      MAIN MODULE                           *
1130 REM *                                                            *
1140 REM * CALL INITIALIZATION                                        *
1150 REM * CALL PROCESS FILE                                          *
1160 REM * CALL WRAP UP                                               *
1170 REM ***************************************************************
1180 GOSUB 2070
1190 GOSUB 3070
1200 GOSUB 4060
1210 STOP
2000 REM ***************************************************************
2010 REM *                  INITIALIZATION MODULE                     *
2020 REM *                                                            *
2030 REM * CALL DISPLAY MENU                                          *
2040 REM * CALL INITIALIZE ACCUMULATORS                              *
2050 REM * CALL PRINT REPORT AND COLUMN HEADINGS                      *
2060 REM ***************************************************************
2070 GOSUB 2240
2080 GOSUB 2430
2090 GOSUB 5030
2100 LET Z$ = " \\        ###  #.##     #  ##,###.##    #,###.##    #,###.##
2110 RETURN
2200 REM ***************************************************************
2210 REM *                  DISPLAY MENU MODULE                       *
2230 REM ***************************************************************
2240 CLS
2250 PRINT
2260 PRINT "          MENU FOR INVENTORY ANALYSIS"
2270 PRINT "          -------------------------------"
2280 PRINT
2290 PRINT "     CODE      FUNCTION"
2300 PRINT "     ----      --------"
2310 PRINT "      1   -   DISPLAY RECORDS AND SUMMARY TOTALS"
2320 PRINT "      2   -   DISPLAY SUMMARY TOTALS"
2330 PRINT
2340 INPUT "     ENTER A CODE OF 1 OR 2"; F
2350 IF F = 1 OR F = 2 THEN 2380
2360    PRINT "     CODE OUT OF RANGE, PLEASE"
2370    GOTO 2340
2380 RETURN
2400 REM ***************************************************************
2410 REM *                INITIIALIZE ACCUMULATORS MODULE             *
2420 REM ***************************************************************
2430 LET P = 0
2440 LET T1 = 0
2450 LET T2 = 0
2460 LET T3 = 0
2470 LET T = 0
2480 RETURN
```

```
3000 REM **********************************************************
3010 REM *                    PROCESS FILE MODULE                 *
3020 REM *                                                        *
3030 REM * CALL COMPUTE                                           *
3040 REM * CALL INCREMENT ACCUMULATORS                            *
3050 REM * CALL PRINT A RECORD                                    *
3060 REM **********************************************************
3070 READ I$, Q, U, K
3080 WHILE I$ <> "EOF"
3090     GOSUB 3250
3100     GOSUB 3530
3110     IF F = 1 THEN GOSUB 3650
3120     READ I$, Q, U, K
3130 WEND
3140 RETURN
3200 REM **********************************************************
3210 REM *                    COMPUTE MODULE                      *
3220 REM *                                                        *
3230 REM * CALL COMPUTE ITEM RETAIL VALUE                         *
3240 REM **********************************************************
3250 LET C = U * Q
3260 GOSUB 3330
3270 LET Z = S - C
3280 RETURN
3300 REM **********************************************************
3310 REM *           COMPUTE ITEM RETAIL VALUE MODULE             *
3320 REM **********************************************************
3330 ON K GOTO 3340, 3360, 3380, 3400
3340     LET M = 0.35
3350 GOTO 3410
3360     LET M = 0.45
3370 GOTO 3410
3380     LET M = 0.55
3390 GOTO 3410
3400     LET M = 0.65
3410 LET S = (1/(1 - M)) * C
3420 RETURN
3500 REM **********************************************************
3510 REM *              INCREMENT ACCUMULATORS MODULE             *
3520 REM **********************************************************
3530 LET T1 = T1 + C
3540 LET T2 = T2 + Z
3550 LET T3 = T3 + S
3560 LET T = T + Q
3570 RETURN
3600 REM **********************************************************
3610 REM *                  PRINT A RECORD MODULE                 *
3620 REM *                                                        *
3630 REM * CALL PRINT REPORT AND COLUMN HEADINGS                  *
3640 REM **********************************************************
3650 IF L >= 6 THEN 3660 ELSE 3690
3660     PRINT
3670     INPUT "PRESS ENTER KEY TO VIEW NEXT PAGE....."; A$
3680     GOSUB 5030
3690 PRINT USING Z$; I$, Q, U, K, S, C, Z
3700 LET L = L + 1
3710 RETURN
```

PROGRAM 6.16
(Continued)

```
4000 REM ********************************************************
4010 REM *                        WRAP UP MODULE                *
4020 REM *                                                      *
4030 REM * CALL COMPUTE AVERAGES                                *
4040 REM * CALL PRINT SUMMARY TOTALS AND AVERAGES               *
4050 REM ********************************************************
4060 GOSUB 4230
4070 GOSUB 4430
4080 RETURN
4200 REM ********************************************************
4210 REM *                 COMPUTE AVERAGES MODULE              *
4220 REM ********************************************************
4230 LET A1 = T1/T
4240 LET A2 = T2/T
4250 LET A3 = T3/T
4260 RETURN
4400 REM ********************************************************
4410 REM *       PRINT SUMMARY TOTALS AND AVERAGES MODULE       *
4420 REM ********************************************************
4430 PRINT
4440 PRINT USING "TOTAL RETAIL VALUE=======> ##,###.##"; T3
4450 PRINT USING "TOTAL WHOLESALE VALUE====> ##,###.##"; T1
4460 PRINT USING "TOTAL PROFIT POTENTIAL===> ##,###.##"; T2
4470 PRINT
4480 PRINT USING "TOTAL NUMBER OF PIECES===> ##,###"; T
4490 PRINT
4500 PRINT USING "AVERAGE RETAIL VALUE=====> ##,###.##"; A3
4510 PRINT USING "AVERAGE WHOLESALE VALUE==> ##,###.##"; A1
4520 PRINT USING "AVERAGE PROFIT POTENTIAL=> ##,###.##"; A2
4530 PRINT
4540 PRINT "JOB COMPLETE"
4550 RETURN
5000 REM ********************************************************
5010 REM *         PRINT REPORT AND COLUMN HEADINGS MODULE      *
5020 REM ********************************************************
5030 CLS
5040 LET P = P + 1
5050 PRINT "                    INVENTORY ANALYSIS           PAGE:";
5060 PRINT USING " ##"; P
5070 PRINT "                    --------------------"
5080 PRINT
5090 IF F = 1 THEN 5100 ELSE 5140
5100 PRINT "                    UNIT   MARGIN  RETAIL   WHOLESALE  PROFIT"
5110 PRINT "ITEM  QUANTITY  COST   CODE    VALUE    VALUE      POTENTIAL"
5120 PRINT "----  --------  ----   ------  ------   ---------  ---------"
5130 LET L = 0
5140 RETURN
6000 REM ********************************************************
6010 REM *                    DATA FOLLOWS                      *
6020 REM ********************************************************
6030 DATA 01, 30, 1.45, 2, 03, 123, 2.34, 3, 05, 34, 1.23, 1
6040 DATA 07, 456, 0.94, 4, 10, 321, 3.56, 2, 14, 81, 5.67, 3
6050 DATA 16, 234, 5.67, 3, 21, 14, 3.45, 4, 25, 124, 1.28, 2
6060 DATA 31, 378, 2.47, 4, 35, 521, 0.34, 4, 47, 200, 3.23, 2
6070 DATA 52, 21, 9.97, 3, 56, 245, 5.89, 1, 67, 398, 6.78, 4
6080 DATA EOF, 0, 0, 0
6090 END

RUN
```

PROGRAM 6.16
(Continued)

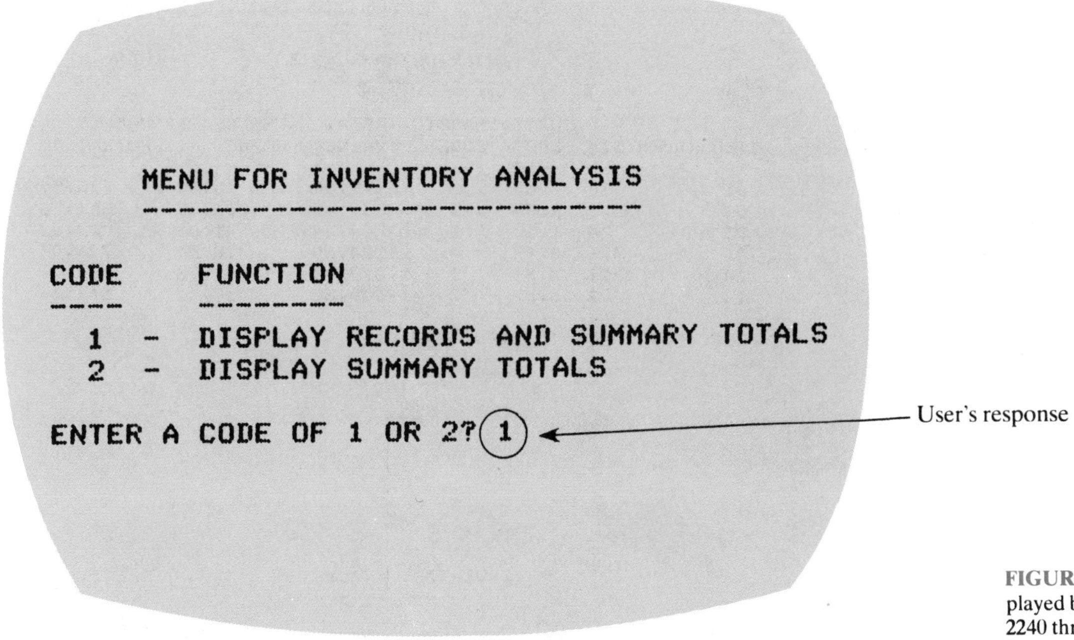

```
MENU FOR INVENTORY ANALYSIS
-------------------------------------

CODE      FUNCTION
----      --------
  1    -  DISPLAY RECORDS AND SUMMARY TOTALS
  2    -  DISPLAY SUMMARY TOTALS

ENTER A CODE OF 1 OR 2? (1)
```
                                            User's response

FIGURE 6.21   Menu displayed by Program 6.16 lines 2240 through 2380.

Line 2110 returns control to line 1190 in the Main module, which in turn transfers control to the Process File module. Line 3070 reads the first record before the system enters the While loop (lines 3080 through 3130). For each record processed, line 3090 transfers control to the Compute module which computes the item's wholesale value, retail value and profit potential.

The RETURN statement in line 3280 transfers control back to line 3100 in the Process File module. Line 3100 then transfers control to the Increment Accumulators module beginning at line 3530. After the system executes this module, control returns to line 3110. Since the function code F is equal to 1, in line 3110 control passes to the Print a Record module beginning at line 3650. The Print a Record module first tests to determine if 6 detail records have been displayed. If line count L is greater than or equal to 6, then line 3670 displays the prompt message: PRESS ENTER KEY TO VIEW NEXT PAGE. . . . . . .? Once the Enter key is pressed, control passes to the Print Report and Column Headings module.

Line 3690 of the Print a Record module displays a detail record before control is transferred back to the Process File module. Following the return of control, the next inventory record is read and the While loop continues until the sentinel record is read. When the sentinel record is processed, control returns to line 1200 in the main module. The GOSUB statement in line 1200 transfers control to the Wrap Up module, which calls upon its subordinates to compute the averages and display the summary totals and averages.

Figure 6.22 illustrates the information generated by Program 6.16 when the user enters a function code of 1. Figure 6.23 shows the results when a function code of 2 is entered.

```
                        INVENTORY ANALYSIS        PAGE:   1
                        -------------------

               UNIT  MARGIN  RETAIL    WHOLESALE  PROFIT
     ITEM  QUANTITY  COST  CODE    VALUE     VALUE      POTENTIAL
     ----  --------  ----  ------  ------    ---------  ---------
      01        30   1.45    2       79.09      43.50     35.59
      03       123   2.34    3      639.60     287.82    351.78
      05        34   1.23    1       64.34      41.82     22.52
      07       456   0.94    4    1,224.68     428.64    796.04
      10       321   3.56    2    2,077.74   1,142.76    934.98
      14        81   5.67    3    1,020.60     459.27    561.33

     PRESS ENTER KEY TO VIEW NEXT PAGE.....?
```

```
                        INVENTORY ANALYSIS        PAGE:   2
                        -------------------

               UNIT  MARGIN  RETAIL    WHOLESALE  PROFIT
     ITEM  QUANTITY  COST  CODE    VALUE     VALUE      POTENTIAL
     ----  --------  ----  ------  ------    ---------  ---------
      16       234   5.67    3    2,948.40   1,326.78  1,621.62
      21        14   3.45    4      138.00      48.30     89.70
      25       124   1.28    2      288.58     158.72    129.86
      31       378   2.47    4    2,667.60     933.66  1,733.94
      35       521   0.34    4      506.11     177.14    328.97
      47       200   3.23    2    1,174.54     646.00    528.54

     PRESS ENTER KEY TO VIEW NEXT PAGE.....?
```

```
                        INVENTORY ANALYSIS        PAGE:   3
                        -------------------

               UNIT  MARGIN  RETAIL    WHOLESALE  PROFIT
     ITEM  QUANTITY  COST  CODE    VALUE     VALUE      POTENTIAL
     ----  --------  ----  ------  ------    ---------  ---------
      52        21   9.97    3      465.27     209.37    255.90
      56       245   5.89    1    2,220.08   1,443.05    777.03
      67       398   6.78    4    7,709.82   2,698.44  5,011.38

     TOTAL RETAIL VALUE=======>  23,224.40
     TOTAL WHOLESALE VALUE====>  10,045.30
     TOTAL PROFIT POTENTIAL===>  13,179.10

     TOTAL NUMBER OF PIECES===>   3,180

     AVERAGE RETAIL VALUE=====>      7.30
     AVERAGE WHOLESALE VALUE==>      3.16
     AVERAGE PROFIT POTENTIAL=>      4.14

     JOB COMPLETE
```

FIGURE 6.22   The display from entering a function code of 1.

```
        MENU FOR INVENTORY ANALYSIS
        ---------------------------

    CODE    FUNCTION
    ----    --------
      1  -  DISPLAY RECORDS AND SUMMARY TOTALS
      2  -  DISPLAY SUMMARY TOTALS

    ENTER A CODE OF 1 OR 2? (2)
```

— User's response

```
              INVENTORY ANALYSIS           PAGE:   1
              ------------------

    TOTAL RETAIL VALUE=======>  23,224.40
    TOTAL WHOLESALE VALUE====>  10,045.30
    TOTAL PROFIT POTENTIAL===>  13,179.10

    TOTAL NUMBER OF PIECES===>   3,180

    AVERAGE RETAIL VALUE=====>       7.30
    AVERAGE WHOLESALE VALUE==>       3.16
    AVERAGE PROFIT POTENTIAL=>       4.14

    JOB COMPLETE
```

FIGURE 6.23 The display from entering a function code of 2.

Another technique that may be used to implement the top-down approach is to write external subroutines that are linked together by the CHAIN statement. The CHAIN statement may be used within a BASIC program to instruct the computer to stop executing the current program, to load another program from auxiliary storage and to start executing it.

The general form of the CHAIN statement is shown in Table 6.10.

6.7 THE CHAIN STATEMENT

TABLE 6.10 **The CHAIN Statement**

General Form:	CHAIN "program name", line number, ALL
	where program name is the name of the program which is loaded from auxiliary storage and executed
	line number is an optional parameter that indicates the line number in the chained-to program where execution begins
	ALL is an optional parameter which, when present, instructs the computer to maintain all the current values of the variables as defined in the chaining program.
Purpose:	Instructs the computer to stop executing the current program, load another program from auxiliary storage and start executing it.

Examples:	`3000 CHAIN "PROG2"`
	 `4000 CHAIN "PROG3", 2000`
	 `5000 CHAIN "MODULE2",, ALL`
	 `6000 CHAIN "MODULE6", 1000, ALL`

Caution:	This statement is not available on all BASIC systems.

In the first example in Table 6.10, the statement

```
3000 CHAIN "PROG2"
```

terminates execution of the current program (the **chaining program**), loads

PROG2 from auxiliary storage, and executes PROG2 at the first executable statement. PROG2 is the **chained-to program**. In this example, the variables defined in the chaining program are not available for the chained-to program.

In the second example, the statement

```
4000 CHAIN 'PROG2', 2000
```

initiates execution at line 2000 in program PROG3. Specifying a line number is a common technique for chaining back to another program that has already partially executed. For example, a program may chain to a subordinate program that carries out a sub-task. When the subordinate program is finished with its task, it chains back to a specified line number in its superior program.

The third example in Table 6.10 shows how a chaining program may pass the current values of all variables to the chained-to program. Note that two commas must be used when the line number is omitted.

The last example also passes the current values of all variables to the chained-to program, but in this case execution begins in the chained-to program at line 1000.

Care should be taken when using the READ and DATA statements in a chained-to program that may be called a multiple number of times. The chained-to program causes the pointer to be moved back to the beginning of the data sequence holding area in a manner similar to the RESTORE statement.

The following example consists of two programs:

PROGRAM 6.17

```
100 REM PROGRAM 6.17
110 REM THE CHAINING PROGRAM
120 REM PROG1
130 REM ********************
140 LET S = 0
150 FOR I = 1 TO 99 STEP 2
160     LET S = S + I
170 NEXT I
180 PRINT 'PROG1 TOTAL ='; S
190 CHAIN 'PROG2',, ALL
200 END
```

PROGRAM 6.18

```
100 REM PROGRAM 6.18
110 REM THE CHAINED-TO PROGRAM
120 REM PROG2
130 REM *********************
140 LET T = 0
150 FOR J = 2 TO 100 STEP 2
160     LET T = T + J
170 NEXT J
180 PRINT 'PROG2 TOTAL ='; T
190 PRINT 'GRAND TOTAL ='; S + T
200 END
```

When the run command is issued, the following displays:

```
RUN

PROG1 TOTAL = 2500
PROG2 TOTAL = 2550
GRAND TOTAL = 5050
```

Examine the output of Programs 6.17 and 6.18 closely—especially the grand total. The ALL parameter in PROG1, line 190, allows the current values of all the variables in PROG1 to become available to PROG2.

Most beginners will probably not have the long, complex programs that require the use of the CHAIN statement, but in the real world of programming, programs like these are sometimes the rule rather than the exception.

1. When two or more conditions are combined by the logical operators AND, OR, XOR, EQV and IMP, the expression is a compound condition.

2. The truth value of the relational expression in a condition is complemented by the logical operator NOT.

3. The logical operator AND requires that both conditions be true for the compound condition to be true.

4. The logical operator OR requires that only one of the two conditions be true for the compound condition to be true. If both conditions are true, the compound condition is also true.

5. The logical operator NOT requires that the relational expression be false for the condition to be true. If the relational expression is true, then the condition is false.

6. Unless parentheses dictate otherwise, reading from left to right, conditions containing relational operators are evaluated first, then those containing NOT operators, then those containing AND operators, and finally those conditions containing OR operators.

7. The XOR (exclusive OR) operator requires that one of the two conditions be true for the compound condition to be true. If both are true, the condition is false.

8. The EQV (equivalence) operator requires that both conditions be true or both conditions be false for the compound condition to be true.

9. The IMP (implication) operator requires that both conditions be true or both conditions be false or the first condition be false and the second true for the compound condition to be true.

10. Data validation is a technique used to ensure that valid data is assigned to a program. Data can be validated, or checked, for reasonableness, range, code and digit.

11. A reasonableness check is a technique used to ensure that data items entered from an external source are legitimate.

12. A range check is a technique used to ensure that data items entered from an external device fall within a range of valid values.

13. A code check is a technique used to ensure that codes entered from an external source are valid.

14. A digit check is a technique used to verify the assignment of a special digit to a number.

15. A check digit is an addition to a number that requires validation; this addition can be used to verify the rest of the digits.

16. The FOR and NEXT statements are used to set up counter-controlled loops.

17. The NEXT statement must have a higher line number than its corresponding FOR statement.

18. The FOR statement may be located anywhere before the corresponding NEXT statement.

19. A valid initial entry into a For loop can only be accomplished by transferring control to the FOR statement.

20. If the range of a For loop includes another For loop, all statements in the range of the inner For loop must also be within the range of the outer For loop.

21. When one For loop is within another, the name of the control variable for each For loop must be different.

22. An internal subroutine is a group of statements within a BASIC program associated with a single programming task.

23. Subroutines, or modules as they can also be called, are useful in solving large, complex problems, because they allow a problem to be subdivided into smaller and more manageable subproblems, which can then be solved with appropriate subroutines.

24. A subroutine may be referenced by either a GOSUB or ON–GOSUB statement.

25. The RETURN statement is always the last statement executed in a subroutine. Its function is to cause control to transfer from the subroutine back to the statement immediately following the corresponding GOSUB or ON–GOSUB statement.

26. The function of the STOP statement is to terminate execution of the program after displaying the message BREAK IN k, where k represents the line number of the STOP

statement. One major use of the STOP statement is to terminate execution of a program containing subroutines, and thereby to prevent a subroutine from being executed as part of the end-of-job routine.

27. A subroutine may call another subroutine, which may in turn call another, and so on.

28. The top-down approach is a popular method of solving large complex problems.

29. A top-down chart is a graphical representation of the task broken down into subtasks.

30. The CHAIN statement is used to instruct the computer to stop executing the current program, to load another program from auxiliary storage and start executing it.

6.9 SELF-TEST EXERCISES

1. Consider the valid programs listed below. What is displayed if each program is executed?

a) Assume that the following data items are entered in sequence as requested: 4, 6, 9, 15, 18.

```
100 REM CHAPTER 6 SELF-TEST 1A
110 LET S = 0
120 FOR I = 1 TO 5
130     INPUT "NEXT VALUE"; A
140     LET S = S + A
150 NEXT I
160 PRINT "THE SUM IS"; S
170 END
```

b)
```
100 REM CHAPTER 6 SELF-TEST 1B
110 LET A = 4
120 LET B = 6
130 LET C = 5
140 LET D = 9
150 IF A < B THEN PRINT A, B ELSE PRINT B, A
160 IF A > B OR C < 6 THEN IF D > C THEN PRINT D, C ELSE 180
170 IF D > C XOR D = 9 THEN PRINT A ELSE PRINT B
180 END
```

c)
```
100 REM CHAPTER 6 SELF-TEST 1C
110 FOR I = 1 TO 20
120     IF 2 * INT(I/2) - I <> 0 THEN 140
130         PRINT I
140 NEXT I
150 END
```

d)
```
100 REM CHAPTER 6 SELF-TEST 1D
110 READ A
120 WHILE A <> -1
130     GOSUB 180
140     GOSUB 200
150     READ A
160 WEND
170 STOP
180 LET X = 2 * A
190 RETURN
200 PRINT A, X
210 RETURN
220 REM ****DATA FOLLOWS****
230 DATA 2, 4, 6, 8, -1
240 END
```

2. Write a sequence of statements, including an IF-THEN-ELSE, to satisfy the logic in this partial flowchart.

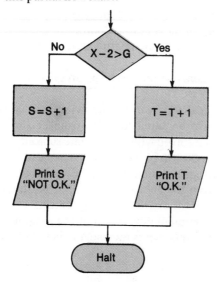

3. Identify the error(s), if any, in each of the following programs.

a)
```
100 REM CHAPTER 6 SELF-TEST 3A
110 FOR I = 10 TO 1
120    PRINT I;
130 NEXT K
```

b)
```
100 REM CHAPTER 6 SELF-TEST 3B
110 LET X = 1
120 WHILE X < 10
130    PRINT X
140 WEND
```

c)
```
100 REM CHAPTER 6 SELF-TEST 3C
110 FOR K = 6 TO 12 STEP 2
120    PRINT K;
130    FOR J = 2 TO 5
140 NEXT K
```

d)
```
100 REM CHAPTER 6 SELF-TEST 3D
110 FOR X = 1 TO 10
120    PRINT X;
140 NEXT X
150 GOTO 120
160 END
```

4. Insert parentheses in each of the following compound conditions to correspond to the evaluation by the BASIC system.

a) $S > 0$ AND NOT $T > 0$ OR $A > 0$

b) $S > 0$ AND $A > 0$ OR NOT $T > 0$

c) $S > 0$ OR $A > 0$ OR $T > 0$

d) $S > 0$ AND $A > 0$ AND NOT $T > 0$

e) $S > 0$ AND $A > 0$ OR $T > 0$ AND $P > 0$

f) $S > 0$ OR $A > 0$ AND $T > 0$ AND $P > 0$

g) $S > 0$ OR $A > 0$ OR $T > 0$ AND $P > 0$

h) NOT $S > 0$ AND $T > 0$ OR $P > 0$

5. A bonus is to be paid to all employees who are over 50 years of age (A) and have been employed (S) for 10 years or more, or are over 60 years of age and have been employed for 5 years or more. Write a single IF-THEN-ELSE statement that will increment a counter C for each employee eligible for a bonus.

6. Consider the following program.
```
100 REM CHAPTER 6 SELF-TEST 6
110 LET K = 0
120 FOR X = 3 TO 1 STEP -1
130    LET P = 0
140    LET K = K + X
150    FOR Y = 1 TO 3
160       LET P = P + Y
170       PRINT X, K, Y, P
180    NEXT Y
190 NEXT X
200 END
```
Indicate in tabular form the values displayed.

7. Which of the following programs computes most efficiently the average F of the data items processed?

a)
```
100 REM CHAPTER 6 SELF-TEST 7A
110 LET T = 0
120 READ X
130 FOR I = 1 TO X
140    READ N
150    LET T = T + N
160 NEXT I
170 LET F = T/X
180 PRINT "THE AVERAGE IS"; F
190 DATA 6, 3, 5, 7, 8, 4, 9
200 END
```

b)
```
100 REM CHAPTER 6 SELF-TEST 7B
110 LET T = 0
120 READ X
130 FOR I = 1 TO X
140    READ N
150    LET T = T + N
160    LET F = T/X
170 NEXT I
180 PRINT "THE AVERAGE IS"; F
190 DATA 6, 3, 5, 7, 8, 4, 9
200 END
```

8. Identify the syntax and logic error(s), if any, in each of the following statements.

a) `100 IF A > 0 LET I = I + 1`

b) `100 IF A NOT < B THEN 600 ELSE 110`

c) `100 IF B < C THEN 100 ELSE 110`

d) `100 IF A > C AND OR C > D THEN 110 ELSE 700`

e) `100 IF A > E AND IF C < B THEN PRINT A ELSE PRINT B`

f) `100 FOR X = 1 TO 10`

g) `100 FOR A$ = 1 TO 5`

h) `100 WHILE X < 10 TO 20`

i) `100 WEND X = 0`

j) `100 ON X GOTO Y, Z, W`

k) `100 FOR A = 1 TO 5 STEP -1`

l) `100 WHILE A < 5 OR B < 10`

9. Write a program that will sum the first 1000 negative integers.

10. Write a single IF-THEN-ELSE statement for each of the following.
    a) When X is greater than Y, or K is less than or equal to 1, increment L by 1.
    b) When X is between 0 and 5 inclusive, or X is between 10 and 20 (not inclusive), transfer control to line 500.
    c) When J is greater than 10 transfer control to line 400; otherwise, if K is less than 5 and M is equal to zero increment P by 1, else transfer control to line 250.

11. Write a program that corresponds to the program flowchart below.
    a) Using For loops.
    b) Using While loops.

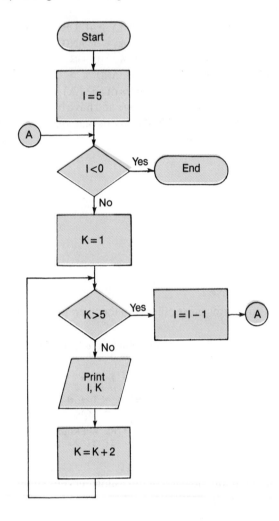

12. Write an IF-THEN-ELSE statement for each of the following partial flowcharts.

a)

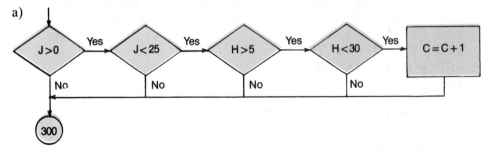

b)

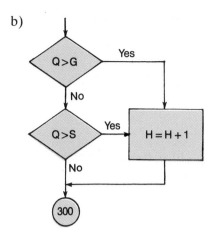

c)

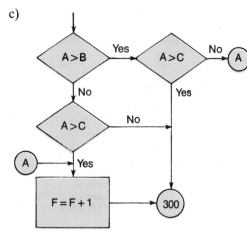

d)

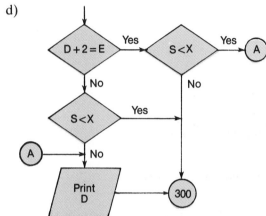

13. Is the following partial program valid or invalid? If it is invalid, indicate why.

```
100 REM CHAPTER 6 SELF-TEST 13
110 REM ***MAIN MODULE***
     .
     .
     .
150 GOSUB 180
160 PRINT X
170 REM ***COMPUTE SQUARE***
180 LET X = X^2
190 RETURN
200 END
```

14. Consider the two programs below. Assume the first program's name is PROG1, and it currently resides both in memory and in auxiliary storage. Assume the second program resides in auxiliary storage under the name PROG2. What is displayed if PROG1 is executed? (Enter the values 1, 3, 5, 7, and 0 in response to the INPUT statement.)

```
100 REM CHAPTER 6 SELF-TEST 14 PROG1
110 INPUT "ENTER A NUMBER"; A
120 IF A <> 0 THEN 130 ELSE 140
130    CHAIN "PROG2",, ALL
140 PRINT "JOB COMPLETE"
150 END
```

```
100 REM CHAPTER 6 SELF-TEST 14 PROG2
110 LET X = A*A*A
120 PRINT A, X
130 CHAIN "PROG1"
140 END
```

6.10
TEST YOUR
BASIC SKILLS

1. Consider the valid programs listed below. What is displayed if each is executed?

a)
```
100 REM EXERCISE 6.1A
110 READ X, Y
120 WHILE X >= 0
130    IF X = Y AND Y >= 10 THEN PRINT Y ELSE PRINT X, Y
140    IF X = Y OR Y >= 10 THEN PRINT 2 * Y ELSE PRINT X, 2 * Y
150    READ X, Y
160 WEND
170 PRINT "END OF JOB"
180 DATA 3, 5, 8, 10, 15, 15, 4, 4, -1, 0
190 END
```

b) Assume B is assigned the following values: 500, −10, 0, 600 and −999999.
```
100 REM EXERCISE 6.1B
110 INPUT "BALANCE"; B
120 WHILE B <> -999999
130    IF B >= 0 AND B <= 550 THEN 160
140        PRINT "BALANCE IS INVALID, PLEASE RE-ENTER"
150    GOTO 170
160        PRINT "INTEREST"; 0.10 * B
170 INPUT "BALANCE"; B
180 WEND
180 PRINT "END OF JOB"
190 END
```

c)
```
100 REM EXERCISE 6.1C
110 LET A = 0
120 LET B = 0
130 LET C = 0
140 READ P
150 FOR I = 1 TO P
160    READ D
170    IF D >= 0 AND D < 50 THEN LET A = A + 1
180    IF D >= 50 AND D < 100 THEN LET B = B + 1
190    IF D >= 100 THEN LET C = C + 1
200 NEXT I
210 PRINT A, B, C
220 DATA 10, 150, 99, 100, 50, 0, 25, 88, 42, 101, 10
230 END
```

d) Assume the following values are entered in sequence as requested: 15, 8, 17, −999999.
```
100 REM EXERCISE 6.1D
110 INPUT "INVENTORY NUMBER"; I1
120 WHILE I1 <> -999999
130    LET C = 0
140    WHILE C = 0
150        READ I2, P
160        IF I2 <> 0 THEN 200
170            PRINT "INVENTORY ITEM NOT FOUND"
180            LET C = 1
190            GOTO 230
200        IF I1 <> I2 THEN 230
210            PRINT "THE PRICE IS"; P
220            LET C = 1
230    WEND
240    RESTORE
250    INPUT "INVENTORY NUMBER"; I1
260 WEND
270 PRINT "JOB COMPLETE"
280 DATA 6, 4.54, 8, 12.96, 15, 14.98, 22, 4.96, 0, 0
290 END
```

2. Given the following:

Employee number E = 500
Salary S = \$700
Job code J = 1
Tax T = \$60
Insurance deduction I = \$40

Determine the truth value of the following compound conditions.

a) $E < 400$ OR $J = 1$

b) $S = 700$ AND $T = 50$

c) $S - T = 640$ AND $J = 1$

d) $T + I = S - 500$ OR $J = 0$

e) NOT $J < 0$

f) NOT $S > 500$ AND NOT $T > 80$

g) NOT $(J = 1$ OR $T = 60)$

h) $J = 1$ XOR $E >= 500$

i) I <> 40 EQV S > 500   l) S < 300 AND (I < 50 OR J = 1)
j) S = 700 IMP T = 60   m) NOT (NOT J = 1)
k) S < 300 AND I < 50 OR J = 1   n) I < 40 OR T = 60 XOR S > 600

3. Assume P and Q are simple conditions. The following logical equivalences are known
   as **DeMorgan's Laws:**

   > NOT (P OR Q) is equivalent to NOT P AND NOT Q
   > NOT (P AND Q) is equivalent to NOT P OR NOT Q

   Use DeMorgan's Laws to find a logical equivalent for each of the following:

   a) NOT (P OR (NOT Q))   c) NOT (NOT P AND Q)
   b) NOT ((NOT P) OR Q)   d) NOT ((NOT P) AND (NOT Q))

4. Construct a partial flowchart for each of the following:

   a) NOT S = Q AND (X > 1 OR C < 3)
   b) (K = 9 AND Q = 2) OR (NOT Z = 3 OR T = 0)

5. Given the following:

   > S = 0
   > Y = 4
   > B = 7
   > T = 8
   > X = 3

   Determine the action taken for each of the following.

   ```
   a) 100 IF S > -1 THEN PRINT S ELSE 500
   b) 100 IF B = 4 OR T > 7 THEN IF X > 1 THEN 400
   c) 100 IF X = 3 OR T > 2 THEN IF Y > 7 THEN 500
   d) 100 IF X + 2 < 5 THEN IF B < Y + X THEN 110 ELSE 500
   e) 100 IF B <> 7 THEN 110 ELSE IF X = 4 THEN 500 ELSE 600
   f) 100 IF S < X THEN IF Y < T THEN 110 ELSE LET T = T + 1
   ```

6. Write a partial program for each of the following situations that request the user to
   enter a value. After the value is entered, validate the value using one IF-THEN-ELSE
   statement. If the value is invalid, display an appropriate diagnostic message and
   transfer control back to the INPUT statement. Begin each partial program with line
   100 and branch to line 140 when the data is valid.

   a) Request a percent P. If the percent is negative or
      greater than 25, request the user to re-enter the
      value.

   b) Request a balance B. Check if the balance is
      between $550.99 and 765.50 inclusive. If the bal-
      ance is outside the range, request the user to
      re-enter the value.

   c) Request a customer code C$. Check to ensure that
      the code is an "A," "D," "E" or "F." If the code is
      invalid, request the user to re-enter the code.

   d) Request a customer number N$ and check to ensure
      that the third digit is a 4. If the third digit is not a 4,
      request the user to re-enter the number.

7. Write a *single* IF-THEN-ELSE statement for each of the following partial flowcharts.
   When appropriate, use logical operators.

   a)

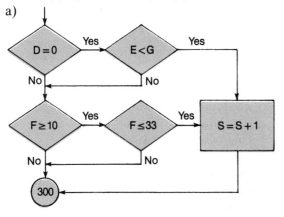

b)

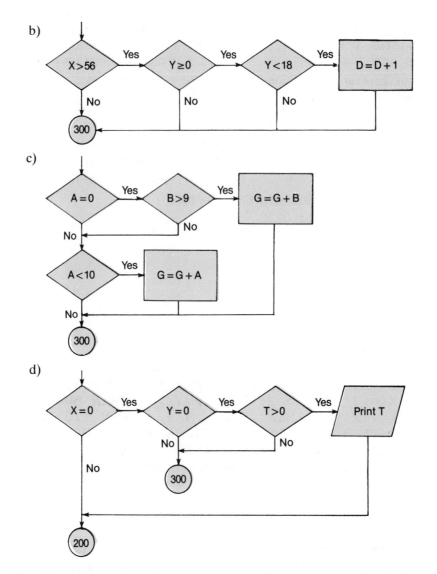

c)

d)

8. Write a short program that corresponds to the program flowchart below.
   a) Using an IF-THEN statement to facilitate looping
   b) Using a For loop
   c) Using a While loop

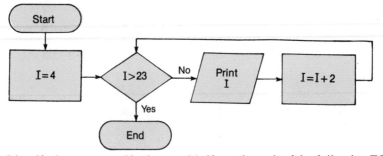

9. Identify the syntax and logic error(s), if any, in each of the following FOR statements.

a) `100 FOR X = 1, 6`   h) `100 FOR X = 10 TO 1`
b) `100 FOR Y = 1 TO 6 STEP -1`   i) `100 FOR P = 1, STEP 1 TO 2`
c) `100 FOR 30 = 5, 10`   j) `100 FOR R = 5 TO 5`
d) `100 FOR X = -1 TO 10 STEP 5` k) `100 FOR X = A TO B STEP -B`
e) `100 FOR A1 = 1 TO 25^(1/2)`   l) `100 FOR Q = 3.9*X TO 4*(B + C) STEP X*Y`
f) `100 FOR A(1) = 1 TO 10`   m) `100 FOR X = 4.7 TO 1.6 STEP -0.1`
g) `100 FOR B$ = 0 TO 7`   n) `100 FOR E = 1 TO 10 STEP 0`

10. Draw a flowchart for the following program.

```
100 REM EXERCISE 6.10
110 FOR I = 1 TO 19 STEP 2
120    LET J = I + 1
130    PRINT I
140 NEXT I
150 PRINT J
160 END
```

11. The following questions pertain to Exercise 10.

    a) How many lines of output are generated by the program?

    b) What value is printed on the last line of output?

    c) How many lines of output are generated if a semicolon is placed after the I in line 130?

    d) If lines 140 and 150 are interchanged, and no other changes are made, how many lines of output are generated by the program?

12. Consider the following program:

```
100 REM EXERCISE 6.12
110 LET F = 0
120 FOR I = 1 TO 3
130    LET G = 0
140    LET F = F + 1
150    FOR J = 1 TO 4
160        LET G = G + F
170        PRINT F, G
180    NEXT J
190 NEXT I
200 END
```

    a) How many lines are displayed?

    b) What is the maximum value of F?

    c) What is the maximum value of G?

13. Identify the error(s), if any, that exist in each of the following programs.

    a)
    ```
    100 REM EXERCISE 6.13A
    110 FOR I = 1 TO 10
    120    FOR K = 2 TO 12
    130        LET J = K + 5
    140    NEXT I
    150    PRINT J
    160 NEXT K
    170 END
    ```

    c)
    ```
    100 REM EXERCISE 6.13C
    110 FOR I = 1 TO 10
    120    LET X = X + 1
    130    LET Y = 2 * X
    140    FOR I = 2 TO 5
    150        LET Z = 2 * Y
    160        PRINT Z
    170    NEXT I
    180 NEXT I
    190 END
    ```

    b)
    ```
    100 REM EXERCISE 6.13B
    110 FOR I = 1 TO 10
    120    FOR K = 5 TO 30 STEP 2
    130        PRINT I, K
    140    NEXT K
    150    FOR L = 0.01 TO 1 STEP 0.01
    160        PRINT L
    170    NEXT L
    180 NEXT I
    190 END
    ```

    d)
    ```
    100 REM EXERCISE 6.13D
    110 LET F = 3000
    120 FOR I = 1 TO 20
    130    GOTO 160
    140    FOR K = 1 TO 3
    150        PRINT F
    160        PRINT K
    170    NEXT K
    180 NEXT I
    190 END
    ```

14. How many lines will be displayed by the following program?

```
100 REM EXERCISE 6.14
110 FOR C = 1 TO 20
120    FOR A = 1 TO 10
130        FOR Q = 1 TO 8
140            PRINT C, A, Q
150        NEXT Q
160    NEXT A
170 NEXT C
180 END
```

15. Write a program for each of the following expressions and display the result.

    a) $2 \times 4 \times 6 \times 8 \times \cdots \times 80$ b) $1 + \dfrac{1}{2} + \dfrac{1}{4} + \dfrac{1}{8} + \cdots + \dfrac{1}{2^{10}}$

    c) $1^1 + 2^2 + 3^3 + 4^4 + 5^5$

16. Write a program that determines the number of negative values N, number of zero values Z, and number of positive values P in the following data set: $4, 2, 3, -9, 0, 0, -4,$

$-6, -8, 3, 2, 0, 0, 8, -3, 4$. Use an INPUT statement to enter the *number* of data items to be processed, in this case 16. Store the data items in a DATA statement and use a For or While loop to process the data.

17. Write a subroutine that will convert a Fahrenheit temperature F to Centigrade C, Kelvin K and Rankine R. Use the following formulas:

C = (F − 32)5/9
K = C + 273
R = F + 460

18. Assume program PROG2 is stored in auxiliary storage and the first executable statement is in line 150. Indicate the differences between the following three CHAIN statements:

```
1120 CHAIN "PROG2"
1120 CHAIN "PROG2", 200
1120 CHAIN "PROG2",, ALL
```

6.11 PROGRAMMING EXERCISES

Exercise 1: Sales Pricing

Purpose: To become familiar with the use of decision statements and data validation.

Problem: A company sells four differently priced items in each line of products. Write a program that determines the gross sales for each different item in the product line and the total number of units sold of each item. Also, compute the total gross sales for the product. The product number and the prices of each item are to be stored in one or more DATA statements. The item number (codes 1, 2, 3, or 4) and the number of units sold are entered into the program via an INPUT statement. The program should only accept valid item numbers (i.e., codes 1, 2, 3 or 4 are valid). −1 indicates end of job.

Input Data: Prepare and use the following sample data:

Product Number: 123

Prices: 0.14, 0.18, 0.22, 0.36 (The prices are in a sequence that corresponds to the item number codes of 1, 2, 3, and 4.)

The item number and number of units sold are:

Item Number	Number of Units Sold
1	255
3	650
4	225
0	123
2	125
4	650
3	725
1	860
2	125
5	780
4	270
1	365
2	124

Output Results: The following partial results are shown:

```
ITEM NUMBER PLEASE? 1
NUMBER OF UNITS SOLD? 255
ITEM NUMBER PLEASE? 3
NUMBER OF UNITS SOLD? 650
ITEM NUMBER PLEASE? 4
NUMBER OF UNITS SOLD? 225
ITEM NUMBER PLEASE? 0
ITEM NO. INVALID TRY AGAIN
        .
        .
        .
ITEM NUMBER PLEASE? 2
NUMBER OF UNITS SOLD? 124
ITEM NUMBER PLEASE? -1
```

```
TOTALS FOR PRODUCT 123

ITEM            TOTAL
NUMBER          UNITS           GROSS SALES
------          -----           -----------
  1             1,480              207.20
  2               374               67.32
  3             1,375              302.50
  4             1,145              412.20

TOTAL GROSS SALES FOR PRODUCT 123 IS  $989.22
```

Purpose: To become familiar with the concepts of aging accounts receivable using Julian Calendar dates (i.e., using a number between 1 and 365 to signify a date).

Exercise 2: Aging Accounts

Problem: Write a program to compute the total amount due and percentage of the total amount of receivables that are:

1) Less than 30 days past due (accounts due < 30 days)
2) Past due between 31 and 60 days ($30 \le$ accounts due ≤ 60)
3) Past due over 60 days (accounts due > 60)

Include in the output the number of accounts in each category. The first input value will be today's Julian date. However, the account number, amount due and the date due for each customer shall be stored in one or more DATA statements.

Input Data: Prepare and use the following sample data. Assume today's Julian date is 155 (i.e., 155th day of the year).

Account Number	Amount Due	Date Due
1168	1495.67	145
2196	3211.16	15
3485	1468.12	130
3612	1896.45	98
7184	5.48	126
8621	965.10	75
9142	613.50	105

Output Results: The following results are displayed:

```
WHAT IS THE JULIAN DATE? 155

ACCOUNTS                NUMBER OF      TOTAL          PERCENT OF
PAST DUE                ACCOUNTS       AMOUNT DUE     TOTAL AMOUNT
---------               ---------      ----------     ------------
LESS THAN 30 DAYS           3          2,969.27         30.7522
30 TO 60 DAYS               2          2,509.95         25.9951
OVER 60 DAYS                2          4,176.26         43.2528

JOB COMPLETE
```

Purpose: To illustrate the concepts of selection and data validation.

Exercise 3: Selecting Eligible Programmers

Problem: An employment agency maintains a prospective employee file. Each record contains a name and codes ("Y" or "N" for each programming language) that indicate the individual's area of expertise. Write a program which will display a list of prospective employees who meet the selection criteria that has been entered via INPUT statements. The names and corresponding codes are to be stored in DATA statements. The user may request, for example, all records that meet these criteria: *Proficient in BASIC, PL/1 and COBOL*. The program should first request the criteria and allow the user to enter "Y" or "N" for each programming language desired. Each entry should be validated to ensure that the user entered a "Y" or "N." Next the program should read a prospective employee record and determine if the record meets the criteria. If the record passes the tests, display the name and increment a counter. If the record fails to pass the tests, read the next record.

Hint: A record passes each programming language test if the user enters an "N" for the language *or* if the user enters a "Y" and the record contains a "Y" for the language.

Input Data: Prepare and use the following prospective employee data:

Employee Name	BASIC	COBOL	FORTRAN	PASCAL	RPG
Quinn, Jack	Y	N	Y	N	Y
Chab, Sarah	N	Y	Y	Y	N
Korman, Liz	Y	Y	N	Y	Y
Jones, David	Y	N	N	Y	N
Albe, Jim	Y	Y	N	Y	N
Biag, John	N	Y	Y	Y	Y
Holk, George	N	Y	Y	Y	N
Lock, Kim	Y	N	Y	N	N
Smyth, Fred	Y	Y	Y	N	N
Lave, Linda	N	N	Y	Y	N

Use the following selection criteria and RUN the program three times.

1) Select all prospective employees whose area of expertise includes COBOL and PASCAL.
2) Select all prospective employees whose area of expertise includes COBOL, FORTRAN, PASCAL and RPG.
3) Select all prospective employees whose area of expertise includes BASIC.

Output Results: The following results are displayed for the first criterion:

```
ENTER 'Y' OR 'N' FOR EACH LANGUAGE AS REQUESTED
BASIC? N
COBOL? Y
FORTRAN? F
INVALID ENTRY, PLEASE ENTER A 'Y' OR 'N'
FORTRAN? N
PASCAL? Y
RPG? N


PROSPECTIVE EMPLOYEES WHO MEET CRITERION
-------------------------------------------
CHAB, SARAH
KORMAN, LIZ
ALBE, JIM
BIAG, JOHN
HOLK, GEORGE

TOTAL NUMBER MEETING CRITERION 5

JOB COMPLETE
```

Exercise 4:
Solution of an Equation

Purpose: To become familiar with the techniques of solving the quadratic equation.

Problem: Construct an efficient program to solve for the roots of the quadratic equation $ax^2 + bx + c = 0$ where $a = 0$, using the quadratic formula

$$x = \frac{-b \pm \sqrt{b^2 - 4ac}}{2a}$$

Read three values for the coefficients a, b, c, respectively. Print the values of the coefficients and the roots on one line. If the roots are equal, print only one root. Assume the coefficient *a* does not have a value of zero and that complex roots do not exist (that is, that $4ac$ is always less than or equal to b^2).

Input Data: Prepare and use the following sample values for the coefficients.

A	B	C
3	−5	−2
1	−4	2
1	6	9
4	−20	2.5
8	0	0
1	80	1

Output Results: The following results are displayed:

```
     A         B         C       ROOT 1    ROOT 2
   -----     -----     -----     ------    ------
    3.00     -5.00     -2.00      2.000    -0.333
    1.00     -4.00      2.00      3.414     0.586
    1.00      6.00      9.00     -3.000
    4.00    -20.00      2.50      4.872     0.128
    8.00      0.00      0.00      0.000
    1.00     80.00      1.00     -0.013   -79.987

  END OF REPORT
```

Purpose: To become familiar with counter-controlled loops.

Exercise 5:
Sum of a Series
of Numbers

Problem:

Part A: Construct a program to compute and display the sum of the following series: $1 + 2 + 3 + \cdots + 100$. Use a For loop to create these integers and sum them.

Part B: Same as in Part A, but instead sum all the even numbers from 2 to 100 inclusive.

Part C: Same as in Part A, but instead input the lower and upper limits.

Part D: Same as in Part A and C, but instead include a variable step.

Input Data: For Parts A and B there is no input. For C, input a lower limit of 15 and an upper limit of 42. For Part D, input a lower limit of 20, an upper limit of 75 and a step of 5.

Output Results: For Part A, the sum is 5050.   For Part C, the sum is 798.
For Part B, the sum is 2550.   For Part D, the sum is 570.

Purpose: To become familiar with counter-controlled loops.

Exercise 6:
Population Growth

Problem: The estimated population of the United States for January 1984 is 234,500,000. Write a program using a For loop that will display the estimated population for years 1985 through 2000. Assume that the annual growth rate is 0.9% and that the rate will remain constant. The algorithm to be employed is the following:

Population 1985 = Population 1984 × (1 + 0.009)
Population 1986 = Population 1985 × (1 + 0.009)

or

New Year Population = Old Year Population × (1 + 0.009)

Construct the For loop so that the initial parameter (beginning year) and limit parameter (ending year) are variables entered prior to the execution of the FOR statement.

Input Data: Prepare and use the following sample data.

    Population   = 234,500,000
    Initial Year = 1985
    Terminal Year = 2000

If your computer system does not allow for nine digits of precision, write the 234,500,000 in exponential notation (try 2.345E08; for other possibilities, see Section 3.2).

Output Results: The following results are displayed:

```
POPULATION GROWTH
YEAR            POPULATION
----            ----------
1985            2.36611E+08
1986            2.3874E+08
1987            2.40889E+08
  .                 .
  .                 .
  .                 .
1997            2.63468E+08
1998            2.65839E+08
1999            2.68232E+08
2000            2.70646E+08

JOB COMPLETE
```

Exercise 7: Breakeven Point Analysis

Purpose: To become familiar with subroutines and the use of For loops to generate a tabular report.

Problem: The Silicon Chip company manufactures memory chips for computers. The company analysts project fixed costs for the next fiscal year at $125,000. They expect sales to approach $435,000. Because of the fluctuation in the inflation rate, the analysts are having a difficult time estimating variable costs. Estimates run between 68 and 77 percent of total sales.

   Write a program that calls upon a subroutine to compute the breakeven point in terms of dollar sales for variable costs between 68 and 77 percent of total sales. The breakeven point is that level of sales which produces neither a loss or a profit. The breakeven point can be computed from the following formula:

$$B = \frac{F}{1 - \dfrac{V}{S}}$$

where B = breakeven point in dollar sales
       F = total fixed cost
       V = variable cost (percent of expected sales)
       S = expected sales

Also determine the profit based on the expected sales of $435,000 for each of the computed breakeven points. Use the formula:

$$P = S - B$$

where S = expected sales
       B = breakeven point in dollar sales
       P = profit

Use a minus sign to the right in the descriptor field to illustrate a deficit in the profit column. See Section 4.5.

Input Data: Use the following sample data: expected sales, $435,000; fixed cost, $125,000; initial variable cost, 68% of sales; terminal variable cost, 77% of sales.

Output Results: The following results are displayed:

```
EXPECTED SALES? 435000
FIXED COST? 125000
INITIAL VARIABLE COST (IN PERCENT)? 68
TERMINAL VARIABLE COST (IN PERCENT)? 77

              BREAKEVEN POINT ANALYSIS
              EXPECTED SALES $ 435000
              FIXED COST $ 125000

VARIABLE COST OF SALES   BREAKEVEN
PERCENT        DOLLARS   POINT          PROFIT
----------------------   ---------      ------
    68         295,800   390,625        44,375
    69         300,150   403,226        31,774
    70         304,500   416,667        18,333
    71         308,850   431,034         3,966
    72         313,200   446,429        11,429-
    73         317,550   462,963        27,963-
    74         321,900   480,769        45,769-
    75         326,250   500,000        65,000-
    76         330,600   520,833        85,833-
    77         334,950   543,478       108,478-

  JOB COMPLETE
```

Purpose: To illustrate a **table look-up** process.

Exercise 8:
Part Cost and
Description Look-up

Problem: Construct a program that requests the user to enter a three-digit part number and display the part cost and part description. Each part cost and description are to be stored in DATA statements along with the corresponding part number.

Following the entry of a part number, via the INPUT statement, and using a For or While loop, the program should search the table of entries using a READ statement and a decision statement. If the part number entered equals a part number in one of the DATA statements, display the cost and description. If the part number entered does not equal any of the part numbers in the DATA statements, display a diagnostic message.

Use the RESTORE statement to reset the pointer in the data holding area for the next part number entered by the user. The program terminates when the user enters a −999999 part number.

Input Data: Prepare and use the following part number table entries:

Part Number	Part Cost	Part Description
122	$79.95	Western Guitar
128	59.95	Jumbo Guitar
130	49.95	Concert-size Guitar
142	69.95	Classic Guitar
154	24.95	Student-size Guitar
161	99.95	Harmonic Distortion

Use the following sample part numbers: 154, 131, 130, 122, −999999

Output Results: The following results are displayed for part numbers 154 and 131:

```
PART NUMBER? 154
PART COST $ 24.95
PART DESCRIPTION -  STUDENT-SIZE GUITAR

PART NUMBER? 131
PART NUMBER IS INVALID
```

Purpose: To become familiar with the use of subroutines and the top-down program approach.

Exercise 9:
Determining the
Mortgage Payment and
Amortization Schedule

Problem: Construct a program to compute and display the monthly payment for a mortgage when the annual interest rate, expressed in *percent*, the amount of the loan and the number of years are entered via INPUT statements. Assume that a payment is made each month.

The monthly payment for the mortgage is computed from the following relationship:

$$\text{PAYMENT} = \left[\frac{r(1 + r)^n}{(1 + r)^n - 1} \right] \times L$$

where L = amount of the loan
   r = monthly interest (Divide r, the % entered, by 1200.)
   n = number of payments (years × 12)

Round the Payment to the nearest cent.

In addition, the program should generate the amortization schedule of this mortgage in tabular form by displaying on each line the payment number, which represents the month, the amount of the monthly payment applied to the interest, the amount of the monthly payment applied to the principal and the balance owed on the loan. Round to two decimal places the values displayed in the amortization schedule.

Develop a solution based on the following top-down chart:

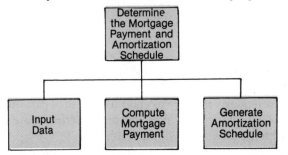

Input Data: Use the following sample data:

   Amount = 8000
   Interest = 9.25%
      Time = 3 years

Output Results: The following results are displayed:

```
AMOUNT? 8000
INTEREST? 9.25
TIME IN YEARS? 3
THE MONTHLY PAYMENT IS $ 255.33

                <-AMOUNT APPLIED TO->       BALANCE
   MONTH        INTEREST      PAYMENT        OWED
   -----        --------      -------       -------
     1            61.67        193.66       7,806.34
     2            60.17        195.16       7,611.18
     3            58.67        196.66       7,414.52
     .              .            .             .
     .              .            .             .
     .              .            .             .
    34             5.81        249.52        504.81
    35             3.89        251.44        253.37
    36             1.95        253.38          0.00

END OF REPORT
```

Exercise 10:
Future Values for
Varying Interest Rates

Purpose: To become familiar with the iterative technique for solving compound interest problems and to illustrate nested For loops.

Problem: Construct a program that requests the user to enter the principal P and the time period T in years and compute the future value of that principal at interest rates R ranging from 5.5% to 11.5% in increments of 2% for years I through T. The future values are to be displayed in tabular form with the percentages as the column headings. The amount A is to be computed for each year and each percentage on an individual basis using the formula $A = P(1 + R)^T$. If a time period of 5 is entered, the program should generate future values for years 1 through 5 at the interest rates specified above.

Hint: See Programming Case Study 12 in Section 6.4.

Input Data: Use the following sample data:

Principal	Time
$5000	7 years
$ 450	6 years
−1	0 (end-of-file condition)

Output Results: The following results are displayed for the first set of the sample data:

```
WHAT IS THE PRINCIPAL? 5000
WHAT IS THE TIME IN YEARS? 7

YEAR      5.5%       7.5%       9.5%      11.5%
----      ----       ----       ----      -----
  1     5,275.00   5,375.00   5,475.00   5,575.00
  2     5,565.12   5,778.13   5,995.13   6,216.13
  3     5,871.21   6,211.49   6,564.66   6,930.98
  4     6,194.12   6,677.35   7,188.31   7,728.04
  5     6,534.80   7,178.15   7,871.19   8,616.77
  6     6,894.21   7,716.51   8,618.96   9,607.69
  7     7,273.39   8,295.25   9,437.76  10,712.58
```

Purpose: To become familiar with the use of subroutines and the top-down approach.

Exercise 11: Declining Balance Depreciation

Problem: There are several methods to compute the depreciation on potential or present capital investments. In Chapter 4, Programming Exercise 5, the straight-line depreciation method was used. In this exercise, we will use another method, called the "declining-balance depreciation" method, which considers the depreciation of an investment to be greatest at the outstart and progressively smaller on a declining basis thereafter.

Using the top-down approach, write a program to compute and display in annual stages the declining-balance depreciation for the purchase of a $15,000 microcomputer system. Display the results (rounded to two decimal places) in tabular form over an eight year period.

To compute the depreciation, multiply the current value of the investment at the beginning of each time period by a depreciation percentage. For this exercise, use a depreciation percentage of 2% per month. The following illustrate the computations involved:

Month 1: $15,000 \times 0.02 = 300.00$ depreciation
Month 2: $14,700 \times 0.02 = 294.00$ depreciation
. . . and so on.

Input Data: Use the following sample data:

Investment = $15,000
Time period = 8 years
Depreciation per month = 2%

Output Results: The following results are displayed:

```
INVESTMENT? 15000
TIME IN YEARS? 8
PERCENT DEPRECIATION PER MONTH? 2

YEAR  DEPRECIATION     VALUE
----  ------------     -----
  1     3,229.25    11,770.75
  2     2,534.04     9,236.71
  3     1,988.50     7,248.21
  4     1,560.42     5,687.79
  5     1,224.49     4,463.30
  6       960.89     3,502.41
  7       754.00     2,748.41
  8       591.68     2,156.72

JOB COMPLETE
```

Exercise 12:
Developing a
Menu Driven Program
Top-Down

Purpose: To illustrate the top-down approach, the CHAIN statement, and menu controlled programs.

Problem: Construct a program to display the menu illustrated below. If the user enters a code of 1, chain to the program solution for Program 5.9 illustrated in Chapter 5 (p. 161). If the user enters a code of 2, chain to the program solution for Programming Exercise 14 in Chapter 5. If the user enters a code fo 3, then terminate execution of the program. Adjust the menus in Program 5.9 and in Programming Exercise 5.14 so that control returns to the main program when a code of 7 is entered for Program 5.9 and code 5 for Programming Exercise 5.14. Create your own test data to evaluate the programs.

```
        AREA AND VOLUME MENU
        -------------------

    CODE    FUNCTION
    ----    --------
      1   - COMPUTE AREAS
      2   - COMPUTE VOLUMES
      3   - END PROGRAM

    ENTER A CODE 1 THROUGH 3?
```

Exercise 13:
The Check Digit
Problem

Purpose: To illustrate the concepts of generating check digits.

Problem: Construct a program similar to Program 6.2 to verify a 6-digit part number by validating the units position for a check digit. The computation of the check digit involves multiplying every other digit of the original number by 2 and adding these values and the remaining digits of the number together. The units digit of the result obtained is then subtracted from 10 to obtain the check digit.

   To illustrate the process used, let us form the part number by computing the check digit for the number 72546. The alternate digits are first multiplied by 2:

$$
\begin{array}{ccc}
7 & 5 & 6 \\
 & & 2 \\
\hline
14 & 10 & 12
\end{array}
$$

Then the remaining digits (2 and 4) are included and all the above digits are added:

$$1 + 4 + 1 + 0 + 1 + 2 + 2 + 4 = 15$$

The 5 is subtracted from 10 to give a check digit of 5, so the part number becomes 725465.

   This algorithm is more sophisticated than the one given in Section 6.3, since it can detect invalid part numbers which have digits reversed, like 752465 (instead of 725465).

Input Data: Prepare and use the following part numbers. Check to see if the rightmost digit is the correct check digit.

725465, 752465, 033332, 098792,
098798, 089798, 000000, 000001,
999999, 999995

Output Results: See Program 6.2 for the format of the output results.

Exercise 14:
Payroll Problem V—
Social Security
Computations

Purpose: To become familiar with the use of subroutines and program modification.

Problem: Modify Payroll Problem IV in Chapter 5 to determine the social security deduction. The social security deduction is equal to 6.70% of the gross pay to a maximum of $2,579.50 (6.70% of $38,500) for the year. Modify the solution to Payroll Problem IV by adding this additional computation as a subroutine. Round the social security tax to the nearest cent.

Input Data: Use the sample data found in Payroll Problem IV and add the following year-to-date social security deductions to the corresponding DATA statements.

Employee Number	Year-to-Date Social Security
123	$ 725.15
124	2,579.50
125	2,573.32
126	100.00

Output Results: The following results are displayed:

```
EMPLOYEE                                              YEAR-TO-DATE
NUMBER    GROSS PAY   FED. TAX   SOC. SEC.   NET PAY   SOC. SEC.
--------  ---------   --------   ---------   -------   ------------
  123     1,000.00     184.62       67.00    748.38        792.15
  124       880.00     168.31        0.00    711.69      2,579.50
  125     1,040.00     200.31        6.18    833.51      2,579.50
  126        90.00       0.00        6.03     83.97        106.03

TOTAL GROSS PAY==============>   3,010.00
TOTAL WITHHOLDING TAX=======>      553.24
TOTAL SOCIAL SECURITY=======>       79.21
TOTAL NET PAY===============>    2,377.55

JOB COMPLETE
```

ARRAYS, SORTING AND TABLE PROCESSING 7

In the previous chapters, the programs used simple variables like A, B1 and X$ to store and access data. Each variable was assigned a single value in an INPUT, LET or READ statement. Another technique which can make a program shorter, easier to code, and more general is the use of arrays. In this chapter we will discuss the advantages of grouping similar data into an array.

An **array** is an ordered set of string or numeric data defined in terms of 1 or more dimensions. In mathematics, an array is sometimes called a **matrix** or a table. Each member of an array is called an **array element**.

In BASIC, an array is a variable allocated a specified number of storage locations, each of which can be assigned a unique value. In other words, an array allows a programmer to store more than one value under the same variable name. Arrays are commonly used for sorting and table processing.

A report is usually easier to work with and more meaningful if the information is generated in some sequence, like first to last, largest to smallest or oldest to newest. Arranging data according to order or sequence is called **sorting**.

In data processing terminology, a **table** is a collection of data in which each item is uniquely identified by a label, by its position relative to other items or by some other means. Income tax tables, insurance tables, airline schedules and telephone directories are example of tables that present data that is concise, yet easy to read and understand. Storing table elements in arrays allows a programmer to organize the entries and to write efficient code for retrieving each individual element.

It is important to understand how arrays are defined in BASIC and how array elements in a program are accessed.

Arrays versus Simple Variables

Arrays permit a programmer to represent many values with one variable name. The variable name assigned to represent an array is called the **array name**. The elements in the array are distinguished from one another by subscripts. In BASIC, the subscript is written inside a set of parentheses and placed immediately to the right of the array name. Recall from Chapter 3, Section 3, that BASIC allows for two different types of variables, simple and subscripted. While simple variables are used to store and reference values that are independent from one another, subscripted variables are used to store and reference values that have been grouped into an array.

Consider the problem of writing a program that is to manipulate the twelve monthly sales for a company and generate a year-end report. Figure 7.1 illustrates the difference between using an array to store the 12 monthly sales and using simple variables.

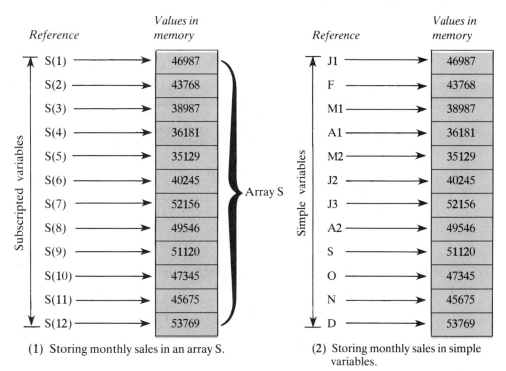

(1) Storing monthly sales in an array S.

(2) Storing monthly sales in simple variables.

FIGURE 7.1   Utilizing an array (1) versus simple variables (2).

The monthly sales stored in an array require the same memory allocation that the sales represented as independent variables do. The difference lies in the programming techniques which can access the different values. For example, the programmer may assign the values of simple variables in a READ statement, like this:

```
150 READ J1, F, M1, A1, M2, J2, J3, A2, S, O, N, D
```

Each simple variable must explicitly appear in a LET or PRINT statement if the monthly sales are to be summed or displayed. Not only is the programming time-consuming, but the variables *must* be properly placed in the program.

The same function can be accomplished by entering all 12 values into array S:

```
140 FOR M = 1 TO 12
150    READ S(M)
160 NEXT M
```

In line 140, the value of M is initialized to 1, and the first value in the data holding area is assigned to S(1) (read "S sub 1"). Then M is incremented to 2, and the next value is assigned to S(2). This continues until S(12) is assigned the 12th value in the data holding area.

S2 and S(2) are different from each other. S2 is a simple variable, no different from K, Y, X or G. On the other hand, S(2), is the second element in array S, and it is called upon in a program in a different fashion than a simple variable is.

**7.2
DECLARING
ARRAYS**

Before arrays can be used, the amount of memory to reserve for them must be declared in the program. This is the purpose of the DIM statement. The keyword DIM is an abbreviation of **dimension**. The DIM statement also declares the **upper bound value**, the limit value, of the subscript.

The DIM Statement

The main function of the DIM statement is to declare to the system the necessary information regarding the allocation of storage locations for arrays used in a program. Good programming practice dictates that every program that utilizes array elements should have a DIM statement that properly defines the arrays.

The general form of the DIM statement is given in Table 7.1. Note that commas are required punctuation between the declared array elements.

TABLE 7.1   The DIM Statement

General Form:	DIM array name (size), . . . , array name (size)
	where **array name** represents a numeric or string variable name, and where **size** represents the upper bound value of each array. The size may be an integer or simple variable for one-dimensional arrays. The size may be a series of integers or a series of simple variables separated by commas for multi-dimensional arrays.
Purpose:	To reserve storage locations for arrays.
Examples:	100 DIM B(4)
	200 DIM M(6), J$(200), L(N), T(20, 20)
	300 DIM X(50), F(10, 45), K$(X, Y, Z), D(2, 25, 7)

To ensure the proper placement of DIM statements, most programmers put them at the beginning of the program.

> **DIM Rule 1:** The DIM statement may be located anywhere before the first use of an array element in a program.

In Table 7.1, line 100 reserves memory for a one-dimensional array B consisting of 5 elements or storage locations. These elements—B(0), B(1), B(2), B(3) and B(4)—can be used in a program much as a simple variable can. For this DIM statement, elements B(5) or B(6) are considered not valid.

Line 200 declares 3 one-dimensional arrays M, J$ and L, and 1 two-dimensional array T. Line 200 reserves space for 7 elements for array M, 201 elements for array J$, N + 1 elements for array L and 441 elements for array T.

Line 300 in Table 7.1 declares 4 arrays. The first array, X, is a one-dimensional array. The second array, F, is a two-dimensional array. The last two, K$ and D, are three-dimensional arrays. Multi-dimensional arrays like F, K$ and D are discussed in Section 7.4.

A single DIM statement will be sufficient for most programs in this chapter. If five different arrays are to be declared, all five arrays can be listed in the same DIM statement:

```
200 DIM A(20), B(15, 28), C(X, Y, Z), D$(25), E(12, 24, 48)
```

Five separate DIM statements can also be used in the program to declare the arrays individually:

```
200 DIM A(20)
210 DIM B(15, 28)
220 DIM C(X, Y, Z)
230 DIM D$(25)
240 DIM E(12, 24, 48)
```

Unless otherwise specified, BASIC allocates the zero element for each one-dimensional array. For two-dimensional arrays an extra row, the zero row, and an extra column, the zero column, are reserved. Thus,

```
130 DIM S(12), T(20, 20)
```

actually reserves 13 elements for array S and 21 rows and 21 columns for array T. The extra array element is S(0) for array S and the extra row and column is the 0th (read "zeroth") row and the 0th column for array T. Although an additional element, row or column is of no problem to your program, many BASIC systems include the OPTION BASE statement which allows the programmer to control the **lower bound** of arrays that are declared. The OPTION BASE statement can be used to set the lower bound value to 1 instead of the default 0, which will avoid wasting memory on unused array elements.

The general form of the OPTION BASE statement is found in Table 7.2.

TABLE 7.2 **The** OPTION BASE **Statement**

General Form:	OPTION BASE n where n is either 0 or 1.
Purpose:	To assign a lower bound of 0 or 1 to all arrays in a program.
Examples:	`100 OPTION BASE 0` `120 OPTION BASE 1`
Caution:	This statement is not available on all BASIC systems.

The OPTION BASE statement can be used only once in a program. The effect of the OPTION BASE statement on arrays and its proper placement in a program are summarized in OPTION BASE Rules 1 and 2.

> OPTION BASE **Rule 1:** The OPTION BASE statement affects all arrays declared in a program.

> OPTION BASE **Rule 2:** The OPTION BASE statement must precede any DIM statement in a program.

In this section several sample programs that manipulate the elements of arrays will be discussed. Before the programs are presented, however, it is important that you understand the syntax and limitations of subscripts.

As indicated in Section 7.1, the elements of an array are referenced by assigning a subscript to the array name. The subscript is written within parentheses and placed immediately to the right of the array name. The subscript may be any valid non-negative number, variable or numeric expression within the **range** of the array. The lower and upper bounds of an array should never be exceeded. For example, if an array G is declared as follows:

```
100 DIM G(50)
```

it is invalid to reference G(51), G(−3) or any others that are outside the lower and upper bounds of the array. Table 7.3 illustrates some additional valid and invalid subscripts.

Non-integer subscripts are rounded to the nearest integer to determine the element to be manipulated.*

---

*Some BASIC systems truncate rather than round.

TABLE 7.3   Valid and Invalid Subscripts

A(1)	Valid.
A(−3)	Invalid. Negative subscripts are not permitted.
A(X + Y)	Valid, provided X + Y is within the range of the array.
A(−X)	Valid, provided −X is within the range of the array.
A(12.3)	Valid, provided the array has been declared to 12 or more elements.
A(0)	Valid, provided the 0th element exists.
A(X ∧ 2)	Valid, provided X ∧ 2 is within the range of the array.
A(X + Y/3 + 5 ∧ X)	Valid, provided X + Y/3 + 5 ∧ X is within the range of the array.

If a particular subscripted variable has a single subscript, then that subscript should not be dropped or replaced by multiple subscripts in a given program. For example, if the array element is S(M), the subscript M should not be dropped to form the name S, and the subscript M should not be replaced by multiple subscripts to form S(M, N) in the same program. You must decide which variables will be subscripted in any program and then use them consistently throughout the program.

Program 7.1 reads data into an array and then displays the value of each element in the array.

```
100 REM PROGRAM 7.1
110 REM MONTHLY SALES ANALYSIS I
120 REM ************************
130 DIM S(12)
140 FOR M = 1 TO 12
150     READ S(M)
160 NEXT M
170 FOR M = 1 TO 12
180     PRINT S(M),
190 NEXT M
200 REM **************DATA FOLLOWS***************
210 DATA 46987, 43768, 38987, 36181, 35129, 40245
220 DATA 52156, 49546, 51120, 47345, 45675, 53769
230 END

RUN

46987        43768        38987        36181        35129
40245        52156        49546        51120        47345
45675        53769
```

PROGRAM 7.1

Line 130 reserves 13 elements or storage locations for array S. Valid subscripts for S range from 0 to 12. In this example S(0) is not used. Line 140 activates the first For loop and assigns M a value of 1. Line 150 reads the first data item, 46987, from the data holding area and assigns it to S(1). Line 160 returns control to the FOR statement in line 140 and M is incremented to 2. The READ statement in line 150 then assigns the second data item to S(2). This loop continues until S(12) is assigned the 12th data item.

Line 170 activates the second For loop and resets M to 1. This For loop then proceeds to display the values assigned to array S as shown.

Summing the Elements of an Array

Many applications call for summing the elements of an array. In Program 7.2 the monthly sales are summed, an average is computed and the sales are displayed, four to a line.

In program 7.2, line 170 is used to sum the values of the array elements. For example, when line 150 activates the For loop, M is assigned the value of 1. Line

```
100 REM PROGRAM 7.2
110 REM MONTHLY SALES ANALYSIS II
120 REM ************************
130 DIM S(12)
140 LET T = 0
150 FOR M = 1 TO 12
160    READ S(M)
170    LET T = T + S(M)
180 NEXT M
190 LET A = T/12
200 PRINT USING "THE AVERAGE MONTHLY SALES IS ###,###.##", A
210 PRINT
220 FOR M = 1 TO 12 STEP 4
230    PRINT S(M), S(M + 1), S(M + 2), S(M + 3)
240 NEXT M
250 PRINT
260 PRINT "JOB COMPLETE"
270 REM **************DATA FOLLOWS***************
280 DATA 46987, 43768, 38987, 36181, 35129, 40245
290 DATA 52156, 49546, 51120, 47345, 45675, 53769
300 END
```

PROGRAM 7.2

```
RUN

THE AVERAGE MONTHLY SALES IS   45,075.60

   46987         43768         38987         36181
   35129         40245         52156         49546
   51120         47345         45675         53769

JOB COMPLETE
```

160 reads the first data item, 46987, and assigns it to S(1). Line 170 increments the running total T by S(1), and line 180 returns control to the FOR statement in line 140, where M is incremented to 2.

After the READ statement, T is assigned the sum of T and S(2). This process continues until the 12th element is added to the sum of the first 11 elements of the array S. Line 190 computes the average, and line 200 displays it.

The For loop found in lines 220 through 240 displays the monthly sales four to a line. The first time through the loop, M is equal to 1, and S(1), S(2), S(3) and S(4) display on one line. The next time through the loop, M is equal to 5 and S(5), S(6), S(7) and S(8) display on the next line. Finally, M is set equal to 9 and S(9), S(10), S(11) and S(12) display on the third line. The subscripts in line 230 are in the form of numeric expressions.

Using Parallel Arrays

Program 7.3 illustrates the selection of elements that meet a certain criterion and the use of parallel arrays. **Parallel arrays** are two or more arrays that have corresponding elements. In Program 7.3, arrays M$ and S are parallel arrays and they are assigned the month names and sales. For each value of I in the range 1 through 12, the value of M$(I) is a monthly name and the value of S(I) is the corresponding monthly sales.

Program 7.3 computes and displays the average monthly sales. It also displays the months where the sales are above average by displaying the month, sales and deviation from the average. Finally, the program selects and displays the month with the highest sales and the month with the lowest sales.

Line 130 reserves 13 elements for the string array M$ and the numeric array S. Lines 140 through 200 are similar to Program 7.2. The For loop loads the arrays with values and sums the monthly sales, line 190 computes the average, and line 200 displays the average monthly sales. The next For loop, lines 260 through 280, tests each of the monthly sales found in array S against the average monthly sales

```
100 REM PROGRAM 7.3
110 REM MONTHLY SALES ANALYSIS III
120 REM *************************
130 DIM M$(12), S(12)
140 LET T = 0
150 FOR I = 1 TO 12
160    READ M$(I), S(I)
170    LET T = T + S(I)
180 NEXT I
190 LET A = T/12
200 PRINT USING "THE AVERAGE MONTHLY SALES IS ###,###.##", A
210 PRINT
220 PRINT
230 PRINT "MONTHS IN WHICH SALES ARE ABOVE AVERAGE"
240 PRINT
250 PRINT "MONTH", "SALES", "DEVIATION"
260 FOR I = 1 TO 12
270    IF S(I) >= A THEN PRINT M$(I), S(I), S(I) - A
280 NEXT I
290 PRINT
300 REM **********************************************************
310 REM * ASSUME FIRST MONTH HAS THE HIGHEST AND LOWEST SALES *
320 REM * J = SUBSCRIPT OF HIGHEST SALES, H = HIGHEST SALES   *
330 REM * K = SUBSCRIPT OF LOWEST SALES, L = LOWEST SALES     *
340 REM **********************************************************
350 LET H = S(1)
360 LET J = 1
370 LET L = S(1)
380 LET K = 1
390 FOR I = 2 TO 12
400    IF S(I) <= H THEN 430
410       LET H = S(I)
420       LET J = I
430    IF S(I) >= L THEN 460
440       LET L = S(I)
450       LET K = I
460 NEXT I
470 PRINT "MONTH OF HIGHEST SALES - "; M$(J)
480 PRINT "MONTH OF LOWEST SALES - "; M$(K)
490 PRINT "JOB COMPLETE"
500 REM *****************DATA FOLLOWS*****************
510 DATA JANUARY, 46987, FEBRUARY, 43768, MARCH, 38987
520 DATA APRIL, 36181, MAY, 35129, JUNE, 40245
530 DATA JULY, 52156, AUGUST, 49546, SEPTEMBER, 51120
540 DATA OCTOBER, 47345, NOVEMBER, 45675, DECEMBER, 53769
550 END

RUN

THE AVERAGE MONTHLY SALES IS  45,075.60


MONTHS IN WHICH SALES ARE ABOVE AVERAGE

MONTH           SALES           DEVIATION
JANUARY         46987           1911.4
JULY            52156           7080.4
AUGUST          49546           4470.4
SEPTEMBER       51120           6044.4
OCTOBER         47345           2269.4
NOVEMBER        45675           599.4
DECEMBER        53769           8693.4

MONTH OF HIGHEST SALES - DECEMBER
MONTH OF LOWEST SALES - MAY
JOB COMPLETE
```

PROGRAM 7.3

A. If the value of an element in the array is greater than or equal to the average, then the computer displays the corresponding monthly name found in array M$, the monthly sales and the monthly sales deviation from the average, $S(I) - A$.

Lines 350 through 480 illustrate a technique that determines the month in which the sales are the highest and the month in which the sales are the lowest. In lines 350 through 380, the first month's sales is assumed to be the highest as well as the lowest. The For loop, lines 390 through 460, tests the remaining months against the highest (lines 400 through 420) and lowest sales (lines 430 through 450). If a month's sales $S(I)$ is less than the current highest sales H, control passes to line 430. If a month's sales is greater than the current highest sales, then it is assigned as the current highest sales H and the variable J is assigned the value of the subscript I. When the For loop is satisfied, J is the subscript that represents the element in array S that has the highest sales, and K is the subscript that represents the elements in array S that has the lowest sales. Since M$ and S are parallel arrays, the corresponding month can be obtained by referencing M$(J).

The following problem and program solution incorporate arrays and other concepts discussed in this chapter.

Programming Case Study 14: Daily Sales Report by Department

Problem

The Twin City retail store has ten departments that submit their daily sales to the store manager. Management has asked the data processing department to generate a daily report that includes the department number, daily sales and what percent of the total sales each department contributes. Management also wants the total company sales displayed at the end of the report. A sample set of sales for the ten departments is found below.

Department Number	Daily Sales
1	$ 800
2	2,250
3	1,450
4	1,280
5	1,690
6	2,460
7	3,880
8	4,690
9	2,250
10	1,360

An analysis of the problem, a flowchart, and a program solution follow.

Program Tasks

1) Sum the department daily sales to determine the total sales T.
2) Since the percent P of total sales for each department cannot be computed until after the total sales for the store have been determined, store the department's daily sales into an array S.
3) Determine the percent of total sales from the following formula:

$$P = \frac{100 \times S(I)}{T}$$

where P = the percent of total sales per department
T = total sales
S(I) = sales of the Ith department

4) Use a For loop to read the department sales into array S and sum the department sales.
5) Use a For loop to determine the percent of total sales and display the results for each department.
6) Display the total sales T prior to termination of the program.

The following points should be noted concerning Program 7.4:

1) The DIM statement in line 140 sets aside 10 storage locations for array S, as illustrated:

0	0	0	0	0	0	0
S(0)	S(1)	S(2)	S(3)	S(4)	S(9)	S(10)

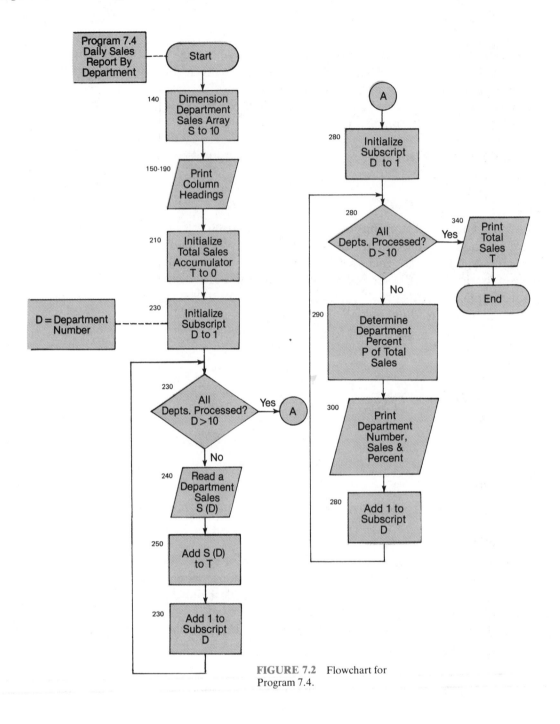

FIGURE 7.2   Flowchart for Program 7.4.

2) The For loop, lines 230 through 260, loads the array S beginning with S(1), as shown below, and accumulates the sum of the sales of the ten departments.

0	800	2250	1450	1280	2250	1360
S(0)	S(1)	S(2)	S(3)	S(4)	S(9)	S(10)

3) The second For loop, lines 280 through 310, computes the various departments' percent of total sales and displays a line each time through the loop.

```
100 REM PROGRAM 7.4
110 REM DAILY SALES REPORT BY DEPARTMENT
120 REM ********************************
130 REM *****DECLARE DEPARTMENT SALES ARRAY S*****
140 DIM S(10)
150 PRINT    "   DAILY SALES REPORT BY DEPARTMENT"
160 PRINT
170 PRINT    "DEPARTMENT      DAILY          % OF"
180 PRINT    "NUMBER          SALES       TOTAL SALES"
190 PRINT    "----------      -----       -----------"
200 LET A$ = "    ##        ##,###.##          ###.##"
210 LET T = 0
220 REM *****READ SALES INTO ARRAY S AND SUM ARRAY*****
230 FOR D = 1 TO 10
240    READ S(D)
250    LET T = T + S(D)
260 NEXT D
270 REM *****DETERMINE DEPT. % OF TOTAL SALES*****
280 FOR D = 1 TO 10
290    LET P = 100 * S(D)/T
300    PRINT USING A$; D, S(D), P
310 NEXT D
320 REM *****DISPLAY TOTAL SALES*****
330 PRINT
340 PRINT USING "TOTAL        ###,###.##"; T
350 REM **********DATA FOLLOWS**********
360 DATA  800, 2250, 1450, 1280, 1690
370 DATA 2460, 3880, 4690, 2250, 1360
380 END
```

PROGRAM 7.4

```
RUN

     DAILY SALES REPORT BY DEPARTMENT

DEPARTMENT      DAILY          % OF
NUMBER          SALES       TOTAL SALES
----------      -----       -----------
    1          800.00          3.62
    2        2,250.00         10.18
    3        1,450.00          6.56
    4        1,280.00          5.79
    5        1,690.00          7.64
    6        2,460.00         11.13
    7        3,880.00         17.55
    8        4,690.00         21.21
    9        2,250.00         10.18
   10        1,360.00          6.15

TOTAL       22,110.00
```

Some applications call for arrays to have their upper bounds assigned **dynamically**. For example, a program may manipulate 60 elements of an array during one run, 100 elements the next time, and so on. Rather than modify the value of the size of a DIM statement each time the number of elements changes, BASIC systems permit the size of an array in a DIM statement to be written as a simple variable, as in:

Dynamic Allocation of Arrays

```
140 DIM S(N)
```

This DIM statement reserves a variable number of elements for the one-dimensional array S.

Usually an INPUT or READ statement is used before the DIM statement to assign a value to the variable N. Once N is assigned a value, the DIM statement allocates the actual number of elements to array S. Any FOR statements involved in the manipulation of the array must contain as their limit parameters the same simple variable N.

Program 7.5 is nearly identical to Program 7.4 except for the addition of lines 123 and 126, the modification of the DIM statement to 140 DIM S (N) to permit dynamic allocation of arrays, and the modification of the FOR statements to include the simple variable N as their limit parameters.

```
100 REM PROGRAM 7.5
110 REM DAILY SALES REPORT BY DEPARTMENT
120 REM ********************************
123 REM *****READ THE NUMBER OF DEPARTMENTS TO PROCESS*****
126 READ N
130 REM *****DECLARE DEPARTMENT SALES ARRAY S*****
140 DIM S(N)
150 PRINT "     DAILY SALES REPORT BY DEPARTMENT"
160 PRINT
170 PRINT "DEPARTMENT       DAILY           % OF"
180 PRINT "NUMBER           SALES       TOTAL SALES"
190 PRINT "----------       -----       -----------"
200 LET A$ = "      ##        ##,###.##          ###.##"
210 LET T = 0
220 REM *****READ SALES INTO ARRAY S AND SUM ARRAY*****
230 FOR D = 1 TO N
240     READ S(D)
250     LET T = T + S(D)
260 NEXT D
270 REM *****DETERMINE DEPT. % OF TOTAL SALES*****
280 FOR D = 1 TO N
290     LET P = 100 * S(D)/T
300     PRINT USING A$; D, S(D), P
310 NEXT D
320 REM *****DISPLAY TOTAL SALES*****
330 PRINT
340 PRINT USING "TOTAL     ###,###.##"; T
350 REM ***********DATA FOLLOWS***********
360 DATA 6
370 DATA 800, 2250, 1450, 1280, 1690, 2460
380 END
```

PROGRAM 7.5

```
RUN

    DAILY SALES REPORT BY DEPARTMENT

DEPARTMENT       DAILY           % OF
NUMBER           SALES       TOTAL SALES
----------       -----       -----------
    1            800.00          8.06
    2          2,250.00         22.66
    3          1,450.00         14.60
    4          1,280.00         12.89
    5          1,690.00         17.02
    6          2,460.00         24.77

TOTAL        9,930.00
```

Program 7.5 generates the same type of report that Program 7.4 does. By changing the value of the size of the array in the DATA statement in line 360, the system can process any number of departments.

In line 126, N is assigned the value of 6. Line 140 then allocates 6 elements to array S. Both For loops are processed 6 times, since N is also the limit parameter for each FOR statement.

7.4 MULTI-DIMENSIONAL ARRAYS

The dimension of an array is the number of subscripts required to reference an element in an array. Up to now, all the arrays were one-dimensional, and an element was referenced by an integer, variable or single expression in the parentheses following the array name. The maximum number of dimensions that an array may have varies among BASIC systems. Some BASIC systems allow only a maximum of two dimensions, while others allow arrays to have up to 255 dimensions. One and two-dimensional arrays are the most common arrays used. Seldom are more than three-dimensional arrays used.

Manipulating Two-Dimensional Arrays

As illustrated in Table 7.1, the number of dimensions is declared in the DIM statement. For example,

140 DIM C(2, 5)

declares an array to be two-dimensional. A two-dimensional array usually takes the form of a table. The first subscript tells how many rows there are and the second subscript tells how many columns. Figure 7.3 shows a 2×5 array (read "2 by 5 array"). $C(1, 1)$—read "C sub one one"—references the element found in the first row and first column. C(2, 3)—read "C sub two three"—references the element found in the second row and third column. Although Figure 7.3 does not show the zero row and zero column, they always exist unless the OPTION BASE statement is used to set the lower bound to 1. That is, the statement

140 DIM C(2, 5)

actually reserves 18 storage locations (3 × 6) unless preceded by the statement:

130 OPTION BASE 1

Let us assume that the elements of array C are assigned values as shown in Figure 7.4.

Columns

	1	2	3	4	5
1	C(1, 1)	C(1, 2)	C(1, 3)	C(1, 4)	C(1, 5)
2	C(2, 1)	C(2, 2)	C(2, 3)	C(2, 4)	C(2, 5)

Rows

FIGURE 7.3 Conceptual view of the storage locations reserved for a 2 × 5 two-dimensional array called C, with the name of each element specified.

Columns

	1	2	3	4	5
1	6	12	−52	3.14	0.56
2	8	2	5	6	2

Rows

FIGURE 7.4 A 2 × 5 array with each element assigned a value.

If the name of the array in Figure 7.4 is C, then the following statements are true:

C(1, 2) is equal to **12**
C(2, 4) is equal to 6
C(2, 2) is equal to 2
C(1, 1) is equal to C(2, 4)
C(3, 5) is outside the range of the array; it does not exist
C(2, 6) is outside the range of the array; it does not exist
C(−2, −5) is outside the range of the array; it does not exist

Two-dimensional arrays are often used to classify data. For example, if a company makes 5 models of a particular product and the production of each model involves a certain amount of processing time on 6 different machines, the processing time can be summarized in a table of 5 rows and 6 columns, as illustrated in Figure 7.5.

Product Processing Time in Minutes		*Machine*					
		1	*2*	*3*	*4*	*5*	*6*
	1	13	30	5	17	12	45
	2	23	12	13	16	0	20
Model Number	*3*	45	12	28	16	10	13
	4	21	16	15	22	19	26
	5	23	50	17	43	15	18

FIGURE 7.5 A table of the processing time each model spends on a machine.

The following statement reserves storage for the two-dimensional array in Figure 7.5:

140 DIM A(5, 6)

If R represents the model number (the *row* of the table) and C represents the machine (the *column* of the table), then the subscripted variable A(R, C) gives the time it takes for a model on a particular machine. The value of R can range from 1 to 5 and the value of C can range from 1 to 6. If R is equal to 4 and C is equal to 5, the table tells us that the product processing time is 19 minutes. That is, model number 4 involves 19 minutes of processing on machine 5.

Programming Case Study 15: Production Planning

The following problem and program solution make use of the table presented in Figure 7.5.

Problem

The plant production supervisor desires that a program be written to allow the production planning clerks to enter a model number and a quantity and generate a report summarizing the amount of time required by each machine as well as the total time required by all machines. The table on the product processing times in Figure 7.5 will be used for the model number and machine. If a production clerk enters model number 3 and a quantity 17, the program should generate the following report:

Machine	Time in Minutes
1	765
2	204
3	476
4	272
5	170
6	221
Total	2,108

The time required on each machine for a given quantity is computed by multiplying the quantity times the proper table entry.

The program should verify that the model number is between 1 and 5, inclusive. The program should also allow the user to terminate the program or process another model number and quantity.

An analysis, a flowchart and a program solution follow.

Program Tasks

1) Define the table by declaring a two-dimensional array A composed of 5 rows and 6 columns.

2) Load the table entries into array A, on a row by row basis. The table entries are initially stored in DATA statements.

3) Request the model number N and the quantity Q be entered using an INPUT statement. Validate the model number. Display a diagnostic message if the model number is invalid and request it to be re-entered.

4) Display appropriate column headings.

5) Initialize the total machine time accumulator S to zero.

6) Determine the time T for each machine from the following formula:

$$T = Q * A(N, C)$$

where

T = machine time
Q = quantity
A = table of product processing times
N = model number
C = machine

using a For loop with a control variable C running from 1 to 6. Also within this

```
100 REM PROGRAM 7.6
110 REM PRODUCTION PLANNING
120 REM A = PRODUCT PROCESSING TIME TABLE FOR MODEL/MACHINE
130 REM *****************************************************
140 DIM A(5, 6)
150 REM *****READ TABLE ENTRIES ROW-WISE INTO ARRAY*****
160 FOR R = 1 TO 5
170    FOR C = 1 TO 6
180       READ A(R, C)
190    NEXT C
200 NEXT R
210 REM *****ACCEPT MODEL NUMBER (N) AND QUANTITY (Q)*****
220 INPUT "MODEL NUMBER (ENTER 1, 2, 3, 4 OR 5)"; N
230 IF N >= 1 AND N <= 5 THEN 260
240    PRINT "MODEL NUMBER INVALID, PLEASE RE-ENTER"
250    GOTO 220
260 INPUT "QUANTITY"; Q
270 PRINT
280 PRINT       "MACHINE      TIME"
290 PRINT       "-------      ----"
300 LET A$ = "     #        #,###"
310 LET B$ = "TOTAL        ##,###"
320 LET S = 0
330 FOR C = 1 TO 6
340    LET T = Q * A(N, C)
350    LET S = S + T
360    PRINT USING A$; C, T
370 NEXT C
380 PRINT
390 PRINT USING B$; S
400 PRINT
410 INPUT "ANOTHER MODEL NUMBER (Y OR N)"; A$
420 IF A$ = "Y" THEN 220
430 PRINT "JOB COMPLETE"
440 REM ***********TABLE ENTRIES***********
450 DATA 13, 30,  5, 17, 12, 45
460 DATA 23, 12, 13, 16,  0, 20
470 DATA 45, 12, 28, 16, 10, 13
480 DATA 21, 16, 15, 22, 19, 26
490 DATA 23, 50, 17, 43, 15, 18
500 END
```

PROGRAM 7.6

```
RUN

MODEL NUMBER (ENTER 1, 2, 3, 4 OR 5)? 3
QUANTITY? 17

MACHINE      TIME
-------      ----
   1         765
   2         204
   3         476
   4         272
   5         170
   6         221

TOTAL      2,108

ANOTHER MODEL NUMBER (Y OR N)? N
JOB COMPLETE
```

loop, increment the total machine time accumulator S and display the machine number C and machine time T.

7) Display the total machine time accumulator S when the looping is satisfied.

8) Determine if the user desires to terminate the program or to continue by entering other model number and quantity.

Program 7.6 includes two important techniques: loading the table values into array A and selecting the elements of the array to generate the report. Lines 160 through 200 load the array with the table values. The values are loaded **row-wise**—row by row—since the control variable C, in the inner block, increases from 1 to 6 for each increment assigned to R.

Lines 330 through 370 select the appropriate table values to multiply by the quantity Q. In line 340, the model number N remains constant. The FOR statement in line 330 initializes C to 1 and then increments C by 1 each time through the loop.

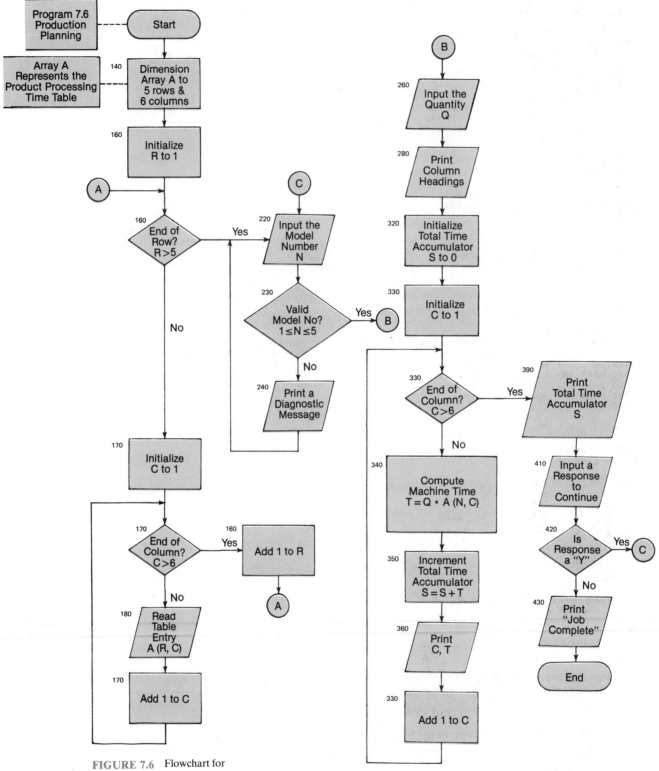

FIGURE 7.6 Flowchart for Program 7.6.

The first time, Q is multiplied by A(3,1). The second time, Q is multiplied by A(3, 2), and so on until Q is multiplied by A(3, 6).

Program 7.6 serves as an introduction to table processing. This important topic is covered in greater detail in Section 7.6.

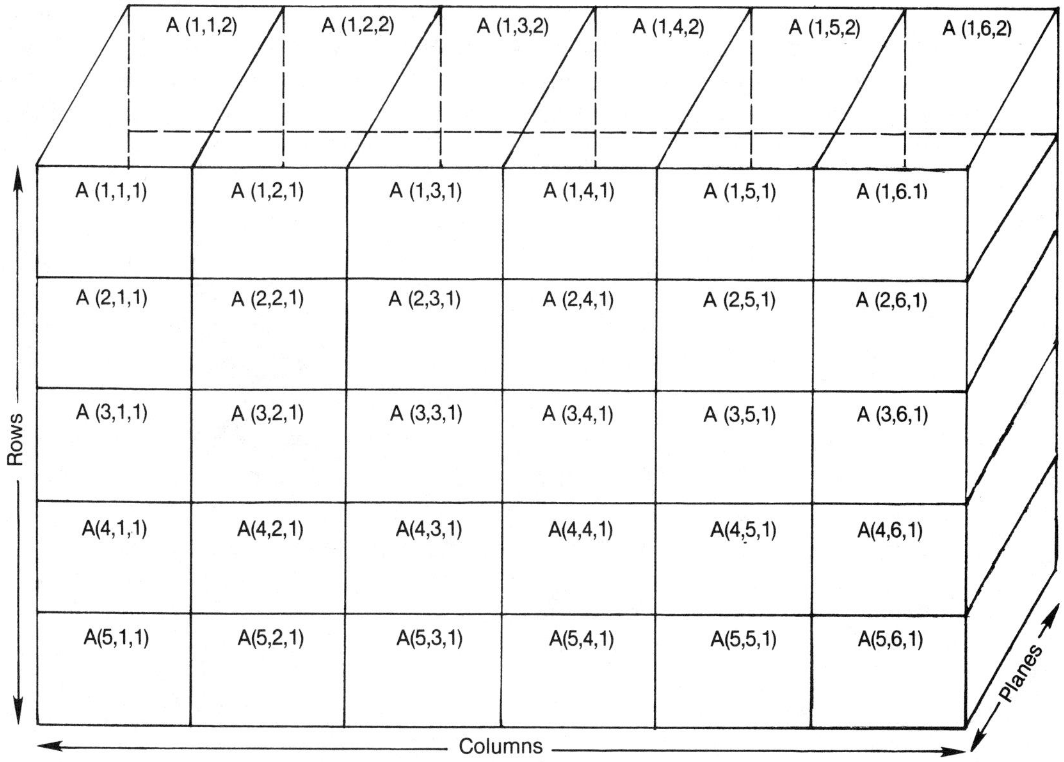

FIGURE 7.7 Conceptual view of some of the storage locations reserved for a 5 × 6 × 2 three-dimensional array called A.

The table in Figure 7.5 is for one product with 5 different models. Now, suppose we want to consider comparable tables for 2 different products, each of which has 5 different model numbers and all utilize the 6 machines. To construct such a table we can modify array A so that it is a three-dimensional array:

Arrays With More Than Two Dimensions

```
140 DIM A(5, 6, 2)
```

Now the subscripted variable A(R, C, P), with P representing the *plane* of the table, refers to the time it takes for model number R on machine C for product P.

Figure 7.7 represents a conceptual view of some of the storage locations for a 5 × 6 × 2 array called A. This three-dimensional array contains five rows, six columns and two planes, for a total of 60 elements.

If we want to take into account the production differences at three different sites, we can make A a four-dimensional array:

```
140 DIM A(5, 6, 2, 3)
```

Now the subscripted variable A(R, C, P, S) refers to the time it takes for model number R on machine C for product P at site S. If more factors besides site, product, model and machine are required, we can add even more dimensions.

The need to sort data into alphabetical or numerical order is one of the more frequent operations carried out in a business data processing environment. It is also a time-consuming operation, especially when there are large amounts of data involved. Computer scientists have spent a great deal of time developing algorithms to speed up the sorting process. Usually, the faster the process, the more complex the algorithm. In this section we will discuss two of the more common sort

7.5 SORTING

algorithms: the bubble sort and the Shell sort. Figure 7.8 illustrates the difference between unsorted data and the same data in ascending and descending sequence. Data that is in sequence from lowest to highest in value is in **ascending sequence**. Data that is in sequence from highest to lowest in value is in **descending sequence**.

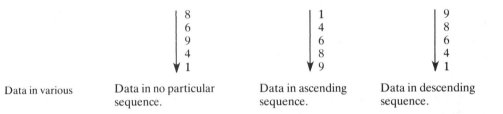

FIGURE 7.8   Data in various sequences.

Data in no particular sequence.

Data in ascending sequence.

Data in descending sequence.

The Bubble Sort   The bubble sort is a straightforward method of sorting data items that have been placed in an array. To illustrate the logic of a bubble sort we will sort the data found in Figure 7.8 into ascending sequence. Assume that the data has been assigned to array B, as illustrated below:

B(1)   8

B(2)   6

B(3)   9   Original order of unsorted data in array B.

B(4)   4

B(5)   1

The bubble sort involves comparing adjacent elements and **swapping** the values of those elements when they are out of order. For example, B(1) is compared to B(2). If B(1) is less than or equal to B(2), no swap occurs. If B(1) is greater than

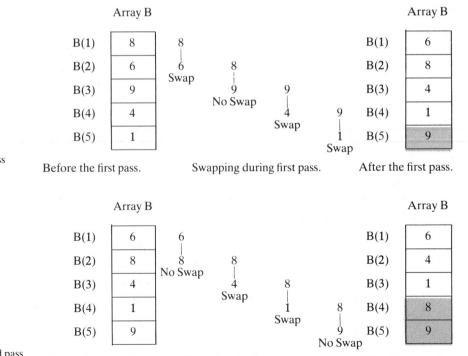

FIGURE 7.9   First pass through array B.

FIGURE 7.10   Second pass through array B.

B(2), the values of the 2 elements are swapped. B(2) is then compared to B(3), and so on until B(4) is compared to B(5). One complete time through the array is called a **pass**. At the end of the first pass, the largest value is in the last element of array B, as illustrated in Figure 7.9. Its box has been shaded to show that it is in its final position and will not move again.

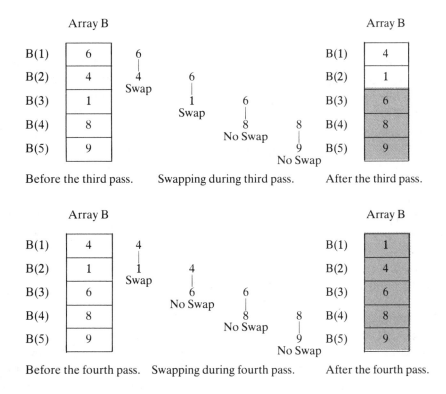

FIGURE 7.11 Third pass through array B.

Before the third pass. Swapping during third pass. After the third pass.

Before the fourth pass. Swapping during fourth pass. After the fourth pass.

FIGURE 7.12 Fourth pass through array B, which is now in ascending sequence.

The maximum number of passes necessary to sort the elements in an array is equal to the number of elements in the array less 1. Since array B has 5 elements, a maximum of four passes are made on the array. Figures 7.10, 7.11 and 7.12 illustrate the second, third and fourth passes made on array B. On the fifth pass no elements are swapped. The swapping pushes the larger values down in the illustrations, and as a side effect, the smaller numbers "bubble" up to the top of the array.

The SWAP statement allows you to write one statement that will exchange the values of two storage locations. It will exchange two variables or two elements of an array. The general form of the SWAP statement is illustrated in Table 7.4.

TABLE 7.4 The SWAP Statement

General Form:	SWAP A, B
	where A and B are variables or elements of an array.
Purpose:	To exchange the values of two variables or two elements of an array.

Examples:	`100 SWAP B(I), B(I + 1)`
	`200 SWAP A, B`
	`300 SWAP C$(I, I), D$(I, I)`

Caution:	Not available on all BASIC systems.

Not all BASIC systems have the SWAP statement. If it is available on your BASIC system, then this partial program sorts array B of Figure 7.9:

```
210 LET S = 0
220 WHILE S = 0
230    LET S = 1
240    FOR I = 1 TO 4
250       IF B(I) <= B(I + 1) THEN 280
260          SWAP B(I), B(I + 1)
270          LET S = 0
280    NEXT I
290 WEND
300 .
      .
      .
```

The variable S controls whether another pass will be done on the array. Line 210 assigns S a value of zero. Since S equals zero, line 220 passes control into the body of the While loop. Line 230 assigns S a value of 1. If S is not modified later in the loop (line 270), the values in the array are in sequence and the next time line 220 is executed, control transfers to line 300.

The FOR statement in line 240 initializes I to 1. The first element B(1) is then compared to B(2). If B(1) is less than or equal to B(2), no swap occurs. If B(1) is greater than B(2), line 260 swaps the values of the two elements and line 270 assigns S a value of zero. Next, B(2) is compared to B(3) and so on. The number of comparisons per pass is equal to 1 minus the number of elements to compare. Since the number of data items to sort is 5, the limit parameter in the FOR statement is set to 4.

In programming, the variable S is called a **switch**, or **flag**, or **indicator**, a variable that usually takes on two values during the duration of a program. When S is 0, the switch is "on," and the loop is executed. When S is 1, the switch is "off," and the loop in lines 220 through 290 is not executed.

If your BASIC system does not have the SWAP statement, then you must use a temporary storage location to complete the swap. The temporary storage location is necessary, since without the SWAP statement two values cannot be switched simultaneously. The following partial program will swap two values on systems that do not have the SWAP statement:

```
210 LET S= 0
220 WHILE S = 0
230    LET S = 1
240    FOR I = 1 TO 4
250       IF B(I) <= B(I + 1) THEN 300
260          LET T = B(I)
270          LET B(I) = B(I + 1)
280          LET B(I + 1) = T
290          LET S = 0
300    NEXT I
310 WEND
320 .
      .
      .
```

Program 7.7 incorporates the logic found in this partial program to sort 8, 6, 9, 4 and 1. Line 130 reserves storage for array B. The For loop made up of lines 150 through 180 loads and displays the unsorted elements of the array. Lines 210 through 310 sort the numeric array without the SWAP statement. Lines 330 through 350 display the elements after the array has been sorted.

Changing the relation in line 250 from "less than or equal to" to "greater than or equal to" causes Program 7.7 to sort the data into descending rather than ascending sequence.

To make the sort algorithm more general, a variable for the size of the array and a variable number of elements can be used. This generalization is illustrated in Program 7.8, which uses the same techniques as Program 7.7 to sort string data items.

```
100 REM PROGRAM 7.7
110 REM SORTING NUMERIC DATA USING THE
115 REM BUBBLE SORT TECHNIQUE
120 REM *****************************
130 DIM B(5)
140 PRINT "UNSORTED -";
150 FOR I = 1 TO 5
160     READ B(I)
170     PRINT B(I);
180 NEXT I
190 PRINT
200 REM *****SORT ROUTINE*****
210 LET S= 0
220 WHILE S = 0
230     LET S = 1
240     FOR I = 1 TO 4
250         IF B(I) <= B(I + 1) THEN 300
260             LET T = B(I)
270             LET B(I) = B(I + 1)
280             LET B(I + 1) = T
290             LET S = 0
300     NEXT I
310 WEND
320 PRINT "SORTED   -";
330 FOR I = 1 TO 5
340     PRINT B(I);
350 NEXT I
360 REM ***DATA FOLLOWS***
370 DATA 8, 6, 9, 4, 1
380 END
```

PROGRAM 7.7

```
RUN

UNSORTED - 8  6  9  4  1
SORTED   - 1  4  6  8  9
```

```
100 REM PROGRAM 7.8
110 REM SORTING STRING DATA USING THE
115 REM BUBBLE SORT TECHNIQUE
120 REM *****************************
125 READ D
130 DIM N$(D)
140 PRINT "UNSORTED - ";
150 FOR I = 1 TO D
160     READ N$(I)
170     PRINT N$(I); " ";
180 NEXT I
190 PRINT
200 REM *****SORT ROUTINE*****
210 LET S= 0
220 WHILE S = 0
230     LET S = 1
240     FOR I = 1 TO D - 1
250         IF N$(I) <= N$(I + 1) THEN 300
260             LET T$ = N$(I)
270             LET N$(I) = N$(I + 1)
280             LET N$(I + 1) = T$
290             LET S = 0
300     NEXT I
310 WEND
320 PRINT "SORTED   - ";
330 FOR I = 1 TO D
340     PRINT N$(I); " ";
350 NEXT I
360 REM ****DATA FOLLOWS*****
370 DATA 8
380 DATA JIM, JOHN, LOUIS, FRAN
390 DATA TOM, ANDY, LOU, MARK
400 END
```

PROGRAM 7.8

```
RUN

UNSORTED - JIM JOHN LOUIS FRAN TOM ANDY LOU MARK
SORTED   - ANDY FRAN JIM JOHN LOU LOUIS MARK TOM
```

In Program 7.8 the string array N\$ is dimensioned to D elements. Line 125 assigns the variable D the number of data items to be sorted. The limit parameter in each of the FOR statements in Program 7.7 (lines 150, 240 and 330) is changed from 5, 4, 5 to D, D − 1 and D. Program 7.8 can sort from 1 to D data items, depending on the value assigned to the variable D.

The sort examples presented thus far have involved only one data item per record. Normally, several data items make up a record. When two records are rearranged, all data items belonging to each record must be swapped. The following problem and program solution make use of parallel arrays to sort records made up of multiple data items.

Problem

Company PUC wants a menu-driven program to sort its salesperson records by name *or* weekly sales in either ascending or descending sequence. The program should read the data items in each record into parallel arrays and display the following menu:

```
            MENU FOR SORTING SALESPERSON FILE
            ------------------------------------

        CODE    FUNCTION
        ----    --------
          1  -  SORT BY NAME IN ASCENDING SEQUENCE
          2  -  SORT BY NAME IN DESCENDING SEQUENCE
          3  -  SORT BY WEEKLY SALES IN ASCENDING SEQUENCE
          4  -  SORT BY WEEKLY SALES IN DESCENDING SEQUENCE
          5  -  END PROGRAM

        ENTER A CODE OF 1 THROUGH 5?
```

Once a code is entered, the program must validate it to ensure that the code corresponds to one of the menu functions. After the selection of the proper function, the program should sort the data items in the parallel arrays and then display the sorted version of the salesperson file. After that, the program should re-display the menu.

For this problem, only six salesperson records will be sorted. The names and weekly sales are shown below:

Salesperson Name	Total Weekly Sales
MALDER, LISA	$14,163
SMITH, JEFF	25,654
RIEL, MARCI	13,211
RALLIS, NIKOLE	28,425
THUME, JODI	26,158
JONES, AMANDA	14,653

A top-down chart (Figure 7.13), an analysis of the problem and a program solution follow.

Program Tasks

1) Assign the value of the number of records to be sorted to a variable R using a READ statement.
2) Declare two parallel one-dimensional arrays containing R elements. Let one array N$ represent the salesperson names and the other array S represent the corresponding weekly sales.
3) Load the data into the arrays using a For loop. The data items are initially stored in DATA statements.
4) Clear the screen and display the menu for sorting salesperson file.

5) Request the operator to enter a code from the menu.
6) Validate the code. Display an appropriate diagnostic message if the code is invalid and request it be re-entered.
7) When a valid code is entered, clear the screen and use an ON-GOSUB statement to transfer control to a subroutine to carry out the requested function.
8) Since there are four different sorts that may be requested, handle each in a separate subroutine. Use the following IF statements in the subroutines:

Sort Subroutine	IF *Statement*
By salesperson name in ascending sequence	IF N$(I) <= N(I + 1) THEN (bypass swap)
By salesperson name in descending sequence	IF N$(I) >= N(I + 1) THEN (bypass swap)
By weekly sales in ascending sequence	IF S(I) <= S(I + 1) THEN (bypass swap)
By weekly sales in descending sequence	IF S(I) >= S(I + 1) THEN (bypass swap)

9) Use the same swap module for all four sort routines. When two records are swapped, both the salesperson name and weekly sales must be swapped.
10) Display the report title and column headings.
11) Use a For loop to display the records in their new sequence.
12) Use the following prompt message to re-display the menu:

        PRESS ENTER KEY TO RETURN TO THE MENU

13) Repeat steps 4 through 12 as necessary.
14) Display the message:

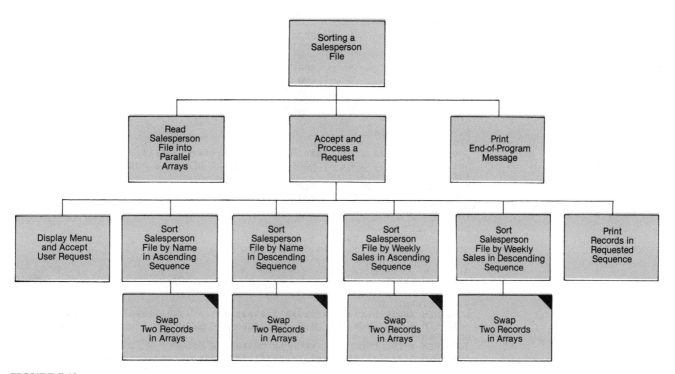

FIGURE 7.13 Top-Down chart for Program 7.9.

```
1000 REM PROGRAM 7.9
1010 REM SORTING A SALESPERSON FILE BY MENU FUNCTIONS
1020 REM C  = FUNCTION CODE
1030 REM N$ = SALESPERSON NAME ARRAY
1040 REM S  = SALESPERSON WEEKLY SALES ARRAY
1050 REM ****************************************************************
1060 REM *                       MAIN MODULE                           *
1070 REM *                                                             *
1080 REM * CALL READ SALESPERSON FILE INTO PARALLEL ARRAYS             *
1090 REM * CALL ACCEPT AND PROCESS A REQUEST                           *
1100 REM ****************************************************************
1110 GOSUB 2030
1120 GOSUB 3100
1130 PRINT
1140 PRINT "    END OF PROGRAM"
1150 STOP
2000 REM ****************************************************************
2010 REM *   READ SALESPERSON FILE INTO PARALLEL ARRAYS MODULE         *
2020 REM ****************************************************************
2030 READ R
2040 DIM N$(R), S(R)
2050 FOR I = 1 TO R
2060    READ N$(I), S(I)
2070 NEXT I
2080 RETURN
3000 REM ****************************************************************
3010 REM *            ACCEPT AND PROCESS A REQUEST MODULE              *
3020 REM *                                                             *
3030 REM * CALL DISPLAY MENU                                           *
3040 REM * CALL SORT BY NAME IN ASCENDING SEQUENCE                     *
3050 REM * CALL SORT BY NAME IN DESCENDING SEQUENCE                    *
3060 REM * CALL SORT BY WEEKLY SALES IN ASCENDING SEQUENCE             *
3070 REM * CALL SORT BY WEEKLY SALES IN DESCENDING SEQUENCE            *
3080 REM * CALL PRINT RECORDS IN REQUESTED SEQUENCE                    *
3090 REM ****************************************************************
3100 GOSUB 4030
3110 WHILE C <> 5
3120    ON C GOSUB 5050, 6050, 7050, 8050
3130    GOSUB 9030
3140    GOSUB 4030
3150 WEND
3160 RETURN
4000 REM ****************************************************************
4010 REM *                 DISPLAY MENU MODULE                         *
4020 REM ****************************************************************
4030 CLS
4040 PRINT
4050 PRINT "           MENU FOR SORTING SALESPERSON FILE"
4060 PRINT "           ------------------------------------"
4070 PRINT
4080 PRINT "     CODE     FUNCTION"
4090 PRINT "     ----     --------"
4100 PRINT "      1  -   SORT BY NAME IN ASCENDING SEQUENCE"
4110 PRINT "      2  -   SORT BY NAME IN DESCENDING SEQUENCE"
4120 PRINT "      3  -   SORT BY WEEKLY SALES IN ASCENDING SEQUENCE"
4130 PRINT "      4  -   SORT BY WEEKLY SALES IN DESCENDING SEQUENCE"
4140 PRINT "      5  -   END PROGRAM"
4150 PRINT
4160 INPUT "    ENTER A CODE OF 1 THROUGH 5"; C
4170 IF C >= 1 AND C <= 5 THEN 4200
4180    PRINT "    CODE OUT OF RANGE, PLEASE"
4190    GOTO 4160
4200 RETURN
5000 REM ****************************************************************
5010 REM *       SORT BY NAME IN ASCENDING SEQUENCE MODULE             *
5020 REM *                                                             *
5030 REM * CALL SWAP TWO RECORDS IN ARRAYS MODULE                      *
5040 REM ****************************************************************
5050 LET W = 0
5060 WHILE W = 0
5070    LET W = 1
5080    FOR I = 1 TO R - 1
5090       IF N$(I) <= N$(I + 1) THEN 5120
5100          GOSUB 9530
5110          LET W = 0
5120    NEXT I
5130 WEND
5140 RETURN
6000 REM ****************************************************************
6010 REM *       SORT BY NAME IN DESCENDING SEQUENCE MODULE            *
6020 REM *                                                             *
6030 REM * CALL SWAP TWO RECORDS IN ARRAYS MODULE                      *
6040 REM ****************************************************************
```

```
6050 LET W = 0
6060 WHILE W = 0
6070    LET W = 1
6080    FOR I = 1 TO R - 1
6090       IF N$(I) >= N$(I + 1) THEN 6120
6100          GOSUB 9530
6110          LET W = 0
6120    NEXT I
6130 WEND
6140 RETURN
7000 REM ******************************************************
7010 REM *    SORT BY WEEKLY SALES IN ASCENDING SEQUENCE MODULE    *
7020 REM *                                                         *
7030 REM * CALL SWAP TWO RECORDS IN ARRAYS MODULE                  *
7040 REM ******************************************************
7050 LET W = 0
7070 WHILE W = 0
7070    LET W = 1
7080    FOR I = 1 TO R - 1
7090       IF S(I) <= S(I + 1) THEN 7120
7100          GOSUB 9530
7110          LET W = 0
7120    NEXT I
7130 WEND
7140 RETURN
8000 REM ******************************************************
8010 REM *    SORT BY WEEKLY SALES IN DESCENDING SEQUENCE MODULE   *
8020 REM *                                                         *
8030 REM * CALL SWAP TWO RECORDS IN ARRAYS MODULE                  *
8040 REM ******************************************************
8050 LET W = 0
8060 WHILE W = 0
8070    LET W = 1
8080    FOR I = 1 TO R - 1
8090       IF S(I) >= S(I + 1) THEN 8120
8100          GOSUB 9530
8110          LET W = 0
8120    NEXT I
8130 WEND
8140 RETURN
9000 REM ******************************************************
9010 REM *         PRINT RECORDS IN REQUESTED SEQUENCE MODULE      *
9020 REM ******************************************************
9030 CLS
9040 PRINT
9050 PRINT    "   SORTED SALESPERSON FILE"
9060 PRINT    "   ------------------------"
9070 PRINT
9080 PRINT    "SALESPERSON      WEEKLY SALES"
9090 PRINT    "-----------      ------------"
9100 LET A$ = "\            \      ##,###.##"
9110 FOR I = 1 TO R
9120    PRINT USING A$; N$(I), S(I)
9130 NEXT I
9140 PRINT
9150 INPUT "PRESS ENTER KEY TO RETURN TO THE MENU"; Z$
9160 RETURN
9500 REM ******************************************************
9510 REM *            SWAP TWO RECORDS IN ARRAYS MODULE           *
9520 REM ******************************************************
9530 LET T$ = N$(I)
9540 LET N$(I) = N$(I + 1)
9550 LET N$(I + 1) = T$
9560 LET T = S(I)
9570 LET S(I) = S(I + 1)
9580 LET S(I + 1) = T
9590 RETURN
9800 REM *******************DATA FOLLOWS*********************
9810 DATA 6
9820 DATA MALDER LISA, 14163
9830 DATA SMITH JEFF, 25654
9840 DATA RIEL MARCI, 13211
9850 DATA RALLIS NIKOLE, 28425
9860 DATA THUME JODI, 26158
9870 DATA JONES AMANDA, 14653
9880 END

RUN
```

PROGRAM 7.9
(Continued)

Figures 7.14 through 7.17 illustrate the sorted results displayed when each code is entered in response to the menu.

```
        SORTED SALESPERSON FILE
        -----------------------

    SALESPERSON        WEEKLY SALES
    -----------        ------------
    JONES AMANDA         14,653.00
    MALDER LISA          14,163.00
    RALLIS NIKOLE        28,425.00
    RIEL MARCI           13,211.00
    SMITH JEFF           25,654.00
    THUME JODI           26,158.00

    PRESS ENTER KEY TO RETURN TO THE MENU?
```

FIGURE 7.14 The display from the selection of code 1 (the salesperson file displayed by name in ascending sequence).

```
        SORTED SALESPERSON FILE
        -----------------------

    SALESPERSON        WEEKLY SALES
    -----------        ------------
    THUME JODI           26,158.00
    SMITH JEFF           25,654.00
    RIEL MARCI           13,211.00
    RALLIS NIKOLE        28,425.00
    MALDER LISA          14,163.00
    JONES AMANDA         14,653.00

    PRESS ENTER KEY TO RETURN TO THE MENU?
```

FIGURE 7.15 The display from the selection of code 2 (the salesperson file displayed by name in descending sequence).

```
        SORTED SALESPERSON FILE
        -----------------------

    SALESPERSON        WEEKLY SALES
    -----------        ------------
    RIEL MARCI           13,211.00
    MALDER LISA          14,163.00
    JONES AMANDA         14,653.00
    SMITH JEFF           25,654.00
    THUME JODI           26,158.00
    RALLIS NIKOLE        28,425.00

    PRESS ENTER KEY TO RETURN TO THE MENU?
```

FIGURE 7.16 The display from the selection of code 3 (the salesperson file displayed by weekly sales in ascending sequence).

```
        SORTED SALESPERSON FILE
        -----------------------

    SALESPERSON        WEEKLY SALES
    -----------        ------------
    RALLIS NIKOLE        28,425.00
    THUME JODI           26,158.00
    SMITH JEFF           25,654.00
    JONES AMANDA         14,653.00
    MALDER LISA          14,163.00
    RIEL MARCI           13,211.00

    PRESS ENTER KEY TO RETURN TO THE MENU?
```

FIGURE 7.17 The display from the selection of code 4 (the salesperson file displayed by weekly sales in descending sequence).

The technique illustrated in Program 7.9 properly sorts any file, provided the size of the program, including the data, does not exceed main memory. Most files in a business environment reside on auxiliary storage and are sorted by sort utilities before the program processes the file. Sort utilities usually swap entire records rather than individual data items.

The advantage to studying sort algorithms is that they raise the question of algorithm efficiency. In the next section, we will discuss the Shell sort, which offers a vast improvement over the bubble sort algorithm.

The Shell Sort

The bubble sort algorithm works well for a small number of data items, but it can take too much processing time for a large number of data items. The problem with this algorithm is that the smaller data items move only one position at a time because only adjacent elements are compared. Named after its author, Donald Shell, the Shell sort provides a faster means of sorting a large number of data items. For example, for 500 items, the Shell sort reduces the processing time by a factor of 5. For 1000 items, it reduces the processing time by a factor of 10. The longer the list to be sorted, the greater the advantage of the Shell sort over the bubble sort.

The Shell sort is similar to the bubble sort except that instead of comparing and swapping adjacent elements $B(I)$ and $B(I + 1)$, it compares and swaps nonadjacent elements $B(I)$ and $B(I + G)$, where G starts out considerably greater than 1.

The variable G is called the **Gap**. The first Gap is one half the length of the array. When a swap is made, a big improvement takes place. When no swap is made on a pass, the Gap G is halved again for the next pass. Finally, the Gap G becomes 1, as in the bubble sort, and adjacent elements are compared and swapped.

```
100 REM PROGRAM 7.10
110 REM SORTING NUMERIC DATA USING THE SHELL SORT TECHNIQUE
120 REM ****************************************************
125 READ D
130 DIM B(D)
140 PRINT 'UNSORTED -';
150 FOR I = 1 TO D
160     READ B(I)
170     PRINT B(I);
180 NEXT I
190 PRINT
200 REM *****SORT ROUTINE*****
203 LET G = INT(D/2)
206 WHILE G <> 0
210     LET S= 0
220     WHILE S = 0
230         LET S = 1
240         FOR I = 1 TO D - G
250             IF B(I) <= B(I + G) THEN 300
260                 LET T = B(I)
270                 LET B(I) = B(I + G)
280                 LET B(I + G) = T
290                 LET S = 0
300         NEXT I
310     WEND
313     LET G  = INT(G/2)
316 WEND
320 PRINT 'SORTED   -';
330 FOR I = 1 TO D
340     PRINT B(I);
350 NEXT I
360 REM ******************DATA FOLLOWS************************
370 DATA 15
380 DATA 18, 13, 6, 4, 19, 12, 67, 1, 11, 13, 27, 32, 2, 17, 55
390 END
```

PROGRAM 7.10

```
RUN

UNSORTED - 18  13   6   4  19  12  67   1  11  13  27  32   2  17  55
SORTED   - 1   2   4   6  11  12  13  13  17  18  19  27  32  55  67
```

The Shell sort is used in Program 7.10 to sort a list of 15 data items. Line 203 begins by assigning the Gap G to one half the size of the list. Line 206 initiates a loop that has as its body the bubble sort with some minor modifications. In lines 240, 250, 270 and 280 the integer 1 has been replaced by G.

**7.6
TABLE
PROCESSING**

Many applications call for the use of data that is arranged in tabular form. One example is the product processing time table used to solve Production Planning Case Study 15. Rates of pay, tax brackets, parts cost and insurance rates are also examples of tables that contain systematically arranged data. Arrays make it easier to write programs for applications involving tables.

**Table
Organization**

Tables are organized based on how the data (also called **table functions**) is to be referenced. Table functions can be accessed by their position in the table in **positionally organized tables**. In **argument organized tables**, table functions are accessed by the value that corresponds to the desired table function.

**Positionally
Organized
Tables**

To illustrate a positionally organized table, a program can be written that displays the name of the month in response to a month number, 1 through 12. Figure 7.18 shows the basic concept behind accessing a table function in a positionally organized table.

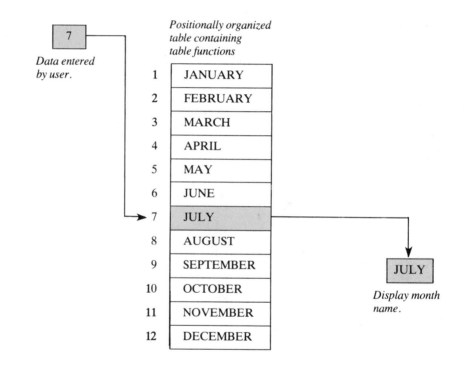

FIGURE 7.18 Accessing a table function in a positionally organized table.

In Figure 7.18, the month name is selected from the table based on its location. A value of 1, entered by the user, equates to January, 2 to February, and so on. To write a program that uses table processing techniques, you must:

1) Define the table by declaring an array.
2) Load the table functions into the array, normally by using a For loop.
3) Write statements to access the table entries.

Program 7.11 illustrates how to declare, load and access the table of month names described in Figure 7.18. Line 140 defines the table by declaring array M$ to 12. Lines 160 through 180 load the table functions—in this case, the month names—into the array. Line 260 accesses the desired table function.

The routine to access the table function in Program 7.11 is rather straight-forward. The user enters a value for N and line 260 references the Nth element of the array containing the table functions.

```
100 REM PROGRAM 7.11
110 REM ACCESSING FUNCTIONS IN A POSITIONALLY
115 REM ORGANIZED TABLE
120 REM ***********************************
130 REM *****DECLARE THE TABLE*****
140 DIM M$(12)
150 REM *****LOAD THE TABLE*****
160 FOR I = 1 TO 12
170    READ M$(I)
180 NEXT I
190 LET A$ = "Y"
200 WHILE A$ = "Y"
210    INPUT "MONTH NUMBER"; N
220    IF N >= 1 AND N <= 12 THEN 260
230       PRINT "MONTH NUMBER INVALID, PLEASE RE-ENTER"
240       GOTO 210
250    REM *****ACCESS THE TABLE FUNCTION*****
260    PRINT "THE MONTH NAME IS "; M$(N)
270    PRINT
280    INPUT "ANOTHER MONTH NUMBER (Y OR N)"; A$
290    PRINT
300 WEND
310 PRINT
320 PRINT "JOB COMPLETE"
330 REM **********TABLE ENTRIES**************
340 DATA JANUARY, FEBRUARY, MARCH, APRIL
350 DATA MAY, JUNE, JULY, AUGUST
360 DATA SEPTEMBER, OCTOBER, NOVEMBER, DECEMBER
370 END

RUN

MONTH NUMBER? 2
THE MONTH NAME IS FEBRUARY

ANOTHER MONTH NUMBER (Y OR N)? Y

MONTH NUMBER? 14
MONTH NUMBER INVALID, PLEASE RE-ENTER
MONTH NUMBER? 8
THE MONTH NAME IS AUGUST

ANOTHER MONTH NUMBER (Y OR N)? Y

MONTH NUMBER? 12
THE MONTH NAME IS DECEMBER

ANOTHER MONTH NUMBER (Y OR N)? N

JOB COMPLETE
```

PROGRAM 7.11

The following problem and program solution provide another example of a positionally organized table.

Programming Case Study 17: Determining the Gross Pay Using a Job Class Table

Problem

Many businesses have job classes that determine the rate of pay an individual earns per hour. For example, job class 1 is assigned a particular hourly rate, job class 2 another, and so on. To write a program that computes the gross pay, given an employee number, hours worked per week and job class, the following table is used:

Job Class	Rate of Pay
01	$5.75
02	6.00
03	6.44
04	6.75
05	7.02
06	8.13
07	8.25
08	8.62
09	9.15

The gross pay is determined as follows:

If Hours $\leq$ 40 then Gross Pay = Rate $\times$ Hours
If Hours > 40 then Gross Pay = 40 $\times$ Rate + 1.5 $\times$ Rate $\times$ (Hours − 40)

The employee file to be processed is found below:

Employee Number	Hours Worked	Job Class
13612	40	05
13916	65	04
14813	45	10
18612	35	09
19138	40	07

Output is to include the employee number, hours worked and gross pay. A test in the program should ensure that an improper job class number results in the display of a diagnostic message. An analysis, flowchart and program solution follow.

Program Tasks

1) Define a one-dimensional array J that will be assigned the table entries.
2) Use a For loop to fill the table before processing any records.
3) Since there is one rate of pay per job class in the table, access the rate of pay based on its relative position in the table.
4) Use the employee job class C as a subscript to determine which element of the array is to be used in the computation of the gross pay G.
5) Display an appropriate diagnostic message if an invalid job class is found in an employee record.
6) Use an IF statement to determine which of the two gross pay formulas is to be used.
7) Display the gross pay before reading the next record and testing for the end-of-file value.

In Program 7.12, line 160 defines the table. Lines 230 through 250 load the table with the rates of pay. Line 280 ensures that the employee job class is valid. If the employee job class is invalid, a diagnostic message is displayed by line 290. Line 310 determines which gross pay formula to use. Either formula accesses the rate of pay by referencing table J using the employee job class C.

Positionally organized tables are not difficult to understand. Unfortunately, few tables can be constructed based on the relative positions of the table functions. Month name, day of the week name and job class tables are examples of systematic data that can be organized into positional tables.

Argument Organized Tables

In most applications, tables are characterized by entries made up of multiple functions. Multiple function entries are accessed by means of a **search argument**. The search argument is entered by the user, much as the month number was in Program 7.11. The search argument is compared to the **table argument**, a table entry, to retrieve the corresponding table function. Figure 7.20 illustrates the composition of a table that is organized by arguments.

The table argument is assigned to a one-dimensional array. Functions are assigned to parallel arrays. Unlike a positionally organized table, in which the value entered is used to obtain the table function, an argument organized table must be searched until the search argument agrees with one of the table arguments. This search is a **table search** or a **table look-up**.

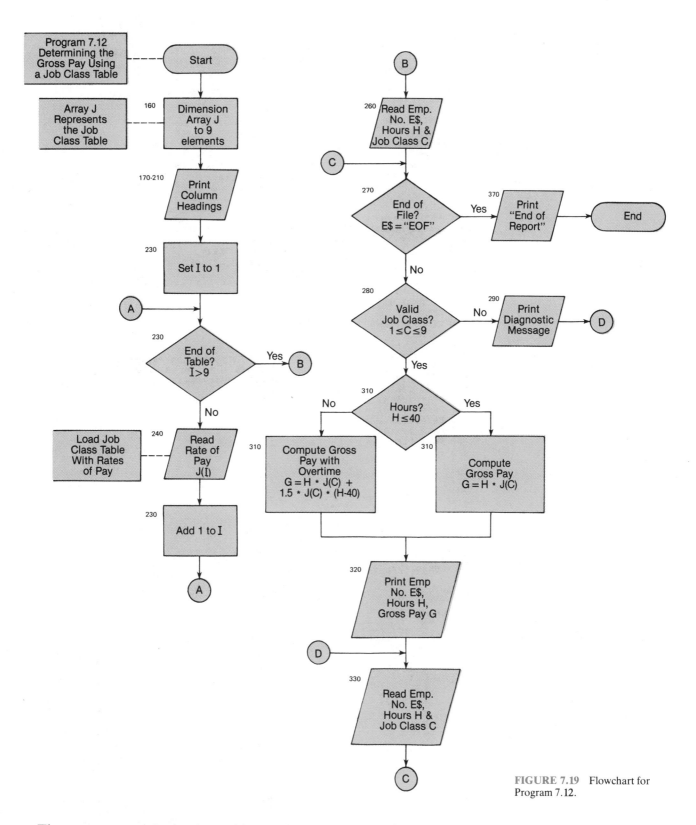

FIGURE 7.19 Flowchart for Program 7.12.

There are two methods of searching a table: the **serial search** and the **binary search**. A serial search begins by comparing the search argument to the first table argument. If the two agree, the search is over. If they do not agree, then the search argument is compared to the second table argument, and so on. In general, a binary search begins the search in the middle of the table and determines whether

```
100 REM PROGRAM 7.12
110 REM DETERMINING THE GROSS PAY USING A JOB CLASS TABLE
120 REM J = JOB CLASS TABLE, E$ = EMPLOYEE NUMBER
130 REM H = HOURS WORKED,     C = JOB CLASS
140 REM G = GROSS PAY
150 REM *************************************************
160 DIM J(9)
170 PRINT TAB(11); "GROSS PAY REPORT"
180 PRINT TAB(11); "----------------"
190 PRINT
200 PRINT    "EMPLOYEE       HOURS      GROSS PAY"
210 PRINT    "--------       -----      ---------"
220 LET A$ = "\       \          ##         $$,###.##"
225 REM ****LOAD THE JOB CLASS TABLE*****
230 FOR I = 1 TO 9
240    READ J(I)
250 NEXT I
260 READ E$, H, C
270 WHILE E$ <> "EOF"
280    IF C >= 1 AND C <= 9 THEN 310
290       PRINT "**ERROR** EMPLOYEE "; E$;
295       PRINT " HAS AN INVALID JOB CLASS OF"; C
300       GOTO 330
310    IF H<=40 THEN LET G = H*J(C) ELSE LET G = 40*J(C)+1.5*J(C)*(H-40)
320    PRINT USING A$; E$, H, G
330    READ E$, H, C
340 WEND
350 REM ****END OF JOB ROUTINE*****
360 PRINT
370 PRINT "END OF REPORT"
380 REM *****************TABLE ENTRIES******************
390 DATA 5.75, 6.00, 6.44, 6.75, 7.02, 8.13, 8.25, 8.62, 9.15
400 REM ****************DATA FOLLOWS********************
410 DATA 13612, 40, 05
420 DATA 13916, 65, 04
430 DATA 14813, 45, 10
440 DATA 18612, 35, 09
450 DATA 19138, 40, 07
460 DATA EOF, 0, 0
470 END
```

PROGRAM 7.12

```
RUN

          GROSS PAY REPORT
          ----------------

EMPLOYEE       HOURS      GROSS PAY
--------       -----      ---------
13612           40          $280.80
13916           65          $523.12
**ERROR** EMPLOYEE 14813 HAS AN INVALID JOB CLASS OF 10
18612           35          $320.25
19138           40          $330.00

END OF REPORT
```

FIGURE 7.20 Conceptual view of an argument organized table.

the table argument that agrees with the search argument is in the upper half or lower half of the table. The half that contains this table argument is then halved. This process continues until there is nothing left to divide in half. At that point the binary search is complete. The binary search will be discussed in greater detail later.

Serial Search   A serial search is a procedure that all of us use in everyday life. Suppose, for example, you have a parts list that contains the part numbers and corresponding part descriptions and part costs. If you have a part number, one method of finding the part description and cost is to read through the part number list until you find the part number you are searching for. You can then read off the description and cost that correspond to the part number. Figure 7.21 illustrates the basic concept of a serial search.

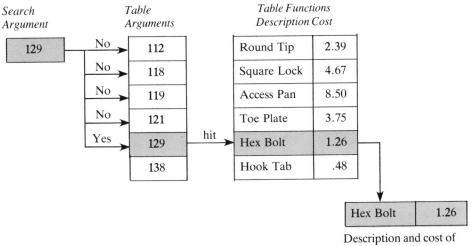

Description and cost of
part number 129

FIGURE 7.21 Conceptual
view of a serial search.

The search argument is tested against each of the table arguments, beginning with the first, until a **hit** is made. At that point, the part description and part cost that correspond to the table argument can be selected from the table.

A program that completes the serial search illustrated in Figure 7.21 first needs to have the table defined. Since each entry is made up of a search argument and two functions, we can declare three parallel arrays—N, D$ and C, as shown below. The variable R will be assigned the number of parts in the parts list.

```
150 REM *****DECLARE THE TABLE*****
160 READ R
170 DIM N(R), D$(R), C(R)
```

Array N can be assigned the part numbers, array D$ the part descriptions and array C the part costs. A For loop is used to load the table, as follows:

```
180 REM *****LOAD THE TABLE*****
190 FOR I = 1 TO R
200    READ N(I), D$(I), C(I)
210 NEXT I
```

Each time the READ statement is executed, one entry is loaded into each of the arrays. Each entry consists of an argument and two functions. A For loop can be used to implement the serial search algorithm. Within the loop, an IF statement compares the part number entered by the user against the part numbers in the table. When the two are equal, the IF statement causes a branch to a statement outside the loop. If the For loop runs through the entire list of arguments without finding a table argument that is equal to the search argument, a diagnostic message will be displayed. The following statements search the table, cause the part description and cost to be displayed and cause a diagnostic message to be displayed.

```
250 REM *****SEARCH THE TABLE*****
260 FOR I = 1 TO R
270    IF P = N(I) THEN 310
280 NEXT I
290 PRINT "**ERROR**"; P; "IS AN INVALID PART NUMBER"
300 GOTO 330
310 PRINT "THE DESCRIPTION IS "; D$(I)
320 PRINT USING "THE COST IS ###.##"; C(I)
330 .
```

The complete program follows.

```
100 REM PROGRAM 7.13
110 REM SERIAL SEARCH OF AN ARGUMENT ORGANIZED TABLE
120 REM N = PART NUMBER ARGUMENTS   D$ = PART DESCRIPTION FUNCTIONS
130 REM C = PART COST FUNCTIONS     R  = NUMBER OF TABLE ENTRIES
140 REM ****************************************************************
150 REM *****DECLARE THE TABLE*****
160 READ R
170 DIM N(R), D$(R), C(R)
180 REM *****LOAD THE TABLE*****
190 FOR I = 1 TO R
200    READ N(I), D$(I), C(I)
210 NEXT I
220 LET A$ = "Y"
230 WHILE A$ = "Y"
240    INPUT "ENTER THE PART NUMBER"; P
250    REM *****SEARCH THE TABLE*****
260    FOR I = 1 TO R
270       IF P = N(I) THEN 310
280    NEXT I
290    PRINT "**ERROR**"; P; "IS AN INVALID PART NUMBER"
300    GOTO 330
310    PRINT "THE DESCRIPTION IS "; D$(I)
320    PRINT USING "THE COST IS ###.##"; C(I)
330    PRINT
340    INPUT "ANOTHER PART NUMBER (Y OR N)"; A$
350 WEND
360 PRINT
370 PRINT "JOB COMPLETE"
380 REM *********************TABLE ENTRIES******************
390 DATA 6
400 DATA 112, ROUND TIP, 2.39, 118, SQUARE LOCK, 4.67
410 DATA 119, ACCESS PAN, 8.50, 121, TOE PLATE, 3.75
420 DATA 129, HEX BOLT, 1.26, 138, HOOK TAB, 0.48
430 END
```

PROGRAM 7.13

```
RUN

ENTER THE PART NUMBER? 129
THE DESCRIPTION IS HEX BOLT
THE COST IS    1.26

ANOTHER PART NUMBER (Y OR N)? Y
ENTER THE PART NUMBER? 119
THE DESCRIPTION IS ACCESS PAN
THE COST IS    8.50

ANOTHER PART NUMBER (Y OR N)? Y
ENTER THE PART NUMBER? 122
**ERROR** 122 IS AN INVALID PART NUMBER

ANOTHER PART NUMBER (Y OR N)? Y
ENTER THE PART NUMBER? 138
THE DESCRIPTION IS HOOK TAB
THE COST IS    0.48

ANOTHER PART NUMBER (Y OR N)? N

JOB COMPLETE
```

Programming Case Study 18: Determining the Federal Withholding Tax From a Tax Table

In many tables, the table argument is a limit to a category, and the search is for a value greater than the search argument rather than equal to it. The following problem incorporates such a search.

Problem

The federal withholding tax is determined by taking an employee's biweekly taxable earnings (Gross Pay $- 38.46 \times$ exemptions) and using it to look up the table entry values that are to be used to compute the tax. The tax table, as shown in Table 7.5, is made up of a series of categories. For example, an employee whose biweekly taxable earnings is between $554.00 and $846.00 pays $79.44 plus 25% of the amount in excess of $554. An employee whose biweekly taxable earnings is between $846.00 and $1,069.00 uses another set of factors to determine the tax to be paid.

Only the table for single wage earners is given here, to simplify this problem. Actually, the Federal Government distributes two tables to companies—one for single wage earners and another for married wage earners.

TABLE 7.5   Tax Table for Single Wage Earners (Biweekly Payroll Period)

If the amount of wages is:		The amount of income tax to be withheld shall be:	
Not over $54		0	
Over—	But not over—		of excess over—
$54	$158	12%	$54
$158	$365	$12.48 plus 15%	$158
$365	$554	$43.53 plus 19%	$365
$554	$846	$79.44 plus 25%	$554
$846	$1,069	$152.44 plus 30%	$846
$1,069	$1,273	$219.34 plus 34%	$1,069
$1,273		$288.70 plus 37%	$1,273

Using Table 7.5, write a program to determine the federal withholding tax for the following group of single employees.

Employee Number	Gross Pay	Dependents
106	$1,550	1
110	85	2
115	525	4
120	4,550	6
125	865	0
127	461	8

Display in columnar form the employee number, gross pay and federal withholding tax. An analysis, a flowchart, and a program solution follow.

Program Tasks

1) Declare four parallel arrays (A, B, P and X) containing 8 elements each. Array A will contain the table arguments (upper limits). Arrays B, P and X will contain the three table functions representing the base tax, percent and in-excess-of, respectively.

2) Load the arrays with the following entries:

Array A (Upper Limit)	Array B (Base Tax)	Array P (Percent)	Array X (In Excess of)
$ 54	$ 0.00	0	$ 0
158	0.00	12	54
365	12.48	15	158
554	43.53	19	365
846	79.44	25	554
1,069	152.44	30	846
1,273	219.34	34	1,069
0	288.70	37	1,273

The last entry in the table, which has an upper limit of zero, is used to compute the tax for employees earning $1,273 or more.

3) Compute the biweekly taxable earnings, which will be the search argument, from the formula:

Biweekly Taxable Earnings = Gross Pay − 38.46 ∗ No. of Dependents

4) Use a For loop to search the table with the value computed in 3, starting with the first element. In a successful search, the biweekly taxable earnings is less than the corresponding table argument in array A. If the For loop runs its normal course, the control variable becomes 8, which implies that the employee earned $1,273 or more.

5) After the proper table entry is determined, compute the withholding tax from the following formula:

$$\text{Withholding Tax} = B(I) + P(I) * (E - X(I))$$

where E = taxable earnings
I = selected entry
B(I) = base tax entry
P(I) = percent entry (in decimal fraction)
E − X(I) = the amount in excess of

6) Display the employee number N$, gross pay G, and federal withholding tax W.

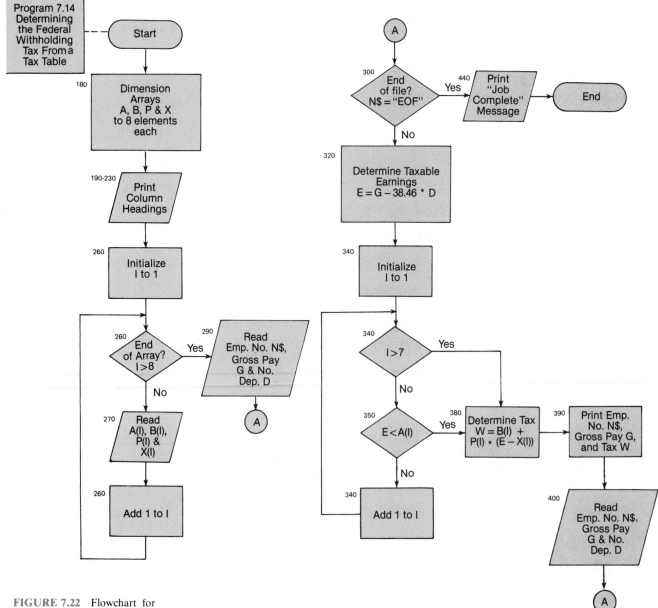

FIGURE 7.22 Flowchart for Program 7.14.

```
100 REM PROGRAM 7.14
110 REM DETERMINING THE FEDERAL WITHHOLDING TAX FROM A TAX TABLE
120 REM A  = ARRAY OF UPPER LIMITS   B  = ARRAY OF BASE TAXES
130 REM P  = ARRAY OF PERCENTS       X  = ARRAY OF 'IN EXCESS OF'
140 REM N$ = EMPLOYEE NUMBER         G  = GROSS PAY
150 REM D  = NUMBER OF DEPENDENTS    E  = TAXABLE INCOME
160 REM W  = FEDERAL WITHHOLDING TAX
170 REM ***************************************************
180 DIM A(8), B(8), P(8), X(8)
190 PRINT TAB(7); "EMPLOYEE TAX REPORT"
200 PRINT
210 PRINT     "EMPLOYEE      GROSS          FEDERAL"
220 PRINT     "NUMBER        PAY            TAX"
230 PRINT     "------        -----          -------"
240 LET A$ = " \ \         #,###.##        #,###.##"
250 REM *****LOAD THE TABLE*****
260 FOR I = 1 TO 8
270     READ A(I), B(I), P(I), X(I)
280 NEXT I
290 READ N$, G, D
300 WHILE N$ <> "EOF"
310     REM *****DETERMINE TAXABLE INCOME*****
320     LET E = G - 38.46 * D
330     REM *****SEARCH TAX TABLE FOR UPPER LIMIT*****
340     FOR I = 1 TO 7
350        IF E < A(I) THEN 380
360     NEXT I
370     REM *****COMPUTE FEDERAL WITHHOLDING TAX*****
380     LET W = B(I) + P(I) * (E - X(I))
390     PRINT USING A$, N$, G, W
400     READ N$, G, D
410 WEND
420 REM *****END OF JOB ROUTINE*****
430 PRINT
440 PRINT "JOB COMPLETE"
450 REM *****************TABLE ENTRIES FOLLOW*****************
460 DATA 54, 0, 0, 0, 158, 0, 0.12, 54, 365, 12.48, 0.15, 158
470 DATA 554, 43.53, 0.19, 365, 846, 79.44, 0.25, 554
480 DATA 1069, 152.44, 0.30, 846, 1273, 219.34, 0.34, 1069
490 DATA 0, 288.70, 0.37, 1273
500 REM ********************DATA FOLLOWS********************
510 DATA 106, 1550, 1, 110, 85, 2
520 DATA 115, 525, 4, 120, 4550, 6
530 DATA 125, 865, 0, 127, 461, 8
540 DATA EOF, 0, 0
550 END
```

RUN   PROGRAM 7.14

```
        EMPLOYEE TAX REPORT

EMPLOYEE      GROSS          FEDERAL
NUMBER        PAY            TAX
------        -----          -------
  106       1,550.00          376.96
  110          85.00            0.00
  115         525.00           44.70
  120       4,550.00        1,415.81
  125         865.00          158.14
  127         461.00           11.92

JOB COMPLETE
```

The table search, in lines 340 through 360, differs from the one presented in Program 7.13 in two ways. First, we are searching for a category that the search argument (taxable earnings) belongs to rather than an exact match. When a table is searched in this fashion it is necessary that the arguments be in sequence. If, for example, the table argument 1273 is placed at the top of the table, most employees would certainly pay the wrong taxes. The IF statement in line 350 terminates the search when the taxable earnings E is less than the table argument A(I).

The second major difference between the search in this program and Program 7.13 is that the tax table is open ended. That is, the last category is used for any employee who has taxable earnings greater than or equal to $1,273. There is no invalid search argument. If the taxable earnings is less than $0, the withholding tax is $0. If the taxable earnings is beyond the last table argument, the last table entry is used. When a For loop runs its normal course, the control variable I is assigned the value that caused the loop to terminate.

Binary Search   A serial search is useful for short tables, but not for long ones. For example, suppose the telephone book names were not listed alphabetically. If there are 15,000 names, it takes on the average 7,500 comparisons to find a specific telephone number. Some numbers might take only a few comparisons, while others might take nearly 15,000. By arranging telephone books alphabetically, it is possible to find a name quickly and easily. When the arguments in a table are in alphabetical or numerical order, an efficient algorithm known as the binary search can be used. A binary search begins the search in the middle of the table. If the search argument is less than the middle table argument, the search continues by halving the lower-valued half of the table. If the search argument is greater than the middle table argument, the search continues by halving the upper higher-valued half of the table. If the search argument is equal to the middle argument, the search is over. The binary search algorithm continues to narrow the table until it finds a match or determines that there is no match.

Figure 7.23 illustrates how the binary search algorithm works with a table of part numbers and corresponding part costs.

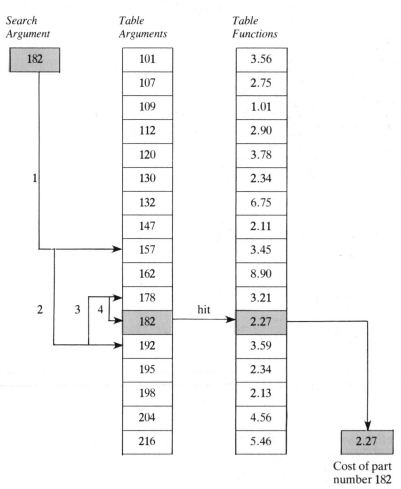

FIGURE 7.23   Conceptual view of a binary search.

Part number 182 is first compared against the 9th element of the 17 element array. Since 182 is greater than 157, the match is located in the higher-valued half of the table. Part number 182 is next compared to the 13th element (halfway between 10 and 17). The part number is less than 192, and the confined area between 10 and 13 is halved again. On the next comparison, 182 is greater than 178 and the area is reduced by half. On the 4th comparison, a match is found. A serial search for part number 182 would have taken 12 comparisons before finding a match. The difference in the number of comparisons between the two algorithms becomes even greater as the size of the table increases.

The following partial program illustrates a binary search.

```
280 LET L = 1
290 LET H = R
300 LET I = 1
310 WHILE P <> N(I) AND L <= H
320    LET I = INT((L + H)/2)
330     IF P < N(I) THEN LET H = I - 1
340     IF P > N(I) THEN LET L = I + 1
350 WEND
360 IF P = N(I) THEN 370 ELSE 390
370    PRINT USING "THE COST IS ###.##"; C(I)
380 GOTO 400
390    PRINT "**ERROR**"; P; "IS AN INVALID PART NUMBER"
400 .
```

The variables L and H point to the beginning and end of the part of the array N to which the search is confined. Line 280 initializes L to 1. Line 290 initializes H to R, which is equal to the number of entries in the table. Line 300 initializes I to 1 to ensure that N(I), in line 310, is within the range of the array.

```
100 REM PROGRAM 7.15
110 REM BINARY SEARCH OF AN ARGUMENT ORGANIZED TABLE
120 REM N = PART NUMBER ARGUMENTS
130 REM C = PART COST FUNCTIONS  R = NUMBER OF TABLE ENTRIES
140 REM ***************************************************
150 REM *****DECLARE THE TABLE*****
160 READ R
170 DIM N(R), C(R)
180 REM *****LOAD THE TABLE*****
190 FOR I = 1 TO R
200    READ N(I), C(I)
210 NEXT I
220 LET Y$ = "Y"
230 WHILE Y$ = "Y"
240    INPUT "ENTER THE PART NUMBER"; P
250    REM *****SEARCH THE TABLE*****
260    REM L = FIRST ELEMENT OF PORTION OF TABLE BEING SEARCHED
270    REM H = LAST ELEMENT OF PORTION OF TABLE BEING SEARCHED
280    LET L = 1
290    LET H = R
300    LET I = 1
310    WHILE P <> N(I) AND L <= H
320       LET I = INT((L + H)/2)
330        IF P < N(I) THEN LET H = I - 1
340        IF P > N(I) THEN LET L = I + 1
350    WEND
360    IF P = N(I) THEN 370 ELSE 390
370       PRINT USING "THE COST IS ###.##"; C(I)
380    GOTO 400
390       PRINT "**ERROR**"; P; "IS AN INVALID PART NUMBER"
400    PRINT
410    INPUT "ANOTHER PART NUMBER (Y OR N)"; A$
420 WEND
430 PRINT
440 PRINT "JOB COMPLETE"
450 REM ******************TABLE ENTRIES********************
460 DATA 17
470 DATA 101, 3.56, 107, 2.75, 109, 1.01, 112, 2.90, 120, 3.78
480 DATA 130, 2.34, 132, 6.75, 147, 2.11, 157, 3.45, 162, 8.90
490 DATA 178, 3.21, 182, 2.27, 192, 3.59, 195, 2.34, 198, 2.13
500 DATA 204, 4.56, 216, 5.46
510 END

RUN

ENTER THE PART NUMBER? 182
THE COST IS    2.27

ANOTHER PART NUMBER (Y OR N)? Y
ENTER THE PART NUMBER? 101
THE COST IS    3.56

ANOTHER PART NUMBER (Y OR N)? Y
ENTER THE PART NUMBER? 163
**ERROR** 163 IS AN INVALID PART NUMBER

ANOTHER PART NUMBER (Y OR N)? Y
ENTER THE PART NUMBER? 132
THE COST IS    6.75

ANOTHER PART NUMBER (Y OR N)? N

JOB COMPLETE
```

PROGRAM 7.15

Lines 310 through 350 carry out the search. The compound condition in line 310 terminates the loop when P is equal to N(I) *sv* when L exceeds H. If the search ends because P is equal to N(I), the search is successful. If the search ends because L exceeds H, the search is unsuccessful. Line 360 tests to determine which of the two conditions caused the loop to terminate.

The first time through the loop, line 320 assigns I a value that points to the middle element of the array. Lines 330 and 340 test the search argument against the Ith element of array N. If P does not equal N(I), one of the two pointers, L or H, is adjusted to shrink the area of the search.

Program 7.15 employs the binary search to search the parts list presented in Figure 7.23.

7.7 WHAT YOU SHOULD KNOW

1. An array is a variable that allocates a specified number of storage locations, each of which can be assigned a unique value.
2. The elements in the array are distinguished from one another by subscripts. The subscript, written in parentheses, can be a numeric constant, numeric variable or a numeric expression.
3. The dimension of an array is the number of subscripts required to reference an element in an array.
4. Before an array can be used in a program, the DIM statement should be used to declare the number of storage locations in main memory to reserve for the array.
5. The DIM statement may be located anywhere before the first appearance of a subscripted variable in a program.
6. Several arrays may be dimensioned in the same DIM statement.
7. The OPTION BASE statement assigns the lower bound of 0 or 1 to all arrays in a program.
8. The subscript that references an array element must be within the range of the array. The range is the number of elements in the array.
9. Non-integer subscripts are rounded to the nearest integer.
10. An array is usually loaded with data using a READ or INPUT statement inside a For loop.
11. Parallel arrays are two or more arrays that have corresponding elements.
12. Some BASIC systems permit arrays to be dynamically allocated. In the DIM statement a variable is placed within the parentheses to indicate the size of the array. Before the DIM statement, the variable is assigned a value to which the array is then dimensioned.
13. A two-dimensional array is one that requires two subscripts to reference any element. The first subscript designates the row and the second subscript the column of that element.
14. Many BASIC systems allow up to 255 dimensions. One and two-dimensional arrays are the most common arrays used.
15. Sorting is arranging data according to some certain order or sequence. Data that is in sequence from lowest to highest is in ascending sequence. Data that is in sequence from highest to lowest is in descending sequence.
16. The bubble and the Shell sort algorithms are the ones most often used.
17. Both the bubble sort and Shell sort algorithms work on arrays containing numeric or string data.
18. Regardless of the sort algorithm used, there are three steps required in a program to sort data—dimension the array, load the array with data and apply an algorithm to manipulate the elements in the array.
19. The SWAP statement allows you to interchange the values of two variables in one statement.
20. Tables are organized based on how the data is to be referenced. In positionally organized tables, table functions can be accessed by their position in the table. In

argument organized tables, table functions are accessed by looking up a desired value that corresponds to them. To retrieve these corresponding table functions, a search argument is compared against table argument. When the search argument matches the table argument, the corresponding table functions are selected and used.

21. To utilize table processing techniques in a program, you must declare the table by dimensioning arrays, load the table entries using a READ or INPUT statement inside a For loop, and code appropriate statements to access the table entries.

22. Serial and binary search methods are normally used to access data stored in tables.

23. A serial search, which normally begins at the top of the table, does not require that the data be in any sequence.

24. A binary search, which begins in the middle of the table, requires that the data be in ascending or descending sequence.

7.8 SELF-TEST EXERCISES

1. Consider the valid programs listed below. What is displayed if each is executed?

a)
```
100 REM CHAPTER7 SELF-TEST 1A
110 DIM A(6)
120 LET S = 0
130 FOR I = 1 TO 6
140    READ A(I)
150    PRINT A(I);
160    LET S = S + A(I)
170 NEXT I
180 PRINT S
190 DATA 4, 2, 3, 9, 4, 1
200 END
```

b)
```
100 REM CHAPTER 7 SELF-TEST 1B
110 DIM A(5), B(5), C(5)
120 FOR I = 1 TO 5
130    READ A(I), B(I)
140 NEXT I
150 FOR I = 1 TO 5
160    LET C(I) = A(I) * B(I)
170    PRINT C(I)
180 NEXT I
190 DATA 1, 4, 2, 3, 4, 4, 2, 4, 3, 5
200 END
```

c)
```
100 REM CHAPTER 7 SELF-TEST 1C
110 READ X, Y
120 DIM A(X, Y)
130 FOR I = 1 TO X
140    FOR J = 1 TO Y
150       READ A(I, J)
160       PRINT A(I, J);
170    NEXT J
180    PRINT
190 NEXT I
200 DATA 4, 3, 2, 1, 6, 9, 5
210 DATA 6, 2, 1, 3, 8, 4, 2
220 END
```

d)
```
100 REM CHAPTER 7 SELF-TEST 1D
110 DIM A(5), B(5)
120 FOR I = 1 TO 5
130    READ A(I), B(I)
140 NEXT I
150 PRINT "A ARRAY -";
160 FOR I = 1 TO 5
170    PRINT A(I);
180 NEXT I
190 PRINT
200 PRINT "B ARRAY -";
210 FOR I = 1 TO 5
220    PRINT B(I);
230 NEXT I
240 PRINT
250 FOR I = 1 TO 5
260    LET T = A(I)
270    LET A(I) = B(I)
280    LET B(I) = T
290 NEXT I
300 PRINT "A ARRAY -";
310 FOR I = 1 TO 5
320    PRINT A(I);
330 NEXT I
340 PRINT
350 PRINT "B ARRAY -";
360 FOR I = 1 TO 5
370    PRINT B(I);
380 NEXT I
390 DATA 0, 1, 2, 3, 4, 5, 6, 7, 8, 9
400 END
```

2. What values will be stored in array B after each of the partial programs are executed?

a)
```
100 REM CHAPTER 7 SELF-TEST 2A
110 DIM B(4, 5)
120 FOR L = 1 TO 4
130    FOR K = 1 TO 5
140       LET B(L, K) = L * K
150    NEXT K
160 NEXT L
```

b)
```
100 REM CHAPTER 7 SELF-TEST 2B
110 DIM B(2, 3)
120 FOR L = 1 TO 2
130    FOR K = 1 TO 3
140       LET B(L, K) = K - L
150    NEXT K
160 NEXT L
```

3. Assume array A contains the following values:

	columns 1	2	3	4	5
r 1	3	1	2	3	0
o 2	2	5	7	1	0
w 3	4	1	5	6	0
s 4	0	0	0	0	0

Indicate the changes, if any, to the above values assigned in array A when the following partial program is executed.

```
100 REM CHAPTER 7 SELF-TEST 3
110 DIM A(4, 5)
120 FOR J = 1 TO 4
130    FOR I = 1 TO 3
140       LET A(4, J) = A(4, J) + A(I, J)
150    NEXT I
160 NEXT J
170 FOR I = 1 TO 4
180    FOR J = 1 TO 4
190       LET A(I, 5) = A(I, 5) + A(I, J)
200    NEXT J
210 NEXT I
```

4. Write a DIM statement to declare array C to have 12 rows and 9 columns and array D to have 6 rows and 9 columns of elements. Assume the statement

```
100 OPTION BASE 1
```

precedes the DIM statement.

5. How many elements are allocated to array C and D in Exercise 4?

6. Write a partial program using a For loop to display the principal diagonal elements of array X. Assume array X is declared in a DIM statement as X(12, 12).

7. Write a partial program that will display the elements of a one-dimensional array, S(200), such that the values of the odd elements display in print zone-1 and the values of the even elements display in print zone-2. For example,

Print Zone 1	*Print Zone 2*
S_1	S_2
S_3	S_4
$\vdots$	$\vdots$
S_{199}	S_{200}

8. Write a partial program that displays the elements of a one-dimensional array, S(200), such that the values of the elements display 5 to a line as shown below:

Print Zone 1	*Print Zone 2*	*Print Zone 3*	*Print Zone 4*	*Print Zone 5*
S_1	S_2	S_3	S_4	S_5
$\vdots$	$\vdots$	$\vdots$	$\vdots$	$\vdots$
S_{196}	S_{197}	S_{198}	S_{199}	S_{200}

9. Write a For loop that reads data into a 10 element array X beginning with the last element, next to last, and so on. The last data item read should be assigned to the first element.

10. What does the following program display when executed?

```
100 REM CHAPTER 7 SELF-TEST 10
110 DIM A (10)
120 FOR I = 1 TO 10
130    READ A(I)
140 NEXT I
150 FOR I = 1 TO 9
160    IF A(I) <= A(I + 1) THEN 180
170       PRINT A(I), A(I + 1), "OUT OF SEQUENCE"
180 NEXT I
190 DATA 6, 9, 12, 15, 14, 18, 12, 20, 23, 21
200 END
```

11. Consider the valid program below. What displays when the program is executed?

```
100 REM CHAPTER 7 SELF-TEST 11
110 DIM F(10)
120 PRINT " N", "NTH FIBONACCI NO."
130 LET F(1) = 1
140 LET F(2) = 1
150 PRINT 1, F(1)
160 PRINT 2, F(2)
170 FOR N = 3 TO 10
180    LET F(N) = F(N - 2) + F(N - 1)
190    PRINT N, F(N)
200 NEXT N
210 END
```

12. Identify the syntax error(s), if any, in each of the following statements.

a) `100 DIM A, F$, C`

b) `200 PRINT X(2, Y)`

c) `300 DIM X(F$)`

d) `400 INPUT A$(C)`

e) `500 LET X = 5 * A(T(Y))`

f) `600 PRINT (5)A, (6)B, (10)C`

g) `700 DIM F$ = 10`

h) `800 IF B$(X) > B$(X + 1) THEN 200`

7.9 TEST YOUR BASIC SKILLS

1. What is displayed if these valid programs are executed?

a) Assume the following data items are entered in response to the INPUT statement in line 170: Earth, Mars, Neptune and Moon.

```
100 REM EXERCISE 7.1A
110 DIM P$(9), D(9)
120 FOR I = 1 TO 9
130    READ P$(I), D(I)
140 NEXT I
150 LET A$ = "Y"
160 WHILE A$ = "Y"
170    INPUT "ENTER THE PLANET NAME"; S$
180    FOR I = 1 TO 9
190       IF S$ = P$(I) THEN 230
200    NEXT I
210    PRINT S$; " IS NOT A PLANET"
220    GOTO 250
230    PRINT "THE DISTANCE FROM THE SUN TO "; S$
240    PRINT "IS"; D(I); "MILLION MILES."
250    INPUT "ANOTHER PLANET (Y OR N)"; A$
260 WEND
270 PRINT "END OF ASTRONOMY LESSON"
280 REM ***************DATA FOLLOWS***************
290 DATA MERCURY, 36, VENUS, 67, EARTH, 93
300 DATA MARS, 142, JUPITER, 483
310 DATA SATURN, 886, URANUS, 1782
320 DATA NEPTUNE, 2793, PLUTO, 3670
330 END
```

b)
```
100 REM EXERCISE 7.1B
110 DIM B$(7)
120 LET A$ = "PROGRAM"
130 FOR I = 1 TO 7
140    LET B$(I) = MID$(A$, I, 1)
150    PRINT B$(I)
160 NEXT I
170 END
```

c)
```
100 REM EXERCISE 7.1C
110 DIM A$(26)
120 FOR I = 1 TO 26
130    READ A$(I)
140 NEXT I
150 LET S = 0
160 IF S <> 0 THEN 260
170    LET S = 1
180    FOR I = 1 TO 25
190       IF A$(I) <= A$(I + 1) THEN 240
200          LET T$ = A$(I)
210          LET A$(I) = A$(I + 1)
220          LET A$(I + 1) = T$
230          LET S = 0
240    NEXT I
250 GOTO 160
260 FOR I = 1 TO 26
270    PRINT " "; A$(I);
280 NEXT I
290 REM ********DATA FOLLOWS*********
300 DATA L, J, A, C, X, Z, N, Q, B, E
310 DATA D, H, O, T, W, Y, F, R, V, I
320 DATA K, M, G, U, S, P
330 END
```

2. Assume array L is declared to have 5 rows and 5 columns and the elements of array L are assigned the following values:

ARRAY L

2	5	14	30	50
7	12	21	70	10
5	15	70	60	0
19	20	30	10	20
22	45	20	40	50

Write the subscripted variable name that references the following values found in array L.

a) 12   b) 70   c) 15   d) 45   e) 60   f) 7   g) 14   h) 22

3. For the array presented in Exercise 2, given:

```
100 REM EXERCISE 7.3
110 LET K = 5
120 FOR I = 1 TO 3
130     LET J = I + 2
140     LET K = I
150 NEXT I
160 LET N = L(K, J)
```

What value is assigned to the variable N?

4. Explain what the following partial program does.

```
100 REM EXERCISE 7.4
110 DIM A(3, 4), B(3, 4)
        .
        .
        .
180 FOR I = 1 TO 3
190     FOR J = 1 TO 4
200         LET B(I, J) = A(I, J)
210     NEXT J
220 NEXT I
```

5. Assume array A has 4 rows and 4 columns and the elements of array A are assigned the following values:

ARRAY A

1	2	3	4
5	6	7	8
9	10	11	12
13	14	15	16

Note: $A(1, 1) = 1$ and $A(3, 2) = 10$.

What will be the final arrangement of array A after the following partial program is executed? Select from the choices below.

```
100 REM EXERCISE 7.5
110 FOR I = 1 TO 4
120     FOR J = 1 TO 4
130         LET A(I, J) = A(J, I)
140     NEXT J
150 NEXT I
```

a)

1	2	3	4
5	6	7	8
9	10	11	12
13	14	15	16

b)

16	15	14	13
12	11	10	9
8	7	6	5
4	3	2	1

c)

1	2	2	4
5	6	6	8
9	10	10	12
13	14	14	16

d)

1	5	9	13
5	6	10	14
9	10	11	15
13	14	15	16

e) None of these.

6. Refer to the initial array A given in Exercise 5. What will be the final arrangement of array A after each of the following partial programs is executed? Select your answer from the choices given in Exercise 5.

a)
```
100 REM EXERCISE 7.6A
110 FOR I = 1 TO 4
120    LET A(I, 3) = A(I, 2)
130 NEXT I
```

b)
```
100 REM EXERCISE 7.6B
110 LET J = 2
120 FOR I = 1 TO 4
130    LET A(I, J + 1) = A(I, J)
140 NEXT I
```

c)
```
100 REM EXERCISE 7.6C
110 FOR I = 1 TO 4
120    LET A(I, I) = A(I - 2, I + 2)
130 NEXT I
```

d)
```
100 REM EXERCISE 7.6D
110 FOR I = 1 TO 4
120    FOR J = 1 TO 4
130       LET A(I, J) = A(I, J)
140    NEXT J
150 NEXT I
```

7. Refer to the initial array A given in Exercise 5. What will be the final arrangement of array A after the following partial program is executed? Select your answer from the choices given in Exercise 5. Assume that array B has been declared the same as array A.

```
100 REM EXERCISE 7.7
110 FOR I = 1 TO 4
120    FOR J = 1 TO 4
130       LET B(I, J) = A(I, J)
140    NEXT J
150 NEXT I
160 LET X = 0
170 FOR I = 4 TO 1 STEP -1
180    LET Y = 0
190    LET X = X + 1
200    FOR J = 4 TO 1 STEP -1
210       LET Y = Y + 1
220       LET A(X, Y) = B(I, J)
230    NEXT J
240 NEXT I
```

8. Given a one-dimensional array N, consisting of 50 elements, write a partial program that will count the number of elements in array N that have a value between 0 and 18 inclusive, between 26 and 29 inclusive, and between 42 and 47. Use the following counters:

   L— count of elements with a value between 0 and 18 inclusive

   M—count of elements with a value between 26 and 29 inclusive

   H—count of elements with a value between 42 and 47

   Use the subscript I to help reference the elements.

9. Given array F declared to have 100 elements, assume each element of array F has been assigned a value. Write a partial program to shift all the values up one location. That is, assign the value of F_1 to F_2, F_2 to F_3 and F_{100} to F_1. Do not use any array other than array F. Be careful not to destroy a value before it is shifted.

10. Given three arrays A, B and C, each declared to 50 elements, assume the elements of arrays A and B have been assigned values. Write a partial program that compares each element of array A to its corresponding element in array B. Assign a 1, 0 or −1 to the corresponding element in array C, as follows:

   1 if A is greater than B
   0 if A is equal to B
   −1 if A is less than B

11. Identify the error(s), if any, in each of the following partial programs:

a)
```
100 REM EXERCISE 7.11A
110 DIM X(300)
120 FOR I = 1 TO 500
130    READ X(I)
140 NEXT I
```

b)
```
100 REM EXERCISE 7.11B
110 DIM X(700)
120 FOR K = 700 TO 1 STEP -1
130    READ X(K)
140 NEXT K
```

12. Identify the error(s), if any, in each of the following variables and their subscripts.

a) F3(8)

b) A(6 − 8)

c) A(K)

d) F(I(K))

e) X(3.7)

f) D(5, 6, 7)

g) Q(K, A)

h) M1$(3)

i) L$(6, 9)

j) Y(I ∗ 3/J, K + M ∧ P)

13. A program utilizes four arrays, B(I), K(J), L(I) and M(Q, J) where the maximum value of I, J and Q are 15, 36 and 29. Write a correct DIM statement.

14. A program utilizes the array element M$(T), where T assumes values from 12 to 46. Write a correct DIM statement.

15. Consider the following partial program:

```
100 REM EXERCISE 7.15
110 DIM P(50)
120 LET S = 0
130 FOR J = 1 TO 50
140    READ P(J)
150    LET S = S + P(J)
160 NEXT J
170 PRINT S
180 FOR I = 1 TO 50 STEP 5
190    PRINT P(I), P(I + 1), P(I + 2), P(I + 3), P(I + 4)
200 NEXT I
```

   a) How many lines of output are displayed?
   b) How many values are displayed?
   c) Briefly describe the function of this program.
   d) Why is the increment 5 instead of 1 in line 180?
   e) Why not use FOR I = 1 TO 10 for the second For loop?

16. Given a one-dimensional array A, consisting of 50 elements, write the DIM statement and the For loop to count the number of elements with negative, positive and zero values in the array.

17. Write a program to find the salesperson who has the greatest total sales for a given period. Assume the total sales is in array A, that the corresponding salesperson's names are in array N$ and that each array has been dimensioned to 50 elements.

18. Write a program to find the salesperson who has the least total sales for a given period. Use the same arrays as in Exercise 17.

19. Write a program to determine the number of times the letter I is the character value of a string array A$ that has been previously dimensioned to 50 elements.

20. Write a program to display the item number and gross sales for all items that have a gross sales greater than $3000. Assume item number is stored in Array A and the corresponding gross sales in array B, and each array is dimensioned to 200.

21. Write a program to display the Centigrade temperature for Farenheit temperatures ranging from $-50°$ to $100°$. Place the output in tabular form.

22. Given two one-dimensional arrays P and Q, each of which has a maximum of 100 elements. Write a program to compute the sum of the products. That is, find:

$$S = \sum_{k=1}^{100} P_k Q_k$$

23. Write a program to generate the first 6 rows of Pascal's Triangle. Each entry in a given row of the triangle is generated by adding the two adjacent entries in the immediately preceding row. For example, the third entry in row 4 is the sum of the second and third entries in row 3. The first 6 rows of Pascal's Triangle are as follows:

```
              1
          1       1
       1      2      1
     1     3     3     1
   1     4     6     4     1
 1    5    10    10    5    1
```

To eliminate the complexity of spacing, display each row starting in column 1.

24. Given two two-dimensional arrays R and S, each of which has 10 rows and 10 columns. Write a program to compute the sum of the products of the elements of the arrays with

common subscripts. That is, find:

$$S = \sum_{j=1}^{10} \left(\sum_{k=1}^{10} R_{jk}S_{jk} \right)$$

25. Specify the value of each of the elements of array S following execution of the partial program below.

```
100 REM EXERCISE 7.25
110 DIM S(2, 3)
120 FOR I = 1 TO 3
130    FOR J = 1 TO 2
140       READ S(J, I)
150    NEXT J
160 NEXT I
170 DATA 1, 2, 3, 4, 5, 6
180 END
```

7.10 PROGRAMMING EXERCISES

Purpose: To become familiar with declaring, loading and searching a table.

Exercise 1: Credit Card Verification

Problem: Write a program that will accept a 6-digit credit card number and verify that this number is in a table. If the credit card number is in the table, display the message "Credit Card Number is Valid." If the credit card number is not in the table, display the message "Credit Card Number Invalid—Alert Your Manager." Declare the credit card number table to N elements. Use the following table of 15 credit card numbers:

131416	238967	384512	583214
172319	345610	410001	672354
194567	351098	518912	691265
210201	372198	562982	

Input Data: Use the following sample data:

```
372198
518912
102002
672354
210200
```

Output Results: The following partial results are shown:

```
CREDIT CARD NUMBER? 372198
CREDIT CARD NUMBER IS VALID

ANOTHER CREDIT CARD NUMBER (Y OR N)? Y
            •
            •
            •
CREDIT CARD NUMBER? 210200
CREDIT CARD NUMBER INVALID - ALERT YOUR MANAGER

ANOTHER CREDIT CARD NUMBER (Y OR N)? N

JOB COMPLETE
```

Purpose: To become familiar with accessing data from a positionally organized table.

Exercise 2: Windchill Table Look-up

Problem: As every resident of Alaska knows, the real enemy is not the near-zero temperatures, but the windchill factor. Meteorologists in Alaska and many other states give both the temperature and the windchill factor. So important is the windchill factor that calm air at $-40°$ Fahrenheit is less likely to cause frostbite than air just below freezing blowing at gale forces. Basically, two factors determine the windchill factor—the velocity of wind and the temperature. Write a program that accepts from the user a temperature between $-20°$ F and 15° F and a wind velocity between 5 mph and 30 mph, both in multiples of five. The program should look up the windchill factor in a positionally organized table and display it. Use the following table of windchill factors:

Table of Windchill Factors

Temperature in Fahrenheit	Wind Velocity in Miles per Hour					
	5	10	15	20	25	30
−20	−26	−46	−58	−67	−74	−79
−15	−21	−40	−51	−60	−66	−71
−10	−15	−34	−45	−53	−59	−64
−5	−10	−27	−38	−46	−51	−56
0	−5	−22	−31	−39	−44	−49
5	0	−15	−25	−31	−36	−41
10	7	−9	−18	−24	−29	−33
15	12	−3	−11	−17	−22	−25

Input Data: Use the following sample data:

Temperature (°F)	Wind Velocity (mph)
−15	10
5	30
−5	40
−40	25
15	10

Output Results: The following partial results are shown:

```
WHAT IS THE TEMPERATURE (BETWEEN −20 AND 15)? −15
WHAT IS THE VELOCITY OF THE WIND (BETWEEN 5 AND 30)? 10
THE WINDCHILL FACTOR IS −40

DO YOU WANT TO DETERMINE ANOTHER WINDCHILL FACTOR (Y OR N)? Y
          .
          .
          .
WHAT IS THE TEMPERATURE (BETWEEN −20 AND 15)? −40
THE TEMPERATURE IS OUT OF RANGE

WHAT IS THE TEMPERATURE (BETWEEN −20 AND 15)? 15
WHAT IS THE VELOCITY OF THE WIND (BETWEEN 5 AND 30)? 10
THE WINDCHILL FACTOR IS −3

DO YOU WANT TO DETERMINE ANOTHER WINDCHILL FACTOR (Y OR N)? N
JOB COMPLETE
```

**Exercise 3:
Week Ending
Department and
Store Receipts**

Purpose: To become familiar with the use of arrays for determining totals.

Problem: Businesses are usually subdivided into smaller units for the purpose of better organization. The Tri-Quality retail store is subdivided into four departments. Each department submits its daily receipts at the end of the day to the store manager. Write a program, using an array consisting of 5 rows and 6 columns, that is assigned the daily sales. Use the 5th row and 6th column to accumulate the totals. After accumulating the totals, display the entire array.

Input Data: Use the following sample data:

Dept.	Monday	Tuesday	Wednesday	Thursday	Friday
1	$2,146	$6,848	$8,132	$8,912	$5,165
2	8,123	9,125	6,159	5,618	9,176
3	4,156	5,612	4,128	4,812	3,685
4	1,288	1,492	1,926	1,225	2,015

Output Results: The following results are displayed:

```
              WEEK ENDING STORE RECEIPTS

DEPT  MONDAY   TUESDAY WEDNESDAY  THURSDAY    FRIDAY      TOTAL
------------------------------------------------------------------
  1   2,146.00  6,848.00  8,132.00  8,912.00  5,165.00  31,203.00
  2   8,123.00  9,125.00  6,159.00  5,618.00  9,176.00  38,201.00
  3   4,156.00  5,612.00  4,128.00  4,812.00  3,685.00  22,393.00
  4   1,288.00  1,492.00  1,926.00  1,225.00  2,015.00   7,946.00
  T  15,713.00 23,077.00 20,345.00 20,567.00 20,041.00 99,743.00
JOB COMPLETE
```

Purpose: To become familiar with the operation of merging.

Exercise 4: Merging Lists

Problem: Merging is the process of combining two sorted lists into a single sorted list. Obviously, one list can be appended to the other and the new list sorted. This process, however, is not always the most efficient. Write a program that merges two arrays, X and Y, into array Z. Assume that arrays X and Y have been pre-sorted and are in ascending sequence. Declare array X to have N elements, array Y to have M elements and array Z to have P elements, where P is equal to N + M. Display the contents of array Z as part of the end-of-job routine.

Hint: Be sure to take into consideration that the two arrays are not the same size. That is, when the shorter of the two arrays has been processed, assign the remaining elements of the longer array to array Z.

Input Data: Use the following sample data:
Array X—15 elements: 6, 9, 12, 15, 22, 33, 44, 66, 72, 84, 87, 92, 96, 98, 99
Array Y—10 elements: 4, 8, 12, 16, 24, 31, 68, 71, 73, 74

Output Results: The following results are displayed:

```
THE MERGED ARRAY, Z, HAS 25 ELEMENTS. THEIR VALUES ARE:
 4   6   8   9  12  12  15  16  22  24  31  33  44  66
68  71  72  73  84  87  92  96  98  99
JOB COMPLETE
```

Purpose: To become familiar with sorting data into ascending or descending sequence and to gain a better understanding of the bubble and Shell sort algorithms.

Exercise 5: Sorting Customer Numbers

Problem: Write a program which requests the selection from a menu of functions for sorting the customer numbers from Programming Exercise 5.9 into either ascending or descending sequence. Use the bubble sort algorithm to sort the customer numbers into ascending sequence. Use the Shell sort algorithm to sort the customer numbers into descending sequence. Declare the customer number array to have N elements.

Input Data: Use the data given in Chapter 5, Programming Exercise 9.

Output results: The following partial results are shown for the ascending sort of the customer numbers:

```
DO YOU WANT THE CUSTOMER NUMBERS SORTED IN:

        1. ASCENDING SEQUENCE
        2. DESCENDING SEQUENCE
        3. EXIT THE PROGRAM

ENTER A 1 OR 2 OR 3? 1

CUSTOMER NUMBERS
  3000
  3012
    .
    .
    .
  3095
  3096

JOB COMPLETE
```

Exercise 6:
Determining
the Mean, Variance
and Standard
Deviation

Purpose: To apply the concepts of array elements to a statistical problem.

Problem: Construct a program to find the mean (average), variance and standard deviation of a variable number of student grades. Use the following relationships
for the mean:

for the mean:
$$M = \frac{\sum\limits_{j=1}^{n} X_j}{n}$$

for the variance:
$$V = \sum\limits_{j=1}^{n} \frac{(X_j - M)^2}{n - 1}$$

for the standard deviation: $SD = \sqrt{V}$

where n is the total number of grades, to be read in first, followed by the student grades, represented by X_j.

Input Data: Enter the following sample data via the INPUT statement:

Number of students: 10
Grades: 97, 90, 87, 93, 96, 88, 78, 95, 96, 87

Output Results: The following partial results are shown:

```
THE MEAN IS 90.7
THE VARIANCE IS 35.1222
THE STANDARD DEVIATION IS 5.9264
```

Exercise 7:
Numeric Sorting
and Z-scores

Purpose: To become familiar with sorting a group of numbers and computing standard scores.

Problem: Construct a program that will sort the data in Exercise 6 and determine the standard score of each data item. Input the mean and standard deviation, which are the output results from Exercise 6. The standard score (Z-score) is a statistic that is used to compare grades on different examinations, where raw scores are sometimes meaningless. The Z-score is computed from the following formula:

$$Z = \frac{\text{raw score} - \text{average}}{\text{standard deviation}}$$

A positive Z-score indicates an above-average score. A negative Z-score represents a below-average performance. The Z-score actually indicates the number of standard deviations a score falls from the mean.

Input Data: Use the READ statement to enter the scores given in Exercise 6. Use the INPUT statement to enter the mean and standard deviation.

Output Results: The following results are shown:

```
WHAT IS THE MEAN? 90.7
WHAT IS THE STANDARD DEVIATION? 5.9264

GRADE           Z-SCORE
-----           -------
 78             -2.14295
 87             -.624325
  .                .
  .                .
  .                .
 96              .894304
 97             1.06304

END OF REPORT
```

Purpose: To become familiar with array manipulation and to determine the correlation coefficient.

Problem: Write a program that will read into two arrays the X and Y scores found below. Use the two arrays to determine the correlation coefficient r, rounded to two decimal places.

The correlation coefficient is a statistical measure that indicates the degree of relationship between two sets of scores where each score in one set has a corresponding score in the other set. The range of r is between -1 and $+1$ inclusive.

The closer r is to a $+1$, the higher the degree of direct relationship between the two sets of scores. That is, a high score in one set will have a corresponding high score in the other set. A negative correlation coefficient points to an inverse relationship. That is, a high score in one set will have a corresponding low score in the other set. A correlation coefficient near or equal to 0 suggests that there is no relationship between the two sets of scores.

The following formulas determine the value of r:

$$ r = \frac{N\Sigma XY - \Sigma X \Sigma Y}{\sqrt{N\Sigma X^2 - (\Sigma X)^2} \; \sqrt{N\Sigma Y^2 - (\Sigma Y)^2}} $$

where

$$ \Sigma XY = X_1 Y_1 + X_2 Y_2 + \cdots + X_n Y_n $$

$$ \Sigma X \Sigma Y = (X_1 + X_2 + \cdots + X_n) \cdot (Y_1 + Y_2 + \cdots + Y_n) $$

$$ \Sigma X^2 = X_1^2 + X_2^2 + X_3^2 + \cdots + X_n^2 $$

$$ (\Sigma X)^2 = (X_1 + X_2 + \cdots + X_n)^2 $$

$N =$ the total number of pairs of X and Y scores.

Input Data: Use the following sample data:

X	Y
67	68
63	66
67	68
64	65
68	69
62	66
70	68
66	65
68	71
67	67
69	68
71	70

Output Results: The following result is displayed:

```
THE CORRELATION COEFFICIENT IS .73
```

Purpose: To become familiar with table utilization and the serial search algorithm.

Problem: Construct a program that will accept the salesperson ID, salesperson name, weekly sales and commission class. The commission is determined by selecting the commission rate that corresponds to the given commission class and multiplying the rate times the sales. Prepare a program table from the following:

Commission Class	Commission Rate (in %)
03	5.5
06	6.5
08	5.6
09	4.5
All others	4.1

3) Display the salesperson ID, salesperson name, weekly sales and commission.

Input Data: Use the following sample data:

Salesperson ID	Salesperson Name	Weekly Sales	Commission Class
14612	DEAN SMITH	$8500.00	06
15678	JOHN FROMMING	5490.00	09
16203	FRED LASP	7450.00	10
18950	JIM FRANKLIN	9995.00	08

Output Results: The following results are displayed:

```
SALESPERSON    SALESPERSON     WEEKLY
ID             NAME            SALES        COMMISSION
-----------    -----------     -----        ----------
  14612        DEAN SMITH      8500           552.5
  15678        JOHN FROMMING   5490           247.05
  16203        FRED LASP       7450           305.45
  18950        JIM FRANKLIN    9995           559.72

END OF REPORT
```

Exercise 10:
Property Tax Rate
Table Look-Up

Purpose: To become familiar with argument organized tables.

Problem: Construct a program that requests the assessed value, searches a table for the tax rate and computes the property tax. The property tax is determined by multiplying the assessed value times the rate. Use the following table to construct the program table. Use the upper limit of each category for the argument. The tax rate will be the corresponding function.

Assessed Value	Tax Rate
$15,000.00 or less	2%
$15,000.01–$25,000.00	2.5%
$25,000.01–$40,000.00	3%
$40,000.01–$50,000.00	3.5%
$50,000.01–$70,000.00	4%
above $70,000.00	4.5%

Input Data: Input the following sample data:

Assessed Value

```
$27,400.00
 32,500.00
 46,800.00
 90,000.00
 14,600.00
```

Output Results: The following results are displayed:

```
WHAT IS THE ASSESSED VALUE? 27400
THE TAX CHARGE IS    822.00
    .
    .
    .
WHAT IS THE ASSESSED VALUE? 14600
THE TAX CHARGE IS    292.00

WHAT IS THE ASSESSED VALUE? -1
END OF REPORT
```

Exercise 11:
Six-Month Moving
Averages

Purpose: To become familiar with manipulating arrays.

Problem: Moving Averages are used in business forecasting, inventory control and accounts received. A moving average is the calculation of successive averages. Each average includes the addition of a new value and the deletion of the oldest value from the previous grouped total.

The Korman Company sales for a twelve month period are:

JANUARY	$15,000	JULY	$49,000
FEBRUARY	18,000	AUGUST	47,000
MARCH	23,000	SEPTEMBER	45,000
APRIL	40,000	OCTOBER	42,000
MAY	45,000	NOVEMBER	39,000
JUNE	50,000	DECEMBER	28,000

Write a program that determines the seven sets of six-month averages beginning with January–June, then February–July, and so on, ending with July–December. Include in the report the total sales for each six-month set. To determine the average of the first set, the sales for the first six months are added and the sum divided by 6. The second set is determined by summing the sales from February to July and dividing the sum by 6. Each new set involves deleting the oldest month and adding the newest month.

Input Data: Use the Korman Company sales shown above.

Output Results: The following results are displayed:

```
              SIX-MONTH MOVING AVERAGE

                           TOTAL
        MONTHS             SALES          AVERAGE
        ------             -----          -------
JANUARY   -   JUNE         191,000         31,833
FEBRUARY  -   JULY         225,000         37,500
MARCH     -   AUGUST       254,000         42,333
APRIL     -   SEPTEMBER    276,000         46,000
MAY       -   OCTOBER      278,000         46,333
JUNE      -   NOVEMBER     272,000         45,333
JULY      -   DECEMBER     250,000         41,667

JOB COMPLETE
```

Purpose: To become familiar with graphical output.

Exercise 12: Plotting a Histogram

Problem: The majority of reports generated thus far have been in tabular form. A computer can also be used to produce information in the form of a graph. A graph gives the user of a report a pictorial view of the information. Consider the following problem that has as its defined output a **histogram** (bar graph). The sales analysis department of company PUC requests from the data processing department, a report in the form of a histogram representing the company's annual sales trend for the ten-year period 1977 to 1986. The annual sales are as follows:

Year	Sales (in millions)
1977	$22
1978	26
1979	28
1980	35
1981	40
1982	43
1983	40
1984	45
1985	50
1986	48

The output must have the following characteristics:

1) The histogram must be displayed horizontally.
2) The column representing the years must be displayed vertically.
3) The sales for each year must be represented by a series of asterisks beginning to the left of the year column and extending to the right.
4) The horizontal axis, representing the amount of sales (in millions) must be marked off in increments of 5 beginning with 0 and ending with 55.

Hint: Use a one-dimensional array containing 55 elements to load and display a bar.

Input Data: Use the ten-year PUC data shown above.

Output Results: The following results are displayed:

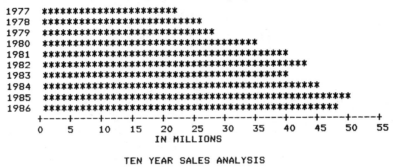

```
1977  ***********************
1978  **************************
1979  *****************************
1980  ************************************
1981  ******************************************
1982  ******************************************
1983  *****************************************
1984  ***********************************************
1985  *****************************************************
1986  ***************************************************
      +----+----+----+----+----+----+----+----+----+----+----+
      0    5    10   15   20   25   30   35   40   45   50   55
                         IN MILLIONS

               TEN YEAR SALES ANALYSIS
```

Exercise 13:
Payroll Problem VI—
Federal Withholding

Purpose: To become familiar with table utilization and program modification.

Problem: Modify Payroll Problem V in Chapter 6 to determine the federal withholding tax from one of two tables dependent upon whether the wage earner is single or married. For single wage earners use the table illustrated in Table 7.5 of Section 7.6. For married wage earners use the following table:

If the amount of wages is:		The amount of income tax to be withheld shall be:	
Not over $92		0	
Over—	But not over—		of excess over—
$92	$369	12%	$92
$369	$738	$33.24 plus 17%	$369
$738	$908	$95.97 plus 22%	$738
$908	$1,112	$133.37 plus 25%	$908
$1,112	$1,315	$184.37 plus 28%	$1,112
$1,315	$1,723	$241.21 plus 33%	$1,315
$1,723		$375.85 plus 37%	$1,723

See Programming Case Study 18 for an example of how the two tables should be implemented in your program and for determining the taxable earnings.

Input Data: Use the sample data described in Payroll Problem V in Chapter 6 and the following type of wage earner code where M means married and S means single.

Employee Number	Type of Wage Earner
123	M
124	S
125	S
126	M

Add the type of wage earner code to the corresponding DATA statements used in Payroll Problem V in chapter 6.

Output Results: The following results are displayed:

```
EMPLOYEE                                            YEAR-TO-DATE
NUMBER   GROSS PAY   FED. TAX   SOC. SEC.   NET PAY  SOC. SEC.
--------  ---------  ---------  ---------   -------  ------------
   123     1,000.00    137.14      67.00    795.86      792.15
   124       880.00    151.33       0.00    728.67    2,579.50
   125     1,040.00    199.10       6.18    834.72    2,579.50
   126        90.00      0.00       6.03     83.97      106.03

TOTAL GROSS PAY=============>   3,010.00
TOTAL WITHHOLDING TAX=======>     487.57
TOTAL SOCIAL SECURITY TAX===>      79.21
TOTAL NET PAY===============>   2,443.22

JOB COMPLETE
```

FILE PROCESSING 8

In the previous chapters, program development was emphasized. Of equal concern are the organization and processing of data in the form of files. This is especially true in a business environment, since:

1) Business applications like payroll, billing, order entry and inventory involve processing vast amounts of data.
2) Data must be continually updated for management reports to be useful.
3) The same data is often required for several applications, like payroll, personnel, pension plans, and insurance reporting.

Computer manufacturers have spent a great deal of effort developing both hardware, like auxiliary storage devices, and software, like file handling statements, to deal directly with the organization and processing of large amounts of data.

In previous exercises, the INPUT statement or the READ and DATA statements were used to enter data into the system. A more efficient and convenient method of organizing data is to store it on an auxiliary storage device, like a floppy diskette, and keep it separate from the programs that will process the data. Data stored in this fashion is a **file**, a group of related records. The number of records making up a file may range from a few to thousands or millions. Each record within the file contains related data items.

Figure 8.1 illustrates a partial list of data items that can be found within the records of a payroll file. Common data items occupy the same position in each record. Order within a record is important for both processing and updating a data file.

Creating a data file which is separate from the program but yet accessible to it means that:

1) Data can be used by different programs without being re-entered each time.
2) Records can be easily updated.

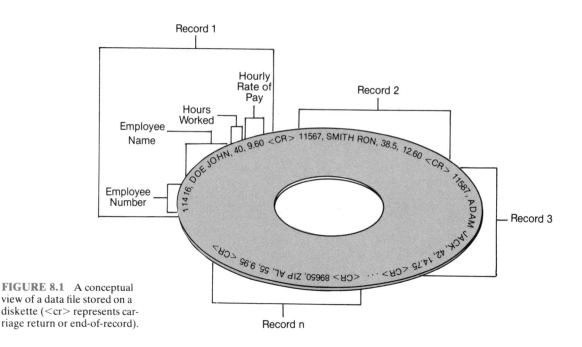

FIGURE 8.1 A conceptual view of a data file stored on a diskette (<cr> represents carriage return or end-of-record).

3) Multiple data files can be processed by a single program.
4) Programs can process a particular data file for one run and another data file the next, provided the data items in the records of the files have some common order.

Nearly all dialects of BASIC include a set of file handling statements that allow a user to:

1) Create data files
2) Define the data files to be used by a program
3) Open a data file
4) Read data from a data file
5) Write data to a data file
6) Test for the end of the data file
7) Close a data file

Unfortunately, the format of these file handling statements varies from one dialect of BASIC to another. In this book the Microsoft version of these statements is used. Microsoft BASIC, or MBASIC, is the most popular BASIC system; it is used with personal computers like the DEC Rainbow, IBM PC, Macintosh and TRS-80.

This chapter presents the general forms of the file handling statements for sequential file processing and the comparable forms for the Apple, COMMO-DORE and DEC VAX-11 systems. No attempt is made to show the variation in random file processing format, since these variations are significant. If you are using an Apple, COMMODORE or VAX-11 and need to create and process random files, check the specifications in the user's manual. Although the particular formats of these statements may vary from one BASIC system to another, the file concepts and problem-solving techniques presented here apply to all dialects of BASIC.

File organization is a method for arranging records on an auxiliary storage device. BASIC systems allow for two types of file organization:

1) Sequential
2) Random

The choice of organization is made during the early stages of development of an application. The type of file organization depends on how the records within the file are to be processed by other programs.

A file organized sequentially is called a **sequential file** and is limited to sequential processing. The records can only be processed in the order in which they are placed in the file. Conceptually, a sequential file is identical to the use of DATA statements within a BASIC program. For example, the 14th record in a sequential file cannot be processed until after the previous 13 records are processed. Similarly, the 14th data item in a DATA statement of a BASIC program cannot be processed until after the previous 13 data items are processed.

Sequential organization may also be used to write reports to auxiliary storage instead of an external device, like a video display device. Once the report is in auxiliary storage, it may be displayed at any time and as often as needed. Writing reports to auxiliary storage is a common practice, especially with programs that generate multiple reports. In such programs, each report is written to a separate file.

A file organized randomly is a **random file**. The sequence of processing a random file has no relationship to the sequence in which the records are stored in it. If the 10th record in a file is required by a program, the record can be directly accessed without processing the previous 9 records. However, the program must indicate to the system the location of the record relative to the beginning of the file. For example, to access the 10th record instead of the 3rd or 4th record, the program must explicitly indicate to the system that the 10th record is requested for processing.

A third type of file organization, known as **indexed**, is also widely used in data processing. This type of organization is not available on most BASIC systems. A file organized by an index is an **indexed file**. An indexed file is organized around a specified data item, the **key**, which is common to each record. In an airline reservation file, the key may be the flight number. In an inventory file, the key may be the part number or a part description.

Indexed files have one advantage over random files: the program need only supply the key of the record to be accessed instead of the record's relative location. Although indexed files are not available with most BASIC systems, this method of organization may be simulated by using both a sequential file and a random file. This is illustrated in Programming Case Study 26.

Indexed files and random files are primarily used for on-line activities where the applications call for random processing of the data. In airline reservation systems, inventory systems, management information systems and customer credit checks, indexed or random organization of a file has important advantages over sequential organization.

A **filename** identifies a file on auxiliary storage. Technically, anything stored in auxiliary storage is a file. This includes BASIC programs, text for text and word processing applications, and data files. A filename consists of a name, from one to eight characters, followed by a period and an **extension**.*The extension may be from one to three characters in length.   Most personal computers also use a **device name** that identifies the device upon which the file is located. The device name and filename are separated by a colon, as shown:

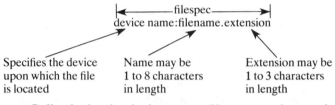

| Specifies the device upon which the file is located | Name may be 1 to 8 characters in length | Extension may be 1 to 3 characters in length |

Collectively, the device name, filename and extension are the **file specification**, or **filespec**. If an extension is used, a period precedes it.

In the selection of a name and extension, the letters of the alphabet, the digits 0 through 9 and certain special characters may be used. Check the specifications of your BASIC system in the user's manual to determine which special characters may be used. Names that are meaningful should be selected. For a payroll file, for example, the name PAYROLL better describes the contents of the file than the names A or Z or R234.

Extensions are used to classify files. The following extensions are used by most programmers:

Extension	Represents a
BAS	— BASIC program
TXT	— Text or word processing file
LIS	— File containing a report
DAT	— Data file
TBL	— File containing tables
SAV	— Backup copy of a file or program

Table 8.1 illustrates several examples of valid filenames.

TABLE 8.1   Valid Filenames

Filename	Comment
B:PARTS.DAT	
A:REPORT1.LIS	
FLIGHT.DAT	BASIC assumes the file is on disk drive A of a personal computer.
ACCOUNTS	BASIC assumes the file is on disk drive A. The period and extension are optional on some BASIC systems.

**8.4
SEQUENTIAL FILE
PROCESSING**

This section presents the file handling statements required to create and process sequential files. Also, sample programs are presented to illustrate how:

    1) Reports can be written to auxiliary storage instead of a video display device or printer.

    2) Data files which other programs can process can be created.

    3) Reports from data located in data files can be generated.

    4) Data files can be updated.

**Opening and Closing
Sequential Files**

Before any file can be read from or written to, it must be opened by the OPEN statement. When a program finishes reading from or writing to a file, it must close the file using the CLOSE statement.

---

*The maximum number of characters in a name vary from system to system.

When executed, the OPEN statement carries out the following five basic functions:

1) It requests the system allocate a **buffer**, a part of main memory, through which data is passed between the program and auxiliary storage.

2) It identifies by name the file to be processed.

3) It indicates whether the file is to be read from or written to.

4) It assigns the file a filenumber.

5) It sets the "pointer" to the beginning of the file.

The CLOSE statement terminates the association between the file and the filenumber assigned in the OPEN statement and de-allocates the part of main memory assigned to the buffer. If a file is being written to, the CLOSE statement ensures that the last record is transfered from the buffer in main memory to auxiliary storage. The general forms of the OPEN and CLOSE statements are shown in Tables 8.2 and 8.3.

TABLE 8.2   The OPEN **Statement for Sequential Files**

General Form:	OPEN mode, #filenumber, filespec
	where **mode** is a string expression equal to one of the following:
	"I" specifies sequential input mode.
	"O" specifies sequential output mode.
	filenumber is a numeric expression whose value is between 1 and 15 and is associated with the file (**filespec**) for as long as it is open. The filenumber may be used by other file handling statements to refer to the specific file.
Purpose:	Allows a program to read records from a sequential file or write records to a sequential file.
Examples:	`100 OPEN "O", #1, "PAYROLL.DAT"`
	`200 OPEN "I", #F, "B:EMPLOYEE.DAT"`
	`300 OPEN M$, #3, "ACCOUNTS"`
	`400 OPEN "I", #1, N$`
Note:	Formats used by some popular computer systems.

Computer System	OPEN *Statement*
Apple	LET D$ = CHR$(4)
	PRINT D$; "OPEN filespec"
	PRINT D$; "mode filespec"
	where mode is READ to read from a file
	WRITE to write to a file
	APPEND to add data to the end of a file
COMMODORE	DOPEN#filenumber, filespec, mode
	where mode is R to read from a file or W to write to a file.
DEC Rainbow IBM PC Macintosh TRS-80 and Microsoft BASIC in general	As indicated above in the General Form. IBM PC also allows for the format indicated for the DEC VAX-11 shown below, with an additional mode option of APPEND.
DEC VAX-11	OPEN filespec FOR mode AS FILE #filenumber where mode is INPUT to read from a file and OUTPUT to write to a file.

As illustrated in Table 8.2, a sequential file may be opened for input or output. Some systems, like the Apple, IBM PC, Macintosh and DEC VAX-11, allow a file to be opened for appending data. If a sequential file is opened for appending data, then the program can only write data to the end of the file.

If a file is opened for input, the program can only read records from the file. For example, the following statement

`500 OPEN "I", #2, "CLASS.DAT"`

opens the file CLASS. DAT so that the program can only read records. An attempt to write a record to CLASS. DAT results in a diagnostic message. The system also displays a diagnostic message if you try to open a file that does not exist.

If a file is opened for output, as shown below in line 600, then the program can only write records to the file.

```
600 OPEN "O", #1, "STUDENT.DAT"
```

Opening a file for output always creates a new file.* If, for example, STUDENT. DAT already exists, then the file is deleted before it is opened.

In all previous examples of the OPEN statement, the filespec was included as a string constant. The filespec may be defined in an OPEN statement as a string variable, provided the filespec is assigned to the string variable before the OPEN statement is executed. For example, the following partial program is valid.

```
700 INPUT "ENTER THE FILESPEC"; N$
710 OPEN "I", #2, N$
```

The OPEN statement in line 710 opens for input the file that corresponds to the string constant assigned to N$ in line 700.

The mode may also be designated as a string variable in the OPEN statement. The following partial program is valid.

```
200 INPUT "OPEN THE FILE FOR INPUT OR OUTPUT (I OR O)"; M$
210 OPEN M$, #3, "ACCOUNTS.DAT"
```

Based on the value of M$ ("I" or "O"), line 210 opens ACCOUNTS. DAT for input or output.

The filenumber may be a numeric variable or numeric expression. For example, in the following partial program the OPEN statement assigns "REPORT. LIS" to the filenumber that is equal to the integer portion of the value of F.

```
400 INPUT "FILENUMBER"; F
410 OPEN "O", #F, "REPORT.LIS"
```

TABLE 8.3 The CLOSE Statement

General Form:	CLOSE #filenumber$_1$, . . . , #filenumber$_n$
Purpose:	Terminates the association between a filenumber and file. If the file is opened for output, the CLOSE statement ensures that the last record is transferred from main memory to auxiliary storage.
	A CLOSE statement with no filenumbers closes all open files.

Examples:	`600 CLOSE #1, #2, #3`
	`700 CLOSE #1`
	`800 CLOSE #2, #1`
	`900 CLOSE`

Note:	Formats used by some popular computer systems.

Computer System	CLOSE Statement
Apple	PRINT CHR$(4); "CLOSE filespec"
COMMODORE	DCLOSE#filenumber
DEC Rainbow, IBM PC, Macintosh, TRS-80, DEC VAX-11 and Microsoft BASIC in general	As indicated in the General Form.

*Apple systems require that an existing file first be deleted before being opened for output. The proper sequence for reusing an existing file is as follows: open the file, delete the file and then open the file again. PRINT D$; "DELETE filespec" deletes the file.

The CLOSE statement terminates access to a file. For example,

```
600 CLOSE #2, #3
```

causes the files assigned to filenumbers 2 and 3 to be closed. Any other files previously opened by the program remain open.

Following the close of a specified file, the filenumber may be assigned again to the same or a different file by an OPEN statement. For example, the following partial program is valid.

```
150 OPEN "I", #1, "INVEN.DAT"
     .
     .
     .
500 CLOSE #1
510 OPEN "I", #1, "INVEN.DAT"
     .
     .
     .
700 CLOSE #1
710 END
```

Line 150 opens INVEN.DAT for input as filenumber 1. Line 500 closes INVEN.DAT. Line 510 reopens INVEN.DAT for input as filenumber 1. Opening and closing a file more than once in a program is quite common. For example, many applications involve reading and processing the records in a file to compute an average. The file is then processed a second time to evaluate each record against the average. In earlier chapters the RESTORE statement was used with data located in DATA statements to process the data set a second time. The term **rewind** is used to describe the technique of closing and then opening the file to begin processing again with the first record.

The following rules summarize the OPEN and CLOSE statements:

CLOSE **Rule 1:** A file must be opened before it can be closed.

OPEN **Rule 1:** A file must be opened before it can be read from or written to.

OPEN **Rule 2:** If a file is opened for input, it must already exist on auxiliary storage.

OPEN **Rule 3:** If a file is opened for output and it exists on auxiliary storage, it is deleted before it is opened.

OPEN **Rule 4:** A filenumber cannot be assigned to more than one file at a time.

Writing Data to a Sequential File

The PRINT #n and PRINT #n, USING statements write data or information to sequential files. The PRINT #n and PRINT #n, USING statements are similar in format to the PRINT and PRINT USING statements from Chapter 4, except that the data or information is written to a file instead of to an external device like a video display device. The general form of the PRINT #n and PRINT #n, USING statements are shown in Tables 8.4 and 8.5.

TABLE 8.4   **The** PRINT #n **Statement**

General Form:	PRINT #n, item pm item pm . . . pm item
	where n is a filenumber assigned to a file defined in an OPEN statement
	    item is one of the following:
	      1) Constant
	      2) Variable
	      3) Expression
	      4) Function reference
	      5) Null
	and where each punctuation mark pm is one of the following:
	      1) Comma
	      2) Semicolon

Purpose:	Provides for the generation of labeled and unlabeled output or of output in a consistent tabular format from the program to a sequential file in auxiliary storage.
| *Examples:* | ```
100 PRINT #1,
200 PRINT #2, A, B; C
300 PRINT #1, TAB(10); "THE ANSWER IS"; A
400 PRINT #2, X + Y/4, C * B
500 PRINT #3, A; ","; B; ","; C$; ","; D
600 PRINT #2, S;
``` |
| *Note:* | With the Apple computer, the number sign and filenumber are not used. Once a file is opened in the WRITE mode, PRINT statements write data to the file instead of to the display device. |

TABLE 8.5   **The** PRINT #n, USING **Statement**

General Form:	PRINT #n, USING string expression; item, item, . . . , item
	where n is a filenumber assigned to a file defined in an OPEN statement
	    string expression is either a string constant or a string variable which is the exact image of the record to be written to the file in auxiliary storage
	    item is one of the following:
	      1) Constant
	      2) Variable
	      3) Expression
	      4) Function reference

Purpose:	Provides for controlling exactly the format of the record written to a sequential file in auxiliary storage.
| *Examples:* | ```
150 PRINT #1, USING "THE AVERAGE IS #,###.##"; A
190 PRINT #2, USING "## IS THE SUM OF # AND #"; S, S1, S2

200 LET A$ = "\        \     ##      ##.##"
210 PRINT #3, USING A$; S$, D, B
``` |
| *Note:* | The PRINT #n, USING statement is not available on the Apple and COM-MODORE. With the DEC VAX-11, a comma instead of a semicolon follows the string expression. |

By now you should know that the statement

```
500 PRINT A, B, C
```

displays the values of A, B and C on a video display device beginning in print zones 1, 2 and 3. Similarly, the statement

```
500 PRINT #1, A, B, C
```

creates and transmits a record image to the sequential file, assigned to filenumber 1, with the values of A, B and C beginning in zones 1, 2 and 3 of the record.

    The following partial program illustrates how an image may be displayed on a video display device and transmitted to a file called REPORT.LIS.

Displays the
values of P, M1
and M2

Writes a record
with the values of
P, M1, and M2
to the file
REPORT.LIS

```
150 OPEN "O", #3, "REPORT.LIS"
     .
     .
     .
400 PRINT USING "## IS THE PRODUCT OF # AND #"; P, M1, M2
410 PRINT #3, USING "## IS THE PRODUCT OF # AND #"; P, M1, M2
```

Line 400 displays the results on a video display device. Line 410 writes a record that
is identical to the line displayed by line 400 to the file REPORT.LIS.

The PRINT #n statement may be used to write data to a file in the format
required by the INPUT #n statement. The format requirement is similar to that of
the READ and DATA statements—all data items must be separated by commas.*

The following PRINT #n statement writes records containing data items that
are in a format required by the INPUT #n statement.

```
500 PRINT #2, A; ","; B; ","; C; ","; D$
```

The technique used in line 500 places a comma between the values of A and B, B
and C, and C and D$. The semicolon separator following A, B, C and each of the
commas, which are string constants, results in the compression of the data items so
that the record has the same appearance in the data file as a DATA statement
without a line number and the keyword DATA. If the list within a PRINT #n or
PRINT #n, USING statement does not end with a comma or semicolon, then a
carriage return is appended to the last data item written to form a record. For
example, if A = 1.5, B = −3, C = 9.8 and D$ = "SHERMAN TANKS," then
line 500 transmits the following record image to the file assigned to filenumber 2 (ƀ
represents a space):

ƀ1.5ƀ,−3ƀ,ƀ9.8ƀ,SHERMANƀTANKS<cr>

Record transmitted to filenumber 2 by line 500.

Some versions of Microsoft BASIC have the WRITE #n statement available to
write records to a file in the format required by the INPUT #n statement. The
WRITE #n statement automatically writes data in the following format:

1) Data items are separated by commas.
2) String data items are surrounded by quotation marks.
3) All leading and trailing spaces are omitted.

For example, the following statement

```
500 WRITE #2, A, B, C, D$
```

transmits the record shown above, omitting the first five spaces (ƀ) and including
quotation marks to surround the value assigned to D$.

Check the specifications on your BASIC system in the user's manual to
determine if the WRITE #n statement may be used to write records to a file in the
format required by the INPUT #n statement. It is recommended that the WRITE
#n statement be used, if it is available, to build files that will be processed at a later
date using the INPUT statement. Since the PRINT #n statement works on nearly
all BASIC systems, the PRINT #n statement will be used in this chapter.

---

*With the Apple, the carriage return character is placed between each data item by writing at
most one data item per PRINT statement.

The following rule summarizes the use of the PRINT #n and PRINT #n, USING statements:

> OUTPUT **Rule 2:** Before the PRINT #n or PRINT #n, USING statement is executed in a program, the filenumber n must be assigned to a file that has been opened for output.

Programming Case Study 8B: Writing the Weekly Payroll and Summary Report to Auxiliary Storage

In Chapter 5 the Weekly Payroll and Summary Report (Programming Case Study 8A) was introduced. In the solution of Program 5.6, the PRINT and PRINT USING statements displayed the report on an external device like a video display device.

Program 8.1 is identical to Program 5.6 except for the inclusion of:

1) Additional comments (lines 115 and 155)
2) An OPEN statement (line 165) and a CLOSE statement (line 395)
3) The filenumber 1 in each PRINT and PRINT USING statement
4) An additional PRINT statement (line 397)

```
100 REM PROGRAM 8.1
110 REM WRITING THE WEEKLY PAYROLL AND SUMMARY REPORT
115 REM TO AUXILIARY STORAGE
120 REM C  = EMPLOYEE COUNT    T = TOTAL GROSS PAY
130 REM E$ = EMPLOYEE NUMBER   H = HOURS WORKED
140 REM R  = RATE OF PAY       B = HOURS GREATER THAN 40
150 REM G  = GROSS PAY         A = AVERAGE GROSS PAY
155 REM REPORT FILE NAME = REPORT.LIS
160 REM ***************************************************
165 OPEN "O", #1, "REPORT.LIS"
170 PRINT #1, TAB(12); "WEEKLY PAYROLL REPORT"
180 PRINT #1,
190 PRINT #1, "EMPLOYEE NO.    HOURS      RATE     GROSS PAY"
200 PRINT #1, "------------    -----      ----     ---------"
210 LET A$ = "    \         \        ###.#     ##.##    ##,###.##"
220 LET C = 0
230 LET T = 0
240 READ E$, H, R
250 REM ****************PROCESS A RECORD****************
260 WHILE E$ <> "EOF"
270    LET C = C + 1
280    LET B = H - 40
290    IF B <= 0 THEN LET G = H*R ELSE LET G = H*R +0.5*B*R
300    LET T = T + G
310    PRINT #1, USING A$; E$, H, R, G
320    READ E$, H, R
330 WEND
340 REM ****************EOF ROUTINE*******************
350 LET A = T/C
360 PRINT #1,
370 PRINT #1, USING "THE TOTAL GROSS PAY IS $$#,###.##"; T
380 PRINT #1, USING "THE TOTAL NUMBER OF EMPLOYEES IS ###"; C
390 PRINT #1, USING "THE AVERAGE GROSS PAY IS $$#,###.##"; A
395 CLOSE #1
397 PRINT "REPORT COMPLETE AND STORED UNDER FILENAME REPORT.LIS"
400 REM ****************DATA FOLLOWS*******************
410 DATA 124, 40, 5.60
420 DATA 126, 56, 5.90
430 DATA 128, 38, 4.60
440 DATA 129, 48.5, 6.10
450 DATA EOF, 0, 0
460 END

RUN

REPORT COMPLETE AND STORED UNDER FILENAME REPORT.LIS
```

PROGRAM 8.1

Program 8.1 writes the report, illustrated in Figure 8.2, to auxiliary storage under the filename REPORT.LIS.

```
              WEEKLY PAYROLL REPORT

EMPLOYEE NO.    HOURS      RATE     GROSS PAY
------------    -----      ----     ---------
    124         40.0       5.60       224.00
    126         56.0       5.90       377.60
    128         38.0       4.60       174.80
    129         48.5       6.10       321.77

THE TOTAL GROSS PAY IS  $1,098.17
THE TOTAL NUMBER OF EMPLOYEES IS    4
THE AVERAGE GROSS PAY IS    $274.54
```

FIGURE 8.2   Results of Program 8.1 written to auxiliary storage under the filename REPORT.LIS.

When the RUN command is issued for Program 8.1, line 165 opens the sequential file REPORT.LIS for output as filenumber 1. Lines 170 through 200 write the report title and column headings to REPORT.LIS. Line 310 writes a detail record to REPORT.LIS for each employee record read. When the trailer record is read, control transfers to line 350 and the total lines are written to REPORT.LIS. Line 395 closes REPORT.LIS and line 397 displays the message

REPORT COMPLETE AND STORED UNDER FILENAME REPORT.LIS.

Following the execution of Program 8.1, the report may be displayed on a video display device or printed on a line printer as often as needed. To view the report on a video display device, use the system command that lists a file, TYPE REPORT.LIS. To print the report on a line printer, use the system command that prints a file, PRINT REPORT.LIS.

The I/O symbol is used to represent the OPEN and CLOSE statements. Therefore, the flowchart symbol

should be placed immediately after the symbol

in Figure 5.7.

Also, the following series of flowchart symbols

should be placed just before the symbol

Figure 5.7, modified as indicated, should then agree with Program 8.1.

The following problem requests the creation of a sequential file.

Programming Case Study 19: Creating a Sequential File

Problem

Company PUC has requested that a sequential file be created from the inventory data listed below. Commas must be included between the data items in each record so that they may be read and processed by other programs using the INPUT #n statement.

In the following inventory data, each line represents an inventory record.

Stock Number	Warehouse Location	Description	Unit Cost	Selling Price	Quantity on Hand
C101	1	Roadhandler	97.56	125.11	25
C204	3	Whitewalls	37.14	99.95	140
C502	2	Tripod	32.50	38.99	10
S209	1	Maxidrill	88.76	109.99	6
S416	2	Normalsaw	152.55	179.40	1
S812	2	Router	48.47	61.15	8
S942	4	Radialsaw	376.04	419.89	3
T615	4	Oxford-Style	26.43	31.50	28
T713	2	Moc-Boot	24.99	29.99	30
T814	2	Work-Boot	22.99	27.99	56

INPUT statements are to be used to request the operator to enter the 6 data items found in each record. A sentinel value of EOF for the stock number S$ indicates all records have been entered.

The end-of-job routine includes the following:

1) Write a trailer record with a stock number of EOF so it may be used by other programs to determine end-of-file.*
2) Close the file.
3) Display a message indicating that file creation is complete.
4) Display the number of records written to the file (do not count the trailer record in the final total).

When Program 8.2 is executed, line 150 opens INVNTORY. DAT for output as filenumber 1. Line 160 and lines 180 through 220 request the operator to enter the data items for the first record. Line 230 writes the record to INVNTORY. DAT in a format that is consistent with the INPUT #n statement. Line 260 requests the stock number of the next record. If S$ is assigned a value of EOF, then line 170 transfers control to the end-of-job routine (lines 280 through 330). If S$ is not assigned the value EOF in line 260, then the While loop continues execution and the remaining data for the next record is requested and written to the file.

As part of the end-of-job routine, line 280 writes the trailer record to INVNTORY. DAT. When line 280 is executed, S$ is set equal to EOF. The variable S$ is also used to assign a description value of EOF to the trailer record.

Figure 8.3 shows the contents of INVNTORY. DAT after Program 8.2 have been executed.

Data validation was purposely left out of the case study to present a clear-cut example of how to create a sequential file. In a production environment, reasonableness checks are always considered for the stock number S$, warehouse location L, unit cost C, selling price P and quantity on hand Q. Data should always be validated before it is placed in a file.

```
C101, 1 ,ROADHANDLER, 97.56 , 125.11 , 25
C204, 3 ,WHITEWALLS, 37.14 , 99.95 , 140
C502, 2 ,TRIPOD, 32.5 , 38.99 , 10
S209, 1 ,MAXIDRILL, 88.76 , 109.99 , 6
S416, 2 ,NORMALSAW, 152.55 , 179.4 , 1
S812, 2 ,ROUTER, 48.47 , 61.15 , 8
S942, 4 ,RADIALSAW, 376.04 , 419.89 , 3
T615, 4 ,OXFORD-STYLE, 26.43 , 31.5 , 28
T713, 2 ,MOC-BOOT, 24.99 , 29.99 , 30
T814, 2 ,WORK-BOOT, 22.99 , 27.99 , 56
EOF, 0 ,EOF, 0, 0, 0
```

FIGURE 8.3 A listing of INVENTORY. DAT created by Program 8.2.

*Later in this section we will discuss the end-of-file mark that is automatically placed at the end of a sequential file and alternative means to test for the end-of-file mark.

```
100 REM PROGRAM 8.2
110 REM CREATING A SEQUENTIAL FILE
120 REM FILE CREATED BY THIS PROGRAM - INVNTORY.DAT
130 REM ********************************************
140 LET R = 0
150 OPEN "O", #1, "INVNTORY.DAT"
160 INPUT "STOCK NUMBER"; S$
170 WHILE S$ <> "EOF"
180     INPUT "WAREHOUSE LOCATION"; L
190     INPUT "DESCRIPTION"; D$
200     INPUT "UNIT COST"; C
210     INPUT "SELLING PRICE"; P
220     INPUT "QUANTITY ON HAND"; Q
230     PRINT #1, S$; ","; L; ","; D$; ","; C; ","; P; ","; Q
240     LET R = R + 1
250     PRINT
260     INPUT "STOCK NUMBER"; S$
270 WEND
280 PRINT #1, S$; ","; 0; ","; S$; ","; 0; ","; 0; ","; 0
290 CLOSE #1
300 PRINT
310 PRINT "CREATION OF SEQUENTIAL FILE INVNTORY.DAT IS COMPLETE."
320 PRINT
330 PRINT "TOTAL NUMBER OF RECORDS IN INVNTORY.DAT IS"; R; "."
340 END
```

PROGRAM 8.2

```
RUN
```

Record 1
```
STOCK NUMBER? C101
WAREHOUSE LOCATION? 1
DESCRIPTION? ROADHANDLER
UNIT COST? 97.56
SELLING PRICE? 125.11
QUANTITY ON HAND? 25
```

.
.
.

Record 10
```
STOCK NUMBER? T814
WAREHOUSE LOCATION? 2
DESCRIPTION? WORK-BOOT
UNIT COST? 22.99
SELLING PRICE? 27.99
QUANTITY ON HAND? 56
```

```
STOCK NUMBER? EOF

CREATION OF SEQUENTIAL FILE INVNTORY.DAT IS COMPLETE.

TOTAL NUMBER OF RECORDS IN INVNTORY.DAT IS 10 .
```

The INPUT #n statement is used to read data from a sequential file and is similar to the READ statement, except that it reads data from a file instead of from DATA statements. Line 250 in the following partial program

The INPUT #n Statement

```
240 OPEN "I", #3, "INVNTORY.DAT"
250 INPUT #3, S$, L, D$, C, P, Q
```

reads six data items from the file INVNTORY. DAT.

For data to be read from a file, the following must be true:

1) The file must already exist.
2) The file must be opened for input.
3) The data items in the file must be separated by a comma or carriage return character.

The general form of the INPUT #n statement is shown in Table 8.6.

The INPUT #n statement causes the variables in its list to be assigned specific values, in order, from the data sequence found in the file assigned to filenumber n. In order to visualize the relationship between the INPUT #n statement and the associated file, you may think of a pointer associated with the data items. When the OPEN statement is executed, this pointer references the first data item in the data

TABLE 8.6   The INPUT #n **Statement**

General Form:	INPUT #n, list of variables
	where n is a filenumber assigned to an existing file that is opened for input.
Purpose:	Reads data items from a sequential file in auxiliary storage and assigns them to variables.

Examples:	`300 INPUT #1, S, F, D$, P`
	`400 INPUT #3, A$`
	`500 INPUT #2, A(I), G, B(4), C(1, 4, T)`

Note:	With the Apple computer, the number sign and filenumber are not used. Once a file is opened in the READ mode, INPUT statements accept data from the file instead of the keyboard.

sequence. Each time an INPUT #n statement is executed, the variables in the "list" are assigned values from the data sequence beginning with the data item indicated by the pointer, and the pointer is advanced, one value per variable. Hence, the pointer points to the next data item to be assigned when the INPUT #n statement is executed.

The system will display a diagnostic message if the data type of the data item to be assigned does not agree with the variable in the INPUT #n statement. It is invalid to assign a string value to a numeric variable.

In determining the actual value of a data item, the system scans in the following manner:

1) For a numeric value—leading spaces and carriage returns ($< cr >$) are ignored. The first character that is not a space or carriage return is assumed to be the start of the numeric data item. A comma, carriage return, or space terminates the numeric value.

2) For string values—leading spaces and carriage returns are ignored. The first character that is not a space or carriage return is assumed to be the start of the string data item. Spaces within a string are valid characters. If the first character is a quotation mark, the string data item will consist of all characters between the first quotation mark and the second. If the first character is a quotation mark, the string may not include a quotation mark. If the string is unquoted, the value terminates with a comma or carriage return.

Recall that any PRINT #n or PRINT #n, USING statement that does not end with a separator writes a carriage return at the end of the record.

Table 8.7 illustrates the assignment of data items to variables in different INPUT #n statements.

TABLE 8.7   Assignment of Data Items to Variables in INPUT #n **Statements**

Statement	*Partial List of Data Items in the File Assigned to Filenumber 3*	*Values Assigned to Variables*
`100 INPUT #3, A, B, C$`	14, −2.3, XY Z$<cr>$	A = 14 B = −2.3 C$ = XY Z
`200 INPUT #3, X$` `300 INPUT #3, A`	ORDER PENDING, 15 $<cr>$	X$ = ORDER PENDING A = 15
`400 INPUT #3, A$, C, D`	CREDIT $<cr>$ 1.22, −38.50 $<cr>$	A$ = CREDIT C = 1.22 D = −38.50

The following rules summarize the material discussed in this section:

> INPUT **Rule 4:** Before the INPUT #n statement is executed, the filenumber n must be assigned to a sequential file that is opened for input.

> INPUT **Rule 5:** The INPUT #n statement requires the data items be separated by commas within a sequential file.

The following problem requires data to be read and processed from the sequential file created by Program 8.2.

Programming Case Study 20: Processing a Sequential File

Problem

INVNTORY.DAT was created by Program 8.2; the contents of the data file are shown in Figure 8.3.

For each record in INVNTORY.DAT, the following is to be displayed:

1) Stock number
2) Description
3) Unit cost
4) Selling price
5) Quantity on hand
6) Total item cost of a stock item (unit cost times quantity on hand)
7) Total selling price of a stock item (unit cost times selling price)

The total inventory cost and total inventory selling price are also displayed.

An analysis of the problem, flowchart and program solution follow.

Program Tasks

1) Initialize total inventory cost S1 and total inventory selling price S2 to zero.

2) Open the sequential file INVNTORY.DAT for input as filenumber 1.

3) Display report and column headings.

4) Read an inventory record. For purposes of consistency, use the same variable names in the list of the INPUT #1 statement as used in the PRINT #1 statement of Program 8.2. That is,

       S$ = Stock number
       L = Warehouse location
       D$ = Description
       C = Unit cost
       P = Selling price
       Q = Quantity on hand

5) Use a While loop to process the records in the file until the trailer record is read. In the While loop, do the following:

   a) Compute T1, the total item cost of a stock item, and T2, the total selling price of a stock item.

   b) Increment the running totals: total inventory cost S1 by T1 and total inventory selling price S2 by T2.

   c) Display the detail record as specified in the problem definition.

   d) Read the next inventory record.

6) Display the running totals S1 and S2, close the file INVNTORY.DAT and display an end-of-job message when the trailer record is read.

```
100 REM PROGRAM 8.3
110 REM PROCESSING A SEQUENTIAL FILE
120 REM S$ = STOCK NUMBER          L  = WAREHOUSE NUMBER
130 REM D$ = DESCRIPTION           C  = UNIT COST
140 REM P  = SELLING PRICE         Q  = QUANTITY ON HAND
150 REM T1 = TOTAL ITEM COST       T2 = TOTAL SELLING PRICE
160 REM S1 = TOTAL INVENTORY COST  S2 = TOTAL INVENTORY SELLING PRICE
170 REM FILE PROCESSED BY THIS PROGRAM - INVNTORY.DAT
180 REM ***********************************************************
190 LET S1 = 0
200 LET S2 = 0
210 OPEN "I", #1, "INVNTORY.DAT"
220 PRINT TAB(21); "INVENTORY ANALYSIS"
230 PRINT TAB(21); "------------------"
240 PRINT
250 PRINT TAB(57); "TOTAL"
260 PRINT    "STOCK                     UNIT SELLING QUANTITY TOTAL          SELLING"
270 PRINT    "NO.    DESCRIPTION         COST PRICE   ON HAND  ITEM COST      PRICE"
280 PRINT    "-----  -----------         ---- ------- -------- ----------     -------"
290 LET A$ = "\   \ \              \ ###.## ####.##      #### ##,###.## ##,###.##"
300 LET B$ = "TOTALS                                        ###,###.## ###,###.##"
310 REM *****PROCESS FILE INVNTORY.DAT*****
320 INPUT #1, S$, L, D$, C, P, Q
330 WHILE S$ <> "EOF"
340    LET T1 = C*Q
350    LET T2 = P*Q
360    LET S1 = S1 + T1
370    LET S2 = S2 + T2
380    PRINT USING A$; S$, D$, C, P, Q, T1, T2
390    INPUT #1, S$, L, D$, C, P, Q
400 WEND
410 REM ********************END OF FILE ROUTINE********************
420 PRINT
430 PRINT USING B$; S1, S2
440 CLOSE #1
470 PRINT "JOB COMPLETE"
480 END
```

PROGRAM 8.3

```
RUN

                    INVENTORY ANALYSIS
                    ------------------

                                                        TOTAL
STOCK                     UNIT SELLING QUANTITY TOTAL   SELLING
NO.    DESCRIPTION        COST PRICE   ON HAND  ITEM COST PRICE
-----  -----------        ---- ------- -------- --------- -------
C101   ROADHANDLER        97.56 125.11      25   2,439.00  3,127.75
C204   WHITEWALLS         37.14  99.95     140   5,199.60 13,993.00
C502   TRIPOD             32.50  38.99      10     325.00    389.90
S209   MAXIDRILL          88.76 109.99       6     532.56    659.94
S416   NORMALSAW         152.55 179.40       1     152.55    179.40
S812   ROUTER             48.47  61.15       8     387.76    489.20
S942   RADIALSAW         376.04 419.89       3   1,128.12  1,259.67
T615   OXFORD-STYLE       26.43  31.50      28     740.04    882.00
T713   MOC-BOOT           24.99  29.99      30     749.70    899.70
T814   WORK-BOOT          22.99  27.99      56   1,287.44  1,567.44

TOTALS                                         12,941.77 23,448.00
JOB COMPLETE
```

The following points should be noted concerning the program flowchart and the program solution represented by Program 8.3:

1) In line 210, the OPEN statement opens INVNTORY.DAT for input as filenumber 1. The remaining file handling statements, lines 320, 390 and 440, reference INVNTORY.DAT by specifying the filenumber 1.

2) The While loop, lines 330 through 400, continues to process records until the trailer record in INVNTORY.DAT is read and S$ is assigned the value EOF.

3) Even though the warehouse location is not manipulated or displayed by Program 8.3, it is necessary to include a variable L representing the warehouse location in the list of the INPUT #n statement, since the data item is part of the record. You cannot be selective and input from a sequential data file only those data items you plan to manipulate or display. All data items within the record must be assigned to variables in the INPUT #n statement as shown in lines 320 and 390.

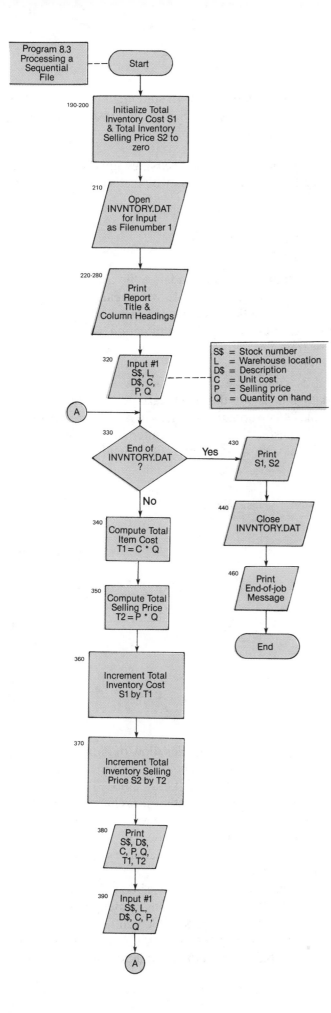

	Program 8.3 Processing a Sequential File

Start

190-200 — Initialize Total Inventory Cost S1 & Total Inventory Selling Price S2 to zero

210 — Open INVNTORY.DAT for Input as Filenumber 1

220-280 — Print Report Title & Column Headings

320 — Input #1 S\$, L, D\$, C, P, Q

S\$ = Stock number
L = Warehouse location
D\$ = Description
C = Unit cost
P = Selling price
Q = Quantity on hand

A

330 — End of INVNTORY.DAT ?

Yes

430 — Print S1, S2

440 — Close INVNTORY.DAT

460 — Print End-of-job Message

End

No

340 — Compute Total Item Cost T1 = C * Q

350 — Compute Total Selling Price T2 = P * Q

360 — Increment Total Inventory Cost S1 by T1

370 — Increment Total Inventory Selling Price S2 by T2

380 — Print S\$, D\$, C, P, Q, T1, T2

390 — Input #1 S\$, L, D\$, C, P, Q

A

FIGURE 8.4 Flowchart for Program 8.3.

317

4) The same variable names used in the INPUT #n statement of Program 8.3 were used in the PRINT #n statement of Program 8.2. Such consistency among programs referencing the same file is good programming practice.

Programming Case Study 21: File Maintenance I– Adding Records by Merging Files

File maintenance is one of the most important activities involved in data processing. Recall from Chapter 1.3 that file maintenance means updating files in one or more of the following ways:

1) *Adding* new records
2) *Deleting* unwanted records
3) *Changing* data within records

The programming techniques that are used to update a file are usually based on the type of file organization under which the file was created. To update sequential files, the record additions, deletions and changes are normally entered into another data file called a **transaction file**. A transaction file, therefore, contains data of a temporary or transient nature. Once the updates are complete, the transaction file can be deleted.

The file that is updated is called the **master file**. A master file (like INVNTORY.DAT) contains data that is for the most part permanent. Current master file refers to the master file before updating and new master file refers to the updated version of the current master file. A file maintenance program that updates a sequential file must deal with at least three files, as illustrated in the **system flowchart** in Figure 8.5.

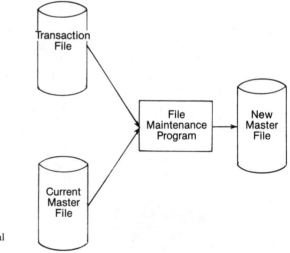

FIGURE 8.5 A system flowchart representing file maintenance of a sequential file.

A system flowchart shows, in graphic form, the files, flow of data, equipment and programs involved in a particular application. The oval symbols in Figure 8.5 symbolize auxiliary storage devices, like floppy diskette units. The rectangle represents a computer system. The arrows in the system flowchart indicate that data is read from two files and the results of the program are written to another file.

To employ the file maintenance technique described in Figure 8.5, it is necessary that both the master and transaction files be in the same sequence. In this case, the two files are in sequence by stock number.

To simplify the presentation of file maintenance, it has been divided into two problems and program solutions. In the first discussion, a method of adding records to the current master file to form a new master file will be illustrated. In Programming Case Study 22, record deletion and changing data within records will be illustrated. Programming Exercise 8.5 requires the completion of all of the file maintenance in one program.

Problem

New stock items are to be added to the inventory master file INVNTORY.DAT created by Program 8.2. The new stock items are shown below and are in file TRNINV.DAT. The program should **merge** the records of the two files to create the new inventory master file. Merging is the process of combining two or more files that are *in the same sequence* into a single file that maintains that same sequence for a given data item found in each record. The two files are each in ascending sequence according to the stock number.

Stock Number	Warehouse Location	Description	Unit Cost	Selling Price	Quantity On Hand
C103	2	Saw-Blades	5.06	6.04	15
C206	1	Square	4.56	5.42	34
S210	3	Microscope	31.50	41.99	8
S941	2	Hip-Boot	26.95	32.50	12
T615	4	Oxford-Style	26.43	31.50	28
T731	1	Sandals	6.75	9.45	52

Assume that this transaction file was created by modifying line 140 in Program 8.2 to

```
140 OPEN "O", #1, "TRNINV.DAT"
```

and executing the modified version of Program 8.2. Also assume that the name of the current master file INVNTORY.DAT has been changed to CURINV.DAT using the command to change filenames. For example,

```
NAME "INVNTORY.DAT" AS "CURINV.DAT"
```

By changing the name of the current master file, a new master file may then be created with the name INVNTORY.DAT.

It is an error for a record in the transaction file to have the same stock number as one in the current master file. If this happens, an appropriate diagnostic message, including the stock number and description, should be displayed. Also, a count of the number of records in the new master file should be displayed before the program is terminated.

An analysis of the problem, including a top-down chart, and program solution follow.

Program Tasks

1) Use the top-down chart illustrated in Figure 8.6.
2) In the Initialization module:
    a) Initialize a counter K to zero. Increment this counter each time a record is written to the new master file.
    b) Open CURINV.DAT and TRNINV.DAT both for input as filenumbers 1 and 2, respectively. Open INVNTORY.DAT for output as filenumber 3.
    c) Read the first record in the current master file and the first record in the transaction file. Use the following variable names:

OLDINV.DAT		TRNINV.DAT	
S$ = Stock number		S1$ = Stock number	
L = Warehouse location		L1 = Warehouse location	
D$ = Description		D1$ = Description	
C = Unit cost		C1 = Unit cost	
P = Selling price		P1 = Selling price	
Q = Quantity on hand		Q1 = Quantity on hand	

3) In the Process Files module:
    a) Compare the stock number S$ from the current master record to the stock number S1$ from the transaction record:

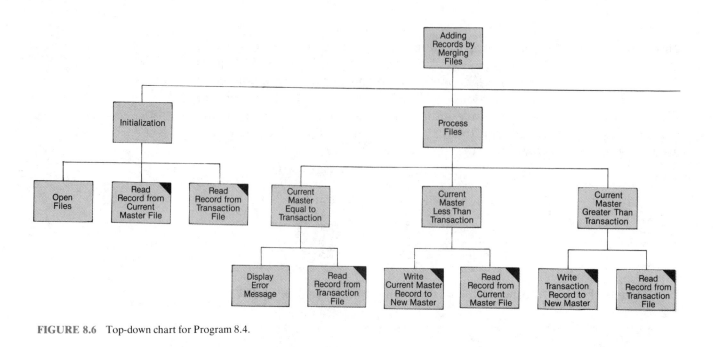

FIGURE 8.6   Top-down chart for Program 8.4.

```
1000 REM PROGRAM 8.4
1010 REM FILE MAINTENANCE I - FILE MERGING
1020 REM CURRENT MASTER FILE - CURINV.DAT      TRANSACTION FILE - TRNINV.DAT
1030 REM ----------------------------------    --------------------------------
1040 REM S$ = STOCK NUMBER                     S1$ = STOCK NUMBER
1050 REM L  = WAREHOUSE LOCATION               L1  = WAREHOUSE LOCATION
1060 REM D$ = DESCRIPTION                      D1$ = DESCRIPTION
1070 REM C  = UNIT COST                        C1  = UNIT COST
1080 REM P  = SELLING PRICE                    P1  = SELLING PRICE
1090 REM Q  = QUANTITY ON HAND                 Q1  = QUANTITY ON HAND
1100 REM NEW MASTER FILE - INVNTORY.DAT
1110 REM K  = COUNT OF RECORDS WRITTEN TO THE NEW MASTER FILE
1120 REM ***********************************************************
1130 REM *                     MAIN MODULE                        *
1140 REM ***********************************************************
1150 GOSUB 2030            'CALL INITIALIZATION
1160 GOSUB 3030            'CALL PROCESS FILES
1170 GOSUB 4030            'CALL WRAP UP
1180 STOP
2000 REM ***********************************************************
2010 REM *              INITIALIZATION MODULE                     *
2020 REM ***********************************************************
2030 LET K = 0
2040 OPEN 'I', #1, 'CURINV.DAT'
2050 OPEN 'I', #2, 'TRNINV.DAT'
2060 OPEN 'O', #3, 'INVNTORY.DAT'
2070 GOSUB 5030            'CALL READ RECORD FROM CURRENT MASTER FILE
2080 GOSUB 6030            'CALL READ RECORD FROM TRANSACTION FILE
2090 RETURN
3000 REM ***********************************************************
3010 REM *               PROCESS FILES MODULE                     *
3020 REM ***********************************************************
3030 WHILE S$ <> 'EOF' AND S1$ <> 'EOF'
3040    IF S$ <> S1$ THEN 3070
3050        GOSUB 3230    'CALL ERROR MODULE
3060        GOTO 3080
3070    IF S$ < S1$ THEN GOSUB 3430 ELSE GOSUB 3630
3080 WEND
3090 RETURN
3200 REM ***********************************************************
3210 REM *                  ERROR MODULE                          *
3220 REM ***********************************************************
3230 PRINT '********** TRANSACTION RECORD ALREADY IN CURRENT MASTER FILE'
3240 PRINT '*  ERROR  * STOCK NUMBER = ', S1$
3250 PRINT '********** DESCRIPTION   = ', D1$
3260 GOSUB 6030            'CALL READ RECORD FROM TRANSACTION FILE
3270 RETURN
3400 REM ***********************************************************
3410 REM *          WRITE RECORD FROM CURRENT MASTER MODULE       *
3420 REM ***********************************************************
```

PROGRAM 8.4

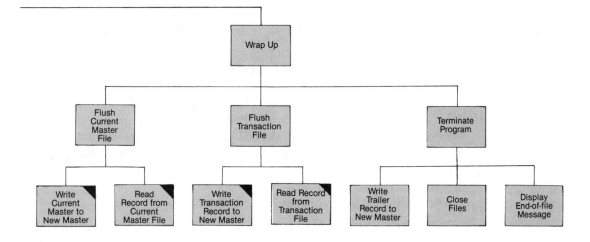

```
3430 PRINT #3, S$; ","; L; ","; D$; ","; C; ","; P; ","; Q
3440 LET K = K + 1
3450 GOSUB 5030          'CALL READ RECORD FROM CURRENT MASTER FILE
3460 RETURN
3600 REM ************************************************************
3610 REM *         WRITE RECORD FROM TRANSACTION FILE MODULE        *
3620 REM ************************************************************
3630 PRINT #3, S1$; ","; L1; ","; D1$; ","; C1; ","; P1; ","; Q1
3640 LET K = K + 1
3650 GOSUB 6030          'CALL READ RECORD FROM TRANSACTION FILE
3660 RETURN
4000 REM ************************************************************
4010 REM *                    WRAP UP MODULE                        *
4020 REM ************************************************************
4030 WHILE S$ <> "EOF"
4040     PRINT #3, S$; ","; L; ","; D$; ","; C; ","; P; ","; Q
4050     LET K = K + 1
4060     GOSUB 5030      'CALL READ RECORD FROM CURRENT MASTER FILE
4070 WEND
4080 WHILE S1$ <> "EOF"
4090     PRINT #3, S1$; ","; L1; ","; D1$; ","; C1; ","; P1; ","; Q1
4100     LET K = K + 1
4110     GOSUB 6030      'CALL READ RECORD FROM TRANSACTION FILE
4120 WEND
4130 PRINT #3, S$; ","; 0; ","; S$; ","; 0; ","; 0; ","; 0
4140 CLOSE #1, #2, #3
4150 PRINT
4160 PRINT "THE NUMBER OF RECORDS IN THE ";
4170 PRINT "NEW MASTER FILE INVNTORY.DAT ="; K
4180 PRINT "INVNTORY.DAT UPDATE COMPLETE"
4190 RETURN
5000 REM ************************************************************
5010 REM *            READ CURRENT MASTER FILE MODULE               *
5020 REM ************************************************************
5030 INPUT #1, S$, L, D$, C, P, Q
5040 RETURN
6000 REM ************************************************************
6010 REM *            READ TRANSACTION FILE MODULE                  *
6020 REM ************************************************************
6030 INPUT #2, S1$, L1, D1$, C1, P1, Q1
6040 RETURN
6050 END

RUN

*********** TRANSACTION RECORD ALREADY IN CURRENT MASTER FILE
*  ERROR  * STOCK NUMBER = T615
*********** DESCRIPTION  = OXFORD-STYLE

THE NUMBER OF RECORDS IN THE NEW MASTER FILE INVNTORY.DAT = 15
INVNTORY.DAT UPDATE COMPLETE
```

PROGRAM 8.4
(continued)

i) If the stock number S$ is equal to the stock number S1$, then display a diagnostic message and read the next transaction record.

ii) If the stock number S$ is less than the stock number S1$, then write the current master record to the new master file, increment counter K by 1 and read the next current master record.

iii) If the stock number S$ is greater than the stock number S1$, then write the transaction record to the new master file, increment counter K by 1 and read the next transaction record.

b) The Process Files module retains control until there are no more records in either the current master file or transaction file.

4) In the Wrap Up module, do the following:

a) One of the two input files may still contain records that need to be written to the new master file. This is often referred to as **flushing** the files.

b) Close all files.

c) Display the value of counter K and the message

INVNTORY.DAT UPDATE COMPLETE.

Because of the complexity involved in merging two files into one, it is recommended that particular attention be paid to the top-down chart in Figure 8.6. Stepping through both the program tasks stated above and the top-down chart will give a better understanding of the algorithm used to merge the two files.

Figures 8.7 and 8.8 show the contents of the current master file, CURINV.DAT, and the transaction file, TRNINV.DAT. When the RUN command is issued for Program 8.4, line 1150 in the Main module calls the Initialization module beginning at line 2030. Lines 2040 and 2050 open the two input files. Line 2060 opens the new master file INVNTORY.DAT. Lines 2070 and 2080 call upon the modules to read the first records in each input file.

```
C101, 1 ,ROADHANDLER, 97.56 , 125.11 , 25
C204, 3 ,WHITEWALLS, 37.14 , 99.95 , 140
C502, 2 ,TRIPOD, 32.5 , 38.99 , 10
S209, 1 ,MAXIDRILL, 88.76 , 109.99 , 6
S416, 2 ,NORMALSAW, 152.55 , 179.4 , 1
S812, 2 ,ROUTER, 48.47 , 61.15 , 8
S942, 4 ,RADIALSAW, 376.04 , 419.89 , 3
T615, 4 ,OXFORD-STYLE, 26.43 , 31.5 , 28
T713, 2 ,MOC-BOOT, 24.99 , 29.99 , 30
T814, 2 ,WORK-BOOT, 22.99 , 27.99 , 56
EOF, 0 ,EOF, 0 , 0 , 0
```

FIGURE 8.7   A list of the records in the current master file CURINV.DAT.

```
C103, 2 ,SAW-BLADES, 5.06 , 6.04 , 15
C206, 1 ,SQUARE, 4.56 , 5.42 , 34
S210, 3 ,MICROSCOPE, 31.5 , 41.99 , 8
S941, 2 ,HIP-BOOT, 26.95 , 32.5 , 12
T615, 4 ,OXFORD-STYLE, 26.43 , 31.5 , 28
T731, 1 ,SANDLES, 6.75 , 9.45 , 52
EOF, 0 ,EOF, 0 , 0 , 0
```

FIGURE 8.8   A list of the records in the transaction file TRNINV.DAT.

Following the return of control to the Main module, line 1160 calls the Process Files module. Within the While loop, lines 3030 through 3080, the stock number S$ from CURINV.DAT is compared to the stock number S1$ from TRNINV.DAT. The comparisons determine which record will next be written to the new master file, INVNTORY.DAT. The logic proceeds as follows:

1) If S$ is equal to S1$, then control transfers to the error module, lines 3230 through 3270, and a diagnostic message is displayed indicating that the record from TRNINV.DAT already exists in CURINV.DAT. The next record in TRNINV.DAT is read before control transfers back to the Process Files module.

2) If S\$ is less than S1\$, then control transfers to the module, lines 3430 through 3460, that writes the record from CURINV.DAT. The counter K is also incremented by 1 and the next record from CURINV.DAT is read before control transfers back to the Process Files module.

3) If S\$ is greater than S1\$, then control transfers to the module, lines 3630 through 3660, that writes the record from TRNINV.DAT. The counter K is incremented by 1 and the next record from TRNINV.DAT is read before control transfers back to the Process Files module.

When the system reads either file's trailer record, then control returns to the Main module. Line 1170 in the Main module transfers control to the Wrap Up module.

If the end-of-file is sensed on TRNINV.DAT, then lines 4030 through 4070 flush any records remaining in CURINV.DAT. If the end-of-file is sensed on CURINV.DAT, then the While loop in lines 4080 through 4120 flush any records that remain in TRNINV.DAT.

A close look at Figures 8.7 and 8.8 reveals that the fifth record in TRNINV.DAT has the same stock number as the eighth record in CURINV.DAT. This causes the display of a diagnostic message below the RUN command.

Figure 8.9 shows the contents of the new master file INVNTORY.DAT created by Program 8.4. To better understand the merging of CURINV.DAT and TRNINV.DAT into INVNTORY.DAT, merge the two files manually using the algorithm illustrated in both the top-down chart in Figure 8.6 and Program 8.4.

```
C101, 1 ,ROADHANDLER, 97.56 , 125.11 , 25
C103, 2 ,SAW-BLADES, 5.06 , 6.04 , 15
C204, 3 ,WHITEWALLS, 37.14 , 99.95 , 140
C206, 1 ,SQUARE, 4.56 , 5.42 , 34
C502, 2 ,TRIPOD, 32.5 , 38.99 , 10
S209, 1 ,MAXIDRILL, 88.76 , 109.99 , 6
S210, 3 ,MICROSCOPE, 31.5 , 41.99 , 8
S416, 2 ,NORMALSAW, 152.55 , 179.4 , 1
S812, 2 ,ROUTER, 48.47 , 61.15 , 8
S941, 2 ,HIP-BOOT, 26.95 , 32.5 , 12
S942, 4 ,RADIALSAW, 376.04 , 419.89 , 3
T615, 4 ,OXFORD-STYLE, 26.43 , 31.5 , 28
T713, 2 ,MOC-BOOT, 24.99 , 29.99 , 30
T731, 1 ,SANDLES, 6.75 , 9.45 , 52
T814, 2 ,WORK-BOOT, 22.99 , 27.99 , 56
EOF, 0 ,EOF, 0 , 0 , 0
```

FIGURE 8.9 A list of the records in the merged new master file INVNTORY.DAT.

In Programming Case Study 21, one category of file maintenance—adding new records to the master file—was introduced. In the following Programming Case Study, the two remaining categories of file maintenance—deletion of unwanted records and changing data within records in the master file—will be introduced. Here again, records will be input from two files, the current master file and a transaction file, and a new master file will be created. A process known as **matching records** will be used. Matching records involves processing two or more related files that are in the same sequence according to a common data item.

Programming Case Study 22: File Maintenance II—Deleting and Changing Records by Matching Records

As records are read from the two related files, the system acts upon them in the following manner:

1) If the stock numbers in both records are equal, then the action indicated on the transaction record is carried out. Either the current master record is deleted by not writing it to the new master file, or the data is changed in the current master record, as indicated on the transaction record, and the modified current master record is written to the new master file.

2) If the stock number in the current master record is less than the stock number in the transaction record (i.e., the transaction file contains no modifications to the current master record), then the current master record is written to the new master file.

3) If the stock number in the current master file is greater than the stock number in the transaction record (i.e., the transaction record has no match), then the transaction record is in error and a diagnostic message should be displayed.

This process of matching records is illustrated in the following problem.

Problem

Given the current master file shown in Figure 8.9 and the transaction file shown below, a program that updates the current master file and creates a new master file will be illustrated. Both the current master file and transaction file are in ascending sequence by stock number.

Stock Number	Transaction Code	Warehouse Location	Description	Unit Cost	Selling Price	Quantity On Hand
C204	D	-1	Null Char.	-1	-1	-1
C402	C	3	Null Char.	33.50	40.50	-1
S812	C	-1	ROUTER-II	-1	-1	12
T615	D	-1	Null Char.	-1	-1	-1
T731	C	-1	Null Char.	6.50	-1	-1

The name of the current master file is CURINV.DAT and the name of the transaction file is TRNINV.DAT. The name of the new master file is to be INVNTORY.DAT.

With respect to the contents of the transaction file TRNINV.DAT:

1) The transaction code D indicates that the corresponding record in the current master file is to be deleted, and the code C indicates changes.

2) Data items that are *not* to be changed in the current master file are designated in the transaction file with a value of -1 if the item is numeric, and by a null character if the item is a string.

3) In order for the INPUT #n statement to read the transaction file properly, all items are assigned a value of either -1 or a null character, including those within records representing a record delete.

```
1000 REM PROGRAM 8.5
1010 REM FILE MAINTENANCE II - DELETING RECORDS AND CHANGING FIELDS
1020 REM BY MATCHING RECORDS
1030 REM CURRENT MASTER FILE - CURINV.DAT    TRANSACTION FILE - TRNINV.DAT
1040 REM --------------------------------    ------------------------------
1050 REM S$ = STOCK NUMBER                   S1$ = STOCK NUMBER
1060 REM L  = WAREHOUSE LOCATION             L1  = WAREHOUSE LOCATION
1070 REM D$ = DESCRIPTION                    D1$ = DESCRIPTION
1080 REM C  = UNIT COST                      C1  = UNIT COST
1090 REM P  = SELLING PRICE                  P1  = SELLING PRICE
1100 REM Q  = QUANTITY ON HAND               Q1  = QUANTITY ON HAND
1110 REM                                     T$  = MAINTENANCE TYPE
1120 REM NEW MASTER FILE - INVNTORY.DAT
1130 REM K1 = DELETION COUNT                 K2  = CHANGE COUNT
1140 REM K3 = COUNT OF RECORDS IN NEW MASTER FILE
1150 REM *****************************************************************
1160 REM *                       MAIN MODULE                            *
1170 REM *****************************************************************
1180 GOSUB 2030          'CALL INITIALIZATION
1190 GOSUB 3030          'CALL PROCESS FILES
1200 GOSUB 4030          'CALL WRAP UP
1210 STOP
2000 REM *****************************************************************
2010 REM *                   INITIALIZATION MODULE                      *
2020 REM *****************************************************************
2030 LET K1 = 0
2040 LET K2 = 0
2050 LET K3 = 0
2060 OPEN "I", #1, "CURINV.DAT"
2070 OPEN "I", #2, "TRNINV.DAT"
2080 OPEN "O", #3, "INVNTORY.DAT"
2090 GOSUB 5030          'CALL READ RECORD FROM CURRENT MASTER FILE
2100 GOSUB 6030          'CALL READ RECORD FROM TRANSACTION FILE
2110 RETURN
```

PROGRAM 8.5

```
3000 REM *****************************************************************
3010 REM *                    PROCESS FILES MODULE                      *
3020 REM *****************************************************************
3030 WHILE S$ <> 'EOF' AND S1$ <> 'EOF'
3040    IF S$ = S1$ THEN 3050 ELSE 3070
3050       IF T$ = 'D' THEN GOSUB 3230 ELSE GOSUB 3430
3060    GOTO 3080
3070       IF S$ < S1$ THEN GOSUB 3630 ELSE GOSUB 3830
3080 WEND
3090 RETURN
3200 REM *****************************************************************
3210 REM *                    DELETE RECORD MODULE                      *
3220 REM *****************************************************************
3230 LET K1 = K1 + 1
3240 GOSUB 5030            'CALL READ RECORD FROM CURRENT MASTER FILE
3250 GOSUB 6030            'CALL READ RECORD FROM TRANSACTION FILE
3260 RETURN
3400 REM *****************************************************************
3410 REM *                    CHANGE RECORD MODULE                      *
3420 REM *****************************************************************
3430 IF L1 <> -1 THEN LET L = L1
3440 IF D1$ <> '' THEN LET D$ = D1$
3450 IF C1 <> -1 THEN LET C = C1
3460 IF P1 <> -1 THEN LET P = P1
3470 IF Q1 <> -1 THEN LET Q = Q1
3480 PRINT #3, S$; ','; L; ','; D$; ','; C; ','; P; ','; Q
3490 LET K2 = K2 + 1
3500 LET K3 = K3 + 1
3510 GOSUB 5030            'CALL READ RECORD FROM CURRENT MASTER FILE
3520 GOSUB 6030            'CALL READ RECORD FROM TRANSACTION FILE
3530 RETURN
3600 REM *****************************************************************
3610 REM *               NO CHANGE TO CURRENT MASTER RECORD            *
3620 REM *****************************************************************
3630 PRINT #3, S$; ','; L; ','; D$; ','; C; ','; P; ','; Q
3640 LET K3 = K3 + 1
3650 GOSUB 5030            'CALL READ RECORD FROM CURRENT MASTER FILE
3660 RETURN
3800 REM *****************************************************************
3810 REM *                    ERROR MODULE                             *
3820 REM *****************************************************************
3830 PRINT '***ERROR*** TRANSACTION RECORD WITH STOCK NUMBER '; S1$;
3840 PRINT ' HAS NO MATCHING RECORD'
3850 GOSUB 6030            'CALL READ RECORD FROM TRANSACTION FILE
3860 RETURN
4000 REM *****************************************************************
4010 REM *                    WRAP UP MODULE                           *
4020 REM *****************************************************************
4030 WHILE S$ <> 'EOF'
4040    PRINT #3, S$; ','; L; ','; D$; ','; C; ','; P; ','; Q
4050    LET K3 = K3 + 1
4060    GOSUB 5030         'CALL READ RECORD FROM CURRENT MASTER RECORD
4070 WEND
4080 WHILE S1$ <> 'EOF'
4090    PRINT '***ERROR*** TRANSACTION RECORD WITH STOCK NUMBER '; S1$;
4100    PRINT ' HAS NO MATCH'
4110    GOSUB 6030         'CALL READ RECORD FROM TRANSACTION FILE
4120 WEND
4130 PRINT #3, S$; ','; 0; ','; S$; ','; 0; ','; 0; ','; 0
4140 CLOSE #1, #2, #3
4150 PRINT
4160 PRINT 'TOTAL NUMBER OF RECORDS DELETED============>'; K1
4170 PRINT 'TOTAL NUMBER OF RECORDS CHANGED============>'; K2
4180 PRINT 'TOTAL NUMBER OF RECORDS IN NEW MASTER=====>'; K3
4190 PRINT 'INVNTORY.DAT UPDATE COMPLETE'
4200 RETURN
5000 REM *****************************************************************
5010 REM *               READ CURRENT MASTER FILE MODULE              *
5020 REM *****************************************************************
5030 INPUT #1, S$, L, D$, C, P, Q
5040 RETURN
6000 REM *****************************************************************
6010 REM *               READ TRANSACTION FILE MODULE                 *
6020 REM *****************************************************************
6030 INPUT #2, S1$, T$, L1, D1$, C1, P1, Q1
6040 RETURN
6050 END
RUN

***ERROR*** TRANSACTION RECORD WITH STOCK NUMBER C402 HAS NO MATCHING RECORD

TOTAL NUMBER OF RECORDS DELETED============> 2
TOTAL NUMBER OF RECORDS CHANGED============> 2
TOTAL NUMBER OF RECORDS IN NEW MASTER=====> 13
INVNTORY.DAT UPDATE COMPLETE
```

PROGRAM 8.5
(continued)

If a record in the TRNINV.DAT file has no matching record in the current master file, then the diagnostic message

```
***ERROR*** TRANSACTION RECORD WITH STOCK NUMBER C402 HAS NO MATCHING RECORD
```

is displayed. As part of the end-of-job routine, the total number of records deleted and the number of records changed should be displayed.

Since the algorithm for matching records is similar to that of merging files presented in Programming Case Study 21, only a discussion of the program solution follows.

When the RUN command is issued for Program 8.5, line 1180 in the Main module transfers control to the Initialization module. Line 2060 opens for input the current master file CURINV.DAT shown in Figure 8.9 as INVNTORY.DAT. Line 2070 opens for input the transaction file TRNINV.DAT, which contains the records shown below:

```
C204,D,-1 ,,-1 ,-1 ,-1
C402,C, 3 ,, 33.50 , 40.50 ,-1
S812,C,-1 ,ROUTER-II,-1 ,-1 , 12
T615,D,-1 ,,-1 ,-1 ,-1
T731,C,-1 ,, 6.50 ,-1 ,-1
EOF,, 0 ,, 0 , 0 , 0
```

Line 2080 opens for output the new master file INVNTORY.DAT.

Lines 2090 and 2100 call upon the modules to read the first current master record and the first transaction record. Control then returns to the Main module.

Line 1190 transfers control to the Process Files module. Within the While loop, lines 3030 through 3080, line 3040 compares the two stock numbers, S$ and S1$. If S$ is equal to S1$, then the transaction represents a change or delete. If S$ does not equal S1$, then the control passes to line 3070. If the transaction represents a change or delete, then control passes to line 3050 and the transaction type is compared to D.

If T$ equals D, then control passes to the Delete Record module, which increments the counter K1 by 1. Deleting the record is handled by *not* writing the corresponding current master record to the new master file. Lines 3240 and 3250 call upon the two modules to read the next current master record and next transaction record before control passes back to the Process Files module.

In line 3050, if T$ does not equal D, then control transfers to the Change Record module.

In the Change Record module, lines 3430 through 3470 test each value assigned to the variables that correspond to the transaction record. If any of the numeric variables L1, C1, P1 or Q1 equal −1, then the corresponding variables in the current master file are *not* changed. If they equal any other value, then the IF statements result in the assignment of new values to the variables making up the current master record. Line 3440 compares D1$ to the null character. The null character signifies that the description field in the current master record is not to be changed. If D1$ does not equal a null character, then D$ is assigned the value of D1$.

After each variable is tested (except for the stock number, which may not be changed), line 3480 writes the modified current master record to the new master file. K2 and K3 are then incremented by 1 before the next current master record and next transaction record are read. Control then returns to the Process Files module.

Let us now go back to line 3040 and discuss what happens if the current master record and transaction record do not match. If S$ does not equal S1$, then control transfers to line 3070. Line 3070 determines if the stock number in the current master record S$ is less than the stock number S1$ in the transaction record. If S$ is less than S1$, then control transfers to the module in lines 3630 through 3660 and the current master record is written to the new master file before K3 is incremented by 1 and the next current master record is read.

In line 3070, if S$ is not less than S1$, then it is greater than S1$. In this case, control transfers to the Error module which displays an appropriate diagnostic message. The diagnostic message states that the transaction record has no corresponding match in the current master file. Line 3850 causes the system to read the next transaction record.

The Process Files module maintains control of the system until end-of-file is sensed on either the current master file or the transaction file. The Wrap Up module then flushes either file that may have records remaining. If records remain in the current master file, then they are written to the new master file. If records remain in the transaction file, then they have no match and are considered to be in error.

In the results displayed following the command RUN, one of the five records in the transaction file, stock number C402, does not have a corresponding match in the current master file. Of the other four transaction records, two call for deleting records and two for modifying the current master records. The new master file contains 13 records plus the trailer record, as shown below.

```
C101, 1 ,ROADHANDLER, 97.56 , 125.11 , 25
C103, 2 ,SAW-BLADES, 5.06 , 6.04 , 15
C206, 1 ,SQUARE, 4.56 , 5.42 , 34
C502, 2 ,TRIPOD, 32.5 , 38.99 , 10
S209, 1 ,MAXIDRILL, 88.76 , 109.99 , 6
S210, 3 ,MICROSCOPE, 31.5 , 41.99 , 8
S416, 2 ,NORMALSAW, 152.55 , 179.4 , 1
S812, 2 ,ROUTER-II, 48.47 , 61.15 , 12
S941, 2 ,HIP-BOOT, 26.95 , 32.5 , 12
S942, 4 ,RADIALSAW, 376.04 , 419.89 , 3
T713, 2 ,MOC-BOOT, 24.99 , 29.99 , 30
T731, 1 ,SANDLES, 6.5 , 9.45 , 52
T814, 2 ,WORK-BOOT, 22.99 , 27.99 , 56
EOF, 0 ,EOF, 0 , 0 , 0
```

Alternative Methods for Detecting End-of-File

Up to this point, a trailer record has been added to the end of a sequential data file to indicate the physical end-of-file. When programs process the file, a test has been made to determine when to branch to an end-of-job routine. It is not necessary to write a trailer record. Each time a CLOSE statement is executed for a sequential file opened for output, the system automatically writes an **end-of-file mark** after the last record.

The method used to test for the end-of-file mark varies between the dialects of BASIC. Since most BASIC systems treat reading past the end-of-file as an error, this error can be trapped and control passed to an end-of-job routine through the use of the ON ERROR GOTO statement. An alternative method, supported by Microsoft BASIC, is to use the function EOF(n) to test for the end-of-file mark. In this section we will discuss the ON ERROR GOTO statement and, later, the use of the function EOF(n).

The ON ERROR GOTO Statement

The ON ERROR GOTO statement enables error trapping and specifies a line number to branch to when an error occurs. The line number may be the beginning of an end-of-job routine. Once the ON ERROR GOTO statement is executed, *all* errors detected cause the system to branch to the specified line number. The user's manual will list the various errors that the ON ERROR GOTO statement can trap.

Most BASIC systems include two special variables named ERR and ERL. When an error is trapped, ERR is assigned an error code. ERL is assigned the line number of the statement that caused the error. Followng the branch to the end-of-job routine, the value of ERR can be tested to determine if the error was caused by reading past end-of-file. If ERR is equal to the correct code, then execution of the end-of-job routine can continue. If ERR does not equal the proper code, then the program should be terminated. The system can be instructed to terminate execution through the use of the statement ON ERROR GOTO 0. When this statement is executed, the system terminates the program.

The general form of the ON ERROR GOTO statement is shown in Table 8.8.

TABLE 8.8   The ON ERROR GOTO **Statement**

General Form:	ON ERROR GOTO line number
Purpose:	Enables error trapping and specifies a line number to branch to when an error occurs. The special variables ERR and ERL may be used to test for the type of error and line number of the statement that caused the error. The statement ON ERROR GOTO 0 may be used to terminate execution of the program if the error is not of the type that can be handled by the routine.
Examples:	`100 ON ERROR GOTO 500` `200 ON ERROR GOTO 0`
Note:	With the Apple, the general form is: ONERR GOTO line number. Also, the special variables ERR and ERL are not available. To determine the error code, use the statement LET E = PEEK(222). The variable E is then assigned the error code. An error code of 5 indicates end-of-file. With the COMMODORE, there is no ON ERROR GOTO statement. However, following a read, comparing the speciable variable STATUS to 64 tests for end-of-file. If STATUS equals 64, then control should be transferred to the end-of-job routine. Listed below is the value assigned to ERR when the ON ERROR statement traps the error for reading past the end-of-file on some popular computer systems.

Computer System	*Value of* ERR *for Reading Past End-of-File*
DEC Rainbow	62
DEC VAX-11	11
IBM PC	62
Macintosh	62
TRS-80	4
In general, systems running Microsoft BASIC	62

The ON ERROR GOTO statement must be placed in a program in such a way that it is executed prior to the lines in which errors are to be trapped. In order to trap an out-of-data error, the ON ERROR GOTO statement must be executed before the INPUT #n statement. The following partial program illustrates the correct placement of the ON ERROR GOTO statement and the use of the special variable ERR.

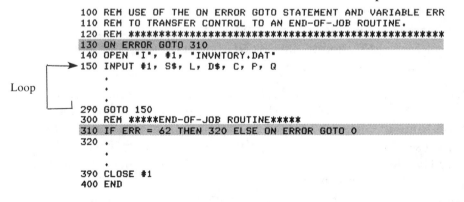

```
100 REM USE OF THE ON ERROR GOTO STATEMENT AND VARIABLE ERR
110 REM TO TRANSFER CONTROL TO AN END-OF-JOB ROUTINE.
120 REM ******************************************
130 ON ERROR GOTO 310
140 OPEN "I", #1, "INVNTORY.DAT"
150 INPUT #1, S$, L, D$, C, P, Q
      .
      .
      .
290 GOTO 150
300 REM *****END-OF-JOB ROUTINE*****
310 IF ERR = 62 THEN 320 ELSE ON ERROR GOTO 0
320 .
      .
      .
390 CLOSE #1
400 END
```
Loop

Line 130 enables error trapping. Line 150 reads the first record. If the file INVNTORY.DAT is empty, then control transfers to line 310. If the file is not empty, the record is processed, line 290 transfers control back to line 150, and the next record is read and processed. The loop continues until there are no more records left in INVNTORY.DAT.

When line 150 attempts to read past end-of-file, control automatically transfers to line 310, which compares ERR to the error code 62. If ERR is equal to 62, then the end-of-job routine is executed. If ERR does not equal 62, then another type of error caused the system to branch to line 310 and the ON ERROR GOTO 0 causes the system to display an appropriate diagnostic message and terminate the program.

Another statement that can be used along with the ON ERROR GOTO statement is the RESUME statement, described in detail in Appendix C. The RESUME statement instructs the system to continue execution at any line number in the program following an error. For example, always closing a file is good programming practice. In the previous partial program, line 310 can be changed to the following to ensure that the file INVNTORY.DAT is closed even if an error other than out-of-data occurs:

```
310 IF ERR = 62 THEN 320 ELSE RESUME 390
```

The following rule summarizes the placement of the ON ERROR GOTO statement in a program.

> ON ERROR GOTO **Rule 1:** The ON ERROR GOTO statement should be executed prior to the lines in which errors are to be trapped.

The Function EOF(n)

The function EOF(n), where n represents the filenumber, tests for end-of-file. Unfortunately, this function is not available on all BASIC systems.* If the function EOF is available, it is preferable to the ON ERROR GOTO statement.

When referenced in a program, the function EOF returns a value of 0 (false) if it is not end-of-file. The function EOF returns a value of −1 (true), when end-of-file has been reached.

The following partial program illustrates how this function may be used to control a loop that reads and processes data found in a file until the end-of-file is detected:

```
           200 OPEN "I", #3, "INVNTORY.DAT"
         ┌→210 WHILE NOT EOF(3)◄──────────────── Function EOF
While    │ 220    INPUT #3, S$, L, D$, C, P, Q    tests for
Loop     │          •                             end-of-file prior
         │          •                             to each attempt to
         │          •                             read data in line 220.
         └──400 WEND
           410 REM ****END OF FILE ROUTINE*****
           420 •
                  •
                  •
```

Line 210 tests for the end-of-file mark *prior to* the execution of the INPUT #n statement in line 220. If INVNTORY.DAT is empty, line 210 transfers control to the end-of-file routine and the statements within the While loop are not executed. If INVNTORY.DAT is not empty, control passes to line 220 and the first record is read and then processed. Before each succeeding pass, the function EOF(3) in line 210 returns a value of 0 (false) or −1 (true). If the function returns a 0, indicating it is

*The function EOF is available on the DEC Rainbow, IBM PC, Macintosh and other computer systems that use Microsoft BASIC.

not end-of-file, then the loop continues. If the function returns a -1, indicating it is end-of-file, then control transfers to the end-of-file routine beginning at line 420.

Note that in line 210, it is not necessary to compare EOF(3) to the numeric value 0. In the previous chapters, all conditions included a relational operator. However, BASIC considers any expression in a WHILE or IF statement false if the expression yields a numeric value of 0, and true if the expression yields *any other value*. That is,

```
200 IF 5 THEN PRINT "TRUE"
```
or
```
300 WHILE -1
```
or
```
400 WHILE X     (where X is not equal to zero)
```

result in true conditions. On the other hand

```
500 IF 0 THEN PRINT X, Y, "FALSE"
```
and
```
600 WHILE 0
```

result in false conditions. Thus, we may write

```
220 WHILE NOT EOF(3)
```

instead of

```
220 WHILE NOT(EOF(3) = 0)
```

although the latter is valid and may be used.

Two additional points concern the function EOF:

1) It is invalid to precede the filenumber by a number sign (#). For example, the following is invalid:

```
220 WHILE NOT EOF(#3)
```
                    ↑ invalid

2) Filenumber n must have been previously opened for input. It is invalid to test for end-of-file on a data file opened for output.

Table 8.9 illustrates several examples of the use of the function EOF.

TABLE 8.9   Examples of the EOF **Function**

Statement
```
200 WHILE NOT EOF(2)
300 IF EOF(1) THEN LET F1$ = "N" ELSE INPUT #1, A, B, C
400 WHILE NOT EOF(2) AND X > 0
500 WHILE NOT EOF(3) AND NOT EOF(1)
600 IF NOT EOF(2) THEN INPUT #2, S$, X, D$
700 WHILE NOT(EOF(3) OR EOF(1))
```

The following rule summarizes the placement of the function EOF in a program.

Function EOF(n) **Rule 1:** The function EOF(n) should test for the end-of-file prior to the execution of an INPUT #n statement.

8.5 RANDOM FILE PROCESSING

Recall from Section 8.2 that the sequence of processing in a file organized randomly has no relationship to the sequence in which the records are stored in the file. Random files have several advantages over sequential files, even though fewer program steps are required to create and access records within sequential files than are required for creating and accessing records within random files. Random files require less space in auxiliary storage because numbers are stored in a compressed format and no commas are required between data items.

Random files may be processed sequentially or randomly, but their main advantage over sequential files is that their records may be processed randomly. To process a record in the middle of the file, it is not necessary to read all the records prior to it. This is true because each record within a random file has a key associated with it. The key indicates the position of the record from the beginning of the random file.

This section presents the file handling statements and functions that are necessary to create and process files that can be accessed randomly. The format of the statements presented follows that of Microsoft BASIC. If you are using some other dialect of BASIC, refer to the user's manual to determine the format of statements comparable to those that are presented here. The *concepts* presented in this section on random files are easily transferable to other dialects of BASIC.

As with sequential files, it is necessary that random files be opened before they are read from or written to. When a program is finished with a random file, it must close the file. The general form of the OPEN statement for random files is shown in Table 8.10. The general form of the CLOSE statement is the same as for sequential files and is shown in Table 8.3.

Opening and Closing Random Files

TABLE 8.10 The OPEN Statement for Random Files

General Form:	OPEN "R", filenumber, filespec, recl
	where R specifies that a file is opened for random processing
	filenumber is a numeric expression whose value is between 1 and 15.
	filespec is the name of the random file
	recl is a value equal to the number of characters in each record
Purpose:	Allows a program to read or write records to a random file.
Examples:	100 OPEN "R", #1, "WAREHSE.DAT", 59
	200 OPEN "R", #2, "ACCOUNT.DAT", R
	300 OPEN M$, #F, N$, R

The two primary differences between opening a random file and a sequential file are:

1) For sequential files, it is necessary that the mode (input or output) of processing be specified. However, random files are always opened for both input and output. Once a random file is opened, a program may read or write records to the file.

2) For random files, it is necessary that in the OPEN statement the record length (i.e., the exact number of characters in each record) be indicated. Failure to do so may result in wasted space in auxiliary storage. The record length may vary between 1 and 32,767 characters and should correspond to the total number of characters defined in the FIELD statement.

The following OPEN statement,

```
200 OPEN "R", #2, "ACCOUNT.DAT", 60
```

opens ACCOUNT.DAT for random processing as filenumber 2. The record length is 60 characters. If ACCOUNT.DAT does not exist in auxiliary storage, then it is created. If ACCOUNT.DAT exists as a random file, the program is terminated after an appropriate diagnostic message is displayed.

When an OPEN statement such as

The FIELD Statement

```
300 OPEN "R", #3, "WAREHSE.DAT", 59
```

is executed, the system establishes in main memory a buffer, 59 positions in length, for sending and receiving data from the random file WAREHSE. DAT. When a program requests a record from WAREHSE. DAT, the system reads the record into the buffer. When a record is written to WAREHSE. DAT, the program must first place the data items of the record into the buffer. When a write statement is executed, the system transfers the contents of the buffer to auxiliary storage.

BASIC includes the FIELD statement so that the program can move the data out of the buffer following a read or store the data into the buffer before a write. The FIELD statement allows data items to be identified with respect to their size and location within the buffer.

Let us assume that the random file WAREHSE. DAT contains a record for each warehouse that our company owns. Each record includes four fields:

Data Item	No. of Characters
Warehouse Name	18
Street Address	17
City State Zip Code	20
Total Square Feet	4

The following FIELD statement may be used to describe each data item within the buffer:

```
310 FIELD #3, 18 AS N$, 17 AS S$, 20 AS C$, 4 AS F$
```

Line 310 allocates the first 18 positions in the buffer to the string variable N$ (warehouse name), the next 17 positions to S$ (street address), the next 20 positions to C$ (city state zip code) and the last 4 positions to F$ (total square feet).

After a record is read into the buffer, the data items may be referenced through the use of N$, S$, C$ and F$. Also, these same variable names may be used to assign data items to the buffer before writing a record.

The general form of the FIELD statement is shown in Table 8.11.

TABLE 8.11   The FIELD Statement

General Form	FIELD #filenumber, list
	each entry in the list is of the form:
	    width AS stringvar
	where width is the number of positions in the buffer allocated to the data item
	    stringvar is the string variable name.

Purpose:	Allocates space for variables in a buffer by defining the location and length (number of characters) of data items and assigns a unique string variable to each data item location. The string variable is used to access or assign a data item in the buffer.
Examples:	100 FIELD #1, 12 AS D$, 36 AS F$, 13 AS U$ 200 FIELD #2, 45 AS T$ 300 FIELD #3, 1 AS G$, 23 AS X$, 200 AS J$

As indicated in Table 8.11, the list that defines a buffer in a FIELD statement can only include simple string variables. The following FIELD statement is invalid

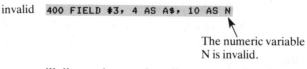

invalid   `400 FIELD #3, 4 AS A$, 10 AS N`

The numeric variable
N is invalid.

Later, we will discuss how to handle numeric data items when dealing with random files.

The placement of the FIELD statement in a program is important. It is necessary that the program open the file before the FIELD statement is executed.

Thus, it is valid to write

```
100 OPEN "R", #1, "WAREHSE.DAT", 59
110 FIELD #1, 18 AS N$, 17 AS S$, 20 AS C$, 4 AS F$
```

and invalid to write

invalid
```
100 FIELD #1, 18 AS N$, 17 AS S$, 20 AS C$, 4 AS F$
110 OPEN "R", #1, "WAREHSE.DAT", 59
```

It is also important that the sum of the widths in the list of a FIELD statement not exceed the record length specified in the OPEN statement.

The following two rules summarize the preceding material:

> FIELD **Rule 1:** A FIELD statement should be executed after the corresponding OPEN statement.

> FIELD **Rule 2:** The sum of the widths in the list of a FIELD statement must not exceed the record length in the OPEN statement.

The buffer of a random file may be defined as often as required. Multiple FIELD statements that refer to the same random file are allowed in the same program. A number of applications, like accounts receivable, inventory control and payroll, are often designed around a single file. The file may contain a number of different types of records, like a **header record** that includes permanent information followed by related transaction records. Each type of record will use a different FIELD statement. A single character in each record identifies it as a header record or transaction record and this is then used to detemine which FIELD statement to use.

The LSET and RSET statements are used to store data in the buffer before writing a record to a random file. LSET stands for left-justify and RSET for right-justify. Given the FIELD statement

The LSET **and** RSET **Statements**

```
310 FIELD #1, 18 AS W$, 17 AS A$, 20 AS C$, 4 AS R$
```

the following series of statements assign data to the buffer:

```
400 LSET W$ = W1$
410 LSET A$ = A1$
420 RSET C$ = C1$
430 LSET R$ = R1$
```

Line 400 left-justifies the value of W1$ in the 18 positions assigned to W$ in the buffer. Likewise, line 410 left-justifies the value of A1$ in the 17 positions assigned to A$ and line 430 the value of R1$ in the 4 positions assigned to R$. Line 420 right-justifies the value of C1$ in the 20 positions assigned in the buffer to C$.

The general forms of the LSET and RSET statements are shown in Table 8.12.

TABLE 8.12   **The** LSET **and** RSET **Statements**

General Forms:	LSET stringvar = string expression RSET stringvar = string expression where stringvar is a string variable defined in the FIELD statement string expression is a value that is assigned to stringvar.
Purpose:	Moves data into a buffer in preparation for writing a random record. LSET left-justifies the string expression in stringvar. RSET right-justifies the string expression in stringvar. If necessary, both statements append spaces to the string expression to ensure that the length of the assignment is equal to the width of stringvar as defined in the FIELD statement.
Examples:	500 LSET X$ = F$ 600 RSET S$ = "MALE" 700 LSET N$ = MKS$(N)

The LSET and RSET statements not only justify a value in the buffer; they also append spaces to ensure that the length of the value is equal to width of the string variable receiving it. If A1$ is equal to 1458 TOD, then it has a length of 8 characters. On the other hand, in the FIELD statement defined earlier by line 310, A$ is defined to have a length of 17 positions. The statement

```
410 LSET A$ = A1$
```

assigns A$ the value 1458bTODbbbbbbbbb where b represents a space. The statement

```
410 RSET A$ = A1$
```

assigns A$ the value bbbbbbbbb1458bTOD.

If the string expression is longer than the width, then both the LSET and RSET statements truncate the excess characters located on the right.

The LSET statement is used more often than the RSET statement. The following rule summarizes the use of the LSET and RSET statements.

> LSET **and** RSET **Rule 1:** Before a record is written to a random file, all values must be stored in the buffer through the use of the LSET or RSET statements. It is invalid to assign variables in a FIELD statement values through the use of the INPUT, LET or READ statements.

The Functions MKS$ and CVS

It is invalid to define a numeric variable in the list of a FIELD statement. So that numeric values may be placed in and removed from a buffer, BASIC includes the functions MKS$ and CVS.* The function MKS$(N) converts the numeric value N to a four-character string value for the purpose of placing the numeric value into the buffer before writing the random record to auxiliary storage. The function CVS(X$) is used to convert the string variable X$, defined in the FIELD statement, to a numeric value following the read of a record from a random file.

Since the function MKS$(N) converts N to a four-character string, string variables defined in a FIELD statement that are assigned numeric values should always be given a width of 4.

Table 8.13 illustrates the use of the two functions.

TABLE 8.13   Examples of the MKS$ and CVS Functions

Given the FIELD *statement:* 200 FIELD 4 AS N$, 4 AS G$

The Statement	Result
300 LSET N$ = MKS$(N1)	The numeric value of N1 is converted to a string value and assigned to N$.
310 LSET G$ = MKS$(G)	The numeric value of G is converted to a string value and assigned to G$.
400 LET N1 = CVS(N$)	The string value assigned to N$ is converted to a numeric value and assigned to N1.
410 LET G = CVS(G$)	The string value assigned to G$ is converted to a numeric value and assigned to G.

Lines 300 and 310 show how the value of a numeric variable can be assigned to a string variable defined in the FIELD statement before a record is written to a random file. Lines 400 and 410 show how the value of a string variable defined in the FIELD statement can be converted to a numeric value following the read of a record from a random file.

---

*The functions MKS$ and CVS are used with single precision variables. The functions MKI$ and CVI are used with integer variables. The functions MKD$ and CVD are used with double-precision variables. In this section we will deal only with single precision variables.

The GET statement reads and transfers a record from a random file to the buffer defined by the corresponding FIELD statement. The PUT statement writes a record from the buffer defined by the corresponding FIELD statement to a random file.

The GET and PUT Statements

The general forms of the GET and PUT statements are shown in Tables 8.14 and 8.15.

TABLE 8.14 The GET Statement

General Form:	GET #n, r
	where n is a filenumber assigned to a random file in an OPEN statement
	r is the number of the record to be read and transferred to the buffer.
Purpose:	To read and transfer a record from a random file to a buffer defined by a corresponding FIELD statement. If the record number r is not included in the GET statement, then the next record in the random file is read and transferred to the buffer.
Examples:	400 GET #1, R
	500 GET #2, 47
	600 GET #F, N
	700 GET #3

The following partial program illustrates the relationship between the OPEN, FIELD and GET statements.

```
150 OPEN "R", #1, "WAREHSE.DAT", 59
160 FIELD #1, 18 AS N$, 17 AS S$, 20 AS C$, 4 AS F$
    •
    •
    •
200 GET #1, R
```

When line 200 is executed, the Rth record is read from WAREHSE.DAT and transferred to the buffer defined by the FIELD statement in line 160.

Records from a random file may be read sequentially beginning at any record in the file. For example, if X is assigned the value 26 before the execution of line 500 in the following partial program

```
500 GET #2, X
    •
    •
    •
600 GET #2
    •
    •
    •
700 GET #2
```

then line 500 reads the 26th record, line 600 the 27th record and line 700 the 28th record. If the first GET following an open has no record number, then the first record in the random file is read and transferred to the buffer. The following partial program reads sequentially a random file with 50 records and sums the numeric value assigned to N$ for each record read.

```
100 LET S = 0
110 OPEN "R", #3, "ACCOUNT.DAT", 41
120 FIELD #3, 14 AS X$, 23 AS A$, 4 AS N$
130 FOR I = 1 TO 50
140    GET #3
150    LET S = S + CVS(N$)
160 NEXT I
170 PRINT "THE SUM IS"; S
```

Line 140 of the For loop reads the next record in the random file. Line 150 increments the variable S by the numeric value of N$ for each record read. Note that CVS(N$) is equal to the numeric value of N$.

TABLE 8.15   **The** PUT **Statement**

General Form:	PUT #n, r
	where n is a filenumber assigned to a random file in an OPEN statement
	r is the number of the record to be written from the buffer to the random file.
Purpose:	To write a record from the buffer defined by a corresponding F IELD statement to a random file. If the record number is not included in the PUT statement, then the next record in the random file is replaced by the contents of the buffer.
Examples:	300 PUT #1, N
	400 PUT #2, 567
	500 PUT #F, T
	600 PUT #3

As indicated in Table 8.15, the PUT statement writes the contents of the buffer to a random file. Thus the statement

```
800 PUT #2, 62
```

writes the contents of the corresponding buffer to filenumber 2 as record 62.

The Functions LOC and LOF

The function LOC(n) returns the record number of the last record read or written to the random file assigned to filenumber n. For example, in the following partial program

```
500 GET #3, X
510 LET L = LOC(3)
```

the variable L is assigned the value of X, since X indicates the record number of the last record read from the random file assigned to filenumber 3. The LOC function may also be used with sequential files to determine the total number of records read and written since it was last opened.

The function LOF (n) returns information regarding the size of the random file assigned to filenumber n. Not all versions of Microsoft are consistent in the form of the information returned. On the IBM PC, the function LOF returns the number which equals the number of characters in the file. This value may then be used to determine the number of records in a random file by dividing whatever the function LOF returns by the record length defined in the OPEN statement. This expression can be important when processing a random file sequentially.

Check the specifications on your BASIC system in the user's manual as to the form of the information returned by the function LOF.

Programming Case Study 23: Creating a Random File

In Programming Case Studies 19 through 22, each record in INVNTORY.DAT includes a number to indicate the warehouse in which the stock item is located. The warehouse location numbers vary between 1 and 4. The following problem creates a random file in which each record includes a warehouse name, address and total number of square feet for each of the four warehouses.

Problem

Company PUC requests a program that creates a random file in which each record represents one of its warehouses. Each record includes the following data items:

Data Item	No. of Characters
Warehouse Name	18
Street Address	17
City State Zip Code	20
Total Square Feet	4

The actual data for each record is shown below:

Warehouse Location	Warehouse Name	Street Address	City State Zip Code	Total Square Feet
1	PUC GYTE WHSE	1498 BARING AVE.	WHITLEY IN 46325	80,000
2	PUC ANDERSON WHSE	612 45TH ST.	CALCITY IL 60618	220,000
3	PUC POTTER WHSE	1329 OLCOT ST.	POINTE IN 46367	85,900
4	PUC PORTER WHSE	15 E 63RD ST.	POLK IN 45323	92,500

The operator enters the warehouse location number to indicate the record to be created. The warehouse location number is *not* to be part of the record. A warehouse location number of −1 terminates the program.

An analysis of the problem and a program solution follow.

Program Tasks

1) Open the file WAREHSE.DAT for random access as filenumber 1 with a record length of 59 characters.

2) Use the following FIELD statement:

   FIELD #1, 18 AS N$, 17 AS S$, 20 AS C$, 4 AS F$

   where N$ = Warehouse name
   S$ = Street address
   C$ = City state zip code
   F$ = Total square feet

3) Clear the screen and display a message describing the function of the program and method of termination.

4) Use the INPUT statement to accept the first warehouse location number N:

```
100 REM PROGRAM 8.6
110 REM CREATING A RANDOM FILE
120 REM N$ = FIELD WAREHOUSE NAME
130 REM S$ = FIELD STREET ADDRESS
140 REM C$ = FIELD CITY STATE ZIP CODE
150 REM F$ = FIELD TOTAL SQUARE FEET
160 REM NAME OF RANDOM FILE CREATED - WAREHSE.DAT
170 REM **************************************
180 OPEN "R", #1, "WAREHSE.DAT", 59
190 FIELD #1, 18 AS N$, 17 AS S$, 20 AS C$, 4 AS F$
200 CLS
210 PRINT "**********************************************************"
220 PRINT "*   THIS PROGRAM CREATES THE RANDOM FILE WAREHSE.DAT   *"
230 PRINT "*                                                      *"
240 PRINT "*   AFTER THE LAST WAREHOUSE RECORD, ENTER A -1 FOR    *"
250 PRINT "*   THE WAREHOUSE NUMBER TO TERMINATE THE PROGRAM.     *"
260 PRINT "**********************************************************"
270 INPUT "WAREHOUSE NUMBER"; N
280 WHILE N <> -1
290    INPUT "WAREHOUSE NAME"; N1$
300    INPUT "STREET ADDRESS"; S1$
310    INPUT "CITY STATE ZIP CODE"; C1$
320    INPUT "TOTAL SQUARE FEET"; F
330    REM *****ASSIGN INPUT VALUES TO BUFFER*****
340    LSET N$ = N1$
350    LSET S$ = S1$
360    LSET C$ = C1$
370    LSET F$ = MKS$(F)
380    REM *****WRITE RANDOM RECORD*****
390    PUT #1, N
400    PRINT
410    INPUT "WAREHOUSE NUMBER"; N
420 WEND
430 REM *****END OF JOB ROUTINE*****
440 CLOSE #1
450 PRINT
460 PRINT "RANDOM FILE WAREHSE.DAT CREATED"
470 PRINT
480 PRINT "JOB COMPLETE"
490 END
```

RUN   PROGRAM 8.6

5) Use a While loop to do the following:
  a) Accept the four data items: warehouse name N1$, street address S1$, city state zip code C1$ and total square feet F.
  b) Use the LSET statement to assign the four data items to the buffer. Use the function MKS$ to convert the numeric value of F to an appropriate string value.
  c) Write the record to random file WAREHSE. DAT using the PUT statement.
  d) Use an INPUT statement to accept the next warehouse location number N.
6) In the end-of-job routine, do the following:
  a) Close the random file WAREHSE. DAT.
  b) Display an end-of-job message.

When the RUN command is issued for Program 8.6, line 180 opens the random file WAREHSE. DAT as filenumber 1. Line 190 defines the buffer for filenumber 1. As shown in Figure 8.10, lines 210 through 260 display an appropriate message to the operator. Lines 270 and 290 through 320 accept the operator's responses. Lines 340 through 370 assign the data items to the buffer. Line 390 writes the record before accepting the next warehouse location number. When a warehouse location number equal to −1 is entered by the operator, the program terminates.

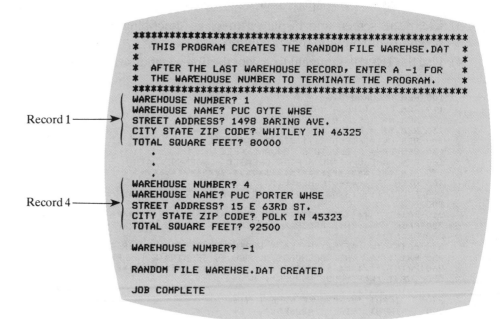

FIGURE 8.10   Partial display from the execution of Program 8.6.

```
*************************************************************
*    THIS PROGRAM CREATES THE RANDOM FILE WAREHSE.DAT     *
*                                                          *
*    AFTER THE LAST WAREHOUSE RECORD, ENTER A -1 FOR       *
*    THE WAREHOUSE NUMBER TO TERMINATE THE PROGRAM.        *
*************************************************************
WAREHOUSE NUMBER? 1
WAREHOUSE NAME? PUC GYTE WHSE
STREET ADDRESS? 1498 BARING AVE.
CITY STATE ZIP CODE? WHITLEY IN 46325
TOTAL SQUARE FEET? 80000
        .
        .
        .
WAREHOUSE NUMBER? 4
WAREHOUSE NAME? PUC PORTER WHSE
STREET ADDRESS? 15 E 63RD ST.
CITY STATE ZIP CODE? POLK IN 45323
TOTAL SQUARE FEET? 92500

WAREHOUSE NUMBER? -1

RANDOM FILE WAREHSE.DAT CREATED

JOB COMPLETE
```

Record 1 →
Record 4 →

Program 8.6 can be rewritten without requiring the operator to enter the warehouse location number N. In the rewritten version, line 390 is modified to 390 PUT #1. A PUT statement without a record number writes the buffer as the next record. However, the operator would then be required to enter the records in sequence. As it stands now, Program 8.6 will properly create the random file regardless of the order the records are entered. Warehouse location number 4 can be entered before warehouse location number 1 in Program 8.6.

Because it requests a warehouse location number, Program 8.6 can later be used to add new warehouse records or modify existing warehouse records. For example, if a fifth warehouse is added by company PUC, Program 8.6 can be used to add this new record. Unlike sequential files, whose contents are automatically deleted when opened for output, on most systems random files exist until deleted by a system command. By slightly modifying the message displayed prior to the While loop, Program 8.6 can be used as a file maintenance program to add or change records.

In the creation of random files, it is not necessary that a record be entered for every record number. It is valid to number warehouses 1, 3, 6 and 10. When a random file like that is created without contiguous record numbers, the system reserves areas for records 2, 4, 5, 7, 8 and 9. These areas are often called **empty cells**.

The following problem shows a program that accesses records in a random file.

Programming Case Study 24: Accessing a Random File

Problem

Company PUC has requested that a program be written to access and display records from the random file WAREHSE. DAT. To view another record, the operator will enter a "Y" in response to the question:

DO YOU WANT TO VIEW ANOTHER RECORD (Y OR N)?

An analysis of the problem and a program solution follow.

Program Tasks

1) Open the file WAREHSE. DAT for random access as filenumber 1 with a record length of 59 characters.
2) Use the FIELD statement found in line 190 of Program 8.6.
3) Clear the screen and display a message describing the function of the program and how to terminate the program.

```
100 REM PROGRAM 8.7
110 REM ACCESSING A RANDOM FILE
120 REM N$ = FIELD WAREHOUSE NAME
130 REM S$ = FIELD STREET ADDRESS
140 REM C$ = FIELD CITY STATE ZIP CODE
150 REM F$ = FIELD TOTAL SQUARE FEET
160 REM NAME OF RANDOM FILE ACCESSED - WAREHSE.DAT
170 REM ****************************************
180 OPEN "R", #1, "WAREHSE.DAT", 59
190 FIELD #1, 18 AS N$, 17 AS S$, 20 AS C$, 4 AS F$
200 CLS
210 PRINT "***********************************************"
220 PRINT "*   THIS PROGRAM ACCESSES THE RANDOM FILE WAREHSE.DAT *"
230 PRINT "*                                             *"
240 PRINT "*   ENTER THE WAREHOUSE NUMBER TO VIEW THE WAREHOUSE   *"
250 PRINT "*   RECORD.  TO TERMINATE THE PROGRAM, ENTER 'N' IN    *"
260 PRINT "*   RESPONSE TO THE QUESTION, 'DO YOU WANT TO VIEW     *"
270 PRINT "*   ANOTHER RECORD?'                          *"
280 PRINT "***********************************************"
290 PRINT
300 PRINT
310 LET A$ = "Y"
320 WHILE A$ = "Y"
330    INPUT "WAREHOUSE NUMBER"; N
340    GET #1, N
350    PRINT
360    PRINT "WAREHOUSE NAME===============> "; N$
370    PRINT "STREET ADDRESS===============> "; S$
380    PRINT "CITY STATE ZIP CODE=========> "; C$
390    PRINT USING "TOTAL SQUARE FEET==========> ###,###"; CVS(F$)
400    PRINT
410    PRINT
420    INPUT "DO YOU WANT TO VIEW ANOTHER RECORD (Y OR N)"; A$
430    IF A$ = "Y" THEN CLS
440 WEND
450 REM *****END OF JOB ROUTINE*****
460 CLOSE #1
470 PRINT
480 PRINT "JOB COMPLETE"
490 END
```

PROGRAM 8.7

4) Set the switch A$ to "Y" to ensure that the program will request at least one warehouse location number.

5) Use a While loop that repeats while the switch A$ is equal to "Y." The While loop should:

   a) Accept a warehouse location number N.

   b) Read the Nth record in WAREHSE . DAT.

   c) Display the warehouse name N$, street address S$, city state and zip code C$ and total square feet CVS (F$) .

   d) Request that the operator enter a "Y" to view another record or "N" to terminate execution of the program. Assign the value to the switch A$.

6) As a part of the end-of-job routine, close filenumber 1 and display the message JOB COMPLETE.

FIGURE 8.11 Results displayed due to entering warehouse location number 4.

FIGURE 8.12 Results displayed due to entering warehouse location number 2.

Figures 8.11 and 8.12 show the results displayed when warehouse location number 4 and 2 are entered. Line 340 in Program 8.7 reads the Nth record, where N is assigned a value in line 330. Lines 360 throgh 380 show that the values found in a record can be displayed by using the variable names in the FIELD statement. It is not necessary to use any special assignment statements like the LSET when displaying the values of variables found in a FIELD statement. In line 390, the function CVS is used to convert the total square feet F$ to a numeric value.

Program 8.7 illustrates the advantages of a random file over a sequential file. When warehouse location number 4 is entered, the program is able to access the record without first reading records 1, 2 and 3. Likewise, when warehouse location number 2 is requested, the program does not have to rewind the file to begin searching from the beginning of the file.

Provided the record number is known, any record can be accessed in a random file. Unfortunately, few applications use integers like 1, 2 and 3 to represent the employee numbers, customer numbers or stock numbers which commonly identify the record to be accessed in a file. More often, these keys are made up of several digits and letters which have no relationship to the location of the record in a random file. However, many applications require random access based on these types of keys.

In many programming languages, like COBOL and PL/I, a third type of file organization, indexed files, allow a relationship between a key and the record location to be automatically established. With most BASIC systems, indexed files are not available, and therefore the relationship between the key and record location must be handled by the programmer.

The following program solutions include an array and a sequential file to store the keys and a random file to store the corresponding data. The solution is divided into two programs. The first program creates an index (for up to 100 keys) and corresponding random file from the sequential file INVNTORY.DAT used in Program 8.5. The second program allows for displaying, adding, changing and deleting records in the file, provided the stock number is known.

8.6 SIMULATED INDEX FILES

Programming Case Study 25: Inventory Retrieval and Update

Problem

The system flowchart in Figure 8.13 illustrates the general logic of creating an index file (Program 8.8) and accessing an index file (Program 8.9).

The first program creates a random file from INVNTORY.DAT and a corresponding stock number index that points to the location of records in the random file. The second program allows for displaying, adding, changing or deleting

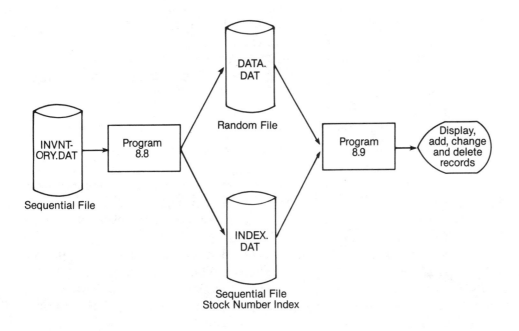

FIGURE 8.13 A system flowchart representing Programs 8.8 and 8.9.

records in the random file. The sequential file INVNTORY.DAT contains the following records:

```
C101, 1 ,ROADHANDLER, 97.56 , 125.11 , 25
C103, 2 ,SAW-BLADES, 5.06 , 6.04 , 15
C206, 1 ,SQUARE, 4.56 , 5.42 , 34
C502, 2 ,TRIPOD, 32.5 , 38.99 , 10
S209, 1 ,MAXIDRILL, 88.76 , 109.99 , 6
S210, 3 ,MICROSCOPE, 31.5 , 41.99 , 8
S416, 2 ,NORMALSAW, 152.55 , 179.4 , 1
S812, 2 ,ROUTER-II, 48.47 , 61.15 , 12
S941, 2 ,HIP-BOOT, 26.95 , 32.5 , 12
S942, 4 ,RADIALSAW, 376.04 , 419.89 , 3
T713, 2 ,MOC-BOOT, 24.99 , 29.99 , 30
T731, 1 ,SANDLES, 6.5 , 9.45 , 52
T814, 2 ,WORK-BOOT, 22.99 , 27.99 , 56
EOF, 0 ,EOF, 0 , 0 , 0
```

An analysis of part 1 of the problem and program solution follow.

Program 1 Tasks—Build Index File

1) Dimension array I\$ to 100 elements.
2) Use a For loop to assign each element in array I\$ the string EMPTY.
3) Open INVENTORY.DAT for input as filenumber 1. Open DATA.DAT for random access as filenumber 2 with a record length of 35.
4) Use the following FIELD statement:

   ```
   FIELD #2, 4 AS S1$, 4 AS L$, 15 AS D1$, 4 AS C$, 4 AS P$, 4 AS Q$
   ```

   where S1\$ is the stock number, L\$ is the warehouse location, D1\$ is the description, C\$ is the unit cost, P\$ is the selling price and Q\$ is the quantity on hand.
5) Initialize the subscript K to zero.
6) Read the first record in the sequential file INVNTORY.DAT.
7) Use a While loop to create the random file DATA.DAT and corresponding index. Within the loop perform the following tasks:
   a) Increment the subscript K by 1.
   b) Set I\$(K) equal to the stock number S\$.
   c) Assign the first record to the buffer.
   d) Write the Kth record to the random file DATA.DAT.
   e) Read the next record in INVNTORY.DAT.
   f) Terminate the While loop when S\$ is equal to EOF.
8) In the end-of-job routine perform the following tasks:
   a) Close the random file DATA.DAT.
   b) Open the sequential file INDEX.DAT for output as filenumber 1.
   c) Use a For loop to write the 100 elements of array I\$ to the sequential file INDEX.DAT.
   d) Close the sequential file INDEX.DAT.
   e) Display the message JOB COMPLETE.

When the RUN command is issued for Program 8.8, lines 230 through 250 initialize all elements of array I\$ to the string EMPTY. In the While loop, each time a data record is written to the random file, the corresponding element in array I\$ is assigned the stock number of the record (line 370). Therefore, a relationship is established such that the Kth element of array I\$ is equal to the stock number of the Kth record in the random file.

As part of the end-of-job routine, array I\$ is written to the sequential file INDEX.DAT. Note that INDEX.DAT contains 100 data items, some of which are equal to stock numbers and others which are equal to the string EMPTY. In Program 8.9 array I\$ is used to determine the location of records with correspond-

```
100 REM PROGRAM 8.8
110 REM CREATE INITIAL INDEX FILE AND RANDOM FILE
120 REM ************************************************************
130 REM *THIS PROGRAM READS THE SEQUENTIAL FILE INVNTORY.DAT AND   *
140 REM *CREATES THE RANDOM FILE DATA.DAT.   THE STOCK NUMBER (KEY) *
150 REM *IS ASSIGNED TO THE ELEMENT IN ARRAY I$ THAT CORRESPONDS   *
160 REM *TO THE RECORD NUMBER. AS PART OF THE END-OF-JOB ROUTINE,  *
170 REM *ARRAY I$ IS WRITTEN TO THE SEQUENTIAL FILE INDEX.DAT.  THE *
180 REM *MAXIMUM NUMBER OF RECORDS THAT DATA.DAT CAN CONTAIN IS 100.*
190 REM ************************************************************
200 REM ****DIMENSION ARRAY I$ WHICH WILL CONTAIN THE RECORD KEYS****
210 DIM I$(100)
220 REM *****SET ELEMENTS OF ARRAY I$ TO THE STRING "EMPTY"*****
230 FOR K = 1 TO 100
240    LET I$(K) = "EMPTY"
250 NEXT K
260 REM *****OPEN SEQUENTIAL FILE INVNTORY.DAT*****
270 OPEN "I", #1, "INVNTORY.DAT"
280 REM *****OPEN RANDOM FILE DATA.DAT*****
290 OPEN "R", #2, "DATA.DAT", 35
300 FIELD #2, 4 AS S1$, 4 AS L$, 15 AS D1$, 4 AS C$, 4 AS P$, 4 AS Q$
310 REM CREATE INITIAL DATA FILE AND CORRESPONDING INDEX IN ARRAY I$
320 LET K = 0
330 INPUT #1, S$, L, D$, C, P, Q
340 WHILE S$ <> "EOF"
350    LET K = K + 1
360    REM *****ASSIGN STOCK NUMBER S$ TO KTH ELEMENT OF ARRAY I$****
370    LET I$(K) = S$
380    REM *****ASSIGN INVENTORY RECORD TO BUFFER*****
390    LSET S1$ = S$
400    LSET L$ = MKS$(L)
410    LSET D1$ = D$
420    LSET C$ = MKS$(C)
430    LSET P$ = MKS$(P)
440    LSET Q$ = MKS$(Q)
450    REM *****WRITE KTH RECORD TO RANDOM FILE DATA.DAT*****
460    PUT #2, K
470    INPUT #1, S$, L, D$, C, P, Q
480 WEND
490 CLOSE #1, #2
500 PRINT "THE NUMBER OF RECORDS IN THE DATA FILE IS"; K
510 REM *****CREATE INDEX FILE INDEX.DAT*****
520 OPEN "O", #1, "INDEX.DAT"
530 FOR K = 1 TO 100
540    PRINT #1, I$(K); ",";
550 NEXT K
560 CLOSE #1
570 PRINT
580 PRINT "JOB COMPLETE"
590 END

RUN

THE NUMBER OF RECORDS IN THE DATA FILE IS 13

JOB COMPLETE
```

PROGRAM 8.8

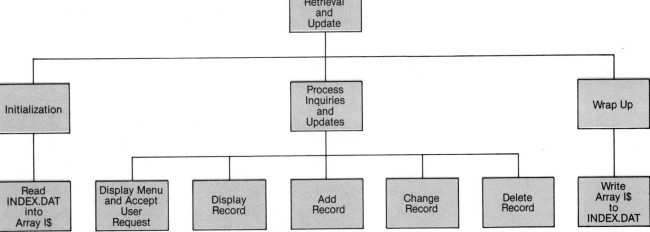

FIGURE 8.14   A top-down chart for Program 8.9.

ing stock numbers. The fact that unused elements of array I$ are equal to the string EMPTY will be helpful for both adding and deleting records.

An analysis of the second part of the problem and program solution follow.

Program 2 Tasks—Process Index File

1) The top-down chart in Figure 8.14 represents the major functions of the second program:

2) The function of the Initialization module is to open DATA. DAT and INDEX. DAT, read the 100 data items in INDEX. DAT into array I$ and close INDEX. DAT.

3) The function of the Process Inquiries and Updates module is to maintain overall control of the program until the user requests the program be terminated. This module calls the Display module, which returns a function code F and a stock number S$. Based on the value of the function code, a GOSUB statement calls the Display Record, Add Record, Change Record or Delete Record module. Following return of control from one of these modules, the Display Menu module is called to initiate the next user request.

4) The function of the Display Menu module is to display a menu, accept a function code F and stock number S$. Both the function code F and stock number S$ must be validated. Valid function codes are as follows:

       1 — Display record
       2 — Add record
       3 — Change record
       4 — Delete record
       5 — End program

    The stock number is validated by comparing it to the elements of array I$. If the function code F equals 1, 3 or 4, then the stock number S$ must equal the value of one of the elements of I$. The subscript of the element of array I$ that is equal to the stock number is used in the Display Record, Change Record and Delete Record modules to get the corresponding record in the random file DATA. DAT.

    If the function code equals 2, then the stock number S$ must not equal the value of an element in array I$.

    Control remains in this module until a valid function code and stock number are entered by the user.

5) The function of the Display Record module is to display the record that corresponds to the stock number entered by the user in the Display Menu module. In this module, do the following:

a) Read the Kth record in the random file DATA. DAT. Recall that K is assigned a value due to the validating of the stock number in the Display Menu module.

b) Display the record read from DATA. DAT.

c) Use the INPUT statement to suspend execution so that the user may view the record before the menu is again displayed.

6) The function of the Add Record module is to add a record to DATA. DAT and a corresponding stock number to array I$. In this module, do the following:

a) Determine the first element of I$ that is equal to the string EMPTY.

b) If no elements of I$ are equal to the string EMPTY, then the array is full, an appropriate diagnostic message is displayed and control is returned to the menu.

c) If an element of I$ equals EMPTY, then request the remaining items that belong to this new record, assign the items to the buffer, assign the stock number S$ to the kth element of I$ and write the Kth record to DATA. DAT. The record is written to DATA. DAT only after the user is given the opportunity to abort the addition.

7) The function of the Change Record module is to allow the user to change any item in the record except the stock number. In this module do the following:

   a) Read the Kth record in the random file DATA. DAT.
   b) Request the user to enter changes. If an item is not to change in the record, then the user responds by entering a −1 for the item in question.
   c) Check each response. If a response is not equal to −1, then assign the item to the buffer.
   d) Write the modified record to DATA. DAT only after the user is given the opportunity to abort the record modification.

8) The function of the Delete module is to delete an unwanted record. To delete an unwanted record, assign the Kth element of I$ the string EMPTY only after giving the user the opportunity to abort the record deletion. Note that nothing is done to the corresponding record in DATA. DAT. However, since the Kth element is assigned the string EMPTY, this element may be used for a record addition at a later date.

9) The function of the Wrap Up module is to write array I$ to the sequential file INDEX. DAT, close the files and terminate the program.

```
1000 REM PROGRAM 8.9
1010 REM INVENTORY RETRIEVAL AND UPDATE PROGRAM
1020 REM ***********************************************************
1030 REM *THIS PROGRAM DISPLAYS OR UPDATES A DATA FILE.  RECORDS ARE  *
1040 REM *ACCESSED RANDOMLY BASED ON A KEY (STOCK NUMBER) ENTERED BY  *
1050 REM *THE USER.  RECORDS MAY BE DISPLAYED, ADDED TO THE FILE,     *
1060 REM *DELETED FROM THE FILE OR CHANGED.                           *
1070 REM *THE INDEX OF KEYS IS LOADED INTO AN ARRAY I$ DURING INITIAL-*
1080 REM *IZATION FROM THE SEQUENTIAL FILE INDEX.DAT. THE ARRAY I$ IS *
1090 REM *WRITTEN BACK TO THE SEQUENTIAL FILE AS PART OF THE END-OF-JOB*
1100 REM *ROUTINE.  THE DATA IS STORED IN A RANDOM FILE DATA.DAT AND  *
1110 REM *ACCESSED BASED ON THE SUBSCRIPT OF ARRAY I$ WHICH CONTAINS  *
1120 REM *THE CORRESPONDING STOCK NUMBER.                             *
1130 REM ***********************************************************
1140 REM
1150 REM
1160 REM ***********************************************************
1170 REM *                     MAIN MODULE                         *
1180 REM ***********************************************************
1190 GOSUB 2030           'CALL INITIALIZATION
1200 GOSUB 3030           'CALL PROCESS INQUIRIES AND UPDATES
1210 GOSUB 9030           'CALL WRAP UP
1220 STOP
2000 REM ***********************************************************
2010 REM *                 INITIALIZATION MODULE                   *
2020 REM ***********************************************************
2030 DIM I$(100)
2040 OPEN 'R', #1, 'DATA.DAT', 35
2050 FIELD #1, 4 AS S1$, 4 AS L$, 15 AS D1$, 4 AS C$, 4 AS P$, 4 AS Q$
2060 OPEN 'I', #2, 'INDEX.DAT'
2070 FOR K = 1 TO 100
2080    INPUT #2, I$(K)
2090 NEXT K
2100 CLOSE #2
2110 RETURN
3000 REM ***********************************************************
3010 REM *             PROCESS INQUIRIES AND UPDATES               *
3020 REM ***********************************************************
3030 GOSUB 4050                        'CALL DISPLAY MENU
3040 WHILE F <> 5
3050    CLS
3060    ON F GOSUB 5030, 6030, 7030, 8030 'CALL DISPLAY,ADD,CHANGE,DELETE
3070    GOSUB 4050                     'CALL DISPLAY MENU
3080 WEND
3090 RETURN
```

```
4000 REM ********************************************************************
4010 REM *                    DISPLAY MENU MODULE                          *
4020 REM *   THIS MODULE DISPLAYS THE MENU, ACCEPTS A CODE F AND STOCK     *
4030 REM *   NUMBER S1$ AND SEARCHES THE ARRAY I$ FOR THE STOCK NUMBER.    *
4040 REM ********************************************************************
4050 LET S = 0
4060 WHILE S = 0
4070    LET S = 1
4080    CLS
4090    PRINT
4100    PRINT "          MENU FOR INVENTORY RETRIEVAL AND UPDATE"
4110    PRINT "          ----------------------------------------"
4120    PRINT
4130    PRINT "                    CODE        FUNCTION"
4140    PRINT "                    ----        --------"
4150    PRINT "                     1     -    DISPLAY RECORD"
4160    PRINT "                     2     -    ADD RECORD"
4170    PRINT "                     3     -    CHANGE RECORD"
4180    PRINT "                     4     -    DELETE RECORD"
4190    PRINT "                     5     -    END PROGRAM"
4200    PRINT
4210    INPUT "               ENTER A CODE OF 1 THROUGH 5"; F
4220    IF F = 1 OR F = 2 OR F = 3 OR F = 3 OR F = 4 OR F = 5 THEN 4250
4230       PRINT "***ERROR***     CODE OUT OF RANGE, PLEASE"
4240       GOTO 4210
4250    IF F = 5 THEN 4430
4260    CLS
4270    INPUT "ENTER THE STOCK NUMBER"; S$
4280    REM *****DETERMINE IF THE STOCK NUMBER S$ IS IN ARRAY I$*****
4290    FOR K = 1 TO 100
4300       IF S$ = I$(K) THEN 4380
4310    NEXT K
4320    IF F = 2 THEN 4430
4330       CLS
4340       LET S = 0
4350       PRINT "STOCK NUMBER "; S$; " IS INVALID"
4360       INPUT "PRESS ENTER KEY TO RETURN TO THE MENU..."; Z$
4370       GOTO 4430
4380    IF F <> 2 THEN 4430
4390       CLS
4400       LET S = 0
4410       PRINT "***ERROR*** STOCK NUMBER "; S$; " ALREADY EXISTS"
4420       INPUT "PRESS ENTER KEY TO RETURN TO THE MENU..."; Z$
4430 WEND
4440 RETURN
5000 REM ********************************************************************
5010 REM *                    DISPLAY RECORD MODULE                        *
5020 REM ********************************************************************
5030 GET #1, K
5040 PRINT "STOCK NUMBER==============> "; S$
5050 PRINT "WAREHOUSE LOCATION=======>"; CVS(L$)
5060 PRINT "DESCRIPTION==============> "; D1$
5070 PRINT USING "UNIT COST================> $$$$.$$"; CVS(C$)
5080 PRINT USING "SELLING PRICE============> $$$$.$$"; CVS(P$)
5090 PRINT USING "QUANTITY ON HAND=========> ####"; CVS(Q$)
5100 PRINT
5110 INPUT "PRESS ENTER KEY TO RETURN TO THE MENU..."; Z$
5120 RETURN
6000 REM ********************************************************************
6010 REM *                    ADD RECORD MODULE                            *
6020 REM ********************************************************************
6030 REM *****SEARCH FOR "EMPTY" ELEMENT IN ARRAY I$*****
6040 FOR K = 1 TO 100
6050    IF I$(K) = "EMPTY" THEN 6100
6060 NEXT K
6070 PRINT "***ERROR***   INDEX IS FULL. NO ROOM LEFT TO ADD "; S$
6080 INPUT "              PRESS ENTER KEY TO RETURN TO THE MENU..."; Z$
6090 GOTO 6270
6100 REM *****REQUEST REMAINING DATA ITEMS*****
6110 PRINT "ENTER REMAINING ITEMS FOR STOCK NUMBER "; S$
6120 INPUT "WAREHOUSE LOCATION"; L
6130 INPUT "DESCRIPTION"; D$
6140 INPUT "UNIT COST"; C
6150 INPUT "SELLING PRICE"; P
6160 INPUT "QUANTITY ON HAND"; Q
6170 INPUT "ENTER 'Y' TO ADD RECORD, ELSE 'N'"; Z$
6180 IF Z$ = "Y" THEN 6190 ELSE 6270
6190    LSET S1$ = S$
6200    LSET L$ = MKS$(L)
6210    LSET D1$ = D$
6220    LSET C$ = MKS$(C)
6230    LSET P$ = MKS$(P)
6240    LSET Q$ = MKS$(Q)
6250    LET I$(K) = S$
6260    PUT #1, K
6270 RETURN
```

PROGRAM 8.9
(continued)

346

```
7000 REM *****************************************************************
7010 REM *                     CHANGE RECORD MODULE                      *
7020 REM *****************************************************************
7030 GET #1, K
7040 PRINT "*****ENTER A -1 IF YOU DO NOT WANT TO CHANGE AN ITEM*****"
7050 PRINT
7060 PRINT "STOCK NUMBER=====> "; S$
7070 INPUT "WAREHOUSE LOCATION"; L
7080 IF L <> -1 THEN LSET L$ = MKS$(L)
7090 INPUT "DESCRIPTION"; D$
7100 IF D$ <> "-1" THEN LSET D1$ = D$
7110 INPUT "UNIT COST"; C
7120 IF C <> -1 THEN LSET C$ = MKS$(C)
7130 INPUT "SELLING PRICE"; P
7140 IF P <> -1 THEN LSET P$ = MKS$(P)
7150 INPUT "QUANTITY ON HAND"; Q
7160 IF Q <> -1 THEN LSET Q$ = MKS$(Q)
7170 INPUT "ENTER 'Y' TO UPDATE RECORD, ELSE 'N'"; Z$
7180 IF Z$ = "Y" THEN PUT #1, K
7190 RETURN
8000 REM *****************************************************************
8010 REM *                     DELETE RECORD MODULE                      *
8020 REM *****************************************************************
8030 PRINT "ARE YOU SURE THAT YOU WANT TO DELETE STOCK NUMBER "; S$
8040 INPUT "ENTER 'Y' TO DELETE, ELSE 'N'"; Z$
8050 IF Z$ = "Y" THEN LET I$(K) = "EMPTY"
8060 RETURN
9000 REM *****************************************************************
9010 REM *                      WRAP UP MODULE                           *
9020 REM *****************************************************************
9030 CLOSE #1
9040 OPEN "O", #2, "INDEX.DAT"
9050 FOR K = 1 TO 100
9060    PRINT #2, I$(K); ",";
9070 NEXT K
9080 CLOSE #2
9090 PRINT "INVENTORY RETRIEVAL AND UPDATE PROGRAM TERMINATED"
9100 PRINT
9110 PRINT "JOB COMPLETE"
9120 END
```

PROGRAM 8.9
(continued)

RUN

When the RUN command is issued for Program 8.9, the menu in Figure 8.15 is displayed:

```
MENU FOR INVENTORY RETRIEVAL AND UPDATE
----------------------------------------

      CODE      FUNCTION
      ----      --------
       1    -   DISPLAY RECORD
       2    -   ADD RECORD
       3    -   CHANGE RECORD
       4    -   DELETE RECORD
       5    -   END PROGRAM

      ENTER A CODE OF 1 THROUGH 5?
```

FIGURE 8.15 Menu displayed for Program 8.9.

If a function code of 1 through 4 is entered, then line 4270 requests the user enter a stock number by displaying the following message:

ENTER THE STOCK NUMBER?

Lines 4290 through 4420 verify the stock number. If a function code of 2 is entered, then the stock number S$ must not equal the value of any of the elements of array I$. If a function code of 1, 3 or 4 is entered, then the stock number S$ must be equal to the value of one of the elements in array I$. An additional function of this validation process, when the function code is 1, 3 or 4, is to establish the record number K of the corresponding record to be displayed, changed or deleted.

If a function code of 1 and stock number S941 are entered by the user, then the Display Record module (lines 5030 through 5120) displays the following:

```
STOCK NUMBER==============> S941
WAREHOUSE LOCATION=======> 2
DESCRIPTION==============> HIP-BOOT
UNIT COST================>   $26.95
SELLING PRICE============>   $32.50
QUANTITY ON HAND=========>    12

PRESS ENTER KEY TO RETURN TO THE MENU...?
```

If a function code of 2 and stock number S429 are entered by the user, then the Add Record module (lines 6030 through 6270) requests the remaining items that make up this new record.

```
ENTER REMAINING ITEMS FOR STOCK NUMBER S429
WAREHOUSE LOCATION? 2
DESCRIPTION? PLIER
UNIT COST? 3.45
SELLING PRICE? 4.55
QUANTITY ON HAND? 13
ENTER 'Y' TO ADD RECORD, ELSE 'N'?
```

Lines 6040 through 6060 determine the first element of I$ that is equal to the string EMPTY. The subscript of this element is then used to indicate the record number in the PUT statement in line 6260. Just before line 6260, line 6250 assigns the stock number S$ to I$(K).

If a function code of 3 and stock number T814 are entered, then the Change Record module (lines 7030 through 7190) reads the Kth record, requests changes and rewrites the record. The following is displayed:

```
*****ENTER A -1 IF YOU DO NOT WANT TO CHANGE AN ITEM*****

STOCK NUMBER=====> T814
WAREHOUSE LOCATION? -1
DESCRIPTION? -1
UNIT COST? -1
SELLING PRICE? 29.95
QUANTITY ON HAND? 32
ENTER 'Y' TO UPDATE RECORD, ELSE 'N'?
```

If a function code of 4 and stock number of C206 are entered, then the Delete Record module (lines 8030 through 8060) assigns the Kth element of I$ the string EMPTY. Note that the data record in DATA. DAT is not changed in any way. Later, when a record is added, the record in DATA. DAT is changed to the new record. The following is displayed:

```
ARE YOU SURE THAT YOU WANT TO DELETE STOCK NUMBER C206
ENTER 'Y' TO DELETE, ELSE 'N'?
```

If a function code of 5 is entered, then the Wrap Up module writes the array I$ to the sequential file INDEX. DAT, closes the files and displays the following:

```
INVENTORY RETRIEVAL AND UPDATE PROGRAM TERMINATED

JOB COMPLETE
```

8.7 WHAT YOU SHOULD KNOW

1. In BASIC, there are four techniques that may be used to integrate data into a program. Data may be read through the use of
   a) The INPUT statement
   b) The READ and DATA statements
   c) The INPUT #n statement
   Finally, data may be directly inserted into statements like the LET statement.
2. A file is a group of related records. Each record within the file contains related data items.
3. BASIC systems allow for two types of file organization—sequential and random. A file organized sequentially is a sequential file and is limited to sequential processing. A file organized randomly is a random file. The sequence of processing a random file has no relationship to the sequence in which the records are stored in it.

4. A third type of organization, indexed, is also widely used in data processing. It is not available on most BASIC systems. Indexed files may be simulated by using both a sequential file and random file.

5. A filename identifies a file in auxiliary storage.

6. Before a file can be read from or written to, it must be opened by the OPEN statement.

7. When a program is finished reading from or writing to a file, it must close the file using the CLOSE statement.

8. A sequential file may be opened for input or output. Some systems also allow a file to be opened for appending data. If a sequential file is opened for input, then a program can only read data from the file. If a sequential file is opened for output, then the program can only write data to it. If a sequential file is opened for appending data, then the program can only write data to the end of the file.

9. The parameters in an OPEN statement may be variable names that are assigned values prior to the execution of the OPEN statement.

10. A filenumber cannot be assigned to more than one file at a time.

11. The PRINT #n and PRINT #n, USING statements write data or information to sequential files.

12. Through the use of the PRINT #n and PRINT #n, USING statements, reports may be written to a file instead of to an external device like a video display device or printer.

13. The PRINT #n statement writes data to a file in the format required by the INPUT #n statement. The format requirement is similar to that of the READ and DATA statements—all data items must be separated by commas.

14. Some systems use the WRITE #n statement. This statement may be used to simplify the task of writing data to a file in the format required by the INPUT #n statement.

15. The INPUT #n statement reads data from a sequential file.

16. File maintenance is the process of updating files in one or more of the following ways:
    a) Adding new records
    b) Deleting unwanted records
    c) Changing data within records

17. A transaction file contains data of a temporary or transient nature.

18. A master file contains data that is, for the most part, permanent.

19. A file maintenance program that updates a sequential file must deal with at least three files: a transaction file, the current master file and a new master file.

20. A system flowchart shows, in graphic form, the files, flow of data, equipment, and programs involved in a particular application.

21. Merging is the process of combining two or more files that are in the same sequence into a single file that maintains that same sequence for a given data item in each record.

22. Matching records involves two or more related files that are in the same sequence according to a common data item. If a record in the transaction file matches a record in the current master file, then the current master record may be updated. If there is no match, then appropriate action must be taken depending on the application.

23. The ON ERROR GOTO statement may be used to transfer control to an end-of-job routine when there are no more records left in a sequential file. Once an ON ERROR GOTO statement is executed, all errors detected cause the system to branch to the specified line number. The special variables ERR and ERL may be used to check the type of error that caused the sytem to transfer control.

24. The statement ON ERROR GOTO 0 instructs the system to display an appropriate diagnostic message before terminating the program. The RESUME statement may be used to transfer control to a line in the program followng the detection of an error by the ON ERROR GOTO statement.

25. The function EOF(n) may be used to test for end-of-file on some BASIC systems. The function EOF(n) must be placed in a program in such a way that the function tests for end-of-file prior to the use of an INPUT #n statement.

26. Like sequential files, random files must be opened before they are read from or written to. When a program finishes with a random file, it must close the file. Unlike sequential files, random files are opened for both input and output at the same time.

27. Whenever a file is opened with a mode of "R," the record length must be specified.

28. The FIELD statement is used to define data items with respect to their size and location within the buffer.

29. Only string variables may be used in a FIELD statement to define the buffer.

30. A random file must be opened before a corresponding FIELD statement is executed.

31. The sum of the widths in the list of a FIELD statement must not exceed the record length specified in the OPEN statement.

32. The LSET and RSET statements are used to store data in the buffer.

33. So that numeric values may be placed in and removed from a buffer, BASIC includes the functions MKS$ and CVS. The function MKS$ (N) converts the numeric value N to a 4-character string value for the purpose of placing the numeric value into the buffer. The function CVS (X$) converts the string variable X$, defined in the FIELD statement, to a numeric value.

34. The GET #n, r statement reads the rth record from the random file assigned to filenumber n.

35. The PUT #n, r statement writes the rth record to the random file assigned to filenumber n.

36. If the second parameter in a GET or PUT statement is not included, then the system reads or writes the next record in sequence in the random file.

37. The function LOC (n) returns the record number of the last record read or written to the random file assigned to filenumber n.

38. The function LOF (n) returns information regarding the size of the random file assigned to filenumber n.

8.8 SELF-TEST EXERCISES

1. Consider the valid programs listed below. Explain the function of each program. Assume the following values are entered in response to the INPUT statements in a and d:

Description	Cost
CUTTER	$5.76
SCRAPER	2.59
SWIVEL	4.32
CARVER	3.78
EOF	

a)
```
100 REM CHAPTER 8 SELF-TEST 1A
110 OPEN "O", #1, "INV.DAT"
120 INPUT "DESCRIPTION"; D$
130 WHILE D$ <> "EOF"
140     INPUT "COST"; C
150     PRINT #1, D$; ","; C
160     INPUT "DESCRIPTION"; D$
170 WEND
180 PRINT #1, "EOF"; ","; 0
190 CLOSE #1
200 PRINT "JOB COMPLETE"
210 END
```

b)
```
100 REM CHAPTER 8 SELF-TEST 1B
110 OPEN "I", #1, "INV.DAT"
120 PRINT "DESCRIPTION", "COST"
130 PRINT "-----------", "----"
140 INPUT #1, D$, C
150 WHILE D$ <> "EOF"
160     PRINT D$, C
170     INPUT #1, D$, C
180 WEND
190 CLOSE #1
200 PRINT
210 PRINT "JOB COMPLETE"
220 END
```

c)
```
100 REM CHAPTER 8 SELF-TEST 1C
110 OPEN "I", #1, "INV.DAT"
120 OPEN "O", #2, "REPORT.DAT"
130 PRINT #2, "DESCRIPTION", "COST"
140 PRINT #2, "-----------", "----"
150 INPUT #1, D$, C
160 WHILE D$ <> "EOF"
170     PRINT #2, D$, C
180     INPUT #1, D$, C
190 WEND
200 PRINT #2,
210 PRINT #2, "JOB COMPLETE"
220 CLOSE #1, #2
230 PRINT
240 PRINT "JOB COMPLETE"
250 END
```

d)
```
100 REM CHAPTER 8 SELF-TEST 1D
110 OPEN "R", #1, "RINV.DAT", 14
120 FIELD #1, 10 AS D1$, 4 AS C$
130 INPUT "DESCRIPTION"; D$
140 WHILE D$ <> "EOF"
150     INPUT "COST"; C
160     LSET D1$ = D$
170     LSET C$ = MKS$(C)
180     PUT #1
190     INPUT "DESCRIPTION"; D$
200 WEND
210 CLOSE #1
220 PRINT "JOB COMPLETE"
230 END
```

2. Find the errors in the following programs.

a)
```
100 REM CHAPTER 8 SELF-TEST 2A
110 OPEN "O", #2, "INV.DAT"
120 INPUT #1, D$, C
130 WHILE D$ <> "EOF"
140    PRINT D$, C
150    INPUT #1, D$, C
160 WEND
170 CLOSE #1
180 END
```

b)
```
100 REM CHAPTER 8 SELF-TEST 2B
110 OPEN "R", #1, "RINV.DAT", 14
120 FIELD #1, 15 AS D1$, 4 AS C$
130 INPUT "RECORD NUMBER"; N
140 WHILE N <> -1
150    INPUT #1, N
160    PRINT D1$, CVS(C$)
170    INPUT "RECORD NUMBER"; N
180 WEND
190 CLOSE #1
200 PRINT "JOB COMPLETE"
210 END
```

3. Describe the following OPEN statements in terms of mode, filenumber and filespec.

a) `100 OPEN "O", #3, "ACCOUNT.DAT"`

b) `200 OPEN "I", #2, "RAWMAT.DAT"`

c) `300 OPEN "R", #2, "TOWNSHIP.DAT", 39`

4. Fill in the following:
   a) A record is composed of related _____.
   b) A file is composed of related _____.
   c) In BASIC, files may be organized _____ or _____.
   d) When a file is opened with mode O, a program can only _____ records to the file.
   e) When a file is opened with mode I, a program can only _____ records to the file.

5. Construct a PRINT #n statement that writes the values of A$, F and T to a sequential file in a manner that is consistent with the format required by the INPUT #n statement. Use filenumber 3.

6. Construct an INPUT #n statement that reads the values assigned to the sequential file in Exercise 5. Use filenumber 3.

7. For the following partial program, describe the OPEN statement in terms of mode, filenumber and filespec. Assume that the following items are entered in response to the INPUT statements in the order given: TIMECARD.DAT, I, 2.
```
100 REM CHAPTER 8 SELF-TEST 7
110 INPUT "FILENAME"; F$
120 INPUT "MODE"; M$
130 INPUT "FILENUMBER"; F
140 OPEN M$, #F, F$
```

8. Consider again Self-Test Exercise 1a which created the sequential file INV.DAT and the following partial program. Explain the function of this partial program.
```
100 REM CHAPTER 8 SELF-TEST 8
110 DIM D1$(4), C1(4)
120 OPEN "I", #2, "INV.DAT"
130 LET I = 1
140 INPUT #2, D$, C
150 WHILE D$ <> "EOF"
160    LET D1$(I) = D$
170    LET C1(I) = C
180    LET I = I + 1
190    INPUT #2, D$, C
200 WEND
```

9. Indicate the record length parameter for the OPEN statements that correspond to each of the following FIELD statements.
```
200 FIELD #2, 12 AS D$, 15 AS F$, 36 AS R$, 4 AS C$
300 FIELD #3, 120 AS L$
```

10. Given:
```
300 FIELD #2, 10 AS G$, 12 AS B$, 4 AS N$
310 LET D$ = "10-12-86"
320 LET H$ = "23956"
330 LET N = 5.67
340 LSET G$ = D$
350 RSET B$ = H$
360 LSET N$ = MKS$(N)
```
What is assigned to G$, B$ and N$? Use a ƀ to indicate a space.

11. Explain the functions of the ON ERROR GOTO statement and function EOF.

1. Consider the valid program listed below. Explain the function of this program. Assume the following values are entered in response to the INPUT statements.

Stock Item	Selling Price	Discount Code
138	$ 78.56	2
421	123.58	3
617	475.65	2
812	23.58	1
917	754.56	4
EOF		

```
100 REM EXERCISE 8.1
110 OPEN "O", #1, "SALES.DAT"
120 INPUT "STOCK ITEM"; S$
130 WHILE S$ <> "EOF"
140     INPUT "SELLING PRICE"; S
150     INPUT "DISCOUNT CODE"; C
160     PRINT #1, S$; ","; S; ","; C
170     INPUT "STOCK ITEM"; S$
180 WEND
190 PRINT #1, "EOF"; ","; 0; ","; 0
200 CLOSE #1
210 PRINT "JOB COMPLETE"
220 END
```

2. Write a program that lists in columns the contents of the sequential file created by the program in Exercise 1. A program that lists the contents of a file is often called a **file list program**. As part of the end-of-job routine, display the total number of records and average selling price.

3. Consider the following valid program which uses the file created in Exercise 1. Explain the function of this program. Assume the following values are entered in response to the INPUT statements.

Stock Item	Selling Price	Discount Code
943	$675.89	3
975	45.98	1
EOF		

```
100 REM EXERCISE 8.3
110 LET K1 = 0
120 LET K2 = 0
130 OPEN "I", #1, "SALES.DAT"
140 OPEN "O", #2, "NEWSALES.DAT"
150 INPUT #1, S$, S, C
160 WHILE S$ <> "EOF"
170     PRINT #2, S$; ","; S; ","; C
180     LET K1 = K1 + 1
190     INPUT #1, S$, S, C
200 WEND
210 CLOSE #1
220 INPUT "STOCK ITEM"; S$
230 WHILE S$ <> "EOF"
240     INPUT "SELLING PRICE"; S
250     INPUT "DISCOUNT CODE"; C
260     PRINT #2, S$; ","; S; ","; C
270     LET K2 = K2 + 1
280     INPUT "STOCK ITEM"; S$
290 WEND
300 PRINT #2, "EOF"; ","; 0; ","; 0
310 CLOSE #2
320 PRINT "NUMBER OF RECORDS IN FILE PRIOR TO ADDITIONS===>"; K1
330 PRINT "NUMBER OF RECORDS APPENDED TO FILE=============>"; K2
340 PRINT "TOTAL NUMBER OF RECORDS IN FILE================>"; K1 + K2
350 PRINT
360 PRINT "JOB COMPLETE"
370 END
```

4. Fill in the following:
   a) A sequential file must be _____ for _____ before a corresponding PRINT #n statement is executed.
   b) A sequential file must be _____ for _____ before a corresponding INPUT #n statement is executed.

c) A file may be opened as often as required provided it is ___ before each subsequent open.

d) A random file is always opened for _____.

e) A _____ statement is used to define the buffer.

f) Values are assigned to the buffer via the _____ and _____ statements.

g) _____ variables are valid in a FIELD statement. _____ variables are invalid in a FIELD statement.

5. List the three methods described in this chapter for determining end-of-file.

6. State the purpose of the ON ERROR GOTO 0 statement and the RESUME statement.

7. State the purpose of the special variables ERR and ERL. What error code corresponds to reading past the end-of-file on *your* BASIC system?

8. A program is required to read records from one of three sequential files, SALES1.DAT, SALES2.DAT and SALES3.DAT. Write an INPUT statement and OPEN statement that allow the program to open any of the three sequential files. Use filenumber 1.

9. Construct a PRINT #n statement that writes the values of A, B, C$ and D to a sequential file in the format required by the INPUT #n statement. Use filenumber 1.

10. Is the following sequence of INPUT #n statements valid for reading data from the sequential file created through the use of the PRINT #n statement in Exercise 9?

```
300 INPUT #1, A
310 INPUT #1, B
320 INPUT #1, C$
330 INPUT #1, D
```

11. A random file COUNT.DAT contains one record. The record contains one data item that corresponds to the number of records in the sequential file TABLE.DAT. Each record in TABLE.DAT contains three numeric values. Write a partial program that reads the record from COUNT.DAT and dynamically dimensions the parallel arrays A, B and C to the value found in the random record. Read the data items found in TABLE.DAT into the parallel arrays A, B and C, respectively. Be sure to include all file handling statements in the partial program.

12. Which of the following are invalid file handling statements? Why?

```
a) 100 OPEN 'FILE1.DAT', 'I', #1          f) 600 INPUT #2, A,
b) 200 OPEN M, #N, N$                     g) 700 CLOSE 'FILE1.DAT'
c) 300 PRINT #1,                          h) 800 ON ERROR GOTO 800
d) 400 PRINT #1, A,                       i) 900 WHILE EOF(#3)
e) 500 PRINT #1 USING '####.##'; A
```

13. State the purpose of the functions MKS$ and CVS.

14. Which of the following are invalid file handling statements? Why?

```
a) 100 OPEN 'R', #1, 'FILEA.DAT', -3      f) 600 LSET N$ = N
b) 200 GET #2                             g) 700 RSET N = N$
c) 300 GET #1, N                          h) 800 GET #1, LOC(1)
d) 400 GET #2, N$                         i) 900 LSET C$ = CVS(C)
e) 500 PUT #3
```

15. State the purpose of the functions LOC and LOF.

16. Rewrite the following invalid programs.

```
a) 100 REM EXERCISE 8.16A          b) 100 REM EXERCISE 8.16B
   110 CLOSE #3                       110 FIELD #3, 4 AS A$, 4 AS B$
   120 OPEN 'O', #1, 'QUARTER.DAT'    120 OPEN 'R', #1, 'RANQUAR.DAT', 6
   130 FOR I = 1 TO 100               130 FOR I = 1 TO 100
   140     INPUT #2, A                140     GET #2, I
   150     PRINT A                    150     PRINT MKS$(A$), MKS$(B$), MKS$(A$) + MKS$(B$)
   160 NEXT I                         160 NEXT I
   170 END                           170 CLOSE #3
                                      180 END
```

17. Describe the three types of file organization discussed in this chapter.

8.10 PROGRAMMING EXERCISES

Exercise 1: Creating a Master File

Purpose: To become familiar with creating a sequential file that is consistent with the format required by the INPUT #n statement.

Problem: Construct a program to create a sequential file named PAYMAST.DAT that represents the payroll master file for company PUC. Each record in the file describes an employee, including the year-to-date (YTD) payroll information, as shown under the Input Data.

Write the data to the file in the format required by the INPUT #n statement. If you do not plan to use the ON ERROR GOTO statement or the function EOF in the later exercises of this chapter, then write a trailer record as the last record to identify end-of-file. As part of the end-of-job routine, display a message indicating the file was created and the total number of records written to the file.

After the program creates the file properly, modify the program to validate the marital status and numeric values. The marital status should be M or S and the numeric values should be non-negative. Validation is discussed in Section 6.3. Select your own data to test the validation routines.

Input Data: Prepare and use the following sample data:

Employee Number	Employee Name	Dependents	Marital Status	Rate of Pay	Year-to-Date Gross Pay	Year-to-Date Federal With. Tax	Year-to-Date Social Security
123	Cole Jim	2	M	$12.50	5,345.23	$1,256.34	$725.15
124	Fiel Don	1	S	18.00	5,910.45	1,546.45	791.90
125	Dit Bill	1	S	13.00	4,115.23	1,035.78	585.72
126	Snow Joe	9	M	4.50	1,510.05	354.34	100.00
134	Hi Frank	0	M	8.75	9,298.65	2,678.25	576.23
167	Brink Ed	3	S	10.40	190.45	17.50	16.76
210	Liss Ted	6	M	8.85	7,098.04	2,120.55	825.35
234	Son Fred	2	M	6.75	0.00	0.00	0.00

Output Results: The sequential file PAYMAST.DAT is created in auxiliary storage. The following partial results are shown:

```
EMPLOYEE NUMBER? 123
EMPLOYEE NAME? COLE JIM
NUMBER OF DEPENDENTS? 2
MARITAL STATUS? M
RATE OF PAY? 12.50
YEAR-TO-DATE GROSS PAY? 5345.23
YEAR-TO-DATE WITHHOLDING TAX? 1256.34
YEAR-TO-DATE SOCIAL SECURITY? 725.15
        .
        .
        .
EMPLOYEE NUMBER? EOF

CREATION OF SEQUENTIAL FILE PAYMAST.DAT IS COMPLETE.
TOTAL NUMBER OF RECORDS WRITTEN TO PAYMAST.DAT IS 8.
JOB COMPLETE
```

Exercise 2: Master File List

Purpose: To become familiar with reading and displaying records in a sequential data file.

Problem: Write a program that displays the data items found in each employee record of the sequential file PAYMAST.DAT created in Programming Exercise 1. As part of the end-of-job routine, display the following totals: employee-record count, YTD gross pay, YTD federal withholding tax, and YTD social security tax.

Input Data: Use the sequential file PAYMAST.DAT created in Programming Exercise 1.

Output Results: The following results are displayed.

```
                 PAYROLL MASTER FILE LIST
                 ------------------------

 EMPLOYEE              MARITAL RATE OF   <-------YEAR-TO-DATE-------->
 NO. NAME        DEP. STATUS  PAY       GROSS PAY WITH. TAX SOC. SEC.
 --- --------    ---- ------- -------   --------- --------- ---------
 123 COLE JIM     2      M     12.50    5,345.23  1,256.34   725.15
 124 FIEL DON     1      S     18.00    5,910.45  1,546.45   791.90
 125 DIT BILL     1      S     13.00    4,115.23  1,035.78   585.72
 126 SNOW JOE     9      M      4.50    1,510.05    354.34   100.00
 134 HI FRANK     0      M      8.75    9,298.65  2,678.25   576.23
 167 BRINK ED     3      S     10.40      190.45     17.50    16.76
 210 LISS TED     6      M      8.85    7,098.04  2,120.55   825.35
 234 SON FRED     2      M      6.75        0.00      0.00     0.00

 TOTAL NUMBER OF RECORDS====================>      8
 TOTAL YEAR-TO-DATE GROSS PAY===============> 33,468.10
 TOTAL YEAR-TO-DATE WITHHOLDING TAX=========>  9,009.21
 TOTAL YEAR-TO-DATE SOCIAL SECURITY TAX=====>  3,621.11

 JOB COMPLETE
```

**Exercise 3:
Writing a Report to
Auxiliary Storage**

Purpose: To become familiar with writing a report to a sequential file.

Problem: Same as Programming Exercise 2, except write the report to the sequential file REPORT. DAT.

Input Data: Use the sequential file PAYMAST. DAT created in Programming Exercise 1.

Output Results: The sequential file REPORT. DAT is created in auxiliary storage. The following results are displayed:

```
REPORT COMPLETE AND STORED UNDER THE FILENAME REPORT.DAT.
JOB COMPLETE
```

**Exercise 4:
Appending Records to
the End of a File**

Purpose: To become familiar with appending records to the end of a sequential file.

Problem: Write a program that will append new employee records to the end of PAYMAST. DAT created in Programming Exercise 1. If your BASIC system allows for a file to be opened in the append mode, you may use this option. If your BASIC system does not allow for the append mode, then you must write all the records in PAYMAST. DAT to another file and add the new employee records before closing this file.
(*Hint:* see Exercise 3 in Section 8.9, Test Your BASIC Skills.)

Input Data: Prepare and use the following sample data:

Employee Number	Employee Name	Dependents	Marital Status	Rate of Pay
345	Lie Jeff	2	M	$6.60
612	Abe Mike	1	S	8.75

Assign all year-to-date items a value of zero.

Output Results: The following results are displayed:

```
EMPLOYEE NUMBER? 345
EMPLOYEE NAME? LIE JEFF
NUMBER OF DEPENDENTS? 2
MARITAL STATUS? M
RATE OF PAY? 6.60

EMPLOYEE NUMBER? 612
EMPLOYEE NAME? ABE MIKE
NUMBER OF DEPENDENTS? 1
MARITAL STATUS? S
RATE OF PAY? 8.75

EMPLOYEE NUMBER? EOF

NUMBER OF EMPLOYEE RECORDS IN ORIGINAL MASTER FILE===> 8
NUMBER OF EMPLOYEE RECORDS APPENDED===================> 2
NUMBER OF EMPLOYEE RECORDS IN NEW MASTER FILE========> 10
```

Purpose: To become familiar with the maintenance of a sequential file.

Problem: Write two programs. The first program should create a transaction file made up of the changes to the payroll master file PAYMAST. DAT. The second program should process the transaction file against the payroll master file.

Use a modified version of the program solution for Programming Exercise 1 to create the transaction file. Each record in the transaction file should include eight data items that correspond to the eight data items in the payroll master file plus one data item (a transaction code) which determines if the transaction record is an add, change or delete. Validate all transaction codes. Also enter the transaction records in ascending sequence by employee number. For changes and deletions use the null character to indicate string items that are not to be changed and use a −1 to indicate numeric items that are not to be changed. See Programming Case Study 22. Call the transaction file PAYTRANS. DAT.

The second program should match and merge the current payroll master file PAYMAST. DAT with the transaction file PAYTRANS. DAT and create a new payroll master file NEWPAYMA. DAT. Include the following diagnostic messages:

```
**ERROR** ADDITION INVALID - EMPLOYEE XXX ALREADY IN FILE
**ERROR** TRANSACTION INVALID - EMPLOYEE XXX NOT IN FILE
```

In the second program, display as part of the end-of-job routine the total number of additions, changes, deletions, errors, transactions and the number of records in the new master file.

Input Data: Use the following sample data. The transaction code A represents an addition, C a record change and D a record delete. "Null" represents the null character. To assign the null character to a variable, press the Enter key in response to the INPUT statement.

Transaction Code	Employee No.	Name	Dependents	Marital Status	Rate of Pay	Gross Pay	Federal With. Tax	Social Security Tax
							Year-to-Date	
C	124	Null	4	Null	−1	$6,345.20	−1	−1
A	126	Fish Joe	1	M	$6.00	0	0	0
D	134	Null	−1	Null	−1	−1	−1	−1
A	143	Byrd Ed	3	S	9.00	0	0	0
C	167	Null	0	Null	−1	−1	−1	−1
C	225	Null	−1	S	−1	−1	−1	−1
D	250	Null	−1	Null	−1	−1	−1	−1

Output Results: The first set of partial results shows the last record entered and the end-of-job messages for the program that creates the transaction file PAYTRANS. DAT.

Program 1 Output Results:

```
TYPE OF MAINTENANCE (A, C, D)? D
EMPLOYEE NUMBER? 250
EMPLOYEE NAME?
NUMBER OF DEPENDENTS? -1
MARITAL STATUS?
RATE OF PAY? -1
YEAR-TO-DATE GROSS PAY? -1
YEAR-TO-DATE WITHHOLDING TAX? -1
YEAR-TO-DATE SOCIAL SECURITY TAX? -1

TYPE OF MAINTENANCE (A, C, D)? EOF

CREATION OF SEQUENTIAL FILE PAYTRANS.DAT IS COMPLETE.
TOTAL NUMBER OF RECORDS WRITTEN TO PAYTRANS.DAT IS 7 .
JOB COMPLETE
```

The second set of results displayed show the diagnostic messages for the program that update the payroll master file. Following the execution of Program 2, display the contents of PAYMAST. DAT and NEWPAYMA. DAT to verify the additions, changes and deletions.

Program 2 Output Results:

```
**ERROR** ADDITION INVALID - EMPLOYEE 126 ALREADY IN FILE
**ERROR** TRANSACTION INVALID - EMPLOYEE 225 NOT IN FILE
**ERROR** TRANSACTION INVALID - EMPLOYEE 250 NOT IN FILE

TOTAL NUMBER OF RECORDS ADDED==============> 1
TOTAL NUMBER OF RECORDS CHANGED===========> 2
TOTAL NUMBER OF RECORDS DELETED===========> 1
TOTAL NUMBER OF TRANSACTION ERRORS========> 3
TOTAL NUMBER OF TRANSACTIONS==============> 7
TOTAL NUMBER OF RECORDS IN NEW MASTER=====> 8
```

Exercise 6:
Creating a Random
File for Quarterly
Payroll Totals

Purpose: To become familiar with creating a random file.

Problem: Write a program that creates a random file with four records. Each record contains payroll information with respect to the following time periods:

Record Number	Time Period
1	January–March
2	April–June
3	July–September
4	October–December

Each record is made up of the following quarterly employee totals: gross pay, withholding tax and social security tax. To ensure accuracy, use double-precision variables. Define the variables in the FIELD statement to have a width of eight and assign values to the buffer using the function MKD$ rather than MKS$. Call the random file PAYQUAR.DAT.

Input Data: Use the following sample data:

Quarter	Gross Pay	Withholding Tax	Social Security
1	$11,231.12	$3,998.34	$1,121.45
2	8,345.23	2,456.23	913.75
3	13,891.75	2,554.64	1,585.11
4	0.00	0.00	0.00

Output Results: The random file PAYQUAR.DAT is created in auxiliary storage. The following is displayed for the first record entered:

```
QUARTER? 1
GROSS PAY? 11231.12
WITHHOLDING TAX? 3998.34
SOCIAL SECURITY? 1121.45
```

Exercise 7:
Random Access
of Quarterly
Payroll Totals

Purpose: To become familiar with accessing records in a random file.

Problem: Write a program that will randomly access any record in PAYQUAR.DAT based upon a user request. If the user enters 2, then the program should display the payroll totals for the second quarter. If the user enters 1, then the program should display the payroll totals for the first quarter. Use the function CVD rather than CVS to convert numeric values from the buffer.

Input Data: Use the random file PAYQUAR.DAT created in Programming Exercise 6.

Output Results: The following results are displayed for quarter 2:

```
QUARTER? 2
GROSS PAY=============>   8,345.23
WITHHOLDING TAX======>   2,456.23
SOCIAL SECURITY TAX==>     913.75
```

Exercise 8:
Employee Record
Retrieval and
Update—An Index File

Purpose: To become familiar with the use of indexed files.

Problem: Construct two programs. The first program is to take the file PAYMAST.DAT described in Programming Exercise 1 and create an index in a sequential file made up of the employee numbers and a corresponding random file made up of the data in PAYMAST.DAT. Declare 200 elements for the array written to the sequential file. See Program 8.8 in Section 8.6.

The second program is to be a menu-driven program that allows the user to display, add, change and delete records on a random basis. The user informs the system of the record to access by entering the employee number. See Program 8.9 in Section 8.6.

The menu-driven program should accept the following function codes:

Code	Function	Code	Function
1	Display record	4	Delete record
2	Add record	5	End program
3	Change record		

Input Data: Update the payroll file with the sample data given in Programming Exercise 5.

Output Results: The program should generate results similar to Program 8.9 presented earlier in this chapter.

Exercise 9:
Payroll Problem VII—
Multiple File
Processing

Purpose: To become familiar with multiple file processing.

Problem: Write two programs. The first program is to create an hours worked sequential file called TIMECARD.DAT made up of records containing an employee number and hours worked for a biweekly payroll period. The employee numbers in this file correspond to the employee numbers in the payroll master file PAYMAST.DAT created in Programming Exercise 1.

The second program is to match the records in TIMECARD.DAT and PAYMAST.DAT and generate a preliminary payroll report similar to that of Payroll Problem VI in Programming Exercise 7.13. Since the data in PAYMAST.DAT differs from that used in Payroll Problem VI the results will not be the same. Use the same formulas to compute the gross pay, federal withholding tax, social security tax and net pay as in Payroll Problem VI.
(*Hint:* Although this problem does not update the master file, the logic regarding matching records is similar to Program 8.5 of Programming Case Study 22.)

Input Data: Use the file created in Programming Exercise 1 for the master file. Use the following data in creating TIMECARD.DAT.

Employee Number	Hours Worked	Employee Number	Hours Worked
123	80	167	68
125	100	168	68
126	20	210	73.5
134	72	234	80

Output Results: The following results are displayed:

```
EMPLOYEE                                          YEAR-TO-DATE
NUMBER   GROSS PAY   FED. TAX   SOC. SEC.   NET PAY   SOC. SEC.
-------- ---------   --------   ---------   -------   ------------
  123     1,000.00    137.14      67.00     795.86      792.15
***NOTE*** EMPLOYEE 124 HAS NO TIME CARD RECORD
  125     1,430.00    266.47      95.81   1,067.72      681.53
  126        90.00      0.00       6.03      83.97      106.03
  134       630.00     77.61      42.21     510.18      618.44
  167       707.20     71.12      47.38     588.70       64.14
***ERROR*** EMPLOYEE 168 HAS NO MASTER RECORD
  210       650.48     41.86      43.58     565.04      868.93
  234       540.00     49.23      36.18     454.59       36.18

TOTAL GROSS PAY===============>   5,047.68
TOTAL WITHHOLDING TAX=======>       643.43
TOTAL SOCIAL SECURITY TAX===>       338.19
TOTAL NET PAY================>    4,066.06

JOB COMPLETE
```

MORE ON STRINGS AND FUNCTIONS 9

Computers were originally built to perform mathematical calculations. Today, they are still used for that purpose. However, more and more applications require computers to process string data as well. Section 3.5 briefly introduced four string functions, LEFT$, MID$, RIGHT$ and LEN, giving some indication of the ability of BASIC to manipulate string data. As you shall see in this chapter, BASIC includes several additional string functions and string statements that place it among the better programming languages for manipulating letters, numbers, words and phrases.

BASIC also includes numeric functions to handle common mathematical calculations. For example, it is often necessary in programming to obtain the square root or the logarithm of a number. In this chapter we will discuss the two numeric functions that handle these two calculations as well as ten others that are frequently found with BASIC systems.

A second type of function that will be discussed in this chapter is the **user-defined function**. With a function that is defined by the user, numeric or string functions can be created to perform an often needed task.

Table 9.1 shows a list of some common string functions discussed in this chapter and their availability on some popular computer systems. Most of the function names are followed by an argument in parentheses. To be used, these functions need only be referred to by name in a LET, PRINT or IF statement and, if necessary, followed by arguments in parentheses.

In the sections that follow, the concatenation operator +, each of the string functions listed in Table 9.1, and the LINE INPUT and MID$ statements will be discussed.

**9.1
INTRODUCTION**

**9.2
STRING
FUNCTIONS AND
STATEMENTS**

TABLE 9.1 String Functions Common to Most BASIC Systems*

Function	Function Value	Apple	COMMO-DORE	DEC Rainbow	DEC VAX-11	IBM PC and Macintosh	TRS-80
ASC(C$)	Returns a two-digit numeric value that is equivalent in ASCII code to the single character C$.	Yes	Yes	Yes	ASCII(C$)	Yes	Yes
CHR$(N)	Returns a single string character that is equivalent in ASCII code to the numeric argument N.	Yes	Yes	Yes	Yes	Yes	Yes
DATE$	Returns the date as a string in the form mm-dd-yyyy.	No	Yes	No	Yes	Yes	Yes
INKEY$	Provides for a program to accept a single character from the keyboard without the Enter key being pressed.	No	GET C$	Yes	No	Yes	Yes
INPUT$(N)	Provides for a program to accept N number of characters from the keyboard without the Enter key being pressed.	GET C$	No	No	No	Yes	No
INSTR(P,X$,S$)	Returns the beginning position of the substring S$ in string X$. P indicates the position the search begins in X$ and may be omitted from the argument list. If the search for S$ in X$ is unsuccessful, INSTR returns a value of 0.	No	No	Yes	Yes	Yes	No
LEFT$(X$, N)	Extracts the leftmost N characters of the string argument X$.	Yes	Yes	Yes	Yes	Yes	Yes
LEN(X$)	Returns the length of the string argument X$.	Yes	Yes	Yes	Yes	Yes	Yes
MID$(X$,P,N)	Extracts N characters of the string argument X$ beginning at position P.	Yes	Yes	Yes	Yes	Yes	Yes
RIGHT$(X$, N)	Extracts the rightmost N characters of the string argument X$.	Yes	Yes	Yes	Yes	Yes	Yes
SPACE$(N)	Returns N number of spaces.	No	No	Yes	Yes	Yes	No
SPC(N)	Displays N spaces. May only be used in a PRINT statement.	Yes	Yes	Yes	No	Yes	No
STR$(N)	Returns the string equivalent of the numeric argument N.	Yes	Yes	Yes	Yes	Yes	Yes
STRING$(N,"C")	Returns N times the character C within quotation marks.	No	No	Yes	Yes	Yes	Yes
TIME$	Returns the time of day in 24-hour notation as a string in the form hh:mm:ss.	No	Yes	No	Yes	Yes	Yes
VAL(X$)	Returns the numeric equivalent of the string argument X$.	Yes	Yes	Yes	Yes	Yes	Yes

*Check the specifications on your BASIC system in the user's manual for the format of the value returned by these functions. Some of the computer systems designated as not having a particular function may in fact have the function under some other operating system.

Concatenation, Substrings and Character Counting Revisited—+, LEN, LEFT$, RIGHT$ and MID$

The extraction of substrings from a large string or the combination of two or more strings are important in manipulating non-numeric data. In Section 3.5 the concatenation operator + and the LEN, LEFT$, RIGHT$ and MID$ functions were briefly introduced. Recall that concatenation is the only string operation allowed in BASIC. It joins two strings to form a new string. For example,

```
500 LET A$ = "ABC" + "DEF"
```

assigns A\$ the value ABCDEF. The second string is joined to the right end of the first string to form the result, which is then assigned to A\$. More than one concatenation operator may appear in a single assignment statement. For example, if X\$ = RESIST⍉ and Y\$ = THE URGE⍉ and Z\$ = TO CODE, then

```
600 LET T$ = X$ + Y$ + Z$
```

assigns T\$ the string RESIST THE URGE TO CODE.

The function LEN returns the length of the argument. The argument may be a string constant, string variable or string expression. Table 9.2 and Program 9.1 illustrate the use of the function LEN.

TABLE 9.2   Examples of the LEN Function

Value of Variable	The Statement	Results In
S\$ = IBM PC	100 LET L1 = LEN(S\$)	L1 = 6
X\$ = APPLE	200 LET L2 = LEN(X\$)	L2 = 5
	300 LET L3 = LEN("TRS-80")	L3 = 6
	400 LET L4 = LEN("")	L4 = 0
Y\$ = null	500 LET L5 = LEN(Y\$)	L5 = 0

```
100 REM PROGRAM 9.1
110 REM EXAMPLES OF THE USE OF THE FUNCTION LEN
120 REM ****************************************
130 LET B$ = "STRUCTURED"
140 LET C$ = "PROGRAMMING"
150 LET L = LEN(B$)
160 PRINT B$; " HAS"; L; "CHARACTERS."
170 PRINT C$; " HAS"; LEN(C$); "CHARACTERS."
180 PRINT B$ + " " + C$; " HAS"; LEN(B$ + " " + C$); "CHARACTERS."
190 END

RUN

STRUCTURED HAS 10 CHARACTERS.
PROGRAMMING HAS 11 CHARACTERS.
STRUCTURED PROGRAMMING HAS 22 CHARACTERS.
```

PROGRAM 9.1

In Program 9.1, LEN (B\$) in line 150 assigns the variable L a value of 10. In line 170, LEN (C\$) is displayed as 11. In line 180, the function LEN returns the length of the string expression B\$ + " " + C\$ as 22.

The string functions LEFT\$, MID\$ and RIGHT\$ may be used to extract **substrings** from a string constant, string variable or string expression. A substring is a part of a string. For example: some substrings of RETURN OF THE JEDI are RETURN, JEDI, OF T and ED. All three functions reference substrings based on the position of characters within the argument string, where the leftmost character of the argument string is position 1 and the next position 2 and so on. For example, in the string RETURN OF THE JEDI, the substring RETURN begins in position 1 and the substring JEDI begins in position 15.

The function LEFT\$ (X\$, N) extracts a substring starting with the leftmost character (position 1) of the string X\$. The length of the substring is determined by the integer value of the length argument N. For example, the following statement assigns a value of RETURN to S\$.

```
300 LET S$ = LEFT$("RETURN OF THE JEDI", 6)
```

RETURN begins in position 1 and has a length of 6. The quotation marks are not part of the string.

The function RIGHT\$ (X\$, N) extracts a substring starting with the rightmost character of the string argument X\$. The length of the substring is determined by the value of the length argument N. For example, if C\$ is equal to the string RAIDERS OF THE LOST ARK, then the following statement assigns G\$ the substring ARK:

```
400 LET G$ = RIGHT$(C$, 3)
```

The function MID$ (X$, P, N) extracts a substring beginning with the character in position P of X$. The length of the substring is determined by the value of the length argument N. For example, if A$ is equal to the string EVERY DOG MUST HAVE HIS DAY, then the following statement assigns V$ the substring DOG MUST HAVE:

```
500 LET V$ = MID$(V$, 7, 13)
```

Table 9.3 illustrates the use of the functions LEFT$, RIGHT$ and MID$.

TABLE 9.3   Examples of the LEFT$, RIGHT$ **and** MID$ **Functions**

Assume S$ is equal to: IF SOMETHING CAN GO WRONG, IT WILL

The Statement	*Results In*
`100 LET C$ = LEFT$(S$, 12)`	C$ = IF SOMETHING
`200 LET F$ = LEFT$(S$, 1.4)`	F$ = I
`300 LET H$ = LEFT$(S$, 0)`	H$ = null
`400 LET J$ = RIGHT$(S$, 7)`	J$ = IT WILL
`500 LET P$ = RIGHT$('TO BE', -1)`	Illegal function call
`600 LET R$ = RIGHT$(S$, 50)`	R$ = S$
`700 LET T$ = MID$(S$, 3 + 4, 6)`	T$ = ETHING
`800 LET U$ = MID$(LEFT$(S$, 4), 2, 1)`	U$ = F
`900 LET V$ = MID$(S$, 75, 4)`	V$ = null
`950 LET X$ = MID$(S$, 18, 200)`	X$ = GO WRONG, IT WILL

In line 200 of Table 9.3, the argument 1.4 is rounded to the value of 1.* In line 300, the numeric argument 0 causes the system to return the null string. In line 500, the negative argument results in an illegal function call. Line 500 is invalid. Lines 600 and 950 of Table 9.3 also show that if the length argument is greater than the length of the string argument, the function returns a substring that begins at the specified position and includes the remaining portion of the string. Line 800 shows that you may include a string function as the string argument. Finally, line 900 illustrates that a null string is returned when the position P specified in the MID$ function is greater than the length of the argument string. BASIC interprets the position argument P and the length argument N of the functions LEFT$, MID$ and RIGHT$ according to the following rules:

String Function Rule 1: If the position argument P or the length argument N is a decimal fraction, the value of N or P is rounded.

String Function Rule 2: If the length argument is 0, then the function returns a null string. If the length argument is less than 0, then the function call is illegal.

String Function Rule 3: If the position argument P for the MID$ function is less than zero, the function returns a substring that begins at position 1.

---

*Some BASIC systems truncate rather than round.

String Function Rule 4: If the position argument P for the MID$ function is greater than the length of the string argument, the function returns a null string.

String Function Rule 5: If the length argument N is greater than the remaining length of the string argument, the function returns a substring that begins at the specified position and includes the remaining portion of the string.

The following program makes use of the functions LEN and MID$. The basic purpose of the program is to search for words in a sentence. Each time a word is found, the program displays it on a separate line. The program assumes that each word, except for the last, is followed by a space.

```
100 REM PROGRAM 9.2
110 REM DISPLAYING EACH WORD IN A SENTENCE
120 REM ********************************
130 PRINT "ENTER THE SENTENCE WITHOUT PUNCTUATION"
140 INPUT X$
150 LET P = 1
160 PRINT
170 PRINT "WORDS IN THE SENTENCE:"
180 FOR I = 1 TO LEN(X$)
190    IF MID$(X$, I, 1) = " " THEN 200 ELSE 220
200       PRINT TAB(23); MID$(X$, P, I - P)
210       LET P = I + 1
220 NEXT I
230 REM *****DISPLAY THE LAST WORD*****
240 PRINT TAB(23); MID$(X$, P, LEN(X$))
250 PRINT "JOB COMPLETE"
260 END

RUN

ENTER THE SENTENCE WITHOUT PUNCTUATION
? IF AN EXPERIMENT WORKS SOMETHING HAS GONE WRONG

WORDS IN THE SENTENCE:
                      IF
                      AN
                      EXPERIMENT
                      WORKS
                      SOMETHING
                      HAS
                      GONE
                      WRONG

JOB COMPLETE
```

PROGRAM 9.2

In line 150 the variable P is assigned a value of 1. This variable is used later in line 200 to indicate the beginning position of each word and in line 240 to display the last word in the sentence. Line 190 in the For loop tests each character in the sentence to determine if it is a space. If a character is a space, then line 200 displays the word beginning at position P with a length of I − P. Line 210 sets P equal to a value which is equivalent to the start of the next word. Since the last word in the sentence does not end with a space, line 240, instead of line 200, is used to display the last word.

Companies that advertise and sell their products by mail rely heavily on computer-generated personalized letters. These letters, which may be several pages in length, are identical except for the receiver's name in various places of the letter. These letters look like they have been personally typed by the sender on individual forms. The following problem involves writing a program to generate letters and mailing labels, depending on the operator's response to a menu.

Programming Case Study 26: Generating Personalized Letters and Mailing Labels

Problem

Given the data file POTCUS. DAT of potential customers:

Full Name of Husband	Street Address	City State Zip Code	First Name of Wife
MR. JOHN CALUM	1122-171ST	HAMMOND, IN 46323	MARY
MR. LOUIS FREE	402 TOD	HOBART, IN 46365	ELLEN
MR. FRANK ELY	312-45TH	EAST CHICAGO, IN 46312	JODI
MR. STEVE HATT	89 OLCOT	GARY, IN 46404	ELLEN

Write a menu-driven program that generates a personalized letter or mailing label for each of the potential customers in the POTCUS. DAT file. The trailer record has EOF in the position normally used for the full name of the husband.*

The general form of the personalized letter is as follows:

Full Name of Husband
Street Address
City State Zip Code
DEAR FIRST NAME OF HUSBAND:

   HOW ARE THE LAST NAME OF HUSBAND S DOING? WE JUST PUT OUR LECTRO VACUUM CLEANER ON SALE FOR $299.95.

   THIS SUPER SCOOPER WILL MAKE AN IDEAL MOTHER'S DAY GIFT FOR WIFE'S FIRST NAME . SHE WILL LOVE YOU ALL THE MORE.

   IF YOU ARE INTERESTED, FIRST NAME OF HUSBAND , OUR FRIENDLY SALES REPRESENTATIVE, RITA, WILL BE IN CITY NAME DURING THE FIRST WEEK OF MAY.

   TO SET UP A PERSONAL APPOINTMENT WITH RITA TO DEMONSTRATE OUR LECTRO SUPER SCOOPER, CALL 1-219-844-0520 AND ASK FOR FRED.

                    SINCERELY YOURS,

The general form of the mailing label is as follows:

Full Name of Husband
Street Address
City State Zip Code

The shaded areas in the output represent personalized information that will change from letter to letter or from label to label.

   Before any records are processed, display the following menu so the operator may choose the output desired:

MENU FOR PERSONALIZED LETTERS AND MAILING LABELS

    CODE   FUNCTION
      1   — DISPLAY PERSONALIZED LETTERS
      2   — DISPLAY MAILING LABELS

    ENTER A CODE OF 1 OR 2?

Verify that the code is a 1 or 2.
An analysis of the problem and a program solution follow.

---

*On some computer systems, the ON ERROR GOTO statement or function EOF may be used to test for the end-of-file mark. In either case, a trailer record is not required. A trailer record is used in this problem to ensure that the overall logic is compatible with all computer systems.

Program Tasks

1) Use the following top-down chart:

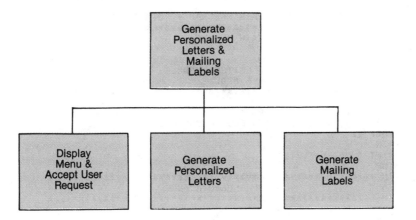

2) Write an internal subroutine to clear the screen, display the menu, request a code, and validate the code entered by the operator.

3) After a valid code is entered, return control to the Main module and perform the following tasks:

a) Open the data file POTCUS.DAT for input.

b) Use an IF statement to call either an internal subroutine for generating the personalized letters or an internal subroutine for generating the mailing labels.

c) After control returns to the Main module, close the data file POTCUS.DAT and display JOB COMPLETE.

4) To generate the personalized letters, perform the following tasks using an internal subroutine:

a) Read the first record from POTCUS.DAT. Use the following variable names:

  N\$ = Full name of husband
  S\$ = Street address
  A\$ = City, state zip code
  W\$ = First name of wife

b) Use a While loop to process the data file.

c) Use the function MID\$ to extract the husband's first and last name, which are separated by a space. Use the function RIGHT\$ to determine if the last name ends with an S. If so, an E must be added to the last name before it is pluralized.

d) Use the function MID\$ to extract the name of the city. Each city terminates with a comma.

e) Clear the screen and display the personalized letter.

f) Following the letter display the message:

  `PRESS ENTER KEY TO VIEW THE NEXT LETTER....`

g) Read the next record from POTCUS.DAT.

5) In the subroutine that generates the mailing labels, do the following:

a) Read the first record from POTCUS.DAT.

b) Use a While loop to process the data file.

c) Within the While loop display mailing labels for four records and then display the following message:

  `PRESS ENTER KEY TO VIEW NEXT SET OF MAILING LABELS....`

```
1000 REM PROGRAM 9.3
1010 REM GENERATING PERSONALIZED LETTERS AND MAILING LABELS
1020 REM N$ = FULL NAME OF HUSBAND    S$ = STREET ADDRESS
1030 REM A$ = CITY, STATE ZIP CODE    W$ = FIRST NAME OF WIFE
1040 REM F$ = FIRST NAME OF HUSBAND   L$ = LAST NAME OF HUSBAND
1050 REM C$ = CITY
1060 REM FILE PROCESSED BY THIS PROGRAM - POTCUS.DAT
1070 REM *********************************************************
1080 REM *                      MAIN MODULE                      *
1090 REM *                                                       *
1100 REM * CALL DISPLAY MENU                                     *
1110 REM * CALL PERSONALIZED LETTERS MODULE                      *
1120 REM * CALL MAILING LABELS MODULE                            *
1130 REM *********************************************************
1140 GOSUB 2030
1150 OPEN "I", #1, "POTCUS.DAT"
1160 IF F = 1 THEN GOSUB 3030 ELSE GOSUB 4030
1170 CLOSE #1
1180 PRINT
1190 PRINT "JOB COMPLETE"
1200 STOP
2000 REM *********************************************************
2010 REM *                  DISPLAY MENU MODULE                  *
2020 REM *********************************************************
2030 CLS
2040 PRINT
2050 PRINT "   MENU FOR PERSONALIZED LETTERS AND MAILING LABELS"
2060 PRINT "   --------------------------------------------------"
2070 PRINT
2080 PRINT "            CODE      FUNCTION"
2090 PRINT "            ----      --------"
2100 PRINT "             1   -    DISPLAY PERSONALIZED LETTERS"
2110 PRINT "             2   -    DISPLAY MAILING LABELS"
2120 PRINT
2130 INPUT "            ENTER A CODE OF 1 OR 2"; F
2140 IF F = 1 OR F = 2 THEN 2170
2150    PRINT "            CODE OUT OF RANGE, PLEASE"
2160    GOTO 2130
2170 RETURN
3000 REM *********************************************************
3010 REM *              PERSONALIZED LETTERS MODULE              *
3020 REM *********************************************************
3030 INPUT #1, N$, S$, A$, W$
3040 WHILE N$ <> "EOF"
3050    REM *****DETERMINE FIRST NAME AND LAST NAME OF HUSBAND*****
3060    FOR I = 5 TO LEN(N$)
3070       IF MID$(N$, I, 1) <> " " THEN 3110
3080          LET F$ = MID$(N$, 5, I - 1)
3090          LET L$ = MID$(N$, I + 1, LEN(N$))
3095          IF RIGHT$(L$, 1) = "S" THEN LET L$ = L$ + "E"
3100          GOTO 3130
3110    NEXT I
3120    REM *****DETERMINE NAME OF CITY*****
3130    FOR I = 1 TO LEN(A$)
3140       IF MID$(A$, I, 1) <> "," THEN 3170
3150          LET C$ = MID$(A$, 1, I - 1)
3160          GOTO 3190
3170    NEXT I
3180    REM *****DISPLAY PERSONALIZED LETTER*****
3190    CLS
3200    PRINT N$
3210    PRINT S$
3220    PRINT A$
3230    PRINT
3240    PRINT "DEAR "; F$; ":"
3250    PRINT
3260    PRINT "    HOW ARE THE "; L$; "S DOING?  WE JUST PUT OUR"
3270    PRINT "LECTRO VACUUM CLEANER ON SALE FOR $299.95."
3280    PRINT
3290    PRINT "    THIS SUPER SCOOPER WILL MAKE AN IDEAL MOTHER'S"
3300    PRINT "DAY GIFT FOR "; W$; ".  SHE WILL LOVE YOU ALL THE MORE."
3310    PRINT
3320    PRINT "    IF YOU ARE INTERESTED, "; F$; ", OUR FRIENDLY SALES"
3330    PRINT "REPRESENTATIVE, RITA, WILL BE IN "; C$; " DURING THE"
3340    PRINT "FIRST WEEK OF MAY."
3350    PRINT
3360    PRINT "    TO SET UP A PERSONAL APPOINTMENT WITH RITA TO"
3370    PRINT "DEMONSTRATE OUR LECTRO SUPER SCOOPER, CALL"
3380    PRINT "1-219-844-0520 AND ASK FOR FRED."
3390    PRINT
3400    PRINT TAB(21); "SINCERELY YOURS,"
3410    PRINT
3420    INPUT "PRESS ENTER KEY TO VIEW THE NEXT LETTER...."; X$
3430    INPUT #1, N$, S$, A$, W$
3440 WEND
```

PROGRAM 9.3

```
3450 RETURN
4000 REM ****************************************************
4010 REM *              MAILING LABELS MODULE               *
4020 REM ****************************************************
4030 CLS
4040 LET C = 0
4050 INPUT #1, N$, S$, A$, W$
4060 WHILE N$ <> "EOF"
4070    PRINT
4080    PRINT
4090    PRINT N$
4100    PRINT S$
4110    PRINT A$
4120    LET C = C + 1
4130    IF C < 4 THEN 4180
4140       PRINT
4150       INPUT "PRESS ENTER KEY TO VIEW NEXT SET OF MAILING LABELS...."; X$
4160       CLS
4170       LET C = 0
4180    INPUT #1, N$, S$, A$, W$
4190 WEND
4200 RETURN
4210 END
RUN
```

PROGRAM 9.3
(continued)

When the RUN command is issued for Program 9.3, line 1140 transfers control
to the Display Menu module lines 2000 through 2170 and the following menu is
displayed:

```
MENU FOR PERSONALIZED LETTERS AND MAILING LABELS
------------------------------------------------

        CODE     FUNCTION
        ----     --------
         1   -   DISPLAY PERSONALIZED LETTERS
         2   -   DISPLAY MAILING LABELS

        ENTER A CODE OF 1 OR 2?
```

If the operator enters a code of 1, then control returns to the Main module and line
1160 transfers control to the Personalized Letters module, which generates a
personalized letter for every record found in POTCUS.DAT. The first For loop in
this module extracts the first and last name of the husband. The first name is
assigned to F$. The last name is assigned to L$. The second For loop extracts the
name of the city and assigns it to C$.

Lines 3200 through 3410 display the personalized letter for the first record as
follows:

```
MR. JOHN CALUM
1122-171ST
HAMMOND, IN 46323

DEAR JOHN:

    HOW ARE THE CALUMS DOING?  WE JUST PUT OUR
LECTRO VACUUM CLEANER ON SALE FOR $299.95.

    THIS SUPER SCOOPER WILL MAKE AN IDEAL MOTHER'S
DAY GIFT FOR MARY.  SHE WILL LOVE YOU ALL THE MORE.

    IF YOU ARE INTERESTED, JOHN, OUR FRIENDLY SALES
REPRESENTATIVE, RITA, WILL BE IN HAMMOND DURING THE
FIRST WEEK OF MAY.

    TO SET UP A PERSONAL APPOINTMENT WITH RITA TO
DEMONSTRATE OUR LECTRO SUPER SCOOPER, CALL
1-219-844-0520 AND ASK FOR FRED.

                    SINCERELY YOURS,

PRESS ENTER KEY TO VIEW THE NEXT LETTER....?
```

The Print Screen key on a personal computer with a printer attached prints the letter displayed on the screen. Shortly, instructions that will eliminate the need for the input prompt message displayed on the last line will be discussed.

If the operator enters a code of 2 following the display of the menu, then line 1160 transfers control to the Mailing Labels module which generates a mailing label for every record found in POTCUS.DAT. The logic used in the Mailing Labels module lines 4000 through 4200 is straightforward. The following mailing labels are generated by this module:

```
MR. JOHN CALUM
1122-171ST
HAMMOND, IN 46323


MR. LOUIS FREE
402 TOD
HOBART, IN 46365


MR. FRANK ELY
312-45TH
EAST CHICAGO, IN 46312


MR. STEVE HATT
89 OLCOT
GARY, IN 46404

PRESS ENTER KEY TO VIEW NEXT SET OF MAILING LABELS....?
```

Substring Searching and Replacement— INSTR Function and MID$ Statement

Some BASIC systems include the function INSTR, which searches the string argument for a particular substring. The function INSTR (P, X$, S$) returns the beginning position of the substring S$ in X$. The search begins at position P of X$.

For example, if V$ is equal to TO BE OR NOT TO BE, the following statement assigns C a value of 4:

```
500 LET C = INSTR(1, V$, "BE")
```

Line 500 assigns C the position of the first character of the substring BE in string V$. If there are no occurrences of the substring, INSTR returns the value zero.

The function INSTR always returns the leftmost position of the first occurrence of the substring. The following statement,

```
600 LET C = INSTR(5, V$, "BE")
```

assigns C a value of 17. The first occurrence of BE is bypassed because the search began at position 5.

The position argument P may be omitted from the list of arguments. For example, the following statement is identical to the previous line 500:

```
500 LET C = INSTR(V$, "BE")
```

That is, the search begins at position 1 (by default) and assigns C a value of 4. Table 9.4 illustrates some additional examples of the function INSTR.

TABLE 9.4   Examples of the INSTR Function

Assume S$ is equal to: RALLY 'ROUND THE FLAG, BOYS, RALLY ONCE AGAIN	
The Statement	*Results In*
`100 LET A = INSTR(1, S$, ",")`	A = 22
`200 LET B = INSTR(A, S$, "RALLY")`	B = 30 (assume A = 22)
`300 LET C = INSTR(S$, "'")`	C = 7

Some BASIC systems also include the MID$ statement for the purpose of substring replacement. Do not confuse the MID$ statement with the function

MID$. The function MID$ returns a substring, but the MID$ statement replaces a series of characters within a string with a designated substring. The general form of the MID$ statement is given in Table 9.5

TABLE 9.5   The MID$ **Statement**

General Form:	MID$(X$, P, N) = S$
	where X$ is the string in which the replacement takes place
	P is the position at which the replacement begins
	N is the number of characters to replace
	S$ is the replacement substring.
Purpose:	To replace a substring within a string.
| *Examples:* | ```
100 MID$(X$, 3, 4) = S$
200 MID$(C$, 1, 5) = "Y"  (only 1 character replaced)
300 MID$(F$, 30, 2) = "ABCDE"  (only 2 characters replaced)
400 MID$(E$, 4, 5) = A$ + B$
``` |
| *Caution:* | This statement is found on systems using Microsoft BASIC. It is not available on the Apple, COMMODORE or DEC VAX-11. |

As illustrated by the general form in Table 9.5, a substring of X$, specified by the beginning position P and the length N, is replaced by the substring S$. For example, if X$ is equal to INPROCMENT and S$ is equal to VEST, then the following statement

```
100 MID$(X$, 3, 4) = S$
```

assigns X$ the value IN**VEST**MENT. The substring VEST replaces the substring PROC.

In Table 9.5 line 200 shows that if the replacement substring is shorter than the substring designated by the length argument in the MID$ statement, then only those characters designated by the replacement substring are actually replaced. For example, if C$ is equal to BEAST, then the statement

```
200 MID$(C$, 1, 5) = "Y"
```

assigns C$ the value YEAST.

If the replacement substring has a length greater than that specified by N in the MID$ statement, then the system replaces only N characters. The rightmost excess characters in the replacement substring are not used.

Program 9.4 modifies a line of text through the use of the function INSTR and the MID$ statement. The program searches for all occurrences of the substring NE. Each time the substring is found, it is replaced with the substring IN.

```
100 REM PROGRAM 9.4
110 REM SEARCHING AND REPLACING STRINGS
120 REM ********************************
130 LET A$ = "THE RANE IN SPANE STAYS MANELY IN THE PLANE"
140 PRINT "OLD TEXT - "; A$
150 LET R = INSTR(A$, "NE")
160 WHILE R <> 0
170    MID$(A$, R, 2) = "IN"
180    LET R = INSTR(R + 2, A$, "NE")
190 WEND
200 PRINT
210 PRINT "NEW TEXT - "; A$
220 END

RUN

OLD TEXT - THE RANE IN SPANE STAYS MANELY IN THE PLANE

NEW TEXT - THE RAIN IN SPAIN STAYS MAINLY IN THE PLAIN
```

PROGRAM 9.4

Line 150 in Program 9.4 assigns R the value 7, which is the beginning position of the first occurrence of the substring NE. Line 170 replaces the substring NE that begins in position 7 with the substring IN. Line 180 searches for the next occurrence
```

of the substring NE. The search begins one position to the right of the previous occurrence. The next occurrence of the substring NE begins at position 16. Therefore, the function INSTR assigns R a value of 16. The loop continues with line 170 making the next replacement.

This process continues until all the occurrences of NE have been changed to IN. At this point, line 180 assigns R a value of zero and the loop terminates. The modified value of A$ is then displayed by line 210.

If A$ is assigned a value without the substring NE, the While loop (lines 160 through 190) will not execute. The function INSTR in line 150 returns a value of zero when the substring is not found. With R equal to zero, the WHILE statement in line 160 causes execution to continue at line 200. In this case, the next text and old text are identical.

Converting Character Codes—ASC and CHR$

The functions ASC and CHR$ facilitate the manipulation of individual characters. The function ASC(C$) returns a two-digit numeric value that corresponds to the ASCII code for the single character argument C$. The function CHR$(N) can be described as the reverse of the function ASC. It returns a single string character that is equivalent in ASCII code to the numeric argument N. Recall from Table 5.5 that each character in BASIC has a corresponding ASCII numeric code that the computer uses for storing the character in main memory or on auxiliary storage. For example, the character "A" has an ASCII code of 65, the character "B" has an ASCII code of 66, and so on.

A total of 256 different characters are represented by the ASCII code.* Only characters with codes in the ranges 32–126 and 128–255 can be entered in response to an INPUT statement or defined as a string constant. The function CHR$ allows you to by-pass this restriction and use any of the 256 characters. For example, the partial program

```
300 FOR I = 1 TO 10
310    PRINT CHR$(7);
320 NEXT I
```

causes the system to beep ten times. That is because the ASCII code 7 corresponds to the character BEL (Bell).

The function ASC is used to convert a single character string into a numeric value which can later be manipulated arithmetically. For example, the following partial program changes the single character string assigned to U$ from uppercase to lowercase:

```
490 LET U$ = "A"
500 LET U = ASC(U$)
510 LET L = U + 32
520 LET L$ = CHR$(L)
530 PRINT "UPPERCASE: "; U$
540 PRINT "LOWERCASE: "; L$
        .
        .
        .

RUN

UPPERCASE: A
LOWERCASE: a
```

In this partial program, the ASCII code for a lowercase character is equal to the corresponding uppercase numeric code plus 32. Line 500 assigns the variable U the numeric value 65 that is equal to the ASCII code for the character "A." Line 510 assigns L the value 97. Line 520 assigns L$ the character "a," which has a ASCII code of 97. Lines 530 and 540 display the values of U$ and L$ respectively.

---

*Some computer systems use only 128 different characters, represented by the numeric codes 0–127.

TABLE 9.6 **Examples of the** ASC **and** CHR$ **Function**

Value of	The Statement	Results In
	100 LET C = ASC("5")	C = 53
C$ = null	200 LET D = ASC(C$)	D = 00
D$ = ABC	300 LET E = ASC(D$)	E = 65
	400 LET X$ = CHR$(75)	X$ = K
D = −3	500 LET Y$ = CHR$(D)	Fatal Error

Table 9.6 illustrates several examples of the functions ASC and CHR$ and the following Programming Case Study makes use of both functions to decipher a coded message.

Messages are often coded by having one letter represent another. The coded message is called a **cryptogram**, and an algorithm is used to decipher the message into readable form.

Programming Case Study 27: Deciphering a Coded Message

The objective of the program illustrated is to take a coded message and have the computer display the corresponding deciphered message. The algorithm calls for subtracting 3 from the numeric code representing each character in the coded message. Obviously the algorithm can be, and usually is, more complex.

The coded message is

W K H # V K D G R Z # N Q R Z V

An analysis of the problem and a program solution follow.

Program Tasks

1) Accept a message from the user.
2) Use a For loop to process each character in the message. The For loop includes the following:
   a) An initial parameter of 1
   b) A limit parameter of LEN (message)
   c) The function MID$ to extract each character
   d) The function ASC to determine the numeric value that is equivalent to the ASCII code of the character extracted
   e) Subtraction of 3 from the numeric value determined in 2.d
   f) The function CHR$ to change the numeric value in 2.e to a character
   g) Display of the character

```
100 REM PROGRAM 9.5
110 REM DECIPHERING A CODED MESSAGE
120 REM ***************************
130 INPUT "CODED MESSAGE"; C$
140 PRINT
150 PRINT "THE MESSAGE IS: ";
160 FOR I = 1 TO LEN(C$)
170     LET N = ASC(MID$(C$, I, 1))
180     LET N = N - 3
190     LET M$ = CHR$(N)
200     PRINT M$;
210 NEXT I
220 PRINT
230 PRINT "----------------"
240 END

RUN

CODED MESSAGE? WKH#VKDGRZ#NQRZV

THE MESSAGE IS: THE SHADOW KNOWS
----------------
```

PROGRAM 9.5

Program 9.5 accepts a coded message, deciphers it one character at a time and displays the corresponding message one character at a time.

In line 160 the function LEN determines the value of the terminal parameter for the For loop. Line 170 determines the numeric value that corresponds to the ASCII code for the character selected by the MID$ function. It is valid to have a string function as part of the argument for another string function. Line 180 subtracts 3 from the value of N and in line 190 the function CHR$ returns the corresponding character.

Program 9.5 can be shortened by replacing lines 170 through 200 with the following statement:

```
170 PRINT CHR$(ASC(MID$(C$, I, 1)) - 3);
```

Modifying Data Types—STR$ and VAL

Chapter 3 mentioned that strings and numeric values are stored differently inside the computer and that the computer cannot add a numeric and string value. The functions STR$ and VAL allow this restriction to be circumvented. The function STR$(N) returns the string equivalent of the numeric value N. The function VAL(X$) returns the numeric equivalent of the string X$. Thus, STR$(52.3) returns the string 52.3 and VAL("310.23") returns the numeric value 310.23. If the argument for the function STR$ is negative, the function returns a leading negative sign. If the argument for the function VAL does not represent a number, the function returns a value of 0. For example, the value returned by the following statement

```
500 LET V = VAL("IBM")
```

is zero.

Table 9.7 illustrates examples of both the STR$ and VAL functions. The functions VAL and STR$ are primarily used in instances where a substring of numeric digits within an identification number, like a credit card number or invoice number, need to be extracted for computational purposes and the result transformed back as a string value.

TABLE 9.7   **Examples of the** STR$ **and** VAL **Function***

Value of	The Statement	Results In
	100 LET A$ = STR$(34)	A$ = 34
B = 64.543	200 LET S$ = STR$(B)	S$ = 64.543
C = −3.21	300 LET Z$ = STR$(C)	Z$ = −3.21
	400 LET F = VAL("766.321")	F = 766.321
K$ = 12E−3	500 LET Q = VAL(K$)	Q = 12E−3
P$ = STR	600 LET W = VAL(P$)	W = 0

*Note that any numeric value assigned to a string variable is actually a string and not a number.

Displaying Spaces—SPC

The function SPC is similar to the space bar on a typewriter. The function SPC is used in a PRINT statement to insert spaces between column headings or other results that are displayed as part of a report. The form of the function SPC is SPC(N) where the argument N may be a numeric constant, variable, expression or function reference. Consider the following:

```
240 PRINT "COLUMN 1"; SPC(3); "COLUMN 2"; SPC(5); "COLUMN 3"
```

The SPC(3) causes the insertion of three spaces between COLUMN 1 and COLUMN 2. The SPC(5) inserts five spaces between COLUMN 2 and COL-

UMN 3. The spaces inserted between results displayed are often called **filler**. The function SPC may be used any number of times in the same PRINT statement. However, the SPC function may only be used in a PRINT statement.

The functions SPACE$ and STRING$ are used to duplicate string data. The function SPACE$ (N) returns N spaces or blank characters. It is similar to the function SPC. For example, the two statements

```
300 PRINT "DEC"; SPC(4); "RAINBOW"
```

and

```
300 PRINT "DEC"; SPACE$(4); "RAINBOW"
```

display identical results. The advantage of the function SPACE$ over the function SPC is that SPACE$ may be used in other statements than PRINT statement. For example, the following statement

```
400 LET A$ = SPACE$(25)
```

assigns A$ a string value of 25 spaces. If the argument is equal to or less than zero, the function returns the null string. The function STRING$ (N, "C") returns the character C, which is within quotation marks, N times. The function STRING$ may be used to duplicate any character. For example, the following statement

```
500 PRINT STRING$(72, "*")
```

displays a line of 72 asterisks. The second argument may also be represented in ASCII code. That is, the statement

```
500 PRINT STRING$(72, 42)
```

is identical to the previous one, since 42 is the ASCII code representation for the asterisk character.

Table 9.8 illustrates examples of both the SPACE$ and STRING$ functions. Program 9.6 also uses the function STRING$.

TABLE 9.8 **Examples of the** SPACE$ **and** STRING$ **Functions**

Value of	The Statement	Comment
N = 50	`100 PRINT SPACE$(N); "A"`	Displays the character A in position 51.
	`200 LET X$ = SPACE$(12)`	Assigns 12 spaces to X$.
	`300 LET Y$ = SPACE$(0)`	Assigns Y$ the null string.
S = 45	`400 PRINT STRING$(S, "-")`	Displays 45 minus signs.
	`500 LET X$ = STRING$(5, 65)`	Assigns X$ the string value AAAAA.
	`600 IF Z$ = SPACE$(15) THEN 900`	Transfers control to line 900 if Z$ is equal to 15 spaces.

Many BASIC systems include the function DATE$ and TIME$. The function DATE$ returns the current system date as a string value in the form mm-dd-yyyy.* The first two characters, mm, represent the month. The fourth and fifth characters, dd, represent the day. The last four characters, yyyy, represent the year. For example, if the system date is initialized to December 25, 1986, then the statement

```
300 LET D$ = DATE$
```

assigns D$ the string 12-25-1986.

---

*Some BASIC systems return the time and date in a different format. For example, the DEC VAX-11 returns the date in the form dd-mmm-yy, where mmm is the first three letters of the month name, and the time in the form hh:mm followed by AM or PM. Check the specifications in the user's manual for how your system returns the time and date.

The function TIME$ returns the time of day, in 24-hour notation, as a string value in the form hh:mm:ss. The first two characters, hh, represent the hours (range 00-23). The fourth and fifth characters, mm, represent the minutes. The last two characters represent the seconds. If the internal clock is equal to 11:35:42 *at the instant* the statement

```
400 PRINT "THE TIME IS "; TIME$
```

executes, then the system displays

```
THE TIME IS 11:35:42
```

The key phrase in the last sentence is "at the instant," since the computer's internal clock automatically maintains the time after it is entered by the operator as part of the start up procedures.

Table 9.9 illustrates examples of both the DATE$ and TIME$ functions.

TABLE 9.9   Examples of the DATE$ and TIME$ Functions*

Assume DATE$ = 09-15-1986 and TIME$ = 15:26:32

The Statement	Results In
`100 LET A$ = DATE$`	A$ = 09-15-1986
`200 LET B$ = TIME$`	B$ = 15:26:32
`300 LET C$ = MID$(DATE$, 1, 2)`	C$ = 09
`400 LET D$ = MID$(DATE$, 4, 2)`	D$ = 15
`500 LET E$ = MID$(DATE$, 9, 2)`	E$ = 86
`600 LET F$ = MID$(TIME$, 1, 2)`	F$ = 15
`700 LET G$ = MID$(TIME$, 4, 2)`	G$ = 26
`800 LET H$ = MID$(TIME$, 7, 2)`	H$ = 32

*Note that any numeric value assigned to a string variable is actually a string and not a number.

The function DATE$ and TIME$ are often used to display the date and time as part of report headings.

The function DATE$ is also used in business-related applications to verify that a payment date, birthdate or hire date is valid. The following problem and program solution offer an example of the use of the function DATE$ for this type of verification.

Programming Case Study 28: Validating Payment Dates

The following program solution illustrates how to verify that a payment date is not in the future. The customer number and payment date are stored in DATA statements. The payment date is in the form mmddyy. Assume that today's date is July 4, 1986 (DATE$ = 07–04–1986).

Discussion

The two dates cannot be compared in their original format. For a comparison, the most significant part of the date (years) must be at the far left, followed by the next most significant (months), followed by the least significant (days). That is, the program must rearrange the two dates before it can compare them, as follows:

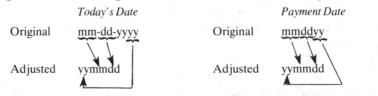

To rearange the substrings, the MID$ function and the concatenation operator may be used. Once the two fields are adjusted, today's date can be compared

```
100 REM PROGRAM 9.6
110 REM VALIDATING PAYMENT DATES
120 REM ************************
130 LET A$ = DATE$
140 LET B$ = MID$(A$, 9, 2) + MID$(A$, 1, 2) + MID$(A$, 4, 2)
150 PRINT "VALIDATING PAYMENT DATES FOR ; A$
160 PRINT STRING$(39, "-")
170 PRINT
180 PRINT "CUSTOMER", "PAYMENT DATE", "COMMENT"
190 PRINT "--------", "------------", "-------"
200 READ C$, D$
210 WHILE C$ <> "EOF"
220    PRINT C$, SPC(3); D$;
230    LET P$ = MID$(D$, 5, 2) + MID$(D$, 1, 2) + MID$(D$, 3, 2)
240    IF B$ >= P$ THEN PRINT "DATE OK" ELSE PRINT "DATE NOT OK"
250    READ C$, D$
260 WEND
270 PRINT
280 PRINT "END OF REPORT"
290 REM ******DATA FOLLOWS******
300 DATA 31245381, 091588
310 DATA 46371230, 070486
320 DATA 71209824, 070686
330 DATA 96012567, 063086
340 DATA EOF, " "
350 END
```

PROGRAM 9.6

```
RUN

VALIDATING PAYMENT DATES FOR 07-04-1986
-----------------------------------------

CUSTOMER        PAYMENT DATE    COMMENT
--------        ------------    -------
31245381          091588        DATE NOT OK
46371230          070486        DATE OK
71209824          070686        DATE NOT OK
96012567          063086        DATE OK

END OF REPORT
```

against the payment date. If today's date is greater than or equal to the payment date, a message indicating that the date is valid will be displayed. Otherwise, a diagnostic message will be displayed.

In Program 9.6, line 130 assigns A\$ today's date. Line 140 rearranges the substrings of A\$ in the format yy-mm-dd and assigns the result to B\$. Line 230 rearranges the substrings of the payment date D\$ into the same format. Line 240 compares today's date to the payment date. If B\$ is greater than or equal to P\$, then the payment date is valid. If B\$ is less than P\$ then the payment date is a future date and the message DATE NOT OK is displayed. Pay particular attention to lines 140 and 230. Rearranging substrings is a common characteristic of programs that validate data items.

Accepting String Data—LINE INPUT Statement and the INKEY\$ and INPUT\$ Functions

Some BASIC systems include an alternative input statement, the LINE INPUT string statement, that accepts a line entered from an external source like a keyboard as the string value and assigns it to a specified string variable. The string value may include quotation marks and commas. That is, if the string value

```
SHE SAID, "TERMINATE THE PROGRAM!"
```

is entered, and the Enter key is pressed in response to the statement

```
300 LINE INPUT "WHAT DID SHE SAY? "; A$
```

then A\$ is assigned the entire string of characters

```
SHE SAID, "TERMINATE THE PROGRAM!"
```

including the comma and quotation marks.

The general form of the LINE INPUT statement is shown in Table 9.10.

TABLE 9.10   The LINE INPUT **Statement.**

General Form:	LINE INPUT string variable or LINE INPUT "input prompt message"; string variable
Purpose:	Provides for the assignment to a string variable of a line, including commas and quotation marks, entered from a source external to the program.
Examples:	

Input Statements	*Data from an External Source*
`100 LINE INPUT A$`	`1 219 844 0520`
`200 LINE INPUT "WHAT? "; S$`	`"DON'T DO IT", SAID AMANDA`
`300 LINE INPUT "WEIGHT? "; W$`	`126.5 LBS.`

Caution:	Not available on the Apple and COMMODORE. On the DEC VAX-11 use the LINPUT statement.

The major differences between the LINE INPUT statement and the INPUT statements are:

1) The LINE INPUT statement does not prompt the user with the question mark and trailing space that the INPUT statement does.

2) The LINE INPUT statement may only have at most one string variable in the list. The INPUT statement may have multiple variables in the list and they may be either numeric or string.

When executed, an INPUT or LINE INPUT statement instructs the system to suspend execution of the program until the Enter key is pressed. That is, with these two statements, we must always signal the system by pressing the Enter key when we have finished entering the data requested.

Some BASIC systems include two functions, INKEY$ and INPUT$, that do not require that the Enter key be pressed for the program to accept input.* The function INKEY$ **does not** suspend execution of the program but instead checks the keyboard to determine if a character is pending—that is, if a key was recently pressed. The function INKEY$ has no argument.

The following statement

```
300 LET A$ = INKEY$
```

assigns A$ the character that corresponds to the last key pressed. If no character is entered, then INKEY$ assigns the null string to A$. Since this function accepts one character from the keyboard but does not suspend execution of the program, the function is normally located in a statement within a loop. For example, the following partial program displays the value of X and 2 * X either until the user presses a key or until the value of X exceeds 1E + 38 (an **arithmetic overflow** occurs):

```
500 LET X = X + 1
510 LET C$ = ""
520 WHILE C$ = ""
530    PRINT X, 2 * X
540    LET X = X + 1
550    LET C$ = INKEY$
560 WEND
```

---

*With the Apple, use the statement GET A$ in place of the function INPUT$. The GET A$ statement only allows for a single character to be entered. The Apple does not have a statement or function that corresponds to the function INKEY$. With the COMMODORE use the statement GET C$ in place of the function INKEY$. The COMMODORE does not have a statement or function that corresponds to the function INPUT$. The DEC VAX-11 has neither function.

Line 510 assigns C$ the null string, which allows control to pass into the While loop. Line 530 displays the value of X and 2 * X. The variable X is incremented by one in line 540. Line 550 checks to determine if the user has recently pressed a key. If no character is pending from the keyboard, C$ is assigned the null string and control once again passes through the loop. The system will continue to execute the loop until the user presses a key or the value of 2 * X causes an arithmetic overflow.

The function INKEY$ is useful for applications that require a program not be interrupted and yet accept responses from the keyboard. This method of processing is essential for video game programs, like Space Invaders or Missile Command, which are moving objects constantly on the display device, but must also constantly check for user input, like the firing of a phaser.

The function INPUT$(N) is even more sophisticated than the function INKEY$, because it accepts N characters from the keyboard. However, unlike INKEY$, INPUT$ suspends execution of the program until the user has pressed N number of keys. For example, the statement

```
300 LET C$ = INPUT$(1)
```

causes the system to suspend execution of the program (like the INPUT and LINE INPUT statements) and wait until a key is pressed. However, the character entered is not displayed on the screen. To display the response, the statement containing INPUT$ must be followed with a PRINT statement. For example,

```
400 LET C$ = INPUT$(5)
410 PRINT C$
```

displays the five characters entered by the user.

Table 9.11 illustrates examples of the functions INKEY$ and INPUT$.

TABLE 9.11 **Examples of the** INKEY$ **and** INPUT$ **Functions**

The Statement	Keyboard Response	Results In
100 LET X$ = INKEY$	J	X$ = J
200 LET V$ = INKEY$	No Response	V$ = null
300 LET W$ = INPUT$(4)	A1B2	W$ = A1B2
400 LET Z$ = INPUT$(1)	3	Z$ = 3

A common use of the function INPUT$ is to suspend the execution of a program at the conclusion of a task so that the information on the screen may be read before it disappears. For example, if a program is displaying a long list of items, you may want to suspend execution of the program after every 20 or so lines are displayed. The message

```
PRESS ANY KEY TO CONTINUE
```

is often used in this situation. The INPUT$ simplifies the entry by not requiring that the Enter key be pressed. The following partial program shows how to incorporate this technique into a BASIC program.

```
1000 PRINT "PRESS ANY KEY TO CONTINUE"
1010 LET A$ = INPUT$(1)
```

In some cases it may be preferable to use the function INPUT$ without a prompt message. For example, in Programming Case Study 26, use of the function INPUT$ without a prompt message would eliminate the last line shown in the output results. Of course, information regarding how the operator continues the program should be included in the menu.

**9.3
NUMERIC
FUNCTIONS**

The most common numeric function supplied with BASIC systems are listed in Table 9.12.

TABLE 9.12   Numeric Functions Common to Most BASIC Systems

Function	Function Value
`ABS(X)`	Returns the absolute value of the argument X.
`ATN(X)`	Returns the angle in radians whose tangent is the value of the argument X.
`COS(X)`	Returns the cosine of the argument X where X is in radians.
`EXP(X)`	Returns e(2.71828···) raised to the argument X.
`FIX(X)`	Returns the integer portion of the argument X.
`INT(X)`	Returns the largest integer that is less than or equal to the argument X.
`LOG(X)`	Returns the natural log of the argument X where X is greater than 0.
`RND`	Returns a random number between 0 (inclusive) and 1 (exclusive).
`SGN(X)`	Returns the sign of the argument X: −1 if the argument X is less than 0; 0 if the argument X is equal to 0; or, +1 if the argument X is greater than 0.
`SIN(X)`	Returns the sine of the argument X where X is in radians.
`SQR(X)`	Returns the positive square root of the argument X.
`TAN(X)`	Returns the tangent of the argument X where X is in radians.

In the discussion that follows, several examples of each numeric function are shown.

**Arithmetic
Functions—ABS, FIX,
INT and SGN**

The functions classified as *arithmetic* include ABS (absolute value), FIX (fixed integer), INT (integer) and SGN (sign).

The function ABS takes any numeric expression and returns its positive value. For example, if X is equal to −4, then ABS (X) is equal to 4. Additional examples of the function ABS are shown in Table 9.13.

The function FIX (X) returns the integer portion of the argument X. For example, if X is equal to 13.45, then FIX (X) returns 13.* When the argument is positive, the function FIX is identical to the function INT. However, when the argument is negative the two functions return a different result. For example, if X is equal to −4.45, then FIX (X) returns −4 and INT (X) returns −5. The function INT returns an integer that is less than or equal to the argument. Additional examples of the function FIX and INT are shown in Table 9.13

The function SGN (X) returns a value of +1 if the argument X is positive; 0 if the argument is 0; and −1 if the argument X is negative. Table 9.13 shows examples of the function SGN.

TABLE 9.13   Examples of the ABS, FIX, INT and SGN Functions

Value of Variable	The Statement	Results In
K = −3	`100 LET P = ABS(K)`	P = 3
Q = 4.5	`200 LET C = ABS(Q)`	C = 4.5
C = 4, D = −6	`300 LET A = C + ABS(D)`	A = 10
G = 25.567	`400 LET F = FIX(G)`	F = 25
G = −25.567	`500 LET F = FIX(G)`	F = −25
G = 25.567	`600 LET I = INT(G)`	I = 25
G = −25.567	`700 LET I = INT(G)`	I = −26
D = 4	`800 LET E = SGN(D)`	E = 1
P = −5	`900 LET F = 5 + SGN(P)`	F = 4

*The function FIX is not available on the Apple or COMMODORE.

The procedure for rounding the result of a computation developed in Section 3.6 can be generalized so that the expression will round to any position. The generalized expression for rounding numbers is:

$$\text{FIX}(N * 10 \wedge E + \text{SGN}(N) * 0.5)/10 \wedge E$$

where N is the result to be rounded

E is the number of decimal places desired

To determine what value should be assigned to E, begin counting from the decimal point, as illustrated below.

For example, if you wish to round a result N to the thousandths place, you assign E a value of 3. The generalized expression becomes:

$$\text{FIX}(N * 1000 + \text{SGN}(N) * 0.5)/1000$$

To round N to the nearest units place assign E a value of 0 and the generalized expression becomes:

$$\text{FIX}(N + \text{SGN}(N) * 0.5)$$

The procedure developed for truncating the result of a computation can also be generalized so that the expression will truncate to any position. The generalized

```
100 REM PROGRAM 9.7
110 REM ROUNDING AND TRUNCATING NUMBERS
120 REM ******************************
130 LET A$ = "Y"
140 WHILE A$ = "Y"
150    INPUT "NUMBER TO BE ADJUSTED"; N
160    INPUT "NUMBER OF DECIMAL PLACES"; E
170    LET A = FIX(N * 10^E + SGN(N) * .5)/10^E
180    PRINT "ROUNDED RESULT======>"; A
190    LET A = FIX(N * 10^E)/10^E
200    PRINT "TRUNCATED RESULT====>"; A
210    PRINT
220    INPUT "ANOTHER NUMBER (Y OR N)"; A$
230 WEND
240 PRINT "JOB COMPLETE"
250 END

RUN

NUMBER TO BE ADJUSTED? 68.567
NUMBER OF DECIMAL PLACES? 2
ROUNDED RESULT======> 68.57
TRUNCATED RESULT====> 68.56

ANOTHER NUMBER (Y OR N)? Y
NUMBER TO BE ADJUSTED? -24.689
NUMBER OF DECIMAL PLACES? 2
ROUNDED RESULT======>-24.69
TRUNCATED RESULT====>-24.68

ANOTHER NUMBER (Y OR N)? Y
NUMBER TO BE ADJUSTED? -24.689
NUMBER OF DECIMAL PLACES? 0
ROUNDED RESULT======>-25
TRUNCATED RESULT====>-24

ANOTHER NUMBER (Y OR N)? Y
NUMBER TO BE ADJUSTED? 68.567
NUMBER OF DECIMAL PLACES? 2
ROUNDED RESULT======> 68.57
TRUNCATED RESULT====> 68.56

ANOTHER NUMBER (Y OR N)? N
JOB COMPLETE
```

PROGRAM 9.7

expression for truncating any number is:

FIX(N * 10 ^)/10 ^ E

where N is the result to be truncated

E is the number of decimal places desired

Program 9.7 illustrates the use of the generalized expression for rounding and truncation.

The program requests the user enter a number N to be rounded and the number of decimal places E required in the result. The first entry shows 68.567 rounded to the hundredths place 68.57, as well as truncated to the hundredths place 68.56. The second entry shows −24.689 rounded and truncated to the nearest hundredths place. The last entry shows −24.689 rounded and truncated to the nearest units position.

Exponential Functions—SQR, EXP and LOG

The functions classified as exponential include the SQR (square root), EXP (exponential) and LOG (logarithmic).

The function SQR (X) computes the square root of the argument X.

Table 9.14 shows several examples of computing the square root of a *non-negative* number.

TABLE 9.14   Examples of the SQR Functions

Value of Variable	The Statement	Results In
Argument = 9	100 LET X = SQR(9)	X = 3
E = 0	110 LET Z = SQR(E)	Z = 0
R = 25	120 LET D = SQR(R)	D = 5
Q(1) = 1.15129	150 LET C = SQR(Q(1))	C = 1.23
X = 3, Y = 4	500 LET P = SQR(X^2 + Y^2)	P = 5
D = −49	650 LET U = SQR(ABS(D))	U = 7

The symbol e in mathematics represents 2.718281828459045 · · · , where the three dots show that the fractional part of the constant is not a repeating sequence of digits. In BASIC, the keyword EXP is used to represent this constant, which is raised to the power given as the argument in parentheses following the function name. The function EXP can be used, for example, to determine the value of $e^{1.4473}$. The following BASIC statement

110 LET Y = EXP(1.4473)

results in a Y value of 3.14159.

The natural log ($\log_e$ or ln) of a number can be determined by using the LOG function. For example, the value of X in the equation

$$e^x = 3$$

can be determined by using the following statement:

110 LET X = LOG(3)

The resulting value of X is 1.09861 and, therefore,

$$e^{1.0961} = 3$$

This function can also be used to determine the logarithm to the base 10 by multiplying the LOG function by .434295. For example, in the statement

110 LET Y = 0.434295 * LOG(3)

Y is assigned the value 0.477122, the base 10 logarithm of 3.

Of the three exponential functions, programmers use the square root function more often than the exponential or logarithmic. However, the latter two functions are essential in some of the advanced applications. The following programming Case Study is an example of the use of the LOG function.

The formula for computing the amount of an investment compounded annually for a given number of years is $A = P(1 + J)^N$ where A is the total amount, P is the initial investment, J is the annual rate of interest and N is the number of years.

Programming Case Study 29: Determining the Time to Double an Investment

This formula can be rewritten to solve for the number of years N:

$$N = \frac{\log \dfrac{A}{P}}{\log (1 + J)}$$

If the number of years it takes to double an investment is to be determined, then the amount A is equal to twice the investment P, or $A = 2P$. The formula for determining the number of years to double an investment can further be simplified to

$$N = \frac{\log 2}{\log (1 + J)}$$

The following problem uses the function LOG to compute the number of years to double an investment.

Problem

The WESAVU National Bank requests that a program be written to display a table of annual interest rates and corresponding years it will take to double an investment compounded annually for integer interests rates from 8 through 18 inclusive. An analysis of the problem and program solution follow.

Program Tasks

1) Display report and column headings
2) Assign LOG(2) to L.
3) Use a For loop to generate the annual interest rates J from 8 through 18. Within the loop perform the following tasks:
   a) Determine the number of years N to double an investment at J percent using the statement: LET N = L/LOG(1 + J/100).
   b) Display the interest rate J and the number of years to double an investment N.
4) Display an end-of-job message.

With slight modifications to the parameters in the FOR statement in Program 9.8, the number of years it takes to double an investment compounded annually can be determined for a variety of interest rates. The argument in the first reference to the LOG function in line 200 can be changed to other numbers, like 3 or 4, to determine how long it takes to triple or quadruple an investment compounded annually. See Programming Exercise 3 at the end of this chapter to determine the number of years to double an investment compounded quarterly.

In BASIC the functions SIN, COS and TAN can be used to determine the sine, cosine, and tangent of the angle X expressed in radians. Since angles are usually expressed in degrees, the following statements relating angles and radians should

Trigonometric Functions—SIN, COS, TAN **and** ATN

```
100 REM PROGRAM 9.8
110 REM DETERMINING THE TIME TO DOUBLE AN INVESTMENT
120 REM ********************************************
130 PRINT    "DOUBLING AN INVESTMENT"
140 PRINT    "_____"
150 PRINT
160 PRINT    "INTEREST      NUMBER"
170 PRINT    "RATE IN %     OF YEARS"
180 PRINT    "_____     _____"
190 LET A$ = "    ##          ##.#"
200 LET L = LOG(2)
210 FOR J = 8 TO 18
220    LET N = L/LOG(1 + J/100)
230    PRINT USING A$; J, N
240 NEXT J
250 PRINT
260 PRINT "END OF REPORT"
270 END
```

PROGRAM 9.8

```
RUN

DOUBLING AN INVESTMENT
_____

INTEREST      NUMBER
RATE IN %     OF YEARS
_____     _____
      8          9.0
      9          8.0
     10          7.3
     11          6.6
     12          6.1
     13          5.7
     14          5.3
     15          5.0
     16          4.7
     17          4.4
     18          4.2

END OF REPORT
```

prove helpful:

$$1 \text{ radian} = 180/\pi \text{ radians} = 180/3.14159 \text{ degrees}$$
$$1 \text{ degree} = \pi/180 \text{ radians} = 3.14159/180 \text{ degrees}$$

When using these three functions remember that if the argument is in units of degrees it must first be multiplied by 3.14159/180 in order to convert it into units of radians before the function can evaluate it. In mathematics, if the equation $X = \sin 30°$ is evaluated, then $X = 0.5$. However, evaluating the same equation in BASIC requires the following:

```
110 LET A = 30 * 3.14159/180
120 LET X = SIN(A)
```

or

```
110 LET X = SIN(30 * 3.14159/180)
```

Most BASIC systems do not have corresponding functions for the cosecant, secant and the cotangent. These three trigonometric functions must be evaluated by combinations of the SIN, COS and TAN functions. Table 9.15 illustrates the combinations.

TABLE 9.15   Determining the Cosecant, Secant and Cotangent

To find the	Use
Cosecant	1/SIN(X)
Secant	1/COS(X)
Cotangent	1/TAN(X)

The fourth trigonometric function available in BASIC is the arctangent. The function ATN returns a value that is the angle (in units of radians) that corresponds to the argument in the function. For example,

```
110 LET V = ATN(1)
```

results in V being assigned the value of .785398 radians. Multiplying this number by 180/3.14159 yields an angle of 45°.

Random Number Function and the RANDOMIZE **Statement**

The function RND is important to the programmer involved in the development of programs simulating situations that are described by a random process. The owners of a shopping mall, for example, may want a program written to simulate the number of cars that will enter their parking lots during a particular period of the day. Or a grocery store may want a program to model unpredictable values that represent people standing in line waiting to check out. The unpredictable values can be supplied by the function RND. Actually, the random numbers generated by the computer are provided by a repeatable process, and for this reason they are often called **pseudo-random numbers**.

The function RND returns an unpredictable decimal fraction number between 0 (inclusive) and 1(exclusive). Each time the function is referenced, any number between 0 and <1 has an equal probability of being returned by the function. For example, the statement

```
100 LET Y = RND
```

assigns Y a random number.* Program 9.9 illustrates the generation of five random numbers.

```
100 REM PROGRAM 9.9
110 REM GENERATING RANDOM NUMBERS
120 REM *************************
130 FOR I = 1 TO 5
140    PRINT RND;
150 NEXT I
160 END

RUN
 .887512      .983185      .496765      .717194      .417542
```

PROGRAM 9.9

Each time the function RND is referenced in line 140 of the loop, Y is assigned a number between 0 and <1.

The functions INT or FIX and RND can be combined to create random digits over a specified range. The following expression allows for the generation of random digits over the range $C \leq n \leq D$:

```
INT((D - C + 1) * RND + C)
```

For example, to generate random digits over the range 1 to 10 inclusive, change line 140 in Program 9.9 to:

```
140 PRINT INT((10 - 1 + 1) * RND + 1)
```

or

```
140 PRINT INT(10 * RND + 1)
```

Program 9.10 simulates tossing a coin twenty times. The expression INT (2 * RND) returns a zero (heads) or one (tails). The expression in line 160 returned 13 zeros (heads) and 7 ones (tails).

Program 9.10 can be enhanced to allow a user to enter the number of simulated coin tosses desired and to display of the total number of heads and tails. This is illustrated in Program 9.11.

---

*With the Apple and COMMODORE, the function RND must be followed to the right with an argument. Check the specifications in the user's manual for the definition of the argument. Also see Table 9.17.

```
100 REM PROGRAM 9.10
110 REM SIMULATION OF COIN TOSSING
120 REM 0 IS A HEAD AND 1 IS A TAIL
130 REM THE COIN IS TOSSED 20 TIMES
140 REM ****************************
150 FOR I = 1 TO 20
160    X = INT(2*RND)
170    PRINT X;
180 NEXT I
190 END
```

PROGRAM 9.10

```
RUN

 1  0  1  0  0  0  0  1  1  0  1  0  0  0  0  1  0  0  1  0  0
```

```
100 REM PROGRAM 9.11
110 REM SIMULATION OF COIN TOSSING
120 REM 0 IS A HEAD AND 1 IS A TAIL
130 REM USER ENTERS NUMBER OF TIMES COIN IS TOSSED
140 REM H = NUMBER OF HEADS, T = NUMBER OF TAILS
150 REM *******************************************
160 LET H = 0
170 LET T = 0
180 INPUT "HOW MANY TOSSES"; N
190 FOR I = 1 TO N
200    LET X = INT(2*RND)
210    IF X = 0 LET H = H + 1 ELSE LET T = T + 1
220 NEXT I
230 PRINT "NUMBER OF HEADS====>"; H
240 PRINT "NUMBER OF TAILS====>"; T
250 END
```

PROGRAM 9.11

```
RUN

HOW MANY TOSSES? 500
NUMBER OF HEADS====> 259
NUMBER OF TAILS====> 241
```

When executed, Program 9.11 requests that the user enter the number of coin tosses to be simulated. Line 210 increments H (head counter) or T (tail counter) by 1 depending upon the value assigned to X. At the conclusion of the For loop, lines 230 and 240 display the total number of heads H and total number of tails T. As illustrated by the results of Program 9.11, out of 500 simulated coin tosses, 259 were heads and 241 tails.

Every time Program 9.11 is executed on the same system, it will display the same results, because the system generates random numbers from a starting value called the **seed**. Unless the seed is changed, the system continues to generate the same set of random numbers in the same sequence each time the same program is executed. Once a program containing the function RND is ready for production, the statement RANDOMIZE can be used to instruct the system to generate random numbers from a different seed each time the program is executed. The general form of the RANDOMIZE statement is shown in Table 9.16.

TABLE 9.16   **The RANDOMIZE Statement**

General Form:	RANDOMIZE
Purpose:	To supply a new seed for the generation of random numbers by the function RND.
Example:	100 RANDOMIZE
Caution:	With the Apple and COMMODORE, a new seed is supplied based on the value of the argument to the right in the function RND. The statement RANDOMIZE is not available with these two systems. With the TRS-80, use the statement RANDOM.
	With the DEC Rainbow, IBM PC, Macintosh and Microsoft BASIC in general, you may include a parameter following the keyword RANDOMIZE. With these systems, if a parameter is not included, the RANDOMIZE statement suspends execution and requests a value. The value must be between −32768 and 32767.

The rule for the execution of the RANDOMIZE statement in a program is

> RANDOMIZE **Rule 1:** The RANDOMIZE statement must be executed prior to any reference to the RND function.

The flowchart in Figure 9.1 and Program 9.12 simulate a popular guessing game in which the player attempts to guess a number between 1 and 100. The RANDOMIZE statement is included so that the function RND will return a new set of random numbers each time the program is executed.

```
100 REM PROGRAM 9.12
110 REM GUESS A NUMBER BETWEEN 1 AND 100
120 REM ******************************
130 RANDOMIZE VAL(MID$(TIME$, 7, 2))
140 LET N = INT(100 * RND + 1)
150 LET C = 1
160 CLS
170 PRINT
180 PRINT "**************************************"
190 PRINT "*                                    *"
200 PRINT "* GUESS A NUMBER BETWEEN 1 AND 100.  *"
210 PRINT "* I WILL TELL YOU IF YOUR GUESS IS   *"
220 PRINT "* TOO HIGH OR TOO LOW.               *"
230 PRINT "*                                    *"
240 PRINT "**************************************"
250 PRINT
260 INPUT "GUESS A NUMBER"; G
270 WHILE G <> N
280    IF G > N THEN PRINT "TOO HIGH" ELSE PRINT "TOO LOW"
290    INPUT "GUESS A NUMBER"; G
300    LET C = C + 1
310 WEND
320 PRINT
330 PRINT "YOUR GUESS IS CORRECT."
340 PRINT "IT TOOK YOU"; C; "GUESSES."
350 END

RUN


**************************************
*                                    *
* GUESS A NUMBER BETWEEN 1 AND 100.  *
* I WILL TELL YOU IF YOUR GUESS IS   *
* TOO HIGH OR TOO LOW.               *
*                                    *
**************************************

GUESS A NUMBER? 50
TOO HIGH
GUESS A NUMBER? 25
TOO HIGH
GUESS A NUMBER? 5
TOO LOW
GUESS A NUMBER? 15
TOO HIGH
GUESS A NUMBER? 10
TOO HIGH
GUESS A NUMBER? 7
TOO LOW
GUESS A NUMBER? 8

YOUR GUESS IS CORRECT.
IT TOOK YOU 7 GUESSES.
```

PROGRAM 9.12

When the RUN command is issued for Program 9.12, line 130 ensures that the program does not generate the same set of random numbers as the last time the program was executed. In line 130, the seed is based on the seconds portion of the function TIME$ and therefore, chances are 1 in 60 that the same seed will be used.

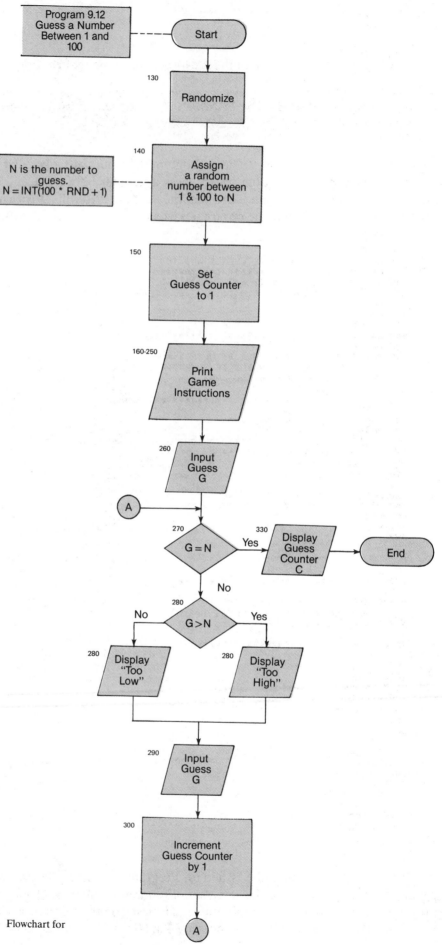

FIGURE 9.1 Flowchart for Program 9.12.

Line 140 assigns N the number to be guessed (8). Line 150 sets a counter C to 1. The counter C keeps track of the number of guesses. Line 160 through 250 display the instructions for the game. Line 260 accepts a guess G from the user. If G is equal to N, the program terminates after 1 guess. If G does not equal N, the system executes the While loop and displays an appropriate message before requesting the next guess and incrementing the counter C. When the user finally guesses the number, control passes to line 320 and a message and the value of C are displayed.

Table 9.17 shows the modifications to Program 9.12 for some popular computer systems.

TABLE 9.17   Variations to the RANDOMIZE **Statement and Function** RND **in Program 9.12**

Computer System	Modification
Apple	Delete line 130 and change the function RND in line 140 to RND(1).
COMMODORE	Delete line 130 and change the function RND in line 140 to RND(−1).
DEC Rainbow, IBM PC, Macintosh and Microsoft BASIC in general	No modifications.
DEC VAX-11	Delete the parameter from the RANDOMIZE statement.
TRS-80	In line 130, replace RANDOMIZE with RANDOM.

9.4 USER-DEFINED FUNCTIONS

In addition to numeric and string functions, BASIC allows you to define new functions that relate to a particular application. This type of function, known as a **user-defined function**, is written as a one-line statement directly into the program.* User-defined functions can be referenced only in the program in which they are included. The BASIC system recognizes a user-defined function by the keyword DEF, which is incorporated in the function statement just to the right of the line number. As an example, the DEF statement

```
150 DEF FNA(X) = X * (X + 1)/2
```

defines a function, $X(X + 1)/2$, whose name is FNA. The parentheses following the name of the function surround a simple variable known as a **function parameter**. The expression to the right of the equal sign indicates the operations that are to be performed with the value of X when the function is referenced in such statements as LET, ON-GOTO and IF.

The DEF statement is non-executable; that is, the system treats the statement in much the same way it treats a DATA statement. It is used only if referenced in another statement. For example, either

```
900 LET B = FNA(R) + 5
```

or

```
910 PRINT FNA(P + 3)
```

found in the same program with line 150 will reference the function FNA.

---

*Some systems allow for multiple line user-defined functions. Check the specifications on your BASIC system in the user's manual.

The DEF Statement   Table 9.18 shows that the DEF statement permits the creation of user-defined functions. The name of the function follows DEF, and it must begin with the two letters FN followed by a variable name that is consistent with the rules used for naming variables.

TABLE 9.18   The DEF Statement

General Form:	DEF FNx(p, . . . , p) = expression where x is a simple variable which must agree in type with the expression p is a simple variable.
Purpose:	To define a function that is relevant to a particular application that can be referenced as often as needed in the program in which it is defined.
| *Examples:* | ```
100 DEF FND(Y) = Y^3
200 DEF FNC$(A$) = MID$(A$, 2, 5)
300 DEF FNG(N, E) = INT(N * 10^E + 0.5 * SGN(N))/10^E
400 DEF FNR(Z) = INT(10 * RND)
``` |
| *Caution:* | With the Apple and COMMODORE, only numeric functions may be defined. |

Table 9.19 lists some invalid DEF statements and some possible valid counterparts.

TABLE 9.19   Invalid DEF Statements and Corresponding Valid DEF Statements

Invalid DEF Statements	*Error in the Invalid DEF Statements*	*Valid DEF Statements*
`100 DEF(X) = X^2`	Missing function name	`100 DEF FNA(X) = X^2`
`150 (X) = X * X + C`	DEF and Name mandatory	`150 DEF FNC(X) = X * X + C`
`220 DEF FN5(V) = V * V * V`	Invalid name.	`220 DEF FNF(V) = V * V * V`
`300 DEF FNA(X$) = LEFT$(X$, 2)`	Function name must have an appended $ since expression is a string.	`300 DEF FNA$(X$) = LEFT$(X$, 2)`

The parameters in a user-defined function are sometimes called **dummy variables**, since they are assigned the values of the corresponding arguments when reference is made to the function. For example, the following partial program contains a user-defined function that rounds the value assigned to the argument X.

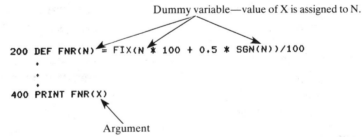

Dummy variable—value of X is assigned to N.

```
200 DEF FNR(N) = FIX(N * 100 + 0.5 * SGN(N))/100
         .
         .
         .
400 PRINT FNR(X)
```

Argument

This partial program displays the value of X rounded to the nearest hundredths place, whether X is positive or negative.

The dummy variables assigned as parameters are local to the function definition. That is, they are distinct from any variables with the same name outside of the function definition. For example, in the following partial program:

```
200 DEF FND(A, B, C) = A * B * C
         .
         .
         .
410 READ A, B, C
```

The dummy variables A, B and C in line 200 *are not affected* when A, B and C are assigned values due to line 410.
```

It is possible to define functions using variables other than the parameters. For example, in the following partial program

```
200 DEF FNC(A) = A * B * C
    .
    .
    .
410 READ A, B, C
```

the variables B and C in line 200 are the same as the variables B and C in line 410. That is, when line 410 is executed, the variables B and C in line 200 are assigned values. The dummy variable A in line 200 however, is not assigned a value when line 410 is executed.

A function that does not use the parameter list in the expression may be defined. Such functions may be used to define constants or expressions that do not require a variable. Each of the following functions includes a parameter that is not used in the expression.

```
100 DEF FNP(Z) = 3.14159
200 DEF FNC(Z) = 2.54
300 DEF FNR(Z) = INT(10 * RND + 1)
```

Line 100 defines FNP equal to pi (π). Line 200 defines FNC equal to the number of centimeters in an inch. Line 300 defines FNR so it returns a random number between 1 and 10. In each case, the parameter Z is not used in the expression. The parameter Z (or any other variable name) is necessary because of the syntax required to write a user-defined function.

The rules regarding DEF statements in a program and error conditions are:

> DEF **Rule 1:** A user-defined function must occur in a lower numbered line than that of the first reference to it.

> DEF **Rule 2:** The same function cannot be defined more than once.

> DEF **Rule 3:** A function definition cannot reference itself.

Referencing User-Defined Functions

User-defined functions may be referenced in statements in the same manner as numeric and string functions. The number of arguments following the reference should agree with the number of dummy variables in the DEF statement.

The following program determines the effective rates of interest for the nominal rates 5.5%, 6.5%, 7.5%, 8.5% and 9.5% using the following formula:

$$R = \left(1 + \frac{J}{C}\right)^C - 1$$

where R is the effective rate
        C is the number of conversions per year
        J is the nominal rate

The program calculates and displays the effective rates for nominal rates converted semiannually, quarterly, monthly and daily (assume 365 days per year). For an in-depth discussion of effective versus nominal rates, see Section 6.4.

The usefulness of DEF statement is apparent in Program 9.13. Rather than code the formula four times to determine the corresponding effective rates for a nominal rate, the DEF statement allows you to code the formula once (line 160), and then reference it four times (line 240). The constant used as the argument in each function reference (line 240) is assigned to the parameter C in the DEF statement. The variable J in the DEF statement is the same as the variable J in the executable statements of the program.

```
100 REM PROGRAM 9.13
110 REM DETERMINING THE EFFECTIVE RATE OF INTEREST
120 REM USING A USER DEFINED FUNCTION
130 REM R = EFFECTIVE RATE,   C = NO. OF CONVERSIONS
140 REM J = NOMINAL RATE
150 REM ********************************************
160 DEF FNE(C) = 100 * ((1 + J/C)^C - 1)
170 PRINT TAB(25); "EFFECTIVE RATES COMPOUNDED"
180 PRINT TAB(15); STRING$(47, "-")
190 PRINT "NOMINAL RATE", "SEMIANNUALLY", "QUARTERLY",
200 PRINT "MONTHLY", "DAILY"
210 PRINT "------------", "------------", "----------",
220 PRINT "-------", "-----"
230 FOR J = 0.055 TO 0.095 STEP 0.01
240     PRINT 100 * J; "%", FNE(2), FNE(4), FNE(12), FNE(365)
250 NEXT J
260 PRINT
270 PRINT "END OF REPORT"
280 END

RUN
```

PROGRAM 9.13

```
                          EFFECTIVE RATES COMPOUNDED
            -----------------------------------------------------
NOMINAL RATE  SEMIANNUALLY  QUARTERLY      MONTHLY      DAILY
------------  ------------  ----------     -------      -----
   5.5 %        5.57559      5.61438       5.64048      5.65126
   6.5 %        6.60558      6.66008       6.69706      6.70428
   7.5 %        7.6406       7.71353       7.76305      7.77586
   8.5 %        8.68056      8.77466       8.83885      8.86142
   9.5 %        9.72559      9.84373       9.92434      9.9556

END OF REPORT
```

Programming Case Study 30: Computer Simulation

The following Programming Case Study incorporates the use of both the function RND and a user-defined function.

Problem

"Beat the House Roller" is a simple but popular dice game, in which the house roller throws a pair of dice. The customer then throws the dice, trying to roll a higher score. If the customer rolls a lower score or the same score as the house roller, the house wins. The bet is $5.00 for each game.

An accumulator is included to keep track of the customer's winnings. Also, the customer's winnings are displayed at the end of each roll. A means of temporarily stopping the game is included so the customer can decide if he or she desires to continue playing. An analysis of the problem, a flowchart and a program solution follow.

Program Tasks

1) Include the RANDOMIZE statement so that a new seed value will be available to the RND function.

2) Use the function RND to generate random numbers to simulate the actual throw of the dice. There are six sides to a die, each with an equal probability of showing up. For each die, provide separate random numbers between 1 and 6. Use the following user-defined function to generate random numbers between 1 and 6:

```
DEF FNR(Z) = INT(6 * RND + 1)
```

3) Reference the user-defined function twice in succession for the house roller. The sum of the two simulated rolls of a die will determine the house roller's score. The customer's score will be determined in the same manner.

4) Determine the winner by comparing the house roller's score and the customer's score. Increment or decrement by $5.00 and display the accumulator A.

5) Use an INPUT statement to determine whether the customer wants to continue playing. A response of YES indicates the customer wants to continue the game.

6) Prior to termination, display a message based on the customer's winnings. If the customer owes money, BETTER LUCK NEXT TIME! will be displayed. If the customer does not owe any money, the system will display YOU ARE PRETTY LUCKY!

The solution to the Computer Simulated Dice Game is represented by the flowchart in Figure 9.2 and Program 9.14, which includes the following significant points.

1) Line 140 defines a function that is referenced four times (lines 190 and 220) for each pass through the While loop. The dummy variable Z is not used in the function's expression.

2) Line 160 ensures at least one pass through the loop by assigning Y$ the value YES, since the condition of the WHILE statement compares Y$ to YES.

3) Line 250 increments or decrements the running total A by $5.00.

4) Lines 320 through 350 display an end-of-game message. The message displayed is dependent on the value of A.

5) Finally, in the flowchart in Figure 9.2, note that the user-defined function is represented by the process symbol.

```
100 REM PROGRAM 9.14
110 REM COMPUTER SIMULATED DICE GAME
120 REM ****************************
130 RANDOMIZE VAL(MID$(TIME$, 7, 2))
140 DEF FNR(Z) = INT(6 * RND + 1)
150 LET A = 0
160 LET Y$ = "YES"
170 WHILE Y$ = "YES"
180     REM *****DETERMINE HOUSE ROLLER SCORE*****
190     LET H = FNR(Z) + FNR(Z)
200     PRINT "THE HOUSE ROLLS=========>"; H
210     REM *****DETERMINE THE CUSTOMER SCORE*****
220     LET C = FNR(Z) + FNR(Z)
230     PRINT "YOUR SCORE===============>"; C
240     REM *****DETERMINE THE WINNER*****
250     IF C > H THEN LET A = A + 5 ELSE LET A = A - 5
260     PRINT USING "YOUR WINNINGS============>$$###.##-"; A
270     PRINT
280     PRINT
290     INPUT "DO YOU WISH TO CONTINUE(ENTER YES OR NO)"; Y$
300 WEND
310 PRINT
320 IF A < 0 THEN 330 ELSE 350
330     PRINT "BETTER LUCK NEXT TIME!"
340 GO TO 360
350     PRINT "YOU ARE PRETTY LUCKY!"
360 END
```

PROGRAM 9.14

```
RUN

THE HOUSE ROLLS=========> 6
YOUR SCORE===============> 9
YOUR WINNINGS============>    $5.00


DO YOU WISH TO CONTINUE(ENTER YES OR NO)? YES
THE HOUSE ROLLS=========> 7
YOUR SCORE===============> 11
YOUR WINNINGS============>   $10.00


DO YOU WISH TO CONTINUE(ENTER YES OR NO)? YES
THE HOUSE ROLLS=========> 12
YOUR SCORE===============> 8
YOUR WINNINGS============>    $5.00


DO YOU WISH TO CONTINUE(ENTER YES OR NO)? NO

YOU ARE PRETTY LUCKY!
```

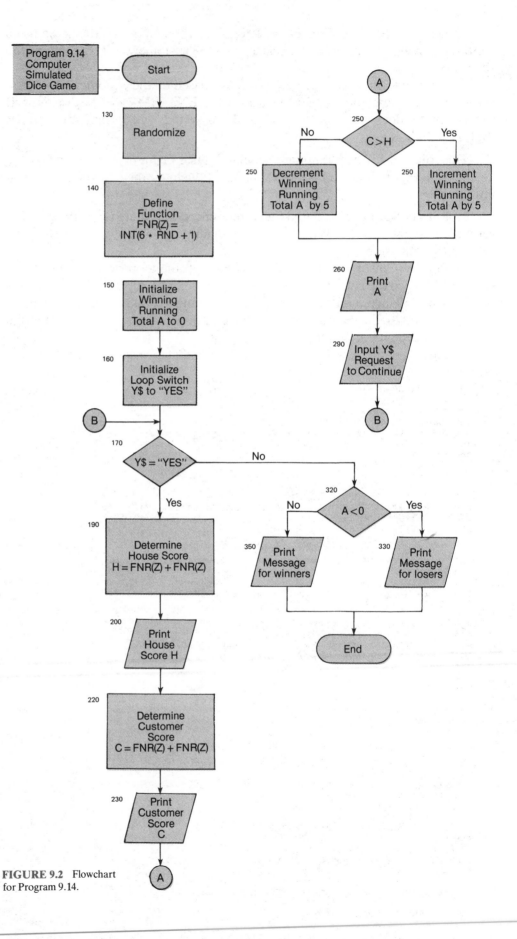

FIGURE 9.2 Flowchart for Program 9.14.

1. BASIC includes several string functions and string statements that place it among the better programming languages for manipulating letters, numbers, words and phrases.

2. The function LEN (X$) returns the length of the string argument X$.

3. The function LEFT$ (X$, N) extracts a substring beginning with the leftmost character (position 1) of the string X$ for a length of N characters.

4. The function RIGHT$ (X$, N) extracts a substring beginning with the rightmost character of the string argument X$ for a length of N characters.

5. The function MID$ (X$, P, N) extracts a substring beginning with the character in position P of X$ for a length of N characters.

6. The function INSTR (P, X$, S$) returns the beginning position of the substring S$ in the string X$. The search begins at position P. If the position argument P is omitted, the system begins the search at position 1 of X$.

7. The string statement MID$ (X$, P, N) = S$ replaces a substring in string X$ beginning at position P for a length of N characters with another substring S$.

8. The function ASC (C$) returns a two-digit numeric value that corresponds to the ASCII code for the single character string C$.

9. The function CHR$ (N) returns a single string character that corresponds to the ASCII code for the numeric value N.

10. The function STR$ (N) returns the string equivalent of the numeric value N.

11. The function VAL (X$) returns the numeric equivalent of the string X$.

12. The function SPC (N) displays N spaces and may only be used in a PRINT statement.

13. The function SPACE$ (N) returns N spaces.

14. The function STRING$ (N, C) returns N times the character "C" within quotation marks.

15. The function DATE$ returns the current system date as a string value in the form mm-dd-yyyy.

16. The function TIME$ returns the current system time of day in 24-hour notation as a string value in the form hh:mm:ss.

17. The string statement LINE INPUT allows you to assign an entered line to a string variable, including quotation marks and commas. The LINE INPUT statement does not display an input prompt.

18. The functions INKEY$ and INPUT$ (N) allow you to write programs that accept input character by character without pressing the Enter key. The INKEY$ does not suspend execution of the program, but instead checks the keyboard to determine if a character is pending. The function INKEY$ returns at most one character. The function INPUT$ (N) returns N characters from the keyboard. Unlike the function INKEY$, INPUT$ (N) suspends execution of the program until N characters are entered from the keyboard.

19. The numeric functions classified as arithmetic include the ABS (absolute value), FIX (fixed integer), INT (integer), and SGN (sign).

20. The numeric functions classified as exponential include the SQR (square root), EXP (exponential) and LOG (logarithmic).

21. The numeric functions classified as trigonometric include the SIN (sine), COS (cosine), TAN (tangent) and ATN (arctangent).

22. The function RND returns an unpredictable decimal fraction number between zero and less than one.

23. The function RND returns random numbers based on the seed. If the seed is not changed, the system returns the same set of random numbers in the same sequence each time the same program is executed. The statement RANDOMIZE, executed before referencing the function RND in a program, changes the seed from which the random numbers are generated.

24. In addition to numeric and string functions, BASIC allows you to define new functions that relate to a particular application. This second type of function, known as a user-defined function, is written as a one-line statement directly into the program. The one-line statement is the DEF statement.

25. All user-defined function names begin with the two letters FN followed by a variable name that is consistent with the rules used for naming variables.

26. User-defined functions are called upon in a LET, PRINT or IF statement the same way that numeric and string functions are called upon.

9.6
SELF-TEST
EXERCISES

1. Consider the valid programs listed below. What is displayed if each is executed?

a)
```
100 REM CHAPTER 9 SELF-TEST 1A
110 LET A$ = "MY PROGRAM HAS BUGS"
120 FOR I = LEN(A$) TO 1 STEP -1
130    PRINT MID$(A$, I, 1)
140 NEXT I
150 END
```

b)
```
100 REM CHAPTER 9 SELF-TEST 1B
110 LET V = 0
120 LET A$ = "COMPUTERS MAKE NO VALUE JUDGEMENTS AND HAVE NO LOYALTIES."
130 LET B$ = "THEY DO PRECISELY WHAT THEY ARE TOLD."
140 LET C$ = A$ + " " + B$
150 FOR I = 1 TO LEN(C$)
160    LET D$ = MID$(C$, I, 1)
170    IF D$="A" OR D$="E" OR D$="I" OR D$="O" OR D$="U" THEN LET V = V + 1
180 NEXT I
190 PRINT A$
200 PRINT B$
210 PRINT "THE NUMBER OF VOWELS IN THE TWO SENTENCES IS"; V
220 END
```

c) Assume JOHN QUINCY ADAMS is entered in response to lines 110 through 130.
```
100 REM CHAPTER 9 SELF-TEST 1C
110 LINE INPUT "ENTER YOUR FIRST NAME"; F$
120 LINE INPUT "ENTER YOUR MIDDLE NAME"; M$
130 LINE INPUT "ENTER YOUR LAST NAME"; L$
140 PRINT
150 PRINT "YOUR INITIALS ARE ";
160 PRINT LEFT$(F$, 1); "."; LEFT$(M$, 1); "."; LEFT$(L$, 1); "."
170 END
```

d)
```
100 REM CHAPTER 9 SELF-TEST 1D
110 DEF FNA(A, B, C) = A * B * C
120 READ L, W, H
130 WHILE L > 0
140    PRINT "THE LENGTH IS"; L
150    PRINT "THE WIDTH IS"; W
160    PRINT "THE HEIGHT IS"; H
170    PRINT "THE AREA IS"; FNA(L, W, H)
180    PRINT
190 WEND
200 PRINT "END OF REPORT"
210 REM ***DATA FOLLOWS***
220 DATA 4, 3, 2, 1, 6, 8, 0, 0, 0
230 END
```

2. Find the errors in the following programs.

a)
```
100 REM CHAPTER 9 SELF-TEST 2A
110 LINE INPUT "WHAT IS THE VALUE"; A
120 LET B = SQR$(A)
130 PRINT "THE SQUARE ROOT OF"; A; "IS"; B
140 LET B$ = INPUT(3) "ENTER 'YES' TO CONTINUE";
150 IF B$ = "YES" THEN 110
160 END
```

b)
```
100 REM CHAPTER 9 SELF-TEST 2B
110 INPUT "WHAT IS THE VALUE"; B
120 LET A = STR$(B)
130 PRINT "THE RESULT IS "; A
140 PRINT "PRESS THE 'Y' KEY TO CONTINUE, ANY OTHER KEY TO TERMINATE"
150 LET C$ = INKEY
160 IF C$ = "" THEN 150
170 IF C$ = "Y" THEN 110
180 END
```

3. Evaluate each of the following:

a) LEN("BASIC")

b) LEFT$("BASIC", 2)

c) RIGHT$("BASIC", 2)

d) MID$("BASIC", 2, 3)

e) INSTR(3, "BASIC", "I")

f) SPACE$(10)

g) MID$("BASIC", 3, 3) = "CAK"

h) ASC("9")

i) CHR$(87)

j) VAL("42.75")

k) STR$(-14.6)

l) STRING(7, "+")

4. Characterize the four methods of accepting data through the keyboard— INPUT, LINE INPUT, INKEY$ and INPUT$ (N) —in terms of suspension of program execution, type of data that may be assigned and whether the Enter key must be pressed.

5. Assume that it is exactly 4:15 P.M. (system time) on July 4, 1986 (system date). Evaluate the following:
   a) `TIME$`
   b) `DATE$`
   c) `MID$(TIME$, 1, 5)`
   d) `MID$(DATE$, 1, 6) + MID$(DATE$, 9, 2)`

6. Write a program that corrects the error in the following string: WORLD WAR II OCCURRED IN THE 19TH CENTURY.

7. What is the range of random numbers assigned to A by the following statement:
   ```
   200 LET A = INT(100 * RND + 1)
   ```

8. Evaluate each of the following:
   a) `ABS(-45)`   d) `INT(1.27)`
   b) `SGN(0)`   e) `SQR(81)`
   c) `SQR(SQR(SQR(256)))` f) `EXP(0)`

9. Write a BASIC statement that will suspend execution of the program, display the message ENTER YOUR FULL NAME, and accept all characters entered before the Enter key is pressed.

10. Write a routine that will suspend program execution and accept eight characters from the keyboard without requiring that the user press the Enter key.

11. What value is assigned to A$ if there is no character pending from the keyboard for the following statement?
    ```
    600 LET A$ = INKEY$
    ```

12. What kind of graphic output displays from the following partial program?
    ```
    390 REM CHAPTER 9 SELF-TEST 12
    400 PRINT STRING$(22, "*")
    410 FOR I = 1 TO 4
    420    PRINT "*"; SPACE$(20); "*"
    430    IF I = 2 THEN PRINT "*"; "   I MADE THIS BOX   "; "*"
    430 NEXT I
    440 PRINT STRING$(22, "*")
    ```

13. Indicate the value displayed due to line 300 in the following partial program:
    ```
    100 REM CHAPTER 9 SELF-TEST 13
    110 DEF FNX(Y) = SQR(ABS(Y))
    120 DEF FNY(X) = INT(FNX(X))
          .
          .
          .
    300 PRINT FNY(-10)
    ```

9.7 TEST YOUR BASIC SKILLS

1. Consider the valid programs listed below. What is displayed if each is executed?
   a)
   ```
   100 REM EXERCISE 9.1A
   110 LET N$ = "MISSISSIPPI"
   120 FOR I = 1 TO LEN(N$)
   130    PRINT LEFT$(N$, I)
   140 NEXT I
   150 END
   ```

   b) Assume that the system time is equal to 15:34:56.
   ```
   100 REM EXERCISE 9.1B
   110 LET B = VAL(MID$(TIME$, 1, 2))
   120 IF B < 12 THEN 130 ELSE 160
   130    LET A$ = "A.M."
   140    IF B = 0 THEN LET B = 12
   150 GOTO 180
   160    LET A$ = "P.M."
   170    IF B <> 12 THEN LET B = B - 12
   180 LET C$ = STR$(B) + MID$(TIME$, 3, 6) + SPACE$(1) + A$
   190 PRINT "THE TIME IS "; C$
   200 END
   ```

```
c)  100 REM EXERCISE 9.1C
    110 LET C$ = "08<NC74NOAA>FN20A45D;;H"
    120 PRINT "CODED MESSAGE:  "; C$
    130 PRINT
    140 PRINT "THE MESSAGE IS: ";
    150 FOR I = 1 TO LEN(C$)
    160    LET N = ASC(MID$(C$, I, 1))
    170    LET N = N + 17
    180    LET M$ = CHR$(N)
    190    PRINT M$;
    200 NEXT I
    210 END
```

```
d)  100 REM EXERCISE 9.1D
    110 LET C$ = "TODAY IS THE TOMORROW YOU WORRIED ABOUT YESTERDAY"
    120 PRINT LEFT$(C$, 1);
    130 FOR I = 2 TO LEN(C$)
    140    LET U = ASC(MID$(C$, I, 1))
    150    IF U <> 32 THEN LET U = U + 32
    160    LET L$ = CHR$(U)
    170    PRINT L$;
    180 NEXT I
    190 PRINT "."
    200 END
```

2. Evaluate each of the following. Assume C$ is equal to the following string: IF I HAVE SEEN FURTHER IT IS BY STANDING UPON THE SHOULDERS OF GIANTS.

   a) `LEN(C$)`   g) `CHR$(71)`
   b) `RIGHT$(C$, 100)`   h) `STRING$(14, "A")`
   c) `LEFT$(C$, 5)`   i) `STR$(-13.691)`
   d) `MID$(C$, 11, 4)`   j) `INSTR(C$, 5, " ")`
   e) `VAL("36.8")`   k) `MID$(C$, 64, 7) = "MIDGETS"`
   f) `ASC(MID$(C$, 4, 1))`   l) `SPACE$(4)`

3. Evaluate each of the following. Assume Y is equal to 2 and A$ is equal to the following string: GOTO IS A FOUR LETTER WORD.

   a) `LEN(A$)`   g) `MID$(A$, Y, 3)`
   b) `RIGHT$(A$, 4)`   h) `MID$(A$, Y^3, 2)`
   c) `RIGHT$(A$, 30)`   i) `MID$(A$, 1, 5 * Y)`
   d) `LEFT$(A$, 50)`   j) `INSTR(A$, "IS")`
   e) `LEFT$(A$, 0)`   k) `INSTR(Y, A$, "T")`
   f) `LEFT$(A$, Y)`   l) `INSTR(2 * Y, A$, "GOTO")`

4. Evaluate each of the following.

   a) `VAL("99")`   f) `CHR$(37)`
   b) `ASC("+")`   g) `ASC(";")`
   c) `CHR$(63)`   h) `VAL("-3.1416")`
   d) `STR$(48.9)`   i) `SPACE$(10)`
   e) `LEN("PROGRAM")`   j) `STRING$(5, " ")`

5. What does the following program display when executed? What value must be assigned to E$ to terminate the program?

```
100 REM EXERCISE 9.5
110 LET C$ = "A"
120 LET E$ = ""
130 WHILE E$ <> "1"
140    FOR I = 1 TO 70
150       PRINT C$;
160    NEXT I
170    PRINT
180    LET E$ = INKEY$
190    IF E$ <> "" THEN LET C$ = E$
200 WEND
210 END
```

6. Write a series of statements that will display the sum of the digits in the customer number N$. Assume that N$ is equal to "1698."

7. Assume that the system time is exactly 11:59:59 P.M. and the system date is September 15, 1986. Evaluate each of the following.

   a) `100 LET A$ = TIME$`
   b) `110 LET B$ = DATE$`

```
c) 300 LET T = 86400*(VAL(MID$(DATE$, 4, 2)) - 1)
   310 LET T = T + 3600*(VAL(MID$(TIME$, 1, 2))
   320 LET T = T + 60*VAL(MID$(TIME$, 4, 2))
   330 LET T = T + VAL(MID$(TIME$, 7, 2))
```

8. What does the following program display when executed? Explain the algorithm used in this program.

```
100 REM EXERCISE 9.8
110 PRINT "PRIME NUMBERS"
120 PRINT "BETWEEN 1 AND 100"
130 PRINT 2
140 FOR I = 3 TO 100
150    LET M = INT(SQR(I))
160    FOR K = 2 TO M
170       IF I = K * INT(I/K) THEN 200
180    NEXT K
190    PRINT I
200 NEXT I
210 END
```

9. What does the following program display when executed?

```
100 REM EXERCISE 9.9
110 FOR K = 1 TO 24
120    FOR J = 1 TO 10
130       PRINT "WAKE UP";
140       FOR I = 1 TO 5
150          PRINT CHR$(7);
160       NEXT I
170    NEXT J
180    PRINT
190 NEXT K
200 END
```

10. Write a single BASIC statement for each of the following. Use numeric functions wherever possible. Assume the value of X is a real number.

    a) $p = \sqrt{a^2 + b^2}$

    b) $b = \sqrt{|\tan X - 0.51|}$

    c) $q = 8 \cos^2 X + 4 \sin X$

    d) $y = e^x + \log_e (1 + X)$

11. What is the numeric value of each of the following?

    a) INT(-18.5)

    b) ABS(-3)

    c) INT(16.9)

    d) ABS(6.7)

    e) EXP(1)

    f) LOG(0)

12. Write a BASIC statement that will

    a) Determine the sign of $2X^3 + 3X + 5$.

    b) Determine the integer part of $4X + 5$.

    c) Round X two decimal places. One decimal place. Use the SGN function so that both positive and negative numbers may be rounded.

13. Write a program that displays the values for X and Sin X where X varies between 0° and 180°. Increment X in steps of 5°.

14. What value displays when the following sequence of statements is executed?

```
100 REM EXERCISE 9.14
110 DEF FNX(B) = B^2 + 5
120 LET C = 20
130 PRINT FNX(C)
140 END
```

15. Write a program that will convert a Farenheit temperature (F) to Centigrade (C), Kelvin (K) and Rankine (R). Employ user-defined functions for the following formulas:

    C = (F − 32) * 5/9

    K = C + 273

    R = F + 460

16. Write a program that will generate and display 100 random numbers between 1 and 52 inclusive.

17. Explain the purpose of the RANDOMIZE statement.

18. Write a user-defined function that will determine a 10% discount on the amount of purchases P in excess of $200.00. The discount applies to the excess and not the entire purchase.

19. What is the difference between a variable found in the parameter list of a user-defined function and a variable used as the argument in a function call?

20. Is the following program valid or invalid? If it is invalid, indicate why.

```
100 REM EXERCISE 9.20
110 DEF FNX(B) = B^2
120 LET B = 5
130 LET C = FNX(B)
140 PRINT C
150 END
```

**9.8
PROGRAMMING
EXERCISES**

Purpose: To become familiar with the use of the functions LEN and MID$ and the LINE INPUT statement.

**Exercise 1:
Palindromes**

Problem: A palindrome is a word or phrase that is the same when read backward or forward. For example, "noon" is a palindrome, but "moon" is not. Write a program that requests the user to enter a string of characters and determines whether the string is a palindrome. The string of characters may include quotation marks. Use a sentinel value of EOE to terminate the program.

Input Data: Use the following sample data

```
I
9876556789
ABLE WAS I ERE I SAW ELBA
"BOB DID BOB"
WOW LIL DID POP
OTTO
RADAR
!@#$$@#!
()
A PROGRAM IS A MIRROR IMAGE OF THE MIND
```

Output Results: The following partial results are shown:

```
STRING? I
I IS A PALINDROME.

STRING? 9876556789
9876556789 IS A PALINDROME.
        .
        .
        .
STRING? WOW LIL DID POP
WOW LIL DID POP IS NOT A PALINDROME.
        .
        .
        .
STRING? EOE
JOB COMPLETE
```

**Exercise 2:
English to Pig Latin
Conversion**

Purpose: To become familiar with string manipulation.

Problem: In Pig Latin a word such as PASCAL is converted to ASCALPAY. For this Programming Exercise, the translation from English to Pig Latin calls for taking the first character of the word and moving it to the end of the word followed by an appended AY. If a word begins with a vowel, then the vowel remains in its beginning position and the string WAY is appended to the end of the word. For example, ADA becomes ADAWAY.

Write a program that displays the Pig Latin translation for a string of English words. Also display the number of words that begin with a vowel, the total number of words in the string and the percentage of words that begin with a vowel. Do not include punctuation.

Input Data: Use the following sample data:

EVERY PROGRAM IS A SELF PORTRAIT OF THE PERSON WHO WROTE IT
AUTOGRAPH YOUR WORK WITH EXCELLENCE

Output Results: The following results are displayed:

```
ENTER THE ENGLISH SENTENCE WITHOUT PUNCTUATION
-----------------------------------------------
? EVERY PROGRAM IS A SELF PORTRAIT OF THE PERSON WHO WROTE IT AUTOGRAPH YOUR WOR
K WITH EXCELLENCE

THE SENTENCE IN PIG LATIN IS:
--------------------------------
EVERYWAY ROGRAMPAY ISWAY AWAY ELFSAY ORTRAITPAY OFWAY HETAY ERSONPAY HOWAY ROTEW
AY ITWAY AUTOGRAPHWAY OURYAY ORKWAY ITHWAY EXCELLENCEWAY

WORDS BEGINNING WITH A VOWEL=========>    7
TOTAL NUMBER OF WORDS================>   17
PERCENTAGE BEGINNING WITH A VOWEL====>  41.2%
```

Exercise 3:
Time to Double
an Investment
Compounded Quarterly

Purpose: To become familiar with the use of numeric functions and user-defined functions.

Problem: Write a program that will determine the time to double an investment compounded quarterly for the following annual interest rates: 6%, 7%, 8% and 9%. The formula for computing the time is:

$$N = \frac{\log 2}{M(\log(1 + J/M))}$$

where N = the time in years
       J = annual interest rate
       M = number of conversion periods

Once the time has been determined for a given interest rate, round the answer to two decimal places. Define the formula in a user-defined function in your program.

Input Data: None

Output Results: The following results are displayed:

```
TIME TO DOUBLE AN INVESTMENT
   COMPOUNDED QUARTERLY
-----------------------------

ANNUAL          YEARS TO
INTEREST        DOUBLE
---------       ---------
  6%            11.64
  7%             9.99
  8%             8.75
  9%             7.79

JOB COMPLETE
```

Exercise 4:
Economic Order
Quantity

Purpose: To become familiar with the use of numeric functions, user-defined functions and economic order quantity.

Problem: From the following formula, the Outland Steel Company determines weekly the quantity of products that it should order:

$$EOQ = \sqrt{\frac{2DC}{PH}}$$

where EOQ = amount to be ordered
       D = average weekly demand
       C = cost of placing an order
       P = unit purchase price
       H = percentage cost of purchase price for inventory overhead

The formula is applied to a product only if B < 2D where B = balance of pieces on hand and D = average weekly demand.

Write a program that employs a user-defined function to round to a whole number the amount of a product to be ordered (EOQ) if B < 2D. Each line of output is to include the product name, amount to order and the balance on hand. Display an appropriate message if a product should not be reordered. Incorporate an EOF test based on the product name.

Input Data: Prepare and use the following sample data:

Item	Demand	Balance	Cost/Order	Purchase Price	Inventory Cost
WIGGLE	2000	2200	$10.50	$ 5.00	0.10%
FLIPPER	500	2000	4.75	12.30	0.20%
PLIXER	1000	1500	2.21	4.75	0.15%

Output Results: The following results are displayed:

```
              INVENTORY REPORT
              ----------------

                 AMOUNT        BALANCE
   ITEM          TO ORDER      ON HAND
   ----          --------      -------
   WIGGLE           2,898        2,200
   FLIPPER     DO NOT ORDER      2,000
   PLIXER             788        1,500

   END OF REPORT
```

Exercise 5:
Order Entry Simulation

Purpose: To become familiar with the use of the random number function and computer simulation.

Problem: Order entry is the process of receiving customer orders and producing shipping orders. The Oldtown Company has three clerks employed in its Order Entry department. On the average, the three clerks can process 197 customer orders a day. Management has requested the data processing department to simulate the activities of the Order Entry department over a four week period (20 working days). The following statistics were compiled over the same four week period during the previous year:

Customer Orders Received	Frequency in Days	Relative Frequency	Cumulative Frequency
185	1	0.05	0.05
190	5	0.25	0.30
195	6	0.30	0.60
200	4	0.20	0.80
205	3	0.15	0.95
210	1	0.05	1.00

Assuming that the four-week period (day 1 through day 20) begins with no backlog order, write a program that will display the simulation of:

1) The number of orders received each day
2) The number of orders processed (the day's order plus backlog orders)
3) The orders not processed
4) The number of days in which orders go unprocessed

The orders received are to be simulated by employing the RND function. The value generated from the RND function should be passed through a series of IF statements, which test to determine if it is less than or equal to the cumulative frequencies for orders compiled from the previous year. The logic for these tests is shown as follows:

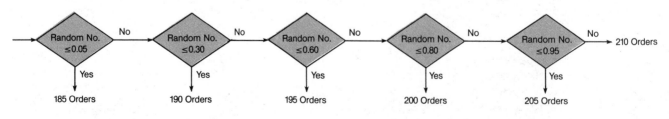

Input Data: None

Output Results: The following illustrates a sample run. Answers will vary, depending upon the random numbers generated by your system.

```
                    ORDER ENTRY SIMULATION
                    ----------------------

                ORDERS        ORDERS        ORDERS
        DAY     RECEIVED      PROCESSED     NOT PROCESSED
        ---     --------      ---------     -------------
         1        195           195              0
         2        190           190              0
         3        195           195              0
         4        205           197              8
         5        195           197              6
         .         .             .               .
         .         .             .               .
         .         .             .               .
        18        200           197              7
        19        195           197              5
        20        190           195              0

    NUMBER OF DAYS ORDERS WENT UNPROCESSED ======> 15
```

Purpose: To become familiar with concatenation, table searching and string manipulation of cryptograms.

Exercise 6: Cryptograms

Problem: In Section 9.2, you were introduced to a method of substituting characters in a coded message and determining the contents of the message. The direct substitution method, based on a table of substitutes, may also be used with cryptograms. Write a program that uses the following table of substitutes to decode a given message. The character Ꞵ represents the space character.

Regular characters— A B C D E F G H I J K L M N O P Q R S T U V W X Y Z – Ꞵ .
Coded characters — 9 G Q 6 V L P N W X A 8 T # H Z J M (U 3) R I S B F K D

Input Data: Use the following sample coded message:

```
LW#6W#PKUNVK6VVZK(WTZ8WQWUWV(KW#K9K
QHTZ8WQ9UV6KQH88VQUWH#KHLKUNW#P(K
UHKGVK6H#VKW(KUNVKQMV9UW)WUSKW#K
ZMHPM9TTW#PKFKND6DTW88(
```

Use the LINE INPUT statement to accept each of the four lines and assign them to four different string variables. Use the concatenation operator to join the four strings.

Output Results: The following is shown for the first line of the coded message:

```
THE MESSAGE IS: FINDING THE DEEP SIMPLICITIES IN A
```

Purpose: To become familiar with character transformation and soundex.

Exercise 7: Soundex Code

Problem: Companies that allow their customers to phone or write for information regarding their account status are often confronted with locating the record in the Account file when only a name is supplied. Situations like this may arise due to illegible handwriting or poor voice communications. In some instances, companies wish to ask as few questions as possible, which gives callers the impression that they are special customers. One method used to transform the sound of a name into a successful search of a record is soundex. The soundex method, developed by M. Odell and R. Russell, involves encoding surnames when a record is first added to the file and placing the soundex code in the record for access purposes. The soundex code for a name is determined from the following rules:

1) Retain the first letter and drop all occurrences of a, e, h, i, o, u, w and y in other positions of the name.

2) Assign the following digits to the remaining letters:

Letters	Digits
b, f, p, v	1
c, g, j, k, q, s, x, z	2
d, t	3
l	4
m, n	5
r	6

3) If two or more letters with the same code are adjacent in the *original* name, drop all but the first one.

4) Convert the name to the form "letter, digit, digit, digit" by adding trailing zeros if there are less than three digits, or by dropping rightmost digits if there ore more than three. The following examples of names have these corresponding soundex codes:

Last Name	Code	Last Name	Code
Case	C200	Knuth	K530
Cash	C200	Smith	S530
Caise	C200	Smyth	S530
Gauss	G200	Smythe	S530

This system does not always work, but it speeds up the searching of many records.

Write a program that builds an account file in which each record contains the customer number, customer name, soundex code and balance due. The program should request from the operator the customer number, name and balance due. From the last name, the program should determine the soundex code and display it. Then the program should write the record to a sequential file which will later be used in Exercise 8.

Input Data: Use the following sample data:

Customer Number	Customer Name	Balance Due
1783	Allen, John	$55.00
1934	Smit, Joe	0.00
2109	Case, Jeff	5.00
2134	Alien, Bill	35.00
2367	Allan, Fred	65.00
2568	Caise, Ed	87.00
3401	Smith, Ron	45.00
3607	Cas, Louis	0.00
4560	Smythe, Al	4.00
5590	Ellen, Boyd	7.80
6498	Caes, Tom	5.30
7591	Kase, Jim	0.00

Output Results: The following partial results are displayed:

```
CUSTOMER NUMBER? 1783
CUSTOMER NAME? ALLEN, JOHN
BALANCE? 55.00

THE SOUNDEX CODE IS A450
```

The records are also written to a sequential file in auxiliary storage.

**Exercise 8:
Browsing a File Using
Soundex**

Purpose: To become familiar with accessing records using the soundex code.

Problem: Write a program that will either access and display a record based on the customer number or access and display all records with the same soundex code. Displaying all records with a common characteristic is *browsing* through the file. The program should initially display a menu with the following selections:

1) Access record by customer number
2) Browse file
3) End program

When the user selects a code of 1, the program accepts the customer number and searches the file sequentially for the corresponding record. If a match is found, all of the information in the record is displayed. If a match is not found, an appropriate message is displayed. In either case, the message: PRESS ANY KEY TO RETURN TO THE MENU... is displayed. When the user selects a code of 2, the program accepts the name, generates the soundex code and displays the customer number and name of all records in the file with that soundex code.

On the lower part of the screen the message: ENTER 'M' TO RETURN TO THE MENU OR A CUSTOMER NUMBER TO DISPLAY THE ENTIRE RECORD is displayed.

If the user enters M, the program returns to the menu. If the user enters a customer number, all the information in the record and the message: PRESS ANY KEY TO RETURN TO THE MENU... are displayed.

Each time the program returns control to the menu, the file must be closed and then reopened.

Input Data: Use the following sample data:

1) Access records by the following customer numbers: 2109, 3607, 6555.

2) Display all records that have customer names that sound alike. Use the following names: Allien, Shmit, Kaise.

3) When the records displayed have the same sound as Shmit, request the display of customer number 4560.

Output Data: The following partial results are shown:

Main Menu

```
        ACCOUNT FILE MENU
        -----------------

    CODE        FUNCTION
    ----        --------
      1         ACCESS BY CUSTOMER NUMBER
      2         BROWSE FILE FOR SIMILAR SOUNDING NAMES
      3         END PROGRAM

    ENTER A NUMBER 1 THROUGH 3?
```

Browse Menu

```
     CUSTOMERS THAT SOUND THE SAME AS SHMIT

            CUSTOMER      CUSTOMER
            NUMBER        NAME
            ------        --------
            1934          SMIT, JOE
            3401          SMITH, RON
            4560          SMYTHE, AL

    ENTER 'M' TO RETURN TO THE MENU OR A CUSTOMER NUMBER
    TO DISPLAY THE ENTIRE RECORD======>4560
```

Record Display

```
    CUSTOMER NUMBER===> 4560
    CUSTOMER NAME=====> SMYTHE, AL
    SOUNDEX CODE======> S530
    BALANCE===========>    $4.00

    PRESS ANY KEY TO RETURN TO THE MENU...
```

Exercise 9:
Payroll
Problem VIII—
Spelling Out
the Net Pay

Purpose: To become familiar with table utilization, the functions INT and STR$, and spelling out numbers.

Problem: Construct a program that spells out the net pay for check writing purposes. For example, the net pay $5,078.45 results in the phrase:

FIVE THOUSAND SEVENTY-EIGHT DOLLARS AND 45 CENTS

Assume that the net pay does not exceed $9,999.99.

Hint: Use the function INT to separate the integer portion of the net pay into single digits. Use the single digits to access the words from one of two positionally organized tables. If the digit represents the thousands, hundreds or units position, then access the word from the following table:

Digit	Word	Digit	Word
0	Null	10	TEN
1	ONE	11	ELEVEN
2	TWO	12	TWELVE
3	THREE	13	THIRTEEN
4	FOUR	14	FOURTEEN
5	FIVE	15	FIFTEEN
6	SIX	16	SIXTEEN
7	SEVEN	17	SEVENTEEN
8	EIGHT	18	EIGHTEEN
9	NINE	19	NINETEEN

If the digit represents the tens position, then access the word from the following table:

Digit	Word	Digit	Word
0	Null	5	FIFTY
1	TEN	6	SIXTY
2	TWENTY	7	SEVENTY
3	THIRTY	8	EIGHTY
4	FORTY	9	NINETY

Use the functions INT and STR$ to determine the fraction portion of the net pay. Use the concatenation operator to string the words together.

Input Data: Use the following sample data:

Employee Number	Net Pay	Employee Number	Net Pay
123	$8,462.34	127	$1,003.39
124	987.23	128	4,037.00
125	78.99	129	4.67
126	6,000.23	130	0.42

Output Results: The following results are displayed:

```
EMPLOYEE
NUMBER    NET PAY   NET PAY SPELLED OUT
--------  -------   -------------------
   123    $8,462.34 EIGHT THOUSAND FOUR HUNDRED SIXTY-TWO DOLLARS AND 34 CENTS
   124     $987.23  NINE HUNDRED EIGHTY-SEVEN DOLLARS AND 23 CENTS
   125      $78.99  SEVENTY-EIGHT DOLLARS AND 99 CENTS
   126    $6,000.23 SIX THOUSAND DOLLARS AND 23 CENTS
   127    $1,003.39 ONE THOUSAND THREE DOLLARS AND 39 CENTS
   128    $4,037.00 FOUR THOUSAND THIRTY-SEVEN DOLLARS AND 0 CENTS
   129       $4.67  FOUR DOLLARS AND 67 CENTS
   130       $0.42  42 CENTS
```

PROGRAM FLOWCHARTING

The main purpose of this appendix is to concentrate on preparing, using and reading program flowcharts. Upon successful completion of this Appendix, you should be able to develop program flowcharts which describe the logic and operations of computer programs.

A **program flowchart** shows in graphic form the algorithm (method of solution) used in a program. A program flowchart also shows how the application or job is to be accomplished by depicting a procedure for arriving at a solution. The term "flowchart" will be used throughout the remainder of this text to mean program flowchart.

Purpose of Flowcharting

A flowchart is used by programmers and analysts as:

1) An aid in developing the logic of a program
2) An aid in breaking the program into smaller units, sometimes called "modules," if a structured, modular approach is used
3) A verification that all possible conditions have been considered in a program
4) A means of communication with others about the program
5) A guide in coding the program
6) Documentation for the program

A programmer prepares a flowchart *before* coding the problem.

Eight basic symbols are commonly used in flowcharting a program. They are given in Table 1.4 with their names, meanings, and some of the BASIC statements that are represented by them (p. 14). In preparing a flowchart, the process, input/output, decision, terminal, connector, and predefined process symbols (see Table 1.4) are connected by solid lines. There are six kinds of solid lines, called **flowline symbols**, that show the direction of flow. The annotation symbol, on the other hand, is connected by a broken line to any one of the other flowchart symbols (including any of the flowline symbols).

One rule that is fundamental to all flowcharts concerns direction. In constructing a flowchart, start at the top (or left-hand corner) of a page. The flow should be top to bottom or left to right. If the flow takes any other course, arrowheads must be used.

Flowchart Notation

Inside each of the symbols, except the flowline symbols write either English-sentence-type notation, mathematical notation, or program language statements. These notations are arbitrary, and their use depends on the kind of program being flowcharted, on the experience of the person constructing the flowchart, and on the standards that are used in the computer installation. One symbol or abbreviated description may represent more than one BASIC statement. The annotation symbol, with comments written inside it, is optional and is used whenever additional information is desired for the sake of clarity.

The first symbol in a flowchart may quite often be a terminal symbol with "Start" written inside it. *This corresponds to no BASIC statement* but is used solely to aid a person unfamiliar with the flowchart to find the beginning point. No flowline symbols are ever drawn curved or diagonally. Also, although arrowheads are shown, they need not be used in this case, since their usage is optional when flow is both left to right and top to bottom.

A glance at Figure A.1 brings forth the logic of Program A.1, which calculates the state income tax. Two versions of the flowchart are given to show that the choice of the written contents placed inside each symbol is an arbitrary matter. Both versions have the same logic, since the number, type, and arrangement of flowchart symbols are identical. The flowchart in FigureA.1 (A) is more like English, and it would be used to communicate with a nonprogrammer, while the flowchart in Figure A.1(B) is more like BASIC and it would be used to communicate with a programmer who is familiar with BASIC. A slight disadvantage in using English-sentence-type notation is that ordinary English can become wordy and, at times, even unclear.

PROGRAM A.1

```
100 REM PROGRAM A.1
110 REM COMPUTATION OF STATE TAX
120 REM ************************
130 INPUT "WHAT IS THE SALARY"; S
140 INPUT "WHAT IS THE NUMBER OF DEPENDENTS"; D
150 LET T = 0.02 * (S - 500 * D)
160 PRINT
170 PRINT "THE STATE TAX IS $"; T
180 END

RUN

WHAT IS THE SALARY? 19500
WHAT IS THE NUMBER OF DEPENDENTS? 5

THE STATE TAX IS $ 340
```

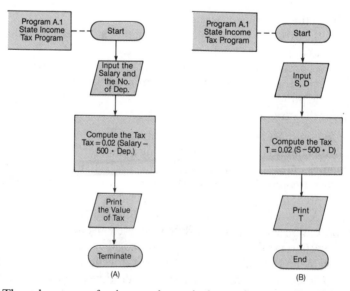

FIGURE A.1 Flowcharts for Program A.1(A). English-like; (B) BASIC-like

The advantage of using mathematical notation over English-like notation is that it permits the description of the operation to be presented in a compact and precise form. For example, the statement 100 LET I = P * R can be stated in the symbol as I = P * R or I ← P * R. (Remember, the symbol ← means "is assigned to" or "is replaced by.") The operation "compare the variable I with the value of 10" can be represented as I:10, where the colon indicates comparison. Table A.1 lists common notations, including mathematical ones, used in flowcharts.

TABLE A.1   Some Common Notations Used in Flowcharts

Symbol or notation	Explanation
+	Addition or positive value
−	Subtraction or negative value
* or ×	Multiplication
/	Division
∧	Exponentiation
←	Is replaced by or is assigned to
=	Is equal to
≠ or =	Is not equal to
:	Comparison
>	Is greater than
≥	Is greater than or equal to
<	Is less than
≤	Is less than or equal to
| |	Absolute value
⌐	Negation
EOF	End of file
LC	Last card
HI	High
LO	Low
EQ	Equal
Yes or Y	
No or N	
On	
Off	Self-explanatory
True or T	
False or F	

Actual program language statements are another means of identifying the operations in a flowchart symbol. Since BASIC is the programming language used in this book, BASIC statements may be used inside flowchart symbols. The advantage of using program language statements in a flowchart is that this type of flowchart can improve communication among programmers who are familiar with the given language. This book, which favors a combination of English-sentence-type, BASIC-type and mathematical-type notation, will use whichever notation renders a given operation clear and unambiguous. For some programs, an English flowchart and a BASIC flowchart will both be presented.

The preparation of flowcharts is still more of an art than a science. There are few formal rules, but some useful approaches can be described.

    Before the flowchart can be drawn, a thorough analysis of the problem, the data, and the desired output results must be performed. The logic required to solve the problem must be determined. On the basis of this analysis, a general flowchart of the main path of the logic can be sketched. This can then be refined until the overall logic is fully determined. Then this general flowchart is used to make one or more detailed flowcharts of the various parts, levels, and exceptions to the main path of logic. After each detailed flowchart has been freed of logical errors and other undesirable features, like unnecessary steps, the actual coding of the program in a computer language can be undertaken.

A.2 GUIDELINES FOR PREPARATION OF FLOWCHARTS

General flowcharts often fit the following straight-line pattern:

    input
      ↓
    process
      ↓
    output

Straight-Line Flowcharts

That is, for the program to output the results, it must process the data. However, before the data can be processed, it must have been made available to the program through input or by some equivalent method like a LET statement.

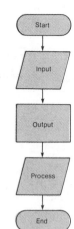

FIGURE A.2   Basic pattern of a straight-line general flow-chart.

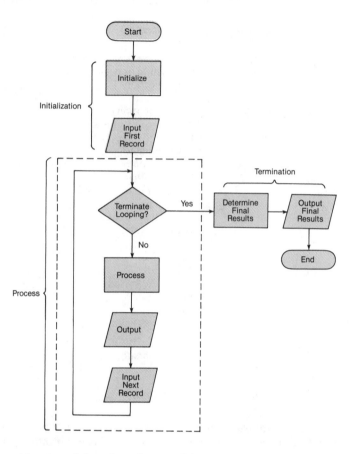

FIGURE A.3   Basic pattern of a general flowchart with looping.

Figure A.2 indicates that this general flowchart is a straight-line flowchart, which is defined as a flowchart in which the symbols are arranged sequentially (one after the other), without any deviations or looping, until the terminal symbol representing the end of the flowchart is reached. Once the operation indicated in any one symbol has been performed, that operation is never repeated.

Straight-line programs are limited, since they can be executed only sequentially, and since they do not have the ability to change the sequence of execution based on conditions encountered in processing the data. The programs discussed in Chapters 2 and 3 are of the straight-line variety.

Flowcharts With Looping   A general flowchart that illustrates an **iterative** or repeating process known as looping is shown in Figure A.3. The program illustrated by this flowchart is in three major parts: initialization, process (the loop), and termination, or finalization. BASIC looping statements are discussed in Chapters 4, 5 and 6. A flowline exits from the bottom symbol in Figure A.3 and enters above the decision symbol that determines whether the loop is to be executed again. This flowline forms part of a loop inside which some operations are repeatedly executed until specified conditions are satisfied. This flowchart shows the input, process, and output pattern; it also uses a decision symbol that shows where the decision is made to continue or stop the looping process. The decision symbol may represent an end-of-file test, a last value test, or a comparison of one condition against another.

The general flowchart also contains two braces that show initialization and termination operations. For example, setting the program counters to zero may represent an initialization operation, and displaying the values of counters may represent a finalization operation.

Like the straight-line flowchart, a flowchart with looping need not have all the symbols, as shown in Figure A.3, or a flowchart can have many more symbols. For example, the process symbol within the loop in Figure A.3, when applied to a particular problem, may expand to include branching forward to bypass a process or backward to redo a process. It is also possible that through the use of decision symbols, the process

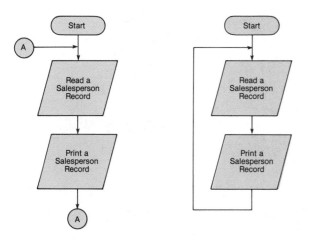

FIGURE A.4 Two methods of representing a loop in a flow-chart.

symbol in Figure A.3 may be shown expanded to several loops, some of which may be independent from each other and some of which may be within other loops.

The main point to remember is that the flowchart shows a process that is carried out. Flowcharts are flexible; they can show any process no matter how complex it may be, and they can show it in whatever detail is needed.

The two flowcharts illustrated in Figure A.4 represent the same program; that is, the program simply reads and then prints a record. Then the program loops back to the reading operation and repeats the sequence, thereby reading and printing for any number of records.

Although the flowcharts in Figure A.4 illustrate two ways a loop can be represented, the particular loop that is shown is an **endless** or **infinite loop**; this type of loop should be avoided in constructing programs. In order to make a program like the one shown in Figure A.4 finite, you must define it so that it will terminate when specified conditions are satisfied. For example, if 15 aging accounts are to be processed, the program can be instructed to process no more than 15 and then to stop. Figure A.5 illustrates the use of a counter C1 in terminating the looping process. Note that the counter is first set to 0 in the initialization step. After an account is read and a message of action printed, the counter is incremented by 1 and tested to find if it is now equal to 15. If the value of the counter is not 15, the looping process continues. If the value of the counter is 15, the looping process terminates.

For the flowchart used in Figure A.5 the exact number of accounts to be processed must be known beforehand. In practice, this will not always be the case, since the number of accounts may be a variable number from one run to the next.

A way to solve this type of problem is shown in Figure A.6, which illustrates the use of an end-of-file test to terminate the looping process. The value of −999999 has been chosen to be the last account number. This kind of value is sometimes known as the sentinel value because it "guards" against reading past the end of file. Also, the numeric item chosen for the last value cannot possibly be confused with a valid item—it is outside the range of the account numbers. Programs using an end-of-file test like the one shown in Figure A.6 are far more flexible and less limited than programs that do not, illustrated in Figures A.4 and A.5. The end-of-file test is illustrated in detail in Chapter 5.

Two more flowcharts with loops are shown in Figures A.7 and 1.12. Figure A.7 illustrates the concept of counting, and Figure 1.12 illustrates the necessary computations required to compute the average commission paid a company's sales personnel. Both flowcharts incorporate the end-of-file test.

The technique of flowcharting may not be very useful in simple computer programs like Program A.1. However, as programs become more complex, with many different paths of execution, a flowchart is not only useful but sometimes a prerequisite for successfully analyzing and coding the program. Indeed, developing the problem solution by arranging and rearranging the flowchart symbols could lead to a more efficient computer program.

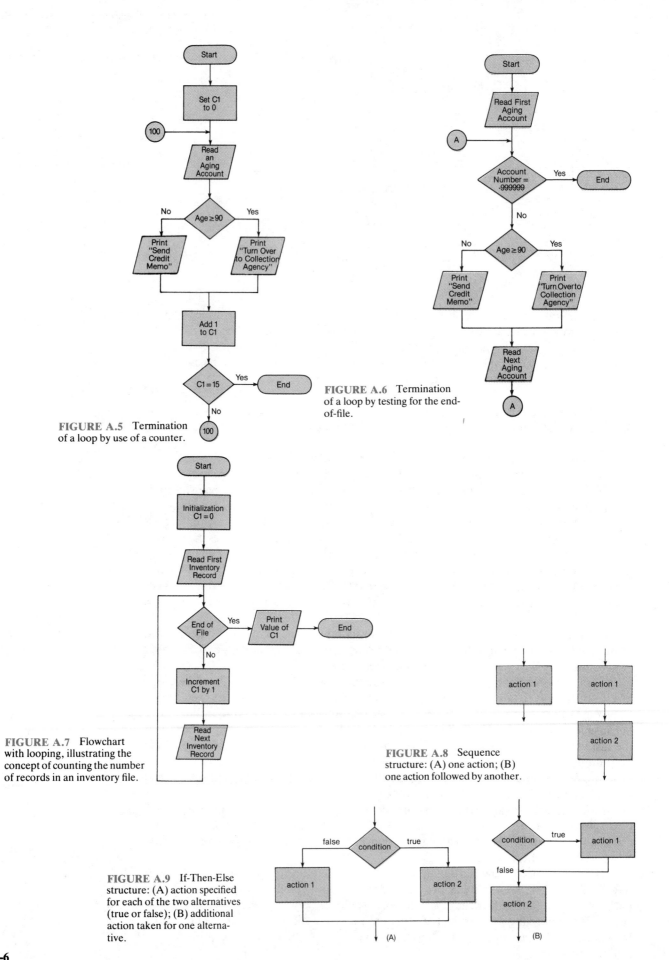

FIGURE A.5 Termination of a loop by use of a counter.

FIGURE A.6 Termination of a loop by testing for the end-of-file.

FIGURE A.7 Flowchart with looping, illustrating the concept of counting the number of records in an inventory file.

FIGURE A.8 Sequence structure: (A) one action; (B) one action followed by another.

FIGURE A.9 If-Then-Else structure: (A) action specified for each of the two alternatives (true or false); (B) additional action taken for one alternative.

Computer scientists agree that good algorithms can be constructed from three basic logic structures, which are:

1) Sequence
2) If-Then-Else or Selection
3) Do-While or Repetition

The following are two common extensions to these logic structures:

4) Do-Until or Repeat-Until
5) Case (an extension of the If-Then-Else logic structure)

The **sequence structure** is used to show one action or one action followed by another and is illustrated in Figure A.8. Every flowchart in this text includes this control structure.

The **If-Then-Else structure** represents a two-way decision with action specified for each of the two alternatives. This logic structure is shown in Figure A.9. The flowcharts presented earlier in Figures A.5 and A.6 include this logic structure. The action can be null for one alternative, as shown in Figure A.9(B).

The **Do-While structure** is the most common logic structure used to create a process that will repeat as long as the condition is true. The Do-While structure is illustrated in Figure A.10 and has been used earlier in Figures A.3, A.6 and A.7. Because the decision to perform the action within the structure is at the *top* of the loop, it is possible that the action may not be done.

The **Do-Until structure** is also used for creating a process that will be repeated. The major differences between the Do-Until and the Do-While structures is that the action within the structure of a Do-Until will always be executed at least once and that the decision to perform the action within the structure is at the *bottom* of the loop. Figure A.11 illustrates the Do-Until structure. The flowchart presented earlier in Figure A.5 included a Do-Until structure.

The **Case structure** is similar to the If-Then-Else structure except that there are more than two alternatives. Figure A.12 illustrates the case structure.

Using only these five logic structures when developing an algorithm will help a program be easy to read, easy to modify and reliable; most important of all, it will help ensure that a program will do what it is intended to do!

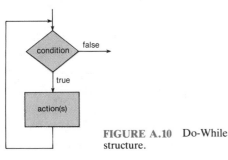

FIGURE A.10 Do-While structure.

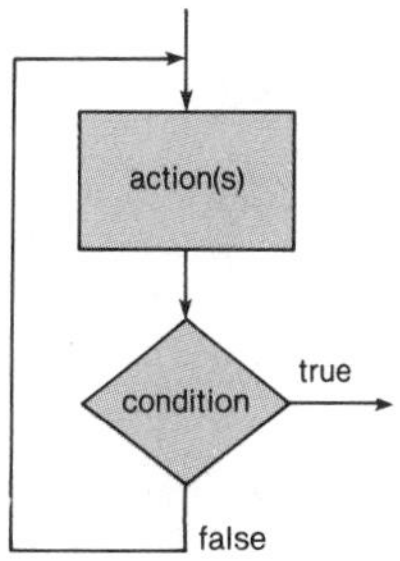

FIGURE A.11 Do-Until structure.

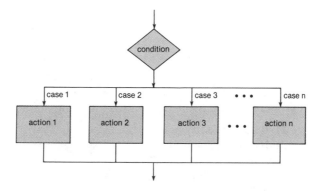

FIGURE A.12 Case structure.

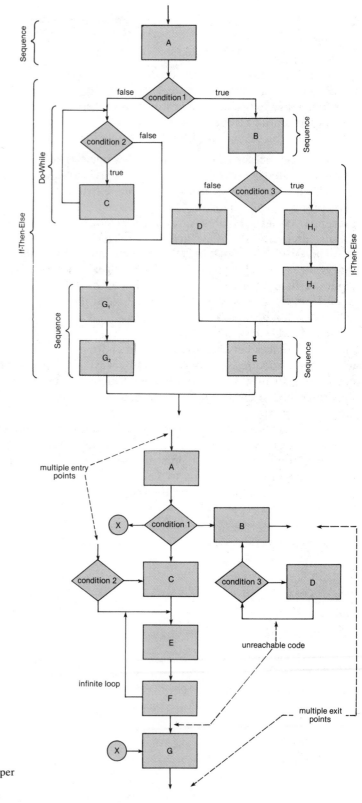

FIGURE A.13 A proper program.

FIGURE A.14 An improper program.

A.4 PROPER PROGRAMS

A **proper program** is one that has the following characteristics:

1) It has one entry point.
2) It has one exit point.
3) It has no unreachable code.
4) It has no infinite loops.

An algorithm constructed using only the five logic structures will form the basis for a proper program. Figure A.13 illustrates the breaking up—the decomposition—of an algorithm into some of the control structures presented in the previous section. On the other hand, Figure A.14 illustrates an algorithm that will result in an improper program.

Shown below are a few flowchart suggestions. These suggestions assume that the input, processing and output of the problem are defined properly.

A.5 FLOWCHARTING TIPS

1) Sketch a general flowchart and the necessary detail flowcharts before coding the problem. Repeat this step until you are satisfied with your flowcharts.
2) Use the control structures described in Section A.3.
3) Put yourself in the position of the reader, keeping in mind that the purpose of the flowchart is to improve communications between one person and another by communicating the method of solution for the problem.
4) Show the flow of processing from top to bottom and from left to right. Use arrowheads as required to indicate the direction of flow.
5) Draw the flowchart so that it is neat and clear. Avoid excessively long flowlines by using the connector symbols.
6) Choose notation and wording that explains the function of each symbol in a clear and precise manner.
7) Do your best to avoid endless loops. Construct loops so that they will be terminated when specific conditions are satisfied.

The reason that flowcharts are so important is simple: the difficulties in programming lie mostly in the realm of logic, not in the realm of the syntax and semantics of the computer language. Thus, most errors when using a computer come from logical mistakes, and a flowchart aids in detecting logical mistakes!

A.6 TEST YOUR BASIC SKILLS

1. What is the first step in solving a problem that uses a computer?
2. Which of the flowchart symbols given are superfluous, in that any program may be flowcharted without using them?
3. Can one flowchart symbol be used to represent, simultaneously, two or more BASIC statements?
4. In the flowchart in Figure A.15 what is the value of I and the value of J at the instant just after the statement $J \leftarrow J + I$ is executed for the fifth time? The value of I and J after the statement $1 \leftarrow I + 2$ is executed the tenth time? (A statement such as $J \leftarrow J + I$ is valid and is read as the "new value of J equals the old value of J plus one" or, equivalently, the "value of J is to be replaced by the value of J plus one.")
5. Consider the flowchart portion in Figure A.16. Given a relatively intelligent person going to work. This individual usually has the car keys but occasionally forgets them. Does the flowchart portion in Figure A.16 incorporate the most efficient method of representing the actions to be taken? If not, redraw the flowchart portion given in Figure A.16.

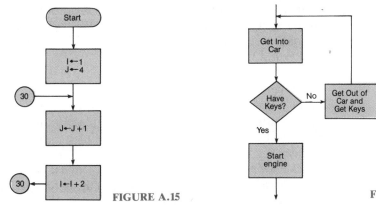

FIGURE A.15   FIGURE A.16

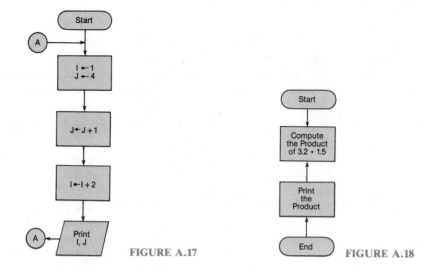

FIGURE A.17

FIGURE A.18

6. In the flowchart in Figure A.17, of a valid though trivial program, what values of I and of J are printed when the output symbol is executed for the fiftieth time?

7. What are the values of I and J just as the output symbol is executed for the thousandth time in the flowchart of Figure A.17?

8. What is wrong with the flowchart in Figure A.18?

9. Two numbers, R and S, located in the main storage of a computer, are to be replaced by their squares. Construct the flowchart to represent this action.

10. Construct an efficient flowchart to solve for the roots of the equation:

$$ax^2 + bx + c = 0$$

using the formula:

$$x = \frac{-b \pm \sqrt{b^2 - 4ac}}{2a}$$

Input three values containing the coefficients a, b and c, respectively. Print the values of the two real roots. If complex roots exist ($b^2 - 4ac < 0$), print a message to that effect. If the roots are equal, print one root. (Assume the coefficient "a" does not have a value of zero, so that an attempted division by zero will not occur.)

11. Two numbers, U and V, located in the main storage, are to be interchanged. Construct the flowchart to represent this interchange.

12. Construct a flowchart for the following problem. Input two values for a and b. If the quotient a/b exists, print its value. If the quotient does not exist, print an appropriate message.

13. Draw one flowchart that will cause the Mechanical Mouse to go through any of the four mazes shown in Figure A.19. At the beginning, an operator will place the mouse on the entry side of the maze, in front of the entry point, facing "up" toward the maze. The instruction "Move to next cell" will put the mouse inside the maze. Each maze has four cells. After that, the job is to move from cell to cell until the mouse emerges on the exit side. If the mouse is instructed to "Move to next cell" when there is a wall in front of it, it will hit the wall and blow up. Obviously, the mouse must be instructed to test if it is "Facing a wall?" before any "Move." The Mechanical Mouse's instruction set consists of the following:

A) *Physical Movement:*
   1) Move to next cell (the mouse will move in the direction it is facing)
   2) Turn right
   3) Turn left
   4) Turn around (all turns are made in place, without moving to another cell)
   5) Halt
B) *Logic:*
   1) Facing a wall? (Through this test, the mouse determines whether there is a wall *immediately* in front of it, that is, on the border of the cell it is occupying and in the direction it is facing.)

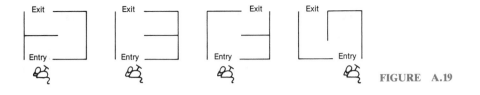

FIGURE   A.19

2) Outside the maze?

If the mouse is outside the maze, it can also make the following decisions:

3) On the entry side?

4) On the exit side?

14. Construct a flowchart for the following problem: input two values P and R, where P represents the amount of a loan and R represents the yearly interest rate. The loan is to be repaid in 12 equal monthly installments, and the total interest to be paid is equal to the product of P and R. Each monthly payment is to reduce the balance owed on the principal by P/12 and the balance owed on the interest by (P) (R)/12.

Print the amount of the monthly payment. For each iteration print the values of N, B and I, where N represents the payment number, B represents the balance owed on the principal, and I represents the balance owed on the interest.

15. An opaque urn contains three diamonds and four worthless rocks. Construct the flowchart describing the following events. Draw a stone from the urn. If it is a diamond, set it aside. Otherwise return it to the urn. Continue until all the diamonds are removed.

16. An opaque urn contains three diamonds, four rubies, and two pearls. Construct the flowchart describing the following events. Draw a gem from the urn. If it is a diamond, lay it aside. If it is not a diamond, return it to the urn. Continue in this fashion until all the diamonds are removed. After all the diamonds are removed, repeat a procedure similar to that above until all the rubies are removed. After all the rubies are removed, continue in the same fashion until all the pearls are removed.

17. In the flowchart represented by Figure A.20, what is the value of I and the value of J at the instant the terminal symbol with the word End is reached?

18. In the flowchart in Figure A.20, if the condition in the first decision symbol is changed from I > J to I = J, what are the values of I and J when control reaches End?

19. In the flowchart in figure A.20, if the condition in the second decision symbol is changed from J > 10 to J ≥ 10, what are the values of I and J when control reaches End?

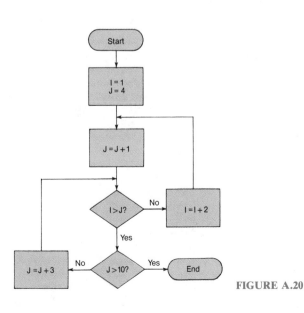

FIGURE A.20

20. In the flowchart in Figure A.21, how many values are read before the value of P is displayed?

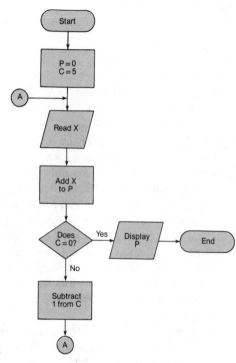

FIGURE A.21

PSEUDOCODE AND OTHER LOGIC DESIGN TOOLS

In recent years, many useful techniques have been developed to aid the problem-solver in the design and documentation of computer programs. Two of these were presented earlier: top-down charts in Chapter 6 and the more traditional program flowcharts in Appendix A. In this Appendix four additional logic tools will be surveyed: pseudocode, Nassi-Shneiderman charts, Warnier-Orr diagrams, and decision tables.

B.1 INTRODUCTION

Pseudocode is a program design technique that uses natural English and resembles BASIC code. It is an intermediate notation that allows for the logic of a program to be formulated without diagrams or charts. Pseudocode resembles BASIC in that specific operations can be expressed:

B.2 PSEUDOCODE

> Read employee record
> Add 1 to male counter
> Display employee record

What makes pseudocode appealing to many is that it has no formal syntactical rules, which allows the programmer to concentrate on the design of the program rather than on the peculiarities of the logic tool itself.

Although pseudocode has no formal rules, the following are commonly-accepted:

1) Begin pseudocode with a program title statement.

   Program: Monthly Sales Analysis Report

2) End pseudocode with a terminal program statement.

   End: Monthly Sales Analysis Report

3) Begin each statement on a new line. Use simple and short imperative sentences containing a single transitive verb and a single object.

   Open employee file
   Subtract 10 from quantity

4) Express assignment as a formula or as an English-like statement.

   Withholding tax = 0.20 × (gross pay − 38.46 × dependents)

   or

   Compute withholding tax

A-13

5) To implement the design, try to avoid using logic structures not available in the programming language to be used.

6) For the If-Then-Else structure, use the following conventions:

a) Align the If and Else vertically.

b) Indent the true and false tasks.

c) Use "End-If" as the structure terminator.

Example 1: If balance ≤ 500 Then
    Display credit ok
Else
    Display credit not ok
End-If

Example 2: If sex code = male Then
    Add 1 to male count
    If age ≥ 21 Then
        Add 1 to male adult count
    Else
        Add 1 to male minor count
Else
    Add 1 to female count
    If age ≥ 21 Then
        Add 1 to female adult count
    Else
        Add 1 to female minor count
End-If

7) For the Do-While structure use the following conventions:

a) If the structure represents a counter-controlled loop, begin the structure with "Do."

b) If the structure does not represent a counter-controlled loop, begin the structure with "Do-While."

c) Specify the condition on the Do-While or Do line.

d) Use "End-Do" at the last statement of the structure.

e) Align the Do-While or Do and the End-Do vertically.

f) Indent the statements within the loop.

Example 3: Program: Employee File List
    Display report and column headings
    Set employee count to 0
    Read first employee record
    Do-While not end-of-file
        Add 1 to employee count
        Display employee record
        Read next employee record
    End-Do
    Display employee count
    Display end-of-job message
    End: Employee File List

Example 4: Program: Sum first 100 Integers
    Set sum to 0
    Do integer = 1 to 100
        Add integer to sum
    End-Do
    Display sum
    Display end-of-job message
    End: Sum first 100 Integers

8) For the Case structure, use the following conventions:

a) Begin the structure with "Case-Start," followed by the variable to be tested.

b) Use "End-Case" as the structure terminator.

c) Align "Case-Start" and "End-Case" vertically.

d) Indent each alternative.

e) Begin each alternative with "Case," followed by the value of the variable that equates to the alternative.

f) Indent the action of each alternative.

Example 5: Case-Start customer code
    Case 100
        Add 1 to high-risk customer count
    Case 200
        Add 1 to risk customer count
    Case 300
        Add 1 to regular customer count
    Case 400
        Add 1 to special customer count
End-Case

Nassi-Shneiderman charts (also called N-S charts) are often refered to as structured flowcharts. Unlike program flowcharts, they contain no flowlines or flowchart symbols and thus have no provision to include a GOTO statement.

   N-S charts are made up of a series of rectangles. Flow of control always runs top to bottom. The sequence structure in an N-S chart is illustrated in the following example:

B.3 NASSI-SHNEIDERMAN CHARTS

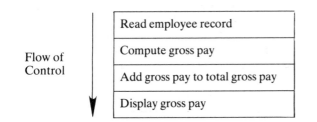

The If-Then-Else structure is shown by three triangles within a rectangle and a vertical line separating the true and false tasks, as shown below:

age ≥ 21	
False True	
Add 1 to minor count	Add 1 to adult count
Display "Minor"	Display "Adult"

The N-S chart indicates a decision (age ≥ 21) and the actions to be taken for an adult and minor. If a person's age is greater than or equal to 21, then the actions specified for the true case are processed. If a person's age is less than 21, then the actions specified for the false case are processed. It is not possible for both the true and false tasks to be processed for the same person.

   The Do-While structure (test at the top of the loop) is referred to by a rectangle within a rectangle, as shown in the following illustration:

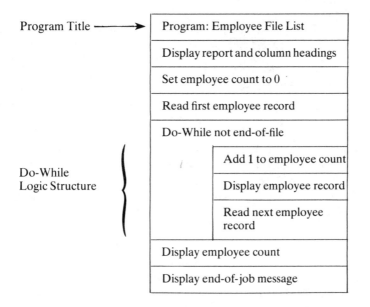

The diagram indicates that the statements within the inner rectangle are to be processed in sequence as long as it is not end-of-file. When the end-of-file is sensed, control passes to the statement below the Do-While structure.

   The Do-Until structure (test at the bottom of the loop) is similarly referred to by a rectangle within a rectangle, as shown at the top of the next page.

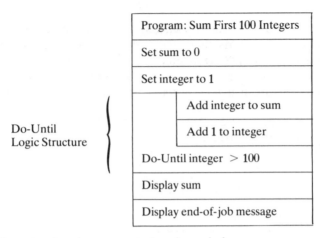

Do-Until
Logic Structure

The Case structure is represented as shown below.

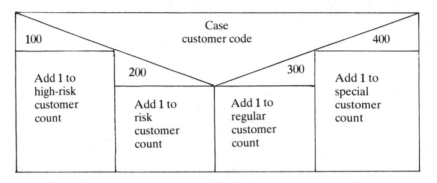

As with the If-Then-Else structure, only one of the actions specified will be processed for each customer.

Those who advocate N-S charts claim they are quite useful in all phases of the program development cycle, expecially for system and program documentation. Nassi and Shneiderman go even further. They write:

> Programmers who first learn to design programs with these symbols never develop the bad habits which other flowchart notation systems permit. . . . Since no more than fifteen or twenty symbols can be drawn on a single sheet of paper, the programmer must modularize his program into meaningful sections. The temptation to use off-page connectors, which lead only to confusion, is eliminated. Finally, the ease with which a structured flowchart can be translated into a structured program is pleasantly surprising.*

Others argue that N-S charts are nothing more than pseudocode with lines and rectangles around it.

B.4
WARNIER-ORR
DIAGRAMS

In some respects, a Warnier-Orr diagram is similar to a top-down chart laid on its side. Both place a heavy emphasis on the idea of hierarchies. Warnier-Orr diagrams, however, go one step further and place an equal emphasis on flow of control.

Recall from Chapter 6 that a top-down chart is primarily used to show functionality or *what* must be done to solve a problem. Once a top-down chart is complete, an intermediate tool, like a program flowchart, N-S chart or pseudocode, must be used to show flow of control or *how* and *when* things are to be done in the framework of a solution. With Warnier-Orr diagrams, no such intermediate step is required.

As with N-S charts, there is no provision within the framework of Warnier-Orr diagrams to show a GOTO statement. Solutions are constructed using the three basic logic structures: sequence, selection (If-Then-Else or Case) and repetition (Do-While or Do-Until).

---

*I. Nassi and B. Shneiderman, "Flowchart Techniques for Structured Programming," SIGPLAN, Notices of the ACM, v. 8, n. 8, August 1973: 12-16.

A Warnier-Orr diagram is made up of a series of left braces, pseudocode-like statements and a few special symbols, as shown in Table B.1.

TABLE B.1   Warnier-Orr Symbols and Their Meanings

Symbol	Meaning
{	The brace is used to enclose logically related events.
(0, 1)	An event is done zero or one time. Notation for selection structure.
(0, n) or (n)	An event is done n times. Notation for Do-While structure.
(1, n)	An event is done one to n times. Notation for Do-Until structure.
blank or (1)	An event is done one time.
⊕	Exclusive OR. Used in conjunction with the notation (0,1) to show a selection structure.

The sequence structure is illustrated in a Warnier-Orr diagram by listing the sequence of events from top to bottom within a brace, as shown below.

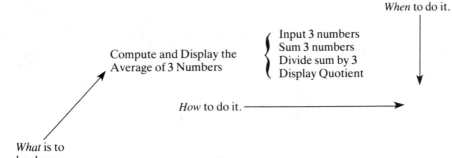

The left brace points to *what* is to be done. Within the brace is the list of events that show *how* to do it and, from top to bottom, when each event is to take place.

The If-Then-Else structure is shown by the use of the notation (0, 1) and the exclusive OR symbol.

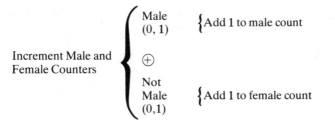

The Case structure is shown in a similar fashion.

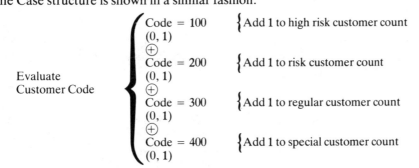

The following Warnier-Orr diagram shows a solution for reading an employee file and computing gross pay for each employee. The solution includes a Do-While structure.

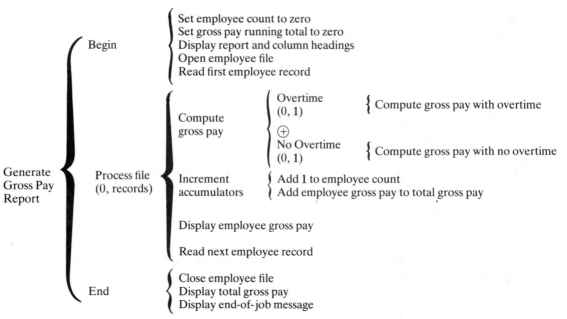

The event "Process file (0,records)" illustrates a Do-While structure. The "0" within parentheses means that the loop can be executed zero times, if, for example, the employee file is empty. The term "records" within parentheses indicates the number of times the loop is to be executed. It is also valid to write the notation for the Do-While structure as "(records)," rather than "(0,records)."

The notation used to represent a Do-Until structure is similar to that of the Do-While structure, except that the notation below the event is written as (1,n) rather than (0,n).

B.5 DECISION TABLES

A decision table can be a powerful aid in describing complex logic. It provides a means for identifying all possible combinations of conditions to ensure each has been considered. A decision table can be helpful in eliminating redundant and meaningless combinations of conditions. Some programmers also find decision tables to be beneficial when presenting a program design for review by a peer group or in discussions with the user who requested the program be written.

Although there are many types of decision tables, only the limited entry decision table will be illustrated here. This table is divided into four sections, as shown below.

Table Title	1	2	3	4	5	6	7	8
condition stub				condition entries				
action stub				action entries				

In the upper left section (condition stub), all conditions are listed. A condition might be SALARY EMPLOYEE? In the upper right section (condition entries), a Y for yes or an N for no is entered in each column. The number of columns of condition entries, often called "rules," depends on the number of conditions in the condition stub. If there is only one condition, then there are two columns of condition entries. If there are two conditions, then there are four columns of condition entries. Each condition increases the number of columns of condition entries by a power of two. Four conditions result in 16 condition entries. Hence, the total number of columns or rules is 2 raised to the power of the number of conditions.

In the lower left section (action stub), the actions are listed. An action might be PAY SPECIAL BONUS. In the lower right section (action entries), an X is used to indicate action and a blank no action.

To illustrate the use of a decision table, let's assume that a company has decided to distribute a year-end bonus to its employees: a special bonus is to be paid to each employee who has 25 years seniority and is either a salary employee or at least 55 years old. All other employees are to receive a regular bonus. There are three conditions:

1) seniority $\geq$ 25 years?
2) salary employee?
3) age $\geq$ 55 years?

Eight columns of condition entries are required to list all possible combinations for three conditions. There are two actions:

1) special bonus
2) regular bonus

The decision table follows.

Bonus Determination	1	2	3	4	5	6	7	8
seniority $\geq$ 25 years	Y	Y	Y	Y	N	N	N	N
salary employee	Y	Y	N	N	Y	Y	N	N
age $\geq$ 55 years	Y	N	Y	N	Y	N	Y	N
pay special bonus	X	X	X					
pay regular bonus				X	X	X	X	X

In order to account for all possibilities, enter the condition entries (Y or N) using a pattern. Take the last condition, age $\geq$ 55 years, and alternate the Y and N beginning with Y. The condition entries become YNYNYNYN. Take the second to the last condition, salary employee, and alternate *pairs* of Ys and Ns. The condition entries become YYNNYYNN. Take the next condition and alternate groups of four Ys and Ns: YYYYNNNN. The upper right section of the table contains all possible combinations for three conditions.

To fill in the action entries it is necessary to construct a logical expression from the problem. The problem corresponds to the following expression:

seniority $\geq$ 25 AND (salary employee OR age $\geq$ 55)

Recalling the definitions of the logical operators AND and OR and the rules of precedence, we can fill in the action entries. The decision table now illustrates all possible combinations and the action to be taken for each combination.

Decision tables are not used to design entire programs, but rather are used in conjunction with other logic tools. They are primarily used to analyze complex If-Then-Else logic structures.

DEBUGGING TECHNIQUES AND PROGRAMMING TIPS

C.1 DEBUGGING TECHNIQUES

Although the top-down approach and structured programming techniques help minimize errors, they by no means guarantee error-free programs.

Due to carelessness or insufficient thought, program portions can be constructed which do not work as anticipated and give erroneous results. When such problems occur, techniques are needed to isolate the errors and correct the erroneous program statements.

Many BASIC systems can detect hundreds of different grammatical errors and display appropriate diagnostic messages. However, there is no BASIC system that can detect all possible errors since literally thousands of possible coding errors can be made. Some of these errors can go undetected by the BASIC system until either an abnormal end occurs during execution or the program terminates with the resulting output in error.

There are several techniques for attempting to discover the portion of the program that is in error. These methods are **debugging techniques.** The errors themselves are **bugs**, and the activity involved in their detection is **debugging**.

Tracing (TRON and TROFF)

Many BASIC systems provide a means of tracing the path of execution through a BASIC program in order to determine which statements are executed.

The most popular trace instructions for personal computers are TRON (**TR**ace **ON**) and TROFF (**TR**ace **OFF**). These instructions may be inserted into a BASIC program as BASIC statements or they may be used as system commands before the RUN command is issued.

The TRON instruction activates tracing and the BASIC system displays the line number of each statement executed. The line numbers appear enclosed in square brackets to prevent them from being confused with other output the program may produce.

For example, if the BASIC system with tracing activated executes a program portion consisting of lines 250, 260, 270 and 280, the output displayed will be as follows:

```
[250][260][270][280]
```

The TROFF instruction deactivates tracing. Both the TRON and TROFF instructions may be used any number of times in a BASIC program, as shown:

```
200  TRON
       .
       .
       .
290  TROFF
       .
       .
       .
550  TRON
       .
       .
       .
700  TROFF
```

Program C.1 has the TRON and TROFF statements in lines 125 and 195. When the RUN command is issued, all statements between lines 125 and 195 are traced, and their line numbers and corresponding output are displayed accordingly.

```
100 REM PROGRAM C.1
110 REM ILLUSTRATING USE OF THE TRACE INSTRUCTIONS
120 REM ******************************************
125 TRON                'SET TRACE ON
130 LET S = 0
140 LET I = 1
150 WHILE I <= 4
160     LET S = S + I
170     LET I = I + 1
180     PRINT S; I
190 WEND
195 TROFF               'SET TRACE OFF
200 END

RUN

[130][140][150][160][170][180] 1   2
[190][160][170][180] 3   3
[190][160][170][180] 6   4
[190][160][170][180] 10   5
[190][195]
```

PROGRAM C.1

Program C.2 is similar to Program C.1. When this program is executed, the computer displays the value of 1 over and over. The program has a bug which results in an infinite loop when the program is run.

```
100 REM PROGRAM C.2
110 REM THIS PROGRAM CONTAINS A BUG
120 REM ***************************
130 LET S = 0
140 LET I = 1
150 WHILE I <= 4
160     LET S = S + I
170     LET T = I + 1     '***ERROR*** - T SHOULD BE I
180     PRINT S
190 WEND
200 END
```

PROGRAM C.2

If the TRON instruction is used as a system command, the following output occurs during tracing:

```
TRON

RUN

[100][110][120][130][140][150][160][170][180] 1
[190][160][170][180] 1
[190][160][170][180] 1
[190][160][170][180] 1
[190]...
```

From the output we can see the repetition of the following sequence of line numbers:

```
[190][160][170][180]
```

This output reveals that the program executes lines 160, 170, 180 and 190 repeatedly in the While loop.

The WHILE statement cannot be satisfied, since the value of I will always be less than four. Line 170 has been incorrectly written. In order to satisfy the WHILE statement, line 170 should be written as:

```
170     LET I = I + 1
```

Another useful debugging technique is to stop a program, examine the values of various variables within the program, and then continue the execution of the program. All this can be accomplished through the use of the STOP, PRINT and CONT (continue) statements.

Examining Values (STOP, PRINT and CONT)

Consider the partial Program C.3:

```
100 REM PROGRAM C.3
110 REM ILLUSTRATING USE OF STOP, PRINT AND CONT
120 REM ****************************************
130 .
      .
      .
300 LET V1 = 10 * 12.15
310 LET A1 = 2 * 24.3
320 LET S1 = 36.9/3
325 STOP
330 .
      .
      .
```

PROGRAM C.3

```
RUN

BREAK IN 325            (Displayed when STOP is executed)

PRINT V1                (Entered by user)

  121.5                 (Displayed result from PRINT statement)

PRINT A1; S1            (Entered by user)

  48.6   12.3           (Displayed result from PRINT statement)


  CONT                  (Entered by user)
```

When the STOP statement is executed in line 325, the program will stop and the message

```
BREAK IN 325
```

will be displayed.

Now the values of various variables can be examined by using a PRINT statement written without a line number.

When a BASIC statement like the PRINT statement is written without a line number, it is executed immediately. This is the **calculator mode** of BASIC; it is also called the **immediate mode**.

After the values of V1, A1, and S1 are displayed, the CONT is issued and the remaining program is executed. CONT should not be placed directly into a BASIC program. Instead, it should be entered as a command from the keyboard by the user.

Intermediate Output   In some instances, including intermediate PRINT statements as a part of the program may be preferable to using STOP statements and displaying the values of variables in calculator mode.

Appropriate PRINT statements are inserted after each one or each group of statements involving computations. This technique is called **source language debugging** or the **intermediate output method**.

Intermediate results are displayed until the specific portion of the program that is in error can be deduced.

If a program produces little output to begin with, the intermediate output method should be used, since the outputs from the intermediate PRINT statements will be easy to distinguish from the regular output. If a program produces a great deal of output, then the technique using the STOP, PRINT and CONT should be used to minimize the amount of output to the display unit.

C.2 TRAPPING USER ERRORS (ON ERROR GOTO AND RESUME)   A thoroughly tested program cannot be guaranteed to be reliable once it is turned over to a user. Most abnormal terminations in a production environment are due to user errors and not programmer errors. This is especially true for programs that interact with the user or are executed on personal computers. User errors fall into two basic categories:

1) Erroneous data entered in response to INPUT statements
2) Not following the instructions in the user's manual

Good programmers will attempt to trap as many user errors as possible. Errors that fall into the first category can be trapped by validating incoming data to ensure it is reasonable or within limits. For example, if a sex code must equal F or M, then the following two partial programs show how the sex code can be validated immediately following its input:

```
100 INPUT "SEX CODE (F OR M)"; S$
110 IF S$ = "F" OR S$ = "M" THEN 140
120    PRINT "SEX CODE "; S$; " IS INVALID, PLEASE RE-ENTER"
130    GOTO 100
```
or
```
100 INPUT "SEX CODE (F OR M)"; S$
110 WHILE S$ <> "F" AND S$ <> "M"
120    PRINT "SEX CODE "; S$; " IS INVALID, PLEASE RE-ENTER"
130    INPUT "SEX CODE (F OR M)"; S$
140 WEND
```

Both partial programs validate the sex code S$ to ensure it is assigned an F or M. For more information on writing programs that reject erroneous input see Section 6.3.

The second category of user errors includes:

1) Not turning on the printer
2) Allowing the printer to run out of paper
3) Not placing a diskette in a disk drive
4) Not closing the door on a disk drive

These types of errors can be trapped through the use of the ON ERROR GOTO statement. Recall from Section 8.4 that the ON ERROR GOTO statement provides a common branch point for any error that occurs following its execution in a program. The branch point and the statements that follow it are an **error-handling routine**.

Once the ON ERROR GOTO statement is inserted in a program, any error that normally terminates execution now causes the system to transfer control to the error-handling routine. BASIC provides two special variables, ERL and ERR, that are automatically assigned values before the ON ERROR GOTO statement transfers control to the routine. ERL is assigned the line number of the statement that caused the error. ERR is assigned an error code. Check the specifications of your BASIC system in the user's manual for the meaning of the error codes, since they vary from one system to another.

Through the use of IF statements, a decision can be made in the error-handling routine to terminate execution or resume execution at some point in the program. The ON ERROR GOTO 0 statement directs the system to terminate execution. The RESUME statement may be used to transfer control to any point in the program to continue execution. If execution is to resume following an error, an error recovery procedure like displaying a message or assigning a value to a variable is performed first. The general form of the ON ERROR GOTO statement and a discussion of the special variables ERL and ERR are given in Table 8.8 of Chapter 8. The general form of the RESUME statement is given in Table C.1.

TABLE C.1   The RESUME Statement

General Form:	RESUME n
	where n may be a blank, zero, line number or the keyword NEXT.
Purpose:	Continues execution of the program after an error-handling routine has been performed. RESUME or RESUME 0 resumes execution at the statement that caused the error. RESUME NEXT resumes execution at the statement immediately following the one which caused the error. RESUME line number resumes execution at the specified line number.
Examples:	200 RESUME 300 RESUME 0 400 RESUME NEXT 500 RESUME 750
Caution:	Not available on all BASIC systems.

The following program uses the ON ERROR GOTO statement to trap user errors. In the error-handling routine, the special variable ERR is tested. If ERR is equal to 24 (printer not ready) or 27 (printer out of paper), a recovery procedure is executed. If ERR equals any other code, then a message is displayed informing the user to copy down the program name, line number in which the error occurred and the error code and transmit this information to the data processing department.

In Program C.4, line 140 activates BASIC's error trapping feature. If an error occurs following line 140, then control transfers to line 250. In line 250, if the error code is equal to 24 or 27, then control passes to line 260 and an appropriate message is displayed. If the error code is not 24 or 27, then control transfers to line 330 and a message is displayed requesting that the user transmit the error code, line number in which the error occurred and the program name to the data processing department.

```
100 REM PROGRAM C.4
110 REM ILLUSTRATING THE USE OF
120 REM THE ON ERROR GOTO STATEMENT
130 REM ****************************
140 ON ERROR GOTO 250
150 LPRINT "NUMBER", "AMOUNT"
160 LPRINT
170 READ N$, A
180 WHILE N$ <> "EOF"
190    LPRINT N$, A
200    READ N$, A
210 WEND
220 LPRINT "JOB COMPLETE"
230 STOP
240 REM *********ERROR-HANDLING ROUTINE**********
250 IF ERR = 24 OR ERR = 27 THEN 260 ELSE 330
260    PRINT "PLEASE CHECK THE PRINTER."
270    PRINT "IT MAY BE TURNED OFF, OUT OF"
280    PRINT "PAPER OR IT IS NOT PROPERLY"
290    PRINT "CONNECTED."
300    PRINT "PRESS THE ENTER KEY WHEN THE"
310    INPUT "PRINTER IS READY.....": Z$
320 RESUME
330    PRINT
340    PRINT "***********PLEASE NOTE************"
350    PRINT "AN IRRECOVERABLE ERROR HAS OCCURRED."
360    PRINT "PLEASE COPY DOWN THE FOLLOWING"
370    PRINT "LINE NUMBER AND ERROR CODE. TRANSMIT"
380    PRINT "THESE AND THE PROGRAM NAME TO THE"
390    PRINT "DATA PROCESSING DEPARTMENT."
400    PRINT "ERROR IN LINE===> "; ERL
410    PRINT "ERROR CODE======> "; ERR
420    PRINT
430    PRINT "              THANK YOU"
440    ON ERROR GOTO 0
450 REM *************DATA FOLLOWS***************
460 DATA 123, 124.89, 126, 145.91, 134, 234.78
470 DATA 210, 567.34, 235, 435.12, 345, 192.45
480 DATA EOF, 0
490 END
```

PROGRAM C.4

C.3 PROGRAMMING TIPS

In BASIC there are many different ways you can code a program and still obtain the same results. This section presents several tips for coding a program to improve its performance, efficiency, structure, and clarity.

Each tip is explained and applied accordingly. You are encouraged to add to the tips in this section.

Tip 1:
Use Simple Arithmetic

On most BASIC systems, addition is performed faster than multiplication, which in turn is faster than division or exponentiation. For example, do the following:

```
150 LET A = B * H * 0.5
160 LET B = S + S
170 LET V = L * L * L
```

instead of:

```
150 LET A = B * H/2
160 LET B = 2 * S
170 LET V = L^3
```

Tip 2:
Avoid Repetitive Evaluation of Expressions

If identical computations are performed in several statements, evaluate the common expression once and save the result in a variable for use in later statements. For example, do the following:

```
200 LET D = SQR(B * B - 4 * A * C)
210 LET R1 = -B + D
220 LET R2 = -B - D
```

instead of:

```
200 LET R1 = -B + SQR(B * B - 4 * A * C)
210 LET R2 = -B - SQR(B * B - 4 * A * C)
```

Do not make unnecessary computations. Remove unnecessary code from a loop, including expressions and statements which do not affect the loop. Place such code outside and before the range of the loop. For example, do the following:

```
300 LET P = 3.14159
310 LET K = 4 * P
320 LET X = Y + 2
330 FOR R = 1 TO 500
340    PRINT K * R * R
350 NEXT R
```

instead of:

```
300 LET P = 3.14159
310 FOR R = 1 TO 500
320    PRINT 4 * P * R * R
330    LET X = Y + 2
340 NEXT R
```

Regardless of the value of R, 4π is always constant. Instead of calculating 4π five hundred times, remove this expression from the loop and compute it once. It is also not necessary to compute the value of X each time through the loop, since the loop never changes the value of X.

Use functions and subroutines wherever possible, since in many cases they conserve main storage and always execute faster than the same capability written in BASIC. For example, do the following:

```
400 LET D = SQR(B * B - 4 * A * C)
```

instead of:

```
400 LET D = (B * B - 4 * A * C)^(0.5)
```

Eliminate unnecessary GOTO statements by reworking the logic in favor of For loops, IF statements, and functions. When GOTO statements are removed, the length of the program usually shortens and a clearer logical structure appears. For example, do the following:

```
500 LET T = 0
510 FOR N = 1 TO 500
520    LET T = T + N
530 NEXT N
540 PRINT T
```

instead of:

```
500 LET T = 0
510 LET N = 1
520 IF N > 500 THEN 560
530    LET T = T + N
540    LET N = N + 1
550 GOTO 520
560 PRINT T
```

Resist the temptation to write clever or tricky code that is difficult to understand. Later modification by someone else may take additional time and may be costly in the long run. For example, do the following:

```
600 FOR R = 1 TO 10
610    FOR C = 1 TO 10
620       IF R <> C THEN LET X(R, C) = 0 ELSE LET X(R, C) = 1
630    NEXT C
640 NEXT R
```

instead of:

```
600 FOR R = 1 TO 10
610    FOR C = 1 TO 10
620       LET X(R, C) = INT(R/C) * INT(C/R)
630    NEXT C
640 NEXT R
```

This section of code generates an array called X where ones are placed on the main diagonal and zeros everywhere else.

You can avoid the need for more IF statements and additional code if you use compound conditions in IF statements and the ELSE clause. For example, do the following:

```
700 IF I = J AND K = L THEN LET A = 99 ELSE LET A = -3
```

instead of:

```
700 IF I = J THEN 720
710 GOTO 730
720 IF K = L THEN 750
730 LET A = -3
740 GOTO 760
750 LET A = 99
760 .
    .
    .
```

When IF statements are placed so the most frequently occurring condition is tested first, extra tests are avoided. A frequency analysis uncovered the following pattern regarding the execution of code:

Type	Name	% Executed
1	Firm Name	0.4
2	Firm Address	0.4
3	Client Name & Address	2.6
4	Client Legal Matter	4.5
5	Legal Costs	12.7
6	Legal Fees	68.1
9	Payments	11.0
	Total Valid	99.7
	Rejects	0.3

In order to code this pattern efficiently, do the following:

```
800 IF T = 6 THEN 1000
810 IF T = 5 THEN 2000
820 IF T = 9 THEN 3000
830 IF T = 4 THEN 4000
840 IF T = 3 THEN 5000
850 IF T = 2 THEN 6000
860 IF T <> 1 THEN 9000
870 LET R1 = R1 + 1
```

instead of:

```
800 IF T = 1 THEN 880
810 IF T = 2 THEN 6000
820 IF T = 3 THEN 5000
830 IF T = 4 THEN 4000
840 IF T = 5 THEN 2000
850 IF T = 6 THEN 1000
860 IF T = 9 THEN 3000
870 GOTO 9000
880 LET R1 = R1 + 1
```

THE BASIC VOCABULARY

Ada A programming language that encourages structured programming and is ideal for use with embedded computer systems. Ada is named in honor of Ada Lovelace, considered by many to be the world's first programmer, a close friend of Charles Babbage, a computer pioneer.

accumulator A numeric variable used to record a total. Also see **counter** and **running total.**

accuracy Exactness or correctness of a result.

address A number used to identify a storage location in main memory.

algorithm A method of solution.

American Standard Code for Information Interchange. See **ASCII Code.**

annotation symbol A flowchart symbol that represents the addition of descriptive or explanatory information and comments.

application program A program written to solve a common problem like payroll or accounts receivable. Also see **software.**

argument An expression surrounded by parentheses following a function name.

argument organized table A table organized so that entries are accessed by comparing a search argument to table arguments. If the search argument agrees with a table argument, then the entry that corresponds to the table agrument is selected.

arithmetic-logic section That part of the central processing unit which performs such operations as addition, subtraction, multiplication, division and logical comparisons. Also see **CPU.**

arithmetic operators A single character that belongs to the following set: + (addition), − (subtraction), * (multiplication), / (division), ∧ (exponentiation).

arithmetic overflow The result of a computation that exceeds the allowable range of numbers that a system can store. The allowable range for most BASIC systems is -1×10^{-38} to $-1 \times 10^{+38}$ and 1×10^{-38} to $1 \times 10^{+38}$.

array or **matrix** A variable allocated a specified number of storage locations, each of which can be assigned a unique value.

array element A member of an array.

array name A variable name or identifier of an array.

ascending sequence of data Data that is in sequence from lowest to highest in value.

ASCII Code The abbreviation for American Standard Code for Information Interchange. Each character, like a number, letter of the alphabet, or special character, is represented by a unique number. See Table 5.5.

audio-response unit An output device that transmits results vocally.

auxiliary storage A subsystem of a computer used to store programs and data for later use. Examples include a magnetic disk and a floppy diskette unit.

BASIC An acronym for the programming language Beginner's All Purpose Symbolic Instruction Code. BASIC is a very simple problem-solving language used interactively with personal computers or with terminals in a timesharing environment.

batch mode A mode of computer operation whereby results are obtained after a delay, often minutes or hours in length.

batch program A program that generates information based on data that has been collected over a period of time.

binary search A method used to search a table. The search begins in the middle of the table to determine if the table argument is in the upper half or lower half of the table. This method continues to divide that portion of the table in which the table argument being sought is located. Also see **serial search**.

blank See **space**.

buffer Adjacent storage locations in main memory assigned to a file when the file is opened.

bugs Program errors.

calculator mode or **immediate mode** A mode of operation which permits the computer to appear to the user as a powerful desk calculator. To use this mode, enter BASIC statements without line numbers.

case logic structure Similar to the **If-Then-Else structure** except that the case logic structure allows more than two alternatives.

chained-to program A program that is loaded into main storage from auxiliary storage and executed due to the execution of a CHAIN statement in another program.

chaining program A program that includes a CHAIN statement.

Chapin charts See **N-S charts**.

character Any letter, symbol or digit that can be entered into the computer. See Table 5.5.

check digit A means of detecting erroneous data. Used to ensure that a number is correct.

COBOL An acronym for the programming language Common Business Oriented Language. COBOL is an English-like language primarily suitable for business data processing applications. It is especially useful for file and table handling and extensive input and output operations.

code check A technique used to ensure that codes entered from an external source are valid.

coding form A specially printed sheet of paper which makes it convenient to write a program. See Figure 2.3.

comma separator A punctuation mark, which allows the production of output from a BASIC program that is automatically positioned in a tabular format as determined by the print zones.

compiler A program that converts a high-level language program to machine language.

compilation The conversion of a source program to an object program.

compilation phase The activity of compiling a program.

complement The negation of a condition. The negation of a condition is formed through the use of the logical operator NOT.

compound condition Two or more simple conditions combined by logical operators.

computer A device that can perform substantial computations, including numerous arithmetic or logic operations, without intervention by a human operator.

concatenation operator An operator (+) used to combine string expressions.

condition A logical expression which may be true or false.

connector symbol A flowchart symbol used to show an entry from or an exit to another part of the flowchart. Also serves as an off-page connector. See Table 1.4.

constant A value that does not change during the execution of a program.

control break A change in the value of a control variable that determines when summaries should be displayed.

control section That part of a central processing unit which directs and coordinates the entire computer system. Also see **CPU**.

control variable Used to determine when a control break occurs. A control variable is assigned a data item that is common to all records in the file. When the value of the control variable changes, a control break occurs. A control variable is also the variable in a FOR statement . Also see **increment parameter**, **initial parameter** and **limit parameter**.

counter An **accumulator** used to count the number of times some action is performed.

counter-controlled loop A loop that is executed repeatedly until a counter attains some predefined value.

CPU Central Processing Unit. That subsystem of a computer that supervises the entire computer system. The CPU is divided into the control section and arithmetic-logic section. Also see **hardware.**

CRT Cathode Ray Tube. See **video display device.**

cryptogram A coded message.

cursor A movable blinking marker, like a line or block, that indicates on the video screen where the next character entry or display will be.

data A group of unorganized facts, like an employee's hours worked and rate of pay in a payroll application.

data sequence holding area An area in main storage in which the data items from all DATA statements in a BASIC program are stored. Also see **pointer.**

data validation The verification that data is within a range to ensure the generation of valid results.

debugging The process of detecting and correcting program errors.

decision-making The process of determining which one of two or more alternative paths should be taken.

decision statement A statement used to control a loop or to cause deviation from sequential execution.

decision symbol A flowchart symbol used to represent a decision that determines which of a number of alternative paths is to be followed. See Table 1.4.

decomposition The process of breaking a large complex problem into smaller problems.

DeMorgan's Laws The following Logical equivalences:

NOT (P OR Q) is equivalent to NOT P AND NOT Q

NOT (P AND Q) is equivalent to NOT P OR NOT Q

descending sequence of data Data that is in sequence from highest to lowest in value.

descriptor field or **field format** or **format field** One or more consecutive format symbols appearing in a string expression. A descriptor field is used with the PRINT USING statement to format output results. See Table 4.8.

desk checking The act of placing yourself in the position of the computer and stepping through a program or the design of a program to determine its correctness.

detail line A line that is displayed for each record processed.

device name A name that identifies the disk drive upon which a program or file is located.

digit check A technique used to verify the assignment of a special digit to a number. See **check digit.**

dimension The number of subscripts required to access an element of an array.

display The transmission of information to a video display device or printer.

documentation The readable description of what a program or procedure within a program is supposed to do.

double precision A format under which numbers are stored to the maximum precision of the computer.

Do-Until logic structure A control structure used for creating a process that will be performed repeatedly until a condition is true. The loop is executed a minimum of one time. Also called **Repeat-Until logic structure.**

Do-While logic structure A control structure used for creating a process that will be performed repeatedly as long as a condition is true. The loop is executed a minimum of zero times. Also called **Repetition logic structure**. Also see **While loop.**

dummy variables The parameters in a user-defined function that are assigned the values of the corresponding arguments when reference is made to the function.

dynamically assigned upper bounds The upper bounds of an array that have been assigned through the use of a variable. For example, DIM A(N) declares A to have N elements.

empty string See **null string.**

endless loop or **infinite loop** A loop which executes continuously.

end-of-file-mark A special character automatically placed at the end of a sequential file when it is closed.

equal sign Used in a LET statement and means "replaced by." The value of the variable to the left of the equal sign is replaced by the final value to the right of the equal sign.

error-handling routine A routine that is executed when an error occurs during the execution of a program.

E-type notation A form of the representation of very large and very small numbers in a program through the use of exponentiation.

evaluation The process of assigning a value to an expression.

execution The actual processing of a program by a computer, such as accepting data, carrying out computations and displaying results.

execution phase The activity of executing a program.

exponent The power to which a number is raised. The number 3 in 10^3 is the exponent.

exponential form or **exponential notation** A form of expressing a number which consists of a signed integer or fixed point constant followed by the letter E and a signed integer. A value expressed as a number (**mantissa**) times ten raised to some power (**exponent**). Also called **E-type notation**.

extension A one- to three-character addition to a filename used to classify files.

fatal error A type of error which causes the system to terminate execution of the program.

field format See **descriptor field.**

file A group of related records.

file list program A program that lists the items in the records that make up a file.

file maintenance Adding records to a file, deleting records from a file or changing records in a file.

filename A sequence of characters that identifies a file on auxiliary storage.

file organization A method of arranging records on an auxiliary storage device. The two types allowed on most BASIC systems are sequential and random organization.

filespec (file specification) The device name, filename and extension of a file.

filler Spaces inserted between results displayed in a line.

fixed point constant A positive or negative real number with a decimal point.

flag See **switch.**

floating point A positive or negative real number written in exponential form.

floppy diskette A plastic disk upon which data and programs can be retrieved or stored for future use.

flowchart A logic diagram or a graphic representation of a program or system.

flowchart template A plastic sheet with cut-out shapes which can be used to draw flowchart symbols.

flowline symbol A flowchart symbol used to represent the sequence of executable operations. See Table 1.4.

flushing a file The process of reading the remaining records in a file.

format field See **descriptor field.**

format symbols Symbols used to define a descriptor field. See Table 4.8.

FORTRAN An acronym for the programming language Formula Translator. FORTRAN is a problem-solving language designed primarily for scientific data processing and process control applications.

function parameter A variable in parentheses following the name of a user-defined function.

GDGI An abbreviation of "Garbage Doesn't Get In." Data validation which does not allow erroneous data to enter the system.

getting on the system. See **logging on.**

GIGO An acronym for "Garbage In—Garbage Out." The generation of inaccurate information because of the input of invalid data.

grammatical errors Errors in spelling or punctuation in a program.

hard copy Results of a program printed on paper by a character or line printer.

hardware The physical aspects of a computer system, like the CPU, main storage unit, a terminal, printer, or magnetic disk unit.

header record A record that includes permanent data followed by records containing temporary data.

hierarchy chart See **top-down chart.**

hierarchy of operations See **precedence, rules of.**

high-level language A programming language, like BASIC and COBOL, which is computer or machine independent.

histogram A bar graph.

If-Then-Else logic structure A control structure that represents a choice between two alternatives. Also called **Selection logic structure.**

immediate mode See **calculator mode.**

implement To write a program that corresponds to a design or method of solution.

increment parameter The value by which the control variable of a For loop is increased each time the loop is executed.

indexed file A file organized around a specified data item, called the **key**, which is common to each record. Records in the file can be accessed directly if the key is known.

infinite loop A loop which has no exit point. Also see **endless loop.**

initial parameter The beginning value of the control variable in a For loop.

Initialization module Usually the first routine executed in a program. Often includes setting variables equal to an initial value, displaying report and column headings and opening files.

initialize or **set** To assign a starting value to a variable.

input device A device that allows programs and data to enter a computer system.

Input/Output symbol A symbol used in flowcharting which represents the request for data or the display of information. See Table 1.4.

input prompt A question mark followed by a space. The input prompt is displayed when the INPUT statement is executed.

input prompt message A displayed message, followed by an input prompt, which requests data from the operator.

instructions Directions or orders to the computer. The basic unit of a program.

integer A positive or negative whole number which does not contain a decimal point and in BASIC is between −32,768 and 32,767.

interactive mode A mode of operation whereby results are obtained immediately or after a short period of time.

interactive program A program which generates information based on data entered by the operator during its execution.

intermediate output method Used in debugging a program. The insertion of PRINT statements in a program to display intermediate results. Also called **source language debugging.**

internal comments Explanatory comments or remarks located within the program itself.

interpreter A machine-language program which, when executed by a computer, will cause a BASIC program to be translated and executed on a line-by-line basis to produce results without the production of an intermediate object program.

key A specified data item around which an indexed file is organized. Also see **indexed file.**

keyboard An input device, similar to the keyboard on a typewriter, used to input data and programs into a computer.

keyword A word which informs BASIC of the type of statement to be executed.

layered structure See **nested If-Then-Else structure.**

leading space A space before a number, which indicates that it is positive.

left-justify To align a result in a column with its leftmost character under the leftmost character of the column heading.

limit parameter A value that a control variable must attain in a FOR statement before the For loop is terminated.

line A line number followed by a statement.

line number An integer between 1 and 32767 that is assigned to every line in a BASIC program.

list A set of distinct elements, each separated from the next by a comma.

logging on or **getting on the system** The process of entering a valid account number and password before being allowed to use the computer.

logic error Program errors that are not detected by the computer or interpreter. Logic errors are the most serious, since they may generate invalid results or cause the abnormal termination of a program.

logical line A line number followed by one of more physical lines which have no line number.

logical operator A keyword like AND, OR or NOT used to combine simple conditions to form compound conditions. Also see **relational operator.**

logic diagram A graphic form of a method of solution, like a flowchart, N-S chart, or Warnier-Orr diagram.

loop A series of statements that are executed repeatedly. A control statement is used to return control to the first of the series of statements that are repeatedly executed.

lower bound value The smallest value that a subscript may be assigned in a subscripted variable.

low-level language A computer- or machine-dependent language. Also see **machine language.**

machine language A set of instructions that a computer can execute directly. Also see **low-level language.**

magnetic disk An auxiliary storage device in which programs and data can be stored for future use. Also see **hardware.**

main memory See **main storage.**

Main module The part of the program that maintains overall control of a program.

main storage or **main memory** That subsystem of a computer in which instructions, data and results are stored during the execution of a program. Also see **hardware.**

mantissa The decimal fraction part of a number expressed in exponential form. In the number 1.23E4, the decimal fraction 1.23 is the mantissa.

master file A file that contains permanent data.

matrix (plural: **matrices**) See **array.**

menu A list of the functions which a program can perform.

mouse An input device used with personal computers to move the cursor on the video display device. The mouse is a hand-sized instrument that moves freely on a flat surface. As the mouse is moved on the surface, the cursor moves on the screen.

merge To combine two or more files that are in sequence into a single file that maintains that same sequence with respect to a given data item found in each record.

microcomputer See **personal computer.**

microprocessor That part of a personal computer which controls the computer and performs the necessary arithmetic and logic operations.

module See **subroutine.**

N-S chart Nassi-Shneiderman chart. A diagram that depicts a method of solution. An alternative to program flowcharts.

nested parenthetical expressions Expressions that are contained within two or more sets of parentheses.

nested If-Then-Else structure An If-Then-Else structure in which the action to be taken for the true or false case includes yet another If-Then-Else structure.

nested IF statement An IF statement in which another IF statement immediately follows the keyword THEN or ELSE.

non-executable statement A statement which is not performed in a program, like a REM or DATA statement.

non-fatal error A type of error which causes the system to supply a predetermined value to an expression.

normal exit The exit out of a For loop or While loop in which the FOR statement or WHILE statement is satisfied. Also see **transferred exit.**

null list A PRINT statement which contains no list of print items.

null string or **empty string** A string with no length.

numeric constant A constant which represents an ordinary number.

numeric expression An expression which consists of one or more numeric constants, numeric variables and numeric function references separated from each other by parentheses and arithmetic operators.

numeric variable A variable which can be assigned a numeric value.

object program A machine-language version of a program written in a higher-level language like BASIC.

operating system A program that has overall control of the computer system.

parallel arrays Two or more arrays that have elements that correspond to one another.

parameter A variable or constant appearing in a FOR statement. Also see **function parameter.**

PASCAL A programming language that allows for the formulations of algorithms and data in a form which clearly exhibits their natural structure. Primarily used for scientific applications and systems programming and, to some extent, in business data processing.

pass Once through a loop.

peer review group A group of programmers and analysts who review and refine the program design before a programmer is allowed to proceed with the development of a program.

personal computer or **microcomputer** A computer which uses a CPU miniaturized on a silicon chip.

physical line A line in a BASIC program which has no line number. Also see **logical line.**

PL/I An abbreviation for the programming language Programming Language I. PL/I incorporates some of the best features of FORTRAN, COBOL and other languages. Used for business and scientific data processing.

pointer A register that keeps track of the next data item to be assigned in the **data sequence holding area** or the next record to be read from a sequential file.

positionally organized table A table in which data is accessed relative to its position in the table.

precedence, rules of or **hierarchy of operations** A set of rules which dictate the order in which arithmetic operations or logic operations are carried out.

precision A measure of correctness. See **double precision** and **single precision.**

predefined process symbol A flowchart symbol which represents a named process consisting of one or more operations or program steps that are specified elsewhere. See Table 1.4.

prime number A whole number that is only divisible by itself and one.

printer spacing chart A chart used to design the format of reports which are to be generated by a computer. See Figure 4.13.

print item Numeric or string constants, variables, expressions, or null items found in the list of a PRINT statement.

print zones A segment, usually 14 or 15 positions in length, of a print line. There are five print zones in each print line.

problem analysis The first step in the **program development cycle.** This step centers on defining the problem.

process symbol A flowchart symbol which represents the process of executing a defined operation or group of operations resulting in a change in value, form, or location of data. See Table 1.4

program The entire series of instructions required to complete a given procedure or task.

program design This step in the **program development cycle** involves devising a method of solution (algorithm), describing the method of solution using logic diagrams, selecting good data and testing the method of solution.

program development cycle A series of steps that a programmer goes through to solve a problem using a computer. See Figure 1.11.

program flowchart Shows in graphic form the algorithm (method of solution) used in a program.

programming The activity of instructing a computer using precise instructions in a specified form in a language the computer understands.

program specifications A short statement of the problem to be solved by a program, which includes suggested input data and the corresponding output results.

proper program A program which has one entry point, one exit point, no unreachable code and no infinite loops.

pseudocode An alternative to program flowcharting, which allows the expression of thoughts as simple imperative English sentences.

pseudo-random number Random numbers generated by the computer using a repeatable process.

random file A file organized in such a way that any record can be directly accessed based upon its relative location from the beginning of the file. Also see **file organization.**

range of a For loop The set of repeatedly executed statements beginning with the FOR statement and continuing up to and including the NEXT statement with the same control variable.

range check A technique used to ensure that data items entered from an external device fall within a range of valid values.

reasonableness check A technique used to ensure that data items entered from an external source are legitimate.

record A group of related data items. Also see **file.**

recursive definition A definition in which the result is defined in terms of itself.

relational operator An operator that belongs to the following set: = (equal to), < (less than), > (greater than), <= (less than or equal to), >= (greater than or equal to), <> (not equal to). Also see **logical operator.**

remark lines Any line in a BASIC program that begins with the keyword REM. Remark lines are used to document a program.

Repeat-Until logic structure See **Do-Until logic structure.**

Repetition logic structure See **Do-While logic structure.**

rewind The technique of closing and then opening a file to begin processing again with the first record.

right-justify To align a result in a column with its rightmost character under the rightmost character of the column heading.

rounding The process of dropping one or more of the least significant digits and adding zero or one to the least significant digit remaining in the number. If the digit to the right of the remaining number is less than five, add zero. If the digit to the right of the remaining number is greater than or equal to five, add one.

RPG An abbreviation for the programming language Report Program Generator. RPG is a popular report generator primarily designed for business data processing applications on small computers.

running total An **accumulator** used to sum the different values that a variable is assigned during the execution of a program.

scientific notation See **exponential form.**

search argument A value used to search a table for a corresponding table argument.

Selection logic structure See **If-Then-Else logic structure.**

semantics The relationship between symbols and their meanings.

semicolon separator A punctuation mark (;) used in a PRINT statement to produce output from a BASIC program in a compressed format.

sentinel record See **trailer record.**

sentinel value The data item selected for the end-of-file test.

Sequence logic structure A control structure that is used to show sequential processing (i.e., one action, or one action followed by another).

sequential file A file organized in such a way that records can only be processed in the order in which they are placed in the file. Also see **file organization** and **pointer.**

serial search A search that begins by comparing the search argument to the first table argument. If the two agree, the search is over. If they do not agree, then the search argument is compared to the second table argument, and so on. Also see **binary search.**

set See **initialize.**

significant digits The digits of a number beginning with the leftmost nonzero digit and extending to the right to include all digits warranted by the accuracy of a measuring device.

silicon chip A wafer of silicon, typically a fraction of an inch long, containing a computer's CPU.

simple variable A variable used to store single values. Also see **variable** and **subscripted variable.**

single precision A format under which numbers are stored in a computer to a prescribed precision. See Table 3.2.

size of an array The upper bound value of an array.

slice of processing time A portion of time allocated by the computer to each of several programs. The computer schedules these slices of time so that each program receives one at short intervals. See **timesharing.**

software A set of programming languages and programs concerned with the operation of a computer system. Software includes both **systems programs** and **application programs.**

sorting Arranging data according to some certain order or sequence.

source language debugging See **intermediate output method.**

source program A program written in a higher-lever language than machine language.

space A character entered by pressing the space bar on a keyboard.

stored program A program placed in auxiliary storage for later use.

straight-line program A program in which statements are executed in sequence one after the other until the last statement of the program is reached.

string constant A sequence of letters, digits or special characters enclosed in quotation marks that is used for non-numeric purposes like representing an employee name, social security number, address or telephone number.

string expression An expression consisting of one or more string constants, string variables and string function references separated by the concatenation operator.

string function A procedure for manipulating strings. BASIC includes several string functions like LEFT$, MID$ and RIGHT$ that are used to extract substrings from a string.

string variable A variable that can be assigned a string of characters.

structured programming A methodology according to which all program logic can be constructed from a combination of the following three basic logic structures: sequence, selection and repetition.

structured style Disciplined and consistent programming. Discipline and consistency help programmers construct readable, maintainable and reliable programs. Often, the style of structured programs is determined by someone in authority, like a supervisor.

structure terminator A line following an IF statement to which control is passed following the execution of the true or false task.

structured walkthrough The evaluation of a program design or system design by a peer review group.

subroutine or **module** A group of statements within a program associated with a single task.

subscripted variable A variable that is associated with an array. For an element in an array to be referenced, the variable name is followed by one or more subscripts enclosed in parentheses.

substring A part of a string. For example DEC is a substring of DEC RAINBOW.

switch or **flag** A variable that usually takes on two values during the execution of a program. A value of zero equates to the switch being off. A value of one equates to the switch being on. A switch is often used to control a looping process.

system command An instruction to the BASIC system to act upon a BASIC program. Examples of system commands are RUN, LIST and NEW. They are entered without line numbers.

system flowchart A diagram that shows in graphic form the files, flow of data, equipment and programs involved in a particular application.

system programs Programs that are usually supplied by the computer manufacturer to perform some specified task.

system prompt A character or series of characters that prompt the user to enter a command.

table A collection of data in which each item is uniquely identified by a label, or by its position relative to other items, or by some other means.

table argument The identification portion of a table entry. Also see **search argument.**

table search or **table look-up** The activity of searching a table by means of comparing a search argument to the table arguments.

terminal symbol A flowchart symbol that represents the beginning, end, or a point of interruption in a program.

timesharing A technique used by some computer systems to share the computer resources among several users.

top-down approach A design technique that calls for devising a solution top-down rather than bottom-up. That is, the higher-level modules are designed before the lower-level modules.

top-down chart A logic diagram made up of process symbols connected by lines to illustrate functionality and to some extent flow of control. In appearance a top-down chart is similar to a company's organization chart. Also called **hierarchy chart** and **VTOC.**

top-down design A design strategy that breaks large, complex problems into smaller, less complex problems and then decomposes each of these into even smaller problems.

top-down programming A coding strategy in which the programmer codes the high-level modules as soon as they are designed and generally before the low-level modules have been designed.

trailer record A record that is added to the end of a date file to identify the end-of-file. Also called **sentinel record.**

transaction file A file that contains data of a temporary or transient nature.

transfer statement A program statement that causes the system to deviate from sequential execution of a program.

transferred exit The exit out of a For loop or While loop due to a transfer statement within the loop. Also see **normal exit.**

truncated The result of dropping the least significant digit(s) in a number.

unconditional branch statement A program statement, like a GOTO statement, that causes the system to deviate from sequential execution irrespective of any conditions within the program.

undefined variable A variable that has not been initialized or assigned a value in the program.

upper bound value The greatest value that a subscript can be assigned in a subscripted variable. The upper bound value is assigned to an array in a DIM statement.

user-defined function A function that has been constructed by the programmer.

variable A storage location in main memory whose value can change as the program is executed.

variable name A series of characters that identifies a variable.

VDT Video Display Tube. See **video display device.**

video display device A television-like device upon which output is displayed. Also called **CRT** or **VDT.**

VTOC Visual Table of Contents. See **top-down chart.**

Warnier-Orr diagram A logic diagram used to depict the design of a program. Warnier-Orr diagrams involve designing programs with a heavy emphasis on hierarachies and flow of control.

While loop A loop that is established in BASIC by the use of the WHILE and WEND statements. Also see **Do-While logic structure.**

Wrap Up module A collection of activities that take place at the conclusion of a program, like displaying final totals, closing files and displaying an end-of-job message.

ANSWERS TO SELF-TEST AND TEST YOUR BASIC SKILLS EXERCISES

CHAPTER 1 **TEST YOUR BASIC SKILLS**

2. The basic subsystems of a computer are input, main storage, central processing unit, auxiliary storage and output.

    Input—a device that allows programs and data to enter into the computer system.

    Main Storage—a subsystem that allows for the storage of programs and data for the **CPU** to process at a given time.

    Central Processing Unit—the **CPU** controls and supervises the entire computer system and performs the actual arithmetic and logical operations on data specified by the stored program.

    Auxiliary Storage—a subsystem that is used to store programs and data for immediate recall.

    Output—a device that allows the computer system to communicate the results of a program to the user.

4. A terminal and a magnetic disk unit both serve as input and output devices.

6. Hardware is the physical equipment of a computer system. The subsystems as described in 2 above are hardware. Software refers to the programs, languages, written procedures and documentation concerned with the operation of a computer system.

8. **BASIC**—processing business or scientific applications in a batch or interactive environment

    RPG—business applications

    FORTRAN—scientific applications

    COBOL—business applications

    PASCAL—scientific applications

    PL/I—business and scientific applications

10. **Compilation Phase**—that phase in which a source program is translated into an object program.

    Execution Phase—that phase in which an object program is executed.

12. No, not at the present state of technology. Computers are completely dependent on the human element. Computers may appear to think to some individuals, because of the stored program concept. However, the program that instructs the computer to perform a task is written by a human being.

14. Answers will vary.

16. a) 7   b) 0   c) 8

Self-Test Exercises   **CHAPTER 2**

1.

Line	W	X	Y	Displayed
100	4	0	0	
110	4	2	0	
120	4	2	6	
130	4	2	6	6 2 4
140	5	2	6	
150	5	30	6	
160	5	30	6	30
170	5	9	6	
180	5	9	4	
190	5	9	4	9 4
200	5	0.09	4	
210	5	0.09	4	.09
220	5	0.09	4	

2.
```
CALCULATE DISCOUNT
ORIGINAL PRICE 4162.5
DISCOUNT 416.25
SALE PRICE 3746.25
END OF PROGRAM
```

3. a) `100 LET T = 3`
   b) `110 LET X = T - 2`
   c) `120 LET P = T * X`
   d) `130 LET T = 3 * T`
   e) `140 LET A = P/X`
   f) `150 LET X = X + 1`
   g) `160 LET R = R^3`
      OR
      `160 LET R = R * R * R`

4. a) line number   b) keyword   c) variables   d) "is replaced by"

5. a) +   b) −   c) *   d) /   e) ^ or ↑

6. The message

   THE SUM OF A AND B IS

   is displayed on a line beginning at the left margin.

7.
```
THE VALUE OF A IS-2
THE VALUE OF B IS -3

THE VALUE OF C IS 6
```

8. a) The INPUT statement should precede the LET statement (see Arithmetic Rule 1).
   b) 1) There is no logical reason to input a value for the variable A, since A is assigned the product of L and W in line 110.
      2) The system command RUN does not begin with a line number.

9.
```
WHAT IS THE LENGTH? 10
WHAT IS THE WIDTH? 8
A RECTANGLE WITH DIMENSIONS 10 AND 8
HAS AN AREA OF 80 .
```

10. 1) Insert the data as constants in the LET statement used to calculate a result.
    2) Assign each data item to a variable. Use these variables in the LET statement to calculate a result.
    3) Use the INPUT statement to assign the data items to variables. Use these variables in the LET statement to calculate a result.

11. Lines 100 and 110.

12. An interactive BASIC system will accept the program. You normally enter BASIC statements in sequence by line number. However, an interactive BASIC system will accept lines out of order and place them in their proper sequence.

13.
```
100 REM CHAPTER 2 SELF-TEST 13
105 LET Y = 5 ^ (1/2)
110 LET X = 2.456 * 3.456 * 716
115 PRINT "THE SQUARE ROOT IS"; Y
120 PRINT "THE PRODUCT IS"; X
125 END
130 END
```

The command NEW *must* be issued before keying in the second program.

Test Your BASIC Skills

2.

D	E	F	Displayed
9	0	0	
9	2	0	
10	2	0	
9	2	0	
9	2	81	
9	92	81	
9	92	72	
9	92	72	
9	92	72	72
9	92	72	9
9	92	72	92
9	92	72	

4. `115 PRINT R`

6. a) `100 LET Y = 21`
   `110 PRINT Y`
   `120 END`

   b) `110 PRINT S`

   c) `120 END`

   d) `105 PRINT S`

   e) `110 PRINT A1`
   `120 END`

   f) `110 PRINT Z`

8. Yes

10. RUN—instructs the computer to execute the current program in main storage.

   LIST—instructs the computer to list the source statements of the current program.

   NEW—instructs the computer to delete the current program.

12. Yes

14. No. Although line 130 displays the correct result, 270, it does not display the value of G. If the rate of pay R or the hours worked H were assigned different values, the program would still display:

   THE GROSS PAY IS 270

   Also, note that in lines 100 and 110, the string constants should not include the question mark and values 40 and 6.75.

16. 120 (and press the Enter key)

18. Press the key twice that is assigned as the DELETE key and enter /9.

CHAPTER 3   Self-Test Exercises

1. a) `A = 6`
   `B =-1`
   `C = 2`

   b) `IS THE AVERAGE 23`
   `OR IS THE AVERAGE 6.2`

   c) `W = 26`

   d) `PRINCIPAL? 100`
   `RATE IN %? 15`
   `THE AMOUNT IS 115`

   e) `6`
   `-2`
   `0`
   `2`

   f) `ENTER SEED NUMBER? 1`
   `2`
   `6`
   `42`
   `1806`

2. a) 1. In line 100 the keyword REM is missing.
   2. In line 110 the comma following the keyword INPUT is invalid.
   3. In line 120 it is invalid to have an expression to the left of the equal sign.
   4. In line 120 it is invalid to have a string variable in a numeric expression.
   5. In line 130 the string THE ANSWER IS should be surrounded by quotation marks.

   b) 1. In line 110 the comma in the constant 42,000 is invalid.
   2. In line 120 the dollar sign in the constant $5.00 is invalid.
   3. In lines 130 and 140 the variable name #A is invalid.

3. Numeric Variables—c, d, g, i.   String Variables—b, f
   Invalid Variables—a, e, h.

4. a) −6⅓   b) 23   c) 1

5. a) 11.2   b) 48.6   c) −1.5   d) −84

6. a) 1E−8 is one possible solution
   b) 356123E3 is one possible solution

7. a) *   b) ∧   c) +

8. a) `100 LET X = (Y + 8)^(1/2)`
   b) `100 LET Y$ = "END OF REPORT"`
   c) `100 LET S = I/(1 + P/50)^H`

9. c, f

10. a) `100 LET A$ = LEFT$(B$, 5)`
    b) `100 LET A$ = MID$(B$, 7, 6)`
    c) `100 LET A$ = RIGHT$(B$, 4)`
    d) `100 LET A$ = LEFT$(B$, 8) + RIGHT$(B$, 5)`

11. a) `100 LET A$ = MID$(B$, 1, 5)`
    b) `100 LET A$ = MID$(B$, 7, 6)`
    c) `100 LET A$ = MID$(B$, 14, 4)`
    d) `100 LET A$ = MID$(B$, 1, 8) + MID$(B$, 13, 5)`

12. `100 LET L = LEN(B$)`

   Note: L is assigned the numeric value 17.

13. a) $8/(2 + 2) + 12$
    b) $8 \wedge (2 - 1)$
    c) None necessary.
    d) $1 \wedge (2 + 1) * 2 * 3/4 - 3/2$
    e) $12 - (2 - 3 - 1) - 4$
    f) $7 * (3 + (4 \wedge 2 - 3)/13$
    g) $3 * (2 - 3) * 4 * (2 + 3)$
    h) $3 * (6 - 3) + 2 + 6 * 4 - 4/(2 \wedge 1)$

Test Your BASIC Skills

2. 8962482E3

   The error is 176.

4. a,f

6. b) The first character of a variable name must be a letter.
   c) The first character of a variable name must be a letter. The appended digit must be an integer from zero through 9, inclusive.
   e) The first character of a variable name must be a letter.
   f) The first character of a variable name must be a letter.
   g) The first character of a variable must be a letter. The optional second character must be an integer from zero through 9, inclusive.

8. The formation of a numeric expression concerns the proper placement of constants, variables, function references, parentheses and arithmetic operators in a numeric expression. The evaluation of a numeric expression is concerned with the manner in which a validly formed numeric expression is to be evaluated by the computer.

10. a) 11   b) 1   c) −.666666   d) 262,144   e) 17   f) 2320

12. a) `110 LET Q = (D + E)^(1/3)`
    b) `120 LET D = (A^2)^3.2`
    c) `130 LET B = 20/(6 - S)`
    d) `140 LET Y = A1 * X + A2 * X^2 + A3 * X^3 + A4 * X^4`
    e) `150 LET E = X + X/(X - Y)`
    f) `160 LET S = 19.2 * X^3`
    g) `170 LET V = 100 - (2/3)^(100 - B)`
    h) `180 LET T = (76234/(2.37 + D))^(1/2)`
    i) `190 LET V = 1234E-4 * M - (.123458^3/(M - N))`
    j) `200 LET Q = ((F - M * 1000)^(2 * B))/(4 * M) - 1/E`

14. a,b,c,d,f,g,i

16. a) D = −1, A and B do not change in value.
    b) A = −2.2, B = 2, E1 = 1, E2 = 3.2, E3 = 5

18. a) Due to lines 110 and 130, the variable A is assigned a value of zero. In line 140, division by zero causes a fatal error. Modify line 110 or line 130 so that A does not equal zero when line 140 is executed.
    b) Due to lines 110 and 120, the numeric expression in line 130 cannot be evaluated by the computer. It is invalid to raise a negative integer to a decimal fraction power. Modify line 110 or 120 so that the computer is not requested to raise a negative integer to a decimal fraction power.

CHAPTER 4   Self-Test Exercises

1. a)
```
1  6  3 -3
4  2  1  4
8  9  3  2
```
    b)
```
OLD VALUE OF X = 4
OLD VALUE OF Y = 6
NEW VALUE OF X = 6
NEW VALUE OF Y = 6

OLD VALUE OF X = 3
OLD VALUE OF Y = 7
NEW VALUE OF X = 7
NEW VALUE OF Y = 7
```

    c)
```
OLD VALUE OF X = 4
OLD VALUE OF Y = 6
NEW VALUE OF X = 6
NEW VALUE OF Y = 4

OLD VALUE OF X = 3
OLD VALUE OF Y = 7
NEW VALUE OF X = 7
NEW VALUE OF Y = 7
```
    d)
```
1  4   9
2  10  19
3  18  31
```

2. a) 1. In line 110 a trailing comma following the READ list is not allowed.
       2. In line 120 there is an unbalanced set of parentheses in the numeric expression.
       3. There is no logical path to line 140. Line number 130 should be changed to a line number between 140 and 150.
       4. The program lacks a DATA statement.
    b) 1. It is invalid to have a numeric constant within the list of a READ statement.
       2. In line 130 the variable B is undefined or zero.
       3. Line 140 should read GOTO 110.

3. a, d, h

4. a) Statement is valid.
    b) The comma following READ is invalid.
    c) The statement is valid provided B isn't zero.
    d) The comma following the last variable N is invalid.
    e) The statement is valid.
    f) The statement is invalid. A READ statement requires a list of variable(s).
    g) The comma following the last variable I is invalid.
    h) The second variable in the list is invalid.
    i) The statement is valid.
    j) The statement is invalid due to the lack of data items.

5.
```
110 PRINT 8 + 4, 6, 6^(8 + 4), "ABC"
```

6.
```
100 INPUT A, B, C
110 PRINT A, A + B, A + B + C
```

7.
```
100 PRINT TAB(26); "BASIC COMPANY"
110 PRINT TAB(26); "-------------"
120 PRINT
130 PRINT , "VALUE OF A", "VALUE OF B", "VALUE OF C"
140 PRINT , "----------", "----------", "----------"
```

8. a) The value of A displays beginning in print position 10. The value of B displays beginning in print position 35.
    b) The value of B displays beginning in print position 20 and the value of C displays beginning in print zone 3. The value of D displays beginning in print position 66.
    c) The value of A displays in print position 35.

9. a)
```
   4.00-
   4.00
 100.06
 100.12
   0.38
   0.77
```
    b)
```
---OUT OF DATA LINE 110
```

10. d and e

11.
```
100 PRINT USING "THE ANSWER IS $$$$.$$-"; A
```

12. a) 5   b) 1   c) 2   d) 3   e) 4   f) 6

13. a)
```
100 PRINT USING "!"; A$
```
    b)
```
100 PRINT USING "&"; A$
```
    c)
```
100 PRINT USING "\    \"; A$
```

Test Your BASIC Skills

2. a)
```
100 REM EXERCISE 4.2A SOLUTION
110 READ S, B
120 LET D = S - B
130 PRINT D
140 DATA 4, 6
150 END
```

b)
```
100 REM EXERCISE 4.2B SOLUTION
110 DATA 1, 2, 5, 6, 8, 7, 1, 3, 2
120 READ X, Y, Z
130 LET X1 = X * Y
140 LET X1 = X1 * Z
150 PRINT X1
160 GOTO 120
170 END
```

4. a) 120 DATA 1, 2, 3, 4, 5
   b) 130 DATA 1, 2
   c) 140 DATA 1, 2, 3, 4
   d) The READ statement is invalid.

6.
```
110 PRINT A
120 PRINT
130 PRINT
140 PRINT B
```

8. b

10. `THE ANSWER TO 5 SQUARED IS 25 .`

12. Use of the READ and DATA statements involves submitting the data item to be processed *prior* to execution of the program. Use of the INPUT statement involves submitting the data items to be processed *during* the execution of the program.

14.
```
100 REM EXERCISE 4.14 SOLUTION
110 INPUT "WHAT VALUE DO YOU WISH TO SQUARE"; W
120 PRINT W; "SQUARED IS"; W^2
130 END
```

16.
```
NET       PAY
        NET PAY

N  E  T     P  A  Y
```

18.
```
  UUUUU
 X     X
 X  O O  X
 X       X
 X   U   X
 X  ( )  X
 X   -   X
  X     X
   XXXXX
```

20. Line 110 assigns A and B the values of 2 and 4, respectively. Line 120 assigns C a value of 8. Line 130 displays the value of C(8). Line 140 transfers control to line 120, which again assigns C the value 8. Line 130 again displays the value 8. This loop continues until the operator intervenes and terminates the program. (Note that line 140 should read 140 GOTO 110.)

CHAPTER 5

Self-Test Exercises

1. a)
```
NUMBER OF EMPLOYEES 5
TOTAL GROSS PAY 2429.47
TOTAL FEDERAL TAX 669.31
```

b)
```
THE NUMBER OF PEOPLE EVALUATED IS 7
THE NUMBER OF ADULTS WEIGHING 120 POUNDS OR MORE IS 5
```

c)
```
204        F        62        80
613        F        43        77

END OF REPORT
```

d) `THE SUM IS 21`

e)
```
JOB CODE AND HOURS, SEPARATED BY A COMMA? 1, 40
GROSS PAY = 190
JOB CODE AND HOURS, SEPARATED BY A COMMA? 3, 25
GROSS PAY = 162.5
JOB CODE AND HOURS, SEPARATED BY A COMMA? 2, 15
GROSS PAY = 85.5
JOB CODE AND HOURS, SEPARATED BY A COMMA? -1, 0
```

2. a) Line 160 should be GOTO 130 in order to read all the data items.
   b) Lines 200 and 210 should each be followed by a GOTO 230.
3. In line 150, the keyword THEN must be followed by a line number or valid statement. In line 180, the GOTO 140 should be replaced by WEND.

4. a)
```
100 IF A > B THEN LET A = A + 1
110 READ X, Y
```

b)
```
100 IF X = Y THEN 130
110 IF Y < Z THEN 130
120 IF C = S THEN 250
130 LET A = A + 1
```

5. a) EQUALS, spelled out, is an invalid relational operator.
   b) It is invalid to compare a string expression to a numeric expression.
   d) THAN is an invalid keyword.
   e) The condition must have an expression on both sides of the relational operator.

f) The keyword THEN must be followed by a line number or statement.

g) WHEREAS is an invalid keyword.

h) It is invalid to compare a numeric expression to a string expression.

i) It is invalid to have more than one relational operator in a single condition.

6. a) x greater than 9.   b) x less than 16.

c) x not equal to negative 5.

7.
```
260 IF X < Y THEN 270 ELSE 290
270    IF Y < Z THEN LET C = C + 1
280 GOTO 300
290    IF X < Z THEN LET B = B + 1 ELSE LET A = A + 1
300
```

8. Yes. Exercise "b" is better because it is easier to read and more efficient than "a." Exercise "b" illustrates a common technique used to assign a variable the greatest or least value among a group of variables.

9.
```
100 IF R/S < X - 1 THEN 110 ELSE 130
110    IF R/S > X + 1 THEN LET E = E + 1 ELSE LET F = F + 1
120 GOTO 140
130    IF R/S = X - 1 THEN LET D = D + 1 ELSE IF R/S >= T THEN C = C + 1
140 LET A = A + 1
```

Test Your BASIC Skills

2.
```
100 LET X = 0
110 LET T = 10
```
a)
```
130 LET X = X + 1
140 LET T = T + 1
```
b)
```
150 LET X = X + 7
160 LET T = T + 7
```
c)
```
170 LET X = X + 2
180 LET T = T + 2
```
d)
```
190 LET X = 2 * X
200 LET T = 2 * T
```
e)
```
210 LET X = X - 1
220 LET T = T - 1
```

4. a) Q value greater than 8

b) Q value greater than or equal to −3

c) Q value less than 27

d) Q value not equal to 3

6. a)
```
200 IF A >= 21 THEN LET C = C + 1
210 LET S = S + 1
```

b)
```
300 IF S$ = "M" THEN LET M = M + 1 ELSE LET F = F + 1
```

8. a)
```
170 IF D$ = "YES" THEN 110
180 PRINT "END OF JOB"
190 END
```

b)
```
120 IF A > B THEN IF B > C THEN IF C > D THEN PRINT "VALUES O.K."
190 END
```

10. 201,000

12. 200,000   −12,345

14. 21

16.
```
190 REM EXERCISE 5.16 SOLUTION
200 IF U < V THEN 210 ELSE 230
210    IF U < W THEN LET S = U ELSE S = W
220 GOTO 240
230    IF V < W THEN LET S = V ELSE S = W
240
```

18 a) X   b) C = 3; S = 320   c) 5   d) 356   e) 4

20.
```
100 REM EXERCISE 5.20 SOLUTION
110 IF C = 0 THEN 120 ELSE 140
120    IF D = 0 THEN LET A = -1 ELSE LET A = -3
130 GOTO 150
140    IF D = 0 THEN LET A = -3 ELSE LET A = -2
150
```

22. *Line 240*

Executed	*D*	*E*	*A*	*B*	*C*	*F*
1st	3	−4	0	0	−4	1
2nd	3	−4	0	4	−4	2
3rd	3	−4	−4	4	−4	3

CHAPTER 6   Self-Test Exercises

1. a)
```
NEXT VALUE? 4
NEXT VALUE? 6
NEXT VALUE? 9
NEXT VALUE? 15
NEXT VALUE? 18
THE SUM IS 52
```
b) 4   6
   9   5
   6
d) 2   4

c) Displays the even numbers between 2 and 20 inclusive (i.e., 2, 4, 6, ⋯, 20)

4	8
6	12
8	16

2.
```
100 IF X - 2 > G THEN 110 ELSE 140
110    LET T = T + 1
120    PRINT T, "O.K."
130 STOP
140    LET S = S + 1
150    PRINT S, "NOT O.K."
160 STOP
```

3. a) 1. Since the increment parameter is not included in line 110, the control variable I is incremented by 1. Therefore, I can never attain the value of the terminal value.

   2. The variable K in the NEXT statement does not correspond to the control variable I in the FOR statement.

   b) The program contains an infinite loop since X is not modified within the While loop.

   c) There is no corresponding NEXT statement for the FOR statement in line 130.

   d) The GOTO statement in line 140 transfers control into the middle of a deactivated For loop.

4. a) $(S > 0$ and (not $T > 0)$) or $A > 0$
   b) $(S > 0$ and $A > 0)$ or (not $T > 0)$
   c) $(S > 0$ or $A >)$ or $T > 0$
   d) $(A > 0$ and $A > 0)$ and (not $T > 0)$
   e) $(S > 0$ and $A > 0)$ or $(T > 0$ and $P > 0)$
   f) $S > 0$ or $((A > 0$ and $T > 0)$ and $P > 0)$
   g) $(S > 0$ or $A > 0)$ or $(T > 0$ and $P > 0)$
   h) $((not S > 0)$ and $T > 0)$ or $P > 0$

5. `100 IF A>50 AND S>=10 OR A>60 AND S>=5 THEN LET C = C + 1`

6.

X	K	Y	P
3	3	1	1
3	3	2	3
3	3	3	6
2	5	1	1
2	5	2	3
2	5	3	6
1	6	1	1
1	6	2	3
1	6	3	6

7. a

8. a) Lacks the keyword THEN.

   b) It is invalid to precede a relational operator with a logical operator. A NOT < B is invalid.

   c) If B is less than C, control transfers back to line 100 and an infinite loop is established.

   d) It is invalid to have two logical operators AND OR adjacent to one another.

   e) It is invalid to have the keyword IF preceded immediately by the logical operator AND.

   f) Valid.

   g) It is invalid to use a string variable as the control variable.

   h) The TO space 20 is invalid.

   i) It is invalid to have an expression in a WEND statement.

   j) It is invalid to have variable names following GOTO.

   k) The increment parameter, negative 1, creates an infinite loop.

   l) Valid.

9.
```
100 REM CHAPTER 6 SELF-TEST 9
110 LET S = 0
120 FOR C = -1 TO -1000 STEP -1
130    LET S = S + C
140 NEXT C
150 PRINT "THE SUM IS "; S
160 END

RUN

THE SUM IS -500500
```

10. a) `100 IF X > Y OR K <= 1 THEN LET L = L + 1`

    b) `100 IF X >= 0 AND X <= 5 OR X > 10 AND X < 20 THEN 500`

    c) `100 IF J>10 THEN 400 ELSE IF K<5 AND M=0 THEN LET P = P + 1 ELSE 250`

11. a)
```
100 REM CHAPTER 6 SELF-TEST 11A
110 FOR I = 5 TO 0 STEP -1
120    FOR K = 1 TO 5 STEP 2
130       PRINT I, K
140    NEXT K
150 NEXT I
160 END
```

b)
```
100 REM CHAPTER 6 SELF-TEST 11B
110 LET I = 5
120 WHILE I >= 0
130    LET K = 1
140    WHILE K <= 5
150       PRINT I, K
160       LET K = K + 2
170    WEND
180    LET I = I - 1
190 WEND
200 END
```

12. a) `290 IF J>0 AND J<25 AND H>5 AND H<30 THEN LET C = C + 1 ELSE 300`

b) `290 IF Q > G OR Q > S THEN LET H = H + 1 ELSE 300`

c) `290 IF A > B XOR A > C THEN LET F = F + 1 ELSE 300`

d) `290 IF D + 2 = E EQV S < X THEN PRINT D ELSE 300`

13. The partial program is invalid. The subroutine is executed due to the GOSUB statement in line 150. The subroutine is again executed when control transfers to line 160 and eventually to line 180. When an attempt is made to execute the RETURN statement in line 190 without having executed a prior corresponding GOSUB statement, a fatal condition results.

14.
```
ENTER A NUMBER? 1
   1           1
ENTER A NUMBER? 3
   3          27
ENTER A NUMBER? 5
   5         125
ENTER A NUMBER? 7
   7         343
ENTER A NUMBER? 0
JOB COMPLETE
```

Test Your BASIC Skills

2. a) True   h) False
   b) False   i) False
   c) True   j) True
   d) False   k) True
   e) True   l) False
   f) True   m) True
   g) False   n) False

4. a)

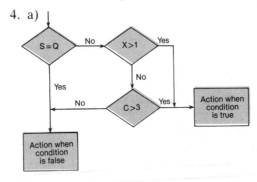

b)

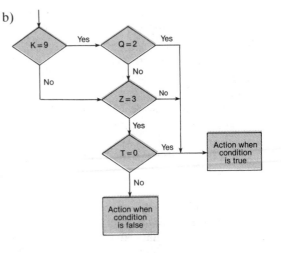

6. a)
```
140 REM EXERCISE 6.6A SOLUTION
150 INPUT "PERCENT"; P
160 IF P > 0 AND P <= 25 THEN 190
170    PRINT "PERCENT INVALID - PLEASE RE-ENTER"
180    GOTO 150
190
```

b)
```
240 REM EXERCISE 6.6B SOLUTION
250 INPUT "BALANCE"; B
260 IF B >= 550.99 AND B <= 765.50 THEN 290
270    PRINT "BALANCE INVALID - PLEASE RE-ENTER"
280    GOTO 250
290
```

c)
```
340 REM EXERCISE 6.6C SOLUTION
350 INPUT "CUSTOMER CODE"; C$
360 IF C$ = "A" OR C$ = "D" OR C$ = "E" OR C$ = "F" THEN 390
370    PRINT "INVALID CUSTOMER CODE - PLEASE RE-ENTER"
380    GOTO 350
390
```

d)
```
440 REM EXERCISE 6.6D SOLUTION
450 INPUT "CUSTOMER NUMBER"; N$
460 IF MID$(N$, 3, 1) = "4" THEN 490
470    PRINT "CUSTOMER NUMBER INVALID - PLEASE RE-ENTER"
480    GOTO 450
490
```

8. a)
```
100 REM EXERCISE 6.8A SOLUTION
110 LET I = 4
120 IF I > 23 THEN 160
130    PRINT I
140    LET I = I + 2
150 GOTO 120
160 END
```

b)
```
200 REM EXERCISE 6.8B SOLUTION
210 FOR I = 4 TO 23 STEP 2
220    PRINT I
230 NEXT I
240 END
```

c)
```
100 REM EXERCISE 6.8C SOLUTION
110 LET I = 4
120 WHILE I <= 23
130    PRINT I
140    LET I = I + 2
150 WEND
160 END
```

10.

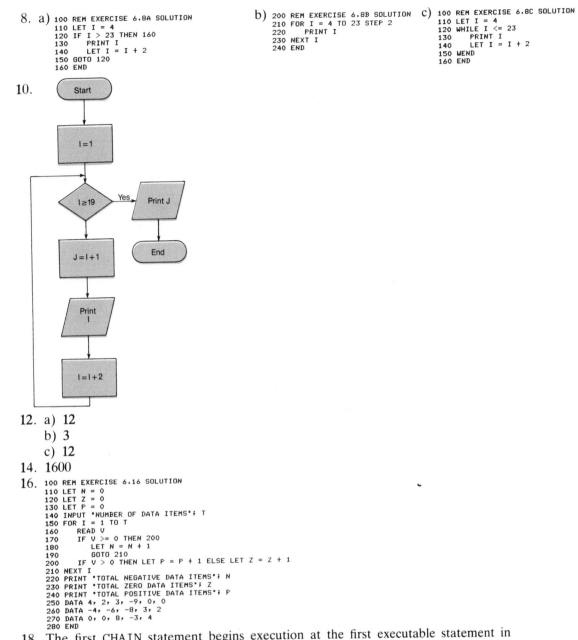

12. a) 12
    b) 3
    c) 12

14. 1600

16.
```
100 REM EXERCISE 6.16 SOLUTION
110 LET N = 0
120 LET Z = 0
130 LET P = 0
140 INPUT "NUMBER OF DATA ITEMS"; T
150 FOR I = 1 TO T
160    READ V
170    IF V >= 0 THEN 200
180       LET N = N + 1
190       GOTO 210
200    IF V > 0 THEN LET P = P + 1 ELSE LET Z = Z + 1
210 NEXT I
220 PRINT "TOTAL NEGATIVE DATA ITEMS"; N
230 PRINT "TOTAL ZERO DATA ITEMS"; Z
240 PRINT "TOTAL POSITIVE DATA ITEMS"; P
250 DATA 4, 2, 3, -9, 0, 0
260 DATA -4, -6, -8, 3, 2
270 DATA 0, 0, 8, -3, 4
280 END
```

18. The first CHAIN statement begins execution at the first executable statement in PROG2. The second CHAIN statement begins execution at line 200 in PROG2. The third CHAIN statement begins execution at the first executable statement in PROG2 and maintains the current values of the variables as defined in the chaining program.

Self-Test Exercises

CHAPTER 7

1. a) 4 2 3 9 4 1 23

   b) 4
       6
       16
       8
       15

   c) 2 1 6
       9 5 6
       2 1 3
       8 4 2

   d) A ARRAY - 0 2 4 6 8
       B ARRAY - 1 3 5 7 9
       A ARRAY - 1 3 5 7 9
       B ARRAY - 0 2 4 6 8

2. a) 1 2 3 4 5
       2 4 6 8 10
       3 6 9 12 15
       4 8 12 16 20

   b)   0 1 2
       -1 0 1

3.

3	1	2	3	9
2	5	7	1	15
4	1	5	6	16
9	7	14	10	40

4. `110 DIM C(12, 9), D(6, 9)`

5. Array C has 108 elements (12×9).
   Array D has 54 elements (6×9).

6.
```
100 REM CHAPTER 7 SELF-TEST 6
110 FOR I = 1 TO 12
120    PRINT X(I, I)
130 NEXT I
```

7.
```
100 REM CHAPTER 7 SELF-TEST 7
110 FOR I = 1 TO 200 STEP 2
120    PRINT S(I), S(I + 1)
130 NEXT I
```

8.
```
100 REM CHAPTER 7 SELF-TEST 8
110 FOR I = 1 TO 200 STEP 5
120    PRINT S(I), S(I + 1), S(I + 2), S(I + 3), S(I + 4)
130 NEXT I
```

9.
```
100 REM CHAPTER 7 SELF-TEST 9
110 FOR I = 10 TO 1 STEP -1
120    READ X(I)
130 NEXT I
```

10.
```
15        14        OUT OF SEQUENCE
18        12        OUT OF SEQUENCE
23        21        OUT OF SEQUENCE
```

11.
```
N              NTH FIBONACCI NO.
1                1
2                1
3                2
4                3
5                5
6                8
7                13
8                21
9                34
10               55
```

12. a) Each array name, A, F4 and C, must be immediately followed by at least an integer or simple variable within parentheses.

   b) Valid.

   c) It is invalid to define the size of an array by a string variable.

   d) Valid.

   e) It is invalid to use a subscripted variable, T(Y), as a subscript.

   f) Array names should precede each item in the list.

   g) The DIM statement is invalid. The following statement dimensions F$ to 10 elements: 700 DIM F$ (10) .

   h) Valid.

Test Your BASIC Skills

2. a) L(2, 2)

   b) L(3, 3)

   c) L(3,2)

   d) L(5, 2)

   e) L(3, 4)

   f) L(2, 1)

   g) L(1, 3)

   h) L(5, 1)

4. Assigns the value of each element of array A to the corresponding element in array B.

6. a) c

   b) c

   c) e, a fatal error is caused by accessing elements outside the range of the array.

   d) a

8.
```
200 REM EXERCISE 7.8 SOLUTION
210 LET L = 0
220 LET M = 0
230 LET H = 0
240 FOR I = 1 TO 50
250    IF N(I) < 0 OR N(I) > 18 THEN 280
260       LET L = L + 1
270       GOTO 330
280    IF N(I) < 26 OR N(I) > 29 THEN 310
290       LET M = M + 1
300       GOTO 330
310    IF N(I) <= 42 OR N(I) >= 47 THEN 330
320       LET H = H + 1
330 NEXT I
```

10.
```
190 REM EXERCISE 7.10 SOLUTION
200 FOR I = 1 TO 50
210    IF A(I) >= B(I) THEN 240
220       LET C(I) = -1
230       GOTO 250
240    IF A(I) = B(I) THEN LET C(I) = 0 ELSE LET C(I) = 1
250 NEXT I
```

12 The following are invalid:

   b) The value of the subscript cannot be negative.

   d) Subscripted subscripts are not permitted.

14.
```
100 DIM M$(46)
```

16.
```
190 REM EXERCISE 7.16 SOLUTION
200 DIM A(50)
210 LET N = 0
220 LET Z = 0
230 LET P = 0
240 FOR I = 1 TO 50
250    IF A(I) >= 0 THEN 280
260       LET N = N + 1
270       GOTO 290
280    IF A(I) > 0 THEN LET P = P + 1 ELSE LET Z = Z + 1
290 NEXT I
```

18.
```
190 REM EXERCISE 7.18 SOLUTION
200 DIM A(50), N$(50)
200 LET L = A(1)
210 LET L$ = N$(1)
220 FOR I = 2 TO 50
230    IF L <= A(I) THEN 260
240       LET L = A(I)
250       LET L$ = N$(I)
260 NEXT I
270 PRINT L$, L
```

20.
```
190 REM EXERCISE 7.20 SOLUTION
200 DIM A(200), B(200)
200 FOR I = 1 TO 200
210    IF B(I) > 3000 THEN PRINT A(I), B(I)
220 NEXT I
```

22.
```
170 REM EXERCISE 7.22 SOLUTION
180 DIM P(100), Q(100)
190 LET S = 0
200 FOR I = 1 TO 100
210    LET S = S + P(I) * Q(I)
220 NEXT I
```

24.
```
100 REM EXERCISE 7.24 SOLUTION
110 DIM R(10, 10), S(10, 10)
120 LET S = 0
130 FOR J = 1 TO 10
140    FOR K = 1 TO 10
150       LET S = S + R(J, K) * S(J, K)
160    NEXT K
170 NEXT J
```

Self-Test Exercises

CHAPTER 8

1. a) Creates the *sequential* file INV. DAT made up of five records, the last of which is the trailer ecord EOF.
   b) Reads the records in INV. DAT and displays the following report:

```
DESCRIPTION   COST
-----------   ----
CUTTER        5.76
SCRAPER       2.59
SWIVEL        4.32
CARVER        3.78

JOB COMPLETE
```

   c) Reads the records from file INV. DAT and creates the report shown in Answer 1b under the filename REPORT. LIS.
   d) Creates the *random* file RINV. DAT.

2. a) 1. In line 110 the mode should be I, since line 120 reads from the sequential file INV. DAT.
      2. In lines 120, 150 and 170, the filenumber should be 2.
   b) 1. In line 120 the sum of the widths do not agree with the record length in the OPEN statement.
      2. In line 150 the GET statement should be used instead of the INPUT statement.

3. a) Open for output the sequential file ACCOUNT. DAT as filenumber 3.
   b) Open for input the sequential file RAWMAT. DAT as filenumber 2.
   c) Open the random file TOWNSHIP. DAT with a record length of 39 as filenumber 2.

4. a) data items   b) records   c) sequentially, randomly
   d) write   e) read

5. `300 PRINT #3, A$; ","; F; ","; T`   6. `400 INPUT #3, A$, F, T`

7. Open for input the sequential file TIMECARD. DAT as filenumber 2.

8. The partial program reads the sequential file INV. DAT and assigns the data items to the parallel arrays D1$ and C1 which may be used for table processing.

9. a) 67   b) 120

10. G$ = "10-12-86b̶b̶"
    B$ = "b̶b̶b̶b̶b̶b̶b̶23956"
    N$ = the string representation for 5.67 left-justified. Actual string representation varies among systems.

11. The ON ERROR GOTO statement may be used to trap errors that otherwise cause termination of a program. When an error occurs, the system transfers control to the specified line number, following the keyword GOTO, which can be an error routine or an end-of-job routine. Two additional statements, the ON ERROR GOTO 0 and RESUME statements, are used in conjunction with the ON ERROR GOTO statement. Two special variables, ERR and ERL, may be used in IF statements to test the type of error that cause the system to transfer control to the error or end-of-job routine.

    If available, the function EOF(n) may be used to test for end-of-file before the execution of the INPUT #n statement. Both the ON ERROR GOTO statement and function EOF(n) allow for detection of end-of-file without the need of placing a trailer record in the sequential file.

Test Your BASIC Skills

2.
```
100 REM EXERCISE 8.2 SOLUTION
110 LET K = 0
120 LET T = 0
130 OPEN "I", #1, "SALES.DAT"
140 PRINT "STOCK", "SELLING", "DISCOUNT"
150 PRINT "-----", "-------", "--------"
160 INPUT #1, S$, S, C
170 WHILE S$ <> "EOF"
180    LET K = K + 1
190    LET T = T + S
200    PRINT S$, S, C
210    INPUT #1, S$, S, C
220 WEND
230 CLOSE #1
240 PRINT
250 PRINT USING "TOTAL NUMBER OF RECORDS====> ###"; K
260 PRINT USING "AVERAGE SELLING PRICE======> ###.##"; T/K
270 PRINT
280 PRINT "JOB COMPLETE"
290 END
```

4.   a) opened, output   b) opened, input   c) closed   d) input and output
e) FIELD   f) LSET, RSET   g) String, Numeric

6. The ON ERROR GOTO 0 statement is used to return control to the system following a branch to an error or end-of-file routine when the branch is due to an unexpected error. The system terminates execution of the program following the display of an appropriate diagnostic message.

Following the detection of an error by an ON ERROR GOTO statement, the RESUME statement is used in an error-handling routine or end-of-job routine to transfer control to any line in a program.

8.
```
200 INPUT "ENTER THE FILENAME"; N$
210 OPEN "I", #1, N$
```

10. Yes.

12. a, the parameters are out of order.

b, the variable M should be M$.

e, a comma should follow the filenumber.

f, the trailing comma is invalid.

g, the keyword CLOSE should be followed by a filenumber.

h, the ON ERROR GOTO statement should not transfer control to itself.

i, the number sign (#) is invalid.

14. a, a negative record length is invalid.

d, a string variable as the second parameter in a GET statement is invalid.

f, it is invalid to assign the value of a numeric variable to a string variable. The statement should read 600 LSET N$ = MKS$ (N) .

g, it is invalid to have a numeric variable to the left of the equal sign in an RSET statement.

i, the function CVS should be replaced by MKS$.

16. a)
```
100 REM EXERCISE 8.16A SOLUTION
110 OPEN "I", #1, "QUARTER.DAT"
120 FOR I = 1 TO 100
130    INPUT #1, A
140    PRINT A
150 NEXT I
160 CLOSE #1
170 END
```

b)
```
100 REM EXERCISE 8.16B SOLUTION
110 OPEN "R", #1, "RANQUAR.DAT", 8
120 FIELD #1, 4 AS A$, 4 AS B$
130 FOR I = 1 TO 100
140    GET #1, I
150    PRINT CVS(A$) + CVS(B$)
160 NEXT I
170 CLOSE #1
180 END
```

CHAPTER 9   Self-Test Exercises

1. a)
```
SGUB SAH MARGORP YM
```

b)
```
COMPUTERS MAKE NO VALUE JUDGEMENTS AND HAVE NO LOYALTIES.
THEY DO PRECISELY WHAT THEY ARE TOLD.
THE NUMBER OF VOWELS IN THE TWO SENTENCES IS 30
```

c)
```
J.Q.A.
```

d)
```
THE LENGTH IS 4
THE WIDTH IS 3
THE HEIGHT IS 2
THE AREA IS 24

THE LENGTH IS 1
THE WIDTH IS 6
THE HEIGHT IS 8
THE AREA IS 48

END OF REPORT
```

2. a) 1. In line 110 it is invalid to request a value for a numeric variable in a LINE INPUT statement.
   2. In line 120 the function name SQR$ is invalid. It should be rewritten as SQR.
   3. In line 140 the function name INPUT is invalid. If the function name is changed to INPUT$, the statement is still invalid because you can not include a prompt message in the INPUT$ function.
 b) 1. In line 120 the STR$ function returns a string value and therefore the numeric variable A is invalid.
   2. In line 150 the function name INKEY is invalid. It should be rewritten as INKEY$.

3. a) 5
   b) "BA"
   c) "IC"
   d) "ASI"
   e) 4
   f) 10 Spaces
   g) "BACAK"
   h) 57
   i) "W"
   j) 42.75
   k) "−14.6"
   l) ++++++

4.

Statement or Function	Suspends Program Execution	Type of Data That May Be Assigned	Must Press Enter Key
INPUT	Yes	Numeric or String	Yes
LINE INPUT	Yes	String	Yes
INKEY$	No	String	No
INPUT$	Yes	String	No

5. a) 16:15:00
   b) 07-04-1986
   c) 16:15
   d) 07-04-86

6.
```
100 REM CHAPTER 9 SELF-TEST 6
110 READ A$
120 PRINT A$
130 LET A$ = MID$(A$, 1, 29) + "20" + MID$(A$, 32, 10)
140 PRINT A$
150 REM ***************DATA FOLLOWS*****************
160 DATA "WORLD WAR II OCCURRED IN THE 19TH CENTURY"
170 END
```
Note: There are several other solutions.

7. The range of random numbers assigned to A is: $1 \leq A \leq 100$

8. a) 45   b) 0   c) 2   d) 1   e) 9   f) 1

9. `100 LINE INPUT "ENTER YOUR FULL NAME"; N$`   10. `500 LET B$ = INPUT$(8)`

11. The null string.

12.
```
************************
*                      *
*                      *
*    I MADE THIS BOX    *
*                      *
*                      *
************************
```

13. 3

Test Your BASIC Skills

2. a) 68
   b) The entire string
   c) IF I⃫ (where ⃫ indicates a blank or space follows I)
   d) SEEN
   e) 36.8
   f) 73
   g) G
   h) AAAAAAAAAAAAA
   i) −13.691
   j) Invalid.
   k) GIANTS is replaced by MIDGETS in C$.
   l) Four spaces.

4. a) 99   c) ?   e) 7   g) 58   i) Ten spaces.
   b) 43   d) 48.9   f) 73   h) −3.1416   j) Five spaces.

6.
```
190 REM EXERCISE 9.6 SOLUTION
200 LET N = VAL(N$)
210 LET D4 = INT(N/1000)
220 LET D3 = INT((P - D4 * 1000)/100)
230 LET D2 = INT((P - D4 * 1000 - D3 * 100)/10)
240 LET D1 = INT(P - D4 * 1000 - D3 * 100 - D2 * 10)
250 LET S = D4 + D3 + D2 + D1
```

8. The program displays the prime numbers between 1 and 100. Any whole number greater than 1 that has no factors other than 1 and the number itself is called a **prime number**. In number theory it can be proved that if a number has no factors between 2 and the square root of the number, then the number is prime. The algorithm utilizes this method of finding the prime numbers between 1 and 100.

10. a) `100 LET P = SQR(A^2 + B^2)`
    b) `200 LET B = SQR(ABS(TAN(X) - 0.51)`
    c) `300 LET Q = 8 * (COS(X))^2 + 4 * SIN(X)`
    d) `400 LET Y = EXP(X) + LOG(1 + X)`

12. a) `500 LET S = SGN(2 * X^2 + 3 * X + 5)`
    b) `600 LET I = INT(4 * X + 5)`
    c) `700 LET A = INT(X * 100 + SGN(X) * 0.50)/100`
       `710 LET A = INT(X * 10 + SGN(X) * 0.50)/10`

14. 405

16.
```
100 REM EXERCISE 9.16 SOLUTION
110 FOR R = 1 TO 52
120    PRINT INT(52 * RND + 1)
130 NEXT R
140 END
```

18. `100 DEF FNX(P) = 0.10 * (P - 200)`

20. The program is valid.

APPENDIX A   **Test Your BASIC Skills**

2. The annotation, terminal and connector symbols.

4. Part I: I = 9, J = 9
   Part II: I = 21, J = 14

6. I = 3, J = 5

8. The arrowheads point the wrong way between the process symbol and output symbol and between the output symbol and the terminal symbol representing End.

10.

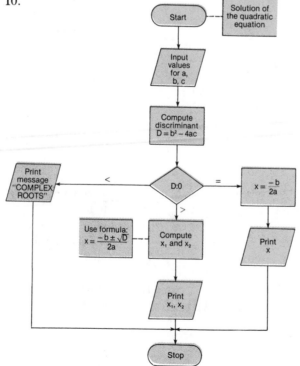

12.

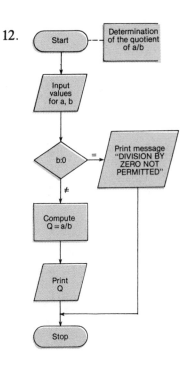

14.

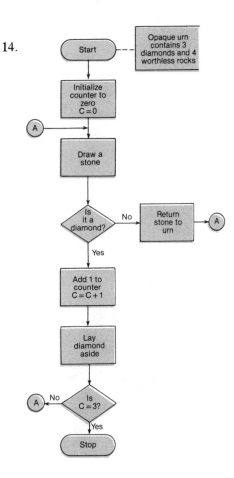

16. I = 17 and J = 16
18. I = 11 and J = 10
20. 6

INDEX